PEARSON
mymanagementlab

mymanagementlab is an online assessment and preparation solution for courses in Principles of Management, Human Resources, Strategy, and Organizational Behavior that help you actively study and prepare material for class. Chapter-by-chapter activities, including built-in pre-tests and post-tests, focus on what you need to learn and to review in order to succeed.

Visit **www.mymanagementlab.com** to learn more.

ELEVENTH EDITION

Management

ELEVENTH EDITION

Management

Stephen P. ROBBINS

San Diego State University

Mary COULTER

Missouri State University

Prentice Hall

Boston   Columbus   Indianapolis   New York   San Francisco   Upper Saddle River
Amsterdam   Cape Town   Dubai   London   Madrid   Milan   Munich   Paris   Montreal   Toronto
Delhi   Mexico City   Sao Paulo   Sydney   Hong Kong   Seoul   Singapore   Taipei   Tokyo

Editorial Director: Sally Yagan
Editor in Chief: Eric Svendsen
Acquisitions Editor: Kim Norbuta
Director of Editorial Services: Ashley Santora
Editorial Project Manager: Claudia Fernandes
Editorial Assistant: Carter Anderson
Director of Marketing: Patrice Lumumba Jones
Marketing Manager: Nikki Ayana Jones
Marketing Assistant: Ian Gold
Senior Managing Editor: Judy Leale
Senior Operations Supervisor: Arnold Vila
Design Development Manager: John Christiana
Art Director: Kathryn Foot
Text and Cover Designer: Kathryn Foot
Photo Development Editor: Nancy Moudry
Editorial Media Project Manager: Denise Vaughn
MyLab Product Manager: Joan Waxman
Media Project Manager: Lisa Rinaldi
Full-Service Project Management: Sharon
    Anderson/BookMasters, Inc.
Composition: Integra Software Services
Printer/Binder: Quebecor World Color/Versailles
Cover Printer: Lehigh-PhoenixColor/Hagerstown
Text Font: 10/12 TimesNewRoman

Credits and acknowledgments borrowed from other sources and reproduced, with permission, in this textbook appear on appropriate page within text.

Library of Congress Cataloging-in-Publication Data

Robbins, Stephen P.
    Management / Stephen P. Robbins, Mary Coulter. — 11th ed.
        p. cm.
    Includes bibliographical references and index.
    ISBN 978-0-13-216384-2
    1. Management.   I. Coulter, Mary K.   II. Title.
    HD31.R5647 2012
    658—dc22
                                   2010035514

10 9 8 7 6 5 4 3 2 1

Prentice Hall
is an imprint of

www.pearsonhighered.com

ISBN 10:   0-13-216384-5
ISBN 13: 978-0-13-216384-2

To my wife, Laura

Steve

....

To my family:
Ron
Sarah and James
Katie and Matt
and our newest addition, Brooklynn

Mary

About *the* Authors

STEPHEN P. ROBBINS (Ph.D., University of Arizona) is professor emeritus of management at San Diego State University and the world's best-selling textbook author in the areas of both management and organizational behavior. His books are used at more than 1,000 U.S. colleges and universities, have been translated into 19 languages, and have adapted editions for Canada, Australia, South Africa, and India. Dr. Robbins is also the author of the best-selling *The Truth About Managing People,* 2nd ed. (Financial Times/Prentice Hall, 2008) and *Decide & Conquer* (Financial Times/Prentice Hall, 2004).

In his "other life," Dr. Robbins actively participates in masters' track competitions. Since turning 50 in 1993, he's won 21 national championships and 12 world titles. He was inducted into the U.S. Masters' Track & Field Hall of Fame in 2005. Dr. Robbins is the current world record holder at 100m (12.37) and 200m (25.20) for men 65 and over.

MARY COULTER (Ph.D., University of Arkansas) is professor emeritus at Missouri State University. Dr. Coulter has published other books with Prentice Hall, including *Strategic Management in Action,* now in its fifth edition, and *Entrepreneurship in Action,* which is in its second edition. During her "free" time, Dr. Coulter enjoys puttering around in her flower garden, trying new recipes on family members (usually successful!), reading a variety of books, and enjoying many different activities with Ron, Sarah and James, Katie and Matt, and first granddaughter, Brooklynn.

Brief Contents

Contents

Part III   Planning

Chapter 7   **Managers as Decision Makers 176**

Preface

You've made a good decision! You're taking a college course ... maybe more than one. Although you may sometimes feel like you're wasting your time being in college, you're not. Yes, it's expensive. Yes, it's even sometimes hard. But what you're doing now will pay off in the long run. In a recent survey of job seekers, a whopping 92 percent said that a major disadvantage in competing for jobs was not having taken college courses. But that's not what you'll face because you *are* enrolled in a college course—the course for which you've purchased this book.

Key Changes to the 11th Edition

Here are some of the main changes we've made in the 11th edition:

▶ Two new chapters: Managing Diversity and Adaptive Organizational Design
▶ Two case applications in each chapter
▶ New *Leader Who Made a Difference* in each chapter
▶ New *By the Numbers* in each chapter
▶ New *Future Vision: The Working World in 2020* in 9 chapters
▶ New *A Manager's Dilemma* in each chapter
▶ 43 percent of the endnotes have been updated with references from 2009 and 2010
▶ New videos—up-to-date videos showing management topics in action, and access to the complete management video library, are available at www.mymanagementlab.com. Visit there to gain access and learn more.

What This Course Is About and Why It's Important

This course and this book are about management and managers. Managers are the one thing that all organizations—no matter the size, kind, or location—need. And there's no doubt that the world managers face has changed, is changing, and will continue to change. The dynamic nature of today's organizations means both rewards *and* challenges for the individuals who will be managing those organizations. Management is a dynamic subject, and a textbook on it should reflect those changes to help prepare you to manage under the current conditions. We've written this 11th edition of *Management* to provide you with the best possible understanding of what it means to be a manager confronting change.

Our Approach

Our approach to management is simple: Management is about people. Managers manage people. Thus, we introduce you to real managers, real people who manage people. We've talked with these real managers and asked them to share their experiences with you. You get to see what being a manager is all about—the problems these real managers have faced and how they have resolved those problems. Not only do you have the benefit of your professor's wisdom and knowledge, you also have access to your very own team of advisors and mentors.

What's Expected of You in This Course

It's simple. Come to class. Read the book. Do your assignments. And . . . study for your exams. If you want to get the most out of the money you've spent for this course and this textbook, that's what you need to do. In addition to writing this book, we have taught management classes. And that's what we expected of our students.

User's Guide

Your management course may be described as a "survey" course because a lot of topics are covered very quickly, and none of the topics are covered in great depth. It can be overwhelming at times! Your classroom professor is your primary source of information and will provide you with an outline of what you're expected to do during the course. That's also the person who will be evaluating your work and assigning you a grade, so pay attention to what is expected of you! View us, your textbook authors, as your supplementary professors. As your partners in this endeavor, we've provided you the best information possible both in the textbook and in the materials on mymanagementlab.com to help you succeed in this course. Now it's up to you to use them!

Getting the Most Out of Your Textbook: Getting a Good Grade in This Course

Professors use a textbook because it provides a compact source of information that you need to know about the course's subject material. Professors like this particular textbook because it presents management from the perspective of the people who actually *do* management—real managers. So take advantage of that and read what these real managers have to say. See how they've handled managerial problems. Learn about their management styles and think about how you might manage.

In addition to what you can learn from these real managers, we provide several ways to help you get a good grade in this course. Use the review and discussion questions at the end of the chapter. They provide a great way to see if you understand the material you've just read. Also, use the materials on mymanagementlab.

Mymanagementlab is a powerful online tool that combines assessment, reporting, and personalized study to help you succeed. Mymanagementlab gives you the opportunity to test yourself on key concepts and skills, track your own progress through the course, and use the personalized study plan activities—all to help achieve success in the classroom.

Finally, we include a wide variety of useful learning experiences both in the textbook and on mymanagementlab. From ethical dilemmas and skill-building exercises to case analyses and hands-on management tasks, we've provided a lot of things to make your management course fun and worthwhile. Your professor will tell you what assignments you will be expected to do. But you don't need to limit your learning experiences to those. Try out some of the other activities, even if they aren't assigned. We know you won't be disappointed!

Student Supplements
CourseSmart eTextbook

CourseSmart is an exciting new choice for students looking to save money. As an alternative to purchasing the print textbook, you can purchase an electronic version of the same content. With a CourseSmart etextbook, you can search the text, make notes online, print out reading assignments that incorporate lecture notes, and bookmark important passages for later review. For more information, or to purchase access to the CourseSmart eTextbook, visit www.coursesmart.com.

mymanagementlab

Mymanagementlab (www.mymanagementlab.com) is an easy to use online tool that personalizes course content and provides robust assessment and reporting to measure individual and class performance. All of the resources that students need for course success are in one place—flexible and easily adapted for your course experience. Some of the resources include an eText version of all chapters, quizzes, video clips, simulations, assessments, and PowerPoint presentations that engage students while helping them study independently.

Self-Assessment Library (S.A.L.)

If you are interested in additional self-assessments, this valuable tool includes 67 individual self-assessment exercises that allow you to assess your knowledge, beliefs, feelings, and actions in regard to a wide range of personal skills, abilities, and interests. Provided scoring keys allow for immediate, individual analysis. S.A.L. is available as a printed workbook, a CD-ROM, and by an access code, so you have a choice of how you want to complete the assessments. S.A.L. ISBN 0-13-608376-5.

Acknowledgments

Every author relies on the comments of reviewers and ours have been very helpful. We want to thank the following people for their insightful comments and suggestions for the 11th edition and previous editions of *Management:*

Suhail Abboushi, *Duquesne State*

Cheryl Adkins, *Longwood College*

Aline Arnold, *Eastern Illinois University*

Joseph Atallah, *DeVry Institute of Technology*

Jayanta Bandyopadhyay, *Central Michigan University*

Robb Bay, *Community College of Southern Nevada*

Henry C. Bohleke, *San Juan College*

Ernest Bourgeois, *Castleton State College*

Jenell Bramlage, *University of Northwestern Ohio*

Jacqueline H. Bull, *Immaculata University*

James F. Cashman, *The University of Alabama*

Rick Castaldi, *San Francisco State University*

Bobbie Chan, *Open University of Hong Kong*

Jim Chimenti, *Jamestown Community College*

Jay Christensen-Szalanski, *University of Iowa*

Thomas Clark, *Xavier University*

Sharon Clinebell, *University of Northern Colorado*

Daniel Cochran, *Mississippi State University*

Augustus B. Colangelo, *Penn State*

Jason Coleman, *Wesley College*

Donald Conlon, *University of Delaware*

Roy Cook, *Fort Lewis College*

Anne C. Cowden, *California State University, Sacramento*

Claudia Daumer, *California State University, Chico*

Kristl Davison, *University of Mississippi*

Thomas Deckleman, *Owens Community College*

R. Dortch, *Austin Peay State University*

Mary Ann Edwards, *College of Mount St. Joseph*

Tan Eng, *Ngee Ann Polytechnic*

Allen D. Engle, Sr., *Eastern Kentucky University*

Judson C. Faurer, *Metro State College*

Dale M. Feinauer, *University of Wisconsin, Oshkosh*

Janice Feldbauer, *Austin Community College*

Diane L. Ferry, *University of Delaware*

Louis Firenze, *Northwood University*

Bruce Fischer, *Elmhurst College*

Phillip Flamm, *Angelo State University*

Robert Foley, *College of St. Joseph*

Barbara Foltz, *Clemson University*

June Freund, *Pittsburgh State University*

Michele Fritz, *DeAnza College*

Charles V. Goodman, *Texas A&M University*

H. Gregg Hamby, *University of Houston*

Frank Hamilton, *University of South Florida*

Robert W. Hanna, *California State University, Northridge*

James C. Hayton, *Utah State University*

Wei He, *Indiana State University*

Phyllis G. Holland, *Valdosta State College*

Phil Holleran, *Mitchell Community College*

Henry Jackson, *Delaware County Community College*

Matrecia James, *Jacksonville University*

Jim Jones, *University of Nebraska, Omaha*

Kathleen Jones, *University of North Dakota*

Marvin Karlins, *University of South Florida*

Andy Kein, *Keller Graduate School of Management*

David Kennedy, *Berkeley School of Business*

Russell Kent, *Georgia Southern University*

William H. Kirchman, *Fayetteville Technical Community College*

John L. Kmetz, *University of Delaware*

Gary Kohut, *University of North Carolina at Charlotte*

William Laing, *Anderson College*

Gary M. Lande, *Montana State University*

Ellis L. Langston, *Texas Tech University*

Les Ledger, *Central Texas College*

David Linthicum, *Cecil College*

W. L. Loh, *Mohawk Valley Community College*

Susan D. Looney, *Delaware Technical and Community College*

James Mazza, *Middlesex Community College*

Lisa McCormick, *Community College of Allegheny*

James McElroy, *Iowa State University*

Carrie Blair Messal, *College of Charleston*

Joseph F. Michlitsch, *Southern Illinois University–Edwardsville*

Sandy J. Miles, *Murray State University*

Lavelle Mills, *West Texas A&M University*

Corey Moore, *Angelo State University*

Rick Moron, *University of California, Berkeley*

Don C. Mosley, Jr., *University of South Alabama*

Anne M. O'Leary-Kelly, *Texas A&M University*

Rhonda Palladi, *Georgia State University*

Shelia Pechinski, *University of Maine*

Victor Preisser, *Golden Gate University*

Michelle Reavis, *University of Alabama, Huntsville*

Clint Relyea, *Arkansas State University, University of Arkansas*

James Robinson, *The College of New Jersey*

Patrick Rogers, *North Carolina A&T University*

James Salvucci, *Curry College*

Elliot M. Ser, *Barry University*

Tracy Huneycutt Sigler, *Western Washington University*

Eva Smith, *Spartanburg Technical College*

James Spee, *The Claremont Graduate School*

Roger R. Stanton, *California State University*

Dena M. Stephenson, *Calhoun Community College*

Charles Stubbart, *Southern Illinois University*

Ram Subramanian, *Grand Valley State University*

Thomas G. Thompson, *University of Maryland, University College*

Frank Tomassi, *Johnson & Wales University*

Isaiah O. Ugboro, *North Carolina A&T State University*

Philip M. VanAuken, *Baylor University*

Carolyn Waits, *Cincinnati State University*

Bill Walsh, *University of Illinois*

Richard C. Warner, *Lehigh Carbon Community College*

Emilia S. Westney, *Texas Tech University*

Gary L. Whaley, *Norfolk State University*

Bobbie Williams, *Georgia Southern University*

Lucia Worthington, *University of Maryland University College*

Wendy Wysocki, *Monroe Community College*

Our team at Prentice Hall has been amazing to work with! This team of editors, production experts, technology gurus, designers, marketing specialists, sales representatives, and warehouse employees works hard to turn our digital files into a bound textbook and to see that it gets to faculty and students. We couldn't do this without all of you! Our sincere thanks to the people who made this book "go" include Kim Norbuta, Nikki Jones, Judy Leale, Claudia Fernandes, Ian Gold, Kathie Foot, Sally Yagan, Nancy Moudry, Sharon Anderson, Suzanne DeWorken, and Cheryl Wilms.

A special thank you goes to Anita Looney who worked very hard to coordinate all the materials and responses from our "real" managers. Anita, you were great, as always! And simple words can't express how much we appreciate those "real" managers who so graciously gave their time to help us put together a textbook that is like no other on the market. Without their contributions, our belief in showing managers as real people would be hard to do. Thank you, thank you, thank you! Mary would also like to thank her department head, Barry Wisdom; and her departmental secretary, Carol Hale, for all their support and encouragement.

Finally, Steve would like to thank his wife, Laura, for her encouragement and support. Mary would like to thank her husband and family for being supportive and understanding and for patiently enduring her many hours at the computer!

ELEVENTH EDITION

Management

Let's Get Real:

Meet the Manager

Lacy Martin
Banking Center Manager
Assistant Vice President
Commerce Bank
Springfield, MO

You'll be hearing more from this real manager throughout the chapter.

MY JOB:

I'm a branch manager for Commerce Bank. I manage a team of individuals who help our customers with solutions to meet all their financial needs.

BEST PART OF MY JOB:

Watching my employees become successful top performers and grow their careers within the company.

Management *and* Organizations

LEARNING OUTCOMES

WORST PART OF MY JOB:
Customers who have had circumstances and decisions that have resulted in putting them in a dire financial state.

BEST MANAGEMENT ADVICE EVER RECEIVED:
A discussion about the importance of open and clear communication that was tied to the famous quote from the 1967 film *Cool Hand Luke*, **"What we've got here is a failure to communicate."**

A Manager's Dilemma

12.7 million. That's the total number of people employed in the restaurant industry according to the National Restaurant Association.[1] Those employees hold jobs ranging from greeting and serving customers to cooking for and cleaning up after customers. There's a lot of action taking place in a restaurant—sometimes calm and sometimes frenetic—as employees work together to provide customers what they want. And overseeing those employees is someone who must ensure that everything runs smoothly.

That someone is a manager. Lisa Greene is one such manager. As the general manager of a popular and very busy restaurant in Springfield, Missouri, she oversees 100 employees. Working long hours, Lisa is expected to lead her team and uphold the company's high standards so employees can do their assigned work efficiently and effectively. Like any hard-working manager, Lisa is continually trying to find ways to cut costs and make her restaurant run a little more smoothly. But her most important challenge comes from looking for ways to make her restaurant a better place to work. Put yourself in Lisa's place.

What Would You Do?

Like many students, maybe you've worked in the restaurant industry at some time or another. It's not an easy job. It can be hot, dirty, and exhausting. Customers can be rude and demanding. And your work experiences, whether in a restaurant or in some other workplace, are likely to have been influenced by the skills and abilities of your manager. Lisa is a good example of what today's successful managers are like and the skills they must have in dealing with the problems and challenges of managing in the twenty-first century. This book is about the important managerial work that Lisa and the millions of other managers like her do. The reality facing today's managers is that the world has changed. In workplaces of all types—restaurants, offices, retail stores, factories, and the like—managers must deal with changing expectations and new ways of managing employees and organizing work. In this chapter, we introduce you to managers and management by looking at why managers are important, who managers are and where they work, and what managers do. Finally, we wrap up the chapter by looking at the factors reshaping and redefining the manager's job and discussing why it's important to study management.

LEARNING OUTCOME
Explain why managers are important to organizations.

1.1

Why Are Managers Important?

" . . . A great boss can change your life, inspiring you to new heights both professionally and personally, and energizing you and your team to together overcome new challenges bigger than any one of you could tackle alone."[2] If you've had the opportunity to work with a manager like this, count yourself lucky. Such a manager can make a job a lot more enjoyable and productive. However, even managers who don't live up to such lofty ideals and expectations are important to organizations. Let's look at three reasons why.

The first reason managers are important is that organizations need their managerial skills and abilities more than ever in these uncertain, complex, and chaotic times. As organizations deal with today's challenges—the worldwide economic climate, changing technology, ever-increasing globalization, and so forth—managers play an important role in identifying critical issues and crafting responses. For example, John Zapp, general manager of several car dealerships in Oklahoma City, has struggled to keep his businesses afloat and profitable in the current economic environment, just as many other car dealers have.[3] However, after four decades in the car business, Zapp understands that he's the one calling the shots and his "call" right now is to focus on selling more used cars. How? By keeping inventory moving and by keeping his salespeople engaged through small cash payment rewards for hitting sales goals. His skills and abilities as a manager have been crucial in guiding his organization through these challenging times.

Another reason managers are important to organizations is that they're critical to getting things done. For instance, in our chapter-opening story, Lisa wasn't the person greeting and seating customers, taking their orders, cooking their meals, or preparing a table for another customer, but she was the person who creates and coordinates the workplace systems and conditions so that others can perform those tasks. Although she often pitches in when and where needed, her job as manager is to ensure that all the employees are getting their jobs done so the organization can do what it's in business to do. If work isn't getting done or isn't getting done as it should be, she's also the one who must find out why and get things back on track.

Finally, *managers do matter* to organizations! How do we know that? The Gallup Organization, which has polled millions of employees and tens of thousands of managers, has found that the single most important variable in employee productivity and loyalty isn't pay or benefits or workplace environment; it's the quality of the relationship between employees and their direct supervisors.[4] In addition, global consulting firm Towers Watson found that the way a company manages and engages its people can significantly affect its financial performance.[5] Also, a recent study of organizational performance found that managerial ability was important in creating organizational value.[6] What can we conclude from such reports? That managers are important and they *do* matter!

Who Are Managers and Where Do They Work?

1.2
LEARNING OUTCOME
Tell who managers are and where they work.

Managers may not be who or what you might expect! Managers can be under the age of 18 to over age 80. They run large corporations as well as entrepreneurial start-ups. They're found in government departments, hospitals, small businesses, not-for-profit agencies, museums, schools, and even such nontraditional organizations as political campaigns and music tours. Managers can also be found doing managerial work in every country on the globe. In addition, some managers are top-level managers while others are first-line managers. And today, managers are just as likely to be women as they are men. However, the number of women in top-level manager positions remains low—only 27 women were CEOs of major U.S. corporations in 2010.[8] But no matter where managers are found or what gender they are, the fact is . . . managers have exciting and challenging jobs!

Who Is a Manager?

It used to be fairly simple to define who managers were: They were the organizational members who told others what to do and how to do it. It was easy to differentiate *managers* from *nonmanagerial employees.* Now, it isn't quite that simple. In many organizations, the changing nature of work has blurred the distinction between managers and nonmanagerial employees. Many traditional nonmanagerial jobs now include managerial activities.[9] For example, at General Cable Corporation's facility in Moose Jaw, Saskatchewan, Canada, managerial responsibilities are shared by managers and team members. Most of the employees at Moose Jaw are cross-trained and multi-skilled. Within a single shift, an employee can be a team leader, equipment operator, maintenance technician, quality inspector, or improvement planner.[10]

So, how *do* we define who managers are? A **manager** is someone who coordinates and oversees the work of other people so that organizational goals can be accomplished. A manager's job is not about *personal* achievement—it's about helping *others* do their work. That may mean coordinating the work of a departmental group, or it might mean supervising a single person. It could involve coordinating the work activities of a team with people from different departments or even people outside the organization, such as temporary employees or individuals who work for the organization's suppliers. Keep in mind, also, that

manager
Someone who coordinates and oversees the work of other people so that organizational goals can be accomplished

by the numbers[7]

8 percent of job applicants say that a good rapport with the manager is most important when considering a new employer.

42 percent of individuals ages 18–34 say they do not want to become a manager.

#1 – the rank of people skills as the most valued skill in job applicants.

28 percent of people would lay off/fire their boss if given the option.

51 percent of workers say they do not have qualified managers.

52 percent of workers say their boss is likable.

3 times—when managers are disengaged from their work, their employees are 3 times as likely to be disengaged from their work.

35 percent of employees who have quit their jobs say it's because of unhappiness with management.

30 percent of white-collar workers think incompetence is what makes for a bad boss.

As brand manager with Little Kids, Inc., Kate Boehnert is a middle manager responsible for the quality and successful promotion of the company's line of bubble toys. In this photo, she demonstrates during a toy trade show how the motorized Bubble Light blows bubbles. Brand managers work with product developers, salespeople, copywriters, and advertising directors to coordinate the production, distribution, and marketing of their product line. They analyze sales figures, set prices, organize advertising campaigns, explore different marketing strategies, and contact retailers to convince them to carry their brands. Successful brand managers may advance to a top management position.

managers may have work duties not related to coordinating and overseeing others' work. For example, an insurance claims supervisor might process claims in addition to coordinating the work activities of other claims clerks.

Is there a way to classify managers in organizations? In traditionally structured organizations (which are often pictured as a pyramid because more employees are at lower organizational levels than at upper organizational levels), managers can be classified as first-line, middle, or top. (See Exhibit 1-1.) At the lowest level of management, **first-line managers** manage the work of nonmanagerial employees who typically are involved with producing the organization's products or servicing the organization's customers. First-line managers may be called *supervisors* or even *shift managers*, *district managers*, *department managers*, or *office managers*. **Middle managers** manage the work of first-line managers and can be found between the lowest and top levels of the organization. They may have titles such as *regional manager*, *project leader*, *store manager*, or *division manager*. In our chapter-opening dilemma, Lisa is a middle manager. As the general manager, she's responsible for how her restaurant performs, but also is one of about 60 general managers company-wide who report to someone at corporate headquarters. At the upper levels of the organization are the **top managers**, who are responsible for making organization-wide decisions and establishing the plans and goals that affect the entire organization. These individuals typically have titles such as *executive vice president*, *president*, *managing director*, *chief operating officer*, or *chief executive officer*.

Not all organizations get work done with a traditional pyramidal form, however. Some organizations, for example, are more loosely configured with work being done by ever-changing teams of employees who move from one project to another as work demands arise. Although it's not as easy to tell who the managers are in these organizations, we do know that someone must fulfill that role—that is, there must be someone who coordinates and oversees the work of others, even if that "someone" changes as work tasks or projects change.

Where Do Managers Work?

It's obvious that managers do their work in organizations. But what is an **organization**? It's a deliberate arrangement of people to accomplish some specific purpose. Your college or university is an organization; so are fraternities and sororities, government departments, churches, Facebook, your neighborhood grocery store, the United Way, the St. Louis Cardinals baseball team, and the Mayo Clinic. All are considered organizations and have three common characteristics. (See Exhibit 1-2.)

First, an organization has a distinct purpose. This purpose is typically expressed through goals that the organization hopes to accomplish. Second, each organization is composed of people. It takes people to perform the work that's necessary for the organization to achieve its goals. Third, all organizations develop some deliberate structure within which members

EXHIBIT 1-1

Levels of Management

EXHIBIT 1-2

Characteristics of Organizations

do their work. That structure may be open and flexible, with no specific job duties or strict adherence to explicit job arrangements. For instance, at Google, most big projects, of which there are hundreds going on at the same time, are tackled by small focused employee teams that set up in an instant and complete work just as quickly.[11] Or the structure may be more traditional—like that of Procter & Gamble or General Electric—with clearly defined rules, regulations, job descriptions, and some members identified as "bosses" who have authority over other members.

Many of today's organizations are structured more like Google, with flexible work arrangements, employee work teams, open communication systems, and supplier alliances. In these organizations, work is defined in terms of tasks to be done. And workdays have no time boundaries since work can—and is—done anywhere, anytime.

FUTURE VISION | The Working World in 2020

A noted inventor once said, "My interest is in the future because I'm going to spend the rest of my life there."[12] While this book presents a fairly accurate description of today's workplace, you're going to spend most of your worklife in the future. What will that worklife look like? How will it be different from today?

Although no one has a perfectly accurate window to the future, certain trends in place today offer insights into what tomorrow holds. We can extrapolate from those trends to sneak a peek at the future. We've arbitrarily chosen to focus on the year 2020 because it's close enough that most of you will be actively in the workforce, yet far enough away that current

managerial practices are likely to have changed because they've become irrelevant or even obsolete.

In 2000, Malcolm Gladwell's popular book *The Tipping Point* looked at how major changes in our society occur. (Even at more than 10 years old, it's an interesting read and we recommend it!) Many demographers have said that 2010 could be a tipping point for the composition of the U.S. population. That's the year it's predicted that "the number of babies born to minorities outnumbers that of babies born to whites." This is yet another trend indicator in which minorities are expected to become the U.S. majority over the next 40 years. Although this demographic shift has been documented

since the early 1990s, it appears that the "tipping point" has been reached. Although this event has numerous societal implications, we're more interested in the implications for the work world that you'll be part of. Implications such as: What will employee hiring and selection processes be like? How will employee training programs change? How will employee reward programs be set up? Who will become the role models and business leaders that guide and shape our businesses? We will look at these types of issues in our Future Vision boxes located in various chapters. So strap on your visionary goggles and enjoy this intriguing look at the future! After all, you're going to be spending the rest of your life there!

first-line managers
Managers at the lowest level of management who manage the work of nonmanagerial employees

middle managers
Managers between the lowest level and top levels of the organization who manage the work of first-line managers

top managers
Managers at or near the upper levels of the organization structure who are responsible for making organization-wide decisions and establishing the goals and plans that affect the entire organization

organization
A deliberate arrangement of people to accomplish some specific purpose

However, no matter what type of approach an organization uses, some deliberate structure is needed so work can get done, with managers overseeing and coordinating that work.

1.3 **What** Do Managers Do?

Simply speaking, management is what managers do. But that simple statement doesn't tell us much, does it? Let's look first at what management is before discussing more specifically what managers do.

Management involves coordinating and overseeing the work activities of others so that their activities are completed efficiently and effectively. We already know that coordinating and overseeing the work of others is what distinguishes a managerial position from a nonmanagerial one. However, this doesn't mean that managers can do what they want anytime, anywhere, or in any way. Instead, management involves ensuring that work activities are completed efficiently and effectively by the people responsible for doing them, or at least that's what managers aspire to do.

Efficiency refers to getting the most output from the least amount of inputs. Because managers deal with scarce inputs—including resources such as people, money, and equipment—they're concerned with the efficient use of those resources. It's often referred to as "doing things right"—that is, not wasting resources. For instance, at the HON Company plant in Cedartown, Georgia, where employees make and assemble office furniture, efficient manufacturing techniques were implemented by doing things such as cutting inventory levels, decreasing the amount of time to manufacture products, and lowering product reject rates. These efficient work practices paid off as the plant reduced costs by more than $7 million in one year.[13]

It's not enough, however, just to be efficient. Management is also concerned with being effective, completing activities so that organizational goals are attained. **Effectiveness** is often described as "doing the right things"—that is, doing those work activities that will help the organization reach its goals. For instance, at the HON factory, goals included meeting customers' rigorous demands, executing world-class manufacturing strategies, and making employee jobs easier and safer. Through various work initiatives, these goals were pursued *and* achieved. Whereas efficiency is concerned with the *means* of getting things done, effectiveness is concerned with the *ends*, or attainment of organizational goals (see Exhibit 1-3). In successful organizations, high efficiency and high effectiveness typically go hand in hand. Poor management (which leads to poor performance) usually involves being inefficient and ineffective or being effective, but inefficient.

Now let's take a more detailed look at what managers do. Describing what managers do isn't easy. Just as no two organizations are alike, no two managers' jobs are alike. In spite of this, management researchers have developed three approaches to describe what managers do: functions, roles, and skills.

Efficiency is important in my job because *customers expect us to be efficient and accurate when conducting their business and it is always important to deliver on the customer's expectation.*

EXHIBIT 1-3

Efficiency and Effectiveness in Management

Efficiency (Means)   Effectiveness (Ends)

Resource Usage   Goal Attainment

Low Waste   High Attainment

Management Strives for:
Low Resource Waste (high efficiency)
High Goal Attainment (high effectiveness)

Management Functions

According to the functions approach, managers perform certain activities or functions as they efficiently and effectively coordinate the work of others. What are these functions? Henri Fayol, a French businessman, first proposed in the early part of the twentieth century that all managers perform five functions: planning, organizing, commanding, coordinating, and controlling.[14] Today, these functions have been condensed to four: planning, organizing, leading, and controlling (see Exhibit 1-4). Let's briefly look at each function.

If you have no particular destination in mind, then any road will do. However, if you have someplace in particular you want to go, you've got to plan the best way to get there. Because organizations exist to achieve some particular purpose, someone must define that purpose and the means for its achievement. Managers are that someone. As managers engage in **planning**, they set goals, establish strategies for achieving those goals, and develop plans to integrate and coordinate activities.

Managers are also responsible for arranging and structuring work to accomplish the organization's goals. We call this function **organizing**. When managers organize, they determine what tasks are to be done, who is to do them, how the tasks are to be grouped, who reports to whom, and where decisions are to be made.

Every organization has people, and a manager's job is to work with and through people to accomplish goals. This is the **leading** function. When managers motivate subordinates, help resolve work group conflicts, influence individuals or teams as they work, select the most effective communication channel, or deal in any way with employee behavior issues, they're leading.

The final management function is **controlling**. After goals and plans are set (planning), tasks and structural arrangements put in place (organizing), and people hired, trained, and motivated (leading), there has to be some evaluation of whether things are going as planned. To ensure that goals are being met and that work is being done as it should be, managers must monitor and evaluate performance. Actual performance must be compared with the set goals. If those goals aren't being achieved, it's the manager's job to get work back on track. This process of monitoring, comparing, and correcting is the controlling function.

Just how well does the functions approach describe what managers do? Do managers always plan, organize, lead, and then control? In reality, what a manager does may not

EXHIBIT 1-4

Four Functions of Management

Planning	Organizing	Leading	Controlling → Lead to	
Setting goals, establishing strategies, and developing plans to coordinate activities	Determining what needs to be done, how it will be done, and who is to do it	Motivating, leading, and any other actions involved in dealing with people	Monitoring activities to ensure that they are accomplished as planned	Achieving the organization's stated purposes

management
Coordinating and overseeing the work activities of others so that their activities are completed efficiently and effectively

efficiency
Doing things right, or getting the most output from the least amount of inputs

effectiveness
Doing the right things, or completing activities so that organizational goals are attained

planning
Management function that involves setting goals, establishing strategies for achieving those goals, and developing plans to integrate and coordinate activities

organizing
Management function that involves arranging and structuring work to accomplish the organization's goals

leading
Management function that involves working with and through people to accomplish organizational goals

controlling
Management function that involves monitoring, comparing, and correcting work performance

Let's Fly Together is the slogan of a merger undertaken by the top managers of United Airlines and Continental Airlines that will form the world's largest airline. United's CEO Glenn Tilton (left) and Continental's CEO Jeff Smisek stated that the merger strategy will achieve the goals of creating a combined airline that is more efficient and better positioned as a strong global competitor, that has the financial strength needed to make investments in improved products and services, and that can achieve and sustain profitability. Plans for the combined airline include flying under the United name and using the logo and colors of Continental.

always happen in this sequence. Regardless of the "order" in which these functions are performed, however, the fact is that managers do plan, organize, lead, and control as they manage. To illustrate, look back at the chapter-opening story. When Lisa is working to keep her employees motivated and engaged, that's leading. As she makes out the week's schedule, that's planning. When she is trying to cut costs, those actions obviously involve controlling. And dealing with unhappy customers is likely to involve leading, controlling, and maybe even planning.

Although the functions approach is popular for describing what managers do, some have argued that it isn't relevant.[15] So let's look at another perspective.

Mintzberg's Managerial Roles and a Contemporary Model of Managing

Henry Mintzberg, a well-known management researcher, studied actual managers at work. In his first comprehensive study, Mintzberg concluded that what managers do can best be described by looking at the managerial roles they engage in at work.[16] The term **managerial roles** refers to specific actions or behaviors expected of and exhibited by a manager. (Think of the different roles you play—such as student, employee, student organization member, volunteer, sibling, and so forth—and the different things you're expected to do in these roles.) When describing what managers do from a roles perspective, we're not looking at a specific person per se, but at the expectations and responsibilities that are associated with being the person in that role—the role of a manager.[17] As shown in Exhibit 1-5, these 10 roles are grouped around interpersonal relationships, the transfer of information, and decision making.

The **interpersonal roles** are ones that involve people (subordinates and persons outside the organization) and other duties that are ceremonial and symbolic in nature. The three interpersonal roles include figurehead, leader, and liaison. The **informational roles** involve collecting, receiving, and disseminating information. The three informational roles include monitor, disseminator, and spokesperson. Finally, the **decisional roles** entail making decisions or choices. The four decisional roles include entrepreneur, disturbance handler, resource allocator, and negotiator.

As managers perform these roles, Mintzberg proposed that their activities included both reflection (thinking) and action (doing).[18] Our manager in the chapter opener would do both as she manages. For instance, reflection would occur when Lisa listens to employees' or customers' problems, while action would occur when she resolves those problems.

EXHIBIT 1-5
Mintzberg's Managerial Roles

Interpersonal Roles

- Figurehead
- Leader
- Liaison

Informational Roles

- Monitor
- Disseminator
- Spokesperson

Decisional Roles

- Entrepreneur
- Disturbance handler
- Resource allocator
- Negotiator

Based on Mintzberg, Henry, *The Nature of Managerial Work,* 1st Edition, © 1980, pp. 93–94.

A number of follow-up studies have tested the validity of Mintzberg's role categories and the evidence generally supports the idea that managers—regardless of the type of organization or level in the organization—perform similar roles.[19] However, the emphasis that managers give to the various roles seems to change with organizational level.[20] At higher levels of the organization, the roles of disseminator, figurehead, negotiator, liaison, and spokesperson are more important; while the leader role (as Mintzberg defined it) is more important for lower-level managers than it is for either middle or top-level managers.

Recently, Mintzberg completed another hands-on and up-close study of managers at work and concluded that, "Basically, managing is about influencing action. It's about helping organizations and units to get things done, which means action."[21] Based on his observations, Mintzberg went on to explain that a manager does this in three ways: (1) by managing actions directly (for instance, negotiating contracts, managing projects, etc.), (2) by managing people who take action (for example, motivating them, building teams, enhance the organization's culture, etc.), or (3) by managing information that propels people to take action (using budgets, goals, task delegation, etc.). The manager at the center of the model has two roles—framing, which defines how a manager

managerial roles
Specific actions or behaviors expected of and exhibited by a manager

interpersonal roles
Managerial roles that involve people and other duties that are ceremonial and symbolic in nature

informational roles
Managerial roles that involve collecting, receiving, and disseminating information

decisional roles
Managerial roles that revolve around making choices

"You can't expect people to do a good job at work if their lives are a mess."[23] That's the philosophy of Panda Express founder and chairman, Andrew Cherng. Together with his wife Peggy, they have built a restaurant empire with more than 1,200 outlets and $1 billion in sales. They believe that a company is only as good as the employees who comprise it. In fact, he says that his company's success doesn't come just from the meals prepared in the kitchen, but because "he cares about the emotional well-being of his employees." With five guiding values—being proactive, showing respect/-having a win-win attitude, pursuing growth, having great operations, and being giving—and a caring and strong management team, this company has prospered. What can you learn from this leader who made a difference?

approaches his or her job; and scheduling, which "brings the frame to life" through the distinct tasks the manager does. A manager enacts these roles while managing action in the three "planes:" with information, through people, and sometimes by taking action directly. It's an interesting perspective on the manager's job and one that adds to our understanding of what it is that managers do.

So which approach is better—managerial functions or Mintzberg's propositions? Although each does a good job of depicting what managers do, the functions approach still seems to be the generally accepted way of describing the manager's job. "The classical functions provide clear and discrete methods of classifying the thousands of activities that managers carry out and the techniques they use in terms of the functions they perform for the achievement of goals."[22] However, Mintzberg's role approach and newly developed model of managing do offer us other insights into managers' work.

Management Skills

Dell Inc. is a company that understands the importance of management skills.[24] It started an intensive five-day offsite skills training program for first-line managers as a way to improve its operations. One of Dell's directors of learning and development thought this was the best way to develop "leaders who can build that strong relationship with their front-line employees." What have the supervisors learned from the skills training? Some things they mentioned were how to communicate more effectively and how to refrain from jumping to conclusions when discussing a problem with a worker.

What types of skills do managers need? Robert L. Katz proposed that managers need three critical skills in managing: technical, human, and conceptual.[25] (Exhibit 1-6 shows the relationships of these skills to managerial levels.) **Technical skills** are the job-specific knowledge and techniques needed to proficiently perform work tasks. These skills tend to be more important for first-line managers because they typically are managing employees who use tools and techniques to produce the organization's products or service the organization's customers. Often, employees with excellent technical skills get promoted to first-line manager. For example, Mark Ryan of Verizon Communications manages almost 100 technicians who service half a million of the company's customers. Before becoming a manager, however, Ryan was a telephone lineman. He says, "The technical side of the business is important, but managing people and rewarding and recognizing the people who do an outstanding job is how we (Verizon) are going to succeed."[26] Ryan is a manager who has technical skills, but also recognizes the importance of **human skills**, which involve the ability to work well with other people both individually and in a group. Because all managers deal with people, these skills are equally important to all levels of management. Managers with good human skills

The skills good managers need *include listening, communication skills, creativity, and a strong sense of teamwork.*

EXHIBIT 1-6

Skills Needed at Different Managerial Levels

EXHIBIT **1-7**

Important Managerial Skills

- Managing human capital
- Inspiring commitment
- Managing change
- Structuring work and getting things done
- Facilitating the psychological and social contexts of work
- Using purposeful networking
- Managing decision-making processes
- Managing strategy and innovation
- Managing logistics and technology

Based on "Dear Workforce: We're Developing Onboarding for New Managers: What Should Be Included?" *Workforce Online,* March 4, 2010; J. R. Ryan, "The Coming Leadership Gap: What You Can Do About It," *Bloomberg BusinessWeek Online,* December 15, 2009; In-Sue Oh and C. M. Berry, "The Five Factor Model of Personality and Managerial Performance: Validity Gains Through the Use of 360 Degree Performance Ratings," *Journal of Applied Psychology,* November 2009, pp. 1498–1513; and R. S. Rubin and E. C. Dierdorff, "How Relevant Is the MBA? Assessing the Alignment of Required Curricula and Required Managerial Competencies," *Academy of Management Learning & Education,* June 2009, pp. 208–224.

get the best out of their people. They know how to communicate, motivate, lead, and inspire enthusiasm and trust. Finally, **conceptual skills** are the skills managers use to think and to conceptualize about abstract and complex situations. Using these skills, managers see the organization as a whole, understand the relationships among various subunits, and visualize how the organization fits into its broader environment. These skills are most important to top managers.

Other important managerial skills that have been identified are listed in Exhibit 1-7. In today's demanding and dynamic workplace, employees who want to be valuable assets must constantly upgrade their skills, and developing management skills can be particularly beneficial in today's workplace. We feel that understanding and developing management skills is so important that we've included a skills feature at the end of each chapter. (The one in this chapter looks at developing your political skill.) In addition, you'll find other material on skill building as well as several interactive skills exercises in our mymanagementlab. As you study the four management functions throughout the rest of the book, you'll be able to start developing some key management skills. Although a simple skill-building exercise won't make you an instant expert, it can provide you an introductory understanding of some of the skills you'll need to master in order to be an effective manager.

How Is the Manager's Job Changing?

1.4

LEARNING OUTCOME
Describe the factors that are reshaping and redefining the manager's job.

"At Best Buy's headquarters, more than 60 percent of the 4,000 employees are now judged only on tasks or results. Salaried people put in as much time as it takes to do their work. Those employees report better relationships with family and friends, more company loyalty, and more focus and energy. Productivity has increased by 35 percent. Employees say they don't know whether they work fewer hours—they've stopped counting. Perhaps more important, they're finding new ways to become efficient."[27] Welcome to the new world of managing!

In today's world, managers are dealing with global economic and political uncertainties, changing workplaces, ethical issues, security threats, and changing technology. For example,

---

technical skills
Job-specific knowledge and techniques needed to proficiently perform work tasks

human skills
The ability to work well with other people individually and in a group

conceptual skills
The ability to think and to conceptualize about abstract and complex situations

Dave Maney, the top manager of Headwaters MB, a Denver-based investment bank, had to fashion a new game plan during the recession. When the company's board of directors gave senior management complete freedom to ensure the company's survival, they made a bold move. All but seven key employees were laid off. Although this doesn't sound very responsible or resourceful, it invited those laid-off employees to form independent member firms. Now, Headwaters steers investment transactions to those firms, while keeping a small percentage for itself. The "restructuring drastically reduced fixed costs and also freed management to do more marketing, rather than day-to-day investment banking transactions." As Maney said, "It was a good strategy for us and positioned us for the future."[28] It's likely that more managers *will* have to manage under such demanding circumstances, and the fact is that *how* managers manage is changing. Exhibit 1-8 shows some of the most important changes facing managers. Throughout the rest of this book, we'll be discussing these and other changes and how they're affecting the way managers plan, organize, lead, and control. We want to highlight three of these changes: the increasing importance of customers, innovation, and sustainability.

Importance of Customers to the Manager's Job

John Chambers, CEO of Cisco Systems, likes to listen to voice mails forwarded to him from dissatisfied customers. He says, "E-mail would be more efficient, but I want to hear the emotion, I want to hear the frustration, I want to hear the caller's level of comfort

EXHIBIT 1-8

Changes Facing Managers

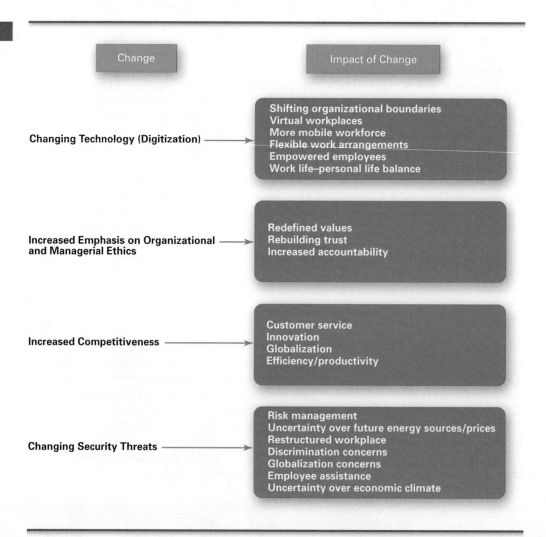

Change

Impact of Change

Changing Technology (Digitization)
- Shifting organizational boundaries
- Virtual workplaces
- More mobile workforce
- Flexible work arrangements
- Empowered employees
- Work life–personal life balance

Increased Emphasis on Organizational and Managerial Ethics
- Redefined values
- Rebuilding trust
- Increased accountability

Increased Competitiveness
- Customer service
- Innovation
- Globalization
- Efficiency/productivity

Changing Security Threats
- Risk management
- Uncertainty over future energy sources/prices
- Restructured workplace
- Discrimination concerns
- Globalization concerns
- Employee assistance
- Uncertainty over economic climate

with the strategy we're employing. I can't get that through e-mail."[29] This manager understands the importance of customers. You need customers. Without them, most organizations would cease to exist. Yet, focusing on the customer has long been thought to be the responsibility of marketing types. "Let the marketers worry about the customers" is how many managers felt. We're discovering, however, that employee attitudes and behaviors play a big role in customer satisfaction. For instance, passengers of Qantas Airways were asked to rate their "essential needs" in air travel. Almost every factor listed was one directly influenced by the actions of company employees—from prompt baggage delivery, to courteous and efficient cabin crews, to assistance with connections, to quick and friendly check-ins.[30]

Today, the majority of employees in developed countries work in service jobs. For instance, some 77 percent of the U.S. labor force is employed in service industries. In Australia, 71 percent work in service industries. In the United Kingdom, Germany, and Japan the percentages are 75, 72, and 75, respectively. Even in developing countries like India and Russia, we find 63 percent and 58 percent of the labor force employed in service jobs.[31] Examples of service jobs include technical support representatives, food servers or fast-food counter workers, sales clerks, teachers, nurses, computer repair technicians, front desk clerks, consultants, purchasing agents, credit representatives, financial planners, and bank tellers. The odds are pretty good that when you graduate you'll go to work for a company that's in a service industry, not in manufacturing or agriculture.

Managers are recognizing that delivering consistent high-quality customer service is essential for survival and success in today's competitive environment and that employees are an important part of that equation.[32] The implication is clear—managers must create a customer-responsive organization where employees are friendly and courteous, accessible, knowledgeable, prompt in responding to customer needs, and willing to do what's necessary to please the customer.[33] We'll look at customer service management in several chapters. Before we leave this topic, though, we want to share one more story that illustrates why it's important for today's managers (all managers, not just those in marketing) to understand what it takes to serve customers. During a broadcasted Stanley Cup playoff game, Comcast subscribers suddenly found themselves staring at a blank screen. Many of those customers got on Twitter to find out why. And it was there, not on a phone system, that they discovered a lightning strike in Atlanta had caused the power outage and that transmission would be restored as quickly as possible. Managers at Comcast understood how to exploit popular communications technology

These kids and teens playing Nintendo's DS portable video game in front of the official Pokemon store in Tokyo illustrates the importance of innovation in the company's worldwide leadership within the interactive entertainment industry. Nintendo continues to create unique video games for young people. But the company's innovation strategy also focuses on exploring new territory to launch new products, such as Wii, that cultivate a new wave of customers. Nintendo plans to further expand the concept of what a video game is, redefining it to include anything that brings people joy, from music to health management.

and the company's smart use of Twitter "underscores what is becoming a staple in modern-day customer service . . . beefing up communications with customers through social-media tools."[34]

Importance of Innovation to the Manager's Job

"Nothing is more risky than not innovating."[35]Innovation means doing things differently, exploring new territory, and taking risks. And innovation isn't just for high-tech or other technologically sophisticated organizations. Innovative efforts can be found in all types of organizations. For instance, the manager of the Best Buy store in Manchester, Connecticut, clearly understood the importance of getting employees to be innovative, a task made particularly challenging because the average Best Buy store is often staffed by young adults in their first or second jobs. "The complexity of the products demands a high level of training, but the many distractions that tempt college-aged employees keep the turnover potential high." However, the store manager tackled the problem by getting employees to suggest new ideas. One idea—a "team close," in which employees scheduled to work at the store's closing time, closed the store together and walked out together as a team—has had a remarkable impact on employee attitudes and commitment.[36] As you'll see throughout the book, innovation is critical throughout all levels and parts of an organization. For example, at Tata of India, the company's top manager, chairman Ratan Tata, told his employees during the bleak aspects of the global economic downturn to "Cut costs. Think out of the box. Even if the world around you is collapsing, be bold, be daring, think big."[37] And his employees obviously got the message. The company's introduction of the $2,000 minicar, the Nano, was the talk of the global automotive industry. As these stories illustrate, innovation is critical. It's so critical to today's organizations and managers that we'll also address this topic in several chapters.

Importance of Sustainability to the Manager's Job

It's the world's largest retailer with more than $408 billion in annual sales, 2.1 million employees, and 7,870 stores. Yes, we're talking about Walmart. And Walmart is probably the last company that you'd think about in a section describing sustainability. However, Walmart announced in early 2010 that it would "cut some 20 million metric tons of greenhouse gas emissions from its supply chain by the end of 2015—the equivalent of removing more than 3.8 million cars from the road for a year."[38] This corporate action affirms that sustainability and green management have become mainstream issues for managers.

What's emerging in the twenty-first century is the concept of managing in a sustainable way, which has had the effect of widening corporate responsibility not only to managing in an efficient and effective way, but also to responding strategically to a wide range of environmental and societal challenges.[39] Although "sustainability" means different things to different people, in essence, according to the World Business Council for Sustainable Development (2005), it is concerned with "meeting the needs of people today without compromising the ability of future generations to meet their own needs." From a business perspective, **sustainability** has been defined as a company's ability to achieve its business goals and increase long-term shareholder value by integrating economic, environmental, and social opportunities into its business strategies.[40] Sustainability issues are now moving up the agenda of business leaders and the boards of thousands of companies. Like the managers at Walmart are discovering, running an organization in a more sustainable way will mean that managers have to make informed business decisions based on thorough communication with various stakeholders, understanding their requirements, and starting to factor economic, environmental, and social aspects into how they pursue their business goals. We'll examine managing for sustainability and its importance to planning, organizing, leading and controlling in several places throughout the book.

Let's Get Real

F2F

My company is going "green" by
providing opportunities for our customers to go "green" and paper-free by using e-statement, online bill pay, and debit cards. We use recycled paper goods.

Why Study Management?

You may be wondering why you need to study management. If you're majoring in accounting or marketing or any field other than management, you may not understand how studying management is going to help you in your career. We can explain the value of studying management by looking at three things: the universality of management, the reality of work, and the rewards and challenges of being a manager.

The Universality of Management

Just how universal is the need for management in organizations? We can say with absolute certainty that management is needed in all types and sizes of organizations, at all organizational levels and in all organizational work areas, and in all organizations, no matter where they're located. This is known as the **universality of management**. (See Exhibit 1-9.) In all these organizations, managers must plan, organize, lead, and control. However, that's not to say that management is done the same way. What a supervisor in a software applications testing group at Microsoft does versus what the CEO of Microsoft does is a matter of degree and emphasis, not of function. Because both are managers, both will plan, organize, lead, and control. How much and how they do so will differ, however.

Management is universally needed in all organizations, so we want to find ways to improve the way organizations are managed. Why? Because we interact with organizations every single day. Are you frustrated when you have to spend two hours in a state government office to get your driver's license renewed? Are you irritated when none of the salespeople in a retail store seems interested in helping you? Is it annoying when you call an airline three times and customer sales representatives quote you three different prices for the same trip? These examples show problems created by poor management. Organizations that are well managed—and we'll share many examples of these throughout the text—develop a loyal customer base, grow, and prosper, even during challenging times. Those that are poorly managed find themselves losing customers and revenues. By studying management, you'll be able to recognize poor management and work to get it corrected. In

EXHIBIT 1-9

Universal Need for Management

addition, you'll be able to recognize and support good management, whether it's in an organization with which you're simply interacting or whether it's in an organization in which you're employed.

The Reality of Work

Another reason for studying management is the reality that for most of you, once you graduate from college and begin your career, you will either manage or be managed. For those who plan to be managers, an understanding of management forms the foundation upon which to build your management skills. For those of you who don't see yourself managing, you're still likely to have to work with managers. Also, assuming that you'll have to work for a living and recognizing that you're very likely to work in an organization, you'll probably have some managerial responsibilities even if you're not a manager. Our experience tells us that you can gain a great deal of insight into the way your boss (and fellow employees) behave and how organizations function by studying management. Our point is that you don't have to aspire to be a manager to gain something valuable from a course in management.

Rewards and Challenges of Being a Manager

We can't leave our discussion here without looking at the rewards and challenges of being a manager. (See Exhibit 1-10.) What *does* it mean to be a manager in today's workplace?

First, there are many challenges. It can be a tough and often thankless job. In addition, a portion of a manager's job (especially at lower organizational levels) may entail duties that are often more clerical (compiling and filing reports, dealing with bureaucratic procedures, or doing paperwork) than managerial.[41] Managers often have to deal with a variety of personalities and have to make do with limited resources. It can be a challenge to motivate workers in the face of uncertainty and chaos, as this recession has illustrated time and time again. And managers may find it difficult to successfully blend the knowledge, skills, ambitions, and experiences of a diverse work group. Finally, as a manager, you're not in full control of your destiny. Your success typically is dependent upon others' work performance.

Despite these challenges, being a manager *can be* rewarding. You're responsible for creating a work environment in which organizational members can do their work to the best of their ability and thus help the organization achieve its goals. You help others find meaning and fulfillment in their work. You get to support, coach, and nurture others and help them make good decisions. In addition, as a manager, you often have the opportunity to think creatively and use your imagination. You'll get to meet and work with a variety of

Let's Get Real

F2F

I find being a manager rewarding because *you can be a guiding hand and voice to another individual's success.*

EXHIBIT 1-10

Rewards and Challenges of Being a Manager

Rewards	Challenges
• Create a work environment in which organizational members can work to the best of their ability	• Do hard work
• Have opportunities to think creatively and use imagination	• May have duties that are more clerical than managerial
• Help others find meaning and fulfillment in work	• Have to deal with a variety of personalities
• Support, coach, and nurture others	• Often have to make do with limited resources
• Work with a variety of people	• Motivate workers in chaotic and uncertain situations
• Receive recognition and status in organization and community	• Blend knowledge, skills, ambitions, and and experiences of a diverse work group
• Play a role in influencing organizational outcomes	• Success depends on others' work performance
• Receive appropriate compensation in the form of salaries, bonuses, and stock options	
• Good managers are needed by organizations	

people—both inside and outside the organization. Other rewards may include receiving recognition and status in your organization and in the community, playing a role in influencing organizational outcomes, and receiving attractive compensation in the form of salaries, bonuses, and stock options. Finally, as we said earlier in the chapter, organizations need good managers. It's through the combined efforts of motivated and passionate people working together that organizations accomplish their goals. As a manager, you can be assured that your efforts, skills, and abilities are needed.

Let's Get Real:

My Response *to A Manager's Dilemma, page 4*

What Would You Do?

A good place to work is one in which employees have the resources they need in order to best fulfill customers' requests and expectations. As companies and managers sometimes look to cut costs and do more with less, they face a fine balance between what employees and customers can have reduced without negative repercussions.

I believe that employee engagement is a critical element in a smooth workplace. If I were in Lisa's situation, I would get the employees involved in brainstorming about areas they see room for cutting costs, ideas on work flows and processes, and what could help all work more efficiently and effectively. Employee engagement is heightened when employees feel like they have a voice in making their workplace a better place to work and that management is in tune with the needs and concerns of front line employees. Also, implementing changes and transitioning employees to a new way of doing business can be easier because employee buy-in is already there if they participated in some of the ground work and ideas.

Lacy Martin
Banking Center
Manager, Assistant
Vice President
**Commerce Bank
Springfield, MO**

CHAPTER SUMMARY
by Learning Outcomes

LEARNING OUTCOME 1.1   **Explain** why managers are important to organizations.

Managers are important to organizations for three reasons. First, organizations need their managerial skills and abilities in uncertain, complex, and chaotic times. Second, managers are critical to getting things done in organizations. Finally, managers contribute to employee productivity and loyalty; the way employees are managed can affect the organization's financial performance; and managerial ability has been shown to be important in creating organizational value.

LEARNING OUTCOME 1.2   **Tell** who managers are and where they work.

Managers coordinate and oversee the work of other people so that organizational goals can be accomplished. Nonmanagerial employees work directly on a job or task and have no one reporting to them. In traditionally structured organizations, managers can be first-line, middle, or top. In other more loosely configured organizations, the managers may not be as readily identifiable, although someone must fulfill that role.

Managers work in an organization, which is a deliberate arrangement of people to accomplish some specific purpose. Organizations have three characteristics: a distinctive purpose, composed of people, and a deliberate structure. Many of today's organizations are structured to be more open, flexible, and responsive to changes.

LEARNING OUTCOME 1.3   **Describe** the functions, roles, and skills of managers.

Broadly speaking, management is what managers do and management involves coordinating and overseeing the efficient and effective completion of others' work activities. Efficiency means doing things right; effectiveness means doing the right things.

The four functions of management include planning (defining goals, establishing strategies, and developing plans), organizing (arranging and structuring work), leading (working with and through people), and controlling (monitoring, comparing, and correcting work performance).

Mintzberg's managerial roles include interpersonal, which involve people and other ceremonial/symbolic duties (figurehead, leader, and liaison); informational, which involve collecting, receiving, and disseminating information (monitor, disseminator, and spokesperson); and decisional, which involve making choices (entrepreneur, disturbance handler, resource allocator, and negotiator). Mintzberg's newest description of what managers do proposes that managing is about influencing action, which managers do in three ways: by managing actions directly, by managing people who take action, and by managing information that impels people to take action.

Katz's managerial skills include technical (job-specific knowledge and techniques), human (ability to work well with people), and conceptual (ability to think and express ideas). Technical skills are most important for lower-level managers while conceptual skills are most important for top managers. Human skills are equally important for all managers. Some other managerial skills also identified include managing human capital, inspiring commitment, managing change, using purposeful networking, and so forth.

LEARNING OUTCOME 1.4   **Describe** the factors that are reshaping and redefining the manager's job.

The changes impacting managers' jobs include global economic and political uncertainties, changing workplaces, ethical issues, security threats, and changing technology. Managers must be concerned with customer service because employee attitudes and behaviors play a big role in customer satisfaction. Managers must also be concerned with innovation because it is important for organizations to be competitive. And finally, managers must be concerned with sustainability as business goals are developed.

Management History Module

enry Ford once said, "History is more or less bunk." Well...he was wrong! History is important because it can put current activities in perspective. In this module, we're going to take a trip back in time to see how the field of study called management has evolved. What you're going to see is that today's managers still use many elements of the historical approaches to management. Focus on the following learning outcomes as you read and study this module.

MH 1
Describe some early management examples.
page 28

MH 2
Explain the various theories in the classical approach.
page 29

MH 3
Discuss the development and uses of the behavioral approach.
page 32

MH 4
Describe the quantitative approach.
page 34

MH 5
Explain the various theories in the contemporary approach.
page 36

LEARNING OUTCOMES

LEARNING OUTCOME
Describe some early
management examples.

MH 1

Early Management

Management has been practiced a long time. Organized endeavors directed by people responsible for planning, organizing, leading, and controlling activities have existed for thousands of years. Let's look at some of the most interesting examples.

The Egyptian pyramids and the Great Wall of China are proof that projects of tremendous scope, employing tens of thousands of people, were completed in ancient times.[1] It took more than 100,000 workers some 20 years to construct a single pyramid. Who told each worker what to do? Who ensured that there would be enough stones at the site to keep workers busy? The answer is *managers.* Someone had to plan what was to be done, organize people and materials to do it, make sure those workers got the work done, and impose some controls to ensure that everything was done as planned.

Another example of early management can be found in the city of Venice, which was a major economic and trade center in the 1400s. The Venetians developed an early form of business enterprise and engaged in many activities common to today's organizations. For instance, at the arsenal of Venice, warships were floated along the canals, and at each stop, materials and riggings were added to the ship.[2] Sounds a lot like a car "floating" along an assembly line, doesn't it? In addition, the Venetians used warehouse and inventory systems to keep track of materials, human resource management functions to manage the labor force (including wine breaks), and an accounting system to keep track of revenues and costs.

In 1776, Adam Smith published *The Wealth of Nations*, in which he argued the economic advantages that organizations and society would gain from the **division of labor** (or **job specialization**)—that is, breaking down jobs into narrow and repetitive tasks. Using the pin industry as an example, Smith claimed that 10 individuals, each doing a specialized task, could produce about 48,000 pins a day among them. However, if each person worked alone performing each task separately, it would be quite an accomplishment to produce even 10 pins a day! Smith concluded that division of labor increased productivity by increasing each worker's skill and dexterity, saving time lost in changing tasks, and creating labor-saving inventions and machinery. Job specialization continues to be popular. For example, think of the specialized tasks performed by members of a hospital surgery team, meal preparation tasks done by workers in restaurant kitchens, or positions played by players on a football team.

Starting in the late eighteenth century when machine power was substituted for human power, a point in history known as the **industrial revolution**, it became more economical to manufacture goods in factories rather than at home. These large efficient factories needed someone to forecast demand, ensure that enough material was on hand to make products, assign tasks to people, direct daily activities, and so forth. That "someone" was a manager: These managers would need formal theories to guide them in running these large organizations. It wasn't until the early 1900s, however, that the first steps toward developing such theories were taken.

EXHIBIT MH-1
Major Approaches to Management

In this module, we'll look at four major approaches to management theory: classical, behavioral, quantitative, and contemporary. (See Exhibit MH-1.) Keep in mind that each approach is concerned with trying to explain management from the perspective of what was important at that time in history and the backgrounds and interests of the researchers. Each of the four approaches contributes to our overall understanding of management, but each is also a limited view of what it is and how to best practice it.

Classical Approach

LEARNING OUTCOME
Explain the various theories in the classical approach.

Although we've seen how management has been used in organized efforts since early history, the formal study of management didn't begin until early in the twentieth century. These first studies of management, often called the **classical approach**, emphasized rationality and making organizations and workers as efficient as possible. Two major theories comprise the classical approach: scientific management and general administrative theory. The two most important contributors to scientific management theory were Frederick W. Taylor and the husband-wife team of Frank and Lillian Gilbreth. The two most important contributors to general administrative theory were Henri Fayol and Max Weber. Let's take a look at each of these important figures in management history.

If you had to pinpoint when modern management theory was born, 1911 might be a good choice. That was when Frederick Winslow Taylor's *Principles of Scientific Management* was published. Its contents were widely embraced by managers around the world. Taylor's book described the theory of **scientific management**: the use of scientific methods to define the "one best way" for a job to be done.

Taylor worked at the Midvale and Bethlehem Steel Companies in Pennsylvania. As a mechanical engineer with a Quaker and Puritan background, he was continually appalled by workers' inefficiencies. Employees used vastly different techniques to do the same job. They often "took it easy" on the job, and Taylor believed that worker output was only about one-third of what was possible. Virtually no work standards existed and workers were placed in jobs with little or no concern for matching their abilities and aptitudes with the tasks they were required to do. Taylor set out to remedy that by applying the scientific method to shop-floor jobs. He spent more than two decades passionately pursuing the "one best way" for such jobs to be done.

EXHIBIT **MH-2**

Taylor's Scientific Management
Principles

1. Develop a science for each element of an individual's work to replace the old rule-of-thumb method.
2. Scientifically select and then train, teach, and develop the worker.
3. Heartily cooperate with the workers so as to ensure that all work is done in accordance with the principles of the science that has been developed.
4. Divide work and responsibility almost equally between management and workers. Management does all work for which it is better suited than the workers.

Taylor's experiences at Midvale led him to define clear guidelines for improving production efficiency. He argued that these four principles of management (see Exhibit MH-2) would result in prosperity for both workers and managers.[3] How did these scientific principles really work? Let's look at an example.

Probably the best known example of Taylor's scientific management efforts was the pig iron experiment. Workers loaded "pigs" of iron (each weighing 92 lbs.) onto rail cars. Their daily average output was 12.5 tons. However, Taylor believed that by scientifically analyzing the job to determine the "one best way" to load pig iron, output could be increased to 47 or 48 tons per day. After scientifically applying different combinations of procedures, techniques, and tools, Taylor succeeded in getting that level of productivity. How? By putting the right person on the job with the correct tools and equipment, having the worker follow his instructions exactly, and motivating the worker with an economic incentive of a significantly higher daily wage. Using similar approaches for other jobs, Taylor was able to define the "one best way" for doing each job. Overall, Taylor achieved consistent productivity improvements in the range of 200 percent or more. Based on his groundbreaking studies of manual work using scientific principles, Taylor became known as the "father" of scientific management. His ideas spread in the United States and to other countries and inspired others to study and develop methods of scientific management. His most prominent followers were Frank and Lillian Gilbreth.

A construction contractor by trade, Frank Gilbreth gave up that career to study scientific management after hearing Taylor speak at a professional meeting. Frank and his wife Lillian, a psychologist, studied work to eliminate inefficient hand-and-body motions. The Gilbreths also experimented with the design and use of the proper tools and equipment for optimizing work performance.[4] Also, as parents of 12 children, the Gilbreths ran their household using scientific management principles and techniques. In fact, two of their children wrote a book, *Cheaper by the Dozen*, which described life with the two masters of efficiency.

Frank is probably best known for his bricklaying experiments. By carefully analyzing the bricklayer's job, he reduced the number of motions in laying exterior brick from 18 to about 5, and in laying interior brick from 18 to 2. Using Gilbreth's techniques, a bricklayer was more productive and less fatigued at the end of the day.

The Gilbreths invented a device called a microchronometer that recorded a worker's hand-and-body motions and the amount of time spent doing each motion. Wasted motions missed by the naked eye could be identified and eliminated. The Gilbreths also devised a classification scheme to label 17 basic hand motions (such as search, grasp, hold), which they called **therbligs** (Gilbreth spelled backward with the *th* transposed). This scheme gave the Gilbreths a more precise way of analyzing a worker's exact hand movements.

How today's managers use scientific management

Many of the guidelines and techniques that Taylor and the Gilbreths devised for improving production efficiency are still used in organizations today. When managers analyze the basic work tasks that must be performed, use time-and-motion study to eliminate wasted motions, hire the best-qualified workers for a job, or design incentive systems based on output, they're using the principles of scientific management.

General administrative theory focused more on what managers do and what constituted good management practice. We introduced Henri Fayol in Chapter 1 because he first identified five functions that managers perform: planning, organizing, commanding, coordinating, and controlling.[5]

Fayol wrote during the same time period as Taylor. While Taylor was concerned with first-line managers and the scientific method, Fayol's attention was directed at the activities of *all* managers. He wrote from his personal experience as the managing director of a large French coal-mining firm.

Fayol described the practice of management as something distinct from accounting, finance, production, distribution, and other typical business functions. His belief that management was an activity common to all business endeavors, government, and even the home led him to develop 14 **principles of management**—fundamental rules of management that could be applied to all organizational situations and taught in schools. These principles are shown in Exhibit MH-3.

EXHIBIT MH-3

Fayol's 14 Principles of Management

1. **Division of Work.** Specialization increases output by making employees more efficient.
2. **Authority.** Managers must be able to give orders, and authority gives them this right.
3. **Discipline.** Employees must obey and respect the rules that govern the organization.
4. **Unity of command.** Every employee should receive orders from only one superior.
5. **Unity of direction.** The organization should have a single plan of action to guide managers and workers.
6. **Subordination of individual interests to the general interest.** The interests of any one employee or group of employees should not take precedence over the interests of the organization as a whole.
7. **Remuneration.** Workers must be paid a fair wage for their services.
8. **Centralization.** This term refers to the degree to which subordinates are involved in decision making.
9. **Scalar chain.** The line of authority from top management to the lowest ranks is the scalar chain.
10. **Order.** People and materials should be in the right place at the right time.
11. **Equity.** Managers should be kind and fair to their subordinates.
12. **Stability of tenure of personnel.** Management should provide orderly personnel planning and ensure that replacements are available to fill vacancies.
13. **Initiative.** Employees who are allowed to originate and carry out plans will exert high levels of effort.
14. **Esprit de corps.** Promoting team spirit will build harmony and unity within the organization.

Weber (pronounced VAY-ber) was a German sociologist who studied organizations.[6] Writing in the early 1900s, he developed a theory of authority structures and relations based on an ideal type of organization he called a **bureaucracy**—a form of organization characterized by division of labor, a clearly defined hierarchy, detailed rules and regulations, and impersonal relationships. (See Exhibit MH-4.) Weber recognized that this "ideal bureaucracy" didn't exist in reality. Instead he intended it as a basis for theorizing about how work could be done in large groups. His theory became the structural design for many of today's large organizations.

Bureaucracy, as described by Weber, is a lot like scientific management in its ideology. Both emphasized rationality, predictability, impersonality, technical competence, and authoritarianism. Although Weber's ideas were less practical than Taylor's, the fact that his "ideal type" still describes many contemporary organizations attests to their importance.

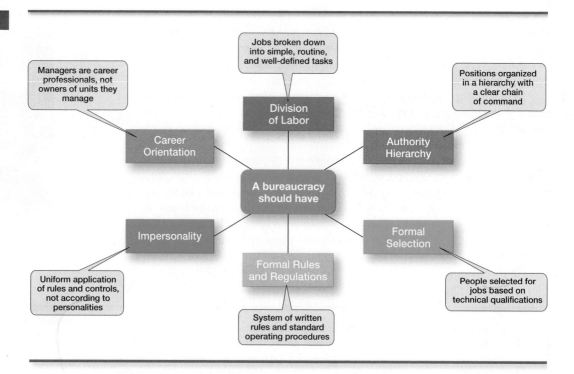

How today's managers use general administrative theory

Several of our current management ideas and practices can be directly traced to the contributions of general administrative theory. For instance, the functional view of the manager's job can be attributed to Fayol. In addition, his 14 principles serve as a frame of reference from which many current management concepts—such as managerial authority, centralized decision making, reporting to only one boss, and so forth—have evolved.

Weber's bureaucracy was an attempt to formulate an ideal prototype for organizations. Although many characteristics of Weber's bureaucracy are still evident in large organizations, his model isn't as popular today as it was in the twentieth century. Many managers feel that a bureaucratic structure hinders individual employees' creativity and limits an organization's ability to respond quickly to an increasingly dynamic environment. However, even in flexible organizations of creative professionals—such as Microsoft, Samsung, General Electric, or Cisco Systems—some bureaucratic mechanisms are necessary to ensure that resources are used efficiently and effectively.

LEARNING OUTCOME
Discuss the development and uses of the behavioral approach.

MH 3

Behavioral Approach

As we know, managers get things done by working with people. This explains why some writers have chosen to look at management by focusing on the organization's people. The field of study that researches the actions (behavior) of people at work is called **organizational behavior (OB)**. Much of what managers do today when managing people—motivating, leading, building trust, working with a team, managing conflict, and so forth—has come out of OB research.

Although a number of individuals in the early twentieth century recognized the importance of people to an organization's success, four stand out as early advocates of the OB approach: Robert Owen, Hugo Munsterberg, Mary Parker

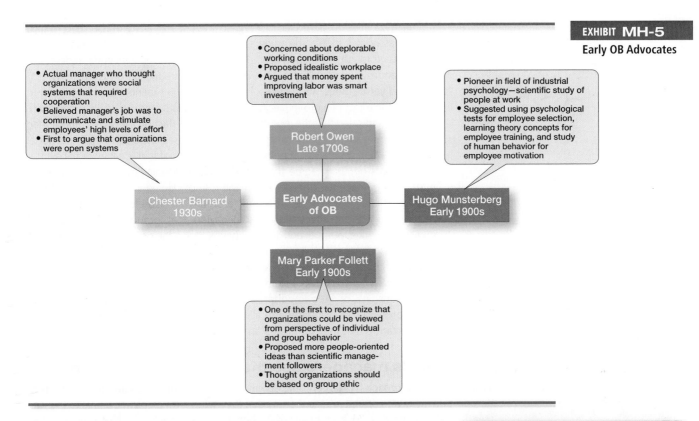

- Actual manager who thought organizations were social systems that required cooperation
- Believed manager's job was to communicate and stimulate employees' high levels of effort
- First to argue that organizations were open systems

- Concerned about deplorable working conditions
- Proposed idealistic workplace
- Argued that money spent improving labor was smart investment

- Pioneer in field of industrial psychology—scientific study of people at work
- Suggested using psychological tests for employee selection, learning theory concepts for employee training, and study of human behavior for employee motivation

Robert Owen
Late 1700s

Chester Barnard
1930s

Early Advocates
of OB

Hugo Munsterberg
Early 1900s

Mary Parker Follett
Early 1900s

- One of the first to recognize that organizations could be viewed from perspective of individual and group behavior
- Proposed more people-oriented ideas than scientific management followers
- Thought organizations should be based on group ethic

Follett, and Chester Barnard. Their contributions were varied and distinct, yet all believed that people were the most important asset of the organization and should be managed accordingly. Their ideas provided the foundation for such management practices as employee selection procedures, motivation programs, and work teams. Exhibit MH-5 summarizes each individual's most important ideas.

Without question, the most important contribution to the OB field came out of the **Hawthorne Studies**, a series of studies conducted at the Western Electric Company Works in Cicero, Illinois. These studies, which started in 1924, were initially designed by Western Electric industrial engineers as a scientific management experiment. They wanted to examine the effect of various lighting levels on worker productivity. Like any good scientific experiment, control and experimental groups were set up with the experimental group being exposed to various lighting intensities, and the control group working under a constant intensity. If you were the industrial engineers in charge of this experiment, what would you have expected to happen? It's logical to think that individual output in the experimental group would be directly related to the intensity of the light. However, they found that as the level of light was increased in the experimental group, output for both groups increased. Then, much to the surprise of the engineers, as the light level was decreased in the experimental group, productivity continued to increase in both groups. In fact, a productivity decrease was observed in the experimental group *only* when the level of light was reduced to that of a moonlit night. What would explain these unexpected results? The engineers weren't sure, but concluded that lighting intensity was not directly related to group productivity, and that something else must have contributed to the results. They weren't able to pinpoint what that "something else" was, though.

In 1927, the Western Electric engineers asked Harvard professor Elton Mayo and his associates to join the study as consultants. Thus began a relationship that would last through 1932 and encompass numerous experiments in the redesign of jobs, changes in workday and workweek length, introduction of rest periods, and individual versus group wage plans.[7] For example, one experiment was designed to evaluate the effect of a group piecework incentive pay system on group productivity. The results indicated that the incentive plan had less effect on a worker's output than did group pressure, acceptance, and security. The researchers concluded that social norms or group standards were the key determinants of individual work behavior.

Scholars generally agree that the Hawthorne Studies had a game-changing impact on management beliefs about the role of people in organizations. Mayo concluded that people's behavior and attitudes are closely related, that group factors significantly affect individual behavior, that group standards establish individual worker output, and that money is less a factor in determining output than are group standards, group attitudes, and security. These conclusions led to a new emphasis on the human behavior factor in the management of organizations.

Although critics attacked the research procedures, analyses of findings, and conclusions, it's of little importance from a historical perspective whether the Hawthorne Studies were academically sound or their conclusions justified.[8] What *is* important is that they stimulated an interest in human behavior in organizations.

How today's managers use the behavioral approach

The behavioral approach has largely shaped how today's organizations are managed. From the way that managers design jobs to the way that they work with employee teams to the way that they communicate, we see elements of the behavioral approach. Much of what the early OB advocates proposed and the conclusions from the Hawthorne studies have provided the foundation for our current theories of motivation, leadership, group behavior and development, and numerous other behavioral approaches.

Quantitative Approach

LEARNING OUTCOME
Describe the quantitative approach.

Although passengers bumping into each other when trying to find their seats on an airplane can be a mild annoyance for them, it's a bigger problem for airlines because lines get backed up, slowing down how quickly the plane can get back in the air. Based on research in space-time geometry, one airline innovated a unique boarding process called "reverse pyramid" that has saved at least 2 minutes in boarding time.[9] This is an example of the **quantitative approach**, which is the use of quantitative techniques to improve decision making. This approach also is known as *management science*.

The quantitative approach evolved from mathematical and statistical solutions developed for military problems during World War II. After the war was over, many of these techniques used for military problems were applied to businesses. For example, one group of military officers, nicknamed the Whiz Kids, joined Ford Motor Company in the mid-1940s and immediately began using statistical methods and quantitative models to improve decision making.

What exactly does the quantitative approach do? It involves applying statistics, optimization models, information models, computer simulations, and other quantitative techniques to management activities. Linear programming, for instance, is a technique that managers use to improve resource allocation decisions. Work scheduling can be more efficient as a result of critical-path scheduling analysis. The economic order quantity model helps managers determine optimum inventory levels.

Each of these is an example of quantitative techniques being applied to improve managerial decision making. Another area where quantitative techniques are used frequently is in total quality management.

A quality revolution swept through both the business and public sectors in the 1980s and 1990s.[10] It was inspired by a small group of quality experts, the most famous being W. Edwards Deming (pictured at right) and Joseph M. Juran. The ideas and techniques they advocated in the 1950s had few supporters in the United States but were enthusiastically embraced by Japanese organizations. As Japanese manufacturers began beating U.S. competitors in quality comparisons, however, Western managers soon took a more serious look at Deming's and Juran's ideas . . . ideas that became the basis for today's quality management programs.

   Total quality management, or **TQM**, is a management philosophy devoted to continual improvement and responding to customer needs and expectations. (See Exhibit MH-6.) The term *customer* includes anyone who interacts with the organization's product or services internally or externally. It encompasses employees and suppliers as well as the people who purchase the organization's goods or services. *Continual improvement* isn't possible without accurate measurements, which require statistical techniques that measure every critical variable in the organization's work processes. These measurements are compared against standards to identify and correct problems.

EXHIBIT MH-6
What Is Quality Management?

1. **Intense focus on the customer.** The customer includes outsiders who buy the organization's products or services and internal customers who interact with and serve others in the organization.
2. **Concern for continual improvement.** Quality management is a commitment to never being satisfied. "Very good" is not good enough. Quality can always be improved.
3. **Process focused.** Quality management focuses on work processes as the quality of goods and services is continually improved.
4. **Improvement in the quality of everything the organization does.** This relates to the final product, how the organization handles deliveries, how rapidly it responds to complaints, how politely the phones are answered, and the like.
5. **Accurate measurement.** Quality management uses statistical techniques to measure every critical variable in the organization's operations. These are compared against standards to identify problems, trace them to their roots, and eliminate their causes.
6. **Empowerment of employees.** Quality management involves the people on the line in the improvement process. Teams are widely used in quality management programs as empowerment vehicles for finding and solving problems.

How today's managers use the quantitative approach

No one likes long lines, especially residents of New York City. If they see a long checkout line, they often go somewhere else. However, at Whole Foods' first gourmet supermarkets in Manhattan, customers found something different—that is, the longer the line, the shorter the wait. When ready to check out, customers are guided into serpentine single lines that feed into numerous checkout lanes. Whole Foods, widely known for its organic food selections, can charge premium prices, which allow it the luxury of staffing all those checkout lanes. And customers are finding that their wait times are shorter than expected.[11] The science of keeping lines moving is known as queue management. And for Whole Foods, this quantitative technique has translated into strong sales at its Manhattan stores.

   The quantitative approach contributes directly to management decision making in the areas of planning and control. For instance, when managers make budgeting, queuing, scheduling, quality control, and similar decisions, they typically rely on quantitative techniques. Specialized software has made the use of these techniques less intimidating for managers, although many still feel anxious about using them.

Contemporary Approaches

As we've seen, many elements of the earlier approaches to management theory continue to influence how managers manage. Most of these earlier approaches focused on managers' concerns *inside* the organization. Starting in the 1960s, management researchers began to look at what was happening in the external environment *outside* the boundaries of the organization. Two contemporary management perspectives—systems and contingency—are part of this approach.

Systems theory is a basic theory in the physical sciences, but had never been applied to organized human efforts. In 1938, Chester Barnard, a telephone company executive, first wrote in his book, *The Functions of an Executive,* that an organization functioned as a cooperative system. However, it wasn't until the 1960s that management researchers began to look more carefully at systems theory and how it related to organizations.

A **system** is a set of interrelated and interdependent parts arranged in a manner that produces a unified whole. The two basic types of systems are closed and open. **Closed systems** are not influenced by and do not interact with their environment. In contrast, **open systems** are influenced by and do interact with their environment. Today, when we describe organizations as systems, we mean open systems. Exhibit MH-7 shows a diagram of an organization from an open systems perspective. As you can see, an organization takes in inputs (resources) from the environment and transforms or processes these resources into outputs that are distributed into the environment. The organization is "open" to and interacts with its environment.

How does the systems approach contribute to our understanding of management? Researchers envisioned an organization as being made up of "interdependent factors, including individuals, groups, attitudes, motives, formal structure, interactions, goals, status, and authority."[12] What this means is that as managers coordinate work activities in the various parts of the organization, they ensure that all these parts are working together so the organization's goals can be achieved. For example, the systems approach recognizes that, no matter how efficient the production department might be, the marketing department must anticipate changes in customer tastes and work with the product development department in creating products customers want or the organization's overall performance will suffer.

EXHIBIT MH-7

Organization as an Open System

Environment		
Organization		
Inputs	**Transformation Process**	**Outputs**
Raw Materials Human Resources Capital Technology Information	Employees' Work Activities Management Activities Technology and Operations Methods	Products and Services Financial Results Information Human Results
	Feedback	
	Environment	

MANAGEMENT HISTORY MODULE

In addition, the systems approach implies that decisions and actions in one organizational area will affect other areas. For example, if the purchasing department doesn't acquire the right quantity and quality of inputs, the production department won't be able to do its job.

Finally, the systems approach recognizes that organizations are not self-contained. They rely on their environment for essential inputs and as outlets to absorb their outputs. No organization can survive for long if it ignores government regulations, supplier relations, or the varied external constituencies upon which it depends.

How relevant is the systems approach to management? Quite relevant. Consider, for example, a shift manager at a Starbucks restaurant who must coordinate the work of employees filling customer orders at the front counter and the drive-through windows, direct the delivery and unloading of food supplies, and address any customer concerns that come up. This manager "manages" all parts of the "system" so that the restaurant meets its daily sales goals.

The early management theorists came up with management principles that they generally assumed to be universally applicable. Later research found exceptions to many of these principles. For example, division of labor is valuable and widely used, but jobs can become *too* specialized. Bureaucracy is desirable in many situations, but in other circumstances, other structural designs are *more* effective. Management is not (and cannot be) based on simplistic principles to be applied in all situations. Different and changing situations require managers to use different approaches and techniques. The **contingency approach** (sometimes called the *situational approach*) says that organizations are different, face different situations (contingencies), and require different ways of managing.

A good way to describe contingency is "if, then." *If* this is the way my situation is, *then* this is the best way for me to manage in this situation. It's intuitively logical because organizations and even units within the same organization differ—in size, goals, work activities, and the like. It would be surprising to find universally applicable management rules that would work in *all* situations. But, of course, it's one thing to say that the way to manage "depends

division of labor (job specialization)
The breakdown of jobs into narrow and repetitive tasks

industrial revolution
A period during the late eighteenth century when machine power was substituted for human power, making it more economical to manufacture goods in factories than at home

classical approach
First studies of management, which emphasized rationality and making organizations and workers as efficient as possible

scientific management
An approach that involves using the scientific method to find the "one best way" for a job to be done

therbligs
A classification scheme for labeling basic hand motions

general administrative theory
An approach to management that focuses on describing what managers do and what constitutes good management practice

principles of management
Fundamental rules of management that could be applied in all organizational situations and taught in schools

bureaucracy
A form of organization characterized by division of labor, a clearly defined hierarchy, detailed rules and regulations, and impersonal relationships

organizational behavior (OB)
The study of the actions of people at work

Hawthorne Studies
A series of studies during the 1920s and 1930s that provided new insights into individual and group behavior

quantitative approach
The use of quantitative techniques to improve decision making

total quality management (TQM)
A philosophy of management that is driven by continuous improvement and responsiveness to customer needs and expectations

system
A set of interrelated and interdependent parts arranged in a manner that produces a unified whole

closed system
Systems that are not influenced by and do not interact with their environment

open system
Systems that interact with their environment

contingency approach
A management approach that recognizes organizations as different, which means they face different situations (contingencies) and require different ways of managing

EXHIBIT MH-8

Popular Contingency Variables

Organization Size. As size increases, so do the problems of coordination. For instance, the type of organization structure appropriate for an organization of 50,000 employees is likely to be inefficient for an organization of 50 employees.

Routineness of Task Technology. To achieve its purpose, an organization uses technology. Routine technologies require organizational structures, leadership styles, and control systems that differ from those required by customized or nonroutine technologies.

Environmental Uncertainty. The degree of uncertainty caused by environmental changes influences the management process. What works best in a stable and predictable environment may be totally inappropriate in a rapidly changing and unpredictable environment.

Individual Differences. Individuals differ in terms of their desire for growth, autonomy, tolerance of ambiguity, and expectations. These and other individual differences are particularly important when managers select motivation techniques, leadership styles, and job designs.

on the situation" and another to say what the situation is. Management researchers continue working to identify these situational variables. Exhibit MH-8 describes four popular contingency variables. Although the list is by no means comprehensive—more than 100 different variables have been identified—it represents those most widely used and gives you an idea of what we mean by the term *contingency variable.* The primary value of the contingency approach is that it stresses there are no simplistic or universal rules for managers to follow.

So what do managers face today when managing? Although the dawn of the information age is said to have begun with Samuel Morse's telegraph in 1837, the most dramatic changes in information technology have occurred in the latter part of the twentieth century and have directly affected the manager's job. Managers now may manage employees who are working from home or working halfway around the world. An organization's computing resources used to be mainframe computers locked away in temperature-controlled rooms and only accessed by the experts. Now, practically everyone in an organization is connected—wired or wireless—with devices no larger than the palm of the hand. Just like the impact of the Industrial Revolution in the 1700s on the emergence of management, the information age has brought dramatic changes that continue to influence the way organizations are managed.

CHAPTER SUMMARY
by Learning Outcomes

Describe some early management examples.

Studying history is important because it helps us see the origins of today's management practices and recognize what has and has not worked. We can see early examples of management practice in the construction of the Egyptian pyramids and in the arsenal of Venice. One important historical event was the publication of Adam Smith's *Wealth of Nations*, in which he argued the benefits of division of labor (job specialization). Another was the industrial revolution where it became more economical to manufacture in factories than at home. Managers were needed to manage these factories and these managers needed formal management theories to guide them.

Explain the various theories in the classical approach.

Frederick W. Taylor, known as the "father" of scientific management, studied manual work using scientific principles—that is, guidelines for improving production efficiency—to find the one best way to do those jobs. The Gilbreths' primary contribution was finding efficient hand-and-body motions and designing proper tools and equipment for optimizing work performance. Fayol believed that the functions of management were common to all business endeavors but also were distinct from other business functions. He developed 14 principles of management from which many current management concepts have evolved. Weber described an ideal type of organization he called a bureaucracy, characteristics that many of today's large organizations still have. Today's managers use the concepts of scientific management when they analyze basic work tasks to be performed, use time-and-motion study to eliminate wasted motions, hire the best qualified workers for a job, and design incentive systems based on output. They use general administrative theory when they perform the functions of management and structure their organizations so that resources are used efficiently and effectively.

Discuss the development and uses of the behavioral approach.

The early OB advocates (Robert Owen, Hugo Munsterberg, Mary Parker Follett, and Chester Barnard) contributed various ideas, but all believed that people were the most important asset of the organization and should be managed accordingly. The Hawthorne Studies dramatically affected management beliefs about the role of people in organizations, leading to a new emphasis on the human behavior factor in managing. The behavioral approach has largely shaped how today's organizations are managed. Many current theories of motivation, leadership, group behavior and development, and other behavioral issues can be traced to the early OB advocates and the conclusions from the Hawthorne Studies.

Describe the quantitative approach.

The quantitative approach involves applications of statistics, optimization models, information models, and computer simulations to management activities. Today's managers use the quantitative approach, especially when making decisions, as they plan and control work activities such as allocating resources, improving quality, scheduling work, or determining optimum inventory levels. Total quality management—a management philosophy devoted to continual improvement and responding to customer needs and expectations—also makes use of quantitative methods to meet its goals.

Explain the various theories in the contemporary approach.

The systems approach says that an organization takes in inputs (resources) from the environment and transforms or processes these resources into outputs that are distributed into the environment. This approach provides a framework to help managers understand how all the interdependent units work together in order to achieve the organization's goals and that decisions and actions taken in one organizational area will affect others. In this way, managers can recognize that organizations are not self-contained, but instead rely on their environment for essential inputs and as outlets to absorb their outputs.

The contingency approach says that organizations are different, face different situations, and require different ways of managing. It helps us understand management because it stresses there are no simplistic or universal rules for managers to follow. Instead, managers must look at their situation and determine that *if* this is the way my situation is, *then* this is the best way for me to manage.

 To check your understanding of learning outcomes – go to **mymanagementlab.com** and try the chapter questions.

REVIEW AND DISCUSSION QUESTIONS

1. Explain why studying management history is important.
2. What early evidence of management practice can you describe?
3. Describe the important contributions made by the classical theorists.
4. What did the early advocates of OB contribute to our understanding of management?
5. Why were the Hawthorne Studies so critical to management history?
6. What kind of workplace would Henri Fayol create? How about Mary Parker Follett? How about Frederick W. Taylor?
7. Explain what the quantitative approach has contributed to the field of management.
8. Describe total quality management.
9. How do systems theory and the contingency approach make managers better at what they do?
10. How do societal trends influence the practice of management? What are the implications for someone studying management?

PREPARING FOR: My Career

MY TURN TO BE A MANAGER

- Choose two nonmanagement classes that you are currently enrolled in or have taken previously. Describe three ideas and concepts from those subject areas that might help you be a better manager.

- Read at least one current business article from any of the popular business periodicals each week for four weeks. Describe what each of the four articles is about and how each relates to any (or all) of the four approaches to management.

- Choose an organization with which you are familiar and describe the job specialization used there. Is it efficient and effective? Why or why not? How could it be improved?

- Can scientific management principles help you be more efficient? Choose a task that you do regularly (such as laundry, fixing dinner, grocery shopping, studying for exams, etc.). Analyze it by writing down the steps involved in completing that task. See if there are activities that could be combined or eliminated. Find the "one best way" to do this task! And the next time you have to do the task, try the scientifically managed way! See if you become more efficient (keeping in mind that changing habits isn't easy to do).

- How do business organizations survive for 100+ years? Obviously, they've seen a lot of historical events come and go! Choose one of these companies and research their history: Coca-Cola, Procter & Gamble, Avon, or General Electric. How has it changed over the years? From your research on this company, what did you learn that could help you be a better manager?

- Find the current top five best-selling management books. Read a review of the book or the book covers (or even the book!). Write a short paragraph describing what each book is about. Also, write about which of the historical management approaches you think the book fits into and how you think it fits into that approach.

- Pick one historical event from this century and do some research on it. Write a paper describing the impact that this event might be having or has had on how workplaces are managed.

- Steve's and Mary's suggested readings: Gary Hamel, *The Future of Management* (Harvard Business School Press, 2007); Malcolm Gladwell, *Blink* (Little, Brown and Company, 2005); James C. Collins, *Good to Great: Why Some Companies Make the Leap . . . and Others Don't* (Harper Business, 2001); Matthew J. Kiernan, *The Eleven Commandments of 21st Century Management* (Prentice Hall, 1996); and James C. Collins and

Jerry I. Porras, *Built to Last: Successful Habits of Visionary Companies* (Harper Business, 1994).

- Come on, admit it. You multitask, don't you? And if not, you probably know people who do. Multitasking is also common in the workplace. But does it make employees more efficient and effective? Pretend you're the manager in charge of a loan processing department. Describe how you would research this issue using each of the following management approaches or theories: scientific management, general administrative theory, quantitative approach, behavioral approach, systems theory, and contingency theory.

- In your own words, write down three things you learned in this module about being a good manager.

- Self-knowledge can be a powerful learning tool. Go to mymanagementlab.com and complete any of these self-assessment exercises: How Well Do I Respond to Turbulent Change? How Well Do I Handle Ambiguity? and What Do I Value? Using the results of your assessments, identify personal strengths and weaknesses. What will you do to reinforce your strengths and improve your weaknesses?

Let's Get Real:

Meet the Manager

Dana Robbins-Murray
Account Director
Caliber Group
Tucson, AZ

You'll be hearing more from this real manager throughout the chapter.

MY JOB:

I am an account director for Caliber Group, a full-service marketing/PR firm. My main responsibility is to work with our clients to determine what type of marketing or public relations they need to create better brand awareness and increase sales for their business.

BEST PART OF MY JOB:

Working with a large, diverse group of businesses that each have their own unique competitive environment, products or services to sell, and management style.

Understanding Management's Context:
Constraints and Challenges

LEARNING OUTCOMES

WORST PART OF MY JOB:

Budgets. In business, as in life, there are always budget limitations that we have to work within and still accomplish our goals.

BEST MANAGEMENT ADVICE EVER RECEIVED:

From my first boss—handle each piece of paper once. In the age of electronic correspondence you can relate this to e-mails as well. Basically the idea is to try to handle everything the first time around, so as not to waste time and energy. It's a hard mantra to practice but it's worthwhile if you can do it, at least most of the time.

"Trial by ice." That's how one analyst described the aftermath of the 2007 Valentine's Day ice and snowstorm that dealt a crushing blow to JetBlue Airways operations.[1] With passengers stranded for hours on its planes stuck on runways and some 1,000 of its flights cancelled, the resulting uproar from customers and from airline regulators forced the company to take a long hard look at itself. It was definitely a low point for JetBlue. Fast forward three years. JetBlue did everything it could to learn from that experience and to make itself better. A critical and significant piece in that process has been the company's culture, which has developed around five key values: safety, caring, integrity, fun, and passion.

CEO Dave Barger (on left in photo) knows how important an organization's culture can be. He says, "The hard product—airplanes, leather seats, satellite TVs, bricks and mortar—as long as you have a checkbook, they can be replicated. It's the culture that can't be replicated. . . . The human side of the equation is the most important thing we're doing." As JetBlue continues to grow, even during rough economic times, how can managers ensure that its culture continues?

Here's a company that recognizes how important culture is! JetBlue created a culture in which employees are treated with respect and are viewed as a core strategic asset. Since that almost catastrophic collapse of its system in 2007, the company has topped all airlines in J.D. Power's annual customer-service survey for five years running. Undoubtedly, its employees and the culture they work in have played a key role in that accomplishment.

In this chapter, we're going to look at culture and other important aspects of management's context. We'll examine the challenges in the external environment and discuss the characteristics of organizational culture. But before we address these topics, we first need to look at two perspectives on how much impact managers actually have on an organization's success or failure.

LEARNING OUTCOME
2.1
Contrast the actions of managers according to the omnipotent and symbolic views.

The Manager:
Omnipotent or Symbolic?

In February 2010, when Ford Motor Company surpassed General Motors in sales for the first time in at least 50 years, GM announced an overhaul in its top managers' ranks. GM's North American president said that "he could see clear as day that the mix and the structure of people weren't right and that these changes were necessary for GM to move faster and win."[2] Such a move shuffling managers is not all that uncommon in the corporate world, but why?

How much difference *does* a manager make in how an organization performs? The dominant view in management theory and society in general is that managers are directly responsible for an organization's success or failure. We call this perspective the **omnipotent view of management**. In contrast, others have argued that much of an organization's success or failure is due to external forces outside managers' control. This perspective is called the **symbolic view of management**. Let's look at each perspective to try and clarify just how much credit or blame managers should get for their organization's performance.

The Omnipotent View

In Chapter 1, we stressed how important managers were to organizations. Differences in an organization's performance are assumed to be due to decisions and actions of its managers. Good managers anticipate change, exploit opportunities, correct poor performance, and lead their organizations. When profits are up, managers take the credit and are rewarded with bonuses, stock options, and the like. When profits are down, top managers are often fired in the belief that "new blood" will bring improved results. For instance, the CEO of Cott Corporation was fired because some of its largest customers were threatening to leave and the company's share prices had declined sharply.[3] In this view, someone has to be held accountable when organizations perform poorly regardless of the reasons, and that "someone" is the manager. Of course, when things go well, managers also get the credit—even if they had little to do with achieving the positive outcomes.

This view of managers as omnipotent is consistent with the stereotypical picture of the take-charge business executive who overcomes any obstacle in seeing that the organization achieves its goals. And this view isn't limited to business organizations. It also explains turnover among college and professional sports coaches, who are considered the "managers" of their teams. Coaches who lose more games than they win are usually fired and replaced by new coaches who are expected to correct the poor performance.

The Symbolic View

In the 1990s, Cisco Systems was the picture of success. Growing rapidly, it was widely praised by analysts for its "brilliant strategy, masterful management of acquisitions and superb customer focus."[4] As Cisco's performance declined during the early part of the twenty-first century, analysts said that its strategy was flawed, its acquisition approach was haphazard, and its customer service was poor. Was declining performance due to the managers' decisions and actions, or was it due to external circumstances beyond their control? The symbolic view would suggest the latter.

The symbolic view says that a manager's ability to affect performance outcomes is influenced and constrained by external factors.[5] According to this view, it's unreasonable to expect managers to significantly affect an organization's performance. Instead, performance is influenced by factors over which managers have little control such as the economy, customers, governmental policies, competitors' actions, industry conditions, and decisions made by previous managers.

This view is labeled "symbolic" because it's based on the belief that managers symbolize control and influence.[6] How do they do that? By developing plans, making decisions, and engaging in other managerial activities to make sense out of random, confusing, and ambiguous situations. However, the actual part that managers play in organizational success or failure is limited according to this view.

In reality, managers are neither all-powerful nor helpless. But their decisions and actions are constrained. As you can see in Exhibit 2-1, external constraints come from the organization's environment and internal constraints come from the organization's culture.

EXHIBIT 2-1

Constraints on Managerial Discretion

LEARNING OUTCOME
Describe the constraints
and challenges facing
managers in today's external
environment.

2.2

The External Environment:
Constraints and Challenges

Despite the fact that appliance sales are expected to climb for the first time in four years, Whirlpool Corporation, which already shut down 10 percent of its production capacity, continues to cut costs and scale down capacity even more.[7] And it's not alone in its protective, defensive actions. The decade from 2000 to 2009 was a challenging one for organizations. For instance, some well-known stand-alone businesses at the beginning of the decade were acquired by other companies during this time, including Compaq (now a part of Hewlett-Packard), Gillette (now a part of Procter & Gamble), Anheuser-Busch (now a part of Anheuser-Busch InBev), and Merrill Lynch (now a part of Bank of America); others disappeared altogether, including Lehman Brothers, Circuit City, and Steve & Barry's (all now bankrupt) and WorldCom and Enron (both done in by ethics scandals).[8] Anyone who doubts the impact the external environment has on managing just needs to look at what's happened during the last decade.

The term **external environment** refers to factors and forces outside the organization that affect its performance. As shown in Exhibit 2-2, it includes several different components. The economic component encompasses factors such as interest rates, inflation, changes in disposable income, stock market fluctuations, and business cycle stages. The demographic component is concerned with trends in population characteristics such as age, race, gender, education level, geographic location, income, and family composition. The political/legal component looks at federal, state, and local laws, as well as global laws and laws of other countries. It also includes a country's political conditions and stability. The sociocultural component is concerned with societal and cultural factors such as values, attitudes, trends, traditions, lifestyles, beliefs, tastes, and patterns of behavior. The technological component is concerned with scientific or industrial innovations. And the global component encompasses those issues associated with globalization and a world economy. Although all these components pose potential constraints on managers' decisions and actions, we're going to take a closer look at two of them—the economic and demographic aspects. Then, we'll look at how changes taking place in those components constrain managers and organizations. We'll wrap up this section by examining environmental uncertainty and stakeholder relationships.

EXHIBIT 2-2

Components of External Environment

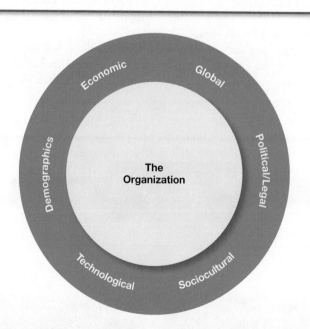

The Working World in 2020

More Diverse Than Ever

Two of the largest changes that we see happening in the makeup of the workforce in 2020 in the United States will be a significant increase in Hispanic and senior-citizen participation.

Hispanic-Americans are the fastest-growing segment of the U.S. population. They currently make up 15 percent of the population, although that number is forecasted to increase to 20 percent by 2025. In the southern part of the United States, the percentages will be higher. In cities such as Los Angeles, Phoenix, Tucson, El Paso, and Miami, more than a third of the population will be Hispanic. These general population percentages should translate equivalently to the labor force. The likelihood that you'll have a coworker whose first language is Spanish will be quite high.

You can also expect to see a graying of the workforce. By 2020, retiring at age 62 or 65 will have become passé. People are living longer and enjoying good health well into their 70s. Those who enjoy being actively engaged in a job won't want to give that up. On the other hand, there also will be those senior citizens who can't afford to retire and have to continue working to avoid financial strains. In fact, we saw this happening in the recession that began in 2008. Individuals who would like to have stepped away from their 8-to-5 jobs were happy to have a job and held onto that job. Now, envision that workplace where you'll also likely be working with many older (age 65+) coworkers.

Again, these two demographic changes foretell a workplace in which as a manager or as coworkers, you're going to be interacting and working with others who may not think or act or do things the way you would.

The Economic Environment

You know the economic context has changed when a blue-ribbon company like General Motors declares bankruptcy; the Organization for Economic Cooperation and Development predicts some 25 million unemployed individuals globally; 8.4 million jobs in the United States vanish; and the economic vocabulary includes terminology such as *toxic assets, collateralized debt obligations, TARP, bailouts, economic stabilization, wraparound mortgages,* and *stress tests.*[9] To understand what this economic environment is like, we need to look at the changes that have taken place and the impact of those changes on the way organizations are managed.

The economic crisis—called the "Great Recession" by some analysts—began with turmoil in home mortgage markets in the United States when many homeowners found themselves unable to make their payments. The problems soon affected businesses as credit markets collapsed. All of a sudden, credit was no longer readily available to fund business activities. It didn't take long for these economic troubles to spread worldwide.

What caused these massive problems? Experts cite a long list of factors that include excessively low interest rates for a long period of time, fundamental flaws in the U.S. housing market, and massive global liquidity. Businesses and consumers became highly leveraged, which wasn't an issue when credit was easily available.[10] However, as liquidity dried up, the worldwide economic system sputtered and very nearly collapsed. Now, massive foreclosures, a huge public debt burden in many countries, and continuing widespread social problems from job losses signal clear changes in the U.S. and global economic environments. Even as global economies began the slow process of recovery, most experts believed that the economic environment facing managers and organizations would not be as it was and would continue to constrain organizational decisions and actions.

The Demographic Environment

Baby Boomers. Gen Y. Post-Millennials. Maybe you've heard or seen these terms before. Population researchers refer to three of the more well-known age groups found in the U.S. population by these terms. Baby Boomers are those individuals born between 1946 and 1964.

Let's Get Real

During the recession, my company *has had to be more aggressive and spend more time selling our services and differentiating ourselves from the competition.*

external environment
Those factors and forces outside the organization that affect its performance

So much is written and reported about "boomers" because there are so many of them. The sheer numbers of people in that cohort means they've significantly affected every aspect of the external environment (from the educational system to entertainment/lifestyle choices to the Social Security system and so forth) as they cycle through the various life stages.

Gen Y (or the "Millennials") is typically considered to encompass those individuals born between 1978 and 1994. As the children of the Baby Boomers, this age group is also large in number and making its imprint on external environmental conditions as well. From technology to clothing styles to work attitudes, Gen Y is affecting organizational workplaces.

Then, we have the Post-Millennials—the youngest identified age group—basically teens and middle-schoolers.[11] This group has also been called the iGeneration, primarily because they've grown up with technology that customizes everything to the individual. Population experts say it's too early to tell whether elementary school-aged children and younger are part of this demographic group or whether the world they live in will be so different that they'll comprise a different demographic cohort.

Demographic age cohorts are important to our study of management because, as we said earlier, large numbers of people at certain stages in the life cycle can constrain decisions and actions taken by businesses, governments, educational institutions, and other organizations. But demographics doesn't only look at current statistics, it also looks to the future. For instance, recent analysis of birth rates shows that more than 80 percent of babies being born worldwide are from Africa and Asia.[12] And here's an interesting fact: India has one of the world's youngest populations with more males under the age of 5 than the entire population of France. And by 2050, it's predicted that China will have more people age 65 and older than the rest of the world combined.[13] Consider the impact of such population trends on organizations and managers in the future.

How the External Environment Affects Managers

Knowing *what* the various components of the external environment are and examining certain aspects of that environment are important to managers. However, understanding *how* the environment affects managers is equally as important. We're going to look at three ways the environment constrains and challenges managers—first, through its impact on jobs and employment; next, through the environmental uncertainty that is present; and finally, through the various stakeholder relationships that exist between an organization and its external constituencies.

JOBS AND EMPLOYMENT   As any or all external environmental conditions (economic, demographic, technological, globalization, etc.) change, one of the most powerful constraints managers face is the impact of such changes on jobs and employment—both in poor conditions and in good conditions. The power of this constraint became painfully obvious during the recent global recession as millions of jobs were eliminated and unemployment rates rose to levels not seen in many years. Economists now predict that about a quarter of the 8.4 million jobs eliminated in the United States during this most recent economic downturn won't be coming back and will instead be replaced by other types of work in growing industries.[14] Other countries face the same issues. Although such readjustments aren't bad in and of themselves, they do create challenges for managers who must balance work demands and having enough of the right types of people with the right skills to do the organization's work.

Not only do changes in external conditions affect the types of jobs that are available, they affect how those jobs are created and managed. For instance, many employers use flexible work arrangements to meet work output demand.[15] For instance, work tasks may be done by freelancers hired to work on an as-needed basis or by temporary workers who work full-time but are not permanent employees or by individuals who share jobs. Keep in mind that such responses have come about because of the constraints from the external environment. As a manager, you'll need to recognize how these work arrangements affect the way you plan, organize, lead, and control. This whole issue of flexible work arrangements has become so prevalent and part of how work is done in organizations that we'll address it in other chapters as well.

EXHIBIT 2-3

Environmental
Uncertainty Matrix

		Degree of Change	
		Stable	**Dynamic**
Degree of Complexity	**Simple**	**Cell 1** Stable and predictable environment Few components in environment Components are somewhat similar and remain basically the same Minimal need for sophisticated knowledge of components	**Cell 2** Dynamic and unpredictable environment Few components in environment Components are somewhat similar but are continually changing Minimal need for sophisticated knowledge of components
	Complex	**Cell 3** Stable and predictable environment Many components in environment Components are not similar to one another and remain basically the same High need for sophisticated knowledge of components	**Cell 4** Dynamic and unpredictable environment Many components in environment Components are not similar to one another and are continually changing High need for sophisticated knowledge of components

ASSESSING ENVIRONMENTAL UNCERTAINTY   Another constraint posed by external environments is the amount of uncertainty found in that environment, which can affect organizational outcomes. **Environmental uncertainty** refers to the degree of change and complexity in an organization's environment. The matrix in Exhibit 2-3 shows these two aspects.

The first dimension of uncertainty is the degree of change. If the components in an organization's environment change frequently, it's a *dynamic* environment. If change is minimal, it's a *stable* one. A stable environment might be one with no new competitors, few technological breakthroughs by current competitors, little activity by pressure groups to influence the organization, and so forth. For instance, Zippo Manufacturing, best known for its Zippo lighters, faces a relatively stable environment, with few competitors and little technological change. The main external concern for the company is probably the declining numbers of tobacco smokers, although the company's lighters have other uses and global markets remain attractive. In contrast, the recorded music industry faces a dynamic (highly uncertain and unpredictable) environment. Digital formats and music-downloading sites turned the industry upside down and brought high levels of uncertainty.

If change is predictable, is that considered dynamic? No. Think of department stores that typically make one-quarter to one-third of their sales in November and December. The drop-off from December to January is significant. But because the change is predictable, the environment isn't considered dynamic. When we talk about degree of change, we mean change that's unpredictable. If change can be accurately anticipated, it's not an uncertainty for managers.

The other dimension of uncertainty describes the degree of **environmental complexity**, which looks at the number of components in an organization's environment and the extent of the knowledge that the organization has about those components. An organization with fewer competitors, customers, suppliers, government agencies, and so forth faces a less complex and uncertain environment. Organizations deal with environmental complexity in various

environmental uncertainty
The degree of change and complexity in an organization's environment

environmental complexity
The number of components in an organization's environment and the extent of the organization's knowledge about those components

LEADER who made a difference

Hot Topic CEO Betsy McLaughlin has a way with words and a way of knowing what an "audience" needs.[16] At the closing session of one of the retailer's annual store manager meetings a few years ago, she rapidly spouted off George Carlin's famous "Seven Dirty Words" . . . something she had practiced for days. Her employees roared in approval! It's probably not too many CEOs that would use that monologue as closing comments even if it was in front of coworkers. But that's McLaughlin's style and her style has propelled her company to retail success. Hot Topic is definitely not mainstream, but neither is McLaughlin. One coworker describes her as "all fun and all business. On a scale of 1 to 10, McLaughlin is an 11 in fun and a 13 in business." One thing that McLaughlin excels at is her ability to take in and read the environment and to understand the demands of various stakeholders. When she travels for work, she is constantly getting inspiration by paying attention to her environment. It's a lesson that all managers can learn from, even if George Carlin isn't your cup of tea!

ways. For example, Hasbro Toy Company simplified its environment by acquiring many of its competitors.

Complexity is also measured in terms of the knowledge an organization needs about its environment. For instance, managers at E*Trade must know a great deal about their Internet service provider's operations if they want to ensure that their Web site is available, reliable, and secure for their customers. On the other hand, managers of college bookstores have a minimal need for sophisticated knowledge about their suppliers.

How does the concept of environmental uncertainty influence managers? Looking again at Exhibit 2-3, each of the four cells represents different combinations of degree of complexity and degree of change. Cell 1 (stable and simple environment) represents the lowest level of environmental uncertainty and cell 4 (dynamic and complex environment) the highest. Not surprisingly, managers have the greatest influence on organizational outcomes in cell 1 and the least in cell 4. Because uncertainty poses a threat to an organization's effectiveness, managers try to minimize it. Given a choice, managers would prefer to operate in the least uncertain environments. However, they rarely control that choice. In addition, the nature of the external environment today is that most industries today are facing more dynamic change, making their environments more uncertain.

MANAGING STAKEHOLDER RELATIONSHIPS What makes MTV a popular cable channel for young adults year after year? One factor is its success in building relationships with its various stakeholders: viewers, music celebrities, advertisers, affiliate TV stations, public service groups, and others. The nature of stakeholder relationships is another way in which the environment influences managers. The more obvious and secure these relationships, the more influence managers will have over organizational outcomes.

Stakeholders are any constituencies in the organization's environment that are affected by an organization's decisions and actions. These groups have a stake in or are significantly influenced by what the organization does. In turn, these groups can influence the organization. For example, think of the groups that might be affected by the decisions and actions of Starbucks—coffee bean farmers, employees, specialty coffee competitors, local communities, and so forth. Some of these stakeholders also, in turn, may influence decisions and actions of Starbucks' managers. The idea that organizations have stakeholders is now widely accepted by both management academics and practicing managers.[17]

Exhibit 2-4 identifies some of an organization's most common stakeholders. Note that these stakeholders include internal and external groups. Why? Because both can affect what an organization does and how it operates.

Why should managers even care about managing stakeholder relationships?[18] For one thing, it can lead to desirable organizational outcomes such as improved predictability of environmental changes, more successful innovations, greater degree of trust among stakeholders, and greater organizational flexibility to reduce the impact of change. But does it affect organizational performance? The answer is yes! Management researchers who have looked at this issue are finding that managers of high-performing companies tend to consider the interests of all major stakeholder groups as they make decisions.[19]

Another reason for managing external stakeholder relationships is that it's the "right" thing to do. Because an organization depends on these external groups as sources of inputs (resources) and as outlets for outputs (goods and services), managers need to consider their

EXHIBIT 2-4
Organizational Stakeholders

Employees

Customers

Unions

Social and Political
Action Groups

Shareholders

Organization

Competitors

Communities

Trade and Industry
Associations

Suppliers

Governments

Media

interests as they make decisions. We'll address this issue in more detail in the chapter on corporate social responsibility.

Organizational Culture:
Constraints and Challenges

LEARNING OUTCOME
Discuss the characteristics
and importance of
organizational culture.

Each of us has a unique personality—traits and characteristics that influence the way we act and interact with others. When we describe someone as warm, open, relaxed, shy, or aggressive, we're describing personality traits. An organization, too, has a personality, which we call its *culture*. And that culture influences the way employees act and interact with others.

What Is Organizational Culture?

Like JetBlue in our chapter opener, W. L. Gore & Associates, a company known for its innovative and high-quality fabrics used in outdoor wear and other products, also understands the importance of organizational culture. Since its founding in 1958, Gore has used employee teams in a flexible, nonhierarchical organizational arrangement to develop its innovative products. Associates (employees) at Gore are committed to four basic principles articulated by company founder Bill Gore: (1) fairness to one another and everyone you come in contact with; (2) freedom to encourage, help, and allow other associates to grow in knowledge, skill, and scope of responsibility; (3) the ability to make your own commitments and keep them; and (4) consulting other associates before taking actions that could affect the company's reputation. After a visit to the company, one analyst reported that an associate told him, "If you tell anybody what to do here, they'll never work for you again." That's the type of independent, people-oriented culture Bill Gore wanted. And it works well for the company—it's earned a position on *Fortune*'s annual list of "100 Best Companies to Work For" every year since the list began in 1998, one of only three companies to achieve that distinction.[20]

Let's Get Real

To me, organizational culture is
the environment and attitudes within the business. It is an organic entity and takes time to change.

stakeholders
Any constituencies in the organization's environment that are affected by an organization's decisions and actions

EXHIBIT 2-5

Dimensions of
Organizational
Culture

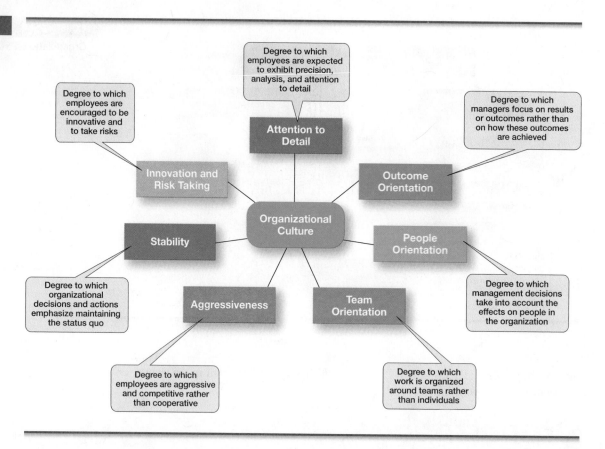

Organizational culture has been described as the shared values, principles, traditions, and ways of doing things that influence the way organizational members act. In most organizations, these shared values and practices have evolved over time and determine, to a large extent, how "things are done around here."[21]

Our definition of culture implies three things. First, culture is a *perception.* It's not something that can be physically touched or seen, but employees perceive it on the basis of what they experience within the organization. Second, organizational culture is *descriptive.* It's concerned with how members perceive the culture and describe it, not with whether they like it. Finally, even though individuals may have different backgrounds or work at different organizational levels, they tend to describe the organization's culture in similar terms. That's the *shared* aspect of culture.

Research suggests seven dimensions that can be used to describe an organization's culture.[22] These dimensions (shown in Exhibit 2-5) range from low to high, meaning it's not very typical of the culture (low) or is very typical of the culture (high). Describing an organization using these seven dimensions gives a composite picture of the organization's culture. In many organizations, one cultural dimension often is emphasized more than the others and essentially shapes the organization's personality and the way organizational members work. For instance, at Sony Corporation the focus is product innovation (innovation and risk taking). The company "lives and breathes" new product development and employees' work behaviors support that goal. In contrast, Southwest Airlines has made its employees a central part of its culture (people orientation). Exhibit 2-6 describes how the dimensions can create significantly different cultures.

Strong Cultures

All organizations have cultures, but not all cultures equally influence employees' behaviors and actions. Strong cultures—those in which the key values are deeply held and widely shared—have a greater influence on employees than do weaker cultures.

EXHIBIT **2-6**
Contrasting Organizational Cultures

Organization A

This organization is a manufacturing firm. Managers are expected to fully document all decisions, and "good managers" are those who can provide detailed data to support their recommendations. Creative decisions that incur significant change or risk are not encouraged. Because managers of failed projects are openly criticized and penalized, managers try not to implement ideas that deviate much from the status quo. One lower-level manager quoted an often-used phrase in the company: "If it ain't broke, don't fix it."

Employees are required to follow extensive rules and regulations in this firm. Managers supervise employees closely to ensure that there are no deviations. Management is concerned with high productivity, regardless of the impact on employee morale or turnover.

Work activities are designed around individuals. There are distinct departments and lines of authority, and employees are expected to minimize formal contact with other employees outside their functional area or line of command. Performance evaluations and rewards emphasize individual effort, although seniority tends to be the primary factor in the determination of pay raises and promotions.

Organization B

This organization is also a manufacturing firm. Here, however, management encourages and rewards risk taking and change. Decisions based on intuition are valued as much as those that are well rationalized. Management prides itself on its history of experimenting with new technologies and its success in regularly introducing innovative products. Managers or employees who have a good idea are encouraged to "run with it," and failures are treated as "learning experiences." The company prides itself on being market driven and rapidly responsive to the changing needs of its customers.

There are few rules and regulations for employees to follow, and supervision is loose because management believes that its employees are hardworking and trustworthy. Management is concerned with high productivity but believes that this comes through treating its people right. The company is proud of its reputation as being a good place to work.

Job activities are designed around work teams, and team members are encouraged to interact with people across functions and authority levels. Employees talk positively about the competition between teams. Individuals and teams have goals, and bonuses are based on achievement of outcomes. Employees are given considerable autonomy in choosing the means by which the goals are attained.

(Exhibit 2-7 contrasts strong and weak cultures.) The more employees accept the organization's key values and the greater their commitment to those values, the stronger the culture is. Most organizations have moderate to strong cultures; that is, there is relatively high agreement on what's important, what defines "good" employee behavior, what it takes to get ahead, and so forth. The stronger a culture becomes, the more it affects the way managers plan, organize, lead, and control.[23]

EXHIBIT **2-7**
Strong Versus Weak Cultures

Strong Cultures	Weak Cultures
Values widely shared	Values limited to a few people—usually top management
Culture conveys consistent messages about what's important	Culture sends contradictory messages about what's important
Most employees can tell stories about company history or heroes	Employees have little knowledge of company history or heroes
Employees strongly identify with culture	Employees have little identification with culture
Strong connection between shared values and behaviors	Little connection between shared values and behaviors

organizational culture
The shared values, principles, traditions, and ways of doing things that influence the way organizational members act

strong cultures
Organizational cultures in which the key values are intensely held and widely shared

EXHIBIT 2-8
Establishing and Maintaining Culture

Why is having a strong culture important? For one thing, in organizations with strong cultures, employees are more loyal than are employees in organizations with weak cultures.[24] Research also suggests that strong cultures are associated with high organizational performance.[25] And it's easy to understand why. After all, if values are clear and widely accepted, employees know what they're supposed to do and what's expected of them, so they can act quickly to take care of problems. However, the drawback is that a strong culture also might prevent employees from trying new approaches especially when conditions are changing rapidly.[26]

Where Culture Comes From and How It Continues

Exhibit 2-8 illustrates how an organization's culture is established and maintained. The original source of the culture usually reflects the vision of the founders. For instance, as we described earlier, W. L. Gore's culture reflects the values of founder Bill Gore. Company founders are not constrained by previous customs or approaches and can establish the early culture by articulating a vision of what they want the organization to be. Also, the small size of most new organizations makes it easier to instill that vision with all organizational members.

Once the culture is in place, however, certain organizational practices help maintain it. For instance, during the employee selection process, managers typically judge job candidates not only on the job requirements, but also on how well they might fit into the organization. At the same time, job candidates find out information about the organization and determine whether they are comfortable with what they see.

The actions of top managers also have a major impact on the organization's culture. For instance, at Best Buy, the company's chief marketing officer would take groups of employees for "regular tours of what the company called its retail hospital." Wearing white lab coats, employees would walk into a room with a row of real hospital beds and patient charts describing the ills affecting each of the company's major competitors. Now that each of those competitors has "succumbed to terminal illness" and is no longer in business, the room is darkened. Just think of the powerful message such a display would have on employees and their work.[27] Through what they say and how they behave, top managers establish norms that filter down through the organization and can have a positive effect on employees' behaviors. For instance, IBM's CEO Sam Palmisano wanted employees to value teamwork so he chose to take several million dollars from his yearly bonus and give it to his top executives based on their teamwork. He said, "If you say you're about a team, you have to be a team. You've got to walk the talk, right?"[28] However, as we've seen in numerous corporate ethics scandals, the actions of top managers also can lead to undesirable outcomes.

Finally, organizations help employees adapt to the culture through **socialization**, a process that helps new employees learn the organization's way of doing things. For instance, new employees at Starbucks stores go through 24 hours of intensive training that helps turn them into brewing consultants (baristas). They learn company philosophy, company jargon, and even how to assist customers with decisions about beans, grind, and espresso machines.

One benefit of socialization is that employees understand the culture and are enthusiastic and knowledgeable with customers.[29] Another benefit is that it minimizes the chance that new employees who are unfamiliar with the organization's culture might disrupt current beliefs and customs.

How Employees Learn Culture

Employees "learn" an organization's culture in a number of ways. The most common are stories, rituals, material symbols, and language.

Our employees learn our company's culture by *observing and interacting.*

STORIES Organizational "stories" typically contain a narrative of significant events or people including such things as the organization's founders, rule breaking, reactions to past mistakes, and so forth.[30] Managers at Southwest Airlines tell stories celebrating employees who perform heroically for customers.[31] Such stories help convey what's important and provide examples that people can learn from. At 3M Company, the product innovation stories are legendary. There's the story about the 3M scientist who spilled chemicals on her tennis shoe and came up with Scotchgard. Then, there's the story about Art Fry, a 3M researcher, who wanted a better way to mark the pages of his church hymnal and invented the Post-It Note. These stories reflect what made 3M great and what it will take to continue that success.[32] To help employees learn the culture, organizational stories anchor the present in the past, provide explanations and legitimacy for current practices, exemplify what is important to the organization, and provide compelling pictures of an organization's goals.[33]

RITUALS In the early days of Facebook, founder Mark Zuckerberg had an artist paint a mural at company headquarters showing children taking over the world with laptops. Also, he would end employee meetings by pumping his fist in the air and leading employees in a chant of "domination." Although the cheering ritual was intended to be something simply fun, other company executives suggested he drop it because it made him seem silly and they feared that competitors might cite it as evidence of monopolistic goals.[34] That's the power that rituals can have in shaping what employees believe is important. Corporate rituals are repetitive sequences of activities that express and reinforce the important values and goals of the organization. One of the best-known corporate rituals is Mary Kay Cosmetics' annual awards ceremony for its sales representatives. Looking like a cross between a circus and a Miss America pageant, the ceremony takes place in a large auditorium, on a stage in front of a large, cheering audience, with all the participants dressed in glamorous evening clothes. Salespeople are rewarded for sales goal achievements with an array of expensive gifts including gold and diamond pins, furs, and pink Cadillacs. This "show" acts as a motivator by publicly acknowledging outstanding sales performance. In addition, the ritual aspect reinforces late founder Mary Kay's determination and optimism, which enabled her to overcome personal hardships, start her own company, and achieve material success. It conveys to her salespeople that reaching their sales goals is important and through hard work and encouragement, they too can achieve success. The contagious enthusiasm and excitement of Mary Kay sales representatives make it obvious that this annual "ritual" plays a significant role in establishing desired levels of motivation and behavioral expectations, which is, after all, what management hopes an organization's culture does.

MATERIAL ARTIFACTS AND SYMBOLS When you walk into different businesses, do you get a "feel" for what type of work environment it is—formal, casual, fun, serious, and so forth? These reactions demonstrate the power of material symbols or artifacts in creating an organization's personality.[35] The layout of an organization's facilities, how employees

At Mary Kay Cosmetics, celebrations honoring employee achievements are rituals that help shape what employees believe is important. In addition to its annual awards ceremony, the company repeatedly honors employees who set personal goals and work hard to achieve them. In this photo, coworkers present a beautiful flower bouquet to Hao Xiaojuan during a party marking her being named National Sales Distributor at the Mary Kay offices in Shanghai, China. These corporate rituals of performance recognition are powerful activities that reinforce the inspirational "You Can Do It" spirit of company founder Mary Kay Ash.

by the numbers [39]

8 percent of executives surveyed said that fostering a shared understanding of values was an important capability.

51 percent of employees polled said they felt there was no clear path toward advancement at their current employer.

43 percent of employees polled said they believed they could only advance if they left their current job.

69 percent of employees polled said their company was taking the right steps to weather the recession.

55 percent of employees polled said that their company would emerge from the recession stronger than it was going into the recession.

78 percent of college freshmen in 2009 said that "to be well-off financially" was very important or essential.

42 percent of college freshmen in 1969 said that "to be well-off financially" was very important or essential.

45 percent of employees surveyed said that their companies' ability to innovate was below average when it came to moving quickly from generating ideas to selling products.

dress, the types of automobiles provided to top executives, and the availability of corporate aircraft are examples of material symbols. Others include the size of offices, the elegance of furnishings, executive "perks" (extra benefits provided to managers such as health club memberships, use of company-owned facilities, and so forth), employee fitness centers or on-site dining facilities, and reserved parking spaces for certain employees. At WorldNow, a business that helps local media companies develop new online distribution channels and revenue streams, an important material symbol is an old dented drill that the founders purchased for $2 at a thrift store. The drill symbolizes the company's culture of "drilling down to solve problems." When an employee is presented with the drill in recognition of outstanding work, he or she is expected to personalize the drill in some way and devise a new rule for caring for it. One employee installed a Bart Simpson trigger; another made the drill wireless by adding an antenna. The company's "icon" carries on the culture even as the organization evolves and changes.[36]

Material symbols convey to employees who is important and the kinds of behavior (for example, risk taking, conservative, authoritarian, participative, individualistic, and so forth) that are expected and appropriate.

LANGUAGE Many organizations and units within organizations use language as a way to identify and unite members of a culture. By learning this language, members attest to their acceptance of the culture and their willingness to help preserve it. For instance, at Cranium, a Seattle board game company, "chiff" is used to remind employees of the need to be incessantly innovative in everything they do. "Chiff" stands for "clever, high-quality, innovative, friendly, fun."[37] At Build-A-Bear Workshop stores, employees are encouraged to use a sales technique called "Strive for Five," in which they work to sell each customer five items. The simple rhyming slogan is fast becoming a powerful tool to drive sales.[38]

Over time, organizations often develop unique terms to describe equipment, key personnel, suppliers, customers, processes, or products related to its business. New employees are frequently overwhelmed with acronyms and jargon that, after a short period of time, become a natural part of their language. Once learned, this language acts as a common denominator that bonds members.

How Culture Affects Managers

Houston-based Apache Corp. has become one of the best performers in the independent oil drilling business because it has fashioned a culture that values risk taking and quick decision making. Potential hires are judged on how much initiative they've shown in getting projects done at other companies. And company employees are handsomely rewarded if they meet profit and production goals.[40] Because an organization's culture constrains what they can and cannot do and how they manage, it's particularly relevant to managers. Such constraints are rarely explicit. They're not written down. It's unlikely they'll even be spoken. But they're there, and all managers quickly learn what to do and not do in their organization. For instance, you won't find the following values written down, but each comes from a real organization.

- ▶ Look busy even if you're not.
- ▶ If you take risks and fail around here, you'll pay dearly for it.
- ▶ Before you make a decision, run it by your boss so that he or she is never surprised.
- ▶ We make our product only as good as the competition forces us to.
- ▶ What made us successful in the past will make us successful in the future.
- ▶ If you want to get to the top here, you have to be a team player.

The link between values such as these and managerial behavior is fairly straight-forward. Take, for example, a so-called "ready-aim-fire" culture. In such an organization, managers will study and analyze proposed projects endlessly before committing to them. However, in a "ready-fire-aim" culture, managers take action and then analyze what has been done. Or, say an organization's culture supports the belief that profits can be increased by cost cutting and that the company's best interests are served by achieving slow but steady increases in quarterly earnings. Managers are unlikely to pursue programs that are innovative, risky, long term, or expansionary. In an organization whose culture conveys a basic distrust of employees, managers are more likely to use an authoritarian leadership style than a democratic one. Why? The culture establishes for managers appropriate and expected behavior. For example, Banco Santander, whose headquarters are located 20 kilometers from downtown Madrid, has been described as a "risk-control freak." The company's managers adhered to "banking's stodgiest virtues—conservatism and patience." However, it's those values that triggered the company's growth from the sixth largest bank in Spain to the largest bank in the euro zone.[41]

As shown in Exhibit 2-9, a manager's decisions are influenced by the culture in which he or she operates. An organization's culture, especially a strong one, influences and constrains the way managers plan, organize, lead, and control.

EXHIBIT 2-9

Managerial Decisions Affected by Culture

Planning
- The degree of risk that plans should contain
- Whether plans should be developed by individuals or teams
- The degree of environmental scanning in which management will engage

Organizing
- How much autonomy should be designed into employees' jobs
- Whether tasks should be done by individuals or in teams
- The degree to which department managers interact with each other

Leading
- The degree to which managers are concerned with increasing employee job satisfaction
- What leadership styles are appropriate
- Whether all disagreements—even constructive ones—should be eliminated

Controlling
- Whether to impose external controls or to allow employees to control their own actions
- What criteria should be emphasized in employee performance evaluations
- What repercussions will occur from exceeding one's budget

2.4

Current Issues
in Organizational Culture

Nordstrom, the specialty retail chain, is renowned for its attention to customers. Nike's innovations in athletic shoe and apparel technology are legendary. Tom's of Maine is known for its commitment to doing things ethically and spiritually. How have these organizations achieved such reputations? Their organizational cultures have played a crucial role. Let's look at three current cultural issues: creating an innovative culture, creating a customer-responsive culture, and nurturing workplace spirituality.

Creating an Innovative Culture

You may not recognize IDEO's name, but you've probably used a number of its products. As a product design firm, it takes the ideas that corporations bring it and turns those ideas into reality. Some of its creations range from the first commercial mouse (for Apple) to the first standup toothpaste tube (for Procter & Gamble) to the handheld personal organizer (for Palm) to the Contour USB glucose meter (for Bayer AG). It's critical that IDEO's culture support creativity and innovation.[42] And you might actually own and use products from another well-known innovative organization—Apple.[43] From its founding in 1976 to today, Apple has been on the forefront of product design and development. They've brought us Mac, iPod, iTunes, iPhone, and the iPad tablet device that is changing the way you read materials such as this textbook. Although both these companies are in industries where innovation is critical to success, the fact is that any successful organization needs a culture that supports innovation. How important is culture to innovation? In a recent survey of senior executives, over half said that the most important driver of innovation for companies was a supportive corporate culture.[44]

What does an innovative culture look like? According to Swedish researcher Goran Ekvall, it would be characterized by the following:

- **Challenge and involvement** – Are employees involved in, motivated by, and committed to long-term goals and success of the organization?
- **Freedom** – Can employees independently define their work, exercise discretion, and take initiative in their day-to-day activities?
- **Trust and openness** – Are employees supportive and respectful to each other?
- **Idea time** – Do individuals have time to elaborate on new ideas before taking action?
- **Playfulness/humor** – Is the workplace spontaneous and fun?
- **Conflict resolution** – Do individuals make decisions and resolve issues based on the good of the organization versus personal interest?
- **Debates** – Are employees allowed to express opinions and put forth ideas for consideration and review?
- **Risk-taking** – Do managers tolerate uncertainty and ambiguity, and are employees rewarded for taking risks?[45]

Creating a Customer-Responsive Culture

Harrah's Entertainment, the world's largest gaming company, is fanatical about customer service and for good reason. Company research showed that customers who were satisfied with the service they received at a Harrah's casino increased their gaming expenditures by 10 percent and those who were extremely satisfied increased their gaming expenditures by 24 percent. When customer service translates into these types of results, of course managers would want to create a customer-responsive culture![46]

What does a customer-responsive culture look like?[47] Exhibit 2-10 describes five characteristics of customer-responsive cultures and offers suggestions as to what managers can do to create that type of culture.

Spirituality and Organizational Culture

What do Southwest Airlines, Chick-fil-A, Ford, Xerox, Timberland, and Hewlett-Packard have in common? They're among a growing number of organizations that have

EXHIBIT **2-10**

Creating a Customer-Responsive Culture

Characteristics of Customer-Responsive Culture	Suggestions for Managers
Type of employee	Hire people with personalities and attitudes consistent with customer service: friendly, attentive, enthusiastic, patient, good listening skills
Type of job environment	Design jobs so employees have as much control as possible to satisfy customers, without rigid rules and procedures
Empowerment	Give service-contact employees the discretion to make day-to-day decisions on job-related activities
Role clarity	Reduce uncertainty about what service-contact employees can and cannot do by continual training on product knowledge, listening, and other behavioral skills
Consistent desire to satisfy and delight customers	Clarify organization's commitment to doing whatever it takes, even if it's outside an employee's normal job requirements

embraced workplace spirituality. What is **workplace spirituality**? It's a culture in which organizational values promote a sense of purpose through meaningful work taking place in the context of community.[48] Organizations with a spiritual culture recognize that people have a mind and a spirit, seek to find meaning and purpose in their work, and desire to connect with other human beings and be part of a community. And such desires aren't limited to workplaces, as a recent study showed that college students also are searching for meaning and purpose in life.[49]

Workplace spirituality seems to be important now for a number of reasons. Employees are looking for ways to cope with the stresses and pressures of a turbulent pace of life. Contemporary lifestyles—single-parent families, geographic mobility, temporary jobs, technologies that create distance between people—underscore the lack of community that

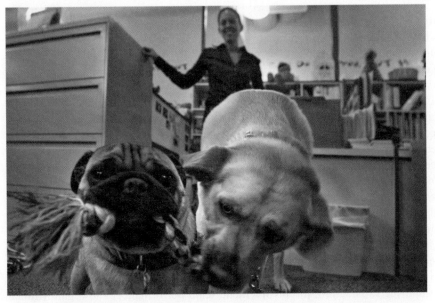

Since starting Build-A-Bear Workshop in 1997, company founder Maxine Clark has worked to create a supportive corporate culture that would inspire employee creativity and innovation. At company headquarters in Overland, Missouri, the work environment is playful, spontaneous, and fun. It's a place where dogs are welcome, bringing joy to employees like Katie Cernuto shown in this photo watching Jack, her yellow lab mix, play tug with Smash, another employee's dog. For a company whose mission is "to bring the Teddy Bear to life," a relaxed dress code and flexible work schedules add to a culture that employees describe as upbeat, happy, busy, and fun.

workplace spirituality
A culture where organizational values promote a sense of purpose through meaningful work that takes place in the context of community

many people feel. As humans, we crave involvement and connection. In addition, as baby boomers navigate mid-life issues, they're looking for something meaningful, something beyond the job. Others wish to integrate their personal life values with their professional lives. For others, formalized religion hasn't worked and they continue to look for anchors to replace a lack of faith and to fill a growing sense of emptiness. What type of culture can do all these things? What differentiates spiritual organizations from their nonspiritual counterparts? Research shows that spiritual organizations tend to have five cultural characteristics.[50]

1. *Strong sense of purpose.* Spiritual organizations build their cultures around a meaningful purpose. While profits are important, they're not the primary values of the organization. For instance, Timberland's slogan is "Boots, Brand, Belief," which embodies the company's intent to use its "resources, energy, and profits as a publicly traded footwear-and-apparel company to combat social ills, help the environment, and improve conditions for laborers around the globe . . . and to create a more productive, efficient, loyal, and committed employee base."[51]

2. *Focus on individual development.* Spiritual organizations recognize the worth and value of individuals. They aren't just providing jobs; they seek to create cultures in which employees can continually grow and learn.

3. *Trust and openness.* Spiritual organizations are characterized by mutual trust, honesty, and openness. Managers aren't afraid to admit mistakes. And they tend to be extremely upfront with employees, customers, and suppliers.

4. *Employee empowerment.* Managers trust employees to make thoughtful and conscientious decisions. For instance, at Southwest Airlines, employees—including flight attendants, baggage handlers, gate agents, and customer service representatives—are encouraged to take whatever action they deem necessary to meet customer needs or help fellow workers, even if it means going against company policies.

5. *Toleration of employee expression.* The final characteristic that differentiates spiritually based organizations is that they don't stifle employee emotions. They allow people to be themselves—to express their moods and feelings without guilt or fear of reprimand.

Critics of the spirituality movement have focused on two issues: legitimacy (Do organizations have the right to impose spiritual values on their employees?) and economics (Are spirituality and profits compatible?).

An emphasis on spirituality clearly has the potential to make some employees uneasy. Critics might argue that secular institutions, especially businesses, have no business imposing spiritual values on employees. This criticism is probably valid when spirituality is defined as bringing religion into the workplace.[52] However, it's less valid when the goal is helping employees find meaning in their work. If concerns about today's lifestyles and pressures truly characterize a growing number of workers, then maybe it is time for organizations to help employees find meaning and purpose in their work and to use the workplace to create a sense of community.

The issue of whether spirituality and profits are compatible is certainly important. Limited evidence suggests that the two may be compatible. One study found that companies that introduced spiritually based techniques improved productivity and significantly reduced turnover.[53] Another found that organizations that provided their employees with opportunities for spiritual development outperformed those that didn't.[54] Others reported that spirituality in organizations was positively related to creativity, ethics, employee satisfaction, job involvement, team performance, and organizational commitment.[55]

What Would You Do?

Let's Get Real:
My Response *to A Manager's Dilemma, page 44*

To ensure the culture continues, it has to be intertwined in every aspect of the business. The managers have to live it, but the employees have to believe it. The hardest challenge for JetBlue will be to steer the culture as the company grows. (I specifically use the word *steer* because I believe that a company culture is an organic entity, which changes with the company. You cannot control it directly but guide its direction.)

- JetBlue needs to continue to reinforce the culture using their five key values. The culture needs to be practiced every day in everything the company does, including the language used in memos and advertising, the hiring and promotion process, and the interaction with customers.

- A company culture cannot just come from the top down. Managers need to engage employees in the whole process. JetBlue should create employee teams who support and believe in the culture to help steer the culture as the company grows.

Management needs to listen to the employees and hear what they are saying, even if they don't want to hear it or don't believe what they hear. Use tools such as anonymous surveys, focus groups, and suggestion "boxes" to engage employees. Hearing the employees will help to gauge the culture of the company.

Dana Robbins-Murray
Account Director
Caliber Group
Tucson, AZ

CHAPTER SUMMARY
by Learning Outcomes

LEARNING OUTCOME **Contrast** the actions of managers according to the omnipotent and symbolic views.

According to the omnipotent view, managers are directly responsible for an organization's success or failure. The symbolic view argues that much of an organization's success or failure is due to external forces outside managers' control. The two constraints on manager's discretion are the organization's culture (internal) and the environment (external). Managers aren't totally constrained by these two factors since they can and do influence their culture and environment.

LEARNING OUTCOME **Describe** the constraints and challenges facing managers in today's external environment.

The external environment includes those factors and forces outside the organization that affect its performance. The main components include economic, demographic, political/legal, sociocultural, technological, and global. Managers face constraints and challenges from these components because of the impact they have on jobs and employment, environmental uncertainty, and stakeholder relationships.

LEARNING OUTCOME **Discuss** the characteristics and importance of organizational culture.

The seven dimensions of culture are attention to detail, outcome orientation, people orientation, team orientation, aggressiveness, stability, and innovation and risk taking. In organizations with strong cultures, employees are more loyal and performance tends to be higher. The stronger a culture becomes, the more it affects the way managers plan, organize, lead, and control. The original source of a culture reflects the vision of organizational founders. A culture is maintained by employee selection practices, the actions of top managers, and socialization processes. Also, culture is transmitted to employees through stories, rituals, material symbols, and language. These elements help employees "learn" what values and behaviors are important as well as who exemplifies those values. The culture affects how managers plan, organize, lead, and control.

LEARNING OUTCOME **Describe** current issues in organizational culture.

The characteristics of an innovative culture are challenge and involvement, freedom, trust and openness, idea time, playfulness/humor, conflict resolution, debates, and risk-taking. A customer-responsive culture has five characteristics: outgoing and friendly employees; jobs with few rigid rules, procedures, and regulations; empowerment; clear roles and expectations; and employees who are conscientious in their desire to please the customer. Workplace spirituality is important because employees are looking for a counterbalance to the stresses and pressures of a turbulent pace of life. Aging baby boomers and other workers are looking for something meaningful in their lives, an involvement and connection that they often don't find in contemporary lifestyles, and to meet the needs that organized religion is not meeting for some of them. Spiritual organizations tend to have five characteristics: strong sense of purpose, focus on individual development, trust and openness, employee empowerment, and toleration of employee expression.

PEARSON mymanagementlab   To check your understanding of learning outcomes **2.1** – **2.4** go to **mymanagementlab.com** and try the chapter questions.

REVIEW AND DISCUSSION QUESTIONS

1. Describe the two perspectives on how much impact managers have on an organization's success or failure.

2. Why is it important for managers to understand the external environmental components?

3. Describe an effective culture for (a) a relatively stable environment and (b) a dynamic environment. Explain your choices.

4. "Businesses are built on relationships." What do you think this statement means? What are the implications for managing the external environment?

5. Refer to Exhibit 2-6. How would a first-line manager's job differ in these two organizations? How about a top-level manager's job?

6. Classrooms have cultures. Describe your classroom culture using the seven dimensions of organizational culture. Does the culture constrain your instructor? How? Does it constrain you as a student? How?

7. Can culture be a liability to an organization? Explain.

8. Discuss the impact of a strong culture on organizations and managers.

9. Using Exhibit 2-8, explain how a culture is formed and maintained.

10. Explain why workplace spirituality seems to be an important concern.

PREPARING FOR: My Career

ETHICS DILEMMA

In many ways, technology has made all of us more productive. However, ethical issues do arise in how and when technology is used. Take the sports arena. All kinds of technologically advanced sports equipment (swimsuits, golf clubs, ski suits, etc.) have been developed that can sometimes give competitors/players an edge over their opponents.[56] We saw it in swim meets at the Beijing summer Olympics and on the ski slopes at the Vancouver winter Olympics. What do you think? Is this an ethical use of technology? What if your school (or country) was competing for a championship and couldn't afford to outfit athletes in such equipment and it affected your ability to compete? Would that make a difference? What ethical guidelines might you suggest for such situations?

SKILLS EXERCISE

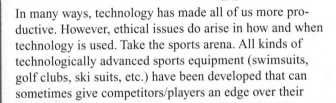

Developing Your Environmental Scanning Skill

About the Skill

Anticipating and interpreting changes that are taking place in the environment is an important skill that managers need. Information that comes from scanning the environment can be used in making decisions and taking actions. And managers at all levels of an organization need to know how to scan the environment for important information and trends.

Steps in Practicing the Skill

You can be more effective at scanning the environment if you use the following suggestions:[57]

1. *Decide which type of environmental information is important to your work.* Perhaps you need to know changes in customers' needs and desires or perhaps you need to know what your competitors are doing. Once you know the type of information that you'd like to have, you can look at the best ways to get that information.

2. *Regularly read and monitor pertinent information.* There is no scarcity of information to scan, but what you need to do is read those information sources that are pertinent. How do you know information sources are pertinent? They're pertinent if they provide you with the information that you identified as important.

3. *Incorporate the information that you get from your environmental scanning into your decisions and actions.* Unless you use the information you're getting, you're wasting your time getting it. Also, the more that you find you're using information from your environmental scanning, the more likely it is that you'll want to continue to invest time and other resources into gathering it. You'll see that this information is important to your being able to manage effectively and efficiently.

4. *Regularly review your environmental scanning activities.* If you find that you're spending too much time getting nonuseful information or if you're not using the pertinent information that you've gathered, you need to make some adjustments.

5. *Encourage your subordinates to be alert to information that is important.* Your employees can be your "eyes and ears" as well. Emphasize to them the importance of gathering and sharing information that may affect your work unit's performance.

Practicing the Skill

The following suggestions are activities you can do to practice and reinforce the behaviors associated with scanning the environment.

1. Select an organization with which you're familiar either as an employee or perhaps as a frequent customer. Assume that you're the top manager in this organization. What types of information from environmental scanning do you think would be important to you? Where would you find this information? Now assume that you're a first-level manager in this organization. Would the types of information you'd get from environmental scanning change? Explain.

2. Assume you're a regional manager for a large bookstore chain. Using the Internet, what types of environmental and competitive information were you able to identify? For each source, what information did you find that might help you do your job better?

WORKING TOGETHER
Team Exercise

Although all organizations face environmental constraints, the components in their external environments differ. Get into a small group with three to four other class members and choose one organization from two different industries.

Describe the external components for each organization. How are your descriptions different for the two organizations? How are they similar? Now, using the same two organizations, see if you can identify the important stakeholders for these organizations. As a group, be prepared to share your information with the class and to explain your choices.

MY TURN TO BE A MANAGER

- Find two current examples in any of the popular business periodicals of the omnipotent and symbolic views of management. Write a paper describing what you found and how the two examples you found represent the views of management.

- Choose an organization with which you're familiar or one that you would like to know more about. Create a table identifying potential stakeholders of this organization. Then, indicate what particular interests or concerns these stakeholders might have.

- Pick two organizations that you interact with frequently (as an employee or as a customer) and assess their culture by looking at the following aspects:
  - *Physical Design* (buildings, furnishings, parking lot, office or store design): Where are they located and why? Where do customers and employees park? What does the office/store layout look like? What activities are encouraged or discouraged by the physical layout? What do these things say about what the organization values?
  - *Symbols* (logos, dress codes, slogans, philosophy statements): What values are highlighted? Where are logos displayed? Whose needs are emphasized?

What concepts are emphasized? What actions are prohibited? Which are encouraged? Are there artifacts that are prominently displayed? What do those artifacts symbolize? What do these things say about what the organization values?

  - *Words* (stories, language, job titles): What stories are repeated? How are employees addressed? What do job titles say about the organization? Are jokes/anecdotes used in conversation? What do these things say about what the organization values?
  - *Policies and Activities* (rituals, ceremonies, financial rewards, policies for how customers or employees are treated) [Note: you may be able to assess this one only if you're an employee or know the organization well.] What activities are rewarded? Ignored? What kinds of people succeed? Fail? What rituals are important? Why? What events get commemorated? Why? What do these things say about what the organization values?

- If you belong to a student organization, evaluate its culture by answering the following: How would you describe the culture? How do new members learn the culture? How is the culture maintained? If you don't belong to a student organization, talk to another student who does and evaluate it using the same questions.

- Steve's and Mary's suggested readings: G. Barna, *Master Leaders* (Barna Books), 2009; Terrence E. Deal and Allan A. Kennedy, *Corporate Culture: The Rites and Rituals of Corporate Life* (Perseus Books Group, 2000); Edgar H. Schein, *The Corporate Culture Survival Guide* (Jossey-Bass, 1999); and Kim S. Cameron and Robert E. Quinn, *Diagnosing and Changing Organizational Culture* (Jossey-Bass, 2005).

- Find one example of a company that represents each of the current issues in organizational culture. Describe

what the company is doing that reflects its commitment to this culture.

- In your own words, write down three things you learned in this chapter about being a good manager.

- Self-knowledge can be a powerful learning tool. Go to mymanagementlab.com and complete any of these self-assessment exercises: What's the Right Organizational Culture for Me? How Well Do I Respond to Turbulent Change? Am I Experiencing Work/Family Conflict? Using the results of your assessments, identify personal strengths and weaknesses. What will you do to reinforce your strengths and improve your weaknesses?

CASE APPLICATION 1
Out of Control

With a worldwide recall of some 8 million cars and 51 deaths that U.S. regulators say have been caused by mechanical failures in its cars, Toyota Motor Corporation faces a corporate crisis of epic proportions.[58] What happened at the car company that had finally achieved the title of world's largest car maker? (It overtook General Motors in 2008.) What factors contributed to the mess it now found itself in?

At the core of Toyota's manufacturing prowess is the Toyota Production System (TPS), which has long been touted and revered as a model of corporate efficiency and quality. Four management principles (the 4P model) were at the core of TPS and guided employees: problem solving, people and partners, process, and philosophy. The idea behind these principles was that "Good Thinking Means Good Product." Taiichi Ohno, a long-time Toyota executive, is widely credited as the innovative genius behind TPS. During the 1950s, Ohno, along with a small core of other Toyota executives, developed several principles of car-making efficiency that became what is now known as lean manufacturing and just-in-time inventory management. "Ohno's ideas not only changed the auto industry, they changed late-twentieth-century manufacturing." At the very core of these concepts were attention to detail and a "noble frugality." However, over the years, it appears that Toyota's executives slowly lost the "purity" of that approach as the once-strong commitment to quality embedded in Toyota's corporate culture became lost in its aggressive moves to grow market share and achieve productivity gains.

From about 1995 to 2009, Toyota embarked on the "most aggressive overseas expansions in automotive history" and at the same time had a laser-like unparalleled focus on cutting costs. Four major cost-cutting and expansion initiatives severely strained organizational processes and employees. One initiative was localized

Toyota Motor Company President Akio Toyoda, grandson of the company's founder, bows in apology during a press conference where he announced a global vehicle recall. Toyoda's gesture of bowing is the Japanese way of publicly expressing remorse as an act of contrition to restore faith in the company's brands.

manufacturing. Starting in the late 1990s, Toyota established manufacturing hubs in Asia, North America, and Europe. Such an approach meant relying more on local suppliers and design teams to tailor cars to local tastes. Another initiative was called Construction of Cost Competitiveness for the 21st Century, or CCC21. It was a massive cost reduction program. Through an ongoing process of redesigning parts and working with suppliers, more than $10 billion of savings were achieved. The Value Innovation initiative was a more ambitious version of CCC21. Under this program, more savings were achieved by making the entire development process cheaper and by further cutting parts and production costs. And finally, the Global 15 initiative was a master global plan for attaining a 15 percent share of the global car market by 2010. As of mid-2010, Toyota had an 11.7 percent share of the worldwide car market. However, this "combination of high-speed global growth and ambitious cost cuts led to the quality lapses that tarnished the once-mighty brand." Toyota's president, Akio Toyoda apologized for the company's actions and said, "We pursued growth over the speed at which we were able to develop our people and our organization. I regret that this has resulted in the safety issues described in the recalls we face today, and I am deeply sorry for any accidents that Toyota drivers have experienced."

So what is Toyota doing to remedy its problems? In addition to the massive recall, the company's president says that it is setting up a system to respond more quickly to complaints. In fact, the automaker has promised to give regional executives a bigger role in issuing recalls based on local consumer complaints, although Mr. Toyoda says that the final decisions regarding recalls will continue to be made in Japan. The company is also holding twice-yearly global quality meetings and more frequent regional quality meetings. And finally, the company is re-committing itself to better training employees in quality control.

Discussion Questions

1. Using Exhibit 2-5 and the information from the case, describe the culture at Toyota Motor Corporation. Why do you think this type of culture might be important to a car maker?

2. How do you think a long-standing culture that had such a strong commitment to quality lost its ability to influence employee behaviors and actions? What lesson can be learned about organizational culture from this?

3. Do you think it was important for Mr. Toyoda to apologize for the company's decisions? Why? (Think in terms of the company's stakeholders.)

4. What could other organizations learn from Toyota's experiences about the importance of organizational culture?

CASE APPLICATION 2

Dressing Up

E ven when times are good, the department store industry is one of the toughest industries to compete in. Like many of its competitors, Kohl's Corporation struggles to find a way to continue its successes even when faced with a drastically changed external environment.[59] Based in Menomonee Falls, Wisconsin, Kohl's has more than 1,050 discount department stores in 49 states. The company has aggressively moved into the western and southern United States, although nearly a quarter of its stores are located in the Midwest. In 2010, the company had revenues of over $17.1 billion and profits of $991 million. One analyst has described Kohl's as "the best-positioned department store in this economy and one of the leading retailers with respect to inventory management, technological innovation, and merchandising and marketing execution." However, to continue its successes, it's important that Kohl's understand its external environment.

The retail shopping environment has changed. Customers became disenchanted with the shopping experience at many retail establishments. Long checkout lines, missing or vague product information, out-of-stock products, incorrect price tags, and scarce and often unknowledgeable sales staff made the shopping experience quite unpleasant. Local shopping malls and their anchor department stores lost much of their popularity with shoppers. Coupled with the economic and demographic shifts taking place, department stores faced big challenges.

Kohl's has done business differently than most department stores. Its approach is built around convenience and price. Its typical store is a box-like structure with one floor of merchandise under inexpensive lighting where shoppers use carts as they browse through the simple racks and shelves of clothing, shoes, and home apparel merchandise. The company is especially selective about its locations. Everything about the way Kohl's does business—who it sells to and how those customers shop—hinges on where it puts its stores. Its goal is to set up shop in the heart of "soccer mom country." It tries to avoid malls when looking at store sites, believing that its target customers—young mothers—typically don't have the time for a long drive to a mall location and certainly don't want the parking hassles when they do go shopping. Kohl's approach has been free-standing buildings with smaller parking lots in retailing power centers (a retailing destination where several large, specialty brand retailers often locate together) and other kinds of strip malls. For instance, the Kohl's store in Springfield, Missouri, is located adjacent to a Walmart Super Center, a Home Depot, a McDonald's, a Michael's hobby and crafts store, and other casual dining restaurants. The company's target market is women ages 25 to 54 who have children and whose annual household income is moderate ranging from $35,000 to $75,000. Even the merchandise selection offered at Kohl's is aimed at this target demographic by selling casual brands (such as Sag Harbor, Villager, Union Bay, Haggar, Jockey, HealthTex, and others) at low prices. To continue attracting this segment, Kohl's added a home furnishings collection called Casa Cristina (named for Cristina Saralegui, the host of a Spanish-language television show on Univision) and its own Food Network brand of dinnerware and cooking tools. In addition, the company has brought on board popular designers—including Vera Wang and Lauren Conrad—with lines of clothing, shoes, and home goods. Kohl's believed that their customers wanted to and were willing to purchase more fashionable merchandise selections. As one retail expert put it, "The chains have decided to design apparel on their own, ensuring that their lower-income customers can buy skinny jeans and satchel bags at the same time as shoppers at higher-end stores."

Although Kohl's has done well so far in a difficult industry, it faces some serious challenges. In addition to the uncertain external environment, competitors ranging from JCPenney and Sears to Macy's have copied its approach. Even specialty retailers such as Old Navy (a unit of Gap, Inc.) and American Eagle have shifted from trendy teenage fashion toward clothing that appeals to moms. And on the discount end, Walmart Stores has added national brands and improved the quality of its apparel.

Discussion Questions

1. According to the case, what external trends did managers at Kohl's have to deal with? In addition to these, what other external components might be important to these managers? (See Exhibit 2-2.) How might they keep track of changes in these components?

2. If you were a manager at Kohl's headquarters, what types of external information might you want? What if you were a manager of a local Kohl's store? What types of external information might you want?

3. Look at Exhibit 2-3. In what cell of the environmental uncertainty matrix would you place Kohl's? Why? How might Kohl's managers "manage" the environmental uncertainty?

4. What stakeholders do you think might be important to a company like Kohl's? What issues/concerns might be important to those stakeholders? Explain your choices.

Let's Get Real:

Meet the Manager

Cheryl Trewatha
Sr. Group Manager Quality Assurance
Target Corp.
Brooklyn Park, MN

You'll be hearing more from this real manager throughout the chapter.

MY JOB:

My team validates that Target branded product shipped from anywhere in the world meets U.S. federal, state, and Target quality, safety, and performance standards.

BEST PART OF MY JOB:

Because my team is responsible for handling the diverse group of products from the more than a dozen countries that we manufacture in, we are always facing new, unique, and ever-changing problems to solve.

Managing *in a* Global Environment

LEARNING OUTCOMES

WORST PART OF MY JOB:

Trying to interpret laws and regulations set by state and federal governing bodies around product manufacturing and compliance and apply them to a worldwide manufacturing base.

BEST MANAGEMENT ADVICE EVER RECEIVED:

Your team is your most valuable resource; be sure to maximize its potential.

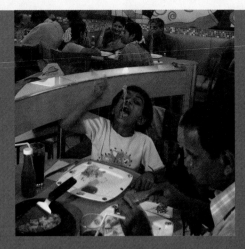

A Manager's Dilemma

Crunchy Taco—Potato. Paneer (cheese) and Potato Burritos.[1] These names may sound strange unless you're a customer at a Taco Bell restaurant in India. Yum Brands Inc. (the parent company of Taco Bell, Pizza Hut, and KFC) opened its first Taco Bell in Bangalore in early 2010. With an increasingly affluent consumer base, India is an attractive market for fast-food chains. Graham Allen, president of Yum's international division, said, "What we're seeing in India is similar to what we saw in China a decade ago. You have a young population with improving standards of living and an enthusiasm to embrace Western brands." However, Yum's push into India puts it into a battle with the other major fast-food companies for the wallets and appetites of consumers in one of the world's most populous countries.

Although 60 percent of Yum's profits now come from overseas markets, Graham Allen and Niren Chaudhary, the managing director of Yum's India business, recognize the challenges that face them in establishing a strong presence in India. One such challenge is understanding the cultural differences in managing employees. How will corporate processes and procedures need to change to accommodate its newly hired Indian employees?

What Would You Do?

Despite their vast experience in global markets, managers at Yum Brands still face challenges as they enter new markets. Even large successful organizations with talented managers (such as Yum Brands) don't always do it right. Despite these challenges, going global is something that most organizations want to do. A study of U.S. manufacturing firms found that companies that operated in multiple countries had twice the sales growth and significantly higher profitability than strictly domestic firms.[2] However, if managers don't closely monitor changes in their global environment or don't consider specific location characteristics as they plan, organize, lead, and control, they may find limited global success. In this chapter, we're going to discuss the issues managers face as they manage in a global environment.

Who Owns What?

One way to see how global the marketplace has become is to consider the country of ownership origin for some familiar products. You might be surprised to find that many products you thought were made by U.S. companies aren't! Take the following quiz[3] and then check your answers at the end of the chapter on page 95.

1. Tombstone and DiGiorno frozen pizzas are products of a company based in:
    a. Italy   b. United States   c. Canada   d. Switzerland

2. Lebedyansky juices are owned by a company based in:
    a. Japan   b. United Kingdom   c. United States   d. Russia

3. Rajah spices are products of a company based in:
    a. United States   b. Brazil   c. India   d. Switzerland

4. Tetley Tea is owned by a company located in:
    a. Great Britain   b. India   c. Japan   d. Spain

5. Volvo cars are products of a company based in:
    a. United States   b. United Kingdom   c. Japan   d. China

6. Dos Equis, Tecate, and Sol beer products are owned by a company based in:
    a. The Netherlands   b. Mexico   c. United States   d. Colombia

7. The company that produces Boboli pizza crust is based in:
    a. United States   b. Mexico   c. Italy   d. Spain

70

8. The parent company of Braun electric shavers is located in:
   a. Switzerland   b. Germany   c. United States   d. Japan

9. The company that owns Sephora Cosmetics retail stores is located in:
   a. Germany   b. Canada   c. France   d. United States

10. The digital ad firm Barbarian Group is owned by a company based in:
    a. United Kingdom   b. United States   c. Greece   d. South Korea

11. Lean Cuisine frozen meals are products of a company based in:
    a. Germany   b. United States   c. Switzerland   d. Brazil

12. The British newspaper, the *Independent,* is owned by a company based in:
    a. Russia   b. United Kingdom   c. South Africa   d. Canada

13. The company that makes French's mustard is based in:
    a. China   b. United Kingdom   c. Japan   d. United States

14. Eight O'Clock Coffee is owned by a company located in:
    a. India   b. Costa Rica   c. United States   d. Canada

15. Frédérick Fekkai & Co. hair care products are marketed by a company based in:
    a. Switzerland   b. United States   c. France   d. Italy

How well did you do? Were you aware of how many products we use every day that are made by companies *not* based in the United States? Probably not! Most of us don't fully appreciate the truly global nature of today's marketplace.

What's Your Global Perspective?

3.1

LEARNING OUTCOME
Contrast ethnocentric, polycentric, and geocentric attitudes toward global business.

It's not unusual for Germans, Italians, or Indonesians to speak three or four languages. "More than half of all primary school children in China now learn English and the number of English speakers in India and China—500 million—now exceeds the total number of mother-tongue English speakers elsewhere in the world." On the other hand, most U.S. children study only English in school—only 24,000 are studying Chinese. And only 22 percent of the population in the United States speaks a language other than English.[4] Americans tend to think of English as the only international business language and don't see a need to study other languages. This could lead to future problems as a major research report commissioned by the British Council says that the "competitiveness of both Britain and the United States is being undermined" by only speaking English.[5]

Monolingualism is one sign that a nation suffers from **parochialism**—viewing the world solely through one's own eyes and perspectives.[6] People with a parochial attitude do not recognize that others have different ways of living and working. They ignore others' values and customs and rigidly apply an attitude of "ours is better than theirs" to foreign cultures. This type of narrow, restricted attitude is one approach that managers might take, but isn't the only one.[7] In fact, there are three possible global attitudes. Let's look at each more closely.

First, an **ethnocentric attitude** is the parochialistic belief that the best work approaches and practices are those of the *home* country (the country in which the company's headquarters are located). Managers with an ethnocentric attitude believe that people in foreign countries don't have the needed skills, expertise, knowledge, or experience to make the best business decisions as people in the home country do. They don't trust foreign employees with key decisions or technology.

parochialism
Viewing the world solely through your own perspectives, leading to an inability to recognize differences between people

ethnocentric attitude
The parochialistic belief that the best work approaches and practices are those of the home country

LEADER who made a difference

She was recently named, for the fourth year straight, the Most Powerful Woman in Business by *Fortune* magazine and was named one of the 100 most powerful women in the world by *Forbes* magazine.[9] "She" is Indra Nooyi, CEO of PepsiCo. Born in India, Ms. Nooyi joined PepsiCo as head of corporate strategy in 1994 and moved quickly up the ladder to become chief executive officer. In 2007, she also assumed the role of chairman of PepsiCo's board of directors. As the CEO of a large American company, Nooyi recognizes how important her company's global business operations are. On a recent trip to China, a critical market for PepsiCo, Nooyi didn't take the usual "CEO tour" of conference rooms, but spent 10 days immersing herself in China. She says, "I wanted to look at how people live, how they eat, what the growth possibilities are." Here's a leader who knows what it will take to succeed in today's global environment.

Next, a **polycentric attitude** is the view that employees in the *host* country (the foreign country in which the organization is doing business) know the best work approaches and practices for running their business. Managers with this attitude view every foreign operation as different and hard to understand. Thus, they're likely to let employees there figure out how best to do things.

The final type of global attitude managers might have is a **geocentric attitude**, a *world-oriented* view that focuses on using the best approaches and people from around the globe. Managers with this type of attitude have a global view and look for the best approaches and people regardless of origin. For instance, Carlos Ghosn, CEO of Nissan and Renault, was born in Brazil to Lebanese parents, educated in France, and speaks four languages fluently. He could very well be the "model of the modern major corporate leader in a globalized world bestraddled by multinational companies."[8] Ghosn's background and perspective have given him a much broader understanding of what it takes to manage in a global environment, something that is characteristic of the geocentric attitude. A geocentric attitude requires eliminating parochial attitudes and developing an understanding of cross-cultural differences. That's the type of approach successful managers will need in today's global environment.

LEARNING OUTCOME
Discuss the importance of
regional trading alliances and
global trade mechanisms.

3.2 Understanding the Global Environment

One important feature of today's global environment is global trade which, if you remember history class, isn't new. Countries and organizations have been trading with each other for centuries.[10] And it continues strong today, as we saw in the chapter-opening quiz. Global trade today is shaped by two forces: regional trading alliances and trade mechanisms that ensure that global trade can happen.

Regional Trading Alliances

Global competition once was considered country against country—the United States versus Japan, France versus Germany, Mexico versus Canada, and so on. Now, global competition is shaped by regional trading agreements including the European Union (EU), North American Free Trade Agreement (NAFTA), the Association of Southeast Asian Nations (ASEAN), and others.

THE EUROPEAN UNION. The **European Union (EU)** is an economic and political partnership of 27 democratic European countries. (See Exhibit 3-1.) Three countries (Croatia, Macedonia, and Turkey) have applied for membership and analysts predict that Croatia will be the next to gain membership in 2012 or 2013.[11] When the 12 original members formed the EU in 1992, the primary motivation was to reassert the region's economic position against the United States and Japan. Before then, each European nation had border controls, taxes, and subsidies; nationalistic policies; and protected industries. These barriers to travel, employment, investment, and trade prevented European companies from developing economic efficiencies. Now with these barriers removed, the economic power represented by the EU is considerable. Its current membership covers a population base of nearly half a billion people and accounts for approximately 31 percent of the world's total economic output.[12]

EXHIBIT **3-1**
European Union
Map

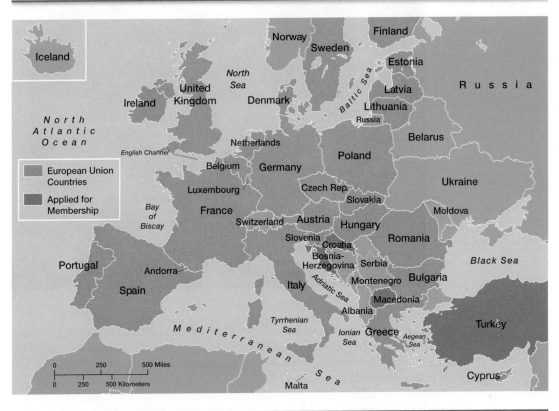

Another step toward full unification occurred when the common European currency, the **euro**, was adopted. The euro is currently in use in 16 of the 27 member states and all new member countries must adopt the euro. Only Denmark, the United Kingdom, and Sweden have been allowed to opt out of using the euro.[13] Another push in unification has been attempts to develop a unified European constitution. EU leaders struggled for nearly a decade to enact a treaty designed to strengthen the EU and give it a full-time president. The so-called Lisbon Treaty (or Reform Treaty) has one remaining hurdle—a signature from the president of the Czech Republic.[14] This treaty would provide EU with a common legal framework and the tools to meet the challenges of a changing world including climatic and demographic changes, globalization, security, and energy. And backers feel the new structure would help strengthen the EU's common foreign policy. Many believe that a more unified Europe could have more power and say in the global arena. As the former Italian prime minister and European Commission president said, "Europe has lost and lost and lost weight in the world."[15]

The last couple of years were difficult economically for the EU and its members, like it was for many global regions. "The traditional concept of 'solidarity' is being undermined by protectionist pressures in some member countries and the rigors of maintaining a common currency for a region that has diverse economic needs."[16] Some analysts believe that the EU is at a pivotal point. "They can spur growth across the region by following through on long-overdue pledges to trim benefits and free up labor markets. Or they can

polycentric attitude
The view that the managers in the host country know the best work approaches and practices for running their business

geocentric attitude
A world-oriented view that focuses on using the best approaches and people from around the globe

European Union (EU)
A union of 27 European nations created as a unified economic and trade entity

euro
A single common European currency

Since NAFTA went into effect in 1994, trade between Mexico and Canada has grown fivefold. Canadian-based aircraft maker Bombardier is boosting Mexico's aerospace industry by adding the country to its global manufacturing network. At a new plant built by Bombardier in Queretaro, Mexico, employees produce electrical harnesses (shown in this photo), fuselages, and flight controls for all Bombardier aircraft in production. The company also plans to build a new facility in Queretaro to make the composite structure for its new Learjet 85 business jet. The plants in Mexico help Bombardier reduce production costs and put the company closer to the growing demand for its aircraft in the Latin American markets.

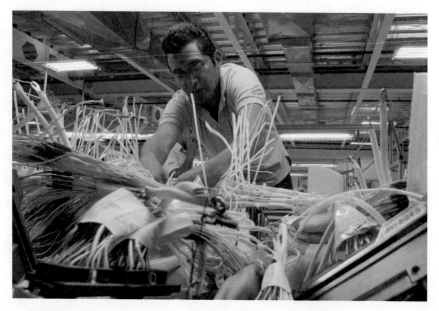

face a decade of economic stagnation."[17] Another major issue faced by the 16 euro zone members—the massive debt crisis in Greece. But leaders bridged sharp philosophical divides and joined forces with the International Monetary Fund to forge an agreement to bail out Greece as its debt troubles intensified.[18]

The euro zone is the world's largest unified economy after the United States and a major source of world demand for goods and services. Therefore, the importance of this regional trading alliance will continue to evolve as EU members work together to assert the region's economic power with successful European businesses continuing to play a crucial role in the global economy.

NORTH AMERICAN FREE TRADE AGREEMENT (NAFTA) AND OTHER LATIN AMERICAN AGREEMENTS. When agreements in key issues covered by the **North American Free Trade Agreement (NAFTA)** were reached by the Mexican, Canadian, and U.S. governments in 1992, a vast economic bloc was created. As of 2010, it remains the largest trade bloc in the world in terms of combined GDP of its members.[19] Between 1994, when NAFTA went into effect, and 2007 (the most recent year for complete statistics), merchandise trade between the United States and Canada and Mexico increased from 4.4 percent to 6.6 percent.[20] Eliminating the barriers to free trade (tariffs, import licensing requirements, customs user fees) strengthened the economic power of all three countries, but not equally. Mexico, especially, has struggled to prosper from free trade. Although Mexico's exports increased dramatically under NAFTA (quintupling to $292 billion during 2008), large numbers of people still migrate to the United States in search of jobs and prosperity. The dream of a richer and more prosperous Mexico has not been realized.[21] And the recent worldwide recession has not helped the situation either. However, despite the criticisms and the challenges, the North American trading bloc remains a powerful force in today's global economy.

Other Latin American nations have become part of free trade blocs, as well. Colombia, Mexico, and Venezuela led the way when all three signed an economic pact in 1994 eliminating import duties and tariffs. Another agreement, the U.S.–Central America Free Trade Agreement (CAFTA), promotes trade liberalization between the United States and five Central American countries: Costa Rica, El Salvador, Guatemala, Honduras, and Nicaragua. However, only El Salvador and Costa Rica have joined. The other countries have yet to change laws to be in line with the agreement.[22] The United States also signed a trade deal with Colombia that is said to be the "largest Washington has concluded with a Latin American country since signing" NAFTA.[23] Also, negotiators from 34 countries in the Western Hemisphere continue work on a Free Trade Area of the

Americas (FTAA) agreement, which was to have been operational no later than 2005, a missed targeted deadline. Leaders of these nations have yet to reach any agreement, leaving the future of the FTAA up in the air.[24] However, another free trade bloc of 10 South American countries known as the Southern Common Market or Mercosur already exists. Some South Americans see Mercosur as an effective way to combine resources to better compete against other global economic powers, especially the EU and NAFTA. With the future of FTAA highly doubtful, this regional alliance could take on new importance.

ASSOCIATION OF SOUTHEAST ASIAN NATIONS (ASEAN). The **Association of Southeast Asian Nations (ASEAN)** is a trading alliance of 10 Southeast Asian nations. (See Exhibit 3-2.) The ASEAN region has a population over 591 million with a combined GDP of US$1.5 trillion.[25] In addition to these 10 nations, leaders from a group dubbed ASEAN+3, which include China, Japan, and South Korea, have met to discuss trade issues. Also, leaders from India, Australia, and New Zealand have participated in trade talks with ASEAN+3 as well. The main issue with creating a trade bloc of all 16 nations has been the lack of any push toward regional integration. Despite the Asian culture's emphasis on consensus building, "ASEAN's biggest problem is that individual members haven't been willing to sacrifice for the common good."[26] Although Southeast Asian leaders agree that closer regional integration would help economic growth, the large differences in wealth among ASEAN members have made it "difficult to create common standards because national standards remain so far apart."[27] However, the challenges brought on by the recent worldwide recession, which adversely affected many countries in this region, triggered greater interest in pushing for integration. In fact, on January 1, 2010, China and ASEAN launched an ambitious free trade agreement, making it the world's third largest trade bloc.[28] In addition to these free trade alliances, it's hoped that by 2015, an established ASEAN economic community will allow goods, skilled workers, and capital to move freely among member countries.

EXHIBIT 3-2

ASEAN Map

Source: Based on J. McClenahen and T. Clark, "ASEAN at Work," *IW*, May 19, 1997, p. 42.

North American Free Trade Agreement (NAFTA)
An agreement among the Mexican, Canadian, and U.S. governments in which barriers to trade have been eliminated

Association of Southeast Asian Nations (ASEAN)
A trading alliance of 10 Southeast Asian nations

Despite the barriers and challenges, progress toward regional integration continues. This fast-growing region means ASEAN and other Asian trade alliances will be increasingly important globally with an impact that eventually could rival that of both NAFTA and the EU.

OTHER TRADE ALLIANCES. Other regions around the world have developed regional trading alliances as well. For instance, the 53-nation African Union (AU), which came into existence in 2002, has the vision of "building an integrated, prosperous and peaceful Africa."[29] Members of this alliance have created an economic development plan to achieve greater unity among Africa's nations. Like members of other trade alliances, these countries hope to gain economic, social, cultural, and trade benefits from their association. Such cooperation couldn't be more important as Africa's economic output is booming like never before. GDP growth rates have been averaging 4.8 percent, the highest rate outside Asia, with most of that growth coming domestically. In addition, Africa has been experiencing a "virtually unprecedented period of political stability with governments steadily deregulating industries and developing infrastructure."[30]

Five east African nations—Burundi, Kenya, Rwanda, Tanzania, and Uganda—have formed a common market called the East African Community (EAC).[31] Under this agreement, goods can be sold across borders without tariffs. The next step for the EAC will be monetary union, although that will take time to implement.

Finally, the South Asian Association for Regional Cooperation (SAARC) composed of eight member states (India, Pakistan, Sri Lanka, Bangladesh, Bhutan, Nepal, the Maldives, and Afghanistan) began eliminating tariffs in 2006.[32] Its aim, like all the other regional trading alliances, is to allow free flow of goods and services.

The preceding discussion indicates that global trade is alive and well. Regional trade alliances continue to be developed in areas where member countries believe it's in their best interest economically and globally to band together and strengthen their economic position.

Global Trade Mechanisms

Global trade among nations doesn't just happen on its own. As trade issues arise, global trade systems ensure that trade continues efficiently and effectively. Indeed, one of the realities of globalization is the interdependence of countries—that is, what happens in one can impact others, good or bad. For example, the financial crisis that started in the United States in 2008 threw the global economy into a tailspin. Although things spiraled precariously out of control, it didn't completely collapse. Why? Because governmental interventions and trade and financial mechanisms helped avert a potential crisis. We're going to look at four important global trade mechanisms: the World Trade Organization, the International Monetary Fund, the World Bank Group, and the Organization for Economic Cooperation and Development.

WORLD TRADE ORGANIZATION. The **World Trade Organization (WTO)** is a global organization of 153 countries that deals with the rules of trade among nations.[33] Formed in 1995, the WTO evolved from the General Agreement on Tariffs and Trade (GATT), a trade agreement in effect since the end of World War II. Today, the WTO is the only *global* organization that deals with trade rules among nations. Its membership consists of 153 member countries and 30 observer governments (which have a specific time frame within which they must apply to become members). The goal of the WTO is to help countries conduct trade through a system of rules. Although critics have staged vocal protests against the WTO claiming that global trade destroys jobs and the natural environment, it appears to play an important role in monitoring, promoting, and protecting global trade. For instance, the WTO recently ruled that the European plane maker Airbus received improper European Union subsidies for the A380 super jumbo jet and several other airplanes, hurting its American rival, Boeing.[34] Airbus has the right to appeal the ruling, but even after appealing, any member ultimately found to have provided improper subsidies is obliged to bring its policies into compliance with global trade rules. Failure to comply could bring trade

Let's Get Real

F2F

It's important to know about global business because *all businesses are impacted by the global market place. If you don't directly import the products or services you sell you are mostly likely competing against an imported product.*

sanctions. In another recent news story, the U.S. government is weighing whether to file a WTO complaint against China's Internet censorship.[35] In addition, the WTO played a pivotal role in keeping global trade active during the global economic crisis. WTO Director-General Pascal Lamy said, "During these difficult times, the multilateral trading system has once again proven its value. WTO rules and principles have assisted governments in keeping markets open and they now provide a platform from which trade can grow as the global economy improves."[36] These examples illustrate the types of trade issues with which the WTO deals. Such issues are best handled by an organization such as the WTO and it has played, without a doubt, an important role in promoting and protecting global trade.

INTERNATIONAL MONETARY FUND AND WORLD BANK GROUP. Two other important and necessary global trade mechanisms include the International Monetary Fund and the World Bank Group. The **International Monetary Fund (IMF)** is an organization of 185 countries that promotes international monetary cooperation and provides member countries with policy advice, temporary loans, and technical assistance to establish and maintain financial stability and to strengthen economies.[37] The **World Bank Group** is a group of five closely associated institutions, all owned by its member countries, that provides vital financial and technical assistance to developing countries around the world. The goal of the World Bank Group is to promote long-term economic development and poverty reduction by providing members with technical and financial support.[38] For instance, during the recent global recession, financial commitments by the World Bank Group reached $100 billion as it helped nations respond to and recover from the economic downturn.[39] Both entities have an important role in supporting and promoting global business.

ORGANIZATION FOR ECONOMIC COOPERATION AND DEVELOPMENT (OECD). The forerunner of the OECD, the Organization for European Economic Cooperation, was formed in 1947 to administer American and Canadian aid under the Marshall Plan for the reconstruction of Europe after World War II. Today, the **Organization for Economic Cooperation and Development (OECD)** is a Paris-based international economic organization whose mission is to help its 30 member countries achieve sustainable economic growth and employment and raise the standard of living in member countries while maintaining financial stability in order to contribute to the development of the world economy.[40] When needed, the OECD gets involved in negotiations with OECD countries so they can agree on "rules of the game" for international cooperation. One current focus is combating small-scale bribery in overseas commerce. The OECD says such "so-called facilitation payments are corrosive . . . particularly on sustainable economic development and the rule of law."[41] With a long history of facilitating economic growth around the globe, the OECD now shares its expertise and accumulated experiences with more than 70 developing and emerging market economies.

Doing Business Globally

Daimler, Nissan Motor, and Renault are part of a strategic partnership that is sharing small-car technology and power trains—an arrangement that all three automakers say will allow them to better compete in an environment where cutting costs is crucial. Until he moved to Japan, Arturo Vega, a Spanish-language teacher, had no idea that the Sofyl brand of yogurt he always bought in his native Mexico was actually made by a Japanese company called Yakult Honsha. Reckitt Benckiser, the U.K.-based maker of consumer products (Lysol, Woolite, and French's mustard are just a few of its products), has operations in more than

---

by the numbers[42]

93 percent of public middle and high schools in the United States offer Spanish; only 4 percent offer Chinese.

32 percent of college graduates surveyed saw themselves using a language other than their first language at work.

70 percent of Americans aged 18 to 24 have not traveled outside the United States in the last three years.

20 percent of U.S. homes house residents who speak a foreign language.

54 percent of business travelers said they're more successful in their career because of global business travel experience.

22 percent of U.S. workers say they "live to work" rather than "work to live".

16 percent of French workers say they "live to work".

3.3

LEARNING OUTCOME
Describe the structures and techniques organizations use as they go international.

World Trade Organization (WTO)
A global organization of 153 countries that deals with the rules of trade among nations

International Monetary Fund (IMF)
An organization of 185 countries that promotes international monetary cooperation and provides advice, loans, and technical assistance

World Bank Group
A group of five closely associated institutions that provides financial and technical assistance to developing countries

Organization for Economic Cooperation and Development (OECD)
An international economic organization that helps its 30 member countries achieve sustainable economic growth and employment

60 countries and its top 400 managers represent 53 different nationalities. The Missouri State Employees' Retirement System pays retirement benefits to recipients in 20 countries outside the United States.[43] As these examples show, organizations in different industries and from different countries do business globally. But *how* do they do so?

Different Types of International Organizations

Companies doing business globally aren't new. DuPont started doing business in China in 1863. H.J. Heinz Company was manufacturing food products in the United Kingdom in 1905. Ford Motor Company set up its first overseas sales branch in France in 1908. By the 1920s, other companies, including Fiat, Unilever, and Royal Dutch/Shell had gone international. But it wasn't until the mid-1960s that international companies became quite common. Today, few companies don't do business internationally. However, there's not a generally accepted approach to describe the different types of international companies; different authors call them different things. We use the terms *multinational, multidomestic, global,* and *transnational.*[44] A **multinational corporation (MNC)** is any type of international company that maintains operations in multiple countries.

One type of MNC is a **multidomestic corporation**, which decentralizes management and other decisions to the local country. This type of globalization reflects the polycentric attitude. A multidomestic corporation doesn't attempt to replicate its domestic successes by managing foreign operations from its home country. Instead, local employees typically are hired to manage the business and marketing strategies are tailored to that country's unique characteristics. For example, Switzerland-based Nestlé is a multidomestic corporation. With operations in almost every country on the globe, its managers match the company's products to its consumers. In parts of Europe, Nestlé sells products that are not available in the United States or Latin America. Another example is Frito-Lay, a division of PepsiCo, which markets a Dorito chip in the British market that differs in both taste and texture from the U.S. and Canadian version. Even the king of retailing, Walmart Stores, has learned that it must "think locally to act globally" as it tailors its inventories and store formats to local tastes.[45] Many consumer product companies organize their global businesses using this approach because they must adapt their products to meet the needs of local markets.

Another type of MNC is a **global company**, which centralizes its management and other decisions in the home country. This approach to globalization reflects the ethnocentric attitude. Global companies treat the world market as an integrated whole and focus on the need for global efficiency and cost savings. Although these companies may have considerable global holdings, management decisions with company-wide implications are made from headquarters in the home country. Some examples of global companies include Sony, Deutsche Bank AG, Starwood Hotels, and Merrill Lynch.

Other companies use an arrangement that eliminates artificial geographical barriers. This type of MNC is often called a **transnational, or borderless, organization** and reflects a geocentric attitude.[46] For example, IBM dropped its organizational structure based on country and reorganized into industry groups. Ford Motor Company is pursuing what it calls the One Ford concept as it integrates its operations around the world. Another company, Thomson SA, which is legally based in France, has eight major locations around the globe. The CEO said, "We don't want people to think we're based anyplace."[47] Managers choose this approach to increase efficiency and effectiveness in a competitive global marketplace.[48]

How Organizations Go International

When organizations do go international, they often use different approaches. (See Exhibit 3-3.) Managers who want to get into a global market with minimal investment may start with **global sourcing** (also called global outsourcing), which is purchasing materials or labor from around the world wherever it is cheapest. The goal: take advantage of lower costs

This baby in Ryazan, Russia, enjoys Nestlé's baby food that may not be available in other parts of the world. That's because Nestlé believes that "food is a local matter." As a multidomestic corporation, Nestlé spans the globe in marketing more than 10,000 products in 130 countries. The company adapts its products to local cultures, tastes, traditions, and consumer needs. Wherever possible, Nestlé produces its products locally and uses local raw materials and components. Even though some Nestlé brands are global, others are marketed in specific geographic areas, such as the Middle East, and many are local to a country or to an area within a country.

EXHIBIT **3-3**
How Organizations Go Global

in order to be more competitive. For instance, Massachusetts General Hospital uses radiologists in India to interpret CT scans.[49] Although global sourcing may be the first step to going international for many companies, they often continue to use this approach because of the competitive advantages it offers. Each successive stage of going international beyond global sourcing, however, requires more investment and thus entails more risk for the organization.

The next step in going international may involve **exporting** the organization's products to other countries—that is, making products domestically and selling them abroad. In addition, an organization might do **importing**, which involves acquiring products made abroad and selling them domestically. Both usually entail minimal investment and risk, which is why many small businesses often use these approaches to doing business globally.

Managers also might use **licensing** or **franchising**, which are similar approaches involving one organization giving another organization the right to use its brand name, technology, or product specifications in return for a lump sum payment or a fee usually based on sales. The only difference is that licensing is primarily used by manufacturing organizations that make or sell another company's products and franchising is primarily used by service organizations that want to use another company's name and operating methods. For example, Chicago consumers can enjoy Guatemalan Pollo Campero fried chicken, South Koreans can indulge in Dunkin' Brands' coffee, Hong Kong residents can dine on Shakey's Pizza, and Malaysians can consume Schlotzky's deli sandwiches—all because of *franchises* in these countries. On the other hand, Anheuser-Busch InBev has *licensed* the right to brew and market its Budweiser beer to brewers such as Kirin in Japan and Crown Beers in India.

When an organization has been doing business internationally for a while and has gained experience in international markets, managers may decide to make more of a direct foreign investment. One way to increase investment is through a **strategic alliance**, which is a partnership between an organization and a foreign company partner or partners in which both share resources and knowledge in developing new products or building production facilities. For example, Honda Motor and General Electric teamed up to produce a new jet engine. A specific type of strategic alliance in which the partners form a separate, independent organization for some business purpose is called a **joint venture**. For example, Hewlett-Packard has had numerous joint ventures with various suppliers around the globe to develop different components for its computer equipment. These partnerships provide a relatively easy way for companies to compete globally.

Finally, managers may choose to directly invest in a foreign country by setting up a **foreign subsidiary** as a separate and independent facility or office. This subsidiary can be managed as a multidomestic organization (local control) or as a global organization (centralized control). As you can probably guess, this arrangement involves the greatest commitment of resources and poses the greatest amount of risk. For instance, United Plastics Group of Westmont, Illinois, built two injection-molding facilities in Suzhou, China. The company's executive vice president for business development said that level of investment was necessary because "it fulfilled our mission of being a global supplier to our global accounts."[50]

LEARNING OUTCOME **3.4**
Explain the relevance of the political/legal, economic, and cultural environments to global business.

Managing in a Global Environment

Assume for a moment that you're a manager going to work for a branch of a global organization in a foreign country. You know that your environment will differ from the one at home, but how? What should you look for?

Any manager who finds himself or herself in a new country faces challenges. In this section, we'll look at some of these challenges. Although our discussion is presented through the eyes of a U.S. manager, this framework could be used by any manager regardless of national origin who manages in a foreign environment.

The Political/Legal Environment

U.S. managers are accustomed to a stable legal and political system. Changes tend to be slow, and legal and political procedures are well established. Elections are held at regular intervals, and even when the political party in power changes after an election, it's unlikely that anything too radical will happen. The stability of laws allows for accurate predictions. However, this certainly isn't true for all countries. Managers must stay informed of the specific laws in countries where they do business. For instance, the president of Zimbabwe is pushing ahead with plans to force foreign companies to sell majority stakes to locals.[51] Such a law would be a major barrier to foreign business investment. In China, foreign businesses are finding a less-than-welcoming climate as government policies are making it more difficult to do business there.[52] And Swedish retailer Ikea has halted further investment in Russia because of continual governmental red tape delays. Per Kaufmann, Ikea's Russia country manager, said the decision was "due to the unpredictability of the administrative processes in some regions."[53]

Also, some countries have risky political climates. Chicago-based Aon Corporation does an annual political risk assessment, and its 2010 report found that businesses faced the highest level of risk in Afghanistan, Congo DRC, Iran, Iraq, North Korea, Somalia, Sudan, Venezuela, Yemen, and Zimbabwe. Company analysts said that political and financial instability remained a feature of the business landscape as a result of the global recession. They also said that "2010 will see elevated political risk levels continue before an overall tendency for improving global business conditions becomes established."[54] Managers of businesses in countries with higher risk levels face dramatically greater uncertainty. In addition, political interference is a fact of life in some regions, especially in some Asian countries such as China.[55]

Keep in mind that a country's political/legal environment doesn't have to be risky or unstable to be a concern to managers. Just the fact that it differs from that of the home country (United States or other) is important. Managers must recognize these differences if they hope to understand the constraints and opportunities that exist.

Let's Get Real

F**2**F

My advice for someone who has little global experience is *research all aspects of that country's culture and find a liaison native to the culture to take as a partner to gain the needed perspective.*

The Economic Environment

Strange as it may sound, 17,000 tons of Parmesan cheese, with an estimated value of $187 million, are being held in the vaults of the Italian bank Credito Emiliano. The cheese is collateral from Italian cheese makers struggling through the recession.[56] Such an example of an economic factor of business may seem peculiar for those of us in the United States, but it's not all that unusual for Italian businesses.

A global manager must be aware of economic issues when doing business in other countries. First, it's important to understand a country's type of economic system. The two major types are a free market economy and a planned economy. A **free market economy** is one in which resources are primarily owned and controlled by the private sector. A **planned economy** is one in which economic decisions are planned by a central government. Actually, no economy is purely free market or planned. For instance, the United States and United Kingdom are toward the free market end of the spectrum but do have governmental intervention and controls. The economies of Vietnam and North Korea are more planned. China is also a more planned economy, but until recently had been moving toward being more free market. Why would managers need to know about a country's economic system? Because it, too, has the potential to constrain decisions. Other economic issues managers need to understand include currency exchange rates, inflation rates, and diverse tax policies.

An MNC's profits can vary dramatically depending on the strength of its home currency and the currencies of the countries in which it operates. For instance, prior to the overall global economic slowdown, the rising value of the euro against both the dollar and the yen had contributed to strong profits for German companies.[57] Any currency exchange revaluations can affect managers' decisions and the level of a company's profits.

Inflation means that prices for products and services are increasing. But it also affects interest rates, exchange rates, the cost of living, and the general confidence in a country's political and economic system. Country inflation rates can, and do, vary widely. The *World Factbook* shows rates ranging from a negative 3.9 percent in Qatar to a positive 34 percent in the Seychelles.[58] Managers need to monitor inflation trends so they can anticipate possible changes in a country's monetary policies and make good business decisions regarding purchasing and pricing.

Finally, tax policies can be a major economic worry. Some countries' tax laws are more restrictive than those in an MNC's home country. Others are more lenient. About the only certainty is that they differ from country to country. Managers need accurate information on tax rules in countries in which they operate to minimize their business's overall tax obligation.

The Cultural Environment

Managing today's talented global workforce can be a challenge![59] A large multinational oil company found that employee productivity in one of its Mexican plants was off 20 percent and sent a U.S. manager to find out why. After talking to several employees, the manager discovered that the company used to have a monthly fiesta in the parking lot for all the employees and their families. Another U.S. manager had canceled the fiestas saying they were a waste of time and money. The message employees were getting was that the company didn't care about their families anymore. When the fiestas were reinstated, productivity and employee morale soared. At Hewlett-Packard, a cross-global team of U.S. and French engineers were assigned to work together on a software project. The U.S. engineers sent long, detailed e-mails to their counterparts in France. The French engineers viewed the lengthy e-mails as patronizing and replied with quick, concise e-mails. This made the U.S. engineers think that the French were hiding something from them. The situation spiraled out of control and negatively affected output until team members went through cultural training.[60]

---

joint venture
A specific type of strategic alliance in which the partners agree to form a separate, independent organization for some business purpose

foreign subsidiary
Directly investing in a foreign country by setting up a separate and independent production facility or office

free market economy
An economic system in which resources are primarily owned and controlled by the private sector

planned economy
An economic system in which economic decisions are planned by a central government

As we know from Chapter 2, organizations have different cultures. Countries have cultures too. **National culture** includes the values and attitudes shared by individuals from a specific country that shape their behavior and their beliefs about what is important.[61]

Which is more important to a manager—national culture or organizational culture? For example, is an IBM facility in Germany more likely to reflect German culture or IBM's corporate culture? Research indicates that national culture has a greater effect on employees than does their organization's culture.[62] German employees at an IBM facility in Munich will be influenced more by German culture than by IBM's culture.

Legal, political, and economic differences among countries are fairly obvious. The Japanese manager who works in the United States or his or her American counterpart who works in Japan can get information about laws or tax policies without too much effort. Getting information about cultural differences isn't quite that easy! The primary reason? It's difficult for natives to explain their country's unique cultural characteristics to someone else. For instance, if you were born and raised in the United States, how would you describe U.S. culture? In other words, what are Americans like? Think about it for a moment and see which characteristics in Exhibit 3-4 you identified.

HOFSTEDE'S FRAMEWORK FOR ASSESSING CULTURES. Geert Hofstede developed one of the most widely referenced approaches to helping managers better understand differences between national cultures. His research found that countries vary on five dimensions of national culture. These dimensions are described in Exhibit 3-5, which also shows some of the countries characterized by those dimensions.

THE GLOBE FRAMEWORK FOR ASSESSING CULTURES. The **Global Leadership and Organizational Behavior Effectiveness (GLOBE)** research program extended Hofstede's work by investigating cross-cultural leadership behaviors and gives managers additional information to help them identify and manage cultural differences. Using data from more than 18,000 managers in 62 countries, the GLOBE research team (led by Robert House) identified nine dimensions on which national cultures

---

EXHIBIT 3-4

What Are Americans Like?

- Americans are *very informal*. They tend to treat people alike even when great differences in age or social standing are evident.
- Americans are *direct*. They don't talk around things. To some foreigners, this may appear as abrupt or even rude behavior.
- Americans are *competitive*. Some foreigners may find Americans assertive or overbearing.
- Americans are *achievers*. They like to keep score, whether at work or at play. They emphasize accomplishments.
- Americans are *independent and individualistic*. They place a high value on freedom and believe that individuals can shape and control their own destiny.
- Americans are *questioners*. They ask a lot of questions, even of someone they have just met. Many may seem pointless ("How ya' doin'?") or personal ("What kind of work do you do?").
- Americans *dislike silence*. They would rather talk about the weather than deal with silence in a conversation.
- Americans *value punctuality*. They keep appointment calendars and live according to schedules and clocks.
- Americans *value cleanliness*. They often seem obsessed with bathing, eliminating body odors, and wearing clean clothes.

Sources: Based on M. Ernest (ed.), *Predeparture Orientation Handbook: For Foreign Students and Scholars Planning to Study in the United States* (Washington, DC: U.S. Information Agency, Bureau of Cultural Affairs, 1984), pp. 103–105; A. Bennett, "American Culture Is Often a Puzzle for Foreign Managers in the U.S.," *Wall Street Journal*, February 12, 1986, p. 29; "Don't Think Our Way's the Only Way," *The Pryor Report*, February 1988, p. 9; and B. J. Wattenberg, "The Attitudes Behind American Exceptionalism," *U.S. News & World Report*, August 7, 1989, p. 25.

EXHIBIT 3-5
Hofstede's Five Dimensions of National Culture

1. *Individualistic*—People look after their own and family interests
   Collectivistic—People expect the group to look after and protect them

   Individualistic ⟷ *Collectivistic*

   United States, Canada, Australia   Japan   Mexico, Thailand

2. *High power distance*—Accepts wide differences in power; great deal of respect for those in authority
   Low power distance—Plays down inequalities: employees are not afraid to approach nor are in awe of the boss

   High power distance ⟷ *Low power distance*

   Mexico, Singapore, France   Italy, Japan   United States, Sweden

3. *High uncertainty avoidance*—Threatened with ambiguity and experience high levels of anxiety
   Low uncertainty avoidance—Comfortable with risks; tolerant of different behavior and opinions

   High uncertainty avoidance ⟷ *Low uncertainty avoidance*

   Italy, Mexico, France   United Kingdom   Canada, United States, Singapore

4. *Achievement*—Values such as assertiveness, acquiring money and goods, and competition prevail
   Nurturing—Values such as relationships and concern for others prevail

   Achievement ⟷ *Nurturing*

   United States, Japan, Mexico   Canada, Greece   France, Sweden

5. *Long-term orientation*—People look to the future and value thrift and persistence
   Short-term orientation—People value tradition and the past

   Short-term orientation ⟷ *Long-term orientation*

   Germany, Australia, United States, Canada   China, Taiwan, Japan

differ.[63] Two dimensions (power distance and uncertainty avoidance) fit directly with Hofstede's. Four are similar to Hofstede's (assertiveness, which is similar to achievement-nurturing; humane orientation, which is similar to the nurturing dimension; future orientation, which is similar to long-term and short-term orientation; and institutional collectivism, which is similar to individualism-collectivism). The remaining three (gender differentiation, in-group collectivism, and performance orientation) offer additional insights into a country's culture. Here are descriptions of these nine dimensions:

▶ **Power distance:** the degree to which members of a society expect power to be unequally shared.
▶ **Uncertainty avoidance:** a society's reliance on social norms and procedures to alleviate the unpredictability of future events.
▶ **Assertiveness:** the extent to which a society encourages people to be tough, confrontational, assertive, and competitive rather than modest and tender.
▶ **Humane orientation:** the degree to which a society encourages and rewards individuals for being fair, altruistic, generous, caring, and kind to others.
▶ **Future orientation:** the extent to which a society encourages and rewards future-oriented behaviors such as planning, investing in the future, and delaying gratification.

national culture
The values and attitudes shared by individuals from a specific country that shape their behavior and beliefs about what is important

Global Leadership and Organizational Behavior Effectiveness (GLOBE) program
The research program that studies cross-cultural leadership behaviors

▶ **Institutional collectivism:** the degree to which individuals are encouraged by societal institutions to be integrated into groups within organizations and society.

▶ **Gender differentiation:** the extent to which a society maximizes gender role differences as measured by how much status and decision-making responsibilities women have.

▶ **In-group collectivism:** the extent to which members of a society take pride in membership in small groups, such as their family and circle of close friends, and the organizations in which they're employed.

▶ **Performance orientation:** the degree to which a society encourages and rewards group members for performance improvement and excellence.

Exhibit 3-6 provides information on how different countries rank on these nine dimensions.

Global Management in Today's World

Doing business globally today isn't easy! As we look at managing in today's global environment, we want to focus on two important aspects. The first aspect involves the challenges associated with globalization, especially in relation to the openness that's part of being global. The second aspect revolves around the challenges of managing a global workforce.

THE CHALLENGE OF OPENNESS. The push to go global has been widespread. Advocates praise the economic and social benefits that come from globalization, but globalization also creates challenges because of the openness that's necessary for it to

---

EXHIBIT 3-6

GLOBE Highlights

Dimension	Countries Rating Low	Countries Rating Moderate	Countries Rating High
Assertiveness	Sweden New Zealand Switzerland	Egypt Ireland Philippines	Spain United States Greece
Future orientation	Russia Argentina Poland	Slovenia Egypt Ireland	Denmark Canada Netherlands
Gender differentiation	Sweden Denmark Slovenia	Italy Brazil Argentina	South Korea Egypt Morocco
Uncertainty avoidance	Russia Hungary Bolivia	Israel United States Mexico	Austria Denmark Germany
Power distance	Denmark Netherlands South Africa	England France Brazil	Russia Spain Thailand
Individualism/collectivism*	Denmark Singapore Japan	Hong Kong United States Egypt	Greece Hungary Germany
In-group collectivism	Denmark Sweden New Zealand	Japan Israel Qatar	Egypt China Morocco
Performance orientation	Russia Argentina Greece	Sweden Israel Spain	United States Taiwan New Zealand
Humane orientation	Germany Spain France	Hong Kong Sweden Taiwan	Indonesia Egypt Malaysia

*A low score is synonymous with collectivism.

Source: M. Javidan and R. J. House, "Cultural Acumen for the Global Manager: Lessons from Project GLOBE," *Organizational Dynamics*, Spring 2001, pp. 289–305. Copyright © 2001. Reprinted with permission from Elsevier.

work. One challenge is the increased threat of terrorism by a truly global terror network. Globalization is meant to open up trade and to break down the geographical barriers separating countries. Yet, opening up means just that—being open to the bad as well as the good. From the Philippines and the United Kingdom to Israel and Pakistan, organizations and employees face the risk of terrorist attacks. Another challenge from openness is the economic interdependence of trading countries. As we saw over the last couple of years, the faltering of one country's economy can have a domino effect on other countries with which it does business. So far, however, the world economy has proved to be quite resilient. And as we discussed earlier, structures that are currently in place, such as the World Trade Organization and the International Monetary Fund, help to isolate and address potential problems.

The far more serious challenge for managers in the openness required by globalization comes from intense underlying and fundamental cultural differences—differences that encompass traditions, history, religious beliefs, and deep-seated values. Managing in such an environment can be extremely complicated. Even though globalization has long been praised for its economic benefits, some individuals think that globalization is simply a euphemism for "Americanization"—that is, the way U.S. cultural values and U.S. business philosophy are said to be slowly taking over the world.[64] At its best, proponents of Americanization hope others will see how progressive, efficient, industrious, and free U.S. society and businesses are and want to emulate that way of doing things. However, critics claim that this attitude of the "almighty American dollar wanting to spread the American way to every single country," has created many problems.[65] Although history is filled with clashes between civilizations, what's unique now is the speed and ease with which misunderstandings and disagreements can erupt and escalate. The Internet, television and other media, and global air travel have brought the good and the bad of American entertainment, products, and behaviors to every corner of the globe. For those who don't like what Americans do, say, or believe, this exposure can lead to resentment, dislike, distrust, and even outright hatred.

CHALLENGES OF MANAGING A GLOBAL WORKFORCE.

▶ "As more Americans go to mainland China to take jobs, more Chinese and Americans are working side by side. These cross-cultural partnerships, while beneficial in many ways, are also highlighting tensions that expose differences in work experience, pay levels, and communication."[66]
▶ Global companies with multicultural work teams are faced with the challenge of managing the cultural differences in work-family relationships. The work-family practices and programs that are appropriate and effective for employees in one country may not be the best solution for employees in other locations.[67]

These examples indicate challenges that are associated with managing a global workforce. As globalization continues to be important for businesses, it's obvious that managers need to understand how to best manage that global workforce. Some researchers have suggested that managers need **cultural intelligence** or cultural awareness and sensitivity skills.[68] Cultural intelligence encompasses three main dimensions: (1) knowledge of culture as a concept—how cultures vary and how they affect behavior; (2) mindfulness—the ability to pay attention to signals and reactions in different cross-cultural situations; and (3) behavioral skills—using one's knowledge and mindfulness to choose appropriate behaviors in those situations.

Other researchers have said that what effective global leaders need is a **global mind-set**, attributes that allow a leader to be effective in cross-cultural environments.[69] Those attributes have three components as shown in Exhibit 3-7.

cultural intelligence
Cultural awareness and sensitivity skills

global mind-set
Attributes that allow a leader to be effective in cross-cultural environments

EXHIBIT 3-7		
A Global Mind-Set		

Intellectual capital:	Knowledge of international business and the capacity to understand how business works on a global scale	
Psychological capital:	Openness to new ideas and experiences	
Social capital:	Ability to form connections and build trusting relationships with people who are different from you	

Source: Based on M. Javidan, M. Teagarden, and D. Bowen, "Making It Overseas," *Harvard Business Review,* April 2010, pp. 109–113; and J. McGregor (ed.), "Testing Managers' Global IQ," *Bloomberg BusinessWeek,* September 28, 2009, p. 68.

Leaders who possess such cross-cultural skills and abilities—whether cultural intelligence or a global mind-set—will be important assets to global organizations. Successfully managing in today's global environment will require incredible sensitivity and understanding. Managers from any country will need to be aware of how their decisions and actions will be viewed, not only by those who may agree, but more importantly, by those who may disagree. They will need to adjust their leadership styles and management approaches to accommodate these diverse views, and at the same time be as efficient and effective as possible in reaching the organization's goals.

Let's Get Real:

My Response *to A Manager's Dilemma, page 70*

All aspects of a country's culture should be researched to understand the dynamics of the culture and their traditions. Some aspects that should be thoroughly understood are:

- Understand the length of a normal workday and local laws surrounding overtime pay and maximum allowable hours in a workweek.
- What transit challenges employees may face and what flexibility may be provided to accommodate mass transit schedules or work shifts that may be set off-cycle from peak traffic times.
- What accommodations employees may prefer such as small kitchens, locker rooms, or prayer space.
- What a competitive benefits package may look like, including health benefits and access to doctors for employees and their families.

These points are important in attracting a qualified workforce, but an understanding of how to reward and motivate employees in a different culture is imperative for retention of your trained workforce.

Understand what types of recognition would be of value and who it should come from. Is recognition between a boss and employee privately or in front of a peer group most valued? What types of awards are most valued: plaques, paid time off or awards of monetary value? How do you make the most of the innovation of your employees? How does the culture affect the chain of command? What is the appropriate way to surface new ideas that may challenge a current process? Provide the appropriate vehicle dictated by the culture to ensure all ideas can be brought forth. Your employees will possess the ideas needed to move your business forward and to implement the changes needed to retain your staff. Be sure not to miss the opportunity to maximize this most valued resource!!

Cheryl Trewatha
Sr. Group Manager
Quality Assurance
Target Corp.
Brooklyn Park, MN

CHAPTER SUMMARY
by Learning Outcomes

LEARNING OUTCOME 3.1 **Contrast** ethnocentric, polycentric, and geocentric attitudes toward global business.

Parochialism is viewing the world solely through your own eyes and perspectives and not recognizing that others have different ways of living and working. An ethnocentric attitude is the parochialistic belief that the best work approaches and practices are those of the home country. A polycentric attitude is the view that the managers in the host country know the best work approaches and practices for running their business. And a geocentric attitude is a world-oriented view that focuses on using the best approaches and people from around the globe.

LEARNING OUTCOME 3.2 **Discuss** the importance of regional trading alliances and global trade mechanisms.

The European Union consists of 27 democratic countries with three countries having applied for membership. Sixteen countries have adopted the euro and all new member countries must adopt it. NAFTA continues to help Canada, Mexico, and the United States strengthen their global economic power. The U.S.–CAFTA alliance is still trying to get off the ground as is the proposed FTAA. Because of the delays for CAFTA and FTAA, Mercosur (Southern Common Market) will likely take on new importance. ASEAN is a trading alliance of ten Southeast Asian nations, a region that remains important in the global economy. The African Union and SAARC are relatively new but will continue to see benefits from their alliances. To counteract some of the risks in global trade, the World Trade Organization (WTO) plays an important role in monitoring and promoting trade relationships. The International Monetary Fund (IMF) and the World Bank Group are two entities that provide monetary support and advice to their member countries. The Organization for Economic Cooperation and Development assists its member countries with financial support in achieving sustainable economic growth and employment.

LEARNING OUTCOME 3.3 **Describe** the structures and techniques organizations use as they go international.

A multinational corporation is an international company that maintains operations in multiple countries. A multidomestic organization is an MNC that decentralizes management and other decisions to the local country (the polycentric attitude). A global organization is an MNC that centralizes management and other decisions in the home country (the ethnocentric attitude). A transnational organization (the geocentric attitude) is an MNC that has eliminated artificial geographical barriers and uses the best work practices and approaches from wherever. Global sourcing is purchasing materials or labor from around the world wherever it is cheapest. Exporting is making products domestically and selling them abroad. Importing is acquiring products made abroad and selling them domestically. Licensing is used by manufacturing organizations that make or sell another company's products and gives that organization the right to use the company's brand name, technology, or product specifications. Franchising is similar but is usually used by service organizations that want to use another company's name and operating methods. A global strategic alliance is a partnership between an organization and foreign company partners in which they share resources and knowledge to develop new products or build facilities. A joint venture is a specific type of strategic alliance in which the partners agree to form a separate, independent organization for some business purpose. A foreign subsidiary is a direct investment in a foreign country that a company creates by establishing a separate and independent facility or office.

Explain the relevance of the political/legal, economic, and cultural environments to global business.

The laws and political stability of a country are issues in the global political/legal environment with which managers must be familiar. Likewise, managers must be aware of a country's economic issues such as currency exchange rates, inflation rates, and tax policies. Geert Hofstede identified five dimensions for assessing a country's culture including individualism-collectivism, power distance, uncertainty avoidance, achievement-nurturing, and long-term/short-term orientation. The GLOBE studies identified nine dimensions for assessing country cultures: power distance, uncertainty avoidance, assertiveness, humane orientation, future orientation, institutional collectivism, gender differentiation, in-group collectivism, and performance orientation. The main challenges of doing business globally in today's world include (1) the openness associated with globalization and the significant cultural differences between countries; and (2) managing a global workforce, which requires cultural intelligence and a global mind-set.

 PEARSON **mymanagementlab** To check your understanding of learning outcomes **3.1** – **3.4** go to **mymanagementlab.com** and try the chapter questions.

REVIEW AND DISCUSSION QUESTIONS

1. Contrast ethnocentric, polycentric, and geocentric attitudes toward global business.

2. Describe the current status of each of the various regional trading alliances.

3. Contrast multinational, multidomestic, global, and transnational organizations.

4. What are the managerial implications of a borderless organization?

5. Describe the different ways organizations can go international.

6. Explain how the global political/legal and economic environments affect managers of global organizations.

7. Can the GLOBE framework presented in this chapter be used to guide managers in a Thai hospital or a government agency in Venezuela? Explain.

8. What challenges might confront a Mexican manager transferred to the United States to manage a manufacturing plant in Tucson, Arizona? Will these issues be the same for a U.S. manager transferred to Guadalajara? Explain.

9. How might the cultural differences in the GLOBE dimensions affect how managers (a) use work groups, (b) develop goals/plans, (c) reward outstanding employee performance, and (d) deal with employee conflict?

10. Is globalization good for business? For consumers? Discuss.

PREPARING FOR: My Career

ETHICS DILEMMA

The "joke" has always been that IBM—the world's top provider of computer products and services—stood for "I've Been Moved" instead of an abbreviation for its corporate name, International Business Machines.[70] That's because employees on their way up in the

company would have to be ready at any time to move where the company wanted them to go. Now, however, that "joke" may not be so funny. A new employee relocation strategy has been raising some eyebrows, especially when thousands of U.S. employees have been laid off. The plan gives the company's U.S. employees the opportunity to move their jobs to emerging market countries, and in turn, the company would foot some of the relocation costs. IBM's U.S. employment fell 5 percent, while emerging market employment rose 15 percent, particularly in high growth markets such as India, China, Brazil, and Russia. What do you think? Why might the company have developed this new program? Does this seem "right" to you? What ethical issues does this strategy raise?

SKILLS EXERCISE
Developing Your Collaboration Skill

About the Skill

Collaboration is the teamwork, synergy, and cooperation used by individuals when they seek a common goal. In many cross-cultural settings, the ability to collaborate is crucial. When all partners must work together to achieve goals, collaboration is critically important to the process.

Steps in Practicing the Skill

1. *Look for common points of interest.* The best way to start working together in a collaborative fashion is to seek commonalities that exist among the parties. Common points of interest enable communications to be more effective.

2. *Listen to others.* Collaboration is a team effort. Everyone has valid points to offer, and each individual should have an opportunity to express his or her ideas.

3. *Check for understanding.* Make sure you understand what the other person is saying. Use feedback when necessary.

4. *Accept diversity.* Not everything in a collaborative effort will "go your way." Be willing to accept different ideas and different ways of doing things. Be open to these ideas and the creativity that surrounds them.

5. *Seek additional information.* Ask individuals to provide additional information. Encourage others to talk and more fully explain suggestions. This brainstorming opportunity can assist in finding creative solutions.

6. *Don't become defensive.* Collaboration requires open communications. Discussions may focus on things you and others may not be doing or need to do better. Don't take the constructive feedback as personal criticism. Focus on the topic being discussed, not on the person delivering the message. Recognize that you cannot always be right!

Practicing the Skill

Interview managers from three different organizations about how they collaborate with others. What specific tips have they discovered for effectively collaborating with others? What problems have they encountered when collaborating? How have they dealt with these problems?

WORKING TOGETHER
Team Exercise

Moving to a foreign country isn't easy, no matter how many times you've done it or how receptive you are to new experiences. Successful global organizations are able to identify the best candidates for global assignments, and one of the ways they do this is through individual assessments prior to assigning people to global facilities. Form groups of three to five individuals. Your newly formed team, the Global Assignment Task Force, has been given the responsibility for developing a global aptitude assessment form for Yum Brands (the company described in the chapter-opening Manager's Dilemma). Because Yum is expanding its global operations significantly, it wants to make sure that it's sending the best possible people to the various global locations. Your team's assignment is to come up with a rough draft of a form to assess people's global aptitude. Think about the characteristics, skills, attitudes, etc. that you think a successful global employee would need. Your team's draft should be at least one-half page but not longer than one page. Be prepared to present your ideas to your classmates and professor.

MY TURN TO BE A MANAGER

- Find two current examples of each of the ways that organizations go international. Write a short paper describing what these companies are doing.

- The U.K.-based company, Kwintessential, has several cultural knowledge "quizzes" on its Web site [http://www.kwintessential.co.uk/resources/culture-tests.html]. Go to the Web site and try two or three of them. Were you surprised at your score? What does your score tell you about your cultural awareness?

- On this Web site, you'll also find Country Etiquette Guides. Pick two countries to study (from different regions) and compare them. How are they the same? Different? How would this information help a manager?

- Interview two or three professors or students at your school who are from other countries. Ask them to describe what the business world is like in their country. Write a short paper describing what you found out.

- Take advantage of opportunities that you might have to travel to other countries, either on personal trips or on school-sponsored trips.

- Create a timeline illustrating the history of the European Union and a timeline illustrating the history of NAFTA.

- Suppose that you were being sent on an overseas assignment to another country (you decide which one). Research that country's economic, political/legal, and cultural environments. Write a report summarizing your findings.

- If you don't have your passport yet, go through the process to get one. (The current fee in the United States is $135.)

- Steve's and Mary's suggested readings: H. L. Sirkin, J. W. Hermerling, and A. K. Bhattacharya, *Globality: Competing with Everyone from Everywhere for Everything* (Boston Consulting Group, Inc., 2008); J. Zogby, *The Way We'll Be* (Random House, 2008); Nancy J. Adler,

International Dimensions of Organizational Behavior, 5th ed. (South-Western Publishing, 2008); Kenichi Ohmae, *The Next Global Stage* (Wharton School Publishing, 2005); John Hooker, *Working Across Cultures* (Stanford Business Books, 2003); and Thomas L. Friedman, *The Lexus and the Olive Tree* (Anchor Books, 2000).

- If you want to better prepare yourself for working in an international setting, take additional classes in international management and international business.

- You've been put in charge of designing a program to prepare your company's managers to go on an overseas assignment. What should (and would) this program include? Be specific. Be thorough. Be creative.

- In your own words, write down three things you learned in this chapter about being a good manager.

- Self-knowledge can be a powerful learning tool. Go to mymanagementlab.com and complete these self-assessment exercises: Am I Well-Suited for a Career as a Global Manager? and What Are My Attitudes Toward Workplace Diversity? Using the results of your assessments, identify personal strengths and weaknesses. What will you do to reinforce your strengths and improve your weaknesses?

CASE APPLICATION 1
Held Hostage

Hostage and *manager*.[71] These are two words that you would not usually expect to hear spoken in the same breath. However, during the first few months of 2009, workers at manufacturing facilities of 3M Company, Sony Corporation, and Caterpillar Inc. in France took managers hostage. Why? To negotiate better severance packages and benefits for laid-off employees.

French workers have long been known for their aggressive and radical responses to what they feel is wrong or oppressive treatment. Says one French executive, "Protest is inscribed in the genes of French culture. In the past, peasants protested against their lords. Today the difference is that the lords are chief executives." Protesting French workers have been known to burn piles of tires in city streets or tie up traffic with caravans of farm tractors. In one instance, striking truckers blockaded roads and highways to highlight their campaign for zretirement at age 55. The labor blockade worked, as the French government relented when food supplies started to run out. And the tactic of taking the boss hostage has been used previously, as well. For instance, in

Nicholas Polutnik, director of Caterpillar's plant near Grenoble, France, sits at his desk while held captive as a hostage by striking employees who protested planned layoffs until management agreed to negotiate with the union over compensation of laid-off workers.

1997, workers at the state-run mortgage bank Credit Foncier de France took their boss hostage for five days to try and prevent the bank's closing even though it had been losing money. Although kidnapping your boss isn't legal, a French sociologist who surveyed 3,000 companies found that 18 of them had experienced an "executive detention" in the prior three years.

These actions by workers, which have been peaceful and more of a symbolic protest, were in response to the economic downturn. Although France wasn't in any worse shape than other big industrialized economies, the country's "strong tradition of egalitarianism triggers strong reactions when people think they are being mistreated or when better-off people appear to flaunt their wealth at a time of general hardship." At Caterpillar's French facility near Grenoble, unhappy workers first went on strike for a day. The next day, they detained the plant director and four other managers for about 24 hours. The managers were released only after the company agreed to resume talks with unions and a government mediator on "how to improve compensation for workers being laid off." The incident at Caterpillar followed others at Sony and 3M, where managers also were held captive by workers angry over being laid off. Although all of the hostage-taking incidents were resolved peacefully, some analysts wonder if more violent actions may be in store, especially if workers feel they have nothing to lose.

Discussion Questions

1. What's your reaction to these events? Do you think your reaction is influenced by the culture, values, and traditions of the country in which you find yourself? Explain.

2. Look at what Hofstede's and the GLOBE findings say about France. How would you explain these workers' actions given these findings?

3. We've said that it's important for managers to be aware of external environmental forces, especially in global settings. Discuss this statement in light of the events described.

4. What might the French managers have done differently leading up to the point at which workers felt they needed to take their managers hostage in order to be heard? Explain.

5. Do you think something like this could happen in the United States? Why or why not?

CASE APPLICATION 2

Global Stumble

It's not always easy to do business globally, as executives at Japanese brokerage firm Nomura Holdings Inc. are discovering.[72] Nomura acquired Lehman's international operations in late 2008 after Lehman's parent company sought Chapter 11 bankruptcy protection, an action that added about 8,000 non-Japanese workers. For Nomura, the time seemed right to strengthen its global expansion strategy. However, since the acquisition, cultural and business differences between the two organizations have been a major stumbling block. Although blending two diverse cultures requires intentional efforts when different organizations merge or are acquired, it's particularly challenging when the key assets in the cross-border acquisition are the people employed by the organization being acquired.

Workplace tensions arose over executive compensation, how quickly decisions were made, and how women were treated. For instance, during Nomura's initial training session for new hires, the men and women were separated. The women—many of whom had earned prestigious degrees from the likes of Harvard—were taught how to wear their hair, serve tea, and choose their clothing according to the season. The company's dress code was strictly interpreted for women, also. Women from Lehman were told to remove highlights from their hair, to wear sleeves no shorter than mid-bicep, and to avoid brightly colored clothing. Several women were sent home from the trading floor for dressing "inappropriately." One said, "I was sent home for wearing a short-sleeve dress, even though I was wearing a jacket." A Nomura spokesperson said, "The dress code is displayed on the company's intranet and is intended to ensure that clients and colleagues don't feel uncomfortable."

Lehman bankers also said they found the process for getting approval on deals was "slower and more difficult than it was at Lehman." Also, at Lehman, clients were categorized, in large part, by the fees they paid. At Nomura, more emphasis was placed on other factors, such as the length of the relationship. The bankers at Nomura said that "their new colleagues were too willing to dump loyal clients for a quick profit."

In its defense, Nomura has tried to blend the two cultures. In offices in Europe and in Asia outside of Japan, there's a mix of nationalities. Also, the company has promoted a handful of non-Japanese employees to high-ranking positions. "To reduce the Tokyo-centric nature of the company, Hiromi Yamaji, head of global investment banking, moved to London, and Naoki Matsuba, global head of equities, moved to New York." Until March 2010, Nomura's executive committee was all Japanese men. However, in an attempt to make the company more globally oriented, an ex-Lehman executive and foreigner, Jasjit "Jesse" Bhattal, a native of India, was promoted to the committee. Nomura's deputy president and chief operating officer, Takumi Shibata, said, "When your business is global, management needs to be global."

Discussion Questions

1. What obvious cultural differences between Nomura and Lehman do you see in this situation?

2. What global attitude do you think characterizes Nomura? Be specific in your description. Do you see any evidence of that changing?

3. Do some cultural research on Japan and the United States. Compare those cultural characteristics. What similarities and differences exist? How might these cultural differences be affecting the situation at Nomura?

4. What could Nomura managers do to support, promote, and encourage cultural awareness among employees? Explain.

5. What do you think the statement, "When your business is global, management needs to be global," is saying? In your opinion, is Nomura doing this? Explain.

Answers to "Who Owns What" Quiz

1. **d. Switzerland**

   Nestlé SA bought both the Tombstone and DiGiorno frozen-pizza brands from Kraft Foods in 2009.

2. **c. United States**

   The maker of Lebedyansky juices was acquired by PepsiCo Inc. and Pepsi Bottling Group Inc. in March 2008.

3. **a. United States**

   Rajah Spices are products of the Lea & Perrins sauce division, which the H.J. Heinz Company acquired in June of 2005.

4. **b. India**

   Tetley Tea is owned by the Tata Tea Group, a subsidiary of Indian conglomerate Tata Group.

5. **d. China**

   Ford Motor Company sold the Volvo brand to Chinese car maker Zhejiang Geely Holding Group Co. in March 2010.

6. **a. The Netherlands**

   Mexico's second-largest beer producer was acquired by Heineken N.V. in January 2010.

7. **b. Mexico**

   Grupo Bimbo, one of the world's largest bakeries, bought the rights to make and distribute Boboli pizza crusts in 2002.

8. **c. United States**

   Braun electric shavers are a part of Global Gillette, which was purchased by the Procter & Gamble Company in October 2005.

9. **c. France**

   LVMH Moët Hennessy Louis Vuitton SA, the world's largest luxury-goods group, owns Sephora.

10. **d. South Korea**

    The Boston-based Barbarian Group was acquired by South Korea's largest advertising agency, Cheil Worldwide, in December 2009.

11. **c. Switzerland**

    Nestlé SA purchased the maker of Lean Cuisine frozen meals in 2002.

12. **a. Russia**

    Russian tycoon Alexander Lebedev acquired the *Independent* in March 2010.

13. **b. United Kingdom**

    French's mustard is a product of Reckitt-Benckiser.

14. **a. India**

    Tata Coffee, a division of Indian conglomerate Tata Group, purchased Eight O'Clock Coffee in 2006.

15. **b. United States**

    Consumer products giant Procter & Gamble purchased the luxury hair-care brand from a private equity firm in 2008.

Let's Get Real:

Meet the Manager

Kim Scartelli
Multiple Franchise Owner and Consultant
Curves for Women
Canton, MI

You'll be hearing more from this real manager throughout the chapter.

MY JOB:

I am a multiple franchise owner for Curves fitness center franchises in southeastern Michigan. I am responsible for the marketing, financials, and operations of my locations.

BEST PART OF MY JOB:

I love the flexibility and satisfaction that comes with owning my own business. I worked in corporate America for six years before starting my own business. It's wonderful to be in control of a large part of the personal success that comes with being your own boss.

Managing Diversity

LEARNING OUTCOMES

WORST PART OF MY JOB:

When a problem arises, I don't always have someone to handle it so it falls on my shoulders. When you are at the top of your own company, there is no one to pass problems "up" to. It often feels like the responsibility is all mine.

BEST MANAGEMENT ADVICE EVER RECEIVED:

Surround yourself with people who have strengths and abilities different from you. They help fill in the gaps of your weaknesses and make your organization more effective.

Companies across Europe have a problem—a large gender gap in leadership.[1] Men far outnumber women in senior business leadership positions. This dismal picture of sexism in Europe exists despite efforts and campaigns to try and ensure equality in the workplace. But one European company is tackling the problem head-on.

Deutsche Telekom, Europe's largest telecommunication company, says that it intends to "more than double the number of women who are managers within five years." In addition, it plans to increase the number of women in senior and middle

management to 30 percent by the end of 2015, up from 12 percent today. With this announcement, the company becomes the first member of the DAX 30 Index of blue-chip German companies to introduce a gender quota. Deutsche's chief executive René Obermann (pictured on right) said, "Taking on more women in management positions is not about the enforcement of misconstrued egalitarianism. Having a greater number of women at the top will quite simply enable us to operate better."

In addition to its plans to intensify recruiting of female university graduates, Deutsche Telekom will need to make changes in its corporate policies and practices to attract and keep women in management positions.

Although Deutsche Telekom's goal of bringing more women into leadership positions is admirable, it's not alone in its inability to diversify its management ranks. Even in the United States, where women have been graduating with advanced professional degrees in record numbers, the number in senior leadership positions remains low—only 3 percent of *Fortune* 500 companies have female CEOs.[2] Clearly, the issue of moving beyond a homogeneous workforce is one that is important for today's managers. In this chapter we'll look closer at managing diversity of all kinds in the workplace.

LEARNING OUTCOME

Define workplace diversity and explain why managing it is so important.

4.1

Diversity 101

Walking through the lobby of one of MGM Mirage's hotels, Brenda Thompson, the company's director of diversity and leadership education notes, "It's amazing all the different languages I can hear. . . . Our guests come from all over the world, and it makes us realize the importance of reflecting that diversity in our workplace." And Thompson has been instrumental in developing a program at MGM that is all "about maximizing 100 percent inclusion of everyone in the organization."[3] Such diversity can be found in many organizational workplaces domestically and globally, and managers in those workplaces are looking for ways to value and develop that diversity, just as Brenda Thompson is doing. However, before we look at what it takes to manage diversity, we first have to know what workplace diversity is and why it's important.

What Is Workplace Diversity?

Look around your classroom (or your workplace). You're likely to see young/old, male/female, tall/short, blonde hair, blue-eyed/dark hair, brown-eyed, any number of races, and any variety of dress styles. You'll see people who speak up in class and others who are content to keep their attention on taking notes or daydreaming. Have you ever noticed your own little world of diversity where you are right now? Many of you may have grown up in an environment around diverse individuals, while others may not have had that experience. We want to focus on *workplace* diversity, so let's look at what it is. By looking at various ways that diversity has been defined, you'll gain a better understanding of it.

Diversity has been "one of the most popular business topics over the last two decades. It ranks with modern business disciplines such as quality, leadership, and ethics. Despite this popularity, it's also one of the most controversial and least understood topics."[4] With its basis in civil rights legislation and social justice, the word *diversity* often invokes a variety of attitudes and emotional responses in people. Diversity has traditionally been considered a term used by human resources departments, associated with fair hiring practices, discrimination, and inequality. But diversity today is considered to be so much more. Exhibit 4-1 illustrates an historical overview of how the concept and meaning of workforce diversity has evolved.

Let's take a look at some of the ways *diversity* has been defined. For instance, at State Farm, the number one provider of auto insurance in the United States, diversity is viewed as "the collective strength of experiences, skills, talents, perspectives, and cultures that each agent and employee brings to State Farm."[5] Dictionary definitions of diversity refer to variety, differences, multiformity (instead of uniformity), or dissimilarities (instead of similarities). The Society for Human Resource Management, an association of human resource professionals, says that "diversity is often used to refer to differences based on ethnicity, gender, age, religion, disability, national origin and sexual orientation," but it also encompasses an "infinite range of unique characteristics and experiences, including communication styles, physical characteristics such as height and weight, and speed of learning and comprehension."[6] Another definition says that diversity is all the ways in which people differ.[7] One final definition of diversity is the "array of physical and cultural differences that constitute the spectrum of human differences."[8] One important thing to note about these diversity definitions is that they focus on *all* the ways in which people can differ. And that's significant because diversity is no longer viewed as simply specific categories like race, gender, age, or disability but has broadened to a more inclusive recognition of the spectrum of differences.

So, what's our definition of **workplace diversity**? We're defining it as the ways in which people in an organization are different from and similar to one another. Notice that our definition not only focuses on the differences, but the similarities of employees.

EXHIBIT 4-1

Timeline of the Evolution of Workforce Diversity

1960s to 1970s	**Focus on complying with laws and regulations:** Title VII of Civil Rights Act; Equal Employment Opportunity Commission; affirmative action policies and programs
Early 1980s	**Focus on assimilating minorities and women into corporate setting:** Corporate programs developed to help improve self-confidence and qualifications of diverse individuals so they can "fit in"
Late 1980s	**Concept of workforce diversity expanded from compliance to an issue of business survival:** Publication of *Workforce 2000* opened business leaders' eyes about the future composition of workforce—that is, more diverse; first use of term *workforce diversity*
Late 1980s to Late 1990s	**Focus on fostering sensitivity:** Shift from compliance and focusing only on women and minorities to including everyone; making employees more aware and sensitive to the needs and differences of others
New Millennium	**Focus on diversity and inclusion for business success:** Workforce diversity seen as core business issue; important to achieve business success, profitability, and growth

Based on Ernst & Young, "The New Global Mindset: Driving Innovation Through Diversity," EYGM Limited, 2010, pp. 5–6; and R. Anand and M. Frances Winters, "A Retrospective View of Corporate Diversity Training from 1964 to the Present," *Academy of Management Learning & Education,* September 2008, pp. 356–372.

workforce diversity
The ways in which people in an organization are different from and similar to one another

This reinforces our belief that managers and organizations should view employees as having qualities in common as well as differences that separate them. It doesn't mean that those differences are any less important, but that our focus as managers is in finding ways to develop strong relationships with and engage our entire workforce.

We want to point out one final thing about our description of "what" workforce diversity is:[9] The demographic characteristics that we tend to think of when we think of diversity—age, race, gender, ethnicity, etc.—are just the tip of the iceberg. These demographic differences reflect **surface-level diversity**, which are easily perceived differences that may trigger certain stereotypes, but that do not necessarily reflect the ways people think or feel. Such surface-level differences in characteristics can affect the way people perceive others, especially when it comes to assumptions or stereotyping. However, as people get to know one another, these surface-level differences become less important and **deep-level diversity**—differences in values, personality, and work preferences—becomes more important. These deep-level differences can affect the way people view organizational work rewards, communicate, react to leaders, negotiate, and generally behave at work.

Why Is Managing Workforce Diversity So Important?

Ranked number 2 on *Diversity Inc.*'s list of top 50 companies for diversity, voice communications services company AT&T recognizes the powerful benefits of diversity. The company's chief diversity officer says, "We know that diverse, talented and dedicated people are critical to AT&T's success. Investing in a well-educated diverse workforce may be the single most important thing we can to do help America remain the leader in a digital, global economy."[10] BP, the British-owned energy company believes that "supplier diversity—that is, using minority or women suppliers—ensures that it gets the best products and services at the lowest price."[11] Many companies besides AT&T and BP are experiencing the benefits that diversity can bring. In this section, we want to look at *why* workforce diversity is so important to organizations. The benefits fall into three main categories: people management, organizational performance, and strategic. (See Exhibit 4-2.)

EXHIBIT 4-2

Benefits of Workforce Diversity

People Management
- Better use of employee talent
- Increased quality of team problem-solving efforts
- Ability to attract and retain employees of diverse backgrounds

Organizational Performance
- Reduced costs associated with high turnover, absenteeism, and lawsuits
- Enhanced problem-solving ability
- Improved system flexibility

Strategic
- Increased understanding of the marketplace, which improves ability to better market to diverse consumers
- Potential to improve sales growth and increase market share
- Potential source of competitive advantage because of improved innovation efforts
- Viewed as moral and ethical; the "right" thing to do

Sources: Based on Ernst & Young, "The New Global Mindset: Driving Innovation Through Diversity," EYGM Limited, 2010; M. P. Bell, M. L. Connerley, and F. K. Cocchiara, "The Case for Mandatory Diversity Education," *Academy of Management Learning & Education*, December 2009, pp. 597–609; E. Kearney, D. Gebert, and S. C. Voelpel, "When and How Diversity Benefits Teams: The Importance of Team Members' Need for Cognition," *Academy of Management Journal*, June 2009, pp. 581–598; J. A. Gonzalez and A. S. DeNisi, "Cross-Level Effects of Demography and Diversity Climate on Organizational Attachment and Firm Effectiveness," *Journal of Organizational Behavior*, January 2009, pp. 21–40; O. C. Richard, "Racial Diversity, Business Strategy, and Firm Performance: A Resource-Based View," *Academy of Management Journal*, April 2000, pp. 164–177; and G. Robinson and K. Dechant, "Building a Business Case for Diversity," *Academy of Management Executive*, August 1997, pp. 21–31.

PEOPLE MANAGEMENT. When all is said and done, diversity *is*, after all, about people, both inside and outside the organization. The people management benefits that organizations get because of their workforce diversity efforts revolve around attracting and retaining a talented workforce. Organizations want a talented workforce because it's the people—their skills, abilities, and experiences—who make an organization successful. Positive and explicit workforce diversity efforts can help organizations attract and keep talented diverse people and make the best of the talents those individuals bring to the workplace. In addition, another important people management benefit is that as companies rely more on employee teams in the workplace, those work teams with diverse backgrounds often bring different and unique perspectives to discussions, which can result in more creative ideas and solutions. However, recent research has indicated that such benefits might be hard to come by in teams performing more interdependent tasks over a long period of time. Such situations also present more opportunities for conflicts and resentments to build.[12] But, as the researchers pointed out, that simply means that those teams may need stronger team training and coaching to facilitate group decision making and conflict resolution.

ORGANIZATIONAL PERFORMANCE The performance benefits that organizations get from workforce diversity include cost savings and improvements in organizational functioning. The cost savings can be significant when organizations that cultivate a diverse workforce reduce employee turnover, absenteeism, and the chance of lawsuits. For instance, the upscale retailer Abercrombie & Fitch paid $50 million to people who alleged in a lawsuit and two class-action suits that it discriminated against minorities and women.[13] That's an amount of money that can seriously affect an organization's bottom line. In 2009, the Equal Employment Opportunity Commission reported 93,277 workplace discrimination claims were filed, the second highest total number of claims ever filed. But more startling than the total number of claims filed was the monetary relief obtained for victims, which totaled more than $376 million.[14] Workforce diversity efforts can reduce the risk of such lawsuits. In addition, a recent report by recruiting firm Korn/Ferry International found that U.S. companies waste $64 billion annually by losing and replacing employees who leave their jobs "solely due to failed diversity management."[15] That same report noted that 34 percent of those who left jobs because of diversity-related issues would have stayed if managers had recognized their abilities. Finally, organizational performance can be enhanced through workforce diversity because of improved problem-solving abilities and system flexibility. An organization with a diverse workforce can tap into the variety of skills and abilities represented and just the fact that its workforce is diverse requires that processes and procedures be more accommodative and inclusive.

Let's Get Real

Diversity is important because *not everyone has a perfect skill set or universal set of life experiences. The more your workplace reflects your customer base, the more successful you can be.*

STRATEGIC Organizations benefit strategically from a diverse workforce, as well. You have to look at managing workforce diversity as the key to extracting the best talent, performance, market share, and suppliers from a diverse country and world. One important strategic benefit is that with a diverse workforce, organizations can better anticipate and respond to changing consumer needs. Diverse employees bring a variety of points of view and approaches to opportunities, which can improve how the organization markets to diverse consumers. For instance, as the Hispanic population has grown, so have organizational efforts to market products and services to that demographic group. Organizations have found their Hispanic employees to be a fertile source of insights that would otherwise not have been available. Food service companies, retailers, financial services companies, and automobile manufacturers are just a few of the industries that have seen sales and market share increases because they paid attention to the needs of diverse consumers using information from employees.

A diverse workforce also can be a powerful source of competitive advantage, primarily because innovation thrives in such an environment. A recent report by Ernst & Young stated

surface-level diversity
Easily perceived differences that may trigger certain stereotypes, but that do not necessarily reflect the ways people think or feel

deep-level diversity
Differences in values, personality, and work preferences

that, "Cultural diversity offers the flexibility and creativity we need to re-create the global economy for the twenty-first century."[16] Innovation is never easy, but in a globalized world, it's even more challenging. Tapping into differing voices and viewpoints can be powerful factors in steering innovation. Companies that want to lead their industries have to find ways to "stir the pot"—to generate the lively debate that can create those new ideas. And research shows that diverse viewpoints can do that. "Diversity powers innovation, helping businesses generate new products and services."[17]

Finally, from an ethical perspective, workforce diversity and effectively managing diversity is the right thing to do. Although many societies have laws that say it's illegal to treat diverse people unfairly, many cultures also exhibit a strong ethical belief that diverse people should have access to equal opportunities and be treated fairly and justly. Businesses do have an ethical imperative to build relationships that value and enable all employees to be successful. Managers need to view workforce diversity as a way to bring different voices to the table and to build an environment based on trusting relationships. If they can do that, good things can happen, as we've noted.

LEARNING OUTCOME
4.2
Describe the changing workplaces in the United States and around the world.

The Changing Workplace

An African American as the chief executive of the United States. A woman heading up the State Department. A Latina sitting on the nation's highest court. Even at the highest levels of the political arena, we see a diverse workplace. In the business world, the once predominantly white male managerial workforce has given way to a more gender-balanced, multiethnic workforce. But it's a workforce still in transition as the overall population changes. In this section, we want to look at some of those changes, focusing on demographic trends by looking first at the characteristics of the U.S. population and then at global diversity trends. These trends will be reflected in a changing workplace, thus making this information important for managers to recognize and understand.

Characteristics of the U.S. Population

Statistics from the 2010 U.S. Census are likely to reinforce what we've already seen happening—we are an increasingly diverse society with some major readjustments occurring that will dramatically change the face of America by the year 2050. Let's look at some of the most dramatic of these changes.[18]

▶ *Total population of the United States:* The total population is projected to increase to 438 million by the year 2050, up from 296 million in 2005; 82 percent of that increase will be due to immigrants and their U.S.-born descendants. Nearly one in five Americans will be an immigrant in 2050, compared with one in eight in 2005.

▶ *Racial/ethnic groups:* In addition to total population changes, the components of that population are projected to change as well. Exhibit 4-3 provides the projected population breakdown. As the projections show, the main changes will be in the percentages of the Hispanic and white population. But the data also indicate that the Asian population will almost double.

EXHIBIT 4-3

Changing Population Makeup of the United States

	2005	2050
Foreign-born	12%	19%
Racial/Ethnic Groups		
White*	67%	47%
Hispanic	14%	29%
Black*	13%	13%
Asian*	5%	9%

*= Non-Hispanic
American Indian/Alaska Native not included.

Sources: H. El Nasser, "U.S. Hispanic Population to Triple by 2050," *USA Today Online* [www.usatoday .com], February 12, 2008; and "U.S. Population Projections: 2005–2050," Pew Research Center [http://pewhispanic.org/reports/], February 11, 2008.

Canada, like the United States, is becoming an increasingly diverse society with population trends that will continue to have a major impact on Canadian workplaces. When Gordon Nixon assumed the leadership of the Royal Bank of Canada as CEO, he created a diversity council as the first step in a drive to effectively manage a workforce that reflects the makeup of the bank's customer base. By actively recruiting women, immigrants, and minorities, RBC has earned a reputation for inclusiveness that helps it attract top female and minority talent and has developed a motivated workforce that results in better customer service and financial performance.

▶ *An aging population.* As a nation, our population is aging. According to the CIA *World Factbook*, the median age of the U.S. population stands at 36.7 years, up from 36.2 years in 2001.[19] That's quite a change, although not unexpected. In the first half of the twentieth century, America was a relatively "young" country, the result of lots of babies being born, declining infant and childhood mortality, and high rates of immigration. By 2050, however, one in every five persons will be aged 65 or over. The "oldest" of this group— those aged 80 and over—will be the most populous age group comprising 8 percent of the entire U.S. population. "Aging will continue to be one of the most important defining characteristics of the population."[20]

As you can probably imagine, such population trends are likely to have a major impact on U.S. workplaces. What workplace changes might we see?

According to the U.S. Bureau of Labor Statistics, by the year 2016, 47 percent of the labor force will be women and 37 percent will be Black, Latino, Asian/Pacific Islander, American Indian, or multiple racial categories.[21] In addition, by 2016, the average age of an employee will be 42.1 years.[22] The immigration issue is also likely to be a factor in a changing workplace. According to a recent analysis released by the U.S. Census Bureau, nearly one in six American workers is foreign-born, the highest proportion since the 1920s.[23] Despite the perception that the surge in immigration, especially over the last two decades, has flooded the United States with low-wage foreign labor, a new analysis of census data indicates that's not the reality. In 14 of the 25 largest metropolitan areas, more immigrants were employed in white-collar occupations than in lower-wage jobs like construction, cleaning, or manufacturing.[24] And now, with the total number of immigrants increasing dramatically, this, too, is likely to affect workplaces. Finally, people now entering the workforce are significantly younger, more ethnically diverse and/or foreign-born. In fact, by the year 2016, it's forecasted that 68 percent of new entrants in the U.S. workforce will be women or people of color.[25] The reality of these trends for businesses is that they'll have to accommodate and embrace such workforce changes. Although America historically has been known as a "melting pot" where people of different nationalities, religions, races, and ethnicities have blended together to become one, that perspective is no longer relevant. Organizations must recognize that they can't expect employees to assimilate into the organization by adopting similar attitudes and values. Instead, there's value in the differences that people bring to the workplace. It's not been easy. The ability of managers and organizations to effectively manage diversity has not kept pace with these population changes, creating challenges for minorities, women, and older employees. But many businesses are excelling at managing diversity and we'll discuss some of their workplace diversity initiatives in a later section of this chapter.

What About Global Workforce Changes?

Some significant worldwide population trends also are likely to affect global workforces. According to United Nations forecasts, "The world is in the midst of an epochal demographic shift that will reshape societies, economies, and markets over the next century."[26] Let's look at two of these trends.[27]

▶ *Total world population.* The total world population in 2010 is estimated at almost 7 billion individuals. However, that number is forecasted to hit 9 billion by 2050, at which point the United Nations predicts the total population will either stabilize or peak after growing for centuries at an ever-accelerating rate. The main reason for this major shift is the decline in birthrates as nations advance economically. However, in developing countries in Africa, Asia, Latin America, the Caribbean, and Oceania, birthrates remain high. One of the benefits is that many of these countries are likely to experience a "demographic dividend: a rising proportion of young people entering the workforce, driving productivity and economic growth."[28]

▶ *An aging population.* This demographic trend is one of critical importance for organizations. How critical? "The world's population is now aging at an *unprecedented rate.*"[29] How much do *you* know about global aging? (Our guess is . . . probably not much!) Take the quiz in Exhibit 4-4—no peeking at the answers beforehand—and see how well you scored. Were you surprised by some of the answers?

When we say the world's population is aging, some of the realities of this trend are hard to even fathom. For instance, people aged 65 and older will soon outnumber children under age 5 for the *first* time in history. Also, the world's population aged 80 and over is projected to increase 233 percent between the years 2008 and 2040. The implications of

---

EXHIBIT 4-4

Global Aging: How Much Do You Know?

1. True or False: The world's children under age 5 outnumber people aged 65 and over.
2. The world's older population (65 and older) increased by approximately how many people each month in 2008?
   a. 75,000
   b. 350,000
   c. 600,000
   d. 870,000
3. Which of the world's developing regions has the highest percentage of older people?
   a. Africa
   b. Latin America
   c. The Caribbean
   d. Asia
4. True or False: More than half of the world's older people live in the industrialized nations of Europe, North America, Japan, and Australia.
5. Which country had the world's highest percentage of older people in 2008?
   a. Sweden
   b. Japan
   c. Spain
   d. Italy

Answers to quiz:

1. *True.* Although the world's population is aging, children still outnumber older people as of 2008. Projections indicate, however, that in fewer than 10 years, older people will outnumber children for the first time in history.
2. *d.* The estimated change in the total size of the world's older population between July 2007 and July 2008 was more than 10.4 million people, an average of 870,000 each month.
3. *c.* The Caribbean, with 7.8 percent of all people aged 65 and over in 2008. Numbers for the other regions: Latin America, 6.4 percent; Asia (excluding Japan), 6.2 percent; and Africa, 3.3 percent.
4. *False.* Although industrialized nations have higher percentages of older people than do most developing countries, 62 percent of all people aged 65 and over now live in the developing regions of Africa, Asia, Latin America, the Caribbean, and Oceania.
5. *b.* Japan, with 22 percent of its population aged 65 or over, has supplanted Italy as the world's oldest major country.

Source: Based on K. Kinsella and W. He, "An Aging World: 2008," U.S. Census Bureau/International Population Reports, June 2009.

these trends for societies and businesses are profound—from changing family structures to shifting patterns of work and retirement to emerging economic challenges based on increasing demands on social entitlement programs, dwindling labor supply, and declining total global savings rates. Such demographic shifts will reshape the global workforce and organizational workplaces. Again, managers and organizations need to understand how such changes are likely to affect future workplace policies and practices.

Types of Workplace Diversity

As we've seen so far, diversity is a big issue, and an important issue, in today's workplaces. What types of dissimilarities—that is, diversity—do we find in those workplaces? Exhibit 4-5 shows several types of workplace diversity. Let's work our way through the different types.

4.3

LEARNING OUTCOME
Explain the different types of diversity found in workplaces.

Age

As we saw in the last section, the aging population is a major critical shift taking place in the workforce. With many of the nearly 85 million baby boomers still employed and active in the workforce, managers must ensure that those employees are not discriminated against because of age. Both Title VII of the Civil Rights Act of 1964 and the Age Discrimination in Employment Act of 1967 prohibit age discrimination. And the Age Discrimination Act also restricts mandatory retirement at specific ages. In addition to complying with these laws, organizations need programs and policies in place that provide for fair and equal treatment of their older employees.

One issue with older workers is the perception that people have of those workers. Perceptions such as they're sick more often and they can't work as hard or as fast as younger employees—perceptions that are inaccurate. Employers have mixed feelings about older workers.[30] On the positive side, they believe that older workers bring a number of good qualities to the job including experience, judgment, a strong work ethic, and a commitment to doing quality work. However, they also view older workers as not being flexible or adaptable and being more resistant to new technology. The challenge for managers is overcoming those misperceptions of older workers and the widespread belief that work performance and work quality decline with age.

Another issue that also supports the need for effectively managing workplace age diversity is that as baby boomers do retire, experts point out that some industries will face severe shortages of qualified employees. "Many of today's growth industries require a higher level

EXHIBIT 4-5

Types of Diversity Found in Workplaces

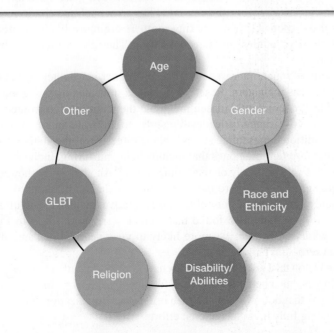

of technical competence in quantitative reasoning, problem solving, and communication skills...and the United States simply does not have enough students who are getting solid math and science education."[31] Organizations that do not plan for such a future may find themselves struggling to find a competent workforce, diverse or not.

Finally, the aging population is not the only age-related issue facing organizations. Some 50 million Generation Xers juggle work and family responsibilities. And now some 76 million members of Generation Y are either already in or poised to enter the workforce.[32] Having grown up in a world where they've had the opportunity to experience many different things, Gen Y workers bring their own ideas and approaches to the workplace. Managers need to ensure that these workers, regardless of age, also are treated fairly and as valuable assets. Effectively managing an organization's diverse age groups can lead to their working well with each other, learning from each other, and taking advantage of the different perspectives and experiences that each has to offer. It can be a win-win situation for all.

Gender

Women (49.8%) and men (50.2%) now each make up almost half of the workforce.[33] Yet, gender diversity issues are still quite prevalent in organizations. Take the gender pay gap. The latest information on the ratio of women's to men's median weekly earnings showed the figure at 80.2; the ratio for median annual earnings stood at 77.1.[34] Other issues involve career start and progress. Although 57 percent of today's college students are women, and women are just as likely to have completed college and hold an advanced degree, inequities persist.[35] Research by Catalyst found that men start their careers at higher levels than do women. And after starting out behind, women don't ever catch up. Men move further up the career ladder and faster as well.[36] Finally, misconceptions, mistaken beliefs, and unsupported opinions still exist about whether women perform their jobs as well as men do. You can see why gender diversity issues are important to attend to. So what *do* we know about differences between men and women in the workplace?

First of all, few, if any, important differences between men and women affect job performance.[37] No consistent male-female differences exist in problem-solving ability, analytical skills, competitive drive, motivation, sociability, or learning ability. Psychological research has found minor differences: Women tend to be more agreeable and willing to conform to authority while men are more aggressive and more likely to have expectations of success.

Another area where we also see differences between genders is in preference for work schedules, especially when the employee has preschool-age children. To accommodate their family responsibilities, working mothers are more likely to prefer part-time work, flexible work schedules, and telecommuting. They also prefer jobs that encourage work–life balance.

One question of much interest as it relates to gender is whether men and women are equally competent as managers. Research evidence indicates that a "good" manager is still perceived as predominantly masculine.[38] But the reality is that women tend to use a broader, more effective range of leadership styles to motivate and engage people. They usually blend traditional masculine styles—being directive, authoritative, and leading by example—with more feminine ones that include being nurturing, inclusive, and collaborative. Men tend to rely primarily on masculine styles.[39] Another study showed that women managers were significantly more likely than their male counterparts to coach and develop others and to create more committed, collaborative, inclusive, and ultimately, more effective, teams. This study also found that women were more likely to foster genuine collaboration while males were far more likely to view negotiations and other business transactions as zero-sum games.[40]

What should you take away from this discussion? Not that either women or men are the superior employees, but a better appreciation for why it's important for organizations to explore the strengths that both women and men bring to an organization and the barriers they face in contributing fully to organizational efforts.

When Kumi Hatsukano joined Nissan Motor, she experienced sexism and harassment at work. Today, she is a manager at a Nissan factory and is reaping the benefits of the automaker's initiative in Japan called "Women in the Driver's Seat: Gender Diversity as a Lever in Japan." Including women as decision makers and in positions of authority resulted from research that identified women as influencers of two-thirds of all car purchases. Nissan's resulting diversity strategy includes female career advisors, career development events, technical training programs, and incorporating the female perspective in the company's design, manufacturing, selling, and customer service operations.

Race and Ethnicity

There's a long and controversial history in the United States and in other parts of the world over race and how people react to and treat others of a different race. Race and ethnicity are important types of diversity in organizations. We're going to define **race** as the biological heritage (including physical characteristics such as one's skin color and associated traits) that people use to identify themselves. Most people identify themselves as part of a racial group. Such racial classifications are an integral part of a country's cultural, social, and legal environments. The racial choices on the 2010 Census included white, black, American Indian or Alaska Native, Asian, Native Hawaiian or other Pacific Islander, and some other race. This last choice, which was on the 2000 Census form for the first time, provided respondents the opportunity to identify themselves as multiracial.[41] The Census Bureau's chief of the racial statistics branch says, "Multiracial Americans are one of the fastest-growing demographic groups in the country."[42] **Ethnicity** is related to race, but it refers to social traits—such as one's cultural background or allegiance—that are shared by a human population.

As we saw earlier in Exhibit 4-3, the racial and ethnic diversity of the U.S. population is increasing at an exponential rate. We're also seeing this same effect in the composition of the workforce. Most of the research on race and ethnicity as they relate to the workplace has looked at hiring decisions, performance evaluations, pay, and workplace discrimination.[43] However, much of that research has focused on the differences in attitudes and outcomes between Whites and African Americans. Minimal study has been done on issues relevant to Asian, Hispanic, and Native American populations. Let's look at a few key findings.

One finding is that individuals in workplaces tend to favor colleagues of their own race in performance evaluations, promotion decisions, and pay raises. Although such effects are small, they are consistent. Next, research shows substantial racial differences in attitudes toward affirmative action, with African Americans favoring such programs to a greater degree than Whites. Other research shows that African Americans generally do worse than Whites in decisions related to the workplace. For instance, in employment interviews, African Americans receive lower ratings. In the job setting, they receive lower job performance ratings, are paid less, and are promoted less frequently. However, no statistically significant differences between the two races are observed in absenteeism rates, applied social skills at work, or accident rates. As you can see, race and ethnicity issues are a key focus for managers in effectively managing workforce diversity.

race
The biological heritage (including skin color and associated traits) that people use to identify themselves

ethnicity
Social traits (such as cultural background or allegiance) that are shared by a human population

Disability/Abilities

1990 was a watershed year for persons with disabilities. That was the year the Americans with Disabilities Act (ADA) became law. ADA prohibits discrimination against persons with disabilities and also requires employers to make reasonable accommodations so their workplaces are accessible to people with physical or mental disabilities and enable them to effectively perform their jobs. With the law's enactment, individuals with disabilities became a more representative and integral part of the U.S. workforce.

One issue facing managers and organizations is that the definition of disability is quite broad. The U.S. Equal Employment Opportunity Commission classifies a person as disabled if he or she has any physical or mental impairment that substantially limits one or more major life activities. For instance, deafness, chronic back pain, AIDS, missing limbs, seizure disorder, schizophrenia, diabetes, and alcoholism would all qualify. However, since these conditions have almost no common features, it's been difficult to study how each condition affects employment. It's obvious that some jobs cannot be accommodated to a disability. For instance, the law recognizes that a visually impaired person could not be an airline pilot, a person with severe cerebral palsy could not be a surgeon, and a person with profound mobility constraints could not be a firefighter. However, computer technology and other adaptive devices have shattered many employment barriers for other employees with disabilities.

Even after 20-plus years of the ADA, organizations and managers still have fears about employing disabled workers. A survey by the U.S. Department of Labor looked at these unfounded fears.[44] Exhibit 4-6 describes some of those fears as well as the reality; that is, what it's really like. Let's look at one company's experience. Walgreen has hired individuals with mental and physical disabilities to work at its distribution center in Anderson, South Carolina.[45] These employees work in one of three departments: case check-in (where merchandise initially comes in), de-trash (where merchandise is unpacked), or picking (where products are sorted into tubs based on individual store orders). Using an innovative approach that included job coaches, automated processes, and comprehensive training, Walgreen now has a capable and trusted workforce. The company's senior vice president of distribution said, "One thing we found is they (the disabled employees) can all do the job. What surprised us is the environment that it's created. It's a building where everybody helps each other out."

In effectively managing a workforce with disabled employees, managers need to create and maintain an environment in which employees feel comfortable disclosing their need

---

Employers' Fears About Disabled Workers

▶ *FEAR: Hiring people with disabilities leads to higher employment costs and lower profit margins*
  • **REALITY:** Absentee rates for sick time are virtually equal between employees with and without disabilities; workers' disabilities are not a factor in formulas calculating insurance costs for workers' compensation

▶ *FEAR: Workers with disabilities lack job skills and experience necessary to perform as well as their abled counterparts*
  • **REALITY:** Commonplace technologies such as the Internet and voice-recognition software have eliminated many of the obstacles for workers with disabilities; many individuals with disabilities have great problem-solving skills from finding creative ways to perform tasks that others may take for granted

▶ *FEAR: Uncertainty over how to take potential disciplinary action with a worker with disabilities*
  • **REALITY:** A person with a disability for whom workplace accommodations have been provided has the same obligations and rights as far as job performance

▶ *FEAR: High costs associated with accommodating disabled employees*
  • **REALITY:** Most workers with disabilities require *no* accommodation but for those who do, more than half of the workplace modifications cost $500 or less

Sources: R. Braum, "Disabled Workers: Employer Fears Are Groundless," *Bloomberg BusinessWeek Online*, October 2, 2009; and U.S. Department of Labor/Office of Disability Employment Policy, "Survey of Employer Perspectives on the Employment of People with Disabilities [http://www.dol.gov/odep/documents/survey_report_jan_09.doc], November 2008.

for accommodation. Those accommodations, by law, need to enable individuals with disabilities to perform their jobs but they also need to be perceived as equitable by those not disabled. That's the balancing act that managers face.

Religion

Hani Khan, a college sophomore, worked for three months as a stock clerk at a Hollister clothing store in San Francisco.[46] One day, she was told by her supervisors to remove the head scarf that she wears in observance of Islam (known as a *hijab*) because it violated the company's "look policy" (which instructs employees on clothing, hair styles, makeup, and accessories they may wear to work). She refused on religious grounds and was fired one week later. Like a number of other Muslim women (425 in 2009 alone), she filed a federal job discrimination complaint. A spokesperson for Abercrombie & Fitch (Hollister's parent company) said, "If any Abercrombie associate identifies a religious conflict with an Abercrombie policy . . . the company will work with the associate in an attempt to find an accommodation." That's a step in the right direction.

Title VII of the Civil Rights Act prohibits discrimination on the basis of religion (as well as race/ethnicity, country of origin, and sex). Today, it seems that the greatest religious diversity issue in the United States revolves around Islam, especially after 9/11.[47] Islam is one of the world's most popular religions and some 2 million Muslims live in the United States. For the most part, U.S. Muslims have attitudes similar to those of other U.S. citizens. However, there are real and perceived differences. For instance, nearly 4 in 10 U.S. adults admit they harbor negative feelings or prejudices toward U.S. Muslims and 52 percent believe U.S. Muslims are not respectful of women.

Religious beliefs also can prohibit or encourage work behaviors. Many conservative Jews believe they should not work on Saturdays. Some Christians do not want to work on Sundays. Religious individuals may believe they have an obligation to express their beliefs in the workplace making it uncomfortable for those who may not share those beliefs. Some pharmacists have refused to give out RU-486 (the "morning after" abortion pill) on the basis of their beliefs.

As you can see, religion and religious beliefs can generate misperceptions and negative feelings. You'd probably not be surprised to find out that the number of religious discrimination claims has been growing in the United States.[48] In accommodating religious diversity, managers need to recognize and be aware of different religions and their beliefs, paying special attention to when certain religious holidays fall. Try to accommodate, when at all possible, employees who have special needs or requests, but do so in a way that other employees don't view it as "special treatment."

GLBT: Sexual Orientation and Gender Identity

The acronym GLBT—which refers to gay, lesbian, bisexual, and transgender people—is being used more frequently and relates to the diversity of sexual orientation and gender identity.[49] Sexual orientation has been called the "last acceptable bias."[50] We want to emphasize that we're not condoning this perspective, but what this comment refers to is that most people understand that racial and ethnic stereotypes are "off-limits," but it's not unusual to hear derogatory comments about gays or lesbians. U.S. federal law does not prohibit discrimination against employees on the basis of sexual orientation, although many states and municipalities do. However, in Europe, the Employment Equality Directive required all European Union member states to introduce legislation making it unlawful to discriminate on grounds of sexual orientation.[51] Despite the progress in making workplaces more accommodating of gays and lesbians, much more needs to be done. One study found more than 40 percent of gay and lesbian employees indicated that they had been unfairly treated, denied a promotion, or pushed to quit their job because of their sexual orientation.[52]

Employers in the United States have taken differing approaches to their treatment of sexual orientation.[53] Many have adopted a variation of the "don't ask, don't tell" policy of the military. Some just flat out do not hire any GLBT employees. However, according to a report from the Human Rights Campaign Foundation, 85 percent of the largest corporations

Let's Get Real

F2F

You can accommodate special needs of different groups without appearing to show favoritism or offending other groups by *implementing fair and consistent company policies that don't give privileges to one group of people over another.*

by the numbers [54]

11 percent—the amount by which women *under-*estimated the performance scores their bosses gave them.

80 percent of women feel that their worth is determined by what their companies choose to pay them.

79 percent of survey respondents believe that there is a definite generation gap.

75 percent of corporate executives believe that having minorities in senior executive positions is important.

78 percent of employees say that their companies do not practice diversity in their workforces as much as they claim publicly.

41 percent of employees say there's more diversity in their workplace than was there 10 years ago.

30 percent of women say that the pay scale for women is the top barrier to women in the workplace.

in the United States now prohibit employment discrimination based on sexual orientation and 35 percent prohibit bias based on gender identity.[55] An increasing number of large companies are implementing policies and practices to protect the rights of GLBT employees in the workplace. For instance, Ernst & Young, S. C. Johnson & Sons, Inc., and Kodak, among others, all provide training to managers on ways to prevent sexual orientation discrimination. A diversity manager at IBM says, "We believe that having strong transgender and gender identification policies is a natural extension of IBM's corporate culture."[56] And more than 57 percent of the largest corporations in the United States now offer their employees health insurance benefits for domestic partners.[57] A recent study analyzed the effect of company GLBT nondiscrimination policies on that company's stock market value. The findings suggest that the stock prices of companies with more progressive GLBT policies outperform those of competitors in the same industry that don't have such policies.[58]

As with most of the types of diversity we've discussed in this section, managers need to look at how best to meet the needs of their GLBT employees. They need to respond to employees' concerns while also creating a safe and productive work environment for all.

Other Types of Diversity

As we said earlier, diversity refers to *any* dissimilarities or differences that might be present in a workplace. Other types of workplace diversity that managers might confront and have to deal with include socioeconomic background (social class and income-related factors), team members from different functional areas or organizational units, physical attractiveness, obesity/thinness, job seniority, or intellectual abilities. Each of these types of diversity also can affect how employees are treated in the workplace. Again, managers need to ensure that all employees—no matter the similarities or dissimilarities—are treated fairly and given the opportunity and support to do their jobs to the best of their abilities.

LEARNING OUTCOME
Discuss the challenges managers face in managing diversity.

4.4

Challenges in Managing Diversity

Although the nooses, racist graffiti, and Confederate battle flags should have been enough to warrant action, it wasn't until an African American employee at a Texas-based plant of Turner Industries Group LLC discovered that he was being paid less as a painter than white workers were being paid finally complained.[59] Soon after filing the complaint, he was fired. His complaints, along with those of seven other employees, "have led to the federal government to conclude there was evidence of racial discrimination." Despite the benefits that we know workforce diversity brings to organizations, managers still face challenges in creating accommodating and safe work environments for diverse employees. In this section, we're going to look at two of those challenges: personal bias and the glass ceiling.

Personal Bias

Smokers. Working mothers. Football players. Blondes. Female president of the United States. Hispanic. What impressions come to mind when you read these words? Based on your background and experiences, you probably have pretty specific ideas and things you would say, maybe even to the point of characteristics you think that all smokers or all working mothers or all Hispanics share. Employees can and do bring such ideas about various groups of people with them into the workplace. Such ideas can lead to prejudice, discrimination, and stereotypes, all of which shape and influence our personal biases.

Bias is a term that describes a tendency or preference toward a particular perspective or ideology. It's generally seen as a "one-sided" perspective. Our personal biases cause us to have preconceived opinions about people or things. Such preconceived opinions can create all kinds of inaccurate judgments and attitudes. Let's take a look at how our personal biases affect the way we view and respond to diversity.

One outcome of our personal biases can be **prejudice**, a preconceived belief, opinion, or judgment toward a person or a group of people. Our prejudice can be based on all the types of diversity we discussed: race, gender, ethnicity, age, disability, religion, sexual orientation, or even other personal characteristics.

A major factor in prejudice is **stereotyping**, which is judging a person on the basis of one's perception of a group to which he or she belongs. For instance, "Married persons are more stable employees than single persons" is an example of stereotyping. Keep in mind, though, that not all stereotypes are inaccurate. For instance, asking someone in accounting about a budgeting problem you're having would be an appropriate assumption and action. However, many stereotypes—red-haired people have a bad temper, elderly drivers are the most dangerous, working mothers aren't as committed to their careers as men are, and so forth—aren't factual and distort our judgment.

Both prejudice and stereotyping can lead to someone treating others who are members of a particular group unequally. That's what we call **discrimination**, which is when someone acts out their prejudicial attitudes toward people who are the targets of their prejudice. You'll find in Exhibit 4-7 definitions and examples of different types of discrimination.

EXHIBIT 4-7

Forms of Discrimination

Type of Discrimination	Definition	Examples from Organizations
Discriminatory policies or practices	Actions taken by representatives of the organization that deny equal opportunity to perform or unequal rewards for performance	Older workers may be targeted for layoffs because they are highly paid and have lucrative benefits.[a]
Sexual harassment	Unwanted sexual advances and other verbal or physical conduct of a sexual nature that create a hostile or offensive work environment	Salespeople at one company went on company-paid visits to strip clubs, brought strippers into the office to celebrate promotions, and fostered pervasive sexual rumors.[b]
Intimidation	Overt threats or bullying directed at members of specific groups of employees	African American employees at some companies have found nooses hanging over their work stations.[c]
Mockery and insults	Jokes or negative stereotypes; sometimes the result of jokes taken too far	Arab Americans have been asked at work whether they were carrying bombs or were members of terrorist organizations.[d]
Exclusion	Exclusion of certain people from job opportunities, social events, discussions, or informal mentoring; can occur unintentionally	Many women in finance claim they are assigned to marginal job roles or are given light workloads that don't lead to promotion.[e]
Incivility	Disrespectful treatment, including behaving in an aggressive manner, interrupting the person, or ignoring his or her opinions	Female lawyers note that male attorneys frequently cut them off or do not adequately address their comments.[f]

Notes:
a. J. Levitz and P. Shishkin, "More Workers Cite Age Bias After Layoffs," *Wall Street Journal*, March 11, 2009, pp. D1–D2.
b. W. M. Bulkeley, "A Data-Storage Titan Confronts Bias Claims," *Wall Street Journal*, September 12, 2007, pp. A1, A16.
c. D. Walker, "Incident with Noose Stirs Old Memories," *McClatchy-Tribune Business News*, June 29, 2008; and D. Solis, "Racial Horror Stories Keep EEOC Busy," *Knight-Ridder Tribune Business News*, July 30, 2005, p. 1.
d. H. Ibish and A. Stewart, *Report on Hate Crimes and Discrimination Against Arab Americans: The Post-September 11 Backlash, September 11, 2001—October 11, 2001* (Washington, DC: American-Arab Anti-Discrimination Committee, 2003).
e. A. Raghavan, "Wall Street's Disappearing Women," *Forbes*, March 16, 2009, pp. 72–78.
f. L. M. Cortina, "Unseen Injustice: Incivility as Modern Discrimination in Organizations."

Source: S. Robbins and T. Judge, *Organizational Behavior*, 14th ed., Prentice Hall, p. 43.

bias
A tendency or preference toward a particular perspective or ideology

prejudice
A preconceived belief, opinion, or judgment toward a person or a group of people

stereotyping
Judging a person based on a perception of a group to which that person belongs

discrimination
When someone acts out their prejudicial attitudes toward people who are the targets of their prejudice

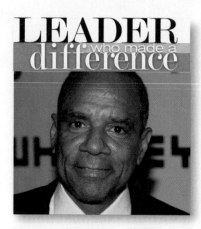

LEADER who made a difference

"To succeed in today's fast-paced work environment, we must understand the needs and expectations of a diverse, multigenerational and global workforce."[60] That's the commitment made by American Express to its employees. Sitting in the top spot at American Express is Kenneth I. Chenault, an African American, who was named by *Black Enterprise* magazine as number one on the list of the 100 most powerful executives in corporate America. Chenault is known for his friendliness and integrity as much as for his discipline and drive. His business acumen is unparalleled having successfully guided his company through the financial meltdown. But he also recognizes the importance of being a leader who knows the importance of attracting and retaining the highest caliber of employees. Chenault meets regularly with the company's employee resource groups, holds senior executives personally responsible for meeting diversity goals, and is a visible supporter of the company's diversity initiatives.

Many of these actions are prohibited by law so you won't find them discussed in employee handbooks or organizational policy statements. However, you can still see these actions in workplaces. "As discrimination has increasingly come under both legal scrutiny and social disapproval, most overt forms have faded, which may have resulted in an increase in more covert forms like incivility or exclusion."[61]

Discrimination, whether intentional or not, can lead to serious negative consequences for employers as illustrated by the example we discussed at the beginning of this section. But it's not just the potential financial consequences organizations and managers face for discriminatory actions. It's the reduced employee productivity, negative and disruptive interpersonal conflicts, increased employee turnover, and overall negative climate that can lead to serious problems for managers. Even if an organization has never had an employment discrimination lawsuit filed against it, managers need to aggressively work to eliminate unfair discrimination.

Glass Ceiling

Pretend that you've just finished your MBA degree. It's not been easy. Your graduate classes were challenging, but you feel well-prepared for and excited about that first post-MBA job. If you're female, that first job for 60 percent of you will be an entry-level position. However, if you're male, only 46 percent of you would start out in an entry-level position.[62] And 2 percent of women would make it to the CEO or senior executive position, although 6 percent of men would. "Although entry into occupations such as accounting, business, and law happens at about the same rate for men and women, evidence is mounting that women's and men's career paths begin to divide soon after."[63] This issue can be seen with minorities as well. Only a small percentage of both male and female Hispanics and African Americans have made it into management positions in the United States. What's going on here? After all these years of "equal opportunity," why do we still see statistics like these?

In the 1980s, the term **glass ceiling**, first used in a *Wall Street Journal* article, refers to the invisible barrier that separates women and minorities from top management positions.[64] The idea of a "ceiling" means that there is something blocking upward movement and the idea of "glass" is that whatever's blocking the way isn't immediately apparent.

Research on the glass ceiling has looked at identifying the organizational practices and interpersonal biases that have blocked women's advancement. Findings from those studies have ranged from lack of mentoring, sex stereotyping, views that associate masculine traits with leader effectiveness, and bosses' perceptions of family–work conflict.[65]

As others have said, it's time to shatter the glass ceiling for all employees. Every employee should have the opportunity to work in a career in which they can use their skills and abilities and to have a career path that allows them to progress however far they want to go. Getting to that end, however, isn't going to be easy. As we'll see in the next section, however, there are a number of workplace diversity initiatives that organizations can implement to work toward that end.

LEARNING OUTCOME **4.5**
Describe various workplace diversity management initiatives.

Workplace Diversity Initiatives

"Marriott International is the textbook definition of a great company for diversity."[66] Bill Marriott, the company's chairman and CEO, is a visible force and advocate for diversity both in the company and externally. He personally signs off on bonuses for his top staff, which are tied to diversity efforts and ability to meet diversity goals, an amount that can account for 13 percent of their compensation. The company also has mandatory diversity training every month and a number of employee resource groups that provide input and advice. Their diversity management efforts have earned the company the number 4 spot on the Top 50 Companies for Diversity list for 2009.

As the Marriott example shows, some businesses *are* effectively managing diversity. In this section we want to look at various workplace diversity initiatives. Before we start discussing these, however, we want to look at the legal framework within which diversity efforts take place.

The Legal Aspect of Workplace Diversity

Would workplaces have evolved to the level of diversity that currently exists without federal legislation and mandates?[67] Although it's an interesting question, the fact is that federal laws *have* contributed to some of the social change we've seen over the last 50-plus years. Exhibit 4-8 describes the major equal employment opportunity laws with which organizations must comply. Failure to do so, as we have seen in some of the examples we've described, can be costly and damaging to an organization's bottom line and reputation. It's important that managers know what they can and cannot do legally and ensure that all employees understand as well.

However, effectively managing workplace diversity needs to be more than understanding and complying with federal laws. Organizations that are successful at managing

Year	Law or Ruling	Description
1963	Equal Pay Act	Prohibits pay differences for equal work based on gender
1964 (amended in 1972)	Civil Rights Act, Title VII	Prohibits discrimination based on race, color, religion, national origin, or gender
1967 (amended in 1978)	Age Discrimination in Employment Act	Prohibits discrimination against employees 40 years and older
1978	Pregnancy Discrimination Act	Prohibits discrimination against women in employment decisions on the basis of pregnancy, childbirth, and related medical decisions
1978	Mandatory Retirement Act	Prohibits the forced retirement of most employees
1990	Americans with Disabilities Act	Prohibits discrimination against individuals who have disabilities or chronic illnesses; also requires reasonable accommodations for these individuals
1991	Civil Rights Act of 1991	Reaffirms and tightens prohibition of discrimination and gives individuals right to sue for punitive damages
1993	Family and Medical Leave Act	Gives employees in organizations with 50 or more employees up to 12 weeks of unpaid leave each year for family or medical reasons
2009	Lilly Ledbetter Fair Pay Act	Changes the statute of limitations on pay discrimination to 180 days from each paycheck

EXHIBIT 4-8

Major Equal Employment Opportunity Laws

glass ceiling
The invisible barrier that separates women and minorities from top management positions

diversity use additional diversity initiatives and programs. We're going to look at four of these including top management commitment, mentoring, diversity skills training, and employee resource groups.

Top Management Commitment to Diversity

Today's increasingly competitive marketplace underscores the reality that creating a diverse workplace has never been more important. It's equally important to make diversity and inclusion an integral part of the organization's culture. "A sustainable diversity and inclusion strategy must play a central role in decision making at the highest leadership level and filter down to every level of the company."[68] How do organizational leaders do that?

One of the first things to do is make sure that diversity and inclusion are part of the organization's purpose, goals, and strategies. Even during economically challenging times, an organization needs a strong commitment to diversity and inclusion programs. Diversity needs to be integrated into every aspect of the business—from the workforce, customers, and suppliers to products, services, and the communities served. Policies and procedures must be in place to ensure that grievances and concerns are addressed immediately. Finally, the organizational culture needs to be one where diversity and inclusion are valued, even to the point where, like Marriott International, individual performance is measured and rewarded on diversity accomplishments.

Mentoring

One of the consequences of having few women and minorities in top corporate leadership positions is that lower-level diverse employees lack someone to turn to for support or advice. That's where a mentoring program can be beneficial. **Mentoring** is a process whereby an experienced organizational member (a mentor) provides advice and guidance to a less-experienced member (a protégé). Mentors usually provide two unique forms of mentoring functions—career development and social support.[69]

Andrea Jung, CEO of Avon Products, the first woman to hold that job in the female-oriented products company, said that her male mentor (previous CEO James Preston) had the most influence on her career.[70] A study by Catalyst of male mentors to women found that men who impeded or who were indifferent to the progress of women viewed the workplace as a zero-sum game where promotion of women came at the expense of men. However, one thing that stood out among males who championed women was a strong sense of fairness.[71]

A good mentoring program would be aimed at all diverse employees with high potential to move up the organization's career ladder. Exhibit 4-9 looks at what a good mentor does. If an organization is serious about its commitment to diversity, it needs to have a mentoring program in place.

EXHIBIT 4-9

What a Good Mentor Does

- Provides instruction
- Offers advice
- Gives constructive criticism
- Helps build appropriate skills
- Shares technical expertise
- Develops a high-quality, close, and supportive relationship with protégé
- Keeps lines of communication open
- Knows when to "let go" and let the protégé prove what he/she can do

Sources: J. Prime and C. A. Moss-Racusin, "Engaging Men in Gender Initiatives: What Change Agents Need to Know," *Catalyst* [www.catalyst.org], 2009; T. J. DeLong, J. J. Gabarro, and R. J. Lees, "Why Mentoring Matters in a Hypercompetitive World," *Harvard Business Review,* January 2008, pp. 115–121; S. N. Mehta, "Why Mentoring Works," *Fortune,* July 9, 2001, p. 119; and D. A. Thomas, "Race Matters: The Truth About Mentoring Minorities," *Harvard Business Review,* April 2001, pp. 99–107.

Diversity Skills Training

"The only thing in human DNA is to discriminate. It's a part of normal human tribal behavior."[72] In a chapter on managing diversity, you might be surprised to find a statement like this. However, the reality is . . . it's reality. Our human nature is to not accept or approach anything that's different from us. But it doesn't make discrimination of any type or form acceptable. And we live and work in a multicultural context. So the challenge for organizations is to find ways for employees to be effective in dealing with others who aren't like them. That's where **diversity skills training**, specialized training to educate employees about the importance of diversity and teach them skills for working in a diverse workplace, comes in. It's estimated that some $80 billion has been spent over the last 10 years on diversity programs, much of it spent on training.[73]

Most diversity skills training programs start with *diversity awareness training*. During this type of training, employees are made aware of the assumptions and biases they may have. Once we recognize that, we can look at increasing our sensitivity and openness to those who are different from us. Sounds simple, but it's not. But if people can be taught to recognize that they're prejudging people and to consciously address that behavior, then the diversity awareness training has been successful. Then, the next step is *diversity skills training*, in which people learn specific skills on how to communicate and work effectively in a diverse work environment. At Sodexho, the food services/facilities management company, employee diversity training is an important part of their diversity management program. The company's chief diversity officer said, "As an organization, we have worked to implement the right policies, but more importantly, empower all our employees to understand issues of diversity and work to ensure change happens at every level of our company."[74]

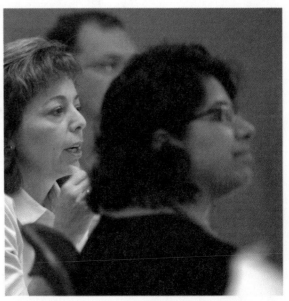

These men and women employed at IBM have the opportunity to participate in employee resource groups for eight constituencies: women, blacks, Hispanics, Asians, Native Americans, people with disabilities, GLBT (gay, lesbian, bisexual, and transgender) and men, as well as another group that focuses on work–life balance. IBM has more than 200 network groups within this framework, 42 of which are women's groups. The company supports these groups of employees who come together voluntarily to help IBM be a better place to work and to help each other become more effective by improving their professional and technical skills.

Employee Resource Groups

Kellogg Company, the cereal company, is a pioneer in workplace diversity. More than 100 years ago, the company's founder, W. K. Kellogg, employed women in the workplace and reached across cultural boundaries. That commitment to diversity continues today. The company's CEO says, "There's no doubt that our success comes from the many different backgrounds, experiences, ideas, and viewpoints that our people contribute to our business."[75] Kellogg's has been very supportive of its various **employee resource groups**, made up of employees connected by some common dimension of diversity. Such groups typically are formed by the employees themselves, not the organizations. However, it's important for organizations to recognize and support these groups.

Employee resource groups (also called employee networks or affinity groups) have become quite popular over the last 10 years.[76] Why are they so popular? The main reason is that diverse groups have the opportunity to see that their existence is acknowledged and that they have the support of people within and outside the group. Individuals in a minority often feel that they're invisible and not important in the overall organizational scheme of things. Employee resource groups provide an opportunity for those individuals to have a voice. For instance, at Kellogg, there's a WOK (Women of Kellogg) group, a KAARG (Kellogg African American Resource Group), !HOLA! (Kellogg's Latino Employee Resource Group), K-MERG (Kellogg Multinational Employee Resource Group), and YP (Kellogg Young Professionals Employee Resource Group). The description for WOK says,

mentoring
A process whereby an experienced organizational member (a mentor) provides advice and guidance to a less-experienced member (a protégé)

diversity skills training
Specialized training to educate employees about the importance of diversity and teach them skills for working in a diverse workplace

employee resource groups
Groups made up of employees connected by some common dimension of diversity

"This community of employees is dedicated to the personal and professional growth and development of the women within Kellogg Company. They work together to project a common voice for the shared experiences, perceptions, and needs of women in the Kellogg workplace and to help members reach their full potential." The statements about the other groups are similar in describing the commitment to empowering, leveraging, and fostering the development of the individual members of the resource group. Through these employee resource groups, those in a minority find that they're not alone. And that can be a powerful means of embracing and including all employees, regardless of their differences.

What Would You Do?

Kim Scartelli
Multiple Franchise
Owner and
Consultant
Curves for Women
Canton, MI

Let's Get Real:

My Response *to A Manager's Dilemma, page 98*

I think it is admirable for the Deutsche Telekom Company to recognize the need for more women in management positions in their company. However, the idea of a quota troubles me. Quotas could backfire and have the negative effect of lowering morale in a company. In this case, for instance, women who are promoted might feel as though they were selected for their gender versus their individual merit, performance, or abilities. Men, on the other hand, might resent being passed over for promotion to meet the arbitrary quota and may leave a company because they feel as if they can never get ahead with the company policies and quota in place.

Deutsche Telekom can keep their goal of increasing women in management but instead of implementing a quota could:

- Research and understand the root causes of the gender gap.
- Provide gender awareness education for all leaders in the company.
- Begin removing the barriers that keep women from reaching these positions.

CHAPTER SUMMARY
by Learning Outcomes

Define workplace diversity and explain why managing it is so important.

Workplace diversity is the ways in which people in an organization are different from and similar to one another. Managing workforce diversity is important for three reasons: (1) people management benefits—better use of employee talent, increased quality of team problem-solving efforts, and ability to attract and retain diverse employees; (2) organizational performance benefits—reduced costs, enhanced problem-solving ability, and improved system flexibility; and (3) strategic benefits—increased understanding of diverse marketplace, potential to improve sales and market share, competitive advantage because of improved innovation efforts, and viewed as moral and ethical.

Describe the changing workplaces in the United States and around the world.

The main changes in the workplace in the United States include the total increase in the population, the changing components of the population especially in relation to racial/ethnic groups, and an aging population. The most important changes in the global population include the total world population and the aging of that population.

Explain the different types of diversity found in workplaces.

The different types of diversity found in workplaces include age (older workers and younger workers), gender (male and female), race and ethnicity (racial and ethnic classifications), disability/abilities (people with a disability that limits major life activities), religion (religious beliefs and religious practices), sexual orientation and gender identity (gay, lesbian, bisexual, and transgender) and other (for instance, socioeconomic background, team members from different functional areas, physical attractiveness, obesity, job seniority, and so forth).

Discuss the challenges managers face in managing diversity.

The two main challenges managers face are personal bias and the glass ceiling. Bias is a tendency or preference toward a particular perspective or ideology. Our biases can lead to prejudice, which is a preconceived belief, opinion, or judgment toward a person or a group of people; stereotyping, which is judging a person on the basis of one's perception of a group to which he or she belongs; and discrimination, which is when someone acts out their prejudicial attitudes toward people who are the targets of their prejudice. The glass ceiling refers to the invisible barrier that separates women and minorities from top management positions.

Describe various workplace diversity management initiatives.

It's important to understand the role of federal laws in diversity. Some of these laws include Title VII of the Civil Rights Act, the Americans with Disabilities Act, and Age Discrimination in Employment Act. Workplace diversity management initiatives include top management commitment to diversity; mentoring, which is a process whereby an experienced organizational member provides advice and guidance to a less-experienced member; diversity skills training; and employee resource groups, which are groups made up of employees connected by some common dimension of diversity.

To check your understanding of learning outcomes **4.1** – **4.5** go to **mymanagementlab.com** and try the chapter questions.

REVIEW AND DISCUSSION QUESTIONS

1. What is workforce diversity and why is managing it so important?

2. Why is it important for an organization to have a clear definition of diversity?

3. Distinguish between surface-level diversity and deep-level diversity. Why is it important to understand the difference between the two?

4. What are the major trends in the changing populations of the United States and the world?

5. Describe the issues associated with each of the types of workforce diversity.

6. Distinguish between race and ethnicity.

7. What challenges do managers face in creating accommodating and safe work environments for employees?

8. Explain the relationship between bias, prejudice, stereotyping, and discrimination.

9. What U.S. federal laws are important to workplace diversity initiatives?

10. Why do you think the glass ceiling has proven to be a barrier to women and minorities?

PREPARING FOR: My Career

ETHICS DILEMMA

In August of 2009, a viral campaign against McDonald's website, 365black.com, began to spread.[77] Anger over the website grew as news commentators discovered an additional McDonald's website targeting the Asian community, called MyInspirAsian.com. One individual said, "Even if the idea was a good one and truly was promoting Black cultural heritage, it really does come off as manipulation and stereotyping." Check out both websites. What do you think? Do you think these targeted sites are manipulative and stereotypical? Why or why not? Is there anything else the company could or should be doing?

SKILLS EXERCISE

Developing Your Valuing Diversity Skill

About the Skill

Understanding and managing people who are similar to us are challenges—but understanding and managing people who are dissimilar from us and from each other can be even tougher.[78] The diversity issues an individual manager might face are many. They may include issues such as communicating with employees whose familiarity with the language may be limited; creating career development programs that fit the skills, needs, and values of a particular group; helping a diverse team cope with a conflict over goals or work assignments; or learning which rewards are valued by different groups.

Steps in Practicing the Skill

1. *Fully accept diversity.* Successfully valuing diversity starts with each individual accepting the principle of diversity. Accept the value of diversity for its own sake—not simply because it's the right thing to do. And it's important that you reflect your acceptance in all you say and do.

2. *Recruit broadly.* When you have job openings, work to get a diverse applicant pool. Although referrals from current employees can be a good source of applicants, that source tends to produce candidates similar to the present workforce.

3. *Select fairly.* Make sure that the selection process doesn't discriminate. One suggestion is to use job-specific tests rather than general aptitude or knowledge tests. Such tests measure specific skills, not subjective characteristics.

4. *Provide orientation and training for diverse employees.* Making the transition from outsider to insider can be particularly difficult for a diverse employee. Provide support either through a group or through a mentoring arrangement.

5. *Sensitize nondiverse employees.* Not only do you personally need to accept and value diversity, as a manager you need to encourage all your employees to do so. Many organizations do this through diversity training programs. In addition, employees can also be part of ongoing discussion groups whose members meet monthly to discuss stereotypes and ways of improving diversity relationships. The most important thing a manager can do is show by his or her actions that diversity is valued.

6. *Strive to be flexible.* Part of valuing diversity is recognizing that different groups have different needs and values. Be flexible in accommodating employee requests.

7. *Seek to motivate individually.* Motivating employees is an important skill for any manager; motivating a diverse workforce has its own special challenges. Managers must strive to be in tune with the background, cultures, and values of employees.

8. *Reinforce employee differences.* Encourage individuals to embrace and value diverse views. Create traditions and ceremonies that promote diversity. Celebrate diversity by accentuating its positive aspects. However, also be prepared to deal with the challenges of diversity such as mistrust, miscommunication, lack of cohesiveness, attitudinal differences, and stress.

Practicing the Skill

Read through the following scenario. Write down some notes about how you would handle the situation described. Be sure to refer to the eight behaviors described for valuing diversity.

Scenario

Read through the descriptions of the following employees who work for the same organization. After reading each description, write a short paragraph describing what you think the goals and priorities of each employee might be. With what types of employee issues might the manager of each employee have to deal? How could these managers show that they value the diversity represented by each?

Lester. Lester is 57 years old, a college graduate, and a vice president of the firm. His two children are married and he is a grandparent of three beautiful grandchildren. He lives in a condo with his wife who does volunteer work and is active in their church. Lester is healthy and likes to stay active, both physically and mentally.

Sanjyot. Sanjyot is a 30-year-old clerical worker who came to the United States from Indonesia 10 years ago. She completed high school after moving to the United States and has begun to attend evening classes at a local community college. Sanjyot is a single parent with two children under the age of 8. Although her health is excellent, one of her children suffers from a severe learning disability.

Yuri. Yuri is a recent immigrant from one of the former Soviet republics. He is 42 years old and his English communication skills are quite limited. He has an engineering degree from his country but since he's not licensed to practice in the United States, he works as a parts clerk. He is unmarried and has no children but feels obligated to send much of his paycheck to relatives back in his home country.

WORKING TOGETHER
Team Exercise

The popularity of employee resource groups continues to climb. Form small groups with three or four other class members. Your task is to research how to form employee resource groups for staff members at your school. Come up with a written plan that discusses the benefits and challenges of employee resource groups, the steps to follow in creating these groups, and suggestions for maintaining the value of such groups for their members. Be prepared to turn in your written report to your professor or to present it in class.

MY TURN TO BE A MANAGER

- Describe your experiences with people from other backgrounds. What challenges have you faced? What have you learned that will help you in understanding the unique needs and challenges of a diverse workplace?

- Go to *DiversityInc.com* [www.diversityinc.com] and find the latest list of Top 50 Companies for Diversity. Select three companies from this list. Describe and evaluate what they're doing as far as workplace diversity.

- Think of times when you may have been treated unfairly because of stereotypical thinking. What stereotypes were being used? How did you respond to the treatment?

- Go to the website of Catalyst [www.catalyst.org] and find the Research & Knowledge tab. Click on "Browse Research & Knowledge." Go through the list and find the research on "Women in Management, Global Comparison." What surprised you the most about the data shown there? Why?

- Find two examples of companies that are doing each of the four workplace diversity initiatives. Write a short description of what each is doing.

- Steve's and Mary's suggested readings: C. Harvey and M. J. Allard, *Understanding and Managing Diversity,* 4th ed. (Upper Saddle River, NJ: Pearson Prentice Hall, 2009); S. Thiederman, *Making Diversity Work: 7 Steps for Defeating Bias in the Workplace,* 2nd ed. (New York: Kaplan Publishing, 2008); A. M. Konrad, P. Prasad, and J. K. Pringle (eds.), *Handbook of Workplace Diversity* (Thousand Oaks, CA: Sage Publications, 2006); and G. N. Powell, *Managing a Diverse Workforce,* 2nd ed. (Thousand Oaks, CA: Sage Publications, 2004).

- Pick one of the laws listed in Exhibit 4-8. Research that law looking for these elements: Whom does the law cover? What does the law prohibit? What are the consequences for violating the law?

- In your own words, write down three things you learned in this chapter about being a good manager.

- Self-knowledge can be a powerful learning tool. Go to mymanagementlab.com and complete any of these self-assessment exercises: What Are My Attitudes Toward Workplace Diversity? Am I Well-Suited for a Career as a Global Manager? What's My Attitude Toward Older People? and What Are My Gender Role Perceptions? Using the results of your assessments, identify personal strengths and weaknesses. What will you do to reinforce your strengths and improve your weaknesses?

CASE APPLICATION 1
Mission Possible: Strategic Diversity

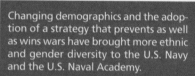

The U.S. Navy and the U.S. Naval Academy, the prestigious undergraduate college of the Navy service in Annapolis, Maryland, might not be places that come to mind when you think of organizations that are superior diversity champions.[79] Yet the Navy is just that. In fact, the enlisted force of the Navy is more than 40 percent diverse.

The Deputy Chief of Naval Operations Vice Admiral says, "We view the diversity imperative as a strategic issue for several reasons." One reason is the changing demographics of the United States. With nearly 70 percent of new workers entering the workforce in our recruitable demographic being women and minorities, the Navy has to pay attention to diversity. Another compelling reason is that the Navy's strategic imperative has evolved over time to include preventing wars, not just winning wars. This approach involves engaging in humanitarian assistance, disaster relief, and building strong maritime partners around the world, all of which benefit from a diverse naval force. For instance, after the Indonesian tsunami in late December 2004, a Navy hospital ship was relocated to that region. During that event, the public opinion of the United States changed in a few short months from 70 percent not liking to 70 percent supporting. Since that time, the hospital ship has been to South America and other places. "We see America's Navy as a force for good around the globe."

Changing demographics and the adoption of a strategy that prevents as well as wins wars have brought more ethnic and gender diversity to the U.S. Navy and the U.S. Naval Academy.

At the Naval Academy, where the military branch's future leaders are educated, applications have increased 57 percent among Black, Latino, and other traditionally underrepresented applicants. The Naval Academy Superintendent Vice Admiral says that, although there's no specific numerical diversity goal, it makes sense to have representation close to the demographics of the country. The faculty/staff at the Naval Academy have seen changes with the new generation of "millennial" midshipmen (the "students" at the Naval Academy) and have adjusted their methods and approaches to accommodate those changes. "How we reach out to them is different. We just have to be smart enough to understand that."

Discussion Questions

1. How are population trends affecting the U.S. Navy's education and operations? What might the organization have to do to adapt to these trends beyond what they're already doing?

2. What challenges might the Navy face in adapting to a more diverse student body at the Naval Academy?

3. Just like the dilemma that businesses face in retaining diverse employees, the Navy has to ensure that once its workforce is trained that those individuals stay with the organization. What can the Navy do to assure this?

4. Would mentoring or employee resource groups be appropriate for a military organization? Explain. How might a mentoring program or employee resource groups be implemented in the Navy?

CASE APPLICATION

Women in Management at Deutsche Telekom: Part 2

Continuing the story from our chapter-opening Manager's Dilemma, what is Deutsche Telekom doing to achieve its goal of bringing more women into management positions? One action the company is taking is to increase and improve recruiting of female university graduates. In fact, the company has committed to having at least 30 percent of the places in executive development programs held by women.

Other steps being taken by the company revolve around the work environment and work–family issues. The company plans to expand its parental-leave programs and introduce more flexible working hours for managers. Right now, fewer than 1 percent of the company's managers work part time. In addition, the company plans to double the number of available places in company child-care programs.

Discussion Questions

1. What do you think of this "quota" approach that Deutsche Telekom is pursuing? What benefits and drawbacks does such an approach have?

2. What issues might Deutsche Telekom face in recruiting female university graduates? How could they address these issues?

3. What issues might the company face in introducing changes in work–family programs? Again, how could they address these issues?

4. What workplace diversity initiatives discussed in the chapter might be appropriate for Deutsche Telekom? What would be involved in implementing these initiatives?

Let's Get Real:

Meet the Manager

John Emerman
Owner
The Stone Oven Bakery & Café
Cleveland, OH

You'll be hearing more from this real manager throughout the chapter.

MY JOB:

I am the owner/manager and founder of The Stone Oven Bakery & Café. I'm involved in every aspect of the business including bookkeeping, marketing/advertising, menu design, hiring/firing, scheduling employees, maintaining and repairing equipment and the furnishings in the store, and serving customers when necessary.

BEST PART OF MY JOB:

The creative aspects. I designed the interior of my store, decided what items to serve, laid out equipment, and so on. Because I wear every hat imaginable, I never get bored. I have an endless list of projects to work on. For example, last month I purchased a new cash register system that I had to program. It was a great learning experience and a creative process—choosing key colors and placement for optimal efficiency.

The other thing I love about the business is the pace. When we have a line to the door at lunchtime I'm a master at weaving quickly through the crowd to bus tables, restock napkins, and expediting orders. It's a real rush.

Managing Social Responsibility *and* Ethics

5.1   **Discuss** what it means to be socially responsible and what factors influence that decision.
page 124

5.2   **Explain** green management and how organizations can go green.
page 127

5.3   **Discuss** the factors that lead to ethical and unethical behavior.
page 129

5.4   **Describe** management's role in encouraging ethical behavior.
page 135

5.5   **Discuss** current social responsibility and ethics issues.
page 139

LEARNING OUTCOMES

WORST PART OF MY JOB:

Owning a business that operates 360 days per year means you are "on-call" every day. Although I only work a couple of hours each weekend day, I may get a call at any hour of the day or night with a problem that needs my immediate attention (one of the delivery vans broke down, the credit card machines stopped working, the walk-in cooler is at 50 degrees, and so on). I always carry the work schedule on my person in case someone doesn't show up and I need to find a replacement.

Because restaurant workers are typically paid less than in other businesses, turnover can be high. It is a continuing effort to find and try to keep workers who have the right combination of brains, personality (sense of humor), and work ethic.

BEST MANAGEMENT ADVICE EVER RECEIVED:

"Don't go into the restaurant business—it's the hardest." I didn't listen.

It's an incredibly simple but potentially world-changing idea.[1] For each pair of shoes sold, a pair is donated to a child in need. That's the business model followed by TOMS Shoes. During a visit to Argentina in 2006 as a contestant on the CBS reality show *The Amazing Race*, Blake Mycoskie, founder of TOMS, "saw lots of kids with no shoes who were suffering from injuries to their feet." Just think what it would be like to be barefoot, not by choice, but from lack of availability and ability to own a pair. He was so moved by the experience that he wanted to do something. That something is what TOMS does now by blending charity with commerce. (The name TOMS is actually short for a "better tomorrow.") And a better tomorrow is what Blake wanted to provide to shoeless children around the world.

Those shoe donations have been central to the success of the TOMS brand, which is popular among tweens, teens, and twenty-somethings. And 400,000 pairs of shoes had been donated as of early 2010. Put yourself in Blake's position. How can he balance being socially responsible *and* being focused on profits?

Deciding how socially responsible an organization needs to be is just one example of the complicated types of ethical and social responsibility issues that managers, such as Blake Mycoskie, may have to cope with as they plan, organize, lead, and control. As managers manage, these issues can and do influence their actions.

LEARNING OUTCOME 5.1
Discuss what it means to be socially responsible and what factors influence that decision.

What Is Social Responsibility?

By using digital technology and file-sharing Web sites, music and video users all over the world often obtain and share many of their favorite recordings for free. Large global corporations lower their costs by outsourcing to countries where human rights are not a high priority and justify it by saying they're bringing in jobs and helping strengthen the local economies. Businesses facing a drastically changed economic environment offer employees reduced hours and early retirement packages. Are these companies being socially responsible? Managers regularly face decisions that have a dimension of social responsibility in areas such as employee relations, philanthropy, pricing, resource conservation, product quality and safety, and doing business in countries that devalue human rights. What does it mean to be socially responsible?

From Obligations to Responsiveness to Responsibility

The concept of *social responsibility* has been described in different ways. For instance, it's been called "profit making only," "going beyond profit making," "any discretionary corporate activity intended to further social welfare," and "improving social or environmental conditions."[2] We can understand it better if we first compare it to two similar concepts: social obligation and social responsiveness.[3] **Social obligation** is when a firm engages in social actions because of its obligation to meet certain economic and legal responsibilities. The organization does what it's obligated to do and nothing more. This idea reflects the **classical view** of social responsibility, which says that management's only social responsibility is to maximize profits. The most outspoken advocate of this approach is economist and Nobel laureate Milton Friedman. He argued that managers' primary responsibility is to operate the business in the best interests of the stockholders, whose primary concerns are financial.[4] He also argued that when managers decide to spend the organization's resources for "social good," they add to the costs of doing business, which have to be passed on to consumers through higher prices or absorbed by stockholders through smaller dividends. You need to understand that Friedman doesn't say that organizations shouldn't be socially responsible. But his interpretation of social responsibility is to maximize profits for stockholders.

The other two concepts—social responsiveness and social responsibility—reflect the **socioeconomic view**, which says that managers' social responsibilities go beyond making profits to include protecting and improving society's welfare. This view is based on the belief that corporations are *not* independent entities responsible only to stockholders, but have an obligation to the larger society. Organizations around the world have embraced this view as shown by a survey of global executives in which 84 percent said that companies must balance obligations to shareholders with obligations to the public good.[5] But how do these two concepts differ?

Social responsiveness is when a company engages in social actions in response to some popular social need. Managers are guided by social norms and values and make practical, market-oriented decisions about their actions.[6] For instance, Ford Motor Company became the first automaker to endorse a federal ban on sending text messages while driving. A company spokesperson said that, "The most complete and most recent research shows that activity that draws drivers' eyes away from the road for an extended period while driving, such as text messaging, substantially increases the risk of accidents."[7] By supporting this ban, company managers "responded" to what they felt was an important social need. When the disastrous earthquake hit Haiti in January 2010, many companies responded to the immense needs in that region. For instance, UPS has a company-wide policy that urges employees to volunteer during natural disasters and other crises. In support of this policy, UPS maintains a 20-person Logistics Emergency Team in Asia, Europe, and the Americas that's trained in humanitarian relief.[8]

A socially *responsible* organization views things differently. It goes beyond what it's obligated to do or chooses to do because of some popular social need and does what it can to help improve society because it's the right thing to do. We define **social responsibility** as a business's intention, beyond its legal and economic obligations, to do the right things and act in ways that are good for society.[9] Our definition assumes that a business obeys the law and cares for its stockholders, but adds an ethical imperative to do those things that make society better and not to do those that make it worse. A socially responsible organization does what is right because it feels it has an ethical responsibility to do so. For example, Abt Electronics in Glenview, Illinois, would be described as socially responsible according to our definition. As one of the largest single-store electronics retailers in the United States, it responded to soaring energy costs and environmental concerns by shutting off lights more frequently and reducing air conditioning and heating. However, an Abt family member said, "These actions weren't just about costs, but about doing the right thing. We don't do everything just because of money."[10]

So, how should we view an organization's social actions? A U.S. business that meets federal pollution control standards or that doesn't discriminate against employees over the age of 40 in job promotion decisions is meeting its social obligation because laws mandate these actions. However, when it provides on-site child-care facilities for employees or packages products using recycled paper, it's being socially responsive. Why? Working parents and environmentalists have voiced these social concerns and demanded such actions.

For many businesses, their social actions are better viewed as being socially responsive than socially responsible (at least according to our definition). However, such actions are still good for society. For example, Walmart sponsored a program to address a serious social problem—hunger. Customers donated money to America's Second Harvest by purchasing puzzle pieces and Walmart matched the first $5 million raised. As part of this program, the company ran advertisements in major newspapers showing the word H_NGER and the tag line, "The problem can't be solved without You."[11]

---

social obligation
When a firm engages in social actions because of its obligation to meet certain economic and legal responsibilities

classical view
The view that management's only social responsibility is to maximize profits

socioeconomic view
The view that management's social responsibility goes beyond making profits to include protecting and improving society's welfare

social responsiveness
When a firm engages in social actions in response to some popular social need

social responsibility
A business's intention, beyond its legal and economic obligations, to do the right things and act in ways that are good for society

Should Organizations Be Socially Involved?

Other than meeting their social obligations (which they *must* do), should organizations be socially involved? One way to look at this question is by examining arguments for and against social involvement. Several points are outlined in Exhibit 5-1.[12]

Numerous studies have examined whether social involvement affects a company's economic performance.[13] Although most found a small positive relationship, no generalizable conclusions can be made because these studies have shown that relationship is affected by various contextual factors such as firm size, industry, economic conditions, and regulatory environment.[14] Another concern was causation. If a study showed that social involvement and economic performance were positively related, this correlation didn't necessarily mean that social involvement *caused* higher economic performance. It could simply mean that high profits afforded companies the "luxury" of being socially involved.[15] Such methodological concerns can't be taken lightly. In fact, one study found that if the flawed empirical analyses in these studies were "corrected," social responsibility had a neutral impact on a company's financial performance.[16] Another found that participating in social issues not related to the organization's primary stakeholders was negatively associated with shareholder value.[17] A re-analysis of several studies concluded that managers can afford to be (and should be) socially responsible.[18]

EXHIBIT 5-1

Arguments For and Against Social Responsibility

For	Against
Public expectations Public opinion now supports businesses pursuing economic and social goals.	**Violation of profit maximization** Business is being socially responsible only when it pursues its economic interests.
Long-run profits Socially responsible companies tend to have more secure long-run profits.	**Dilution of purpose** Pursuing social goals dilutes business's primary purpose—economic productivity.
Ethical obligation Businesses should be socially responsible because responsible actions are the right thing to do.	**Costs** Many socially responsible actions do not cover their costs and someone must pay those costs.
Public image Businesses can create a favorable public image by pursuing social goals.	**Too much power** Businesses have a lot of power already and if they pursue social goals they will have even more.
Better environment Business involvement can help solve difficult social problems.	**Lack of skills** Business leaders lack the necessary skills to address social issues.
Discouragement of further governmental regulation By becoming socially responsible, businesses can expect less government regulation.	**Lack of accountability** There are no direct lines of accountability for social actions.
Balance of responsibility and power Businesses have a lot of power and an equally large amount of responsibility is needed to balance against that power.	
Stockholder interests Social responsibility will improve a business's stock price in the long run.	
Possession of resources Businesses have the resources to support public and charitable projects that need assistance.	
Superiority of prevention over cures Businesses should address social problems before they become serious and costly to correct.	

Another way to view social involvement and economic performance is by looking at socially responsible investing (SRI) funds, which provide a way for individual investors to support socially responsible companies. (You can find a list of SRI funds at [www.socialfunds.com].) Typically, these funds use some type of **social screening**; that is, they apply social and environmental criteria to investment decisions. For instance, SRI funds usually will not invest in companies that are involved in liquor, gambling, tobacco, nuclear power, weapons, price fixing, fraud, or in companies that have poor product safety, employee relations, and environmental track records. The number of socially screened mutual funds has grown from 55 to 260 and assets in these funds have grown to more than $2.7 trillion—about 11 percent of total assets in managed funds in the United States.[19] But more important than the total amount invested in these funds is that the Social Investment Forum reports that the performance of most SRI funds is comparable to that of non-SRI funds.[20]

So, what can we conclude about social involvement and economic performance? It appears that a company's social actions *don't hurt* its economic performance. Given political and societal pressures to be socially involved, managers probably need to take social issues and goals into consideration as they plan, organize, lead, and control.

Green Management and Sustainability 5.2

LEARNING OUTCOME
Explain green management
and how organizations
can go green.

Coca-Cola, the world's largest soft drink company, announced that 100 percent of its new vending machines and coolers would be hydrofluorocarbon-free (HFC-free) by 2015. This initiative alone would have the same effect on global carbon emissions as taking 11 million cars off the road for a single year.[21] The Fairmont Hotel chain has generated a lot of buzz over its decision to set up rooftop beehives to try and help strengthen the population of honeybees, which have been mysteriously abandoning their hives and dying off by the millions worldwide. This Colony Collapse Disorder could have potentially disastrous consequences since one-third of the food we eat comes from plants that depend on bee pollination. At Toronto's Fairmont Royal York, six hives are home to some 360,000 bees that forage in and around the city *and* produce a supply of award-winning honey.[22] In 2004, top executives at General Electric Company voted against CEO Jeffrey Immelt's plan for a green business initiative. However, Immelt refused to take "no" for an answer and today that initiative, called Ecomagination, is one of the most widely recognized corporate green programs. It led to $100 million in cost savings and reduced the company's greenhouse emissions by 30 percent. And the program fostered the development of 80 new products and services that generate some $17 billion in annual revenue. Immelt said, "Going green has been 10 times better than I ever imagined."[23] Being green is in!

Until the late 1960s, few people (and organizations) paid attention to the environmental consequences of their decisions and actions. Although some groups were concerned with conserving natural resources, about the only reference to saving the environment was the ubiquitous printed request "Please Don't Litter." However, a number of environmental disasters brought a new spirit of environmentalism to individuals, groups, and organizations. Increasingly, managers have begun to consider the impact of their organization on the natural environment, which we call **green management**. What do managers need to know about going green?

How Organizations Go Green

Managers and organizations can do many things to protect and preserve the natural environment.[24] Some do no more than what is required by law—that is, they fulfill their social obligation. However, others have radically changed their products and production processes. For instance, Fiji Water is using renewable energy sources, preserving forests,

---

social screening
Applying social criteria (screens) to investment
decisions

green management
Managers consider the impact of their
organization on the natural environment

LEADER *who made a* **difference**

Yvon Chouinard is a self-taught blacksmith who, in 1957, started crafting mountain climbing pitons used by himself and other climbing enthusiasts as anchors on risky climbs.[26] His hardware became so popular that he would go on to found the outdoor-clothing company Patagonia. As his company grew, Chouinard realized that everything his company did had an effect—mostly negative—on the environment. Today, he defines the company's mission in eco-driven terms: "To use business to inspire and implement solutions to the environmental crisis." Chouinard has put environmental activism at the forefront of his company. Since 1985, Patagonia has donated 1 percent of its annual sales to grassroots environmental groups and has gotten more than 1,200 companies to follow its lead as part of its "1% for the Planet" group. He recognizes that "every product, no matter how much thought goes into it, has a destructive impact on Earth." But nonetheless, he keeps doing what he does because "it's the right thing to do."

and conserving water. Carpet-maker Mohawk Industries uses recycled plastic containers to produce fiber used in its carpets. Google and Intel initiated an effort to get computer makers and customers to adopt technologies that reduce energy consumption. Paris-based TOTAL, SA, one of the world's largest integrated oil companies, is going green by implementing tough new rules on oil tanker safety and working with groups such as Global Witness and Greenpeace. UPS, the world's largest package delivery company, has done several things—from retrofitting its aircraft with advanced technology and fuel-efficient engines to developing a computer network that efficiently dispatches its fleet of brown trucks to using alternative fuel to run those trucks. Although interesting, these examples don't tell us much about how organizations go green. One model uses the terms *shades of green* to describe the different environmental approaches that organizations may take.[25] (See Exhibit 5-2.)

The first approach, the *legal (or light green) approach,* is simply doing what is required legally. In this approach, which illustrates social obligation, organizations exhibit little environmental sensitivity. They obey laws, rules, and regulations without legal challenge and that's the extent of their being green.

As an organization becomes more sensitive to environmental issues, it may adopt the *market approach*, and respond to environmental preferences of customers. Whatever customers demand in terms of environmentally friendly products will be what the organization provides. For example, DuPont developed a new type of herbicide that helped farmers around the world reduce their annual use of chemicals by more than 45 million pounds. By developing this product, the company was responding to the demands of its customers (farmers) who wanted to minimize the use of chemicals on their crops. This is a good example of social responsiveness, as is the next approach.

In the *stakeholder approach*, an organization works to meet the environmental demands of multiple stakeholders such as employees, suppliers, or community. For instance, Hewlett-Packard has several corporate environmental programs in place for its supply chain (suppliers), product design and product recycling (customers and society), and work operations (employees and community).

Finally, if an organization pursues an *activist (or dark green) approach*, it looks for ways to protect the earth's natural resources. The activist approach reflects the highest degree of environmental sensitivity and illustrates social responsibility. For example, Belgian company Ecover produces ecological cleaning products in a near-zero-emissions factory. This factory (the world's first ecological one) is an engineering marvel with a huge grass roof that keeps things cool in summer and warm in winter and a water treatment system that runs on wind and solar energy. The company chose to build this facility because of its deep commitment to the environment.

EXHIBIT 5-2

Green **Approaches**

Source: Based on R. E. Freeman, J. Pierce, and R. Dodd, *Shades of Green: Business Ethics and the Environment* (New York: Oxford University Press, 1995).

Low	Environmental Sensitivity		High
Legal Approach (Light Green)	Market Approach	Stakeholder Approach	Activist Approach (Dark Green)

At New Zealand's largest wind farm, these wind turbines made by Siemens Windpower generate clean electricity for 100,000 households. One of the most sustainable corporations in the world, Germany-based Siemens pursues an activist approach to the environment from its factories and buildings that consume only small amounts of power to its power plants that generate electricity from the sun. As a good corporate citizen and as a business enterprise, Siemens management and employees are committed to provide products, systems, and technologies that protect the environment, foster human health, and help conserve natural resources.

Evaluating Green Management Actions

As businesses become "greener," they often release detailed reports on their environmental performance. More than 1,300 companies around the globe voluntarily report their efforts in promoting environmental sustainability using the guidelines developed by the Global Reporting Initiative (GRI). These reports, which can be found on the GRI Web site [www.globalreporting.org], describe the numerous green actions of these organizations.

Another way that organizations show their commitment to being green is through pursuing standards developed by the nongovernmental International Organization for Standardization (ISO). Although ISO has developed more than 18,000 international standards, it's probably best known for its ISO 9000 (quality management) and ISO 14000 (environmental management) standards. Organizations that want to become ISO 14000 compliant must develop a total management system for meeting environmental challenges. In other words, it must minimize the effects of its activities on the environment and continually improve its environmental performance. If an organization can meet these standards, it can state that it's ISO 14000 compliant, an accomplishment that organizations in 155 countries have achieved.

One final way to evaluate a company's green actions is to use the Global 100 list of the most sustainable corporations in the world [www.global100.org].[27] To be named to this list, which is announced each year at the renowned World Economic Forum in Davos, Switzerland, a company has displayed a superior ability to effectively manage environmental and social factors. In 2010, the United Kingdom led the list with 21 Global 100 companies. The United States followed with 12, and both Australia and Canada had 9 companies on the list. Some companies on the 2010 list included Siemens (Germany), Pearson PLC (U.K.), Westpac Banking Corp. (Australia), Encana Corp. (Canada), and Starbucks (U.S.).

Managers and Ethical Behavior

5.3

LEARNING OUTCOME
Discuss the factors that lead to ethical and unethical behavior.

One hundred fifty years. That was the maximum prison sentence handed to financier Bernard Madoff, who stole billions of dollars from his clients, by a U.S. district judge who called his crimes "evil." In Britain, which has been characterized by some critics as a "nanny state because of its purported high level of social control and surveillance," a controversy is brewing over the monitoring of garbage cans. Many local governments have installed monitoring chips in municipally distributed trash bans. These chips match cans with owners and can be used to track the weight of the bins, leading some critics to fear that the country is moving to a pay-as-you go system, which they believe will discriminate against large families. A government report says that Iceland, hit hard by both the global economic meltdown and a pesky volcano, was "victimized by politicians, bankers, and regulators who engaged in acts of extreme negligence."[28] When you hear about such behaviors—especially after the high-profile financial misconduct at companies such as Enron, Worldcom, Lehman Brothers, and others—you might conclude that businesses aren't ethical. Although that's not the case, managers—at all levels, in all areas, in all sizes, and in all kinds of organizations—do face ethical issues and dilemmas. For instance, is it ethical for a sales representative to bribe a purchasing agent as an inducement to buy? Would it make a difference if the bribe came out of the sales rep's commission? Is it ethical for someone to use a company car for private use? How about using company e-mail for personal correspondence or using the company phone to make personal phone calls? What if you managed an employee who worked all weekend on an emergency situation and you told him to take off two days sometime later and mark it down as "sick days" because your company had a clear policy that overtime would not be compensated for any reason?[29] Would that be okay? How will you handle such situations? As managers plan, organize, lead, and control, they must consider ethical dimensions.

What do we mean by **ethics**? We're defining it as the principles, values, and beliefs that define right and wrong decisions and behavior.[30] Many decisions that managers make require them to consider both the process and who's affected by the result.[31] To better understand the ethical issues involved in such decisions, let's look at the factors that determine whether a person acts ethically or unethically.

Factors That Determine Ethical and Unethical Behavior

Whether someone behaves ethically or unethically when faced with an ethical dilemma is influenced by several things: his or her stage of moral development and other moderating variables including individual characteristics, the organization's structural design, the organization's culture, and the intensity of the ethical issue. (See Exhibit 5-3.) People who lack a strong moral sense are much less likely to do the wrong things if they're constrained by rules, policies, job descriptions, or strong cultural norms that disapprove of such behaviors. Conversely, intensely moral individuals can be corrupted by an organizational structure and culture that permits or encourages unethical practices. Let's look more closely at these factors.

STAGE OF MORAL DEVELOPMENT.   Research divides moral development into three levels, each having two stages.[32] At each successive stage, an individual's moral judgment becomes less dependent on outside influences and more internalized.

At the first level, the *preconventional* level, a person's choice between right or wrong is based on personal consequences from outside sources, such as physical punishment, reward, or exchange of favors. At the second level, the *conventional* level, ethical decisions rely on maintaining expected standards and living up to the expectations of others. At the *principled* level, individuals define moral values apart from the authority of the groups to which they belong or society in general. The three levels and six stages are described in Exhibit 5-4.

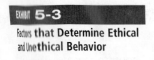

EXHIBIT 5-3

Factors **that Determine Ethical** and Un**ethical Behavior**

EXHIBIT 5-4

Stages of Moral Development

Source: Based on L. Kohlberg, "Moral Stages and Moralization: The Cognitive-Development Approach," in T. Lickona (ed.), *Moral Development and Behavior: Theory, Research, and Social Issues* (New York: Holt, Rinehart & Winston, 1976), pp. 34–35.

Level	Description of Stage
Principled	6. Following self-chosen ethical principles even if they violate the law
	5. Valuing rights of others and upholding absolute values and rights regardless of the majority's opinion
Conventional	4. Maintaining conventional order by fulfilling obligations to which you have agreed
	3. Living up to what is expected by people close to you
Preconventional	2. Following rules only when doing so is in your immediate interest
	1. Sticking to rules to avoid physical punishment

What can we conclude about moral development?[33] First, people proceed through the six stages sequentially. Second, there is no guarantee of continued moral development. Third, the majority of adults are at Stage 4: They're limited to obeying the rules and will be inclined to behave ethically, although for different reasons. A manager at stage 3 is likely to make decisions based on peer approval; a manager at stage 4 will try to be a "good corporate citizen" by making decisions that respect the organization's rules and procedures; and a stage 5 manager is likely to challenge organizational practices that he or she believes to be wrong.

INDIVIDUAL CHARACTERISTICS. Two individual characteristics—values and personality—play a role in determining whether a person behaves ethically. Each person comes to an organization with a relatively entrenched set of personal **values**, which represent basic convictions about what is right and wrong. Our values develop from a young age based on what we see and hear from parents, teachers, friends, and others. Thus, employees in the same organization often possess very different values.[34] Although *values* and *stage of moral development* may seem similar, they're not. Values are broad and cover a wide range of issues; the stage of moral development is a measure of independence from outside influences.

Two personality variables have been found to influence an individual's actions according to his or her beliefs about what is right or wrong: ego strength and locus of control. **Ego strength** measures the strength of a person's convictions. People with high ego strength are likely to resist impulses to act unethically and instead follow their convictions. That is, individuals high in ego strength are more likely to do what they think is right and be more consistent in their moral judgments and actions than those with low ego strength.

Locus of control is the degree to which people believe they control their own fate. People with an *internal* locus of control believe they control their own destinies. They're more likely to take responsibility for consequences and rely on their own internal standards of right and wrong to guide their behavior. They're also more likely to be consistent in their moral judgments and actions. People with an *external* locus believe what happens to them is due to luck or chance. They're less likely to take personal responsibility for the consequences of their behavior and more likely to rely on external forces.[35]

STRUCTURAL VARIABLES. An organization's structural design can influence whether employees behave ethically. Those structures that minimize ambiguity and uncertainty with

ethics
Principles, values, and beliefs that define what is right and wrong behavior

values
Basic convictions about what is right and wrong

ego strength
A personality measure of the strength of a person's convictions

locus of control
A personality attribute that measures the degree to which people believe they control their own fate

Let's Get Real

My company's values include
supporting local nonprofit organizations and groups by donating leftover food and gift certificates.

formal rules and regulations and those that continuously remind employees of what is ethical are more likely to encourage ethical behavior. Other structural variables that influence ethical choices include goals, performance appraisal systems, and reward allocation procedures.

Although many organizations use goals to guide and motivate employees, those goals can create some unexpected problems. One study found that people who don't reach set goals are more likely to engage in unethical behavior, even if they do or don't have economic incentives to do so. The researchers concluded that "goal setting can lead to unethical behavior."[36] Examples of such behaviors abound—from companies shipping unfinished products just to reach sales goals or "managing earnings" to meet financial analysts' expectations, to schools excluding certain groups of students when reporting standardized test scores to make their "pass" rate look better.[37]

An organization's performance appraisal system also can influence ethical behavior. Some systems focus exclusively on outcomes, while others evaluate means as well as ends. When employees are evaluated only on outcomes, they may be pressured to do whatever is necessary to look good on the outcomes, and not be concerned with how they got those results. Research suggests that "success may serve to excuse unethical behaviors."[38] The danger of such thinking is that if managers are more lenient in correcting unethical behaviors of successful employees, other employees will model their behavior on what they see.

Closely related to the organization's appraisal system is how rewards are allocated. The more that rewards or punishment depend on specific goal outcomes, the more employees are pressured to do whatever they must to reach those goals, perhaps to the point of compromising their ethical standards.

ORGANIZATION'S CULTURE. As Exhibit 5-3 showed, the content and strength of an organization's culture also influence ethical behavior.[40] We learned in Chapter 2 that an organization's culture consists of the shared organizational values. These values reflect what the organization stands for and what it believes in as well as create an environment that influences employee behavior ethically or unethically. When it comes to ethical behavior, a culture most likely to encourage high ethical standards is one that's high in risk tolerance, control, and conflict tolerance. Employees in such a culture are encouraged to be aggressive and innovative, are aware that unethical practices will be discovered, and feel free to openly challenge expectations they consider to be unrealistic or personally undesirable.

Because shared values can be powerful influences, many organizations are using **values-based management**, in which the organization's values guide employees in the way they do their jobs. For instance, Timberland is an example of a company using values-based management. With a simple statement, "Make It Better," employees at Timberland know what's expected and valued; that is, find ways to "make it better"—whether it's creating quality products for customers, performing community service activities, designing employee training programs, or figuring out ways to make the company's packaging more environmentally friendly. As CEO Jeffrey Swartz says on the company's Web site, "Everything we do at Timberland grows out of our relentless pursuit to find a way to make it better." At Corning, one of the core values guiding employee behavior is integrity. Employees are expected to work in ways that are honest, decent, and fair. Timberland and Corning aren't alone in their use of values-based management. A survey of global companies found that a large number (more than 89%) said they had a written corporate values statement.[41] This survey also found that most of the companies believed that their values influenced relationships and reputation, the top-performing companies consciously connected values with the way employees did their work, and top managers were important to reinforcing the importance of the values throughout the organization.

Thus, an organization's managers do play an important role here. They're responsible for creating an environment that encourages employees to embrace the culture and the desired values as they do their jobs. In fact, research shows that the behavior of managers is the single most important influence on an individual's decision to act ethically or unethically.[42] People look to see what those in authority are doing and use that as a benchmark for acceptable practices and expectations.

More than 7,700 corporate participants and stakeholders from over 130 countries have signed the Compact, making it the world's largest voluntary corporate citizenship initiative.[50] The goal of the Compact is a more sustainable and inclusive global economy. Organizations making this commitment do so because they believe that the world business community plays a significant role in improving economic and social conditions. In addition, the Organization for Economic Co-operation and Development (OECD) has made fighting bribery and corruption in international business a high priority. The centerpiece of its efforts is the Anti-Bribery Convention (or set of rules and guidelines), which was the first global instrument to combat corruption in cross-border business deals. To date, significant gains have been made in fighting corruption in the 38 countries that have ratified it.[51]

Encouraging Ethical Behavior

5.4

LEARNING OUTCOME
Describe management's role in encouraging ethical behavior.

At a Senate hearing exploring the accusations that Wall Street firm Goldman Sachs deceived its clients during the housing-market meltdown, Arizona senator John McCain said, "I don't know if Goldman has done anything illegal, but there's no doubt their behavior was unethical."[52] You have to wonder what the firm's managers were thinking or doing while such ethically questionable decisions and actions were occurring.

Managers can do a number of things if they're serious about encouraging ethical behaviors—hire employees with high ethical standards, establish codes of ethics, lead by example, and so forth. By themselves, such actions won't have much of an impact. But if an organization has a comprehensive ethics program in place, it can potentially improve an organization's ethical climate. The key variable, however, is *potentially*. There are no guarantees that a well-designed ethics program will lead to the desired outcome. Sometimes corporate ethics programs are little more than public relations gestures that do little to influence managers and employees. For instance, Sears had a long history of encouraging ethical business practices through its corporate Office of Ethics and Business Practices. However, its ethics programs didn't stop managers from illegally trying to collect payments from bankrupt charge account holders or from routinely deceiving automotive service center customers into thinking they needed unnecessary repairs. Even Enron, often referred to as the "poster child" of corporate wrongdoing, outlined values in its final annual report that most would consider ethical—communication, respect, integrity, and excellence. Yet the way top managers behaved didn't reflect those values at all.[53] Let's look at some specific ways that managers can encourage ethical behavior and create a comprehensive ethics program.

Employee Selection

The selection process (interviews, tests, background checks, and so forth) should be viewed as an opportunity to learn about an individual's level of moral development, personal values, ego strength, and locus of control.[54] However, a carefully designed selection process isn't foolproof and, even under the best circumstances, individuals with questionable standards of right and wrong may be hired. Such an issue can be overcome if other ethics controls are in place.

Codes of Ethics and Decision Rules

George David, former CEO and chairman of Hartford, Connecticut-based United Technologies Corporation, believed in the power of a code of ethics. That's why UTC has always had one that was quite explicit and detailed. Employees know the behavioral expectations, especially when it comes to ethics. UBS AG, the Swiss bank, also has an explicit employee code crafted by CEO Oswald Grübel that bans staff from helping clients cheat on their taxes.[55] However, not all organizations have such explicit ethical guidelines.

Uncertainty about what is and is not ethical can be a problem for employees. A **code of ethics**, a formal statement of an organization's values and the ethical rules it expects employees to follow, is a popular choice for reducing that ambiguity. Research shows that 97 percent of organizations with more than 10,000 employees have a written code of ethics. Even in smaller organizations, nearly 93 percent have one.[56] And codes of ethics are becoming more popular globally. Research by the Institute for Global Ethics says that shared values such as honesty, fairness, respect, responsibility, and caring are pretty much universally embraced.[57] In addition, a survey of businesses in 22 countries found that 78 percent have formally stated ethics standards and codes of ethics; and more than 85 percent of *Fortune* Global 200 companies have a business code of ethics.[58]

What should a code of ethics look like? It should be specific enough to show employees the spirit in which they're supposed to do things yet loose enough to allow for freedom of judgment. A survey of companies' codes of ethics found their content tended to fall into three categories as shown in Exhibit 5-7.[59]

Unfortunately, codes of ethics may not work as well as we think they should. A survey of employees in U.S. businesses found that 49 percent of those surveyed had observed ethical or legal violations in the previous 12 months including such things as conflicts of interest,

---

EXHIBIT 5-7

Codes of Ethics

Cluster 1. Be a Dependable Organizational Citizen

1. Comply with safety, health, and security regulations.
2. Demonstrate courtesy, respect, honesty, and fairness.
3. Illegal drugs and alcohol at work are prohibited.
4. Manage personal finances well.
5. Exhibit good attendance and punctuality.
6. Follow directives of supervisors.
7. Do not use abusive language.
8. Dress in business attire.
9. Firearms at work are prohibited.

Cluster 2. Do Not Do Anything Unlawful or Improper That Will Harm the Organization

1. Conduct business in compliance with all laws.
2. Payments for unlawful purposes are prohibited.
3. Bribes are prohibited.
4. Avoid outside activities that impair duties.
5. Maintain confidentiality of records.
6. Comply with all antitrust and trade regulations.
7. Comply with all accounting rules and controls.
8. Do not use company property for personal benefit.
9. Employees are personally accountable for company funds.
10. Do not propagate false or misleading information.
11. Make decisions without regard for personal gain.

Cluster 3. Be Good to Customers

1. Convey true claims in product advertisements.
2. Perform assigned duties to the best of your ability.
3. Provide products and services of the highest quality.

Source: F. R. David, "An Empirical Study of Codes of Business Ethics: A Strategic Perspective," paper presented at the 48th Annual Academy of Management Conference, Anaheim, California, August 1988. Used with permission of Fred David.

EXHIBIT 5-8
A Process for Addressing Ethical Dilemmas

Step 1: What is the **ethical dilemma**?

Step 2: Who are the **affected stakeholders**?

Step 3: What **personal**, **organizational**, and **external factors** are important in this decision?

Step 4: What are possible **alternatives**?

Step 5: What is my **decision** and how will I act on it?

abusive or intimidating behavior, and lying to employees. And 37 percent of those employees didn't report observed misconduct.[60] Does this mean that codes of ethics shouldn't be developed? No. However, in doing so, managers should use these suggestions:[61]

1. Organizational leaders should model appropriate behavior and reward those who act ethically.
2. All managers should continually reaffirm the importance of the ethics code and consistently discipline those who break it.
3. The organization's stakeholders (employees, customers, and so forth) should be considered as an ethics code is developed or improved.
4. Managers should communicate and reinforce the ethics code regularly.
5. Managers should use the five-step process (see Exhibit 5-8) to guide employees when faced with ethical dilemmas.

Leadership

In 2007, Peter Löscher was hired as CEO of German company Siemens to clean up a global bribery scandal that cost the company a record-setting $1.34 billion in fines. His approach: "Stick to your principles. Have a clear ethical north. Be trusted and be the role model of your company . . . true leaders have a set of core values they publicly commit to and live by in good times and bad."[62] Doing business ethically requires a commitment from top managers. Why? Because they're the ones who uphold the shared values and set the cultural tone. They're role models in terms of both words and actions, though what they *do* is far more important than what they *say*. If top managers, for example, take company resources for their personal use, inflate their expense accounts, or give favored treatment to friends, they imply that such behavior is acceptable for all employees.

Top managers also set the tone by their reward and punishment practices. The choices of whom and what are rewarded with pay increases and promotions send a strong signal to employees. As we said earlier, when an employee is rewarded for achieving impressive results in an ethically questionable manner, it indicates to others that those ways are acceptable. When an employee does something unethical, managers must punish the offender and publicize the fact by making the outcome visible to everyone in the organization. This practice sends a message that doing wrong has a price and it's not in employees' best interests to act unethically!

Let's Get Real

An ethical leader is one who *acts ethically, that is, one who makes decisions that are consistent with his or her belief system.*

Job Goals and Performance Appraisal

Employees in three Internal Revenue Service offices were found in the bathrooms flushing tax returns and other related documents down the toilets. When questioned, they openly admitted doing it, but offered an interesting explanation for their behavior. The employees' supervisors had been pressuring them to complete more work in less time. If the piles of tax returns weren't processed and moved off their desks more quickly, they were told their performance reviews and salary raises would be adversely affected. Frustrated by few resources

code of ethics
A formal statement of an organization's primary values and the ethical rules it expects its employees to follow

and an overworked computer system, the employees decided to "flush away" the paperwork on their desks. Although these employees knew what they did was wrong, it illustrates how powerful unrealistic goals and performance appraisals can be.[63] Under the stress of unrealistic goals, otherwise ethical employees may feel they have no choice but to do whatever is necessary to meet those goals. Also, goal achievement is usually a key issue in performance appraisal. If performance appraisals focus only on economic goals, ends will begin to justify means. To encourage ethical behavior, both ends *and* means should be evaluated. For example, a manager's annual review of employees might include a point-by-point evaluation of how their decisions measured up against the company's code of ethics as well as how well goals were met.

Ethics Training

More organizations are setting up seminars, workshops, and similar ethics training programs to encourage ethical behavior. Such training programs aren't without controversy as the primary concern is whether ethics can be taught. Critics stress that the effort is pointless because people establish their individual value systems when they're young. Proponents note, however, several studies have shown that values can be learned after early childhood. In addition, they cite evidence that shows that teaching ethical problem solving can make an actual difference in ethical behaviors;[64] that training has increased individuals' level of moral development;[65] and that, if nothing else, ethics training increases awareness of ethical issues in business.[66]

How can ethics be taught? Let's look at an example involving global defense contractor Lockheed Martin, one of the pioneers in the case-based approach to ethics training.[67] Lockheed Martin's employees take annual ethics training courses delivered by their managers. The main focus of these short courses is Lockheed Martin–specific case situations "chosen for their relevance to department or job-specific issues." In each department, employee teams review and discuss the cases and then apply an "Ethics Meter" to "rate whether the real-life decisions were ethical, unethical, or somewhere in between." For example, one of the possible ratings on the Ethics Meter, "On Thin Ice," is explained as "bordering on unethical and should raise a red flag." After the teams have applied their ratings, managers lead discussions about the ratings and examine "which of the company's core ethics principles were applied or ignored in the cases." In addition to its ethics training, Lockheed Martin has a widely used written code of ethics, an ethics helpline that employees can call for guidance on ethical issues, and ethics officers based in the company's various business units.

Cisco Systems' ethics training program teaches employees such as the software engineers in this photo how to deal with ethical problems they encounter every day. Based on its own risk analysis and designed to fit the company's corporate culture, the training parodies the *American Idol* TV show. The Web-based program shows cartoon contestants singing about various ethical workplace scenarios included in Cisco's Code of Business Conduct and then poses questions to employees as to which judge's answer they agree with. Employees can provide feedback, see how other employees respond, and view the official Cisco answer to help them learn how to make good ethical decisions that apply to their day-to-day jobs.

Independent Social Audits

The fear of being caught can be an important deterrent to unethical behavior. Independent social audits, which evaluate decisions and management practices in terms of the organization's code of ethics, increase that likelihood. Such audits can be regular evaluations or they can occur randomly with no prior announcement. An effective ethics program probably needs both. To maintain integrity, auditors should be responsible to the company's board of directors and present their findings directly to the board. This arrangement gives the auditors clout and lessens the opportunity for retaliation from those being audited. Because the Sarbanes-Oxley Act holds businesses to more rigorous standards of financial disclosure and corporate governance, more organizations are finding the idea of independent social audits appealing. As the publisher of *Business Ethics* magazine stated, "The debate has shifted from *whether* to be ethical to *how* to be ethical."[68]

Protective Mechanisms

Employees who face ethical dilemmas need protective mechanisms so they can do what's right without fear of reprimand. An organization might designate ethical counselors for employees facing an ethics dilemma. These advisors also might advocate the ethically "right" alternatives. Other organizations have appointed ethics officers who design, direct, and modify the organization's ethics programs as needed.[69] The Ethics and Compliance Officer Association is the world's largest group of ethics and compliance practitioners with a total membership topping 1,100 (including more than half of the *Fortune* 100 companies) and covering several countries including, among others, the United States, Germany, India, Japan, and Canada.[70]

Social Responsibility and Ethics Issues in Today's World

5.5

LEARNING OUTCOME
Discuss current social responsibility and ethics issues.

Today's managers continue to face challenges in being socially responsible and ethical. Next we examine three current issues: managing ethical lapses and social irresponsibility, social entrepreneurship, and promoting positive social change.

Managing Ethical Lapses and Social Irresponsibility

Even after public outrage over the Enron-era misdeeds, irresponsible and unethical practices by managers in all kinds of organizations haven't gone away, as you've observed with some of the questionable behaviors that took place at financial services firms such as Goldman Sachs and Lehman Brothers. But what's more alarming is what's going on "in the trenches" in offices, warehouses, and stores. One survey reported that among 5,000 employees: 45 percent admitted falling asleep at work; 22 percent said they spread a rumor about a coworker; 18 percent said they snooped after hours; and 2 percent said they took credit for someone else's work.[71]

Unfortunately, it's not just at work that we see such behaviors. They're prevalent throughout society. Studies conducted by the Center for Academic Integrity showed that 26 percent of college and university business majors admitted to "serious cheating" on exams and 54 percent admitted to cheating on written assignments. But business students weren't the worst cheaters—that distinction belonged to journalism majors, of whom 27 percent said they had cheated.[72] And a survey by Students in Free Enterprise (SIFE) found that only 19 percent of students would report a classmate who cheated.[73] But even more frightening is what today's teenagers say is "acceptable." In a survey, 23 percent said they thought violence toward another person is acceptable on some level.[74] What do such statistics say about what managers may have to deal with in the future? It's not too far-fetched to say that organizations may have difficulty upholding high ethical standards when their future employees so readily accept unethical behavior.

What can managers do? Two actions seem to be particularly important: ethical leadership and protecting those who report wrongdoing.

ETHICAL LEADERSHIP.   Not long after Herb Baum took over as CEO of Dial Corporation, he got a call from Reuben Mark, the CEO of competitor Colgate-Palmolive, who told him he had a copy of Dial's strategic marketing plan that had come from a former Dial salesperson who recently had joined Colgate-Palmolive. Mark told Baum that he had not looked at it, didn't intend to look at, and was returning it. In addition, he himself was going to deal appropriately with the new salesperson.[75] As this example illustrates, managers must provide ethical leadership. As we said earlier, what managers *do* has a strong influence on employees' decisions whether to behave ethically. When managers cheat, lie, steal, manipulate, take advantage of situations or people, or treat others unfairly, what kind of signal are they sending to employees (or other stakeholders)? Probably not the one they want to send. Exhibit 5-9 gives some suggestions on how managers can provide ethical leadership.

PROTECTION OF EMPLOYEES WHO RAISE ETHICAL ISSUES.   What would you do if you saw other employees doing something illegal, immoral, or unethical? Would you step forward? Many of us wouldn't because of the perceived risks. That's why it's important for managers to assure employees who raise ethical concerns or issues that they will face no personal or career risks. These individuals, often called **whistle-blowers**, can be a key part of any company's ethics program. For example, Sherron Watkins, who was a vice president at Enron, clearly outlined her concerns about the company's accounting practices in a letter to chairman Ken Lay. Her statement that, "I am incredibly nervous that we will implode in a wave of accounting scandals" couldn't have been more prophetic.[76] However, surveys show that most observers of wrongdoing don't report it and that's the attitude managers have to address.[77] How can they protect employees so they're willing to step up if they see unethical or illegal things occurring?

One way is to set up toll-free ethics hotlines. For instance, Dell has an ethics hotline that employees can call anonymously to report infractions that the company will then investigate.[78] In addition, managers need to create a culture where bad news can be heard and acted on before it's too late. Michael Josephson, founder of the Josephson Institute of Ethics [www.josephsoninstitute.org] said, "It is absolutely and unequivocally important to establish a culture where it is possible for employees to complain and protest and to get heard."[79] Even if some whistle-blowers have a personal agenda they're pursuing, it's important to take them seriously. Finally, the federal legislation Sarbanes-Oxley offers some legal protection. Any manager who retaliates against an employee for reporting violations faces a stiff penalty: a 10-year jail sentence.[80] Unfortunately, despite this protection, hundreds of employees who have stepped forward and revealed wrongdoings at their companies have been fired or let go from their jobs.[81] So at the present time, it's not a perfect solution, but is a step in the right direction.

Social Entrepreneurship

The world's social problems are many and viable solutions are few. But numerous people and organizations are trying to do something. For instance, Reed Paget, founder and CEO

EXHIBIT 5-9

Being an Ethical Leader

- Be a good role model by being ethical and honest.
  - Tell the truth always.
  - Don't hide or manipulate information.
  - Be willing to admit your failures.
- Share your personal values by regularly communicating them to employees.
- Stress the organization's or team's important shared values.
- Use the reward system to hold everyone accountable to the values.

CHAPTER SUMMARY
by Learning Outcomes

Discuss what it means to be socially responsible and what factors influence that decision.

Social obligation, which reflects the classical view of social responsibility, is when a firm engages in social actions because of its obligation to meet certain economic and legal responsibilities. Social responsiveness is when a firm engages in social actions in response to some popular social need. Social responsibility is a business's intention, beyond its economic and legal obligations, to pursue long-term goals that are good for society. Both of these reflect the socioeconomic view of social responsibility. Determining whether organizations should be socially involved can be done by looking at arguments for and against it. Other ways are to assess the impact of social involvement on a company's economic performance and evaluate the performance of SRI funds versus non-SRI funds. We can conclude that a company's being socially responsible doesn't appear to hurt its economic performance.

Explain green management and how organizations can go green.

Green management is when managers consider the impact of their organization on the natural environment. Organizations can "go green" in different ways. The light green approach is doing what is required legally, which is social obligation. Using the market approach, organizations respond to the environmental preferences of their customers. Using the stakeholder approach, organizations respond to the environmental demands of multiple stakeholders. Both the market and stakeholder approaches can be viewed as social responsiveness. With an activist or dark green approach, an organization looks for ways to respect and preserve the earth and its natural resources, which can be viewed as social responsibility.

Green actions can be evaluated by examining reports that companies compile about their environmental performance, by looking for compliance with global standards for environmental management (ISO 14000), and by using the Global 100 list of the most sustainable corporations in the world.

Discuss the factors that lead to ethical and unethical behavior.

Ethics refers to the principles, values, and beliefs that define right and wrong decisions and behavior. The factors that affect ethical and unethical behavior include an individual's level of moral development (preconventional, conventional, or principled), individual characteristics (values and personality variables—ego strength and locus of control), structural variables (structural design, use of goals, performance appraisal systems, and reward allocation procedures), organizational culture (shared values and cultural strength), and issue intensity (greatness of harm, consensus of wrong, probability of harm, immediacy of consequences, proximity to victims, and concentration of effect).

Since ethical standards aren't universal, managers should know what they can and cannot do legally as defined by the Foreign Corrupt Practices Act. It's also important to recognize any cultural differences and to clarify ethical guidelines for employees working in different global locations. Finally, managers should know about the principles of the Global Compact and the Anti-Bribery Convention.

Describe management's role in encouraging ethical behavior.

The behavior of managers is the single most important influence on an individual's decision to act ethically or unethically. Some specific ways managers can encourage ethical behavior include paying attention to employee selection, having and using a code of ethics, recognizing the important ethical leadership role they play and how what they do is far more important than what they say, making sure that goals and the performance appraisal process don't reward goal achievement without taking into account how those goals were achieved, using ethics training and independent social audits, and establishing protective mechanisms.

LEARNING OUTCOME **5.5** **Discuss** current social responsibility and ethics issues.

Managers can manage ethical lapses and social irresponsibility by being strong ethical leaders and by protecting employees who raise ethical issues. The example set by managers has a strong influence on whether employees behave ethically. Ethical leaders also are honest, share their values, stress important shared values, and use the reward system appropriately. Managers can protect whistle-blowers (employees who raise ethical issues or concerns) by encouraging them to come forward, by setting up toll-free ethics hotlines, and by establishing a culture in which employees can complain and be heard without fear of reprisal. Social entrepreneurs play an important role in solving social problems by seeking out opportunities to improve society by using practical, innovative, and sustainable approaches. Social entrepreneurs want to make the world a better place and have a driving passion to make that happen. Businesses can promote positive social change through corporate philanthropy and employee volunteering efforts.

PEARSON mymanagementlab™ To check your understanding of learning outcomes **5.1** – **5.5** go to **mymanagementlab.com** and try the chapter questions.

REVIEW AND DISCUSSION QUESTIONS

1. Differentiate between social obligation, social responsiveness, and social responsibility.

2. What does social responsibility mean to you personally? Do *you* think business organizations should be socially responsible? Explain.

3. What is green management and how can organizations go green?

4. What factors influence whether a person behaves ethically or unethically? Explain all relevant factors.

5. Do you think values-based management is just a "do-gooder" ploy? Explain your answer.

6. Discuss specific ways managers can encourage ethical behavior.

7. Internet file sharing programs are popular among college students. These programs work by allowing non-organizational users to access any local network where desired files are located. Because these types of file sharing programs tend to clog bandwidth, local users' ability to access and use a local network is reduced. What ethical and social responsibilities does a university have in this situation? To whom do they have a responsibility? What guidelines might you suggest for university decision makers?

8. What are some problems that could be associated with employee whistle-blowing for (a) the whistle-blower and (b) the organization?

9. Describe the characteristics and behaviors of someone you consider to be an ethical person. How could the types of decisions and actions this person engages in be encouraged in a workplace?

10. Explain the ethical and social responsibility issues facing managers today.

ETHICS DILEMMA

"Apple's chief takes a medical leave after months of denial that his health is declining; many feel because he is so closely linked with the firm's creative vision, Steve Jobs should be required to release more medical information." What do you think? Do the heads of publicly traded firms have a right to medical privacy? What ethical issues might arise in such a situation?[93]

SKILLS EXERCISE

Developing Your
Developing Trust Skill

About the Skill

Trust plays an important role in the manager's relationships with his or her employees.[94] Given the importance of trust in setting a good ethical example for employees, today's managers should actively seek to develop it within their work group.

Steps in Practicing the Skill

1. *Practice openness.* Mistrust comes as much from what people don't know as from what they do. Being open with employees leads to confidence and trust. Keep people informed. Make clear the criteria you use in making decisions. Explain the rationale for your decisions. Be forthright and candid about problems. Fully disclose all relevant information.

2. *Be fair.* Before making decisions or taking actions, consider how others will perceive them in terms of objectivity and fairness. Give credit where credit is due. Be objective and impartial in performance appraisals. Pay attention to equity perceptions in distributing rewards.

3. *Speak your feelings.* Managers who convey only hard facts come across as cold, distant, and unfeeling. When you share your feelings, others will see that you are real and human. They will know you for who you are and their respect for you is likely to increase.

4. *Tell the truth.* Being trustworthy means being credible. If honesty is critical to credibility, then you must be perceived as someone who tells the truth. Employees are more tolerant of hearing something "they don't want to hear" than of finding out that their manager lied to them.

5. *Be consistent.* People want predictability. Mistrust comes from not knowing what to expect. Take the time to think about your values and beliefs and let those values and beliefs consistently guide your decisions. When you know what's important to you, your actions will follow, and you will project a consistency that earns trust.

6. *Fulfill your promises.* Trust requires that people believe that you are dependable. You need to ensure that you keep your word. Promises made must be promises kept.

7. *Maintain confidences.* You trust those whom you believe to be discreet and those on whom you can rely. If people open up to you and make themselves vulnerable by telling you something in confidence, they need to feel assured you won't discuss it with others or betray that confidence. If people perceive you as someone who leaks personal confidences or someone who can't be depended on, you've lost their trust.

8. *Demonstrate competence.* Develop the admiration and respect of others by demonstrating technical and professional ability. Pay particular attention to developing and displaying your communication, negotiation, and other interpersonal skills.

Practicing the Skill

Read through the following scenario. Write a paper describing how you would handle the situation. Be sure to refer to the eight behaviors described for developing trust.

Scenario

Donna Romines is the shipping department manager at Tastefully Tempting, a gourmet candy company based in Phoenix. Orders for the company's candy come from around the world. Your six-member team processes these orders. Needless to say, the two months before Christmas are quite hectic. Everybody counts the days until December 24 when the phones finally stop ringing off the wall, at least for a couple of days. You and all of your team members breathe a sigh of relief as the last box of candy is sent on its way out the door.

When the company was first founded five years ago, after the holiday rush, the owners would shut down Tastefully Tempting for two weeks after Christmas. However, as the business has grown and moved into Internet sales, that practice has become too costly. There's too much business to be able to afford that luxury. And the rush for Valentine's Day orders start pouring in the week after Christmas. Although the two-week post-holiday company-wide shutdown has been phased out formally, some departments have found it difficult to get employees to gear up once again after the Christmas break. The employees who come to work after Christmas usually accomplish little. This year, though, things have got to change. You know that the cultural "tradition" won't be easy to overcome, but your shipping team needs to be ready to tackle the orders that have piled up. After all, Tastefully Tempting's customers want their orders filled promptly and correctly!

WORKING TOGETHER
Team Exercise

In an effort to be (or at least appear to be) socially responsible, many organizations donate money to philanthropic and charitable causes. In addition, many organizations ask their employees to make individual donations to these causes. Suppose you're the manager of a work team, and you know that several of your employees can't afford to pledge money right now because of personal or financial problems. You've also been told by your supervisor that the CEO has been known to check the list of individual contributors to see who is and is not "supporting these very important causes." Working together in a small group of three or four, answer the following questions:

- How would you handle this situation?

- What ethical guidelines might you suggest for individual and organizational contributions in such a situation?

- Create a company policy statement that expresses your ethical guidelines.

MY TURN TO BE A MANAGER

- Find five different examples of organizational codes of ethics. Using Exhibit 5-7, describe what each contains. Compare and contrast the examples.

- Using the examples of codes of ethics you found, create what you feel would be an appropriate and effective organizational code of ethics. In addition, create your own *personal code of ethics* that you can use as a guide to ethical dilemmas.

- Take advantage of volunteer opportunities. Be sure to include these on your résumé. If possible, try to do things in these volunteer positions that will improve your managerial skills in planning, organizing, leading, or controlling.

- Go to the Global Reporting Initiative Web site [www.globalreporting.org] and choose three businesses from the list that have filed reports. Look at those reports and describe/evaluate what's in them. In addition, identify the stakeholders that might be affected and how they might be affected by the company's actions.

- Make a list of what green management things your school is doing. If you're working, make a list of what green management things your employer is doing. Do some research on being green. Are there additional things your school or employer could be doing? Write a report to each describing any suggestions. (Look for ways that you could use these suggestions to be more "green" in your personal life.)

- Over the course of two weeks, see what ethical "dilemmas" you observe. These could be ones that you personally face or they could be ones that others (friends, colleagues, other students talking in the hallway or before class starts, or so forth) face. Write these dilemmas down and think about what you might do if faced with that dilemma.

- Interview two different managers about how they encourage their employees to be ethical. Write down their comments and discuss how these ideas might help you be a better manager.

- Steve's and Mary's suggested readings: Bethany McLean and Peter Elkind, *The Smartest Guys in the Room: The Amazing Rise and Scandalous Fall of Enron* (Portfolio, 2003); Barbara Ley Toffler, *Final Accounting: Ambition, Greed, and the Fall of Arthur Andersen* (Broadway Books, 2003); Joseph L. Badaracco, Jr., *Leading Quietly: An Unorthodox Guide to Doing the Right Thing* (Harvard Business School Press, 2002); and Kenneth Blanchard and Norman Vincent Peale, *The Power of Ethical Management* (Morrow, 1988).

- If you have the opportunity, take a class on business or managerial ethics or on social responsibility—often called business and society—or both. Not only will this look good on your résumé, it could help you personally grapple with some of the tough issues managers face in being ethical and responsible.

- In your own words, write down three things you learned in this chapter about being a good manager.

- Self-knowledge can be a powerful learning tool. Go to mymanagementlab.com and complete these self-assessment exercises: What Do I Value? How Do My Ethics Rate? Do I Trust Others? and Do Others See Me as Trusting? Using the results of your assessments, identify personal strengths and weaknesses. What will you do to reinforce your strengths and improve your weaknesses?

CASE APPLICATION 1
Lessons from Lehman Brothers: Will We Ever Learn?

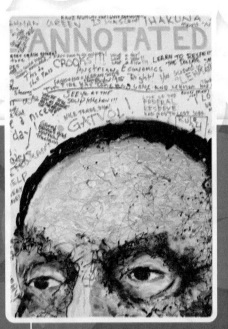

On September 15, 2008, financial services firm Lehman Brothers filed for bankruptcy with the U.S. Bankruptcy Court in the Southern District of New York.[95] That action—the largest Chapter 11 filing in financial history—unleashed a "crisis of confidence that threw financial markets worldwide into turmoil, sparking the worst crisis since the Great Depression." The fall of this Wall Street icon is, unfortunately, not a new one, as we've seen in the stories of Enron, WorldCom, and others. In a report released by bankruptcy court-appointed examiner Anton Valukas, Lehman executives and the firm's auditor, Ernst & Young, were lambasted for actions that led to the firm's collapse. He said, "Lehman repeatedly exceeded its own internal risk limits and controls, and a wide range of bad calls by its management led to the bank's failure." Let's look behind the scenes at some of the issues.

"Greed" and "Crooks" are a sampling of comments recorded on a rendering of Lehman's chief executive Richard Fuld by artist Geoffrey Raymond, who placed his painting outside of Lehman's New York City offices and handed out markers to employees and pedestrians so they could write a message regarding the firm's announcement that it was filing for bankruptcy.

One of the major problems at Lehman was its culture and reward structure. Excessive risk taking by employees was openly lauded and rewarded handsomely. Individuals making questionable deals were hailed and treated as "conquering heroes." On the other hand, anyone who questioned decisions was often ignored or overruled. For instance, Oliver Budde, who served as an associate general counsel at Lehman for nine years, was responsible for preparing the firm's public filings on executive compensation. Infuriated by what he felt was the firm's "intentional under-representation of how much top executives were paid," Budde argued with his bosses for years about that matter, to no avail. Then, one time he objected to a tax deal that an outside accounting firm had proposed to lower medical insurance costs saying, "My gut feeling was that this was just reshuffling some papers to get an expense off the balance sheet. It was not the right thing, and I told them." However, Budde's bosses disagreed and okayed the deal.

Another problem at Lehman was the firm's top leadership. Valukas's report was highly critical of Lehman's executives who "should have done more, done better." He pointed out that the executives made the company's problems worse by their conduct, which ranged from "serious but nonculpable errors of business judgment to actionable balance sheet manipulation." Valukas went on to say that "former chief executive Richard Fuld was at least grossly negligent in causing Lehman to file misleading periodic reports." These reports were part of an accounting device called "Repo 105." Lehman used this device to get some $50 billion of undesirable assets off its balance sheet at the end of the first and second quarters of 2008, instead of selling those assets at a loss. The examiner's report "included e-mails from Lehman's global financial controller confirming that the only purpose or motive for Repo 105 transactions was reduction in the balance sheet, adding that there was no substance to the transactions." Lehman's auditor was aware of the use of Repo 105 but did not challenge or question it. Sufficient evidence indicated that Fuld knew about the use of it as well; however, he signed off on quarterly reports that made no mention of it. Fuld's attorney said, "Mr. Fuld did not know what these transactions were—he didn't structure or negotiate them, nor was he aware of their accounting treatment." A spokesperson from Ernst & Young (the auditor) said that, "Lehman's bankruptcy was the result of a series of unprecedented adverse events in the financial markets."

Discussion Questions

1. Describe the situation at Lehman Brothers from an ethics perspective. What's your opinion of what happened here?

2. What was the culture at Lehman Brothers like? How did this culture contribute to the company's downfall?

3. What role did Lehman's executives play in the company's collapse? Were they being responsible and ethical? Discuss.

4. Could anything have been done differently at Lehman Brothers to prevent what happened? Explain.

5. After all the public uproar over Enron and then the passage of the Sarbanes-Oxley Act to protect shareholders, why do you think we still continue to see these types of situations? Is it unreasonable to expect that businesses can and should act ethically?

CASE APPLICATION 2
Green Up on Aisle Two

It's probably the last company that you'd think of as going green.[96] As the world's largest retailer with more than 8,400 stores globally, Walmart moves massive amounts of products and uses massive amounts of power and other resources to operate its business. But it's also striving to transform itself into a company that's seen as environmentally friendly. That's why the company's announcement that it would cut some 20 million metric tons of greenhouse gas emissions from its supply chain—the equivalent of removing more than 3.8 million cars from the road for a year—got widespread attention. This announcement came a few months after the company said that it would be creating a sustainability index of just how green its products are.

The first part of Walmart's three-phase plan was getting information from its more than 100,000 suppliers using a 15-question survey about their greenhouse gas emissions, water and solid waste reduction efforts, and other details about business practices. That information was received by October 2009, and the second-phase process of entering it into a massive database began. The third phase involves getting all that data eventually condensed into an easily understood universal rating system, similar to a nutrition label but focused on details about environmental and social sustainability. However, it's likely that this effort won't be complete until 2013.

This isn't the company's first push toward being green. Walmart has started many environmental initiatives in recent years including improving the efficiency of its truck fleet and working with 20th Century Fox Home Entertainment, which produces DVDs, to cut greenhouse gas emissions by eliminating the plastic knob in the center of its CD cases. The most difficult part of this latest green initiative has been persuading its suppliers to spend the time and money tracking and lessening their environmental impact. Essentially, suppliers are being asked to "examine the carbon lifecycle of their products, from the raw materials used in manufacturing all the way through to the recycling phase." Although supplier participation was not mandatory, Walmart made it clear that it was interested in doing business only with suppliers that shared its goals. The company is also collaborating with organizations such as the Environmental Defense Fund, ClearCarbon, the Applied Sustainability Center at the University of Arkansas, and the Carbon Disclosure Project. These groups will advise Walmart and its suppliers and help in evaluating and measuring reductions.

Discussion Questions

1. What do you think of Walmart's green initiatives? Will it ever be able to achieve the reputation of being environmentally friendly? Discuss.

2. Why do you think suppliers might be reluctant to be involved in this initiative? How might that reluctance be addressed? Although it said supplier participation was not mandatory, does Walmart appear to be "forcing" suppliers to participate?

3. Why do you think it's important for Walmart to collaborate with other green-minded organizations?

4. What could other organizations learn from Walmart's green initiatives?

Let's Get Real:

Meet the Manager

Reginald Lo
Vice President of Professional Services
Third Sky, Inc.
Alameda, CA

You'll be hearing more from this real manager throughout the chapter.

MY JOB:

I'm vice president for professional services at Third Sky, Inc. Third Sky is a consulting company that helps IT organizations deliver better service to their customers. Third Sky provides education on industry best practices, consulting services for planning and executing improvement initiatives, and technology implementation services to enable the adoption of best practices. I play a dual role at Third Sky: I manage all of Third Sky's consultants and oversee the development of new service offerings; and I am a consultant who goes to customers' sites to help them improve.

BEST PART OF MY JOB:

The thanks I receive from customers when we teach them industry best practices and help them adopt these practices. We have made their lives less hectic and enabled them to provide better service to their customers, who in turn thank them.

Managing Change *and* Innovation

LEARNING OUTCOMES

WORST PART OF MY JOB:

The "administrivia." Unfortunately, one must do certain activities in order to maintain good control of an organization (e.g. reviewing and approving timesheets and expense reports, triggering invoicing, etc.).

BEST MANAGEMENT ADVICE EVER RECEIVED:

There are three types of people in an organization: the change agent, the change participant, and the change resister. The change agents are the happiest because they control their own destiny. The change resisters aren't going to be around for very long.

A Manager's Dilemma

After 29 years of flight, NASA's space shuttle program is expected to end in 2010.[1] Over that time span, we've seen highs and lows, triumphs and tragedies. Dismantling a program of this magnitude involves massive changes for managers and employees.

One change that managers must deal with is how the agency will be structured to revitalize the space program—a decision that's not theirs to make. Because it is a governmental agency, lawmakers will make the decision. Congress wants to continue with NASA's existing space exploration program, Constellation. But the president thinks it is too expensive and flawed and wants to use private enterprise until NASA can develop more advanced space vehicles. The reputation of the United States as a leader in space exploration, being the only country to put people on the moon, is at stake. But there's more than national pride. "Losing the lead in space has national security and industrial consequences."

The most critical change facing NASA's managers is what to do with its workforce of highly trained and skilled individuals while the future of its space

exploration program is debated and decided. How will they keep employees focused during this change?

What Would You Do?

The managerial challenges facing NASA'S leaders in encouraging continued innovative efforts among all the agency's employees during uncertain times is certainly not unique. Big companies and small businesses, universities and colleges, state and city governments, and even the military are forced to be innovative. Although innovation has always been a part of the manager's job, it has become even more important in recent years. We'll describe why innovation is important and how managers can manage innovation in this chapter. Because innovation is often closely tied to an organization's change efforts, we'll start by looking at change and how managers manage change.

LEARNING OUTCOME 6.1
Compare and contrast views on the change process.

The Change Process

When John Lechleiter assumed the CEO's job at Eli Lilly, he sent each of his senior executives a gift—"a digital clock counting down, second by second, to October 23, 2011. That's the day Lilly's $5 billion-a-year schizophrenia pill, Zyprexa, is no longer under patent." Between 2010 and the end of 2016, Lilly stands to lose $10 billion in annual revenues as patents on three of its key drugs expire. Needless to say, the company has had to make some organizational changes as it picks up the pace of drug development.[2] Lilly's managers are doing what managers everywhere must do—implement change!

If it weren't for change, a manager's job would be relatively easy. Planning would be simple because tomorrow would be no different from today. The issue of effective organizational design would also be resolved because the environment would not be uncertain and there would be no need to redesign the structure. Similarly, decision making would be dramatically streamlined because the outcome of each alternative could be predicted with almost certain accuracy. But that's not the way it is. Change is an organizational reality.[3] Organizations face change because external and internal factors create the need for change (see Exhibit 6-1). When managers recognize that change is needed, then what? How do they respond?

Two Views of the Change Process

Two very different metaphors can be used to describe the change process.[4] One metaphor envisions the organization as a large ship crossing a calm sea. The ship's captain and crew know exactly where they're going because they've made the trip many times before. Change comes in the form of an occasional storm, a brief distraction in an otherwise calm and predictable trip.

EXHIBIT **6-1**

External and Internal Forces for Change

External

- Changing consumer needs and wants
- New governmental laws
- Changing technology
- Economic changes

Internal

- New organizational strategy
- Change in composition of workforce
- New equipment
- Changing employee attitudes

In the calm waters metaphor, change is seen as an occasional disruption in the normal flow of events. In the other metaphor, the organization is seen as a small raft navigating a raging river with uninterrupted white-water rapids. Aboard the raft are half-a-dozen people who have never worked together before, who are totally unfamiliar with the river, who are unsure of their eventual destination, and who, as if things weren't bad enough, are traveling at night. In the white-water rapids metaphor, change is normal and expected and managing it is a continual process. These two metaphors present very different approaches to understanding and responding to change. Let's take a closer look at each one.

THE CALM WATERS METAPHOR.   At one time, the calm waters metaphor was fairly descriptive of the situation that managers faced. It's best discussed using Kurt Lewin's three-step change process.[5] (See Exhibit 6-2.)

According to Lewin, successful change can be planned and requires *unfreezing* the status quo, *changing* to a new state, and *refreezing* to make the change permanent. The status quo is considered equilibrium. To move away from this equilibrium, unfreezing is necessary. Unfreezing can be thought of as preparing for the needed change. It can be done by increasing the *driving forces,* which are forces pushing for change; by decreasing the *restraining forces*, which are forces that resist change; or by combining the two approaches.

Once unfreezing is done, the change itself can be implemented. However, merely introducing change doesn't ensure that it will take hold. The new situation needs to be *refrozen* so that it can be sustained over time. Unless this last step is done, there's a strong chance that employees will revert back to the old equilibrium state—that is, the old ways of doing things. The objective of refreezing, then, is to stabilize the new situation by reinforcing the new behaviors.

Lewin's three-step process treats change as a move away from the organization's current equilibrium state. It's a calm waters scenario where an occasional disruption (a "storm") means changing to deal with the disruption. Once the disruption has been dealt with, however, things can continue on under the new changed situation. This type of environment isn't what most managers face today.

EXHIBIT **6-2**

The Three-Step Change Process

Unfreezing | Changing | Refreezing

WHITE-WATER RAPIDS METAPHOR. Susan Whiting is CEO of Nielsen Media Research, the company best known for its television ratings, which are frequently used to determine how much advertisers pay for TV commercials. The media research business isn't what it used to be, however, as the Internet, video on demand, cell phones, iPods, digital video recorders, and other changing technologies have made data collection much more challenging. Whiting says, "If you look at a typical week I have, it's a combination of trying to lead a company in change in an industry in change."[6] That's a pretty accurate description of what change is like in our second change metaphor—white-water rapids. It's also consistent with a world that's increasingly dominated by information, ideas, and knowledge.[7]

To get a feeling of what managing change might be like in a white-water rapids environment, consider attending a college that had the following rules: Courses vary in length. When you sign up, you don't know how long a course will run. It might go for 2 weeks or 15 weeks. Furthermore, the instructor can end a course at any time with no prior warning. If that isn't challenging enough, the length of the class changes each time it meets: Sometimes the class lasts 20 minutes; other times it runs for 3 hours. And the time of the next class meeting is set by the instructor during this class. There's one more thing: All exams are unannounced, so you have to be ready for a test at any time. To succeed in this type of environment, you'd have to respond quickly to changing conditions. Students who are overly structured or uncomfortable with change wouldn't succeed.

Increasingly, managers are realizing that their job is much like what a student would face in such a college. The stability and predictability of the calm waters metaphor don't exist. Disruptions in the status quo are not occasional and temporary, and they are not followed by a return to calm waters. Many managers never get out of the rapids. Like Susan Whiting, they face constant change.

Is the white-water rapids metaphor an exaggeration? Probably not! Although you'd expect a chaotic and dynamic environment in high-tech industries, even organizations in non-high-tech industries are faced with constant change. Take the case of Swedish home appliance company Electrolux. You might think that the home appliances industry couldn't be all that difficult—after all, most households need the products, which are fairly uncomplicated—but that impression would be wrong. Electrolux's chief executive Hans Straberg has had several challenges to confront.[8] First, there's the challenge of developing products that will appeal to a wide range of global customers. Then, there's the challenge of cheaper alternatives flooding the market. In addition, Electrolux faces intense competition in the United States, where it gets 40 percent of its sales. Because approximately 80 percent of the workforce in Sweden belongs to a labor union, companies certainly face expectations as far as how they treat their employees. However, Straberg recognized that his company was going to have to change if it was going to survive and prosper. One thing he did was to shift production to lower-cost facilities in Asia and Eastern Europe. Then, to better grasp what today's consumers are thinking, the company held in-depth interviews with 160,000 customers from around the world. Using this information, a group of Electrolux employees gathered in Stockholm for a weeklong brainstorming session to search for insights on what hot new products to pursue. Finally, to make the new product development process speedier, Straberg eliminated the structural divisions between departments. Designers, engineers, and marketers have to work together to come up with ideas. These changes were essential if Electrolux wanted to survive the white-water rapids environment in which it operated.

Today, any organization that treats change as the occasional disturbance in an otherwise calm and stable world runs a great risk. Too much is changing too fast for an organization or its managers to be complacent. It's no longer business as usual. And managers must be ready to efficiently and effectively manage the changes facing their organization or their work area.

Let's Get Real

F2F

"Calm waters" or "white-water rapids"? *Our company is definitely a "white-water rapids" environment. We strive to continually increase our rate of change by improving our team, the way we work, and our equipment so we can navigate the waters successfully.*

6.2

LEARNING OUTCOME
Classify types of organizational

Types of Organizational Change

Managers at Verizon Wireless know what change is all about. "Even in an industry where rapid change is the status quo, it takes a special kind of company to handle the challenges posed by a major corporate acquisition and massive product rollout."[9] Verizon was up for the challenges and focused its change efforts on its people and processes.

The fact that almost everything a manager does involves making decisions doesn't mean that decisions are always time-consuming, complex, or evident to an outside observer. Most decision making is routine. For instance, every day of the year you make a decision about what to eat for dinner. It's no big deal. You've made the decision thousands of times before. It's a pretty simple decision and can usually be handled quickly. It's the type of decision you almost forget *is* a decision. And managers also make dozens of these routine decisions every day, such as, for example, which employee will work what shift next week, what information should be included in a report, or how to resolve a customer's complaint. Keep in mind that even though a decision seems easy or has been faced by a manager a number of times before, it still is a decision. Let's look at four perspectives on how managers make decisions.

Making Decisions: Rationality

When Hewlett-Packard (HP) acquired Compaq, the company did no research on how customers viewed Compaq products until "months after then-CEO Carly Fiorina publicly announced the deal and privately warned her top management team that she didn't want to hear any dissent pertaining to the acquisition."[8] By the time they discovered that customers perceived Compaq products as inferior—just the opposite of what customers felt about HP products—it was too late. HP's performance suffered and Fiorina lost her job.

We assume that managers will use **rational decision making**; that is, they'll make logical and consistent choices to maximize value.[9] After all, managers have all sorts of tools and techniques to help them be rational decision makers. But as the HP example illustrates, managers aren't always rational. What does it mean to be a "rational" decision maker?

ASSUMPTIONS OF RATIONALITY. A rational decision maker would be fully objective and logical. The problem faced would be clear and unambiguous, and the decision maker would have a clear and specific goal and know all possible alternatives and consequences. Finally, making decisions rationally would consistently lead to selecting the alternative that maximizes the likelihood of achieving that goal. These assumptions apply to any decision—personal or managerial. However, for managerial decision making, we need to add one additional assumption—decisions are made in the best interests of the organization. These assumptions of rationality aren't very realistic, but the next concept can help explain how most decisions get made in organizations.

Making Decisions: Bounded Rationality

Despite the unrealistic assumptions, managers *are* expected to be rational when making decisions.[10] They understand that "good" decision makers are supposed to do certain things and exhibit good decision-making behaviors as they identify problems, consider alternatives, gather information, and act decisively but prudently. When they do so, they show others that they're competent and that their decisions are the result of intelligent deliberation. However, a more realistic approach to describing how managers make decisions is the concept of **bounded rationality**, which says that managers make decisions rationally, but are limited (bounded) by their ability to process information.[11] Because they can't possibly analyze all information on all alternatives, managers **satisfice**, rather than maximize. That is, they accept solutions that are "good enough." They're being rational within the limits (bounds) of their ability to process information. Let's look at an example.

Suppose that you're a finance major and upon graduation you want a job, preferably as a personal financial planner, with a minimum salary of $35,000 and within a hundred miles of your hometown. You accept a job offer as a business credit analyst—not exactly a personal

---

rational decision making
Describes choices that are logical and consistent and maximize value

bounded rationality
Decision making that's rational, but limited (bounded) by an individual's ability to process information

satisfice
Accept solutions that are "good enough"

financial planner but still in the finance field—at a bank 50 miles from home at a starting salary of $34,000. If you had done a more comprehensive job search, you would have discovered a job in personal financial planning at a trust company only 25 miles from your hometown and starting at a salary of $38,000. You weren't a perfectly rational decision maker because you didn't maximize your decision by searching all possible alternatives and then choosing the best. But because the first job offer was satisfactory (or "good enough"), you behaved in a bounded rationality manner by accepting it.

Most decisions that managers make don't fit the assumptions of perfect rationality, so they satisfice. However, keep in mind that their decision making is also likely influenced by the organization's culture, internal politics, power considerations, and by a phenomenon called **escalation of commitment**, which is an increased commitment to a previous decision despite evidence that it may have been wrong.[12] The *Challenger* space shuttle disaster is often used as an example of escalation of commitment. Decision makers chose to launch the shuttle that day even though the decision was questioned by several individuals who believed that it was a bad one. Why would decision makers escalate commitment to a bad decision? Because they don't want to admit that their initial decision may have been flawed. Rather than search for new alternatives, they simply increase their commitment to the original solution.

Making good decisions is hard because *every decision carries some sort of risk. You have to own the decision you are making and not go back on your thoughts. Make it and stick to it because if you change your mind too often, it can confuse your employees.*

Making Decisions: The Role of Intuition

When managers at stapler-maker Swingline saw the company's market share declining, they used a logical scientific approach to address the issue. For three years, they exhaustively researched stapler users before deciding what new products to develop. However, at Accentra, Inc., founder Todd Moses used a more intuitive decision approach to come up with his line of unique PaperPro staplers.[13]

Like Todd Moses, managers often use their intuition to help their decision making. What is **intuitive decision making**? It's making decisions on the basis of experience, feelings, and accumulated judgment. Researchers studying managers' use of intuitive decision making have identified five different aspects of intuition, which are described in Exhibit 7-6.[14] How common is intuitive decision making? One survey found that almost half of the executives surveyed "used intuition more often than formal analysis to run their companies."[15]

EXHIBIT 7-6

What Is Intuition?

Source: Based on L. A. Burke and M. K. Miller, "Taking the Mystery Out of Intuitive Decision Making," *Academy of Management Executive*, October 1999, pp. 91–99.

Intuitive decision making can complement both rational and bounded rational decision making.[16] First of all, a manager who has had experience with a similar type of problem or situation often can act quickly with what appears to be limited information because of that past experience. In addition, a recent study found that individuals who experienced intense feelings and emotions when making decisions actually achieved higher decision-making performance, especially when they understood their feelings as they were making decisions. The old belief that managers should ignore emotions when making decisions may not be the best advice.[17]

Making Decisions: The Role of Evidence-Based Management

Suppose you were exhibiting some strange, puzzling physical symptoms. In order to make the best decisions about proper diagnosis and treatment, wouldn't you want your doctor to base her decisions on the best available evidence? Now suppose that you're a manager faced with putting together an employee recognition program. Wouldn't you want those decisions also to be based on the best available evidence? "Any decision-making process is likely to be enhanced through the use of relevant and reliable evidence, whether it's buying someone a birthday present or wondering which new washing machine to buy."[18] That's the premise behind **evidence-based management (EBMgt)**, which is the "systematic use of the best available evidence to improve management practice."[19]

EBMgt is quite relevant to managerial decision making. The four essential elements of EBMgt are the decision maker's expertise and judgment; external evidence that's been evaluated by the decision maker; opinions, preferences, and values of those who have a stake in the decision; and relevant organizational (internal) factors such as context, circumstances, and organizational members. The strength or influence of each of these elements on a decision will vary with each decision. Sometimes, the decision maker's intuition (judgment) might be given greater emphasis in the decision; other times it might be the opinions of stakeholders; and at other times, it might be ethical considerations (organizational context). The key for managers is to recognize and understand the mindful, conscious choice as to which element(s) are most important and should be emphasized in making a decision.

Types of Decisions and Decision-Making Conditions

7.3

LEARNING OUTCOME
Classify decisions and decision-making conditions.

Restaurant managers in New York City make routine decisions weekly about purchasing food supplies and scheduling employee work shifts. It's something they've done numerous times. But now they're facing a different kind of decision—one they've never encountered—how to adapt to the new law requiring that nutritional information be posted.

Types of Decisions

Such situations aren't all that unusual. Managers in all kinds of organizations face different types of problems and decisions as they do their jobs. Depending on the nature of the problem, a manager can use one of two different types of decisions.

STRUCTURED PROBLEMS AND PROGRAMMED DECISIONS. Some problems are straightforward. The decision maker's goal is clear, the problem is familiar, and information about the problem is easily defined and complete. Examples might include when a

---

escalation of commitment
An increased commitment to a previous decision despite evidence it may have been wrong

intuitive decision making
Making decisions on the basis of experience, feelings, and accumulated judgment

evidence-based management (EBMgt)
The systematic use of the best available evidence to improve management practice

customer returns a purchase to a store, when a supplier is late with an important delivery, a news team's response to a fast-breaking event, or a college's handling of a student wanting to drop a class. Such situations are called **structured problems** because they're straightforward, familiar, and easily defined. For instance, a server spills a drink on a customer's coat. The customer is upset and the manager needs to do something. Because it's not an unusual occurrence, there's probably some standardized routine for handling it. For example, the manager offers to have the coat cleaned at the restaurant's expense. This is what we call a **programmed decision**, a repetitive decision that can be handled by a routine approach. Because the problem is structured, the manager doesn't have to go to the trouble and expense of going through an involved decision process. The "develop-the-alternatives" stage of the decision-making process either doesn't exist or is given little attention. Why? Because once the structured problem is defined, the solution is usually self-evident or at least reduced to a few alternatives that are familiar and have proved successful in the past. The spilled drink on the customer's coat doesn't require the restaurant manager to identify and weight decision criteria or to develop a long list of possible solutions. Instead, the manager relies on one of three types of programmed decisions: procedure, rule, or policy.

A **procedure** is a series of sequential steps a manager uses to respond to a structured problem. The only difficulty is identifying the problem. Once it's clear, so is the procedure. For instance, a purchasing manager receives a request from a warehouse manager for 15 PDA handhelds for the inventory clerks. The purchasing manager knows how to make this decision by following the established purchasing procedure.

A **rule** is an explicit statement that tells a manager what can or cannot be done. Rules are frequently used because they're simple to follow and ensure consistency. For example, rules about lateness and absenteeism permit supervisors to make disciplinary decisions rapidly and fairly.

The third type of programmed decisions is a **policy**, which is a guideline for making a decision. In contrast to a rule, a policy establishes general parameters for the decision maker rather than specifically stating what should or should not be done. Policies typically contain an ambiguous term that leaves interpretation up to the decision maker. Here are some sample policy statements:

▶ The customer always comes first and should always be *satisfied*.
▶ We promote from within, *whenever possible*.
▶ Employee wages shall be *competitive* within community standards.

Notice that the terms *satisfied, whenever possible,* and *competitive* require interpretation. For instance, the policy of paying competitive wages doesn't tell a company's human resources manager the exact amount he or she should pay, but it does guide them in making the decision.

UNSTRUCTURED PROBLEMS AND NONPROGRAMMED DECISIONS. Not all the problems managers face can be solved using programmed decisions. Many organizational situations involve **unstructured problems**, which are problems that are new or unusual and for which information is ambiguous or incomplete. Whether to build a new manufacturing facility in China is an example of an unstructured problem. So, too, is the problem facing restaurant managers in New York City who must decide how to modify their businesses to comply with the new law. When problems are unstructured, managers must rely on nonprogrammed decision making in order to develop unique solutions. **Nonprogrammed decisions** are unique and nonrecurring and involve custom-made solutions.

Exhibit 7-7 describes the differences between programmed and nonprogrammed decisions. Lower-level managers mostly rely on programmed decisions (procedures, rules, and policies) because they confront familiar and repetitive problems. As managers move up the organizational hierarchy, the problems they confront become more unstructured. Why? Because lower-level managers handle the routine decisions and let upper-level managers deal with the unusual or difficult decisions. Also, upper-level managers delegate routine decisions to their subordinates so they can deal with more difficult issues.[20] Thus, few managerial decisions in the real world are either fully programmed or nonprogrammed. Most fall somewhere in between.

Characteristic	Programmed Decisions	Nonprogrammed Decisions
Type of problem	Structured	Unstructured
Managerial level	Lower levels	Upper levels
Frequency	Repetitive, routine	New, unusual
Information	Readily available	Ambiguous or incomplete
Goals	Clear, specific	Vague
Time frame for solution	Short	Relatively long
Solution relies on . . .	Procedures, rules, policies	Judgment and creativity

EXHIBIT 7-7
Programmed Versus
Nonprogrammed Decisions

Decision-Making Conditions

When making decisions, managers may face three different conditions: certainty, risk, and uncertainty. Let's look at the characteristics of each.

CERTAINTY.   The ideal situation for making decisions is one of **certainty**, which is a situation where a manager can make accurate decisions because the outcome of every alternative is known. For example, when North Dakota's state treasurer decides where to deposit excess state funds, he knows exactly the interest rate being offered by each bank and the amount that will be earned on the funds. He is certain about the outcomes of each alternative. As you might expect, most managerial decisions aren't like this.

RISK.   A far more common situation is one of **risk**, conditions in which the decision maker is able to estimate the likelihood of certain outcomes. Under risk, managers have historical data from past personal experiences or secondary information that lets them assign probabilities to different alternatives. Let's do an example.

FUTURE VISION | The Working World in 2020

Artificial intelligence software will be available to approach problems the way the human brain does—by trying to recognize patterns that underlie a complex set of data.[21] Like people, this software will "learn" to pick out subtle patterns. In so doing, it will be able to perform a number of decision-making tasks.

Just as today's computers allow you to access information quickly from sources such as spreadsheets or search engines, most of the routine decisions that employees now do on the job are likely to be delegated to a software program. For instance, much of the diagnostic work now done by doctors will be done by software. Patients will describe their symptoms to a computer in a medical kiosk, possibly at their neighborhood drugstore, and from answers that the patient provides, the computer will render a decision. Similarly many hiring decisions will be made by software that is programmed to simulate the successful decision processes used by recruiters and managers. Welcome to the future of decision making!

structured problems
Straightforward, familiar, and easily defined problems

programmed decision
A repetitive decision that can be handled by a routine approach

procedure
A series of sequential steps used to respond to a well-structured problem

rule
An explicit statement that tells managers what can or cannot be done

policy
A guideline for making decisions

unstructured problems
Problems that are new or unusual and for which information is ambiguous or incomplete

nonprogrammed decisions
Unique and nonrecurring decisions that require a custom-made solution

certainty
A situation in which a manager can make accurate decisions because all outcomes are known

risk
A situation in which the decision maker is able to estimate the likelihood of certain outcomes

EXHIBIT 7-8

Expected Value

Event	Expected Revenues	x	Probability	=	Expected Value of Each Alternative
Heavy snowfall	$850,000		0.3		$255,000
Normal snowfall	725,000		0.5		362,500
Light snowfall	350,000		0.2		70,000
					$687,500

Suppose that you manage a Colorado ski resort and you're thinking about adding another lift. Obviously, your decision will be influenced by the additional revenue that the new lift would generate, which depends on snowfall. You have fairly reliable weather data from the last 10 years on snowfall levels in your area—three years of heavy snowfall, five years of normal snowfall, and two years of light snow. And you have good information on the amount of revenues generated during each level of snow. You can use this information to help you make your decision by calculating expected value—the expected return from each possible outcome—by multiplying expected revenues by snowfall probabilities. The result is the average revenue you can expect over time if the given probabilities hold. As Exhibit 7-8 shows, the expected revenue from adding a new ski lift is $687,500. Of course, whether that's enough to justify a decision to build depends on the costs involved in generating that revenue.

UNCERTAINTY.   What happens if you face a decision where you're not certain about the outcomes and can't even make reasonable probability estimates? We call this condition **uncertainty**. Managers do face decision-making situations of uncertainty. Under these conditions, the choice of alternative is influenced by the limited amount of available information and by the psychological orientation of the decision maker. An optimistic manager will follow a *maximax* choice (maximizing the maximum possible payoff); a pessimist will follow a *maximin* choice (maximizing the minimum possible payoff); and a manager who desires to minimize his maximum "regret" will opt for a *minimax* choice. Let's look at these different choice approaches using an example.

A marketing manager at Visa has determined four possible strategies (S_1, S_2, S_3, and S_4) for promoting the Visa card throughout the West Coast region of the United States. The marketing manager also knows that major competitor MasterCard has three competitive

Influenced by his optimism and intuition, Richard Branson (left), founder of The Virgin Group, unveiled a new online gaming venture based on his hunch that gamers want something new, interactive, and fun. A convergence of video games, social networking, and competitive gaming, Virgin Gaming enables players from around the world to meet and challenge each other in matches for cash and prizes. Although launched during a time of global economic uncertainty, Branson sees an enormous potential of an online community of 40 million daily users. Unlike competitors that target professionals, Virgin Gaming is designed for gamers of all skill levels. Shown here with Branson are (from left) Virgin Gaming president and cofounder William Levy, vice president of gaming operations, and cofounder Zack Zeldin, and CEO Rob Segal.

EXHIBIT 7-9
Payoff Matrix

Visa Marketing Strategy (in millions of dollars)	MasterCard's Competitive Action		
	CA₁	CA₂	CA₃
S₁	13	14	11
S₂	9	15	18
S₃	24	21	15
S₄	18	14	28

actions (CA_1, CA_2, CA_3) it's using to promote its card in the same region. For this example, we'll assume that the Visa manager had no previous knowledge that would allow her to determine probabilities of success of any of the four strategies. She formulates the matrix shown in Exhibit 7-9 to show the various Visa strategies and the resulting profit depending on the competitive action used by MasterCard.

In this example, if our Visa manager is an optimist, she'll choose strategy 4 (S_4) because that could produce the largest possible gain: $28 million. Note that this choice maximizes the maximum possible gain (maximax choice).

If our manager is a pessimist, she'll assume that only the worst can occur. The worst outcome for each strategy is as follows: S_1 = $11 million; S_2 = $9 million; S_3 = $15 million; S_4 = $14 million. These are the most pessimistic outcomes from each strategy. Following the *maximin* choice, she would maximize the minimum payoff; in other words, she'd select S_3 ($15 million is the largest of the minimum payoffs).

In the third approach, managers recognize that once a decision is made, it will not necessarily result in the most profitable payoff. There may be a "regret" of profits given up—*regret* referring to the amount of money that could have been made had a different strategy been used. Managers calculate regret by subtracting all possible payoffs in each category from the maximum possible payoff for each given event, in this case for each competitive action. For our Visa manager, the highest payoff, given that MasterCard engages in CA_1, CA_2, or CA_3, is $24 million, $21 million, or $28 million, respectively (the highest number in each column). Subtracting the payoffs in Exhibit 7-9 from those figures produces the results shown in Exhibit 7-10.

The maximum regrets are S_1 = $17 million, S_2 = $15 million, S_3 = $13 million, and S_4 = $7 million. The *minimax* choice minimizes the maximum regret, so our Visa manager would choose S_4. By making this choice, she'll never have a regret of profits given up of more than $7 million. This result contrasts, for example, with a regret of $15 million had she chosen S_2 and MasterCard had taken CA_1.

Although managers try to quantify a decision when possible by using payoff and regret matrices, uncertainty often forces them to rely more on intuition, creativity, hunches, and "gut feel."

As a business owner in Russia, Mikhail D. Prokhorov has had to make a lot of risky decisions.[22] He's president of Onexim Group, a company with businesses in metal, gold, and real estate. And he's worth an estimated $17.9 billion. He says, "Doing business in Russia in the early 1990s was cowboy territory with no sheriff." That's an interesting and probably fairly accurate description of risk. And it's a good thing he's comfortable with risk because he's now made another risky decision, this time in the United States. He's become an NBA league owner. As the new majority owner of the New Jersey Nets, he says "I am real excited to take the worst team of the league and turn it into the best." The basketball-loving Russian billionaire hopes his latest decision is a slam dunk!

uncertainty
A situation in which a decision maker has neither certainty nor reasonable probability estimates available

EXHIBIT 7-10

Regret Matrix

(in millions of dollars) Visa Marketing Strategy	MasterCard's Competitive Action		
	CA₁	CA₂	CA₃
S_1	11	7	17
S_2	15	6	10
S_3	0	0	13
S_4	6	7	0

LEARNING OUTCOME **7.4**
Describe different decision-making styles and discuss how biases affect decision making.

Decision-Making Styles

William D. Perez's tenure as Nike's CEO lasted a short and turbulent 13 months. Analysts attributed his abrupt dismissal to a difference in decision-making approaches between him and Nike co-founder Phil Knight. Perez tended to rely more on data and facts when making decisions, whereas Knight highly valued, and had always used, his judgment and feelings to make decisions.[23] As this example clearly shows, managers have different styles when it comes to making decisions.

Linear–Nonlinear Thinking Style Profile

Suppose that you're a new manager. How will you make decisions? Recent research done with four distinct groups of people says that the way a person approaches decision making is likely affected by his or her thinking style.[24] Your thinking style reflects two things: (1) the source of information you tend to use (external data and facts OR internal sources such as feelings and intuition), and (2) whether you process that information in a linear way (rational, logical, analytical) OR a nonlinear way (intuitive, creative, insightful). These four dimensions are collapsed into two styles. The first, **linear thinking style**, is characterized by a person's preference for using external data and facts and processing this information through rational, logical thinking to guide decisions and actions. The second, **nonlinear thinking style**, is characterized by a preference for internal sources of information (feelings and intuition) and processing this information with internal insights, feelings, and hunches to guide decisions and actions. Look back at the earlier Nike example and you'll see both styles described.

Managers need to recognize that their employees may use different decision-making styles. Some employees may take their time weighing alternatives and relying on how they feel about it while others rely on external data before logically making a decision. These differences don't make one person's approach better than the other. It just means that their decision making styles are different.

Decision-Making Biases and Errors

When managers make decisions, they not only use their own particular style, they may use "rules of thumb," or **heuristics**, to simplify their decision making. Rules of thumb can be useful because they help make sense of complex, uncertain, and ambiguous information.[25] Even though managers may use rules of thumb, that doesn't mean those rules are reliable. Why? Because they may lead to errors and biases in processing and evaluating information. Exhibit 7-11 identifies twelve common decision errors and biases that managers make. Let's look at each.[26]

When decision makers tend to think they know more than they do or hold unrealistically positive views of themselves and their performance, they're exhibiting the *overconfidence bias*. The *immediate gratification bias* describes decision makers who tend to want immediate rewards and to avoid immediate costs. For these individuals, decision choices that provide quick payoffs are more appealing than those with payoffs in the future. The *anchoring effect* describes how decision makers fixate on initial information as a

Let's Get Real

Good decision-making skills include
not acting too fast, but actually evaluating all pros and cons, then writing it out or walking through it to get the right decision made. Talking it out with other assistants or teammates is helpful too because you they might be able to provide a different perspective. When you are the manager, you are expected to make the decision . . . so you need to be assertive.

EXHIBIT 7-11
Common Decision-Making Biases

starting point and then, once set, fail to adequately adjust for subsequent information. First impressions, ideas, prices, and estimates carry unwarranted weight relative to information received later. When decision makers selectively organize and interpret events based on their biased perceptions, they're using the *selective perception bias*. This influences the information they pay attention to, the problems they identify, and the alternatives they develop. Decision makers who seek out information that reaffirms their past choices and discount information that contradicts past judgments exhibit the *confirmation bias*. These people tend to accept at face value information that confirms their preconceived views and are critical and skeptical of information that challenges these views. The *framing bias* is when decision makers select and highlight certain aspects of a situation while excluding others. By drawing attention to specific aspects of a situation and highlighting them, while at the same time downplaying or omitting other aspects, they distort what they see and create incorrect reference points. The *availability bias* happens when decisions makers tend to remember events that are the most recent and vivid in their memory. The result? It distorts their ability to recall events in an objective manner and results in distorted judgments and probability estimates. When decision makers assess the likelihood of an event based on how closely it resembles other events or sets of events, that's the *representation bias*. Managers exhibiting this bias draw analogies and see identical situations where they don't exist. The *randomness bias* describes the actions of decision makers who try to create meaning out of random events. They do this because most decision makers have difficulty dealing with chance even though random events happen to everyone and there's nothing that can be done to predict them. The *sunk costs error* occurs when decision makers forget that current choices can't correct the past. They incorrectly fixate on past expenditures of time, money, or effort in assessing choices rather than on future consequences. Instead of ignoring sunk costs, they can't forget them. Decision makers who are quick to take credit for their successes and to blame failure on outside factors are exhibiting the *self-serving bias*. Finally, the *hindsight bias* is the tendency for decision makers to falsely believe that they would have accurately predicted the outcome of an event once that outcome is actually known.

linear thinking style
Decision style characterized by a person's preference for using external data and facts and processing this information through rational, logical thinking

nonlinear thinking style
Decision style characterized by a person's preference for internal sources of information and processing this information with internal insights, feelings, and hunches

heuristics
Rules of thumb that managers use to simplify decision making

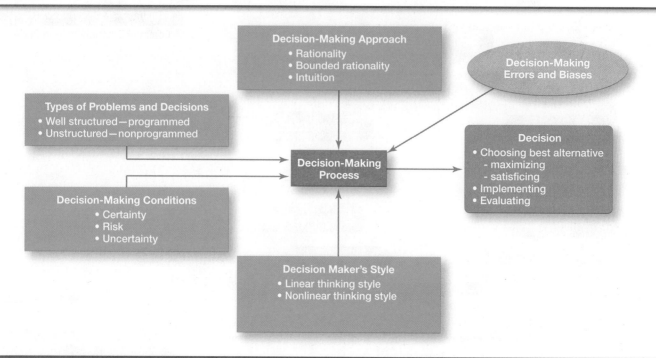

EXHIBIT 7-12

Overview of Managerial
Decision Making

Managers avoid the negative effects of these decision errors and biases by being aware
of them and then not using them! Beyond that, managers also should pay attention to "how"
they make decisions and try to identify the heuristics they typically use and critically evaluate how appropriate those heuristics are. Finally, managers might want to ask trusted individuals around them to help them identify weaknesses in their decision-making style and try
to improve on those weaknesses.

Overview of Managerial Decision Making

Exhibit 7-12 provides an overview of managerial decision making. Because it's in their best
interests, managers *want* to make good decisions—that is, choose the "best" alternative,
implement it, and determine whether it takes care of the problem, which is the reason the
decision was needed in the first place. Their decision-making process is affected by four factors: the decision-making approach, the type of problem, decision-making conditions, and
their decision-making style. In addition, certain decision-making errors and biases may
impact the process. Each factor plays a role in determining how the manager makes a decision. So whether that decision involves addressing an employee's habitual tardiness, resolving a product quality problem, or determining whether to enter a new market, remember
that it has been shaped by a number of factors.

LEARNING OUTCOME
Identify effective decision-
making techniques.

7.5

Effective Decision Making in Today's World

Per Carlsson, a product development manager at IKEA, "spends his days creating Volvo-
style kitchens at Yugo prices." His job is to take the "problems" identified by the company's
product-strategy council (a group of globe-trotting senior managers that monitors consumer
trends and establishes product priorities) and turn them into furniture that customers around
the world want to buy. One "problem" recently identified by the council: the kitchen has
replaced the living room as the social and entertaining center in the home. Customers are
looking for kitchens that convey comfort and cleanliness while still allowing them to

pursue their gourmet aspirations. Carlsson must take this information and make things happen. There are a lot of decisions to make—programmed and nonprogrammed—and the fact that IKEA is a global company makes it even more challenging. Comfort in Asia means small, cozy appliances and spaces, while North American customers want oversized glassware and giant refrigerators. His ability to make good decisions quickly has significant implications for IKEA's success.[27]

Today's business world revolves around making decisions, often risky ones, usually with incomplete or inadequate information, and under intense time pressure. Most managers make one decision after another; and as if that weren't challenging enough, more is at stake than ever before. Bad decisions can cost millions. What do managers need to do to make effective decisions in today's fast-moving world? Here are some guidelines.

▶ *Understand cultural differences.* Managers everywhere want to make good decisions. However, is there only one "best" way worldwide to make decisions? Or does the "best way depend on the values, beliefs, attitudes, and behavioral patterns of the people involved?"[28]

▶ *Know when it's time to call it quits.* When it's evident that a decision isn't working, don't be afraid to pull the plug. For instance, the CEO of L.L.Bean pulled the plug on building a new customer call center in Waterville, Maine—"literally stopping the bulldozers in their tracks"—after T-Mobile said it was building its own call center right next door. He was afraid that the city would not have enough qualified workers for both companies and so decided to build 55 miles away in Bangor.[30] He knew when it was time to call it quits. However, as we said earlier, many decision makers block or distort negative information because they don't want to believe that their decision was bad. They become so attached to a decision that they refuse to recognize when it's time to move on. In today's dynamic environment, this type of thinking simply won't work.

▶ *Use an effective decision-making process.* Experts say an effective decision-making process has these six characteristics: (1) It focuses on what's important; (2) It's logical and consistent; (3) It acknowledges both subjective and objective thinking and blends analytical with intuitive thinking; (4) It requires only as much information and analysis as is necessary to resolve a particular dilemma; (5) It encourages and guides the gathering of relevant information and informed opinion; and (6) It's straightforward, reliable, easy to use, and flexible."[31]

▶ *Build an organization that can spot the unexpected and quickly adapt to the changed environment.* This suggestion comes from Karl Weick, an organizational psychologist, who has made a career of studying organizations and how people work.[32] He calls such organizations *highly reliable organizations* (HROs) and says they share five habits. (1) They're *not tricked by their success.* HROs are preoccupied with their failures. They're alert to the smallest deviations and react quickly to anything that doesn't fit with their expectations. He talks about Navy aviators who describe "leemers—a gut feeling that something isn't right." Typically, these leemers turn out to be accurate. Something, in fact, is wrong. Organizations need to create climates where people feel safe trusting their leemers. (2) They *defer to the experts on the front line.* Frontline workers—those who interact day in and day out with customers, products, suppliers, and so forth—have firsthand knowledge of what can and cannot be done, what will and will not work. Get their input. Let them make decisions. (3) They *let unexpected circumstances provide the solution.* One of Weick's better-known works is his study of the Mann Gulch fire in Montana that killed 13 smoke jumpers in 1949. The event was a massive, tragic organizational failure. However, the reaction of the foreman illustrates how effective decision makers respond to unexpected circumstances. When the fire was nearly on top of his men, he invented the escape fire—a small fire that consumed all the brush around the team, leaving an area where the larger fire couldn't burn. His action was contrary to everything firefighters are taught (that is, you don't start fires—you extinguish them), but at the time it was the best decision. (4) They *embrace complexity.* Because business is

by the numbers[29]

90 percent of people believe they are just a little more competent, smarter, or kinder than average.

91 percent of U.S. companies use teams and groups to solve specific problems.

40 About 40 percent more ideas are generated with electronic brainstorming than with individuals brainstorming alone.

59 percent of employees say that a key obstacle to their job is that more attention is paid to placing blame than to solving problems.

77 percent of managers said that the number of decisions they made during a typical workday had increased.

43 percent of managers said that the amount of time given to each decision had decreased.

RPS In Asia, RPS (rock, paper, scissors) is more recognized as a decision tiebreaker than it is in the United States.

20 percent of American adults said that they think most creatively in their cars.

complex, these organizations recognize that it "takes complexity to sense complexity." Rather than simplifying data, which we instinctively try to do when faced with complexity, these organizations aim for deeper understanding of the situation. They ask "why" and keep asking why as they probe more deeply into the causes of the problem and possible solutions. (5) Finally, they *anticipate, but also recognize their limits*. These organizations do try to anticipate as much as possible, but they recognize that they can't anticipate everything. As Weick says, they don't "think, then act. They think by acting. By actually doing things, you'll find out what works and what doesn't."

Making decisions in today's fast-moving world isn't easy. Successful managers need good decision-making skills to plan, organize, lead, and control.

What Would You Do?

Tiffany
Eulinger
Area Manager
Buckle
Kansas City, MO

Let's Get Real:
My Response *to A Manager's Dilemma, page 178*

I believe that guest satisfaction and attendance are what will show whether this was a "slam dunk" decision. You won't know in the first year of the attraction whether it was a success because of all of the hype leading up to the theme park. It will be the continued success and attendance at the park that will prove it to be a great idea. I'm sure that when the final Harry Potter movie comes out in November 2010, the park will see a surge in attendance and excitement.

Measuring attendance each year, as well as the cost to run and maintain the park would be important. I would measure success based on "sales" like we do in retail. Usually a new store will start out great because of advertising for the new store opening. It is the consistent growth each year on top of the previous year's sales that truly proves whether the store was a "success."

CHAPTER SUMMARY
by Learning Outcomes

Describe the eight steps in the decision-making process.

A decision is a choice. The decision-making process consists of eight steps: (1) identify problem; (2) identify decision criteria; (3) weight the criteria; (4) develop alternatives; (5) analyze alternatives; (6) select alternative; (7) implement alternative; and (8) evaluate decision effectiveness.

Explain the four ways managers make decisions.

The assumptions of rationality are as follows: the problem is clear and unambiguous; a single, well-defined goal is to be achieved; all alternatives and consequences are known; and the final choice will maximize the payoff. Bounded rationality says that managers make rational decisions but are bounded (limited) by their ability to process information. Satisficing happens when decision makers accept solutions that are good enough. With escalation of commitment, managers increase commitment to a decision even when they have evidence it may have been a wrong decision. Intuitive decision making means making decisions on the basis of experience, feelings, and accumulated judgment. Using evidence-based management, a manager makes decisions based on the best available evidence.

Classify decisions and decision-making conditions.

Programmed decisions are repetitive decisions that can be handled by a routine approach and are used when the problem being resolved is straightforward, familiar, and easily defined (structured). Nonprogrammed decisions are unique decisions that require a custom-made solution and are used when the problems are new or unusual (unstructured) and for which information is ambiguous or incomplete. Certainty is a situation in which a manager can make accurate decisions because all outcomes are known. Risk is a situation in which a manager can estimate the likelihood of certain outcomes. Uncertainty is a situation in which a manager is not certain about the outcomes and can't even make reasonable probability estimates. When decision makers face uncertainty, their psychological orientation will determine whether they follow a maximax choice (maximizing the maximum possible payoff); a maximin choice (maximizing the minimum possible payoff); or a minimax choice (minimizing the maximum regret—amount of money that could have been made if a different decision had been made).

Describe different decision-making styles and discuss how biases affect decision making.

A person's thinking style reflects two things: the source of information you tend to use (external or internal) and how you process that information (linear or nonlinear). These four dimensions were collapsed into two styles. The linear thinking style is characterized by a person's preference for using external data and processing this information through rational, logical thinking. The nonlinear thinking style is characterized by a preference for internal sources of information and processing this information with internal insights, feelings, and hunches. The 12 common decision-making errors and biases include overconfidence, immediate gratification, anchoring, selective perception, confirmation, framing, availability, representation, randomness, sunk costs, self-serving bias, and hindsight. The managerial decision making model helps explain how the decision-making process is used to choose the best alternative(s) either through maximizing or satisficing and then implement and evaluate the alternative. It also helps explain what factors affect the decision-making process including the decision-making approach (rationality, bounded rationality, intuition), the types of problems and decisions (well structured and programmed or unstructured and nonprogrammed), the decision-making conditions (certainty, risk, uncertainty), and the decision maker's style (linear or nonlinear).

LEARNING
OUTCOME **7.5**   **Identify** effective decision-making techniques.

Managers can make effective decisions by understanding cultural differences in decision making, knowing when it's time to call it quits, using an effective decision-making process, and building an organization that can spot the unexpected and quickly adapt to the changed environment. An effective decision-making process (1) focuses on what's important; (2) is logical and consistent; (3) acknowledges both subjective and objective thinking and blends both analytical and intuitive approaches; (4) requires only "enough" information as is necessary to resolve a problem; (5) encourages and guides gathering relevant information and informed opinions; and (6) is straightforward, reliable, easy to use, and flexible. The five habits of highly reliable organizations are (1) not being tricked by their successes; (2) deferring to experts on the front line; (3) letting unexpected circumstances provide the solution; (4) embracing complexity; and (5) anticipating, but also recognizing, limits.

PEARSON
mymanagementlab   To check your understanding of learning outcomes **7.1** — **7.5** go to **mymanagementlab.com** and try the chapter questions.

REVIEW AND DISCUSSION QUESTIONS

1. Why is decision making often described as the essence of a manager's job?

2. Describe the eight steps in the decision-making process.

3. Compare and contrast the four ways managers make decisions.

4. How might an organization's culture influence the way managers make decisions?

5. Explain the two types of problems and decisions. Contrast the three decision-making conditions.

6. All of us bring biases to the decisions we make. What would be the drawbacks of having biases? Could there be any advantages to having biases? Explain. What are the implications for managerial decision making?

7. Would you call yourself a linear or nonlinear thinker? What are the decision-making implications of these labels? What are the implications for choosing where you want to work?

8. "As managers use computers and software tools more often, they'll be able to make more rational decisions." Do you agree or disagree with this statement? Why?

9. How can managers blend the guidelines for making effective decisions in today's world with the rationality and bounded rationality models of decision making, or can they? Explain.

10. Is there a difference between wrong decisions and bad decisions? Why do good managers sometimes make wrong decisions? Bad decisions? How can managers improve their decision-making skills?

PREPARING FOR: My Career

ETHICS DILEMMA

The 75 employees of Atomic Games worked nearly four years creating a realistic video game called Six Days in Fallujah, "weaving in real war footage and interviews with Marines who had fought there."[33] Now, relatives of dead Marines are angry. Said one mom whose son was killed by a sniper in Fallujah, "By making it something people play for fun, they are trivializing the battle."

Company executive Peter Tamte relied on the advice of a number of Fallujah veterans and calls the video game a "documentary-style reconstruction that will be so true to the original battle, gamers will almost feel what it was like to fight in Fallujah in November 2004." What do you think? What ethical issues do you see here? Should the company proceed with the game's release? Why or why not?

SKILLS EXERCISE
Developing Your Creativity Skill

About the Skill

Creativity is a frame of mind. You need to open your mind to new ideas. Every individual has the ability to be creative, but many people simply don't try to develop that ability. In contemporary organizations, such people may have difficulty achieving success. Dynamic environments and managerial chaos require that managers look for new and innovative ways to attain their goals as well as those of the organization.[34]

Steps in Practicing the Skill

1. **Think of yourself as creative.** Although it's a simple suggestion, research shows that if you think you can't be creative, you won't be. Believing in yourself is the first step in becoming more creative.

2. **Pay attention to your intuition.** Every individual's subconscious mind works well. Sometimes answers come to you when least expected. For example, when you are about to go to sleep, your relaxed mind sometimes whispers a solution to a problem you're facing. Listen to that voice. In fact, most creative people keep a notepad near their bed and write down those great ideas when they occur. That way, they don't forget them.

3. **Move away from your comfort zone.** Every individual has a comfort zone in which certainty exists. But creativity and the known often do not mix. To be creative, you need to move away from the status quo and focus your mind on something new.

4. **Engage in activities that put you outside your comfort zone.** You not only must think differently; you need to do things differently and, thus, challenge yourself.

Learning to play a musical instrument or learning a foreign language, for example, opens your mind to a new challenge.

5. **Seek a change of scenery.** People are often creatures of habit. Creative people force themselves out of their habits by changing their scenery, which may mean going into a quiet and serene area where you can be alone with your thoughts.

6. **Find several right answers.** In the discussion of bounded rationality, we said that people seek solutions that are good enough. Being creative means continuing to look for other solutions even when you think you have solved the problem. A better, more creative solution just might be found.

7. **Play your own devil's advocate.** Challenging yourself to defend your solutions helps you to develop confidence in your creative efforts. Second-guessing yourself may also help you find more creative solutions.

8. **Believe in finding a workable solution.** Like believing in yourself, you also need to believe in your ideas. If you don't think you can find a solution, you probably won't.

9. **Brainstorm with others.** Being creative is not a solitary activity. Bouncing ideas off others creates a synergistic effect.

10. **Turn creative ideas into action.** Coming up with ideas is only half the process. Once the ideas are generated, they must be implemented. Keeping great ideas in your mind or on paper that no one will read does little to expand your creative abilities.

Practicing the Skill

How many words can you make using the letters in the word *brainstorm*? There are at least 95.

WORKING TOGETHER
Team Exercise

Being effective in decision making is something that managers obviously want. What's involved with being a good decision maker? Form groups of three to four students. Discuss your experiences making decisions—for example, buying a car or some other purchase, choosing classes and professors, making summer or spring break plans, and so forth. Each of you should share times when you felt you made good decisions. Analyze what happened during that decision-making process that contributed to it being a good decision. Then, consider some decisions that you felt were bad. What happened to make them bad? What common characteristics, if any, did you identify among the good decisions? The bad decisions? Come up with a bulleted list of practical suggestions for making good decisions. As a group, be prepared to share your list with the class.

MY TURN TO BE A MANAGER

- For one week, pay close attention to the decisions you make and how you make them. Write a description of five of those decisions using the steps in the decision-making process as your guide. Also, describe whether you relied on external or internal sources of information to help you make the decision and whether you think you were more linear or nonlinear in how you processed that information.

- When you feel you haven't made a good decision, assess how you could have made a better decision.

- Find two examples of a procedure, a rule, and a policy. Bring a description of these examples to class and be prepared to share them.

- Write a procedure, a rule, and a policy for your instructor to use in your class. Be sure that each one is clear and understandable. And be sure to explain how it fits the characteristics of being a procedure, a rule, or a policy.

- Find three examples of managerial decisions described in any of the popular business periodicals (*Wall Street Journal, BusinessWeek, Fortune,* etc.). Write a paper describing each decision and any other information such as what led to the decision, what happened as a result of the decision, etc. What did you learn about decision making from these examples?

- Interview two managers and ask them for suggestions on what it takes to be a good decision maker. Write down their suggestions and be prepared to present them in class.

- Steve's and Mary's suggested readings: Noel M. Tichy and Warren G. Bennis, *Judgment: How Winning Leaders Make Great Calls* (Portfolio, 2007); Gerd Gigerenzer, *Gut Feelings: The Intelligence of the Unconscious* (Viking, 2007); Stephen P. Robbins, *Decide & Conquer: Make Winning Decisions and Take Control of Your Life* (Financial Times Press, 2004); and John S. Hammond, Ralph L. Keeney, and Howard Raiffa, *Smart Choices: A Practical Guide to Making Better Decisions* (Harvard Business School Press, 1999).

- Do a Web search on the phrase "101 dumbest moments in business." Get the most current version of this end-of-year list. Pick three of the examples and describe what happened. What's your reaction to the example? How could the managers have made better decisions?

- In your own words, write down three things you learned in this chapter about being a good manager.

- Self-knowledge can be a powerful learning tool. Go to mymanagementlab.com and complete these self-assessment exercises: How Well Do I Handle Ambiguity? How Well Do I Respond to Turbulent Change? and What's My Decision-Making Style? Using the results of your assessments, identify personal strengths and weaknesses. What will you do to reinforce your strengths and improve your weaknesses?

CASE APPLICATION **1**
The Curtain Falls

I t's been called one of "the entertainment industry's biggest programming debacles."[35] Jay Leno moved from host of the "Tonight
Show" to his own talk show, "The Jay Leno Show," which aired at
the 10 p.m. weeknight time slot. Conan O'Brien was brought on as
Leno's replacement on the "Tonight Show," which has always aired
after the local news.

The Jay Leno–Conan O'Brien fiasco started with a decision by
NBC executives to save some money by giving Leno one of the oldest formats in TV programming: a comedy-variety show with a comedian, a
stage, guests, and in-show ads. But that decision was also a radical experiment based on a single show airing every single weeknight during prime
time on a major broadcast network. This format was cheaper to produce for
an entire week than 60 minutes of the pricey scripted dramas that are usually broadcast during that time period. Jeff Gaspin, chairman of television
entertainment at NBC Universal, said, "I don't think it's wrong to take
chances. . . . Sometimes they work. Sometimes they don't." And this decision wasn't working.

"The Tonight Show" host Jay Leno
(right) interviews his replacement
Conan O'Brien during Leno's final
taping as host of the show before he
began his own primetime talk show,
an NBC management decision to cut
costs and dubbed as one of "the
entertainment industry's biggest programming debacles."

It all started to unravel when ratings for Leno's talk show were low and continued to sink. One media analyst
said, "Nobody's happy—the talent isn't happy, the advertisers aren't happy, and the audience isn't happy."
Local network affiliates that rely on that 10 p.m. slot to lead people into the late local news rebelled. Those
affiliates threatened to preempt Leno's show with other programming. But that wasn't NBC's only problem.
O'Brien's "Tonight Show" also was doing poorly in its time slot, losing resoundingly to "Late Show with David
Letterman" on CBS for the first time in 15 years.

NBC executives continued to struggle with decision making. It took nearly two weeks of a very public
spectacle for them to craft a solution in which Leno returned to his gig at the "Tonight Show" and O'Brien left
with a $40 million agreement to walk away from "his dream job." And so the curtain closes on a story NBC
executives wish had never been written.

Discussion Questions

1. Would you characterize television programming decisions as structured or unstructured?
   Explain. What type of decision-making condition would you consider this to be? Explain.

2. What criteria did NBC use in evaluating its initial decision to move Leno and O'Brien? Was
   that criteria appropriate? Why or why not?

3. Evaluate Jeff Gaspin's statement, "I don't think it's wrong to take chances. . . . Sometimes they work. Sometimes they don't." What does it say about his decision-making
   style?

4. Describe how NBC executives could have used each of the following to make better
   decisions: (a) rationality, (b) bounded rationality, (c) intuition, and (d) evidence-based
   management.

CASE APPLICATION 2

Underwater Chaos

It would be a claustrophobic's worst nightmare—trapped subsea in the 31-mile Eurotunnel beneath the English Channel on the Eurostar train that travels between Britain and the European mainland.[36] A series of breakdowns on five London-bound trains from Brussels, which began December 18, 2009, left more than 2,000 passengers stranded for up to 16 hours. Many of those passengers trapped in the dark and overheated tunnel endured serious distress. "Parents had to remove their children's clothes, leaving them in underwear and diapers. Some passengers suffered stress and panic attacks. Others started feeling ill due to the heat." Was this just an unfortunate incident for the unlucky passengers who happened to be on those trains or did poor managerial decision making about the operation of both the train and the channel tunnel also play a role?

An independent review of the incident blamed Eurostar and the operator of the tunnel for being unprepared for severe winter weather. The report said that Eurostar had failed to adequately maintain and winterize its high-speed trains to protect sensitive components from malfunctioning due to excessive snow and moisture buildup. At the time of the Eurostar train breakdowns, severe winter weather had been wreaking havoc on Europe. Airlines, car and truck drivers, and other rail operators across Europe were also suffering from a winter that was on course to be the coldest in more than 30 years. Freezing weather and snow had caused travel problems for days in Northern Europe. In addition, the report criticized Eurotunnel (the operator of the channel tunnel) for having unsatisfactory communications systems in place inside the tunnel, which could have given its employees direct contact with train drivers and other Eurostar staff. "If a train breaks down and passengers have to be rescued and evacuated, this must be done with greater speed and consideration. In an emergency, passengers need to have prompt information and regular updates."

Although the severe weather conditions undoubtedly played a role in this fiasco, there's no doubt that managers could have done a better job of making decisions in preparing for such scenarios.

Discussion Questions

1. What's your reaction to this story? What does it illustrate about decision making?
2. How could the decision-making process have helped in both the response to the crisis situation and in preventing it from happening?
3. Could procedures, policies, and rules play any role in future crisis situations like this one? If so, how? If not, why not?
4. What could other organizations learn from this incident?

Let's Get Real:

Meet the Manager

Chuck Pick
President
Chuck's Parking Service, Inc.
Sherman Oaks, CA

You'll be hearing more from this real manager throughout the chapter.

MY JOB:

I'm the president and owner of Chuck's Parking Service, Inc. We are a full-service valet parking and transportation company that provides both valet parking and shuttle services for commercial locations and important events in Los Angeles and the surrounding area. I am personally involved in every facet of the company and its operations.

BEST PART OF MY JOB:

My greatest satisfaction comes from meeting a new client with a particularly challenging parking situation, designing and implementing a sound operational plan, and seeing my talented management team and employees execute every detail exactly as planned. It's a thrill to work with some of the most important people and events in the world, from standing U.S. presidents to the Academy Awards.

Foundations *of* Planning

8.1 **Define** the nature and purposes of planning. *page 204*

8.2 **Classify** the types of goals organizations might have and the plans they use. *page 205*

8.3 **Compare** and contrast approaches to goal setting and planning. *page 208*

8.4 **Discuss** contemporary issues in planning. *page 212*

LEARNING OUTCOMES

WORST PART OF MY JOB:

As the owner of a service industry business, there is no downtime. We are working when most people are not (weekends, evenings, and holidays). Although I surround myself with competent managers and supervisors, it's impossible to ever completely clear my mind of the business. Late-night calls regarding damages or other unforeseen problems are especially unpleasant.

BEST MANAGEMENT ADVICE EVER RECEIVED:

You can't cheat on service! Either provide a great service or don't provide a service at all. Avoid the temptation of cutting service to fit a client's budget and don't lower your standards to the level of your competition. I constantly tell myself that you can't do every event.

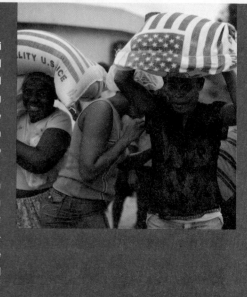
You may think that "planning" isn't something that's relevant to you right now. But when you figure out your class schedule for the next term or when you decide what you need to do to finish a class project on time, you're planning. And planning is something that all managers, such as Lou Policastro and others who responded to the Haiti relief effort, need to do. Although what they plan and how they plan may differ, it's still important that they do plan. In this chapter we present the basics: what planning is, why managers plan, and how they plan.

LEARNING OUTCOME
8.1
Define the nature and purposes of planning.

The What and Why of Planning

Boeing called its new 787 aircraft the Dreamliner, but the project turned into more of a nightmare for managers. The new plane was the company's most popular product ever, mostly because of its innovations, especially in fuel efficiency. However, the plane is two and a half years behind schedule. The first airplanes are scheduled to be delivered to ANA (All Nippon Airways) in the fourth quarter of 2010. Boeing admitted that the project's timeline was way too ambitious even though every detail had been meticulously planned.[2] Some customers (the airlines who ordered the jets)—around 60 in total—got tired of waiting or responded to the changing economic environment and canceled their orders. Could Boeing's managers have planned better?

What Is Planning?

As we stated in Chapter 1, **planning** involves defining the organization's goals, establishing strategies for achieving those goals, and developing plans to integrate and coordinate work activities. It's concerned with both ends (what) and means (how).

When we use the term *planning*, we mean *formal* planning. In formal planning, specific goals covering a specific time period are defined. These goals are written and shared with organizational members to reduce ambiguity and create a common understanding about what needs to be done. Finally, specific plans exist for achieving these goals.

Why Do Managers Plan?

Planning seems to take a lot of effort. So why should managers plan? We can give you at least four reasons. First, planning *provides direction* to managers and nonmanagers alike. When employees know what their organization or work unit is trying to accomplish and what they must contribute to reach goals, they can coordinate their activities, cooperate with each other, and do what it takes to accomplish those goals. Without planning, departments and individuals might work at cross-purposes and prevent the organization from efficiently achieving its goals.

Next, planning *reduces uncertainty* by forcing managers to look ahead, anticipate change, consider the impact of change, and develop appropriate responses. Although planning won't eliminate uncertainty, managers plan so they can respond effectively.

In addition, planning *minimizes waste and redundancy*. When work activities are coordinated around plans, inefficiencies become obvious and can be corrected or eliminated.

Finally, planning *establishes the goals or standards used in controlling*. When managers plan, they develop goals and plans. When they control, they see whether the plans have been carried out and the goals met. Without planning, there would be no goals against which to measure work effort.

Planning and Performance

Is planning worthwhile? Numerous studies have looked at the relationship between planning and performance.[3] Although most showed generally positive relationships, we can't say that organizations that formally plan *always* outperform those that don't plan. What *can* we conclude?

First, generally speaking, formal planning is associated with positive financial results—higher profits, higher return on assets, and so forth. Second, it seems that doing a good job planning and implementing those plans play a bigger part in high performance than does how much planning is done. Next, in those studies where formal planning didn't lead to higher performance, the external environment often was the culprit. When external forces—think governmental regulations or powerful labor unions—constrain managers' options, it reduces the impact planning has on an organization's performance. Finally, the planning-performance relationship seems to be influenced by the planning time frame. It seems that at least four years of formal planning is required before it begins to affect performance.

Goals and Plans

8.2

LEARNING OUTCOME
Classify the types of goals organizations might have and the plans they use.

Planning is often called the primary management function because it establishes the basis for all the other things managers do as they organize, lead, and control. It involves two important aspects: goals and plans.

Goals (objectives) are desired outcomes or targets.[4] They guide management decisions and form the criterion against which work results are measured. That's why they're often described as the essential elements of planning. You have to know the desired target or outcome before you can establish plans for reaching it. **Plans** are documents that outline how goals are going to be met. They usually include resource allocations, schedules, and other necessary actions to accomplish the goals. As managers plan, they develop both goals and plans.

planning
Defining the organization's goals, establishing strategies for achieving those goals, and developing plans to integrate and coordinate work activities

goals (objectives)
Desired outcomes or targets

plans
Documents that outline how goals are going to be met

The goal that guides management decisions at Sykes Enterprises is that every client will be more efficient, more profitable, and have stronger loyalty to the company brands due to the services provided by Sykes. As a global outsourcing and consulting service, Sykes operates more than 40 technical help and customer support centers in the Americas, Asia, Europe, and Africa. One of the plans Sykes has for achieving its goal is to employ the best individuals in the industry and to reward them for their commitment to excellence. For example, the well-trained technicians shown here at Sykes' multilingual call center in Manila speak fluent English in responding to clients' questions and providing comprehensive service that ensures customer satisfaction.

Types of Goals

It might seem that organizations have a single goal. Businesses want to make a profit and not-for-profit organizations want to meet the needs of some constituent group(s). However, a single goal can't adequately define an organization's success. And if managers emphasize only one goal, other goals essential for long-term success are ignored. Also, as we discussed in Chapter 5, using a single goal such as profit may result in unethical behaviors because managers and employees will ignore other aspects of their jobs in order to look good on that one measure.[5] In reality, all organizations have multiple goals. For instance, businesses may want to increase market share, keep employees enthused about working for the organization, and work toward more environmentally sustainable practices. And a church provides a place for religious practices, but also assists economically disadvantaged individuals in its community and acts as a social gathering place for church members.

We can classify most company's goals as either strategic or financial. Financial goals are related to the financial performance of the organization, while strategic goals are related to all other areas of an organization's performance. For instance, McDonald's states that its financial targets are 3 to 5 percent average annual sales and revenue growth, 6 to 7 percent average annual operating income growth, and returns on invested capital in the high teens.[6] Here's an example of a strategic goal from Bloomberg L.P.: "We want to be the world's most influential news organization."[7]

The goals just described are **stated goals**—official statements of what an organization says, and what it wants its stakeholders to believe, its goals are. However, stated goals—which can be found in an organization's charter, annual report, public relations announcements, or in public statements made by managers—are often conflicting and influenced by what various stakeholders think organizations should do. For instance, Nike's goal is "delivering inspiration and innovation to every athlete." Canadian company EnCana's vision is to "be the world's high performance benchmark independent oil and gas company." Deutsche Bank's goal is "to be the leading global provider of financial solutions, creating lasting value for our clients, our shareholders and people and the communities in which we operate."[8] Such statements are vague and probably better represent management's public relations skills than being meaningful guides to what the organization is actually trying to accomplish. It shouldn't be surprising then to find that an organization's stated goals are often irrelevant to what actually goes on.[9]

If you want to know an organization's **real goals**—those goals an organization actually pursues—observe what organizational members are doing. Actions define priorities. For example, universities may say their goal is limiting class sizes, facilitating close student-faculty relations, and actively involving students in the learning process, but then they put students into 300+ student lecture classes! Knowing that real and stated goals may differ is important for recognizing what you might otherwise think are inconsistencies.

Let's Get Real

F 2 F

Goals are important because *they set priorities for which managers and employees should strive. Goals are often set higher than expectations, making a clear and concise plan even more important.*

EXHIBIT 8-1
Types of Plans

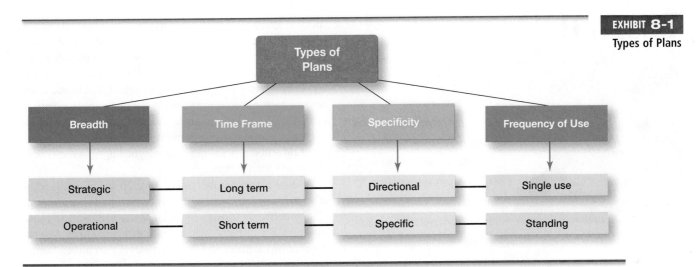

Types of Plans

The most popular ways to describe organizational plans are breadth (strategic versus operational), time frame (short term versus long term), specificity (directional versus specific), and frequency of use (single use versus standing). As Exhibit 8-1 shows, these types of plans aren't independent. That is, strategic plans are usually long term, directional, and single use whereas operational plans are usually short term, specific, and standing. What does each include?

Strategic plans are plans that apply to the entire organization and establish the organization's overall goals. Plans that encompass a particular operational area of the organization are called **operational plans**. These two types of plans differ because strategic plans are broad while operational plans are narrow.

The number of years used to define short-term and long-term plans has declined considerably because of environmental uncertainty. Long-term used to mean anything over seven years. Try to imagine what you're likely to be doing in seven years and you can begin to appreciate how difficult it would be for managers to establish plans that far in the future. We define **long-term plans** as those with a time frame beyond three years.[10] **Short-term plans** cover one year or less. Any time period in between would be an intermediate plan. Although these time classifications are fairly common, an organization can use any planning time frame it wants.

Intuitively, it would seem that specific plans would be preferable to directional, or loosely guided, plans. **Specific plans** are clearly defined and leave no room for interpretation. A specific plan states its objectives in a way that eliminates ambiguity and problems with misunderstanding. For example, a manager who seeks to increase his or her unit's work output by 8 percent over a given 12-month period might establish specific procedures, budget allocations, and schedules of activities to reach that goal.

However, when uncertainty is high and managers must be flexible in order to respond to unexpected changes, directional plans are preferable. **Directional plans** are flexible plans that set out general guidelines. They provide focus but don't lock managers into

stated goals
Official statements of what an organization says, and what it wants its various stakeholders to believe, its goals are

real goals
Goals that an organization actually pursues, as defined by the actions of its members

strategic plans
Plans that apply to the entire organization and establish the organization's overall goals

operational plans
Plans that encompass a particular operational area of the organization

long-term plans
Plans with a time frame beyond three years

short-term plans
Plans covering one year or less

specific plans
Plans that are clearly defined and leave no room for interpretation

directional plans
Plans that are flexible and set out general guidelines

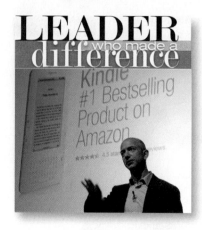

Jeff Bezos, founder and CEO of Amazon.com, understands the importance of goals and plans. As a leader, he exudes energy, enthusiasm, and drive.[12] He's fun loving (his legendary laugh has been described as a flock of Canadian geese on nitrous oxide) but has pursued his vision for Amazon with serious intensity and has demonstrated an ability to inspire his employees through the ups and downs of a rapidly growing company. When Bezos founded the company as on online bookstore, his goal was to be the leader in online retailing. Now fifteen years later, Amazon is quickly becoming the world's general store, selling not only books, CDs, and DVDs, but LEGOs, power drills, and Jackalope Buck taxidermy mounts, to name a few of the thousands of products you can buy.

specific goals or courses of action. For example, Sylvia Rhone, president of Motown Records, said she has a simple goal—to "sign great artists."[11] So instead of creating a specific plan to produce and market 10 albums from new artists this year, she might formulate a directional plan to use a network of people around the world to alert her to new and promising talent so she can increase the number of new artists she has under contract. Keep in mind, however, that the flexibility of directional plans must be weighed against the lack of clarity of specific plans.

Some plans that managers develop are ongoing while others are used only once. A **single-use plan** is a one-time plan specifically designed to meet the needs of a unique situation. For instance, when Walmart wanted to expand the number of its stores in China, top-level executives formulated a single-use plan as a guide. In contrast, **standing plans** are ongoing plans that provide guidance for activities performed repeatedly. Standing plans include policies, rules, and procedures, which we defined in Chapter 7. An example of a standing plan is the sexual harassment policy developed by the University of Arizona. It provides guidance to university administrators, faculty, and staff as they make hiring plans.

LEARNING OUTCOME 8.3
Compare and contrast approaches to goal setting and planning.

Setting Goals and Developing Plans

Taylor Haines has just been elected president of her business school's honorary fraternity. She wants the organization to be more actively involved in the business school than it has been. Francisco Garza graduated from Tecnologico de Monterrey with a degree in marketing and computers three years ago and went to work for a regional consulting services firm. He recently was promoted to manager of an eight-person e-business development team and hopes to strengthen the team's financial contributions to the firm. What should Taylor and Francisco do now? Their first step should be to set goals.

Approaches to Setting Goals

As we stated earlier, goals provide the direction for all management decisions and actions and form the criterion against which actual accomplishments are measured. Everything organizational members do should be oriented toward achieving goals. These goals can be set either through a traditional process or by using management by objectives.

In **traditional goal setting**, goals set by top managers flow down through the organization and become subgoals for each organizational area. This traditional perspective assumes that top managers know what's best because they see the "big picture." And the goals passed down to each succeeding level guide individual employees as they work to achieve those assigned goals. If Taylor were to use this approach, she would see what goals the dean or director of the school of business had set and develop goals for her group that would contribute to achieving those goals. Or take a manufacturing business, for example. The president tells the vice president of production what he expects manufacturing costs to be for the coming year and tells the marketing vice president what level he expects sales to reach for the year. These goals are passed to the next organizational level and written to reflect the responsibilities of that level, passed to the next level, and so forth. Then, at some later time, performance is evaluated to determine whether the assigned goals have been achieved. Although the process is supposed to happen in this way, in reality it doesn't always do so. Turning broad strategic goals into departmental, team, and individual goals can be a difficult and frustrating process.

Another problem with traditional goal setting is that when top managers define the organization's goals in broad terms—such as achieving "sufficient" profits or increasing "market

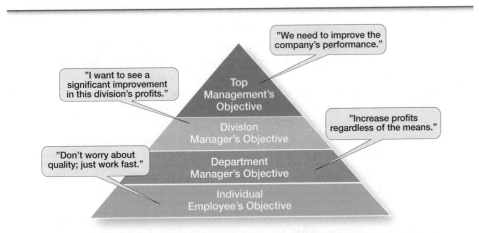

EXHIBIT 8-2
The Downside of Traditional Goal
Setting

leadership"—these ambiguous goals have to be made more specific as they flow down through the organization. Managers at each level define the goals and apply their own interpretations and biases as they make them more specific. However, what often happens is that clarity is lost as the goals make their way down from the top of the organization to lower levels. Exhibit 8-2 illustrates what can happen. But it doesn't have to be that way. For example, at the Carrier-Carlyle Compressor Facility in Stone Mountain, Georgia, employees and managers focus their work efforts around goals. Those goals encompass meeting and exceeding customer needs, concentrating on continuous improvement efforts, and engaging the workforce. To keep everyone focused on those goals, a "thermostat"—a 3-foot-by-4-foot metric indicator—found at the employee entrance communicates what factory performance is at any given time and where attention is needed. "The thermostat outlines plant goals across a range of metrics as well as monthly performance against those goals." Company executives state, "We have found that well-executed pre-planning drives improved results." Does their goal approach work? In the past three years, the facility has experienced a nearly 76 percent reduction in customer reject rates and a 54.5 percent reduction in OSHA-recordable injury and illness cases.[13]

When the hierarchy of organizational goals *is* clearly defined, as it is at Carrier-Carlyle Compressor, it forms an integrated network of goals, or a **means-ends chain**. Higher-level goals (or ends) are linked to lower-level goals, which serve as the means for their accomplishment. In other words, the goals achieved at lower levels become the means to reach the goals (ends) at the next level. And the accomplishment of goals at that level becomes the means to achieve the goals (ends) at the next level and on up through the different organizational levels. That's how traditional goal setting is supposed to work.

Instead of using traditional goal setting, many organizations use **management by objectives (MBO)**, a process of setting mutually agreed-upon goals and using those goals to evaluate employee performance. If Francisco were to use this approach, he would sit down with each member of his team and set goals and periodically review whether progress was being made toward achieving those goals. MBO programs have four elements: goal specificity, participative decision making, an explicit time period, and performance feedback.[14] Instead of using goals to make sure employees are doing what they're supposed to be doing,

EXHIBIT 8-3

Steps in MBO

1. The organization's *overall objectives and strategies* are formulated.
2. Major objectives are allocated among *divisional and departmental units*.
3. Unit managers *collaboratively set specific objectives* for their units with their managers.
4. Specific objectives are collaboratively set with *all department members*.
5. *Action plans*, defining how objectives are to be achieved, are specified and agreed upon by managers and employees.
6. The action plans are *implemented*.
7. Progress toward objectives is *periodically reviewed*, and *feedback is provided*.
8. Successful achievement of objectives is reinforced by *performance-based rewards*.

MBO uses goals to motivate them as well. The appeal is that it focuses on employees working to accomplish goals they've had a hand in setting. Exhibit 8-3 lists the steps in a typical MBO program.

Does MBO work? Studies have shown that it can increase employee performance and organizational productivity. For example, one review of MBO programs found productivity gains in almost all of them.[15] But is MBO relevant for today's organizations? If it's viewed as a way of setting goals, then yes, because research shows that goal setting can be an effective approach to motivating employees.[16]

Let's Get Real

F2F

I set goals by *carefully studying historic business data and realistically exceeding our past performance by adding incentives and making use of new and innovative marketing approaches.*

CHARACTERISTICS OF WELL-WRITTEN GOALS. Goals aren't all written the same way. Some are better than others at making the desired outcomes clear. For instance, the CEO of Procter & Gamble said that he wants to see the company add close to 548,000 new customers a day, every day, for the next five years.[17] It's an ambitious but specific goal. Managers should be able to write well-written goals. What makes a "well-written" goal?[18] Exhibit 8-4 lists the characteristics.

STEPS IN GOAL SETTING. Managers should follow five steps when setting goals.

1. *Review the organization's* **mission**, *or purpose*. A mission is a broad statement of an organization's purpose that provides an overall guide to what organizational members think is important. Managers should review the mission before writing goals because goals should reflect that mission.
2. *Evaluate available resources*. You don't want to set goals that are impossible to achieve given your available resources. Even though goals should be challenging, they should be realistic. After all, if the resources you have to work with won't allow you to achieve a goal no matter how hard you try or how much effort is exerted, you shouldn't set that goal. That would be like the person with a $50,000 annual income and no other financial resources setting a goal of building an investment portfolio worth $1 million in three years. No matter how hard he or she works at it, it's not going to happen.
3. *Determine the goals individually or with input from others*. The goals reflect desired outcomes and should be congruent with the organizational mission and goals in other organizational areas. These goals should be measurable, specific, and include a time frame for accomplishment.

EXHIBIT 8-4

Well-Written Goals

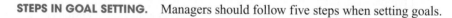

- Written in terms of outcomes rather than actions
- Measurable and quantifiable
- Clear as to a time frame
- Challenging yet attainable
- Written down
- Communicated to all necessary organizational members

4. *Write down the goals and communicate them to all who need to know.* Writing down and communicating goals forces people to think them through. The written goals also become visible evidence of the importance of working toward something.

5. *Review results and whether goals are being met.* If goals aren't being met, change them as needed.

Once the goals have been established, written down, and communicated, a manager is ready to develop plans for pursuing the goals.

Developing Plans

The process of developing plans is influenced by three contingency factors and by the planning approach followed.

CONTINGENCY FACTORS IN PLANNING. Look back at our chapter-opening "A Manager's Dilemma." How will Lou Policastro and other aid relief managers know what types of plans to develop for what needs to get done in responding to the Haiti disaster? Three contingency factors affect the choice of plans: organizational level, degree of environmental uncertainty, and length of future commitments.[20]

Exhibit 8-5 shows the relationship between a manager's level in the organization and the type of planning done. For the most part, lower-level managers do operational planning while upper-level managers do strategic planning.

The second contingency factor is environmental uncertainty, a factor that was quite obvious in the chapter-opening Haitian relief effort example. When uncertainty is high, plans should be specific, but flexible. Managers must be prepared to change or amend plans as they're implemented. At times, they may even have to abandon the plans.[21] For example, prior to Continental Airlines' merger with United Airlines, the former CEO and his management team established a specific goal of focusing on what customers wanted most—on-time flights—to help the company become more competitive in the highly uncertain airline industry. Because of the high level of uncertainty, the management team identified a "destination, but not a flight plan," and changed plans as necessary to achieve that goal of on-time service.

The last contingency factor also is related to the time frame of plans. The **commitment concept** says that plans should extend far enough to meet those commitments made when the plans were developed. Planning for too long or too short a time period is inefficient and ineffective. What happened at AT&T with the iPhone is a good example of why it's important to

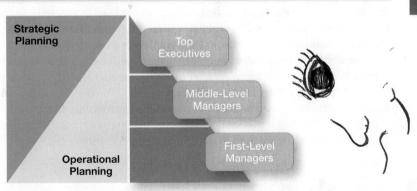

EXHIBIT 8-5
Planning and Organizational Level

mission
The purpose of an organization

commitment concept
Plans should extend far enough to meet those commitments made when the plans were developed

understand the commitment concept. When it secured exclusive rights to support the iPhone on its wireless network in June 2007, both Apple and AT&T vastly underestimated the phone's popularity—some 42.4 million have been sold. And then there's all those apps—at least 140,000 different ones that have been downloaded some 3 billion times—many of which consume bandwidth. AT&T's network "simply can't handle the traffic." AT&T's Operations president John Stankey said, "We missed on our usage estimates." As the company discovered, the bandwidth-hungry super-phone has created serious challenges.[22] How does this illustrate the commitment concept? In becoming the primary provider of the iPhone, AT&T "committed" to whatever future expenses are generated by that planned decision. And they have to live with the decision and its consequences, good and bad.

Approaches to Planning

Federal, state, and local government officials are working together on a plan to boost populations of wild salmon in the northwestern United States. Managers in the Global Fleet Graphics division of the 3M Company are developing detailed plans to satisfy increasingly demanding customers and to battle more aggressive competitors. Emilio Azcárraga Jean, chairman, president, and CEO of Grupo Televisa, gets input from many different people before setting company goals and then turns over the planning for achieving the goals to various executives. In each of these situations, planning is done a little differently. *How* an organization plans can best be understood by looking at *who* does the planning.

In the traditional approach, planning is done entirely by top-level managers who often are assisted by a **formal planning department**, a group of planning specialists whose sole responsibility is to help write the various organizational plans. Under this approach, plans developed by top-level managers flow down through other organizational levels, much like the traditional approach to goal-setting. As they flow down through the organization, the plans are tailored to the particular needs of each level. Although this approach makes managerial planning thorough, systematic, and coordinated, all too often the focus is on developing "the plan," a thick binder (or binders) full of meaningless information that's stuck away on a shelf and never used by anyone for guiding or coordinating work efforts. In fact, in a survey of managers about formal top-down organizational planning processes, over 75 percent said that their company's planning approach was unsatisfactory.[23] A common complaint was that, "plans are documents that you prepare for the corporate planning staff and later forget." Although this traditional top-down approach to planning is used by many organizations, it can be effective only if managers understand the importance of creating documents that organizational members actually use, not documents that look impressive but are never used.

Another approach to planning is to involve more organizational members in the process. In this approach, plans aren't handed down from one level to the next, but instead are developed by organizational members at the various levels and in the various work units to meet their specific needs. For instance, at Dell, employees from production, supply management, and channel management meet weekly to make plans based on current product demand and supply. In addition, work teams set their own daily schedules and track their progress against those schedules. If a team falls behind, team members develop "recovery" plans to try to get back on schedule.[24] When organizational members are more actively involved in planning, they see that the plans are more than just something written down on paper. They can actually see that the plans are used in directing and coordinating work.

8.4

Contemporary Issues in Planning

The second floor of the 21-story Hyundai Motor headquarters buzzes with data 24 hours a day. That's where you'd find the company's Global Command and Control Center (GCCC), which is modeled after the CNN newsroom with "dozens of computer screens relaying video and data keeping watch on Hyundai operations around the world." Managers get information on parts shipments from suppliers to factories. Cameras watch assembly lines and "keep a close watch on Hyundai's giant Ulsan, Korea, plant, the world's largest integrated auto factory" looking for competitors' spies and any hints of labor unrest. The GCCC also keeps tabs on the company's R&D activities in Europe, Japan, and North America. Hyundai can identify problems in an instant and react quickly. The company is all about aggressiveness and speed and is representative of how a successful twenty-first-century company approaches planning.[25]

We conclude this chapter by addressing two contemporary issues in planning. Specifically, we're going to look at planning effectively in dynamic environments and then at how managers can use environmental scanning, especially competitive intelligence.

How Can Managers Plan Effectively in Dynamic Environments?

As we saw in Chapter 2, the external environment is continually changing. For instance, cloud computing storage is revolutionizing all kinds of industries from financial services to health care to engineering.[26] Social networking sites are being used by companies to connect with customers, employees, and potential employees. Amounts spent on eating out instead of cooking at home are predicted to decline. And experts believe that China and India are transforming the twenty-first-century global economy.

How can managers effectively plan when the external environment is continually changing? We already discussed uncertain environments as one of the contingency factors that affect the types of plans managers develop. Because dynamic environments are more the norm than the exception, let's look at how managers can effectively plan in such environments.

In an uncertain environment, managers should develop plans that are specific, but flexible. Although this may seem contradictory, it's not. To be useful, plans need some specificity, but the plans should not be set in stone. Managers need to recognize that planning is an ongoing process. The plans serve as a road map although the destination may change due to dynamic market conditions. They should be ready to change directions if environmental conditions warrant. This flexibility is particularly important as plans are implemented. Managers need to stay alert to environmental changes that may impact implementation and respond as needed. Keep in mind, also, that even when the environment is highly uncertain, it's important to continue formal planning in order to see any effect on organizational performance. It's the persistence in planning that contributes to significant performance improvement. Why? It seems that, as with most activities, managers "learn to plan" and the quality of their planning improves when they continue to do it.[27] Finally, make the organizational hierarchy flatter to effectively plan in dynamic environments. This means allowing lower organizational levels to set goals and develop plans because there's little time for goals and plans to flow down from the top. Managers should teach their employees how to set goals and to plan and then trust them to do it. And you need look no further than Bangalore, India, to find a company that effectively understands this. Just a decade ago, Wipro Limited was "an anonymous conglomerate selling cooking oil and personal computers, mostly in India." Today, it's a $6 billion-a-year global company with much of its business coming from information-technology services.[28] Accenture, Hewlett-Packard, IBM, and the big U.S. accounting firms know all too well the competitive threat Wipro represents. Not only are Wipro's employees economical, they're knowledgeable and skilled. And they play an important role in the company's planning. Because the information services industry is continually changing, employees are taught to analyze situations and to define the scale and scope of a client's problems in order to offer the best solutions. These employees are the ones on the front line with the clients and it's their responsibility to establish what to do and how to do it. It's an approach that positions Wipro for success no matter how the industry changes.

formal planning department
A group of planning specialists whose sole responsibility is helping to write organizational plans

Scanning the environment helps Toyota Motor Corporation managers detect emerging trends that influence the company's future plans. Based on trends in computing and communications technology plus demographic trends such as a rapidly aging population and a decreasing birthrate in Japan and other developing nations, Toyota sees robotics as a key business in coming years. Its violin-playing robot, with 17 joints in each hand and arm, has the precise control and coordination to achieve humanlike agility for performing domestic chores like folding laundry and medical tasks such as dispensing medicine. Toyota and competitors such as Honda and Hitachi are racing to build robots that will serve the needs of the elderly in Japan, where 40 percent of the population is expected to be older than 65 by 2055, and in other global markets.

How Can Managers Use Environmental Scanning?

Crammed into a small Shanghai apartment that houses four generations of a Chinese family, Indra Nooyi, Chairman and CEO of PepsiCo Inc., asked the inhabitants several questions about "China's rapid development, their shopping habits, and how they feel about Western brands." This visit was part of an "immersion" tour of China for Ms. Nooyi, who hopes to strengthen PepsiCo's business in emerging markets. She said, "I wanted to look at how people live, how they eat, what the growth possibilities are."[29] The information gleaned from her research—a prime example of environmental scanning up close and personal—will help in establishing PepsiCo's future goals and plans.

A manager's analysis of the external environment may be improved by **environmental scanning**, which involves screening information to detect emerging trends. One of the fastest-growing forms of environmental scanning is **competitor intelligence**, which is gathering information about competitors that allows managers to anticipate competitors' actions rather than merely react to them.[30] It seeks basic information about competitors: Who are they? What are they doing? How will what they're doing affect us?

Many who study competitive intelligence suggest that much of the competitor-related information managers need to make crucial strategic decisions is available and accessible to the public.[31] In other words, competitive intelligence isn't corporate espionage. Advertisements, promotional materials, press releases, reports filed with government agencies, annual reports, want ads, newspaper reports, information on the Internet, and industry studies are readily accessible sources of information. Specific information on an industry and associated organizations is increasingly available through electronic databases. Managers can literally tap into this wealth of competitive information by purchasing access to databases. Attending trade shows and debriefing your own sales staff also can be good sources of information on competitors. In addition, many organizations even regularly buy competitors' products and ask their own employees to evaluate them to learn about new technical innovations.[32]

In a changing global business environment, environmental scanning and obtaining competitive intelligence can be quite complex, especially since information must be gathered

environmental scanning
Screening information to detect emerging trends

competitor intelligence
Gathering information about competitors that allows managers to anticipate competitors' actions rather than merely react to them

from around the world. However, one thing managers could do is subscribe to news services that review newspapers and magazines from around the globe and provide summaries to client companies.

Managers do need to be careful about the way information, especially competitive intelligence, is gathered to prevent any concerns about whether it's legal or ethical.[33] For instance, Starwood Hotels recently sued Hilton Hotels alleging that two former employees stole trade secrets and helped Hilton develop a new line of luxury, trendy hotels designed to appeal to a young demographic.[34] The court filing said, "This is the clearest imaginable case of corporate espionage, theft of trade secrets, unfair competition, and computer fraud." Competitive intelligence becomes illegal corporate spying when it involves the theft of proprietary materials or trade secrets by any means. The Economic Espionage Act makes it a crime in the United States to engage in economic espionage or to steal a trade secret. Difficult decisions about competitive intelligence arise because often there's a fine line between what's considered *legal and ethical* and what's considered *legal but unethical*. Although the top manager at one competitive intelligence firm contends that 99.9 percent of intelligence gathering is legal, there's no question that some people or companies will go to any lengths—some unethical—to get information about competitors.[35]

Let's Get Real:

My Response *to A Manager's Dilemma, page 204*

A crisis the magnitude of the Haitian earthquake requires a global response, which is exactly what happened. The timing of the disaster on a holiday weekend was unfortunate, but no one can fault the herculean efforts of the WFP in their response to the crisis. In the shadow of Hurricane Katrina, agencies such as the WFP were intensely scrutinized and obviously had fairly well laid out action plans for disasters such as this. That being said, no amount of planning can prepare for the devastation that the relief teams found in Haiti.

Getting the military involved from the outset was a key factor. They are at a constant state of readiness and are trained first responders. The military command should take control of damage assessment, procuring local equipment, and mobilizing shipments of additional equipment necessary to get runways repaired and open and seaports in working order. The WFP should immediately take the lead and begin centralizing food and relief supplies from the myriad of relief agencies across the country and begin scheduling shipments accordingly.

In general, the actual relief operation was impressive and efficient and argues well for the effectiveness of good planning.

What Would You Do?

Chuck Pick
President
Chuck's Parking
Service, Inc.
Sherman Oaks, CA

CHAPTER SUMMARY
by Learning Outcomes

LEARNING OUTCOME 8.1 **Define** the nature and purposes of planning.

Planning involves defining the organization's goals, establishing an overall strategy for achieving those goals, and developing plans for organizational work activities. The four purposes of planning include providing direction, reducing uncertainty, minimizing waste and redundancy, and establishing the goals or standards used in controlling. Studies of the planning-performance relationship have concluded that formal planning is associated with positive financial performance, for the most part; it's more important to do a good job of planning and implementing the plans than doing more extensive planning; the external environment is usually the reason why companies that plan don't achieve high levels of performance; and the planning-performance relationship seems to be influenced by the planning time frame.

LEARNING OUTCOME 8.2 **Classify** the types of goals organizations might have and the plans they use.

Goals are desired outcomes. Plans are documents that outline how goals are going to be met. Goals might be strategic or financial and they might be stated or real. Strategic plans apply to the entire organization while operational plans encompass a particular functional area. Long-term plans are those with a time frame beyond three years. Short-term plans cover one year or less. Specific plans are clearly defined and leave no room for interpretation. Directional plans are flexible and set out general guidelines. A single-use plan is a one-time plan designed to meet the needs of a unique situation. Standing plans are ongoing plans that provide guidance for activities performed repeatedly.

LEARNING OUTCOME 8.3 **Compare** and contrast approaches to goal setting and planning.

In traditional goal setting, goals are set at the top of the organization and then become subgoals for each organizational area. MBO (management by objectives) is a process of setting mutually agreed-upon goals and using those goals to evaluate employee performance. Well-written goals have six characteristics: (1) written in terms of outcomes, (2) measurable and quantifiable, (3) clear as to time frame, (4) challenging but attainable, (5) written down, and (6) communicated to all organizational members who need to know them. Goal setting involves these steps: review the organization's mission; evaluate available resources; determine the goals individually or with input from others; write down the goals and communicate them to all who need to know them; and review results and change goals as needed. The contingency factors that affect planning include the manager's level in the organization, the degree of environmental uncertainty, and the length of future commitments. The two main approaches to planning include the traditional approach, which has plans developed by top managers that flow down through other organizational levels and which may use a formal planning department. The other approach is to involve more organizational members in the planning process.

LEARNING OUTCOME 8.4 **Discuss** contemporary issues in planning.

One contemporary planning issue is planning in dynamic environments, which usually means developing plans that are specific but flexible. Also, it's important to continue planning even when the environment is highly uncertain. Finally, because there's little time in a dynamic environment for goals and plans to flow down from the top, lower organizational levels should be allowed to set goals and develop plans. Another contemporary planning issue involves using environmental scanning to help do a better analysis of the external environment. One form of environmental scanning, competitive intelligence, can be especially helpful in finding out what competitors are doing.

PEARSON mymanagementlab To check your understanding of learning outcomes **8.1** – **8.4** go to **mymanagementlab.com** and try the chapter questions.

REVIEW AND DISCUSSION QUESTIONS

1. Explain what studies have shown about the relationship between planning and performance.
2. Discuss the contingency factors that affect planning.
3. Describe how managers can effectively plan in today's dynamic environment.
4. Will planning become more or less important to managers in the future? Why?
5. If planning is so crucial, why do some managers choose not to do it? What would you tell these managers?
6. Explain how planning involves making decisions today that will have an impact later.
7. How might planning in a not-for-profit organization such as the American Cancer Society differ from planning in a for-profit organization such as Coca-Cola?
8. What types of planning do you do in your personal life? Describe these plans in terms of being (a) strategic or operational, (b) short term or long term, and (c) specific or directional.
9. The late Peter Drucker, an eminent management author, coined the SMART format for setting goals back in 1954: S (specific), M (measurable), A (attainable), R (relevant), and T (time-bound). Are these still relevant today? Discuss.
10. Many companies have a goal of becoming more environmentally sustainable. One of the most important steps they can take is controlling paper waste. Choose a company—any type, any size. You've been put in charge of creating a program to do this for your company. Set goals and develop plans. Prepare a report for your boss (that is, your professor) outlining these goals and plans.

PREPARING FOR: My Career

ETHICS DILEMMA

As companies prepared plans to keep their businesses operating if the H1N1 (swine) flu pandemic materialized, thorny issues arose. At one small business, for example, the boss sent two employees home on "indefinite leave" after the employees' children's school was closed down because of an H1N1 outbreak there. Neither of their children had flu symptoms, nor did the employees. Now they're out of paid sick day leaves and are losing pay. At

Procter & Gamble, executives asked company doctors whether it should try to secure a private stash of Tamiflu for its staff. One of the company's medical leaders responded, "How ethical would it be if we were holding supplies that the general public didn't have access to but badly needed?"[36] What do you think? Is it ethical for a business to be overly cautious in protecting employees? Is it ethical for a company to protect its own employees at the expense of public protection? What would you do in this situation?

SKILLS EXERCISE

Developing Your Goal Setting Skill

About the Skill

Employees should have a clear understanding of what they're attempting to accomplish. In addition, managers have the responsibility for seeing that this is done by helping employees set work goals. Setting goals is a skill every manager needs to develop.

Steps in Practicing the Skill

You can be more effective at setting goals if you use the following eight suggestions.

1. *Identify an employee's key job tasks.* Goal setting begins by defining what it is that you want your employees to accomplish. The best source for this information is each employee's job description.

2. *Establish specific and challenging goals for each key task.* Identify the level of performance expected of each employee. Specify the target toward which the employee is working.

3. *Specify the deadlines for each goal.* Putting deadlines on each goal reduces ambiguity. Deadlines, however, should not be set arbitrarily. Rather, they need to be realistic given the tasks to be completed.

4. *Allow the employee to actively participate.* When employees participate in goal setting, they're more likely to accept the goals. However, it must be sincere participation. That is, employees must perceive that you are truly seeking their input, not just going through the motions.

5. *Prioritize goals.* When you give someone more than one goal, it's important for you to rank the goals in order of importance. The purpose of prioritizing is to encourage the employee to take action and expend effort on each goal in proportion to its importance.

6. *Rate goals for difficulty and importance.* Goal setting should not encourage people to choose easy goals. Instead, goals should be rated for their difficulty and importance. When goals are rated, individuals can be given credit for trying difficult goals, even if they don't fully achieve them.

7. *Build in feedback mechanisms to assess goal progress.* Feedback lets employees know whether their level of effort is sufficient to attain the goal. Feedback should be both self-generated and supervisor generated. In either case, feedback should be frequent and recurring.

8. *Link rewards to goal attainment.* It's natural for employees to ask, "What's in it for me?" Linking rewards to the achievement of goals will help answer that question.

Practicing the Skill

1. Where do you want to be in five years? Do you have specific five-year goals? Establish three goals you want to achieve in five years. Make sure these goals are specific, challenging, and measurable.

2. Set personal and academic goals you want to achieve by the end of this college term. Prioritize and rate them for difficulty.

WORKING TOGETHER
Team Exercise

Form small groups of three to four individuals and read through the following scenario. Complete the work that's called for. Be sure that your goals are well designed and that your plans are descriptive.

Scenario

Facing dire budget predictions, many school districts are moving to a four-day week. Of nearly 15,000-plus districts nationwide, more than 100 in at least 17 states have moved to the four-day system.[37] Suppose that you are employed by a school district in San Antonio, Texas, that is going to move to a four-day week by the start of the next school year. What type of planning would need to be done as your school district embarked on this process? Identify three or four primary goals for accomplishing this action. Then, describe what plans would be needed to ensure that those goals are met.

MY TURN TO BE A MANAGER

- Practice setting goals for various aspects of your personal life such as academics, career preparation, family, hobbies, and so forth. Set at least two short-term goals and at least two long-term goals for each area.

- For these goals that you have set, write out plans for achieving those goals. Think in terms of what you will have to do to accomplish each. For instance, if one of your academic goals is to improve your grade-point average, what will you have to do to reach it?

- Write a personal mission statement. Although this may sound simple to do, it's not going to be simple or easy. Our hope is that it will be something that you'll want to keep, use, and revise when necessary, and that it will help you be the person you'd like to be and live the life you'd like to live. Start by doing some research on personal mission statements. There are some wonderful Web resources that can guide you. Good luck!

- Interview three managers about the types of planning they do. Ask them for suggestions on how to be a better planner. Write a report describing and comparing your findings.

- Choose two companies, preferably in different industries. Research the companies' Web sites and find examples of goals that they have stated. (Hint: A company's annual report is often a good place to start.) Evaluate these goals. Are they well-written? Rewrite those that don't exhibit the characteristics of well-written goals so that they do.

- Steve's and Mary's suggested readings: Atul Gawande, *The Checklist Manifesto: How to Get Things Right* (Metropolitan Books, 2009); Peter F. Drucker, *Management: Tasks, Responsibilities, Practices* (Harper Business, 1974); Peter F. Drucker, *The Executive in Action; Managing for Results* (Harper Business, 1967); and Peter F. Drucker, *The Practice of Management* (HarperCollins, 1954).

- What does it take to be a good planner? Do some research on this issue. As part of your research, talk to professors and other professionals. Make a bulleted list of suggestions. Be sure to cite your sources.

- In your own words, write down three things you learned in this chapter about being a good manager.

- Self-knowledge can be a powerful learning tool. Go to mymanagementlab.com and complete these self-assessment exercises: What's My Attitude Toward Achievement? What Are My Course Performance Goals? What Time of Day Am I Most Productive? and How Good Am I at Personal Planning? Using the results of your assessments, identify personal strengths and weaknesses. What will you do to reinforce your strengths and improve your weaknesses?

CASE APPLICATION 1
Icelandic Volcano, 1; Global Commerce, 0

This volcano has a funny name—Eyjafjallajokull—but its impact was not so funny to global businesses, both large and small.[38] When it erupted on April 14, 2010, the plume of volcanic ash that spread across thousands of miles disrupted air travel and global commerce for a number of days.

As thousands of flights were canceled across Europe, tens of thousands of air travelers couldn't get to their destination. For example, Marthin De Beer, vice president of emerging technologies at Cisco Systems, was headed to Oslo to discuss the final aspects of its acquisition of Tandberg, a Norwegian teleconferencing company. However, when his flight was canceled, he and Tandberg's CEO, Fredrik Halvorsen, used their merged companies' equipment to hold a virtual press conference. Other businesses weren't as lucky, especially those with high-value, highly perishable products such as berries, fresh fish and flowers, and medicines and pharmaceuticals. African farmers, European fresh-produce importers, and flower traders from Kenya to the Netherlands found their businesses threatened by the air traffic shutdown. Even manufacturers were affected. For instance, BMW had to scale back work hours and had even prepared for possibly shutting down production at its Spartanburg, South Carolina, plant because it depended on trans-Atlantic flights to bring transmissions and other components from German factories by air. A spokesperson at another automobile company, Mercedes-Benz, said, "There has been disruption in our parts supply. We expect that there may be shortages of some parts or delays in some instances."

A flight information screen at an airport outside of Paris lists commercial airline cancellations in cities across northern Europe as a result of the drifting plume of ash that spread thousands of miles from the Icelandic volcano eruption, disrupting air travel and global commerce.

Discussion Questions

1. Could a company even plan for this type of situation? If yes, how? If not, why not?

2. Would goals be useful in this type of situation? What types of goals might a manufacturing company like BMW have in such a situation? How about a global airline? How about a small flower grower in Kenya?

3. What types of plans could companies use in this type of situation? Explain why you think these plans would be important.

4. What lessons about planning can managers learn from this crisis?

CASE APPLICATION
Building a Future

Habitat for Humanity is a nonprofit, ecumenical Christian housing ministry whose mission is to "eliminate poverty and homelessness from the world and to make decent shelter a matter of conscience and action."[39] The organization was founded by Millard and Linda Fuller in 1976 in Americus, Georgia. More than 300,000 Habitat houses have been built, sheltering more than 1.5 million people around the world. These houses can be found in all 50 states of the United States, the District of Columbia, Guam, Puerto Rico, and more than 90 countries around the world. "Thousands of low-income families have found new hope in this form of affordable housing."

Habitat's approach is simple. Families in need of decent housing apply to local Habitat for Humanity affiliates. Homeowners are chosen based on their level of need, their willingness to become partners in the program, and their ability to repay the loan. And that's the unique thing about Habitat's approach. It's not a giveaway program. Families chosen to become homeowners have to make a down payment and monthly mortgage payments, and invest hundreds of hours of their own labor into building their Habitat home and helping build other Habitat houses. Habitat volunteers provide labor and donations of money and materials as well. (Maybe some of you have helped in a Habitat build.)

In 2009, J. Ronald Terwilliger, a former CEO of housing developer Trammell Crow Residential Co., who also has been a long-time member of Habitat's board of directors, made a $100 million commitment to Habitat. He says that "through his work with Habitat and in the private sector, he's witnessed the depths of poverty, seeing people living in cardboard shacks and unspeakable filth, as well as the struggle for middle-class families to find affordable housing." According to the Center on Philanthropy at Indiana University, "It's one of the largest gifts in recent years to a group devoted to social services." Terwilliger's gift is intended to give people a helping hand toward a decent, safe clean home. And it's intended to send a message to other philanthropists to "step up their giving." As for Habitat, its CEO, Jonathan Reckford, said, "This is a chance to have a really deep impact." Having that type of impact when the needs now are greater than ever is a definite planning challenge for the organization and its managers.

Discussion Questions

1. What role do you think goals would play in planning for the wise use of this gift? List some goals you think might be important. (Make sure these goals have the characteristics of well-written goals.)

2. What types of plans would be needed in wisely using this gift? (For instance, long-term or short-term, or both?) Explain why you think these plans would be important.

3. What contingency factors might affect the planning Habitat executives have to do for the wise use of this gift? How might those contingency factors affect the planning?

4. What planning challenges do you think Habitat executives face with getting the most use out of this gift? How should they cope with those challenges?

Let's Get Real:

Meet the Manager

Sid Gokhale
President
Dowden Custom Media
Montvale, NJ

You'll be hearing more from this real manager throughout the chapter.

MY JOB:
I'm the president of a strategic health care communications company.

BEST PART OF MY JOB:
Working with a diverse group of people and tapping into their expertise and talents. You need to leverage your employees' strengths. I know that I'm not an expert in all aspects of the business, which is why we have specialists in editorial, design, Internet technology, and project management—all working toward a common goal.

Strategic
Management

LEARNING OUTCOMES

WORST PART OF MY JOB:

To say no, especially because of forces beyond your control. You always want to go the extra mile to please your stakeholders, who include your employees and customers. When you can't because of environmental factors or other limitations, it's tough.

BEST MANAGEMENT ADVICE EVER RECEIVED:

Listen first, speak later. In order to understand the market, your customers, and your employees, you need to hear what they have to say and then work toward crafting a solution for their needs.

A Manager's Dilemma

Shut Up Kanye (published soon after the MTV VMAs) and *Where's the Naughty Governor?* (published just after South Carolina governor Mark Sanford admitted to having an affair) are just two of the online games offered by MTV Network's subsidiary AddictingGames.[1]

As vice president of Addicting-Games, the largest free online-games site for teens, Kate Connally is responsible for managing the subsidiary that was acquired by MTV Networks in 2005. Keeping 15.3 million unique monthly visitors happy and coming back is a real challenge. To do so,

"Connally taps a network of 1,000 Flash developers, publishing a new game every day and 12 on Fridays." Those developers are found globally from Canada to India. Having access to such a globally connected network is how the company is able to respond almost overnight to current events like Kanye's outburst at the VMAs and Governor Sanford's affair disclosure.

Now, Connelly is overseeing a major strategic change—bringing those online games to the iPhone. She said, "Media companies need to provide experiences wherever their audiences are, and the iPhone is really where we're seeing the audience go." How could SWOT analysis help her?

What Would You Do?

The importance of having good strategies can be seen by what Kate Connally has accomplished with AddictingGames. By recognizing game opportunities in current news stories and in new formats and formulating effective strategies to exploit these opportunities, her company has become the leader in online gaming. As she continues expanding access to those games, strategic management will continue to play an important role in the company's ability to continue to be the most popular online games site. An underlying theme in this chapter is that effective strategies result in high organizational performance.

LEARNING OUTCOME 9.1
Define strategic management and explain why it's important.

Strategic Management

- ▶ Vente-privee.com, one of Europe's top e-tailers, is looking to expand in Europe, but not in the United States, where competition from outlet malls and discounters is too great.
- ▶ Facing intense pressure from users over privacy issues, Facebook CEO Mark Zuckerberg unveiled a new set of controls to help people better understand what information they are sharing online.
- ▶ Charles Schwab, chairman and founder of his namesake financial services company, is worried about his customers, especially since his company's success depends on his financial advisers' ability to keep those customers "engaged" in equities markets.
- ▶ The private equity firm, C. Dean Metropoulos & Company, has reached an agreement to buy Pabst Blue Ribbon, a once-popular beer brand, with hopes of rebuilding its share in a competitive market.[2]

These are just a few of the business news stories from a single week, and each one is about a company's strategies. Strategic management is very much a part of what managers do. In this section, we want to look at what strategic management is and why it's important.

What Is Strategic Management?

The discount retail industry is a good place to see what strategic management is all about. Walmart and Kmart Corporation (now part of Sears Holdings) have battled for market dominance since 1962, the year both companies were founded. The two chains have other similarities: store atmosphere, names, markets served, and organizational purpose. Yet, Walmart's performance (financial and otherwise) has far surpassed that of Kmart. Walmart is the world's largest retailer and Kmart was the largest retailer ever to seek Chapter 11 bankruptcy protection. Why the difference in performance? Because

224

of different strategies and competitive abilities.[3] Walmart has excelled by using strategic management effectively while Kmart has struggled by failing to use strategic management effectively.

Strategic management is what managers do to develop the organization's strategies. It's an important task involving all the basic management functions—planning, organizing, leading, and controlling. What are an organization's **strategies**? They're the plans for how the organization will do whatever it's in business to do, how it will compete successfully, and how it will attract and satisfy its customers in order to achieve its goals.[4]

One term often used in strategic management is **business model**, which simply is how a company is going to make money. It focuses on two things: (1) whether customers will value what the company is providing, and (2) whether the company can make any money doing that.[5] For instance, Dell pioneered a new business model for selling computers to consumers directly online instead of selling through computer retailers like other manufacturers. Did customers "value" that? Absolutely! Did Dell make money doing it that way? Absolutely! As managers think about strategies, they need to think about the economic viability of their company's business model.

Why Is Strategic Management Important?

In the summer of 2002, a British television show spin-off called *American Idol* became one of the biggest shows in American television history. Nine seasons later, it's still the most-watched show on television although its audience has declined for four seasons. However, the show's executive producer said, "If we're smart about it, there's no reason why 'Idol' wouldn't keep going. Just look at 'Price is Right.' It's been on for over 35 years."[6] The managers behind *Idol* seem to understand the importance of strategic management as they've developed and exploited every aspect of the *Idol* business—the television show, the music, the concerts, and all the other associated licensed products. Now, their challenge is to keep the franchise a strong presence in the market by making strategic changes.

Why is strategic management so important? There are three reasons. The most significant one is that it can make a difference in how well an organization performs. Why do some

Wang Chuanfu recognizes the importance of strategic management to improve organizational performance. Chuanfu is the CEO of BYD, a firm he started in 1995 in Shenzhen, China, to make and sell rechargeable batteries for computers. Today BYD is a top battery supplier to both computer and cell phone makers. Recognizing an opportunity to build profits by entering a new market, Chuanfu bought a struggling car company in China and applied his core technology of rechargeable batteries to producing electric cars. Chuanfu, shown here with his e6 fuel-efficient and environmentally friendly electric car, hopes to capture a good part of the worldwide global market for electric cars that's predicted to be as big as 10 million cars per year by 2016.

strategic management
What managers do to develop the organization's strategies

strategies
The plans for how the organization will do what it's in business to do, how it will compete successfully, and how it will attract and satisfy its customers in order to achieve its goals

business model
How a company is going to make money

businesses succeed and others fail, even when faced with the same environmental conditions? (Remember our Walmart and Kmart example.) Research has found a generally positive relationship between strategic planning and performance.[7] In other words, it appears that organizations that use strategic management do have higher levels of performance. And that fact makes it pretty important for managers!

Another reason it's important has to do with the fact that managers in organizations of all types and sizes face continually changing situations (as we discussed in Chapter 6). They cope with this uncertainty by using the strategic management process to examine relevant factors and decide what actions to take. For instance, as business executives across a wide spectrum of industries coped with the global recession, they focused on making their strategies more flexible. At Office Depot, for example, store managers throughout the company told CEO Steve Odland that cash-strapped consumers no longer wanted to buy pens or printer paper in bulk. So the company created special displays promoting single Sharpie pens and introduced five-ream packages of paper, half the size of the normal big box of paper.[8]

Finally, strategic management is important because organizations are complex and diverse. Each part needs to work together toward achieving the organization's goals; strategic management helps do this. For example, with more than 2.1 million employees worldwide working in various departments, functional areas, and stores, Walmart Stores, Inc., uses strategic management to help coordinate and focus employees' efforts on what's important as determined by its goals.

Today, both business organizations and not-for-profit organizations use strategic management. For instance, the U.S. Postal Service (USPS) is locked in competitive battles with overnight package delivery companies, telecommunications companies' e-mail and text messaging services, and private mailing facilities. In 2006, 213 billion pieces of mail were handled by the postal service. In 2009, that total had dropped to 177 billion, a decline of almost 17 percent. John Potter, USPS's CEO (the U.S. Postmaster General), is using strategic management to come up with a response. One possible action plan, which many critics consider drastic, is discontinuing Saturday mail delivery. However, some strategic changes are needed as the USPS faces losses of $238 billion over the next decade.[9] Strategic management will continue to be important to its operation. Check out the organization's *Vision 2013*, which outlines its internal plan for the future.[10] Although strategic management in not-for-profits hasn't been as well researched as it has in for-profit organizations, we know it's important for these organizations as well.

LEARNING OUTCOME 9.2
Explain what managers do during the six steps of the strategic management process.

The Strategic Management Process

The **strategic management process** (see Exhibit 9-1) is a six-step process that encompasses strategy planning, implementation, and evaluation. Although the first four steps describe the planning that must take place, implementation and evaluation are just as important! Even the best strategies can fail if management doesn't implement or evaluate them properly.

EXHIBIT 9-1

Strategic Management Process

Identify the organization's current mission, goals, and strategies → SWOT Analysis [External Analysis • Opportunities • Threats / Internal Analysis • Strengths • Weaknesses] → Formulate Strategies → Implement Strategies → Evaluate Results

Step 1: Identifying the Organization's Current Mission, Goals, and Strategies

Every organization needs a **mission**—a statement of its purpose. Defining the mission forces managers to identify what it's in business to do. For instance, the mission of Avon is "To be the company that best understands and satisfies the product, service, and self-fulfillment needs of women on a global level." The mission of Facebook is "a social utility that connects you with the people around you." The mission of the National Heart Foundation of Australia is to "reduce suffering and death from heart, stroke, and blood vessel disease in Australia." These statements provide clues to what these organizations see as their purpose. What should a mission statement include? Exhibit 9-2 describes some typical components.

Step 2: Doing an External Analysis

What impact might the following trends have for businesses?

▶ With the passage of the national health care legislation, every big restaurant chain will now be required to post calorie information on their menus and drive-through signs.

▶ Cell phones are now used by customers more for data transmittal and retrieval than for phone calls.

▶ The share of new high-school graduates enrolled in college hit a record high in 2009 and continues to climb.[11]

We described the external environment in Chapter 2 as an important constraint on a manager's actions. Analyzing that environment is a critical step in the strategic management process. Managers do an external analysis so they know, for instance, what the competition is doing, what pending legislation might affect the organization, or what the labor supply is like in locations where it operates. In an external analysis, managers should examine the economic, demographic, political/legal, sociocultural, technological, and global components to see the trends and changes.

Once they've analyzed the environment, managers need to pinpoint opportunities that the organization can exploit and threats that it must counteract or buffer against. **Opportunities** are positive trends in the external environment; **threats** are negative trends.

EXHIBIT 9-2

Components of a Mission Statement

Customers: Who are the firm's customers?

Markets: Where does the firm compete geographically?

Concern for survival, growth, and profitability: Is the firm committed to growth and financial stability?

Philosophy: What are the firm's basic beliefs, values, and ethical priorities?

Concern for public image: How responsive is the firm to societal and environmental concerns?

Products or services: What are the firm's major products or services?

Technology: Is the firm technologically current?

Self-concept: What are the firm's major competitive advantage and core competencies?

Concern for employees: Are employees a valuable asset of the firm?

Source: Based on F. David, *Strategic Management*, 13th ed. (Upper Saddle River, NJ: Prentice Hall, 2011), p. 51.

---

strategic management process
A six-step process that encompasses strategic planning, implementation, and evaluation

mission
A statement of an organization's purpose

opportunities
Positive trends in the external environment

threats
Negative trends in the external environment

Step 3: Doing an Internal Analysis

Now we move to the internal analysis, which provides important information about an organization's specific resources and capabilities. An organization's **resources** are its assets—financial, physical, human, and intangible—that it uses to develop, manufacture, and deliver products to its customers. They're "what" the organization has. On the other hand, its **capabilities** are its skills and abilities in doing the work activities needed in its business—"how" it does its work. The major value-creating capabilities of the organization are known as its **core competencies**.[12] Both resources and core competencies determine the organization's competitive weapons.

After completing an internal analysis, managers should be able to identify organizational strengths and weaknesses. Any activities the organization does well or any unique resources that it has are called **strengths**. **Weaknesses** are activities the organization doesn't do well or resources it needs but doesn't possess.

The combined external and internal analyses are called the **SWOT analysis**, which is an analysis of the organization's *s*trengths, *w*eaknesses, *o*pportunities, and *t*hreats. After completing the SWOT analysis, managers are ready to formulate appropriate strategies—that is, strategies that (1) exploit an organization's strengths and external opportunities, (2) buffer or protect the organization from external threats, or (3) correct critical weaknesses.

Step 4: Formulating Strategies

As managers formulate strategies, they should consider the realities of the external environment and their available resources and capabilities in order to design strategies that will help an organization achieve its goals. The three main types of strategies managers will formulate include corporate, competitive, and functional. We'll describe each shortly.

Step 5: Implementing Strategies

Once strategies are formulated, they must be implemented. No matter how effectively an organization has planned its strategies, performance will suffer if the strategies aren't implemented properly.

Step 6: Evaluating Results

The final step in the strategic management process is evaluating results. How effective have the strategies been at helping the organization reach its goals? What adjustments are necessary? After assessing the results of previous strategies and determining that changes were needed, Ursula Burns, Xerox's CEO, made strategic adjustments to regain market share and improve her company's bottom line. The company cut jobs, sold assets, and reorganized management. (See Leader Who Made a Difference box on p. 230.)

LEARNING OUTCOME **9.3**
Describe the three types of corporate strategies.

Corporate Strategies

As we said earlier, organizations use three types of strategies: corporate, competitive, and functional. (See Exhibit 9-3.) Top-level managers typically are responsible for corporate strategies, middle-level managers for competitive strategies, and lower-level managers for the functional strategies. In this section, we'll look at corporate strategies.

What Is Corporate Strategy?

A **corporate strategy** is one that determines what businesses a company is in or wants to be in, and what it wants to do with those businesses. It's based on the mission and goals of the organization and the roles that each business unit of the organization will play. We can see both of these aspects with PepsiCo, for instance. Its mission: To be the world's premier consumer products company focused on convenient foods and beverages. It pursues that mission with a

EXHIBIT 9-3
Types of
Organizational
Strategies

corporate strategy that has put it in different businesses including PepsiCo Americas Beverages (which includes Pepsi, Gatorade, and other beverages), PepsiCo Americas Foods (which includes Frito-Lay North America, Quaker Foods North America, and Latin American Foods), and PepsiCo International (which includes all PepsiCo's other international products). The other part of corporate strategy is when top managers decide what to do with those businesses: grow them, keep them the same, or renew them.

What Are the Types of Corporate Strategy?

The three main types of corporate strategies are growth, stability, and renewal. Let's look at each type.

GROWTH.   Even though Walmart is the world's largest retailer, it continues to grow internationally and in the United States. A **growth strategy** is when an organization expands the number of markets served or products offered, either through its current business(es) or through new business(es). Because of its growth strategy, an organization may increase revenues, number of employees, or market share. Organizations grow by using concentration, vertical integration, horizontal integration, or diversification.

An organization that grows using *concentration* focuses on its primary line of business and increases the number of products offered or markets served in this primary business. For instance, Beckman Coulter, Inc., a Fullerton, California-based organization with annual revenues over $3.2 billion, has used concentration to become one of the world's largest medical diagnostics and research equipment companies. Another example of a company using concentration is Bose Corporation of Framingham, Massachusetts, which focuses on developing innovative audio products and has become one of the world's leading manufacturers of speakers for home entertainment, automotive, and pro audio markets with sales of more than $2 billion.

A company also might choose to grow by *vertical integration*, either backward, forward, or both. In backward vertical integration, the organization becomes its own supplier so it can control its inputs. For instance, eBay owns an online payment business that helps it provide more secure transactions and control one of its most critical processes. In forward vertical integration, the organization becomes its own distributor and is able to control its outputs. For example, Apple has more than 287 retail stores worldwide to distribute its product.

In *horizontal integration*, a company grows by combining with competitors. For instance, French cosmetics giant L'Oreal acquired The Body Shop. Another example is Live Nation,

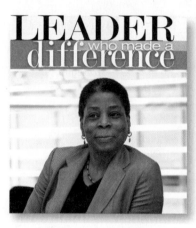

LEADER who made a difference

She's the first African American woman to lead a *Fortune* 500 company.[13] Ursula Burns, who joined Xerox as a summer engineering intern more than 30 years ago, has a reputation for being bold. As a mechanical engineer, she got noticed at Xerox because she wasn't afraid to speak up bluntly in a culture that's known more for being polite, courteous, and discreet than for being outspoken. But that bold approach is serving Burns well in a challenging environment. Just weeks after taking over as CEO, she announced the biggest deal in the firm's history—a $6.4 billion acquisition of Affiliated Computer Services, an outsourcing firm that most people had never heard of. Although the action was criticized, Burns recognized that Xerox needed dramatic action. Her challenge at Xerox is crafting strategies that will help it prosper and be an industry leader in a digital age where change is continual.

the largest concert promoter in the United States, which combined operations with competitor HOB Entertainment, the operator of the House of Blues Clubs. Horizontal integration has been used in a number of industries in the last few years—financial services, consumer products, airlines, department stores, and software, among others. The U.S. Federal Trade Commission usually scrutinizes these combinations closely to see if consumers might be harmed by decreased competition. Other countries may have similar restrictions. For instance, the European Commission, the "watchdog" for the European Union, conducted an in-depth investigation into Unilever's acquisition of the body and laundry care units of Sara Lee.

Finally, an organization can grow through *diversification*, either related or unrelated. Related diversification happens when a company combines with other companies in different, but related, industries. For example, American Standard Cos., based in Piscataway, New Jersey, is in a variety of businesses including bathroom fixtures, air conditioning and heating units, plumbing parts, and pneumatic brakes for trucks. Although this mix of businesses seems odd, the company's "strategic fit" is the efficiency-oriented manufacturing techniques developed in its primary business of bathroom fixtures, which it has transferred to all its other businesses. Unrelated diversification is when a company combines with firms in different and unrelated industries. For instance, the Tata Group of India has businesses in chemicals, communications and IT, consumer products, energy, engineering, materials, and services. Again, an odd mix. But in this case, there's no strategic fit among the businesses.

STABILITY. As the global recession dragged on and U.S. sales of candy and chocolate slowed down, Cadbury Schweppes—with almost half of its confectionary sales coming from chocolate—is maintaining things as they are. A **stability strategy** is a corporate strategy in which an organization continues to do what it is currently doing. Examples of this strategy include continuing to serve the same clients by offering the same product or service, maintaining market share, and sustaining the organization's current business operations. The organization doesn't grow, but doesn't fall behind, either.

RENEWAL. In 2009, Symantec lost $6.7 billion. Sprint-Nextel lost $2.4 billion, and many financial services and real-estate-related companies faced serious financial issues with huge losses. When an organization is in trouble, something needs to be done. Managers need to develop strategies, called **renewal strategies**, that address declining performance. The two main types of renewal strategies are retrenchment and turnaround strategies. A *retrenchment strategy* is a short-run renewal strategy used for minor performance problems. This strategy helps an organization stabilize operations, revitalize organizational resources and capabilities, and prepare to compete once again. When an organization's problems are more serious, more drastic action—the *turnaround strategy*—is needed. Managers do two things for both renewal strategies: cut costs and restructure organizational operations. However, in a turnaround strategy, these measures are more extensive than in a retrenchment strategy.

How Are Corporate Strategies Managed?

When an organization's corporate strategy encompasses a number of businesses, managers can manage this collection, or portfolio, of businesses using a tool called a corporate portfolio matrix. This matrix provides a framework for understanding diverse businesses and helps managers establish priorities for allocating resources.[14] The first portfolio matrix—the **BCG matrix**—was developed by the Boston Consulting Group and introduced the idea that an organization's various businesses could be evaluated and plotted using a 2 × 2 matrix

EXHIBIT **9-4**

BCG Matrix

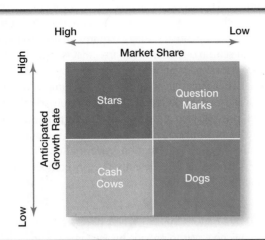

(see Exhibit 9-4) to identify which ones offered high potential and which were a drain on organizational resources.[15] The horizontal axis represents market share (low or high) and the vertical axis indicates anticipated market growth (low or high). A business unit is evaluated using a SWOT analysis and placed in one of the four categories.

What are the strategic implications of the BCG matrix? The dogs should be sold off or liquidated as they have low market share in markets with low growth potential. Managers should "milk" cash cows for as much as they can, limit any new investment in them, and use the large amounts of cash generated to invest in stars and question marks with strong potential to improve market share. Heavy investment in stars will help take advantage of the market's growth and help maintain high market share. The stars, of course, will eventually develop into cash cows as their markets mature and sales growth slows. The hardest decision for managers relates to the question marks. After careful analysis, some will be sold off and others strategically nurtured into stars.

Competitive Strategies

A **competitive strategy** is a strategy for how an organization will compete in its business(es). For a small organization in only one line of business or a large organization that has not diversified into different products or markets, its competitive strategy describes how it will compete in its primary or main market. For organizations in multiple businesses, however, each business will have its own competitive strategy that defines its competitive advantage, the products or services it will offer, the customers it wants to reach, and the like. For example, the French company LVMH-Moët Hennessy Louis Vuitton SA has different competitive strategies for its businesses, which include Donna Karan fashions, Louis Vuitton leather goods, Guerlain perfume, TAG Heuer watches, Dom Perignon champagne, and other luxury products. When an organization is in several different businesses, those single businesses that are independent and that have their own competitive strategies are referred to as **strategic business units (SBUs)**.

9.4

LEARNING OUTCOME
Describe competitive advantage and the competitive strategies organizations use to get it.

The Role of Competitive Advantage

Michelin has mastered a complex technological process for making superior radial tires. Coca-Cola has created the world's best and most powerful brand using specialized marketing and

---

stability strategy
A corporate strategy in which an organization continues to do what it is currently doing

renewal strategy
A corporate strategy designed to address declining performance

BCG matrix
A strategy tool that guides resource allocation decisions on the basis of market share and growth rate of SBUs

competitive strategy
An organizational strategy for how an organization will compete in its business(es)

strategic business unit (SBU)
The single independent businesses of an organization that formulate their own competitive strategies

merchandising capabilities.[16] The Ritz Carlton hotels have a unique ability to deliver personalized customer service. Each of these companies has created a competitive advantage.

Developing an effective competitive strategy requires an understanding of **competitive advantage**, which is what sets an organization apart—that is, its distinctive edge.[17] That distinctive edge can come from the organization's core competencies by doing something that others cannot do or doing it better than others can do it. For example, Southwest Airlines has a competitive advantage because of its skills at giving passengers what they want—convenient and inexpensive air passenger service. Or competitive advantage can come from the company's resources because the organization has something that its competitors do not have. For instance, Walmart's state-of-the-art information system allows it to monitor and control inventories and supplier relations more efficiently than its competitors, which Walmart has turned into a cost advantage.

QUALITY AS A COMPETITIVE ADVANTAGE.   When W. K. Kellogg started manufacturing his cornflake cereal in 1906, his goal was to provide his customers with a high-quality, nutritious product that was enjoyable to eat. That emphasis on quality is still important today. Every employee has a responsibility to maintain the high quality of Kellogg products. If implemented properly, quality can be a way for an organization to create a sustainable competitive advantage.[18] That's why many organizations apply quality management concepts in an attempt to set themselves apart from competitors. If a business is able to continuously improve the quality and reliability of its products, it may have a competitive advantage that can't be taken away.[19]

SUSTAINING COMPETITIVE ADVANTAGE.   Every organization has resources (assets) and capabilities (how work gets done). So what makes some organizations more successful than others? Why do some professional baseball teams consistently win championships or draw large crowds? Why do some organizations have consistent and continuous growth in revenues and profits? Why do some colleges, universities, or departments experience continually increasing enrollments? Why do some companies consistently appear at the top of lists ranking the "best," or the "most admired," or the "most profitable"? The answer is that not every organization is able to effectively exploit its resources and to develop the core competencies that can provide it with a competitive advantage. And it's not enough simply to create a competitive advantage. The organization must be able to sustain that advantage; that is, to keep its edge despite competitors' actions or evolutionary changes in the industry. But that's not easy to do! Market instabilities, new technology, and other changes can challenge managers' attempts at creating a long-term, sustainable competitive advantage. However, by using strategic management, managers can better position their organizations to get a sustainable competitive advantage.

Many important ideas in strategic management have come from the work of Michael Porter.[20] One of his major contributions was explaining how managers can create a sustainable competitive advantage. An important part of doing this is an industry analysis, which is done using the five forces model.

Kellogg has developed a competitive advantage by creating and maintaining high-quality products for more than a century. Quality management at Kellogg includes making each employee responsible for maintaining quality and conducting quality control tests of the company's raw materials, processing, and packaging operations. Quality assurance personnel regularly visit suppliers' plants to assure that proper sanitation procedures are followed and that raw materials meet Kellogg's rigid specifications. A Quality Division at company headquarters establishes quality practices that are carried out by employees at the manufacturing facilities.

EXHIBIT 9-5

Five Forces Model

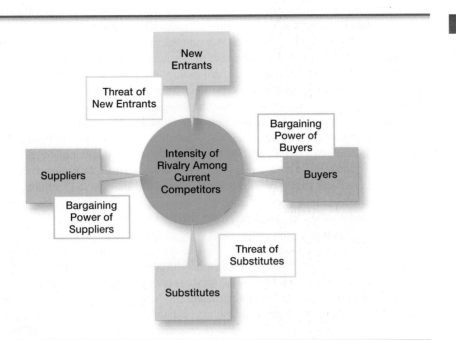

Source: Based on M. E. Porter, *Competitive Strategy: Techniques for Analyzing Industries and Competitors.*
New York: The Free Press, 1980.

FIVE FORCES MODEL.   In any industry, five competitive forces dictate the rules of competition. Together, these five forces (see Exhibit 9-5) determine industry attractiveness and profitability, which managers assess using these five factors:

1. *Threat of new entrants.* How likely is it that new competitors will come into the industry?
2. *Threat of substitutes.* How likely is it that other industries' products can be substituted for our industry's products?
3. *Bargaining power of buyers.* How much bargaining power do buyers (customers) have?
4. *Bargaining power of suppliers.* How much bargaining power do suppliers have?
5. *Current rivalry.* How intense is the rivalry among current industry competitors?

Choosing a Competitive Strategy

Once managers have assessed the five forces and done a SWOT analysis, they're ready to select an appropriate competitive strategy—that is, one that fits the competitive strengths (resources and capabilities) of the organization and the industry it's in. According to Porter, no firm can be successful by trying to be all things to all people. He proposed that managers select a strategy that will give the organization a competitive advantage, either from having lower costs than all other industry competitors or by being significantly different from competitors.

When an organization competes on the basis of having the lowest costs (costs or expenses, not prices) in its industry, it's following a *cost leadership strategy*. A low-cost leader is highly efficient. Overhead is kept to a minimum, and the firm does everything it can to cut costs. You won't find expensive art or interior décor at offices of low-cost leaders. For example, at Walmart's headquarters in Bentonville, Arkansas, office furnishings are functional, not elaborate, maybe not what you'd expect for the world's largest retailer. Although a low-cost leader doesn't place a lot of emphasis on "frills," its product must be perceived as comparable in quality to that offered by rivals or at least be acceptable to buyers.

competitive advantage
What sets an organization apart; its distinctive edge

A company that competes by offering unique products that are widely valued by customers is following a *differentiation strategy*. Product differences might come from exceptionally high quality, extraordinary service, innovative design, technological capability, or an unusually positive brand image. Practically any successful consumer product or service can be identified as an example of the differentiation strategy; for instance, Nordstrom (customer service); 3M Corporation (product quality and innovative design); Coach (design and brand image); and Apple (product design).

Although these two competitive strategies are aimed at the broad market, the final type of competitive strategy—the *focus strategy*—involves a cost advantage (cost focus) or a differentiation advantage (differentiation focus) in a narrow segment or niche. Segments can be based on product variety, customer type, distribution channel, or geographical location. For example, Denmark's Bang & Olufsen, whose revenues are over $527 million, focuses on high-end audio equipment sales. Whether a focus strategy is feasible depends on the size of the segment and whether the organization can make money serving that segment.

What happens if an organization can't develop a cost or a differentiation advantage? Porter called that being *stuck in the middle* and warned that's not a good place to be. An organization becomes stuck in the middle when its costs are too high to compete with the low-cost leader or when its products and services aren't differentiated enough to compete with the differentiator. Getting unstuck means choosing which competitive advantage to pursue and then doing so by aligning resource, capabilities, and core competencies.

Although Porter said that you had to pursue either the low cost or the differentiation advantage to prevent being stuck in the middle, more recent research has shown that organizations *can* successfully pursue both a low cost and a differentiation advantage and achieve high performance.[22] Needless to say, it's not easy to pull off! You have to keep costs low *and* be truly differentiated. But companies such as Hewlett-Packard, FedEx, Intel, and Coca-Cola have been able to do it.

Before we leave this section, we want to point out the final type of organizational strategy, the **functional strategies**, which are the strategies used by an organization's various functional departments to support the competitive strategy. For example, when R. R. Donnelley & Sons Company, a Chicago-based printer, wanted to become more competitive and invested in high-tech digital printing methods, its marketing department had to develop new sales plans and promotional pieces, the production department had to incorporate the digital equipment in the printing plants, and the human resources department had to update its employee selection and training programs. We don't cover specific functional strategies in this book because you'll cover them in other business courses you take.

LEARNING OUTCOME
Discuss current strategic management issues.

9.5

Current Strategic Management Issues

There's no better example of the strategic challenges faced by managers in today's environment than the recorded music industry. Overall sales of CDs have plummeted in the last decade and are down about 50 percent from their peak. Not only has this trend impacted the music companies, but it's affected music retailers as well. "Retailers have been forced to adjust, often by devoting some shelf space to other products." For instance, Best Buy, the national electronics retailer, decided to experiment with selling musical instruments. During spring 2010, the company opened its 100th musical instrument department. Other major music retailers, such as Walmart, have shifted selling space used for CDs to other departments. "At music specialty stores, however, diversification has become a matter of survival." Managers are struggling to find strategies that will help their organizations succeed in such an environment. Many have had to shift into whole new areas of business.[23] But it isn't just the music industry that's dealing with strategic challenges. Managers everywhere face increasingly intense global competition and high performance expectations by investors and customers. How have they responded to these new realities? In this section we look at three current strategic management issues including the need for strategic leadership, the need for strategic flexibility, and how managers design strategies to emphasize e-business, customer service, and innovation.

The Need for Strategic Leadership

Pablo Isa, CEO of Spain's Inditex (owner of clothing chain Zara), is overseeing an aggressive expansion. The company is adding as many as 450 stores a year, including a three-level store on Chicago's Michigan Avenue. With so much prime retail space available in the United States, Isa is exploiting the opportunity to negotiate better deals.[24]

An organization's strategies are usually developed and overseen by its top managers. An organization's top manager is typically the CEO (chief executive officer). This individual usually works with a top management team that includes other executive or senior managers such as a COO (chief operating officer), CFO (chief financial officer), CIO (chief information officer), and other individuals who may have various titles. Traditional descriptions of the CEO's role in strategic management include being the "chief" strategist, structural architect, and developer of the organization's information/control systems.[25] Other descriptions of the strategic role of the "chief executive" include key decision maker, visionary leader, political actor, monitor and interpreter of environment changes, and strategy designer.[26]

No matter how top management's job is described, you can be certain that from their perspective at the organization's upper levels, it's like no other job in the organization. By definition, top managers are ultimately responsible for every decision and action of every organizational employee. One important role that top managers play is that of strategic leader. Organizational researchers study leadership in relation to strategic management because an organization's top managers must provide effective strategic leadership. What is **strategic leadership**? It's the ability to anticipate, envision, maintain flexibility, think strategically, and work with others in the organization to initiate changes that will create a viable and valuable future for the organization.[27] How can top managers provide effective strategic leadership? Eight key dimensions have been identified.[28] (See Exhibit 9-6.) These dimensions include determining the organization's purpose or vision, exploiting and maintaining the organization's core

EXHIBIT 9-6

Effective Strategic Leadership

Sources: Based on J. P. Wallman, "Strategic Transactions and Managing the Future: A Druckerian Perspective," *Management Decision*, vol. 48, no. 4, 2010, pp. 485–499; D. E. Zand, "Drucker's Strategic Thinking Process: Three Key Techniques," *Strategy & Leadership*, vol. 38, no. 3, 2010, pp. 23–28; and R. D. Ireland and M. A. Hitt, "Achieving and Maintaining Strategic Competitiveness in the 21st Century: The Role of Strategic Leadership," *Academy of Management Executive*, February 1999, pp. 43–57.

functional strategy
The strategies used by an organization's various functional departments to support the competitive strategy

strategic leadership
The ability to anticipate, envision, maintain flexibility, think strategically, and work with others in the organization to initiate changes that will create a viable and valuable future for the organization

competencies, developing the organization's human capital, creating and sustaining a strong organizational culture, creating and maintaining organizational relationships, reframing prevailing views by asking penetrating questions and questioning assumptions, emphasizing ethical organizational decisions and practices, and establishing appropriately balanced organizational controls. Each dimension encompasses an important part of the strategic management process.

The Need for Strategic Flexibility

Not surprisingly, the economic recession changed the way that many companies approached strategic planning.[29] For instance, at Spartan Motors, a maker of specialty vehicles, managers used to draft a one-year strategic plan and a three-year financial plan, reviewing each one every financial quarter. However, CEO John Sztykiel said, "that relatively inflexible method bears some of the blame for Spartan's sharp drop in sales and gross profit." He also said that the company didn't "respond quickly enough to shifting demand." Now, the company uses a three-year strategic plan that the top management team updates every month. And at J.C. Penney Company, an ambitious five-year strategic growth plan rolled out in 2007 had to be put on hold as the economy floundered.[30] In its place, CEO Mike Ullman III crafted a tentative "bridge" plan to guide the company. This plan worked as the company improved its profit margins and did not have to lay off any employees.

Jürgen Schrempp, former CEO of Daimler AG, stated, "My principle always was... move as fast as you can and [if] you indeed make mistakes, you have to correct them.... It's much better to move fast, and make mistakes occasionally, than move too slowly."[31] You wouldn't think that smart individuals who are paid lots of money to manage organizations would make mistakes when it comes to strategic decisions. But even when managers use the strategic management process, there's no guarantee that the chosen strategies will lead to positive outcomes. Reading any of the current business periodicals would certainly support this assertion! But the key is responding quickly when it's obvious that the strategy isn't working. In other words, they need **strategic flexibility**—that is, the ability to recognize major external changes, to quickly commit resources, and to recognize when a strategic decision isn't working. Given the highly uncertain environment that managers face today, strategic flexibility seems absolutely necessary! Exhibit 9-7 provides suggestions for developing such strategic flexibility.

Important Organizational Strategies for Today's Environment

ESPN.com gets more than 16 million unique users a month. 16 million! That's almost twice the population of New York City. And its popular online business is just one of many businesses that ESPN is in. Originally founded as a television channel, ESPN is now into original programming,

EXHIBIT 9-7

Developing Strategic Flexibility

- *Encourage leadership unity* by making sure everyone is on the same page.
- *Keep resources fluid* and move them as circumstances warrant.
- *Have the right mindset* to explore and understand issues and challenges.
- Know what's happening with strategies currently being used by *monitoring and measuring results.*
- Encourage employees to *be open about disclosing and sharing negative information.*
- *Get new ideas and perspectives from outside* the organization.
- Have *multiple alternatives* when making strategic decisions.
- *Learn from mistakes.*

Sources: Based on Y. L. Doz and M. Kosonen, "Embedding Strategic Agility: A Leadership Agenda for Accelerating Business Model Renewal," *Long Range Planning*, April 2010, pp. 370–382; E. Lewis, D. Romanaggi, and A. Chapple, "Successfully Managing Change During Uncertain Times," *Strategic HR Review*, vol. 9, no. 2, 2010, pp. 12–18; and K. Shimizu and M. Hitt, "Strategic Flexibility: Organizational Preparedness to Reverse Ineffective Strategic Decisions," *Academy of Management Executive*, November 2004, pp. 44–59.

radio, online, publishing, gaming, X games, ESPY awards, ESPN Zones, global, and is looking to move into more local sports coverage.[32] Company president George Bodenheimer "runs one of the most successful and envied franchises in entertainment," and obviously understands how to successfully manage its various strategies in today's environment! We think three strategies are important in today's environment: e-business, customer service, and innovation.

e-BUSINESS STRATEGIES.   Managers use e-business strategies to develop a sustainable competitive advantage.[33] A cost leader can use e-business to lower costs in a variety of ways. For instance, it might use online bidding and order processing to eliminate the need for sales calls and to decrease sales force expenses; it could use Web-based inventory control systems that reduce storage costs; or it might use online testing and evaluation of job applicants.

A differentiator needs to offer products or services that customers perceive and value as unique. For instance, a business might use Internet-based knowledge systems to shorten customer response times, provide rapid online responses to service requests, or automate purchasing and payment systems so that customers have detailed status reports and purchasing histories.

Finally, because the focuser targets a narrow market segment with customized products, it might provide chat rooms or discussion boards for customers to interact with others who have common interests, design niche Web sites that target specific groups with specific interests, or use Web sites to perform standardized office functions such as payroll or budgeting.

Research also has shown that an important e-business strategy might be a clicks-and-bricks strategy. A clicks-and-bricks firm is one that uses both online (clicks) and traditional stand-alone locations (bricks).[34] For example, Walgreen's established an online site for ordering prescriptions, but some 90 percent of its customers who placed orders on the Web preferred to pick up their prescriptions at a nearby store rather than have them shipped to their home. So its "clicks-and-bricks" strategy has worked well!

CUSTOMER SERVICE STRATEGIES.   Companies emphasizing excellent customer service need strategies that cultivate that atmosphere from top to bottom. Such strategies involve giving customers what they want, communicating effectively with them, and providing employees with customer service training. Let's look first at the strategy of giving customers what they want.

It shouldn't surprise you that an important customer service strategy is giving customers what they want, which is a major aspect of an organization's overall marketing strategy. For

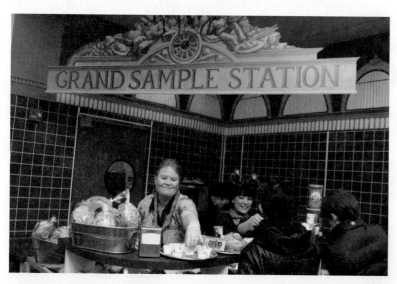

Trader Joe's customer service strategy centers on giving customers what they want and having an effective customer communication system. The specialty grocery uses face-to-face conversations, listening to customers and getting their feedback. Spending most of their day on the retail floor, store managers are available to interact with customers, and the company gives them authority to set up their store to meet local needs. Trader Joe's lets employees open products shoppers want to taste and encourages them to recommend products they like and to be honest about products they don't like. At Trader Joe's, a permanent store section that offers free samples also gives employees another chance to listen and respond to what customers want.

strategic flexibility
The ability to recognize major external changes, to quickly commit resources, and to recognize when a strategic decision was a mistake

instance, New Balance Athletic Shoes gives customers a truly unique product: shoes in varying widths. No other athletic shoe manufacturer has shoes for narrow or wide feet and in practically any size.[35]

Having an effective customer communication system is an important customer service strategy. Managers should know what's going on with customers. They need to find out what customers liked and didn't like about their purchase encounter—from their interactions with employees to their experience with the actual product or service. It's also important to let customers know what's going on with the company that might affect future purchase decisions. For instance, Retailer Hot Topic is fanatical about customer feedback, which it gets in the form of shopper "report cards." The company's CEO, Betsy McLaughlin, pores over more than 1,000 of them each week.[36]

Finally, an organization's culture is important to providing excellent customer service. This typically requires that employees be trained to provide exceptional customer service. For example, Singapore Airlines is well-known for its customer treatment. "On everything facing the customer, they do not scrimp," says an analyst based in Singapore.[37] Employees are expected to "get service right," leaving employees with no doubt about the expectations as far as how to treat customers.

INNOVATION STRATEGIES.   When Procter & Gamble purchased the Iams pet-food business, it did what it always does—used its renowned research division to look for ways to transfer technology from its other divisions to make new products.[38] One outcome of this cross-divisional combination: a new tartar-fighting ingredient from toothpaste that's included in all of its dry adult pet foods.

As this example shows, innovation strategies aren't necessarily focused on just the radical, breakthrough products. They can include applying existing technology to new uses. And organizations have successfully used both approaches. What types of innovation strategies do organizations need in today's environment? Those strategies should reflect their innovation philosophy, which is shaped by two strategic decisions: innovation emphasis and innovation timing.

Managers must first decide where the emphasis of their innovation efforts will be. Is the organization going to focus on basic scientific research, product development, or process improvement? Basic scientific research requires the most resource commitment because it involves the nuts-and-bolts work of scientific research. In numerous industries (for instance, genetics engineering, pharmaceuticals, information technology, or cosmetics), an organization's expertise in basic research is the key to a sustainable competitive advantage. However, not every organization requires this extensive commitment to scientific research to achieve high performance levels. Instead, many depend on product development strategies. Although this strategy also requires a significant resource investment, it's not in areas associated with scientific research. Instead, the organization takes existing technology and improves on it or applies it in new ways, just as Procter & Gamble did when it applied tartar-fighting knowledge to pet food products. Both of these first two strategic approaches to innovation (basic scientific research and product development) can help an organization achieve high levels of differentiation, which can be a significant source of competitive advantage.

Finally, the last strategic approach to innovation emphasis is a focus on process development. Using this strategy, an organization looks for ways to improve and enhance its work processes. The organization innovates new and improved ways for employees to do their work in all organizational areas. This innovation strategy can lead to lower costs, which, as we know, also can be a significant source of competitive advantage.

Once managers have determined the focus of their innovation efforts, they must decide their innovation timing strategy. Some organizations want to be the first with innovations whereas others are content to follow or mimic the innovations. An organization that's first to bring a product innovation to the market or to use a new process innovation is called a **first mover**. Being a

Advantages	Disadvantages
• Reputation for being innovative and industry leader • Cost and learning benefits • Control over scarce resources and keeping competitors from having access to them • Opportunity to begin building customer relationships and customer loyalty	• Uncertainty over exact direction technology and market will go • Risk of competitors imitating innovations • Financial and strategic risks • High development costs

EXHIBIT 9-8

First-Mover Advantages and Disadvantages

first mover has certain strategic advantages and disadvantages as shown in Exhibit 9-8. Some organizations pursue this route, hoping to develop a sustainable competitive advantage. Others have successfully developed a sustainable competitive advantage by being the followers in the industry. They let the first movers pioneer the innovations and then mimic their products or processes. Which approach managers choose depends on their organization's innovation philosophy and specific resources and capabilities.

Let's Get Real:

My Response *to A Manager's Dilemma, page 224*

We need to get our strategic leaders together to analyze our SWOT to see how we can leverage ourselves in this marketplace. Since we don't have experience with iPhones, we need to gain expertise in that area—the technical area, perhaps tapping into our current global technological network. Action steps include:

- Forming a focus group of our core users to see how they would use the iPhone (if at all)
  - Do our current customers (teens) use iPhones and how can we retain their loyalty in the future?
- Examining how other companies are bringing games/applications to the iPhone
- Testing games with heavy iPhone users to see what appeals to them
  - Are iPhone users looking for convenience and are they in the working environment?

What Would You Do?

Sid Gokhale
President
Dowden Custom Media
Montvale, NJ

CHAPTER SUMMARY
by Learning Outcomes

LEARNING OUTCOME 9.1 **Explain** strategic management and explain why it's important.

Strategic management is what managers do to develop the organization's strategies. Strategies are the plans for how the organization will do whatever it's in business to do, how it will compete successfully, and how it will attract and satisfy its customers in order to achieve its goals. A business model is how a company is going to make money. Strategic management is important for three reasons. First, it makes a difference in how well organizations perform. Second, it's important for helping managers cope with continually changing situations. Finally, strategic management helps coordinate and focus employee efforts on what's important.

LEARNING OUTCOME 9.2 **Explain** what managers do during the six steps of the strategic management process.

The six steps in the strategic management process encompass strategy planning, implementation, and evaluation. These steps include the following: (1) identify the current mission, goals, and strategies; (2) do an external analysis; (3) do an internal analysis (steps 2 and 3 collectively are known as SWOT analysis); (4) formulate strategies; (5) implement strategies; and (6) evaluate strategies. Strengths are any activities the organization does well or unique resources that it has. Weaknesses are activities the organization doesn't do well or resources it needs but doesn't have. Opportunities are positive trends in the external environment. Threats are negative trends.

LEARNING OUTCOME 9.3 **Describe** the three types of corporate strategies.

A growth strategy is when an organization expands the number of markets served or products offered, either through current or new businesses. The types of growth strategies include concentration, vertical integration (backward and forward), horizontal integration, and diversification (related and unrelated). A stability strategy is when an organization makes no significant changes in what it's doing. Both renewal strategies—retrenchment and turnaround—address organizational weaknesses that are leading to performance declines. The BCG matrix is a way to analyze a company's portfolio of businesses by looking at a business's market share and its industry's anticipated growth rate. The four categories of the BCG matrix are cash cows, stars, question marks, and dogs.

LEARNING OUTCOME 9.4 **Describe** competitive advantage and the competitive strategies organizations use to get it.

An organization's competitive advantage is what sets it apart, its distinctive edge. A company's competitive advantage becomes the basis for choosing an appropriate competitive strategy. Porter's five forces model assesses the five competitive forces that dictate the rules of competition in an industry: threat of new entrants, threat of substitutes, bargaining power of buyers, bargaining power of suppliers, and current rivalry. Porter's three competitive strategies are as follows: cost leadership (competing on the basis of having the lowest costs in the industry), differentiation (competing on the basis of having unique products that are widely valued by customers), and focus (competing in a narrow segment with either a cost advantage or a differentiation advantage).

Discuss current strategic management issues.

Managers face three current strategic management issues: strategic leadership, strategic flexibility, and important types of strategies for today's environment. Strategic leadership is the ability to anticipate, envision, maintain flexibility, think strategically, and work with others in the organization to initiate changes that will create a viable and valuable future for the organization and includes eight key dimensions. Strategic flexibility—that is, the ability to recognize major external environmental changes, to quickly commit resources, and to recognize when a strategic decision isn't working—is important because managers often face highly uncertain environments. Managers can use e-business strategies to reduce costs, to differentiate their firm's products and services, to target (focus on) specific customer groups, or to lower costs by standardizing certain office functions. Another important e-business strategy is the clicks-and-bricks strategy, which combines online and traditional stand-alone locations. Strategies managers can use to become more customer oriented include giving customers what they want, communicating effectively with them, and having a culture that emphasizes customer service. Strategies managers can use to become more innovative include deciding their organization's innovation emphasis (basic scientific research, product development, or process development) and its innovation timing (first mover or follower).

 PEARSON mymanagementlab

To check your understanding of learning outcomes 9.1 – 9.5 go to **mymanagementlab.com** and try the chapter questions.

REVIEW AND DISCUSSION QUESTIONS

1. Explain why strategic management is important.
2. Describe the six steps in the strategic management process.
3. How could the Internet be helpful to managers as they follow the steps in the strategic management process?
4. How might the process of strategy formulation, implementation, and evaluation differ for (a) large businesses, (b) small businesses, (c) not-for-profit organizations, and (d) global businesses?
5. Should ethical considerations be included in analyses of an organization's internal and external environments? Why or why not?
6. Describe the three major types of corporate strategies and how the BCG matrix is used to manage those corporate strategies.

7. Describe the role of competitive advantage and how Porter's competitive strategies help an organization develop competitive advantage.
8. "The concept of competitive advantage is as important for not-for-profit organizations as it is for for-profit organizations." Do you agree or disagree with this statement? Explain, using examples to make your case.
9. Explain why strategic leadership and strategic flexibility are important.
10. Describe e-business, customer service, and innovation strategies.

PREPARING FOR: My Career

ETHICS DILEMMA

"Nearly two weeks after the largest killer whale in captivity killed one of its trainers, SeaWorld Parks and Entertainment is still wrestling with the dilemma of what to do with its most prized asset." Orcas are big business. As the headline acts at SeaWorld parks in Orlando, San Diego, and San Antonio, they draw a combined 12.2 million visitors annually. And the animals represent a huge investment. "A killer whale can bring almost $10 million on the open market, and years of preparation are necessary for an orca to perform in a show."[39] What do you think? What ethical dilemmas are involved with this strategic decision about a valuable organizational asset? What factors would influence the decision? (Think in terms of the various stakeholders who might be affected by this decision.)

SKILLS EXERCISE

Developing Your
Business Planning Skill

About the Skill

An important step in starting a business or in determining a new strategic direction is preparing a business plan.[40] Not only does the business plan aid in thinking about what to do and how to do it but it can be a sound basis from which to obtain funding and resources.

Steps in Practicing the Skill

1. **Describe your company's background and purpose.** Provide the history of the company. Briefly describe the company's history and what this company does that's unique. Describe what your product or service will be, how you intend to market it, and what you need to bring your product or service to the market.

2. **Identify your short- and long-term goals.** What is your intended goal for this organization? Clearly, for a new company three broad objectives are relevant: creation, survival, and profitability. Specific objectives can include such things as sales, market share, product quality, employee morale, and social responsibility. Identify how you plan to achieve each objective, how you intend to determine whether you met the objective, and when you intend the objective to be met (e.g., short or long term).

3. **Do a thorough market analysis.** You need to convince readers that you understand what you are doing, what your market is, and what competitive pressures you'll face. In this analysis, you'll need to describe the overall market trends, the specific market you intend to compete in, and who the competitors are. In essence, in this section you'll perform your SWOT analysis.

4. **Describe your development and production emphasis.** Explain how you're going to produce your product or service. Include time frames from start to finish. Describe the difficulties you may encounter in this stage as well as how much you believe activities in this stage will cost. Provide an explanation of what decisions (e.g., make or buy?) you will face and what you intend to do.

5. **Describe how you'll market your product or service.** What is your selling strategy? How do you intend to reach your customers? In this section, you'll want to describe your product or service in terms of your competitive advantage and demonstrate how you'll exploit your competitors' weaknesses. In addition to the market analysis, you'll also want to provide sales forecasts in terms of the size of the market, how much of the market you can realistically capture, and how you'll price your product or service.

6. **Put together your financial statements.** What's your bottom line? Investors want to know this information. In the financial section, you'll need to provide projected profit-and-loss statements (income statements) for approximately three to five years. You'll also need to include a cash flow analysis as well as the company's projected balance sheets. In the financial section, you should also give thought to how much start-up costs will be as well as to developing a financial strategy—how you intend to use funds received from a financial institution and how you'll control and monitor the financial well-being of the company.

7. **Provide an overview of the organization and its management.** Identify the key executives, summarizing their education, experience, and any relevant qualifications. Identify their positions in the organization and their job roles. Explain how much salary they intend to earn initially. Identify others who may assist the organization's management (e.g., company lawyer, accountant, board of directors). This section should also include, if relevant, a section on how you intend to deal with employees. For example, how will employees be paid, what benefits will be offered, and how will employee performance be assessed?

8. **Describe the legal form of the business.** Identify the legal form of the business. For example, is it a sole proprietor, a partnership, a corporation? Depending on the legal form, you may need to provide information regarding equity positions, shares of stock issued, and the like.

9. **Identify the critical risks and contingencies facing the organization.** In this section you'll want to identify what you'll do if problems arise. For instance, if you don't meet sales forecasts, what then? Similar responses to such questions as problems with suppliers, inability to hire qualified employees, poor-quality products, and so on should be addressed. Readers want to see if you've anticipated potential problems and if you have contingency plans. This is the what-if section.

10. **Put the business plan together.** Using the information you've gathered from the previous nine steps, it's now time to put the business plan together into a well-organized document. A business plan should contain a cover page that shows the company name, address, contact person, and numbers at which the individual can be reached. The cover page should also contain the date the business was established and, if one exists, the company logo. The next page of the business plan should be a table of contents. Here you'll want to list and identify the location of each major section and subsection in the business plan. Remember to use proper outlining techniques. Next comes the executive summary, the first section the readers will actually read. Thus, it's one of the more critical elements of the business plan, because

if the executive summary is poorly done, readers may not read any further. In a two- to three-page summary, highlight information about the company, its management, its market and competition, the funds requested, how the funds will be used, financial history (if available), financial projections, and when investors can expect to get their money back (called the exit). Next come the main sections of your business plan; that is, the material you've researched and written about in steps 1 through 9. Close out the business plan with a section that summarizes the highlights of what you've just presented. Finally, if you have charts, exhibits, photographs, tables, and the like, you might want to include an appendix in the back of the business plan. If you do, remember to cross-reference this material to the relevant section of the report.

Practicing the Skill

You have a great idea for a business and need to create a business plan to present to a bank. Choose one of the following products or services and draft the part of your plan that describes how you will price and market it (see step 5).

1. Haircuts at home (you make house calls)
2. Olympic snowboarding computer game
3. Online apartment rental listing
4. Voice-activated house alarm

Now choose a different product or service from the list and identify critical risks and contingencies (see step 9).

WORKING TOGETHER
Team Exercise

Organizational mission statements. Are they a promise, a commitment, or just a bunch of hot air? Form small groups of three to four individuals and find examples of three different organizational mission statements. Your first task is to evaluate the mission statements. How do they compare to

the items listed in Exhibit 9-2? Would you describe each as an effective mission statement? Why or why not? How might you rewrite each mission statement to make it better? Your second task is to use the mission statements to describe the types of corporate and competitive strategies each organization might use to fulfill that mission statement. Explain your rationale for choosing each strategy.

MY TURN TO BE A MANAGER

- Do a personal SWOT analysis. Assess your personal strengths and weaknesses (skills, talents, abilities). What are you good at? What are you not so good at? What do you enjoy doing? What don't you enjoy doing? Then, identify career opportunities and threats by researching job prospects in the industry you're interested in. Look at trends and projections. You might want to check out the Bureau of Labor Statistics information on job prospects. Once you have all this information, write a specific career action plan. Outline five-year career goals and what you need to do to achieve those goals.

- Using current business periodicals, find two examples of each of the corporate and competitive strategies. Write a description of what these businesses are doing and how it represents that particular strategy.

- Pick five companies from the latest version of *Fortune*'s "Most Admired Companies" list. Research these companies and identify their (a) mission statement, (b) strategic goals, and (c) strategies being used.

- Steve's and Mary's suggested readings: Adrian Slywotzky and Richard Wise, *How to Grow When Markets*

Don't (Warner Business Books, 2003); Jim Collins, *Good to Great: Why Some Companies Make the Leap... and Others Don't* (Harper Business, 2001); Michael E. Porter, *On Competition* (Harvard Business School Press, 1998); James C. Collins and Jerry I. Porras, *Built to Last: Successful Habits of Visionary Companies* (Harper Business, 1994); and Gary Hamel and C. K. Prahalad, *Competing for the Future* (Harvard Business School Press, 1994).

- Customer service, e-business, and innovation strategies are particularly important to managers today. We described in the chapter specific ways that companies can pursue these strategies. Your task is to pick customer service, e-business, or innovation and find one example for each of the specific approaches in that category. For instance, if you choose customer service, find an example of (a) giving customers what they want, (b) communicating effectively with them, and (c) providing employees with customer service training. Write a report describing your examples.

- In your own words, write down three things you learned in this chapter about being a good manager.

- Self-knowledge can be a powerful learning tool. Go to mymanagementlab.com and complete these self-assessment exercises: How Well Do I Handle Ambiguity? How Creative Am I? How Well Do I Respond to Turbulent Change? Using the results of your assessments, identify personal strengths and weaknesses. What will you do to reinforce your strengths and improve your weaknesses?

CASE APPLICATION 1
Gaga Over Gaga

Just now in her mid-twenties, Lady Gaga has taken the music world by storm with a unique blend of business savvy, interesting hair and wardrobe choices, and a fabulous sound with a "spacey Euro vibe."[41] Five years ago, Lady Gaga did not exist. But the individual who is Lady Gaga, Stefani Germanotta, was waitressing and singing in drab and dingy New York clubs. She was ambitious and had bigger goals. After being signed and dropped from one label, Def Jam (turns out that may not have been the best decision by them), she joined forces with a hand-picked core team of creative advisers she called "Haus of Gaga." Behind all that glitz, glamour, and unusual fashion choices is a "case study of what it takes to succeed in the music business today."

Gaga's impact on the music world in the span of a year has been nothing short of phenomenal. Writing her own material, she's sold more than 10 million albums. Her debut album generated four No.1 songs. She also topped the digital sales chart in 2009 with 15.3 million tracks sold, most on iTunes. She's had more than 1 billion Web views. Some 3.8 million "Little Monsters"—Gaga's nickname for her fans—follow her on Twitter and she has over 6.4 million "fans" on Facebook. She was the most-Googled image in 2009. And then in recognition of the fact that she's been deemed worthy of the success she's had, she opened the Grammy's award show in early 2010 with music legend Sir Elton John. She "reigns over a brand that spans music, video, design, and marketing." One advertising executive said, "No other artist commands the kind of attention that Gaga does. If she does something with your brand, it's like *bam!*—a million eyeballs." For instance, together with MAC Cosmetics, she created a shade of Viva Glam lipstick that has raised $2.2 million for AIDS awareness—Viva Glam's most successful launch ever. What strategies has she used to navigate the turbulent industry and become a star?

Lady Gaga and her team of creative advisors crafted a strategy consisting of a unique persona, a 360-degree deal, and the use of digital media to achieve phenomenal success in the music industry and extreme loyalty from millions of Little Monsters to her brand that spans music, video, design, and marketing.

One important component to her success is her savvy awareness of the power of digital media and her exceptional ability to exploit it. "Her persona is built for the online generation." Even though much of Gaga's audience has got her music online legally for free, "being embedded on the Web can pay dividends in exposure and the loyalty of fans." Gaga keeps her Little Monsters engaged with personal musings and real-time thank-yous.

Another important aspect to Gaga's success is what's called in the music business the 360-degree deal. The major upheaval in the music industry over the last decade led major record companies to look for ways to replace declining revenues. In a 360-degree deal, a label invests more money upfront—on marketing, for example—but in return, gets a piece of merchandise sales, touring revenue, and other earnings artists usually kept for themselves. This arrangement has been wildly successful for Gaga.

Finally, Gaga's persona has been a calculated strategy. "Gaga's allure is that of a misfit run amok in the system, a role that has helped her cut across disparate subcultures, including teens, finicky hipsters and gays." Her look isn't considered shocking like it was say, for instance, when rockers Alice Cooper or Gene Simmons first appeared. It's unique and keeps her audiences eager to see what her next image might be.

Gaga is determined to not be a niche artist. However, her "now-trendy sound won't last forever." Her ability to remain a music industry mainstay will depend on her ability to evolve.

Discussion Questions

1. How is strategic management illustrated by this case story?

2. How might SWOT analysis be helpful to Lady Gaga as she and her advisors manage her career?

3. What competitive advantage do you think Lady Gaga is pursuing? How is she exploiting that competitive advantage?

4. Do you think Lady Gaga's success is due to external or internal factors or both? Explain.

5. What strategic implications does the suggestion that her ability to remain a music industry mainstay depends on her ability to evolve have?

CASE APPLICATION

Faded Signal

As the world's biggest maker of mobile phones, Nokia, the Finnish company, is a "powerhouse in Europe, Asia, and Latin America, with market shares regularly topping 30 percent."[42] However, in the United States, Nokia phones have lost popularity over the last few years. In March 2002, Nokia led the American market with 35 percent market share. By June of 2009, its share was only 7 percent. What happened and more importantly, what is Nokia doing about it?

As mobile phone usage skyrocketed, Nokia was the most popular choice. It was the "cool" phone—the one that everyone, from business executive to high school student to stay-at-home-mom wanted. In 2005, Nokia had just launched the N series, an innovative new line with a Web browser, video, music, and pictures in a single phone. That device moved Nokia a generation ahead in the race to build the first real smart phone. The "forecast for Nokia was as sunny and clear as an endless Finnish summer day." Then came Apple and its iPhone with its clever touch screen and sophisticated software and services. With rave reviews and a reputation for being cool, customers flocked to buy one. However, Nokia executives dismissed the iPhone, saying they were "unimpressed by its engineering."

Now, three years after Apple introduced the iPhone in 2007, Nokia still has no alternative. It did not anticipate changes in American consumer tastes, like flip phones or touch screens. Another major strategic blunder was that its models were based on a European communications standard called GSM when roughly half the United States market used the CDMA (code division multiple access) format. One former Nokia executive said, "Nokia, at the height of its success, decided not to adapt its phones for the U.S. market. That was a mistake and they're still trying to recover from this." An executive at a North American network operator said, "The attitude at Nokia was basically: Here is a phone. Do you want it? Nokia wouldn't play by the rules here, and they have paid a price." That arrogant attitude and the global economic slowdown have continued to hurt the company's sales and earnings.

Meanwhile, Nokia set up liaison offices in Atlanta, Dallas, Seattle, and Parsippany, New Jersey, cities where the top American operators have big business units. And it has recently revamped its U.S. operations to collaborate more closely with those major operators. For example, AT&T has begun billing its customers who use Nokia services, keeping those customers from receiving a second bill from Nokia. Best Buy began carrying a Nokia netbook, which is a model for its new collaborative strategy. Nokia also forged a deal with Qualcomm, the largest maker of mobile phone chips for CDMA devices in the United States. It also struck a deal with Microsoft to design Windows Office Mobile software applications for phones that use Nokia's Symbian operating system. Despite these efforts, however, some industry executives remain unimpressed. One analyst said, "They claim they get it and understand the U.S. market. But the execution still is not there." Mark Louison, president of Nokia's North American unit, who has a seat on Nokia's global management board, said, "In the past, we had a one-size-fits-all mentality that worked well on a global basis but did not help us in this market. That has changed now." The company recognized that its former strategy had not worked in North America and began trying to lay the groundwork for long-term success. Louison says, "Everything you see us doing is to build the broad set of capabilities to take us broader and deeper into the U.S. market."

Discussion Questions

1. What strategic mistakes did Nokia make in the U.S. market?
2. Why do you think a "smart" company makes "dumb" mistakes?
3. What strategies is Nokia using to revitalize its North American business?
4. How could Nokia have done better at using strategic management? What does this case story tell you about strategic management?

Planning Tools *and* Techniques Module

Managers in baseball team front offices have discovered certain factors dictate whether they can charge more for tickets— namely, weather reports, winning streaks, and a big factor: pitching matchups.[1] The San Francisco Giants are the first Major League Baseball team to try and ride these shifts in demand by repricing tickets daily, a technique known as dynamic pricing. How well does it work? In 2009, the Giants were able to earn an extra $500,000 in revenue from dynamic pricing. In 2010, revenues increased about 6 percent.

As this example shows, managers use planning tools and techniques to help their organizations be more efficient and effective. In this module, we discuss three categories of basic planning tools and techniques: techniques for assessing the environment, techniques for allocating resources, and contemporary planning techniques.

Techniques for Assessing the Environment

Leigh Knopf, former senior manager for strategic planning at the AICPA, says that many larger accounting firms have set up external analysis departments to "study the wider environment in which they, and their clients, operate." These organizations have recognized that, "What happens in India in today's environment may have an impact on an American accounting firm in North Dakota."[2] In our description of the strategic management process in Chapter 9, we discussed the importance of assessing the organization's environment. Three techniques help managers do that: environmental scanning, forecasting, and benchmarking.

Environmental Scanning

How important is environmental scanning? While looking around on competitor Google's company Web site, Bill Gates found a help-wanted page with descriptions of all the open jobs. What piqued his interest, however, was that many of these posted job qualifications were identical to Microsoft's job requirements. He began to wonder why Google—a Web search company—would be posting job openings for software engineers with backgrounds that "had nothing to do with web searches and everything to do with Microsoft's core business of operating-system design, compiler optimization, and distributed-systems architecture." Gates e-mailed an urgent message to some of his top executives saying that Microsoft had better be on its toes because it sure looked like Google was preparing to move into being more of a software company.[3]

How can managers become aware of significant environmental changes such as a new law in Germany permitting shopping for "tourist items" on Sunday; the increased trend of counterfeit consumer products in South Africa; the precipitous decline in the working-age populations in Japan, Germany, Italy, and Russia; or the decrease in family size in Mexico? Managers in both small and large organizations use **environmental scanning**, which is the screening of large amounts of information to anticipate and interpret changes in the environment. Extensive environmental scanning is likely to reveal issues and concerns that could affect an organization's current or planned activities. Research has shown that companies that use environmental scanning have higher performance.[4] Organizations that don't keep on top of environmental changes are likely to experience the opposite!

COMPETITOR INTELLIGENCE. A fast-growing area of environmental scanning is competitor intelligence.[5] It's a process by which organizations gather information about their competitors and get answers to questions such as Who are they? What are they doing? How will what they're doing affect us? Let's look at an example of how one organization used competitor intelligence in its planning. Dun & Bradstreet (D&B), a leading provider of business information, has an active business intelligence division. The division manager received a call from an assistant vice president for sales in one of the company's geographic territories. This person had been on a sales call with a major customer and the customer happened to mention in passing that another company had visited and made a major presentation about its services. What was interesting was that, although D&B had plenty of competitors, this particular company wasn't one of them. The manager gathered together a team that sifted through dozens of sources (research services, Internet, personal contacts, and other external sources) and quickly became convinced that there was something to this; that this company was "aiming its guns right at us." Managers at D&B jumped into action to develop plans to counteract this competitive attack.[6]

Competitor intelligence experts suggest that 80 percent of what managers need to know about competitors can be found out from their own employees, suppliers, and customers.[7] Competitor intelligence doesn't have to involve spying. Advertisements, promotional materials, press releases, reports filed with government agencies, annual reports, want ads, newspaper reports, and industry studies are examples of readily accessible sources of information. Attending trade shows and debriefing the company's salesforce can be other good sources of competitor information. Many firms regularly buy competitors' products and have their own engineers study them (through a process called *reverse engineering*) to learn about new technical innovations. In addition, the Internet has opened up vast sources of competitor intelligence as many corporate Web pages include new product information and other press releases.

Managers need to be careful about the way competitor information is gathered to prevent any concerns about whether it's legal or ethical. For instance, at Procter & Gamble, executives hired competitive intelligence firms to spy on its competitors in the hair-care business. At least one of these firms misrepresented themselves to competitor Unilever's employees, trespassed at Unilever's hair-care headquarters in Chicago, and went through trash dumpsters to gain information. When P&G's CEO found out, he immediately fired the

individuals responsible and apologized to Unilever.[8] Competitor intelligence becomes illegal corporate spying when it involves the theft of proprietary materials or trade secrets by any means. The Economic Espionage Act makes it a crime in the United States to engage in economic espionage or to steal a trade secret.[9] The difficult decisions about competitive intelligence arise because often there's a fine line between what's considered *legal and ethical* and what's considered *legal but unethical*. Although the top manager at one competitive intelligence firm contends that 99.9 percent of intelligence gathering is legal, there's no question that some people or companies will go to any lengths—some unethical—to get information about competitors.[10]

GLOBAL SCANNING. One type of environmental scanning that's particularly important is global scanning. Because world markets are complex and dynamic, managers have expanded the scope of their scanning efforts to gain vital information on global forces that might affect their organizations.[11] The value of global scanning to managers, of course, largely depends on the extent of the organization's global activities. For a company that has significant global interests, global scanning can be quite valuable. For instance, Sealed Air Corporation of Elmwood Park, New Jersey—you've probably seen and used its most popular product, Bubble Wrap—tracks global demographic changes. Company managers found that as countries move from agriculture-based societies to industrial ones, the population tends to eat out more and favor prepackaged foods, which translates to more sales of its food packaging products.[12]

Because the sources that managers use for scanning the domestic environment are too limited for global scanning, managers must globalize their perspectives. For instance, they can subscribe to information clipping services that review world newspapers and business periodicals and provide summaries of desired information. Also, there are numerous electronic services that provide topic searches and automatic updates in global areas of special interest to managers.

Forecasting

The second technique managers can use to assess the environment is forecasting. Forecasting is an important part of planning and managers need forecasts that will allow them to predict future events effectively and in a timely manner. Environmental scanning establishes the basis for **forecasts**, which are predictions of outcomes. Virtually any component in an organization's environment can be forecasted. Let's look at how managers forecast and the effectiveness of those forecasts.

---

environmental scanning
The screening of large amounts of information to anticipate and interpret changes in the environment

competitor intelligence
Environmental scanning activity by which organizations gather information about competitors

forecasts
Predictions of outcome

FORECASTING TECHNIQUES. Forecasting techniques fall into two categories: quantitative and qualitative. **Quantitative forecasting** applies a set of mathematical rules to a series of past data to predict outcomes. These techniques are preferred when managers have sufficient hard data that can be used. **Qualitative forecasting**, in contrast, uses the judgment and opinions of knowledgeable individuals to predict outcomes. Qualitative techniques typically are used when precise data are limited or hard to obtain. Exhibit PM-1 describes some popular forecasting techniques.

Today, many organizations collaborate on forecasts using an approach known as CPFR, which stands for collaborative planning, forecasting, and replenishment.[13] CPFR provides a framework for the flow of information, goods, and services between retailers and manufacturers. Each organization relies on its own data to calculate a demand forecast for a particular product. If their respective forecasts differ by a certain amount (say 10%), the retailer and manufacturer exchange data and written comments until they arrive at a more accurate forecast. Such collaborative forecasting helps both organizations do a better job of planning.

FORECASTING EFFECTIVENESS. The goal of forecasting is to provide managers with information that will facilitate decision making. Despite its importance to planning, managers have had mixed success with it.[14] For instance, prior to a holiday weekend at the Procter & Gamble factory in Lima, Ohio, managers were preparing to shut down the facility early so as not to have to pay employees for just sitting around and to give them some extra time off. The move seemed to make sense since an analysis of purchase orders and historical sales trends indicated that the factory had already produced enough cases of Liquid Tide detergent to meet laundry demand over the holiday. However, managers got a real surprise. One of the company's largest retail customers placed a sizable—and unforeseen—order. They had to reopen the plant, pay the workers overtime, and schedule emergency shipments to meet the retailer's request.[15] As this example shows, managers' forecasts aren't always accurate. In a survey of financial managers in the United States, United Kingdom, France, and Germany, 84 percent of the respondents said their financial forecasts were inaccurate by 5 percent or more; 54 percent of the respondents reported inaccuracy of 10 percent or more.[16] Results of another survey showed that 39 percent of financial executives said they could reliably forecast revenues only one quarter out. Even more disturbing is that 16 percent of those executives said they were "in the dark" about revenue forecasts.[17] But it is

EXHIBIT **PM-1**	Technique	Description	Application
Forecasting Techniques	**Quantitative**		
	Time series analysis	Fits a trend line to a mathematical equation and projects into the future by means of this equation	Predicting next quarter's sales on the basis of 4 years of previous sales data
	Regression models	Predicts one variable on the basis of known or assumed other variables	Seeking factors that will predict a certain level of sales (e.g., price, advertising expenditures)
	Econometric models	Uses a set of regression equations to simulate segments of the economy	Predicting change in car sales as a result of changes in tax laws
	Economic indicators	Uses one or more economic indicators to predict a future state of the economy	Using change in GNP to predict discretionary income
	Substitution effect	Uses a mathematical formula to predict how, when, and under what circumstances a new product or technology will replace an existing one	Predicting the effect of DVD players on the sale of VHS players
	Qualitative		
	Jury of opinion	Combines and averages the opinions of experts	Polling the company's human resource managers to predict next year's college recruitment needs
	Salesforce composition	Combines estimates from field sales personnel of customers' expected purchases	Predicting next year's sales of industrial lasers
	Customer evaluation	Combines estimates from established customers' purchases	Surveying major car dealers by a car manufacturer to determine types and quantities of products desired

important to try to make forecasting as effective as possible, because research shows that a company's forecasting ability can be a distinctive competence.[18] Here are some suggestions for making forecasting more effective.[19]

First, it's important to understand that forecasting techniques are most accurate when the environment is not rapidly changing. The more dynamic the environment, the more likely managers are to forecast ineffectively. Also, forecasting is relatively ineffective in predicting nonseasonal events such as recessions, unusual occurrences, discontinued operations, and the actions or reactions of competitors. Next, use simple forecasting methods. They tend to do as well as, and often better than, complex methods that may mistakenly confuse random data for meaningful information. For instance, at St. Louis–based Emerson Electric, chairman emeritus Chuck Knight found that forecasts developed as part of the company's planning process indicated that the competition wasn't just domestic anymore, but global. He didn't use any complex mathematical techniques to come to this conclusion but instead relied on the information already collected as part of his company's planning process. Next, look at involving more people in the process. At *Fortune* 100 companies, it's not unusual to have 1,000 to 5,000 managers providing forecasting input. These businesses are finding that as more people are involved in the process, the more the reliability of the outcomes improves.[20] Next, compare every forecast with "no change." A no change forecast is accurate approximately half the time. Next, use *rolling* forecasts that look 12 to 18 months ahead, instead of using a single, static forecast. These types of forecasts can help managers spot trends better and help their organizations be more adaptive in changing environments.[21] It's also important to not rely on a single forecasting method. Make forecasts with several models and average them, especially when making longer-range forecasts. Next, don't assume that you can accurately identify turning points in a trend. What is typically perceived as a significant turning point often turns out to be simply a random event. And, finally, remember that forecasting *is* a managerial skill and as such can be practiced and improved. Forecasting software has made the task somewhat less mathematically challenging, although the "number crunching" is only a small part of the activity. Interpreting the forecast and incorporating that information into planning decisions is the challenge facing managers.

Benchmarking

Suppose that you're a talented pianist or gymnast. To make yourself better, you want to learn from the best so you watch outstanding musicians or athletes for motions and techniques they use as they perform. That same approach is involved in the final technique for assessing the environment we're going to discuss—**benchmarking**, the search for the best practices among competitors or noncompetitors that lead to their superior performance.[22] Does benchmarking work? Studies show that users have achieved 69 percent faster growth and 45 percent greater productivity.[23]

The basic idea behind benchmarking is that managers can improve performance by analyzing and then copying the methods of the leaders in various fields. Organizations such as Nissan, Payless Shoe Source, the U.S. military, General Mills, United Airlines, and Volvo Construction Equipment have used benchmarking as a tool in improving performance. In fact, some companies have chosen some pretty unusual benchmarking partners! IBM studied Las Vegas casinos for ways to discourage employee theft. Many hospitals have benchmarked their admissions processes against Marriott Hotels. And Giordano Holdings Ltd., a Hong Kong–based manufacturer and retailer of mass-market casual wear, borrowed its "good quality, good value" concept from Marks & Spencer, used Limited Brands to benchmark its point-of-sales computerized information system, and modeled its simplified product offerings on McDonald's menu.[24]

What does benchmarking involve? Exhibit PM-2 illustrates the four steps typically used in benchmarking.

Techniques for Allocating Resources

Once an organization's goals have been established, it's important to determine how those goals are going to be accomplished. Before managers can organize and lead as goals are implemented, they must have **resources**, which are the assets of the organization (financial, physical, human, and intangible). How can managers allocate these resources effectively and efficiently so that organizational goals are met? Although managers can choose from a number of techniques for allocating resources (many of which are covered in courses on accounting, finance, and operations management), we'll discuss four techniques here: budgeting, scheduling, breakeven analysis, and linear programming.

quantitative forecasting
Forecasting that applies a set of mathematical rules to a series of past data to predict outcome

qualitative forecasting
Forecasting that uses the judgment and opinions of knowledgeable individuals to predict outcomes

benchmarking
The search for the best practices among competitors or noncompetitors that lead to their superior performance

resources
The assets of the organization including financial, physical, human, intangible, and structural/cultural

EXHIBIT PM-2

Steps in Benchmarking

Source: Based on Y. K. Shetty, "Aiming High: Competitive Benchmarking for Superior Performance," *Long Range Planning*, February 1993, p. 42.

Budgeting

Most of us have had some experience, as limited as it might be, with budgets. We probably learned at an early age that unless we allocated our "revenues" carefully, our weekly allowance was spent on "expenses" before the week was half over.

A **budget** is a numerical plan for allocating resources to specific activities. Managers typically prepare budgets for revenues, expenses, and large capital expenditures such as equipment. It's not unusual, though, for budgets to be used for improving time, space, and use of material resources. These types of budgets substitute nondollar numbers for dollar amounts. Such items as person-hours, capacity utilization, or units of production can be budgeted for daily, weekly, or monthly activities. Exhibit PM-3 describes the different types of budgets that managers might use.

Why are budgets so popular? Probably because they're applicable to a wide variety of organizations and work activities within organizations. We live in a world in which almost everything is expressed in monetary units. Dollars, rupees, pesos, euros, yuan, yen, and the like are used as a common measuring unit within a country. That's why monetary budgets are a useful tool for allocating resources and guiding work in such diverse departments as manufacturing and information systems or at various levels in an organization. Budgets are one planning technique that most managers, regardless of organizational level, use. It's an important managerial activity because it forces financial discipline and structure

EXHIBIT PM-3

Types of Budgets

Source: Based on R. S. Russell and B. W. Taylor III, *Production and Operations Management* (Upper Saddle River, NJ: Prentice Hall, 1995), p. 287.

- Collaborate and communicate.
- Be flexible.
- Goals should drive budgets—budgets should not determine goals.
- Coordinate budgeting throughout the organization.
- Use budgeting/planning software when appropriate.
- Remember that budgets are tools.
- Remember that profits result from smart management, not because you budgeted for them.

throughout the organization. However, many managers don't like preparing budgets because they feel the process is time consuming, inflexible, inefficient, and ineffective.[25] How can the budgeting process be improved? Exhibit PM-4 provides some suggestions. Organizations such as Texas Instruments, IKEA, Hendrick Motorsports, Volvo, and Svenska Handelsbanken have incorporated several of these suggestions as they revamped their budgeting processes.

Scheduling

Jackie is a manager at a Chico's store in San Francisco. Every week, she determines employees' work hours and the store area where each employee will be working. If you observed any group of supervisors or department managers for a few days, you would see them doing much the same—allocating resources by detailing what activities have to be done, the order in which they are to be completed, who is to do each, and when they are to be completed. These managers are **scheduling**. In this section, we'll review some useful scheduling devices including Gantt charts, load charts, and PERT network analysis.

GANTT CHARTS. The **Gantt chart** was developed during the early 1900s by Henry Gantt, an associate of Frederick Taylor, the scientific management expert. The idea behind a Gantt chart is simple. It's essentially a bar graph with time on the horizontal axis and the activities to be scheduled on the vertical axis. The bars show output, both planned and actual, over a period of time. The Gantt chart visually shows when tasks are supposed to be done and compares those projections with the actual progress on each task. It's a simple but important device that lets managers detail easily what has yet to be done to complete a job or project and to assess whether an activity is ahead of, behind, or on schedule.

Exhibit PM-5 depicts a simplified Gantt chart for book production developed by a manager in a publishing company. Time is expressed in months across the top of the chart. The major work activities are listed down the left side. Planning involves deciding what activities need to be done to get the book finished, the order in which those activities need to be completed, and the time that should be allocated to each activity. Where a box sits within a time frame reflects its planned sequence. The shading represents actual progress. The chart also serves as a control tool because the manager can see deviations from the plan. In this example, both the design of the cover and the review of first pages are running behind schedule. Cover design is

budget
A numerical plan for allocating resources to specific activities

scheduling
Detailing what activities have to be done, the order in which they are to be completed, who is to do each, and when they are to be completed

Gantt chart
A scheduling chart developed by Henry Gantt that shows actual and planned output over a period of time

about three weeks behind (note that there has been no actual progress—shown by blue color line—as of the reporting date), and first pages review is about two weeks behind schedule (note that as of the report date, actual progress—shown by blue color line—is about six weeks, out of a goal of completing in two months). Given this information, the manager might need to take some action to either make up for the two lost weeks or to ensure that no further delays will occur. At this point, the manager can expect that the book will be published at least two weeks later than planned if no action is taken.

LOAD CHARTS. A **load chart** is a modified Gantt chart. Instead of listing activities on the vertical axis, load charts list either entire departments or specific resources. This arrangement allows managers to plan and control capacity utilization. In other words, load charts schedule capacity by work areas.

For example, Exhibit PM-6 shows a load chart for six production editors at the same publishing company. Each editor supervises the production and design of several books. By reviewing a load chart, the executive editor, who supervises the six production editors, can see who is free to take on a new book. If everyone is fully scheduled, the executive editor might decide not to accept any new projects, to accept new projects and delay others, to make the editors work overtime, or to employ more production editors. As this exhibit shows, only Antonio and Maurice are completely scheduled for the next six months. The other editors have some unassigned time and might be able to accept new projects or be available to help other editors who get behind.

PERT NETWORK ANALYSIS. Gantt and load charts are useful as long as the activities being scheduled are few in number and independent of each other. But what if a manager had to plan a large project such as a departmental reorganization, the implementation of a cost-reduction program, or the development of a new product that required coordinating inputs from marketing, manufacturing, and product design? Such projects require coordinating hundreds and even thousands of activities, some of which must be done simultaneously and some of which can't begin until preceding activities have been completed. If you're constructing a building, you obviously can't start putting up the walls until the foundation is laid. How can managers schedule such a complex project? The program evaluation and review technique (PERT) is highly appropriate for such projects.

A **PERT network** is a flowchart diagram that depicts the sequence of activities needed to complete a project and the time or costs associated with each activity. With a PERT network, a manager must think through what has to be done, determine which events depend on one another, and identify potential trouble spots. PERT also makes it easy to compare the effects alternative actions might have on scheduling and costs. Thus, PERT allows managers to monitor a project's progress, identify possible bottlenecks, and shift resources as necessary to keep the project on schedule.

To understand how to construct a PERT network, you need to know four terms. **Events** are end points that represent the completion of major activities. **Activities** represent the time or resources required to progress from one event to another. **Slack time** is the amount of time an individual activity can be delayed without delaying the whole project. The **critical path** is the longest or most time-consuming sequence of events and activities in a PERT network. Any delay in completing events on this path would delay completion of the entire project. In other words, activities on the critical path have zero slack time.

Developing a PERT network requires that a manager identify all key activities needed to complete a project, rank them in order of occurrence, and estimate each activity's completion time. Exhibit PM-7 explains the steps in this process.

Most PERT projects are complicated and include numerous activities. Such complicated computations can be done with specialized PERT software. However, let's work through a simple example. Assume that you're the superintendent at a construction company and have been assigned to oversee the construction of an office building. Because time really is money in your business, you must determine how long it will take to get the building completed. You've determined the

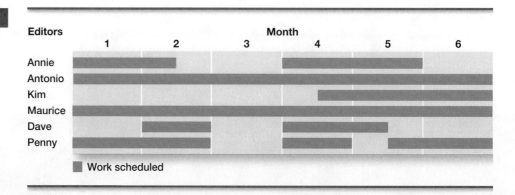

EXHIBIT PM-6
A Load Chart

1. *Identify every significant activity that must be achieved for a project to be completed.* The accomplishment of each activity results in a set of events or outcomes.
2. *Determine the order in which these events must be completed.*
3. *Diagram the flow of activities from start to finish, identifying each activity and its relationship to all other activities.* Use circles to indicate events and arrows to represent activities. This results in a flowchart diagram called a PERT network.
4. *Compute a time estimate for completing each activity.* This is done with a weighted average that uses an *optimistic* time estimate (t_o) of how long the activity would take under ideal conditions, a *most likely* estimate (t_m) of the time the activity normally should take, and a *pessimistic* estimate (t_p) that represents the time that an activity should take under the worst possible conditions. The formula for calculating the expected time (t_e) is then

$$t_e = \frac{t_o + 4t_m + t_p}{6}$$

5. *Using the network diagram that contains time estimates for each activity, determine a schedule for the start and finish dates of each activity and for the entire project.* Any delays that occur along the critical path require the most attention because they can delay the whole project.

EXHIBIT PM-7

Steps in Developing a PERT Network

specific activities and events. Exhibit PM-8 outlines the major events in the construction project and your estimate of the expected time to complete each. Exhibit PM-9 shows the actual PERT network based on the data in Exhibit PM-8. You've also calculated the length of time that each path of activities will take:

A-B-C-D-I-J-K (44 weeks)
A-B-C-D-G-H-J-K (50 weeks)
A-B-C-E-G-H-J-K (47 weeks)
A-B-C-F-G-H-J-K (47 weeks)

Your PERT network shows that if everything goes as planned, the total project completion time will be 50 weeks. This is calculated by tracing the project's critical path (the longest sequence of activities): A-B-C-D-G-H-J-K and adding up the times. You know that any delay in completing the events on this path would delay the completion of the entire project. Taking six weeks instead of four to put in the floor covering and paneling (Event I) would have no effect on the final completion date. Why? Because that event isn't on the critical path. However, taking seven weeks instead of

Event	Description	Expected Time (in weeks)	Preceding Event
A	Approve design and get permits	10	None
B	Dig subterranean garage	6	A
C	Erect frame and siding	14	B
D	Construct floor	6	C
E	Install windows	3	C
F	Put on roof	3	C
G	Install internal wiring	5	D, E, F
H	Install elevator	5	G
I	Put in floor covering and paneling	4	D
J	Put in doors and interior decorative trim	3	I, H
K	Turn over to building management group	1	J

EXHIBIT PM-8

Events and Activities in Constructing an Office Building

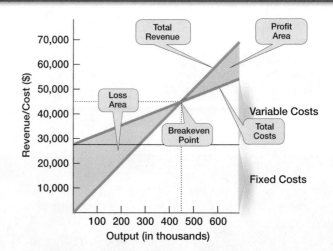

six to dig the subterranean garage (Event B) would likely delay the total project. A manager who needed to get back on schedule or to cut the 50-week completion time would want to concentrate on those activities along the critical path that could be completed faster. How might the manager do this? He or she could look to see if any of the other activities *not* on the critical path had slack time in which resources could be transferred to activities that *were* on the critical path.

Breakeven Analysis

Managers at Glory Foods want to know how many units of their new sensibly seasoned canned vegetables must be sold in order to break even—that is, the point at which total revenue is just sufficient to cover total costs. **Breakeven analysis** is a widely used resource allocation technique to help managers determine breakeven point.[26]

Breakeven analysis is a simple calculation, yet it's valuable to managers because it points out the relationship between revenues, costs, and profits. To compute breakeven point *(BE)*, a manager needs to know the unit price of the product being sold *(P)*, the variable cost per unit *(VC)*, and total fixed costs *(TFC)*. An organization breaks even when its total revenue is just enough to equal its total costs. But total cost has two parts: fixed and variable. *Fixed costs* are expenses that do not change regardless of volume. Examples include insurance premiums, rent, and property taxes.

Variable costs change in proportion to output and include raw materials, labor costs, and energy costs.

Breakeven point can be computed graphically or by using the following formula:

$$BE = \frac{TFC}{P - VC}$$

This formula tells us that (1) total revenue will equal total cost when we sell enough units at a price that covers all variable unit costs, and (2) the difference between price and variable costs, when multiplied by the number of units sold, equals the fixed costs. Let's work through an example.

Assume that Randy's Photocopying Service charges $0.10 per photocopy. If fixed costs are $27,000 a year and variable costs are $0.04 per copy, Randy can compute his breakeven point as follows: $27,000 ÷ ($0.10 − $0.04) = 450,000 copies, or when annual revenues are $45,000 (450,000 copies × $0.10). This same relationship is shown graphically in Exhibit PM-10.

As a planning tool, breakeven analysis could help Randy set his sales goal. For example, he could determine his profit goal and then calculate what sales level is needed to reach that goal. Breakeven analysis could also tell Randy how much volume has to increase to break even if he's currently operating at a loss or how much volume he can afford to lose and still break even.

Linear Programming

Maria Sanchez manages a manufacturing plant that produces two kinds of cinnamon-scented home fragrance products: wax candles and a woodchip potpourri sold in bags. Business is good, and she can sell all of the products she can produce. Her dilemma: Given that the bags of potpourri and the wax candles are manufactured in the same facility, how many of each product should she produce to maximize profits? Maria can use **linear programming** to solve her resource allocation problem.

Although linear programming can be used here, it can't be applied to all resource allocation problems because it requires that resources be limited, that the goal be outcome optimization, that resources can be combined in alternative ways to produce a number of output mixes, and that a linear relationship exist between variables (a change in one variable must be accompanied by an exactly proportional change in the other).[27] For Maria's business, that last condition would be met if it took exactly twice the amount of raw materials and hours of labor to produce two of a given home fragrance product as it took to produce one.

What kinds of problems can be solved with linear programming? Some applications include selecting transportation routes that minimize shipping costs, allocating a limited advertising budget among various product brands, making the optimal assignment of people among projects, and determining how much of each product to make with a limited number of resources. Let's return to Maria's problem and see how linear programming could help her solve it. Fortunately, her problem is relatively simple, so we can solve it rather quickly. For complex linear programming problems, managers can use computer software programs designed specifically to help develop optimizing solutions.

First, we need to establish some facts about Maria's business. She has computed the profit margins on her home fragrance products at $10 for a bag of potpourri and $18 for a scented candle. These numbers establish the basis for Maria to be able to express her *objective function* as maximum profit $= \$10P + \$18S$, where P is the number of bags of potpourri produced and S is the number of scented candles produced. The objective function is simply a mathematical equation that can predict the outcome of all proposed alternatives. In addition, Maria knows how much time each fragrance product must spend in production and the monthly production capacity (1,200 hours in manufacturing and 900 hours in assembly) for manufacturing and assembly. (See Exhibit PM-11.) The production capacity numbers act as *constraints* on her overall capacity. Now Maria can establish her constraint equations:

$$2P + 4S \leq 1{,}200$$
$$2P + 2S \leq 900$$

Of course, Maria can also state that $P \geq 0$ and $S \geq 0$ because neither fragrance product can be produced in a volume less than zero.

Maria has graphed her solution in Exhibit PM-12. The shaded area represents the options that don't exceed the capacity of either department. What does this mean? Well, let's look first at the manufacturing constraint line BE. We know that total manufacturing capacity is 1,200 hours, so if Maria decides to produce all potpourri bags, the maximum she can produce is 600 (1,200 hours ÷ 2 hours required to produce a bag of potpourri). If she decides to produce all scented candles, the maximum she can produce is 300 (1,200 hours ÷ 4 hours required to produce a scented candle). The other constraint Maria faces is that of assembly, shown by line DF. If Maria decides to produce all potpourri bags, the maximum she can assemble is 450 (900 hours production capacity ÷ 2 hours required to assemble). Likewise, if Maria decides to produce all scented candles, the maximum she can assemble is also 450 because the scented candles also take 2 hours to assemble. The constraints imposed by these capacity limits establish Maria's *feasibility region*. Her optimal resource allocation will be defined at one of the corners within this feasibility region. Point C provides the maximum profits within the constraints stated. How do we know? At point A, profits would be 0 (no production of either potpourri bags or scented candles). At point B, profits would be $5,400 (300 scented candles

Department	Number of Hours Required (per unit)		Monthly Production Capacity (in hours)
	Potpourri Bags	Scented Candles	
Manufacturing	2	4	1,200
Assembly	2	2	900
Profit per unit	$10	$18	

EXHIBIT PM-11

Production Data for Cinnamon-Scented Products

× $18 profit and 0 potpourri bags produced = $5,400). At point D, profits would be $4,500 (450 potpourri bags produced × $10 profit and 0 scented candles produced = $4,500). At point C, however, profits would be $5,700 (150 scented candles produced × $18 profit and 300 potpourri bags produced × $10 profit = $5,700).

Contemporary Planning Techniques

Lowest home mortgage rates since 1950s. H1N1 flu pandemic. Chemical/biological attacks. Recession/inflation worries. Category 4 or 5 hurricanes. Changing competition. Today's managers face the challenges of planning in an environment that's both dynamic and complex. Two planning techniques that are appropriate for this type of environment are project management and scenarios. Both techniques emphasize *flexibility*, something that's important to making planning more effective and efficient in this type of organizational environment.

Project Management

Different types of organizations, from manufacturers such as Coleman and Boeing to software design firms such as SAS and Microsoft, use projects. A **project** is a one-time-only set of activities that has a definite beginning and ending point in time.[28] Projects vary in size and scope—from Boston's "big dig" downtown traffic tunnel to a sorority's holiday formal. **Project management** is the task of getting a project's activities done on time, within budget, and according to specifications.[29]

More and more organizations are using project management because the approach fits well with the need for flexibility and rapid response to perceived market opportunities. When organizations undertake projects that are unique, have specific deadlines, contain complex interrelated tasks requiring specialized skills, and are temporary in nature, these projects often do not fit into the standardized planning procedures that guide an organization's other routine work activities. Instead, managers use project management techniques to effectively and efficiently accomplish the project's goals. What does the project management process involve?

PROJECT MANAGEMENT PROCESS. In the typical project, work is done by a project team whose members are assigned from their respective work areas to the project and who report to a project manager. The project manager coordinates the project's activities with other departments. When the project team accomplishes its goals, it disbands and members move on to other projects or back to their permanent work area.

The essential features of the project planning process are shown in Exhibit PM-13. The process begins by clearly defining the project's goals. This step is necessary because the manager and the team members need to know what's expected. All activities in the project and the resources needed to do them must then be identified. What materials and labor are needed to complete the project? This step may be time-consuming and complex, particularly if the project is unique and the managers have no history or experience with similar projects. Once the activities have been identified, the sequence of completion needs to be determined. What activities must be completed before others can begin? Which can be done simultaneously? This step often uses flowchart diagrams such as a Gantt chart, a load chart, or a PERT network. Next, the project activities need to be scheduled. Time estimates for each activity are done, and these estimates are used to develop an overall project schedule and completion date. Then the project schedule

Source: Based on R. S. Russell and B. W. Taylor III, *Production and Operations Management* (Upper Saddle River, NJ: Prentice Hall, 1995), p. 287.

is compared to the goals, and any necessary adjustments are made. If the project completion time is too long, the manager might assign more resources to critical activities so they can be completed faster.

Today, the project management process can take place online as a number of Web-based software packages are available. These packages cover aspects from project accounting and estimating to project scheduling and bug and defect tracking.[30]

THE ROLE OF THE PROJECT MANAGER. The temporary nature of projects makes managing them different from, say, overseeing a production line or preparing a weekly tally of costs on an ongoing basis. The one-shot nature of the work makes project managers the organizational equivalent of a hired gunman. There's a job to be done. It has to be defined—in detail. And the project manager is responsible for how it's done. At J.B. Hunt Transport Services, the head of project management trains project managers on both technical and interpersonal skills so that they know how to "... run a project effectively."[31]

Even with the availability of sophisticated computerized and online scheduling programs and other project management tools, the role of project manager remains difficult because he or she is managing people who typically are still assigned to their permanent work areas. The only real influence project managers have is their communication skills and their power of persuasion. To make matters worse, team members seldom work on just one project. They're usually assigned to two or three at any given time. So project managers end up competing with each other to focus a worker's attention on his or her particular project.

Scenario Planning

During the 1990s, business was so good at Colgate-Palmolive that then-chairman Reuben Mark worried about what "might go wrong." He installed an "early-warning system

to flag problems before they blew up into company-wrecking crises." For instance, a red-flag report alerted Mark "that officials in Baddi, India, had questions about how a plant treated wastewater." Mark's response was to quickly assign an engineering team to check it out and prevent potential problems.[32]

We already know how important it is that today's managers do what Reuben Mark was doing—monitor and assess the external environment for trends and changes. As they assess the environment, issues and concerns that could affect their organization's current or planned operations are likely to be revealed. All of these issues won't be equally important, so it's usually necessary to focus on a limited set that are most important and to develop scenarios based on each.

A **scenario** is a consistent view of what the future is likely to be. Developing scenarios also can be described as *contingency planning*; that is, if this event happens, then we need to take these actions. If, for instance, environmental scanning reveals increasing interest by the U.S. Congress for raising the national minimum wage, managers at Subway could create multiple scenarios to assess the possible consequences of such an action. What would be the implications for its labor costs if the minimum wage was raised to $10 an hour? How about $12 an hour? What effect would these changes have on the chain's bottom line? How might competitors respond? Different assumptions lead to different outcomes. The intent of scenario planning is not to try to predict the future but to reduce uncertainty by playing out potential situations under different specified conditions.[33] Subway could, for example, develop a set of scenarios ranging from optimistic to pessimistic in terms of the minimum wage issue. It would then be prepared to implement new strategies to get and keep a competitive advantage. An expert in scenario planning said, "Just the process of doing scenarios causes executives to rethink and clarify the essence of the business environment in ways they almost certainly have never done before."[34]

---

project
A one-time-only set of activities that has a definite beginning and ending point in time

project management
The task of getting a project's activities done on time, within budget, and according to specifications

scenario
A consistent view of what the future is likely to be

Although scenario planning is useful in anticipating events that *can be* anticipated, it's difficult to forecast random events—the major surprises and aberrations that can't be foreseen. For instance, an outbreak of deadly and devastating tornadoes in southwest Missouri on January 7, 2008, was a scenario that could be anticipated. The disaster recovery planning that took place after the storms was effective because this type of scenario had been experienced before. A response had already been planned and people knew what to do. But the planning challenge comes from those totally random and unexpected events. For instance, the 9/11 terrorist attacks in New York and Washington, D.C., were random, unexpected, and a total shock to many organizations. Scenario planning was of little use because no one could have envisioned this scenario. As difficult as it may be for managers to anticipate and deal with these random events, they're not totally vulnerable to the consequences.

One suggestion that has been identified by risk experts as particularly important is to have an early warning system in place. (A similar idea is the tsunami warning systems in the Pacific and in Alaska, which alert officials to potentially dangerous tsunamis and give them time to take action.) Early warning indicators for organizations can give managers advance notice of potential problems and changes—such as it did Reuben Mark at Colgate-Palmolive—so they, too, can take action. Then, managers need to have appropriate responses (plans) in place if these unexpected events occur.

Planning tools and techniques can help managers prepare confidently for the future. But they should remember that all the tools we've described in this chapter are just that—tools. They will never replace the manager's skills and capabilities in using the information gained to develop effective and efficient plans.

REVIEW AND DISCUSSION QUESTIONS

1. Describe the different approaches to assessing the environment.

2. Describe the four techniques for allocating resources.

3. How does PERT network analysis work?

4. Why is flexibility so important to today's planning techniques?

5. What is project management, and what are the steps managers use in planning projects?

6. "It's a waste of time and other resources to develop a set of sophisticated scenarios for situations that may never occur." Do you agree or disagree? Support your position.

7. Do intuition and creativity have any relevance in quantitative planning tools and techniques? Explain.

8. The *Wall Street Journal* and other business periodicals often carry reports of companies that have not met their sales or profit forecasts. What are some reasons a company might not meet its forecast? What suggestions could you make for improving the effectiveness of forecasting?

9. In what ways is managing a project different from managing a department or other structured work area? In what ways are they the same?

10. What might be some early warning signs of (a) a new competitor coming into your market, (b) an employee work stoppage, or (c) a new technology that could change demand for your product?

Let's Get Real:

Meet the Manager

Cindy Brewer
Customer Contact Channel Manager
Sears Holdings Corporation
Loves Park, IL

You'll be hearing more from this real manager throughout the chapter.

MY JOB:

I am a customer contact channel manager at Sears Holdings Corporation, and my main focus is on process improvement.

BEST PART OF MY JOB:

Being able to drive process improvements that positively impact the customer and employee experience as well as increase revenue and reduce costs.

Basic Organizational Design

LEARNING OUTCOMES

WORST PART OF MY JOB:
The inability to fix everything at once.

BEST MANAGEMENT ADVICE EVER RECEIVED:
The definition of insanity is doing the same thing over and over while expecting different results. Also, tell the truth always and be responsible.

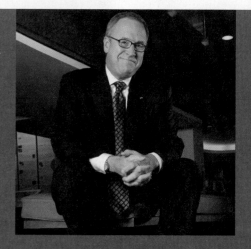

$10 billion. That's how much Eli Lilly & Co. stands to lose in annual revenues between now and 2016 as three of its major drug patents expire.[1] Replacing that revenue is high on the list of "must-do's" for CEO John Lechleiter. The solution is speeding up the pace of drug development, but his challenge is how?

Unlike its global competitors that have addressed similar product development challenges by using large-scale mergers and acquisitions, Lechleiter's focus has been on acquiring smaller drug companies. He said large-scale combinations "provide short-term relief but don't fundamentally address the issue of innovation and how to make (product development) pipelines more productive." Developing new products and moving them forward as quickly as possible on the thorough and mandatory approval process, which can be agonizingly slow, is critical to the company's present and future success.

One action Lechleiter took was revamping the company's operational structure into five global business units: oncology, diabetes, established markets, emerging markets, and animal health. Part of the restructuring also involved creating an improved product research and development center. Now, what other organizational design elements might Lechleiter use to ensure that Lilly achieves its goal of speeding up its product development process?

What Would You Do?

Replacing $10 billion in revenue can't and won't be easy. However, Lilly's CEO, John Lechleiter, understands the importance of organizational structure and design, especially when it comes to the difficult product development challenges facing his company. His initial restructuring actions are ones that many companies undergo when faced with radical environmental challenges in an attempt to become a stronger, more successful organization. His actions also illustrate the importance of designing or redesigning a structure that helps an organization accomplish its goals efficiently and effectively. In this chapter, we'll look at what's involved with that.

LEARNING OUTCOME
Describe six key elements in organizational design.

10.1 Designing Organizational Structure

A short distance south of McAlester, Oklahoma, employees in a vast factory complex make products that must be perfect. These people "are so good at what they do and have been doing it for so long that they have a 100 percent market share."[2] They make bombs for the U.S. military and doing so requires a work environment that's an interesting mix of the mundane, structured, and disciplined, coupled with high levels of risk and emotion. The work gets done efficiently and effectively here. Work also gets done efficiently and effectively at Cisco Systems although not in such a structured and formal way. At Cisco, some 70 percent of the employees work from home at least 20 percent of the time.[3] Both of these organizations get needed work done although each does so using a different structure.

Few topics in management have undergone as much change in the past few years as that of organizing and organizational structure. Managers are reevaluating traditional approaches to find new structural designs that best support and facilitate employees' doing the organization's work—designs that can achieve efficiency but are also flexible.

The basic concepts of organization design formulated by early management writers, such as Henri Fayol and Max Weber, offered structural principles for managers to follow. (Those principles are described on pp. 31–32.) Over 90 years have passed since many of those principles were originally proposed. Given that length of time and all the changes that have taken place, you'd think that those principles would be pretty worthless today. Surprisingly, they're not. For the most part, they still provide valuable insights into designing effective and efficient organizations. Of course, we've also gained a great deal of knowledge over the years as to their limitations.

EXHIBIT 10-1

Purposes of Organizing

- Divides work to be done into specific jobs and departments.
- Assigns tasks and responsibilities associated with individual jobs.
- Coordinates diverse organizational tasks.
- Clusters jobs into units.
- Establishes relationships among individuals, groups, and departments.
- Establishes formal lines of authority.
- Allocates and deploys organizational resources.

In Chapter 1 we defined **organizing** as arranging and structuring work to accomplish organizational goals. It's an important process during which managers design an organization's structure. **Organizational structure** is the formal arrangement of jobs within an organization. This structure, which can be shown visually in an **organizational chart**, also serves many purposes. (See Exhibit 10-1.) When managers create or change the structure, they're engaged in **organizational design**, a process that involves decisions about six key elements: work specialization, departmentalization, chain of command, span of control, centralization and decentralization, and formalization.[4]

Work Specialization

At the Wilson Sporting Goods factory in Ada, Ohio, 150 workers (with an average tenure exceeding 20 years) make every football used in the National Football League and most of those used in college and high school football games. To meet daily output goals, the workers specialize in job tasks such as molding, stitching and sewing, lacing, and so forth.[5] This is an example of **work specialization**, which is dividing work activities into separate job tasks. Individual employees "specialize" in doing part of an activity rather than the entire activity in order to increase work output. It's also known as division of labor, a concept we introduced in the management history module.

Work specialization makes efficient use of the diversity of skills that workers have. In most organizations, some tasks require highly developed skills; others can be performed by employees with lower skill levels. If all workers were engaged in all the steps of, say, a manufacturing process, all would need the skills necessary to perform both the most demanding and the least demanding jobs. Thus, except when performing the most highly skilled or highly sophisticated tasks, employees would be working below their skill levels. In addition, skilled workers are paid more than unskilled workers, and, because wages tend to reflect the highest level of skill, all workers would be paid at highly skilled rates to do easy tasks—an inefficient use of resources. This concept explains why you rarely find a cardiac surgeon closing up a patient after surgery. Instead, doctors doing their residencies in open-heart surgery and learning the skill usually stitch and staple the patient after the surgeon has finished the surgery.

Early proponents of work specialization believed that it could lead to great increases in productivity. At the beginning of the twentieth century, that generalization was reasonable. Because specialization was not widely practiced, its introduction almost always generated higher productivity. But, as Exhibit 10-2 illustrates, a good thing can be carried too far. At some point, the human diseconomies from division of labor—boredom, fatigue, stress, low productivity, poor quality, increased absenteeism, and high turnover—exceed the economic advantages.[6]

organizing
Arranging and structuring work to accomplish the organization's goals

organizational structure
The formal arrangement of jobs within an organization

organizational chart
The visual representation of an organization's structure

organizational design
Creating or changing an organization's structure

work specialization
Dividing work activities into separate job tasks

EXHIBIT 10-2
Economies and Diseconomies of
Work Specialization

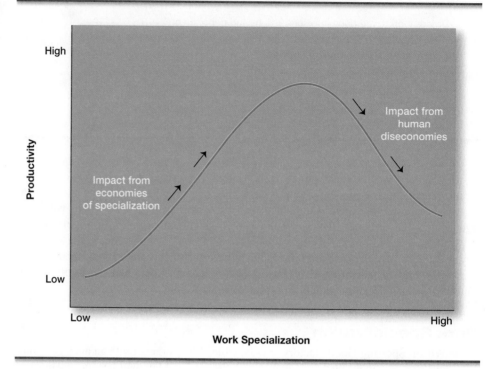

TODAY'S VIEW. Most managers today continue to see work specialization as important because it helps employees be more efficient. For example, McDonald's uses high work specialization to get its products made and delivered to customers efficiently and quickly—that's why it's called "fast" food. One person takes orders at the drive-through window, others cook and assemble the hamburgers, another works the fryer, another gets the drinks, another bags orders, and so forth. Such single-minded focus on maximizing efficiency has contributed to increasing productivity. In fact, at many McDonald's, you'll see a clock that times how long it takes employees to fill the order; look closer and you'll probably see posted somewhere an order fulfillment time goal. At some point, however, work specialization no longer leads to productivity. That's why companies such as Avery-Dennison, Ford Australia, Hallmark, and American Express use minimal work specialization and instead give employees a broad range of tasks to do.

Departmentalization

Does your college have a department of student services or financial aid department? Are you taking this course through a management department? After deciding what job tasks will be done by whom, common work activities need to be grouped back together so work gets done in a coordinated and integrated way. How jobs are grouped together is called **departmentalization**. Five common forms of departmentalization are used, although an organization may develop its own unique classification. (For instance, a hotel might have departments such as front desk operations, sales and catering, housekeeping and laundry, and maintenance.) Exhibit 10-3 illustrates each type of departmentalization as well as the advantages and disadvantages of each.

TODAY'S VIEW. Most large organizations continue to use combinations of most or all of these types of departmentalization. For example, a major Japanese electronics firm organizes its divisions along functional lines, its manufacturing units around processes, its sales units around seven geographic regions, and its sales regions into four customer groupings. Black & Decker organizes its divisions along functional lines, its manufacturing units around processes, its sales around geographic regions, and its sales regions around customer groupings.

EXHIBIT **10-3**

The Five Common
Forms of
Departmentalization

FUNCTIONAL DEPARTMENALIZATION—Groups Jobs According to Function

Plant Manager

| Manager, Engineering | Manager, Accounting | Manager, Manufacturing | Manager, Human Resources | Manager, Purchasing |

+ Efficiencies from putting together similar specialties and people with common skills, knowledge, and orientations
+ Coordination within functional area
+ In-depth specialization
− Poor communication across functional areas
− Limited view of organizational goals

GEOGRAPHICAL DEPARTMENTALIZATION—Groups Jobs According to Geographic Region

Vice President for Sales

| Sales Director, Western Region | Sales Director, Southern Region | Sales Director, Midwestern Region | Sales Director, Eastern Region |

+ More effective and efficient handling of specific regional issues that arise
+ Serve needs of unique geographic markets better
− Duplication of functions
− Can feel isolated from other organizational areas

PRODUCT DEPARTMENTALIZATION—Groups Jobs by Product Line

Source: Bombardier Annual Report.

Bombardier, Ltd.

| Mass Transit Sector | Recreational and Utility Vehicles Sector | Rail Products Sector |

| Mass Transit Division | Bombardier–Rotax (Vienna) | | Rail and Diesel Products Division |

| Recreational Products Division | Logistic Equipment Division | Industrial Equipment Division | Bombardier–Rotax (Gunskirchen) |

+ Allows specialization in particular products and services
+ Managers can become experts in their industry
+ Closer to customers
− Duplication of functions
− Limited view of organizational goals

PROCESS DEPARTMENTALIZATION—Groups Jobs on the Basis of Product or Customer Flow

Plant Superintendent

| Sawing Department Manager | Planing and Milling Department Manager | Assembling Department Manager | Lacquering and Sanding Department Manager | Finishing Department Manager | Inspection and Shipping Department Manager |

+ More efficient flow of work activities
− Can only be used with certain types of products

CUSTOMER DEPARTMENTALIZATION—Groups Jobs on the Basis of Specific and Unique Customers Who Have Common Needs

Director of Sales

| Manager, Retail Accounts | Manager, Wholesale Accounts | Manager, Government Accounts |

+ Customers' needs and problems can be met by specialists
− Duplication of functions
− Limited view of organizational goals

departmentalization
The basis by which jobs are grouped together

One popular departmentalization trend is the increasing use of customer departmentalization. Because getting and keeping customers is essential for success, this approach works well because it emphasizes monitoring and responding to changes in customers' needs. Another popular trend is the use of teams, especially as work tasks have become more complex and diverse skills are needed to accomplish those tasks. One specific type of team that more organizations are using is a **cross-functional team**, which is a work team composed of individuals from various functional specialties. For instance, at Ford's material planning and logistics division, a cross-functional team of employees from the company's finance, purchasing, engineering, and quality control areas, along with representatives from outside logistics suppliers, has developed several work improvement ideas.[7] We'll discuss cross-functional teams (and all types of teams) more fully in Chapter 13.

Chain of Command

Suppose you were at work and had a problem with some issue that came up. What would you do? Who would you go to help you resolve that issue? People need to know who their boss is. That's what the chain of command is all about. The **chain of command** is the line of authority extending from upper organizational levels to lower levels, which clarifies who reports to whom. Managers need to consider it when organizing work because it helps employees with questions such as "Who do I report to?" or "Who do I go to if I have a problem?" To understand the chain of command, you have to understand three other important concepts: authority, responsibility, and unity of command. Let's look first at authority.

AUTHORITY. Authority was a major concept discussed by the early management writers; they viewed it as the glue that held an organization together. **Authority** refers to the rights inherent in a managerial position to tell people what to do and to expect them to do it.[8] Managers in the chain of command had authority to do their job of coordinating and overseeing the work of others. Authority could be delegated downward to lower-level managers, giving them certain rights while also prescribing certain limits within which to operate. These writers emphasized that authority was related to one's position within an organization and had nothing to do with the personal characteristics of an individual manager. They assumed that the rights and power inherent in one's formal organizational position were the sole source of influence and that if an order was given, it would be obeyed.

Another early management writer, Chester Barnard, proposed another perspective on authority. This view, called the **acceptance theory of authority**, says that authority comes from the willingness of subordinates to accept it.[9] If an employee didn't accept a manager's

Early management writer Chester Barnard proposed that authority comes from the willingness of subordinates to accept it. The Jamba Juice employees shown here (in white T-shirts) illustrate Barnard's acceptance theory of authority by putting their raised hands together with their manager as a sign of unity following a business meeting. Barnard's view of authority contends that subordinates will accept orders when they understand the order, when they view the order as being consistent with the organization's purpose, when the orders do not conflict with their personal beliefs, and when they are able to perform the task as directed.

order, there was no authority. Barnard contended that subordinates *will* accept orders only if the following conditions are satisfied:

1. They understand the order.
2. They feel the order is consistent with the organization's purpose.
3. The order does not conflict with their personal beliefs.
4. They are able to perform the task as directed.

Barnard's view of authority seems to make sense, especially when it comes to an employee's ability to do what he or she is being told to do. For instance, if my manager (my department chair) came into my classroom and told me to do open-heart surgery on one of my students, the traditional view of authority said that I would have to follow that order. Barnard's view would say, instead, that I would talk to my manager about my lack of education and experience to do what he's asked me to do and that it's probably not in the best interests of the student (or our department) for me to follow that order. Yes, this is an extreme—and highly unrealistic—example. However, it does point out that simply viewing a manager's authority as total control over what an employee does or doesn't do is unrealistic also, except in certain circumstances like the military where soldiers are expected to follow their commander's orders. However, do understand that Barnard believed most employees would do what their managers asked them to do if they were able to do so.

The early management writers also distinguished between two forms of authority: line authority and staff authority. **Line authority** entitles a manager to direct the work of an employee. It is the employer–employee authority relationship that extends from the top of the organization to the lowest echelon, according to the chain of command, as shown in Exhibit 10-4. As a link in the chain of command, a manager with line authority has the right to direct the work of employees and to make certain decisions without consulting anyone. Of course, in the chain of command, every manager is also subject to the authority or direction of his or her superior.

EXHIBIT 10-4

Chain of Command and Line Authority

cross-functional team
A work team composed of individuals from various functional specialties

chain of command
The line of authority extending from upper organizational levels to the lowest levels, which clarifies who reports to whom

authority
The rights inherent in a managerial position to tell people what to do and to expect them to do it

acceptance theory of authority
The view that authority comes from the willingness of subordinates to accept it

line authority
Authority that entitles a manager to direct the work of an employee

Keep in mind that sometimes the term *line* is used to differentiate line managers from staff managers. In this context, *line* refers to managers whose organizational function contributes directly to the achievement of organizational objectives. In a manufacturing firm, line managers are typically in the production and sales functions, whereas managers in human resources and payroll are considered staff managers with staff authority. Whether a manager's function is classified as line or staff depends on the organization's objectives. For example, at Staff Builders, a supplier of temporary employees, interviewers have a line function. Similarly, at the payroll firm of ADP, payroll is a line function.

As organizations get larger and more complex, line managers find that they do not have the time, expertise, or resources to get their jobs done effectively. In response, they create **staff authority** functions to support, assist, advise, and generally reduce some of their informational burdens. For instance, a hospital administrator who cannot effectively handle the purchasing of all the supplies the hospital needs creates a purchasing department, which is a staff function. Of course, the head of the purchasing department has line authority over the purchasing agents who work for him. The hospital administrator might also find that she is overburdened and needs an assistant, a position that would be classified as a staff position. Exhibit 10-5 illustrates line and staff authority.

RESPONSIBILITY.   When managers use their authority to assign work to employees, those employees take on an obligation to perform those assigned duties. This obligation or expectation to perform is known as **responsibility**. And employees should be held accountable for their performance! Assigning work authority without responsibility and accountability can create opportunities for abuse. Likewise, no one should be held responsible or accountable for work tasks over which he or she has no authority to complete those tasks.

UNITY OF COMMAND.   Finally, the **unity of command** principle (one of Fayol's 14 management principles) states that a person should report to only one manager. Without unity of command, conflicting demands from multiple bosses may create problems as it did for Damian Birkel, a merchandising manager in the Fuller Brands division of CPAC, Inc. He found himself reporting to two bosses—one in charge of the department-store business and the other in charge of discount chains. Birkel tried to minimize the conflict by making a combined to-do list that he would update and change as work tasks changed.[10]

TODAY'S VIEW.   Although early management theorists (Fayol, Weber, Taylor, Barnard, and others) believed that chain of command, authority (line and staff), responsibility, and unity of

EXHIBIT 10-5

Line Versus Staff Authority

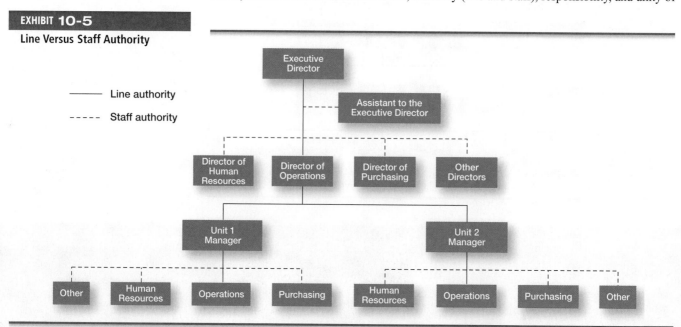

command were essential, times have changed.[11] Those elements are far less important today. For example, at the Michelin plant in Tours, France, managers have replaced the top-down chain of command with "birdhouse" meetings, in which employees meet for five minutes at regular intervals throughout the day at a column on the shop floor and study simple tables and charts to identify production bottlenecks. Instead of being bosses, shop managers are enablers.[12] Information technology also has made such concepts less relevant today. Employees can access information that used to be available only to managers in a matter of a few seconds. It also means that employees can communicate with anyone else in the organization without going through the chain of command. Also, many employees, especially in organizations where work revolves around projects, find themselves reporting to more than one boss, thus violating the unity of command principle. However, such arrangements can and do work if communication, conflict, and other issues are managed well by all involved parties.

Span of Control

How many employees can a manager efficiently and effectively manage? That's what **span of control** is all about. The traditional view was that managers could not—and should not—directly supervise more than five or six subordinates. Determining the span of control is important because to a large degree, it determines the number of levels and managers in an organization—an important consideration in how efficient an organization will be. All other things being equal, the wider or larger the span, the more efficient an organization is. Here's why.

Assume two organizations, both of which have approximately 4,100 employees. As Exhibit 10-6 shows, if one organization has a span of four and the other a span of eight, the organization with the wider span will have two fewer levels and approximately 800 fewer managers. At an average manager's salary of $42,000 a year, the organization with the wider span would save over $33 million a year! Obviously, wider spans are more efficient in terms of cost. However, at some point, wider spans may reduce effectiveness if employee performance worsens because managers no longer have the time to lead effectively.

TODAY'S VIEW.   The contemporary view of span of control recognizes that there is no magic number. Many factors influence the number of employees that a manager can efficiently and effectively manage. These factors include the skills and abilities of the manager and the

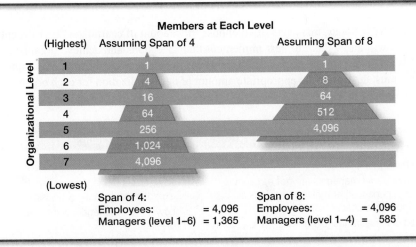

EXHIBIT 10-6

Contrasting Spans of Control

employees, and the characteristics of the work being done. For instance, managers with well-trained and experienced employees can function well with a wider span. Other contingency variables that determine the appropriate span include similarity and complexity of employee tasks, the physical proximity of subordinates, the degree to which standardized procedures are in place, the sophistication of the organization's information system, the strength of the organization's culture, and the preferred style of the manager.[13]

Let's Get Real

F2F

My span of control is *zero—I have no associates who report directly to me.*

The trend in recent years has been toward larger spans of control, which is consistent with managers' efforts to speed up decision making, increase flexibility, get closer to customers, empower employees, and reduce costs. Managers are beginning to recognize that they can handle a wider span when employees know their jobs well and when those employees understand organizational processes. For instance, at PepsiCo's Gamesa cookie plant in Mexico, 56 employees now report to each manager. However, to ensure that performance doesn't suffer because of these wider spans, employees were thoroughly briefed on company goals and processes. Also, new pay systems reward quality, service, productivity, and teamwork.[14]

Centralization and Decentralization

One of the questions that needs to be answered when organizing is "At what organizational level are decisions made?" **Centralization** is the degree to which decision making takes place at upper levels of the organization. If top managers make key decisions with little input from below, then the organization is more centralized. On the other hand, the more that lower-level employees provide input or actually make decisions, the more **decentralization** there is. Keep in mind that centralization-decentralization is not an either-or concept. The decision is relative, not absolute—that is, an organization is never completely centralized or decentralized.

Early management writers proposed that the degree of centralization in an organization depended on the situation.[15] Their goal was the optimum and efficient use of employees. Traditional organizations were structured in a pyramid, with power and authority concentrated near the top of the organization. Given this structure, historically centralized decisions were the most prominent, but organizations today have become more complex and responsive to dynamic changes in their environments. As such, many managers believe that decisions need to be made by those individuals closest to the problems, regardless of their organizational level. In fact, the trend over the past several decades—at least in U.S. and Canadian organizations—has been a movement toward more decentralization in organizations.[16] Exhibit 10-7 lists some of the factors that affect an organization's use of centralization or decentralization.[17]

TODAY'S VIEW. Today, managers often choose the amount of centralization or decentralization that will allow them to best implement their decisions and achieve organizational goals.[18] What works in one organization, however, won't necessarily work in another, so managers must determine the appropriate amount of decentralization for each organization and work units within it.

EXHIBIT 10-7

Centralization or Decentralization

More Centralization	More Decentralization
• Environment is stable.	• Environment is complex, uncertain.
• Lower-level managers are not as capable or experienced at making decisions as upper-level managers.	• Lower-level managers are capable and experienced at making decisions.
• Lower-level managers do not want a say in decisions.	• Lower-level managers want a voice in decisions.
• Decisions are relatively minor.	• Decisions are significant.
• Organization is facing a crisis or the risk of company failure.	• Corporate culture is open to allowing managers a say in what happens.
• Company is large.	• Company is geographically dispersed.
• Effective implementation of company strategies depends on managers retaining say over what happens.	• Effective implementation of company strategies depends on managers having involvement and flexibility to make decisions.

As organizations have become more flexible and responsive to environmental trends, there's been a distinct shift toward decentralized decision making.[19] This trend, also known as **employee empowerment**, gives employees more authority (power) to make decisions. (We'll address this concept more thoroughly in our discussion of leadership in Chapter 17.) In large companies especially, lower-level managers are "closer to the action" and typically have more detailed knowledge about problems and how best to solve them than do top managers. For instance, at Terex Corporation, CEO Ron Defeo, a big proponent of decentralized management, tells his managers that, "You gotta run the company you're given." And they have! The company generated revenues of over $4 billion in 2009 with about 16,000 employees worldwide and a small corporate headquarters staff.[20] Another example can be seen at the General Cable plant in Piedras Negras, Coahuila, Mexico, where employees are responsible for managing nearly 6,000 active raw material SKUs (stock-keeping units) in inventory and on the plant floor. And company managers continue to look for ways to place more responsibility in the hands of workers.[21]

Formalization

Formalization refers to how standardized an organization's jobs are and the extent to which employee behavior is guided by rules and procedures. In highly formalized organizations, there are explicit job descriptions, numerous organizational rules, and clearly defined procedures covering work processes. Employees have little discretion over what's done, when it's done, and how it's done. However, where formalization is low, employees have more discretion in how they do their work.

TODAY'S VIEW. Although some formalization is necessary for consistency and control, many organizations today rely less on strict rules and standardization to guide and regulate employee behavior. For instance, consider the following situation:

> A customer comes into a branch of a large national drug store and drops off a role of film for same-day developing 37 minutes after the store policy cut-off time. Although the sales clerk knows he's supposed to follow rules, he also knows he could get the film developed with no problem and wants to accommodate the customer. So he accepts the film, violating policy, hoping that his manager won't find out.[22]

Has this employee done something wrong? He did "break" the rule. But by "breaking" the rule, he actually brought in revenue and provided good customer service.

Considering there are numerous situations where rules may be too restrictive, many organizations have allowed employees some latitude, giving them sufficient autonomy to make those decisions that they feel are best under the circumstances. It doesn't mean throwing out all organizational rules because there *will* be rules that are important for employees to follow—and these rules should be explained so employees understand why it's important to adhere to them. But for other rules, employees may be given some leeway.[23]

Mechanistic and Organic Structures ⑩.2

LEARNING OUTCOME
Contrast mechanistic and organic structures.

Stocking extra swimsuits in retail stores near water parks seems to make sense, right? And if size 11 women's shoes have been big sellers in Chicago, then stocking more size 11s seems to be a no-brainer. After suffering through 16 months of declining same-store sales, Macy's CEO Terry Lundgren decided it was time to restructure the organization to

by the numbers[24]

34 percent of HR executives said that they had retrained employees for new positions over the last six months.

68 percent of organizations say they've increased centralization in the last five years.

51 percent of white-collar workers say that teleworking is a good idea.

42 percent of U.S. companies offer some form of telework arrangement.

55 percent of workers believe that their work quality is perceived the same when working remotely as when working in the office.

centralization
The degree to which decision making is concentrated at upper levels of the organization

decentralization
The degree to which lower-level employees provide input or actually make decisions

employee empowerment
Giving employees more authority (power) to make decisions

formalization
How standardized an organization's jobs are and the extent to which employee behavior is guided by rules and procedures

EXHIBIT 10-8

Mechanistic Versus Organic Organizations

Mechanistic
- High specialization
- Rigid departmentalization
- Clear chain of command
- Narrow spans of control
- Centralization
- High formalization

Organic
- Cross-functional teams
- Cross-hierarchical teams
- Free flow of information
- Wide spans of control
- Decentralization
- Low formalization

make sure that these types of smart retail decisions are made.[25] He's making the company both more centralized and more locally focused. Although that may seem a contradiction, the redesign seems to be working. Lundgren centralized Macy's purchasing, planning, and marketing operations from seven regional offices to one office at headquarters in New York. He also replaced regional merchandise managers with more local managers—each responsible for a dozen stores—who spend more time figuring out what's selling. Designing (or redesigning) an organizational structure that works is important. Basic organizational design revolves around two organizational forms that are described in Exhibit 10-8.[26]

The **mechanistic organization** (or bureaucracy) was the natural result of combining the six elements of structure. Adhering to the chain-of-command principle ensured the existence of a formal hierarchy of authority, with each person controlled and supervised by one superior. Keeping the span of control small at increasingly higher levels in the organization created tall, impersonal structures. As the distance between the top and the bottom of the organization expanded, top management would increasingly impose rules and regulations. Because top managers couldn't control lower-level activities through direct observation and ensure the use of standard practices, they substituted rules and regulations. The early management writers' belief in a high degree of work specialization created jobs that were simple, routine, and standardized. Further specialization through the use of departmentalization increased impersonality and the need for multiple layers of management to coordinate the specialized departments.

The **organic organization** is a highly adaptive form that is as loose and flexible as the mechanistic organization is rigid and stable. Rather than having standardized jobs and regulations, the organic organization's loose structure allows it to change rapidly as required.[27] It has division of labor, but the jobs people do are not standardized. Employees tend to be professionals who are technically proficient and trained to handle diverse problems. They need few formal rules and little direct supervision because their training has instilled in them standards of professional conduct. For instance, a petroleum engineer doesn't need to follow specific procedures on how to locate oil sources miles offshore. The engineer can solve most problems alone or after conferring with colleagues. Professional standards guide his or her behavior. The organic organization is low in centralization so that the professional can respond quickly to problems and because top-level managers cannot be expected to possess the expertise to make necessary decisions.

Let's Get Real

My organization is *definitely mechanistic. We're a large, multidivisional organization.*

LEARNING OUTCOME **10.3**

Discuss the contingency factors that favor either the mechanistic model or the organic model of organizational design.

Contingency Factors Affecting Structural Choice

When Carol Bartz took over the CEO position at Yahoo! from cofounder Jerry Yang, she found a company "hobbled by slow decision making and ineffective execution on those decisions."[28] Bartz said, "There's plenty that has bogged this company down." For a company that was once the darling of Web search, Yahoo! seemed to have lost its way, a serious misstep in an industry where change is continual and rapid. Bartz implemented a new streamlined structure that was intended to "make the company a lot faster on its feet." Top managers typically put a lot of thought into designing an appropriate organizational structure. What that appropriate structure is depends on four contingency variables: the organization's strategy, size, technology, and degree of environmental uncertainty.

Strategy and Structure

An organization's structure should facilitate goal achievement. Because goals are an important part of the organization's strategies, it's only logical that strategy and structure are closely linked. Alfred Chandler initially researched this relationship.[29] He studied several large U.S. companies and concluded that changes in corporate strategy led to changes in an organization's structure that support the strategy.

Research has shown that certain structural designs work best with different organizational strategies.[30] For instance, the flexibility and free-flowing information of the organic structure works well when an organization is pursuing meaningful and unique innovations. The mechanistic organization with its efficiency, stability, and tight controls works best for companies wanting to tightly control costs.

Size and Structure

There's considerable evidence that an organization's size affects its structure.[31] Large organizations—typically considered to be those with more than 2,000 employees—tend to have more specialization, departmentalization, centralization, and rules and regulations than do small organizations. However, once an organization grows past a certain size, size has less influence on structure. Why? Essentially, once there are around 2,000 employees, it's already fairly mechanistic. Adding another 500 employees won't impact the structure much. On the other hand, adding 500 employees to an organization that has only 300 employees is likely to make it more mechanistic.

Technology and Structure

Every organization uses some form of technology to convert its inputs into outputs. For instance, workers at Whirlpool's Manaus, Brazil, facility build microwave ovens and air conditioners on a standardized assembly line. Employees at FedEx Kinko's Office and Print Services produce custom design and print jobs for individual customers.

Typically organizations with a routine technology adapt a mechanistic structure and those with a nonroutine technology adapt an organic structure. With a more routine technology for transforming inputs into outputs, firms such as insurance companies and banks most often have a mechanistic structure. The bank teller shown here, serving a customer at Nuestro Banco, processes routine transactions such as cashing checks and making deposits, withdrawals, and loan payments. The bank's structure is characterized by rules and regulations, a high degree of work specialization, a formal hierarchy, a small span of control, and departments organized by functions.

mechanistic organization
An organizational design that's rigid and tightly controlled

organic organization
An organizational design that's highly adaptive and flexible

LEADER who made a difference

"On the wall behind the desk of Andrea Jung, the CEO of Avon, a beauty company, hangs a plaque labeled 'The Evolution of Leadership.' It displays four footprints: that of an ape, then a barefoot man, then a man's shoe and finally a high-heeled shoe."[35] It's an interesting symbol, and it wasn't put there by Jung. No, it was hanging in the office of the previous CEO, James Preston. As the first female CEO of Avon, Jung has held that position for a decade—the most-tenured female CEO in the *Fortune* 500. And she's faced numerous managerial challenges head-on. She clearly understands the importance of organizational design in helping her global company prosper in good times and bad. That aspect of her job is particularly challenging given the fact that 70 percent of the company's sales are in developing countries. But she's made the tough decisions to restructure, refocus, and redefine the company's strategies and created an organizational design to help it continue its success as the leading women's beauty products company.

And employees at Bayer's facility in Karachi, Pakistan, are involved in producing pharmaceuticals on a continuous-flow production line.

The initial research on technology's effect on structure can be traced to Joan Woodward, who studied small manufacturing firms in southern England to determine the extent to which structural design elements were related to organizational success.[32] She couldn't find any consistent pattern until she divided the firms into three distinct technologies that had increasing levels of complexity and sophistication. The first category, **unit production**, described the production of items in units or small batches. The second category, **mass production**, described large-batch manufacturing. Finally, the third and most technically complex group, **process production**, included continuous-process production. A summary of her findings is shown in Exhibit 10-9.

Other studies also have shown that organizations adapt their structures to their technology depending on how routine their technology is for transforming inputs into outputs.[33] In general, the more routine the technology, the more mechanistic the structure can be, and organizations with more nonroutine technology are more likely to have organic structures.[34]

Environmental Uncertainty and Structure

Some organizations face stable and simple environments with little uncertainty; others face dynamic and complex environments with a lot of uncertainty. Managers try to minimize environmental uncertainty by adjusting the organization's structure.[36] In stable and simple environments, mechanistic designs can be more effective. On the other hand, the greater the uncertainty, the more an organization needs the flexibility of an organic design. For example, the uncertain nature of the oil industry means that oil companies need to be flexible. Soon after being named CEO of Royal Dutch Shell PLC, Jeroen van der Veer streamlined the corporate structure to counteract some of the industry volatility. One thing he did was eliminate the company's cumbersome, overly analytical process of making deals with OPEC countries and other major oil producers.[37]

TODAY'S VIEW. The evidence on the environment-structure relationship helps explain why so many managers today are restructuring their organizations to be lean, fast, and flexible. Worldwide economic downturns, global competition, accelerated product innovation by competitors, and increased demands from customers for high quality and faster deliveries are examples of dynamic environmental forces.

EXHIBIT 10-9

Woodward's Findings on Technology and Structure

	Unit Production	Mass Production	Process Production
Structural characteristics:	Low vertical differentiation	Moderate vertical differentiation	High vertical differentiation
	Low horizontal differentiation	High horizontal differentiation	Low horizontal differentiation
	Low formalization	High formalization	Low formalization
Most effective structure:	Organic	Mechanistic	Organic

Mechanistic organizations are not equipped to respond to rapid environmental change and environmental uncertainty. As a result, we're seeing organizations become more organic.

Traditional Organizational Designs ⑩.⁴

They're a big hit with the elementary-school crowd and millions of them have been sold every month. Ever heard of Silly Bandz?[38] If you're over the age of 10, you probably haven't! These colorful rubber bands retain the shapes they're twisted in and kids love them. The small business that created Silly Bands—BCP Imports of Toledo, Ohio—increased its employee count from 20 to 200 over the last year and recently added 22 phone lines to keep up with inquiries. The person behind those organizing decisions is company president Robert Croak. In making structural decisions, managers have some common designs from which to choose. In this chapter, we're going to describe the traditional organizational designs. In the next chapter, we'll be looking at more contemporary types of organizational designs.

When designing a structure, managers may choose one of the traditional organizational designs. These structures tend to be more mechanistic in nature. A summary of the strengths and weaknesses of each can be found in Exhibit 10-10.

Simple Structure

Most companies start as entrepreneurial ventures using a **simple structure**, which is an organizational design with low departmentalization, wide spans of control, authority centralized in a single person, and little formalization.[39] As employees are added, however, most don't remain as simple structures. The structure tends to become more specialized and formalized. Rules and regulations are introduced, work becomes specialized, departments are created, levels of management are added, and the organization becomes increasingly bureaucratic. At this point, managers might choose a functional structure or a divisional structure.

EXHIBIT 10-10
Traditional Organizational Designs

Simple Structure
- Strengths: Fast; flexible; inexpensive to maintain; clear accountability.
- Weaknesses: Not appropriate as organization grows; reliance on one person is risky.

Functional Structure
- Strengths: Cost-saving advantages from specialization (economies of scale, minimal duplication of people and equipment); employees are grouped with others who have similar tasks.
- Weaknesses: Pursuit of functional goals can cause managers to lose sight of what's best for the overall organization; functional specialists become insulated and have little understanding of what other units are doing.

Divisional Structure
- Strengths: Focuses on results—division managers are responsible for what happens to their products and services.
- Weaknesses: Duplication of activities and resources increases costs and reduces efficiency.

unit production
The production of items in units or small batches
mass production
The production of items in large batches
process production
The production of items in continuous processes
simple structure
An organizational design with low departmentalization, wide spans of control, centralized authority, and little formalization

Functional Structure

A **functional structure** is an organizational design that groups similar or related occupational specialties together. You can think of this structure as functional departmentalization applied to the entire organization.

Divisional Structure

The **divisional structure** is an organizational structure made up of separate business units or divisions.[40] In this structure, each division has limited autonomy, with a division manager who has authority over his or her unit and is responsible for performance. In divisional structures, however, the parent corporation typically acts as an external overseer to coordinate and control the various divisions, and often provides support services such as financial and legal. Walmart, for example, has two divisions: retail (Walmart Stores, International, Sam's Clubs, and others) and support (distribution centers).

Hopefully, you've seen in this chapter that organizational structure and design (or redesign) are important managerial tasks. Also, we hope that you recognize that organizing decisions aren't only important for upper-level managers. Managers at all levels may have to deal with work specialization or authority or span of control decisions. In the next chapter, we'll continue our discussion of the organizing function by looking at contemporary organizational designs.

functional structure
An organizational design that groups together similar or related occupational specialties

divisional structure
An organizational structure made up of separate, semiautonomous units or divisions

What Would You Do?

Let's Get Real:
My Response *to A Manager's Dilemma, page 264*

With Lechleiter's revamping of the company's operational structure, he needs to consider how to organize each of these departments.

- Create a divisional structure for each of the five global business units.
- Utilize a more organic structure for the teams that will be developing the new products in the product research and development center.
- Employ a more mechanistic structure for those associates who will be driving the products through the mandatory approval process.
- Create cross-functional teams across the business units to share best practices and key learning to increase the product development process.

Cindy Brewer
Customer Contact
Channel Manager
**Sears Holdings
Corporation
Loves Park, IL**

CHAPTER SUMMARY
by Learning Outcomes

LEARNING OUTCOME **Describe** six key elements in organizational design.

The key elements in organizational design are work specialization, chain of command, span of control, departmentalization, centralization-decentralization, and formalization. Traditionally, work specialization was viewed as a way to divide work activities into separate job tasks. Today's view is that it is an important organizing mechanism but it can lead to problems. The chain of command and its companion concepts—authority, responsibility, and unity of command—were viewed as important ways of maintaining control in organizations. The contemporary view is that they are less relevant in today's organizations. The traditional view of span of control was that managers should directly supervise no more than five to six individuals. The contemporary view is that the span of control depends on the skills and abilities of the manager and the employees and on the characteristics of the situation.

The various forms of departmentalization are as follows: *Functional* groups jobs by functions performed; *product* groups jobs by product lines; *geographical* groups jobs by geographical region; *process* groups jobs on product or customer flow; and *customer* groups jobs on specific and unique customer groups.

Authority refers to the rights inherent in a managerial position to tell people what to do and to expect them to do it. The acceptance view of authority says that authority comes from the willingness of subordinates to accept it. Line authority entitles a manager to direct the work of an employee. Staff authority refers to functions that support, assist, advise, and generally reduce some of managers' informational burdens. Responsibility is the obligation or expectation to perform assigned duties. Unity of command states that a person should report to only one manager. Centralization-decentralization is a structural decision about who makes decisions—upper-level managers or lower-level employees. Formalization concerns the organization's use of standardization and strict rules to provide consistency and control.

LEARNING OUTCOME **Contrast** mechanistic and organic structures.

A mechanistic organization is a rigid and tightly controlled structure. An organic organization is highly adaptive and flexible.

LEARNING OUTCOME **Discuss** the contingency factors that favor either the mechanistic model or the organic model of organizational design.

An organization's structure should support the strategy. If the strategy changes, the structure also should change. An organization's size can affect its structure up to a certain point. Once an organization reaches a certain size (usually around 2,000 employees), it's fairly mechanistic. An organization's technology can affect its structure. An organic structure is most effective with unit production and process production technology. A mechanistic structure is most effective with mass production technology. The more uncertain an organization's environment, the more it needs the flexibility of an organic design.

LEARNING OUTCOME **Describe** traditional organizational designs.

A simple structure is one with low departmentalization, wide spans of control, authority centralized in a single person, and little formalization. A functional structure groups similar or related occupational specialties together. A divisional structure is made up of separate business units or divisions.

To check your understanding of learning outcomes 10.1 – 10.4 go to **mymanagementlab.com** and try the chapter questions.

REVIEW AND DISCUSSION QUESTIONS

1. Discuss the traditional and contemporary views of each of the six key elements of organizational design.

2. Can an organization's structure be changed quickly? Why or why not? Should it be changed quickly? Explain.

3. Contrast mechanistic and organic organizations.

4. Would you rather work in a mechanistic or an organic organization? Why?

5. Explain the contingency factors that affect organizational design.

6. Contrast the three traditional organizational designs.

7. With the availability of advanced information technology that allows an organization's work to be done anywhere at any time, is organizing still an important managerial function? Why or why not?

8. Researchers are now saying that efforts to simplify work tasks actually have negative results for both companies and their employees. Do you agree? Why or why not?

PREPARING FOR: My Career

ETHICS DILEMMA

"As British Petroleum (BP) continues to try to stop the oil gushing into the Gulf of Mexico, the energy giant is also dealing with a public relations nightmare."[41] One step the company has taken is buying the Web search terms such as "oil spill" and "oil spill claims" on Google and Yahoo! A company spokeswoman says "the strategy is to assist those who are most impacted and help them find the right forms and the right people quickly and effectively." One consultant who handles crisis management says, "I do it with all of my clients, because if we aren't buying the terms, somebody else is." Another individual who teaches crisis management says, "Most companies that are smart are buying relevant search terms to increase their visibility on the Internet. As long as they are providing factual and timely information in a transparent way and doing interviews with other media sources as well, I don't see any reason why they shouldn't be buying search terms." What do you think? Is this even an ethical issue? (Not the ramifications of the spill itself, but purchasing the search terms.) What ethical concerns do you see in BP doing this? What stakeholders might be affected by BP's actions (buying the search terms)? In what ways might these stakeholders be affected?

SKILLS EXERCISE

Developing Your Empowering People (Delegating) Skill

About the Skill

Managers get things done through other people. Because there are limits to any manager's time and knowledge, effective managers need to understand how to delegate.[42] Delegation is the assignment of authority to another person to carry out specific duties. It allows an employee to make decisions. Delegation should not be confused with participation. In participative decision making, authority is shared. In delegation, employees make decisions on their own.

Steps in Practicing the Skill

A number of actions differentiate the effective delegator from the ineffective delegator. The following five behaviors are used by effective delegators.

1. *Clarify the assignment.* Determine *what* is to be delegated and *to whom.* You need to identify the person who's most capable of doing the task and then determine whether he or she has the time and motivation to do the task. If you have a willing and able employee, it's your responsibility to provide clear information on what is being delegated, the results you expect, and any time or performance expectations you may have. Unless there's an overriding need to adhere to specific methods, you should delegate only the results expected. Get agreement on what is to be

done and the results expected, but let the employee decide the best way to complete the task.

2. *Specify the employee's range of discretion.* Every situation of delegation comes with constraints. Although you're delegating to an employee the authority to perform some task or tasks, you're not delegating unlimited authority. You are delegating authority to act on certain issues within certain parameters. You need to specify what those parameters are so that employees know, without any doubt, the range of their discretion.

3. *Allow the employee to participate.* One of the best ways to decide how much authority will be necessary to accomplish a task is to allow the employee who will be held accountable for that task to participate in that decision. Be aware, however, that allowing employees to participate can present its own set of potential problems as a result of employees' self-interests and biases in evaluating their own abilities.

4. *Inform others that delegation has occurred.* Delegation shouldn't take place behind the scenes. Not only do the manager and employee need to know specifically what has been delegated and how much authority has been given, but so does anyone else who's likely to be affected by the employee's decisions and actions. This includes people inside and outside the organization. Essentially, you need to communicate what has been delegated (the task and amount of authority) and to whom.

5. *Establish feedback channels.* To delegate without establishing feedback controls is inviting problems. The establishment of controls to monitor the employee's performance increases the likelihood that important problems will be identified and that the task will be completed on time and to the desired specifications.

Ideally, these controls should be determined at the time of the initial assignment. Agree on a specific time for the completion of the task and then set progress dates when the employee will report back on how well he or she is doing and any major problems that may have arisen. These controls can be supplemented with periodic checks to ensure that authority guidelines aren't being abused, organizational policies are being followed, proper procedures are being met, and the like.

Practicing the Skill

Read through the following scenario. Write a paper describing how you would handle the situation described. Be sure to refer to the five behaviors described for delegating.

Scenario

Ricky Lee is the manager of the contracts group of a large regional office supply distributor. His boss, Anne Zumwalt, has asked him to prepare by the end of the month the department's new procedures manual that will outline the steps followed in negotiating contracts with office products manufacturers who supply the organization's products. Because Ricky has another major project he's working on, he went to Anne and asked her if it would be possible to assign the rewriting of the procedures manual to Bill Harmon, one of his employees who's worked in the contracts group for about three years. Anne said she had no problems with Ricky reassigning the project as long as Bill knew the parameters and the expectations for the completion of the project. Ricky is preparing for his meeting in the morning with Bill regarding this assignment.

WORKING TOGETHER
Team Exercise

An organization chart can be a useful tool for understanding certain aspects of an organization's structure. Form small groups of three to four individuals. Among yourselves, choose an organization with which one of you is familiar (where you work, a student organization to which you belong, your college or university, etc.). Draw an organization chart of this organization. Be careful to show departments (or groups) and especially be careful to get the chain of command correct. Be prepared to share your chart with the class.

MY TURN TO BE A MANAGER

- Find three different examples of an organizational chart. (Company's annual reports are a good place to look.) In a report, describe each of these. Try to decipher the organization's use of organizational design elements, especially departmentalization, chain of command, centralization-decentralization, and formalization.

- Survey at least 10 different managers as to how many employees they supervise. Also ask them whether they feel they could supervise more employees or whether they feel the number they supervise is too many. Graph your survey results and write a report describing what you found. Draw some conclusions about span of control.

- Using the organizational chart you created in the team exercise, redesign the structure. What structural changes might make this organization more efficient and effective? Write a report describing what you would do and why. Be sure to include an example of the original organizational chart as well as a chart of your proposed revision of the organizational structure.

- Steve's and Mary's suggested readings: Gary Hamel, *The Future of Management* (Harvard Business School Press, 2007); Thomas Friedman, *The World Is Flat 3.0* (Picador, 2007); Harold J. Leavitt, *Top Down: Why Hierarchies Are Here to Stay and How to Manage Them More Effectively* (Harvard Business School Press, 2005); and Thomas W. Malone, *The Future of Work* (Harvard Business School Press, 2004).

- In your own words, write down three things you learned in this chapter about being a good manager.

- Self-knowledge can be a powerful learning tool. Go to mymanagementlab.com and complete these self-assessment exercises: How Well Do I Handle Ambiguity? What Type of Organizational Structure Do I Prefer? Do I Like Bureaucracy? How Good Am I at Playing Politics? How Willing Am I to Delegate? Using the results of your assessments, identify personal strengths and weaknesses. What will you do to reinforce your strengths and improve your weaknesses?

CASE APPLICATION 1
Ask Chuck

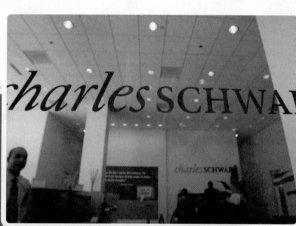

The Charles Schwab Corporation (Charles Schwab) is a San Francisco-based financial services company.[43] Like many companies in that industry, Charles Schwab struggled during the economic recession.

Founded in 1971 by its namesake as a discount brokerage, the company has now "grown up" into a full-service traditional brokerage firm, with more than 300 offices in some 45 states and in London and Hong Kong. It still offers discount brokerage services, but also financial research, advice, and planning; retirement plans; investment management; and proprietary financial products including mutual funds, mortgages, CDs, and other banking products through its Charles Schwab Bank unit. However, its primary business is still making stock trades for investors who make their own financial decisions. The company has a reputation for being conservative, which helped it avoid the financial meltdown suffered by other investment firms. Founder Charles R. Schwab has a black bowling ball perched on his desk. "It's a memento of the long-forgotten bubble of 1961, when shares of bowling-pin companies, shoemakers, chalk manufacturers, and lane operators were thought to be can't-miss plays on the limitless potential of suburbia—and turned out to be duds." He keeps the ball as a reminder not to "buy into hype or take excessive risks."

Effective communication with customers plays an important role in Charles Schwab's customer service strategy. Managers of the company's offices receive daily customer feedback reports and empower employees to respond quickly to customer concerns.

Like many companies, Charles Schwab is fanatical about customer service. By empowering front-line employees to respond fast to customer issues and concerns, Cheryl Pasquale, a manager at one of Schwab's branches, is on the front line of Schwab's efforts to prosper in a "resource-challenged economy." Every workday morning, she pulls up a customer feedback report for her branch generated by a brief survey the investment firm e-mails out daily. The report allows her to review how well her six financial consultants handled the previous day's transactions. She's able to see comments of customers who gave both high and low marks and whether a particular transaction garnered praise or complaint. On one particular day, she notices that several customers commented on how difficult it was to use the branch's in-house information kiosks. "She decides she'll ask her team for insights about this in their weekly meeting." One thing that she pays particular attention to is a "manager alert—a special notice triggered by a client who has given Schwab a poor rating for a delay in posting a transaction to his account." And she's not alone. Every day, Pasquale and the managers at all the company's branches receive this type of customer feedback.

Discussion Questions

1. Describe and evaluate what Charles Schwab is doing.
2. How might the company's culture of not buying into hype and not taking excessive risks affect its organizational structural design?
3. What structural implications—good and bad—might Schwab's intense focus on customer feedback have?
4. Do you think this arrangement would work for other types of organizations? Why or why not?

CASE APPLICATION

A New Kind of Structure

Admit it. Sometimes the projects you're working on (school, work, or both) can get pretty boring and monotonous. Wouldn't it be great to have a magic button you could push to get someone else to do that boring, time-consuming stuff? At Pfizer, that "magic button" is a reality for a large number of employees.[44]

As a global pharmaceutical company, Pfizer is continually looking for ways to help employees be more efficient and effective. The company's senior director of organizational effectiveness found that the "Harvard MBA staff we hired to develop strategies and innovate were instead Googling and making PowerPoints." Indeed, internal studies conducted to find out just how much time its valuable talent was spending on menial tasks was startling. The average Pfizer employee was spending 20 percent to 40 percent of his or her time on support work (creating documents, typing notes, doing research, manipulating data, scheduling meetings) and only 60 percent to 80 percent on knowledge work (strategy, innovation, networking, collaborating, critical thinking). And the problem wasn't just at lower levels. Even the highest-level employees were affected. Take, for instance, David Cain, an executive director for global engineering. He enjoys his job—assessing environmental real estate risks, managing facilities, and controlling a multimillion-dollar budget. But he didn't so much enjoy having to go through spreadsheets and put together PowerPoints. Now, however, with Pfizer's "magic button," those tasks are passed off to individuals outside the organization.

Just what is this "magic button?" Originally called the Office of the Future (OOF), the renamed PfizerWorks allows employees to shift tedious and time-consuming tasks with the click of a single button on their computer desktop. They describe what they need on an online form, which is then sent to one of two Indian service-outsourcing firms. When a request is received, a team member in India calls the Pfizer employee to clarify what's needed and by when. The team member then e-mails back a cost specification for the requested work. If the Pfizer employee decides to proceed, the costs involved are charged to the employee's department. About this unique arrangement, Cain said that he relishes working with what he prefers to call his "personal consulting organization."

The number 66,500 illustrates just how beneficial PfizerWorks has been for the company. That's the number of work hours estimated to have been saved by employees who've used PfizerWorks. What about Joe Cain's experiences? When he gave the Indian team a complex project researching strategic actions that worked when consolidating company facilities, the team put the report together in a month, something that would have taken him six months to do alone. He says, "Pfizer pays me not to work tactically, but to work strategically."

Discussion Questions

1. Describe and evaluate what Pfizer is doing with its PfizerWorks.

2. What structural implications—good and bad—does this approach have? (Think in terms of the six organizational design elements.)

3. Do you think this arrangement would work for other types of organizations? Why or why not? What types of organizations might it also work for?

4. What role do you think organizational structure plays in an organization's efficiency and effectiveness? Explain.

Let's Get Real:

Meet the Manager

Richard "Dickie" Townley
Sr. Manager Product Terminals and Marketing
Holly Energy Partners, L.P.
Artesia, NM

You'll be hearing more from this real manager throughout the chapter.

MY JOB:
I'm the senior manager of product terminals and marketing for Holly Energy Partners, L.P. My primary responsibility is to oversee the day-to-day operation of multi-state fossil fuel product terminals.

BEST PART OF MY JOB:
Being part of an industry that is vital to the economic stability of the country.

Adaptive Organizational Design

11.1
Describe contemporary organizational designs.
page 288

11.2
Discuss how organizations organize for collaboration.
page 293

11.3
Explain flexible work arrangements used by organizations.
page 297

11.4
Discuss organizing issues associated with a contingent workforce.
page 299

11.5
Describe today's organizational design challenges.
page 300

LEARNING OUTCOMES

WORST PART OF MY JOB:
Working in an industry that has a black eye for its environmental impact, and the general public not understanding the efforts being taken by the industry to mitigate the environmental impact while still providing the energy the country needs.

BEST MANAGEMENT ADVICE EVER RECEIVED:
Value what you do, and add value by what you do.

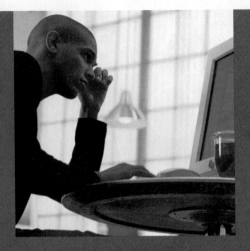

They're individuals you might never have thought of as being part of an organization's structure, but for many organizations, volunteers provide a much-needed source of labor.[1] Maybe you've volunteered at a Habitat build, a homeless shelter, or some nonprofit organization. However, what if the volunteer assignment was at a for-profit business and the job description read like this: "Spend a few hours a day, at your computer, supplying answers online to customer questions about technical matters like how to set up an Internet home network or how to program a new high-definition television," all for no pay. At Verizon's high-speed fiber optic Internet, television, and telephone service, "volunteers" do just that. Many large corporations, start-up companies, and venture capitalists are betting that this "emerging corps of Web-savvy helpers will transform the field of customer service."

As director of Verizon's e-commerce unit, Mark Studness was familiar with Web sites where users offered tips and answered questions. His challenge? Find a way to use that potential resource for customer service. His solution? "Super" or passionate users—that is, users who provided the best answers and dialogue in Web forums. How should Verizon's managers deal with the structural challenges of this unique type of work arrangement?

What Would You Do?

Welcome to the fascinating world of organizational structure and design in the twenty-first century! Did you ever consider that a business might actually have work tasks completed by someone other than employees . . . for free? Mark Studness and Verizon were open to trying new ways to do what they're in business to do and the unusual structural experiment seems to be working well. He describes the company-sponsored customer-service site as a "very productive tool, partly because it absorbs many thousands of questions that would otherwise be expensive calls to a Verizon call center."

In the last chapter, we introduced the basic concepts of traditional organizational design including the six building blocks of an organization's structure: work specialization, departmentalization, chain of command, span of control, centralization and decentralization, and formalization. In this chapter, we're going to explore contemporary aspects of organizational design as organizations adapt to the demands of today's environment. We're going to first look at some contemporary organizational designs and then move on to discussing how organizations are coping with those demands through collaborative work efforts, flexible work arrangements, and a contingent workforce. We'll wrap up the chapter by describing some organizational design challenges facing today's managers.

LEARNING OUTCOME
Describe contemporary
organizational designs.

11.1

Contemporary Organizational Designs

Microsoft's Windows 7 was the outcome of a three-year project marked by close collaboration among the thousands of people working on various aspects of the product.[2] This approach contrasted sharply with the development of Windows Vista, where the development team had evolved into "a rigid set of silos—each responsible for specific technical features—that didn't share their plans widely." With Vista, programming code created by each group might have worked fine on its own, but it caused technical problems when integrated with code created by other groups. Those design issues, as well as internal communications breakdowns, contributed to numerous product delays and defects. CEO Steve Ballmer was adamant about not repeating that mistake. Thus, to "rebuild Windows, Microsoft razed walls"—that is, organizational structure walls that acted as barriers and impediments to efficient and effective work.

EXHIBIT 11-1

Contemporary Organizational Designs

Team Structure

- What it is: A structure in which the entire organization is made up of work groups or teams.

- Advantages: Employees are more involved and empowered.
  Reduced barriers among functional areas.

- Disadvantages: No clear chain of command.
  Pressure on teams to perform.

Matrix-Project Structure

- What it is: Matrix is a structure that assigns specialists from different functional areas to work on projects who then return to their areas when the project is completed. Project is a structure in which employees continuously work on projects. As one project is completed, employees move on to the next project.

- Advantages: Fluid and flexible design that can respond to environmental changes.
  Faster decision making.

- Disadvantages: Complexity of assigning people to projects.
  Task and personality conflicts.

Boundaryless Structure

- What it is: A structure that is not defined by or limited to artificial horizontal, vertical, or external boundaries; includes *virtual* and *network* types of organizations.

- Advantages: Highly flexible and responsive.
  Utilizes talent wherever it's found.

- Disadvantages: Lack of control.
  Communication difficulties.

Learning Structure

- What it is: A structure in which employees continually acquire and share new knowledge and apply that knowledge.

- Advantages: Sharing of knowledge throughout organization. Sustainable source of competitive advantage.

- Disadvantages: Reluctance on part of employees to share knowledge for fear of losing their power.
  Large numbers of experienced employees on the verge of retiring.

Like Steve Ballmer, many managers are finding that the traditional designs (discussed on pp. 277–278) often aren't appropriate for today's increasingly dynamic and complex environment. Instead, organizations need to be lean, flexible, and innovative; that is, they need to be more organic. So managers are finding creative ways to structure and organize work. These contemporary designs include team structures, matrix and project structures, boundaryless organizations, and learning organizations. (See Exhibit 11-1 for a summary of these designs.)

Team Structures

Larry Page and Sergey Brin, cofounders of Google, created a corporate structure that "tackles most big projects in small, tightly focused teams."[3] A **team structure** is one in which the entire organization is made up of work teams that do the organization's work.[4] In this structure, employee empowerment is crucial because no line of managerial authority flows from top to bottom. Rather, employee teams design and do work in the way they think is best, but the teams are also held responsible for all work performance results in their respective areas.

team structure
An organizational structure in which the entire organization is made up of work teams

In large organizations, the team structure complements what is typically a functional or divisional structure and allows the organization to have the efficiency of a bureaucracy *and* the flexibility that teams provide. Companies such as Amazon, Boeing, Hewlett-Packard, Louis Vuitton, Motorola, and Xerox, for instance, extensively use employee teams to improve productivity.

Matrix and Project Structures

Other popular contemporary designs are the matrix and project structures. The **matrix structure** assigns specialists from different functional departments to work on projects being led by a project manager. (See Exhibit 11-2.) One unique aspect of this design is that it creates a *dual chain of command* because employees in a matrix organization have two managers: their functional area manager and their product or project manager, who share authority. The project manager has authority over the functional members who are part of his or her project team in areas related to the project's goals. However, any decisions about promotions, salary recommendations, and annual reviews typically remain the functional manager's responsibility. The matrix design "violates" the unity of command principle, which says that each person should report to only one boss. Despite that, it can, and does, work effectively if both managers communicate regularly, coordinate work demands on employees, and resolve conflicts together.

Many organizations use a **project structure**, in which employees continuously work on projects. Unlike the matrix structure, a project structure has no formal departments where employees return at the completion of a project. Instead, employees take their specific skills, abilities, and experiences to other projects. Also, all work in project structures is performed by teams of employees. For instance, at design firm IDEO, project teams form, disband, and form again as the work requires. Employees "join" project teams because they bring needed skills and abilities to that project. Once a project is completed, however, they move on to the next one.[5]

Project structures tend to be more flexible organizational designs, without the departmentalization or rigid organizational hierarchy that can slow down making decisions or taking action. In this structure, managers serve as facilitators, mentors, and coaches. They eliminate or minimize organizational obstacles and ensure that teams have the resources they need to effectively and efficiently complete their work.

The Boundaryless Organization

The Large Hadron Collider is a $6 billion particle accelerator lying in a tunnel that's 27 kilometers (17 miles) in circumference and 175 meters (574 feet) below ground near Geneva, Switzerland. "The atom smasher is so large that a brief status report lists

Example of a Matrix Organization

2,900 authors, so complex that scientists in 34 countries have readied 100,000 computers to process its data, and so fragile that a bird dropping a bread crust can short-circuit its power supply." [6] But exploiting the collider's potential to expand the frontiers of knowledge has required that scientists around the world cut across "boundaries of place, organization, and technical specialty to conduct ever more ambitious experiments."

The structural arrangement for getting work done that has developed around the massive collider is an example of another contemporary organizational design called the **boundaryless organization**, which is an organization whose design is not defined by, or limited to, the horizontal, vertical, or external boundaries imposed by a predefined structure. [7] Former GE chairman Jack Welch coined the term because he wanted to eliminate vertical and horizontal boundaries within GE and break down external barriers between the company and its customers and suppliers. Although the idea of eliminating boundaries may seem odd, many of today's most successful organizations are finding that they can operate most effectively by remaining flexible and *un*structured: that the ideal structure for them is *not* having a rigid, bounded, and predefined structure. [8]

What do we mean by *boundaries*? There are two types: (1) *internal*—the horizontal ones imposed by work specialization and departmentalization and the vertical ones that separate employees into organizational levels and hierarchies; and (2) *external*—the boundaries that separate the organization from its customers, suppliers, and other stakeholders. To minimize or eliminate these boundaries, managers might use virtual or network structural designs.

VIRTUAL ORGANIZATIONS. Is an internship something you've ever thought about doing (or maybe have done)? How about an internship that you could do, not in a workplace cubicle, but from your couch using your computer? [9] Such virtual internships are becoming quite popular, especially with smaller and midsize companies and, of course, with online businesses. The type of work virtual interns do typically involves "researching, sales, marketing, and social-media development"—tasks that can be done anywhere with a computer and online access. Some organizations are structured in a way that allows most employees to be virtual employees.

A **virtual organization** typically consists of a small core of full-time employees and outside specialists temporarily hired as needed to work on projects. [10] An example is StrawberryFrog, a global advertising agency with offices in Amsterdam, New York, São Paulo, and Mumbai. It does its work with a relatively small administrative staff but has a global network of virtual freelance employees who are hired to work as needed on client projects. By relying on these virtual employees, the company enjoys a network of talent without all the unnecessary overhead and structural complexity. [11]

NETWORK ORGANIZATIONS. Food marketer Smart Balance Inc. helps people stay trim and lean with its heart-healthy products. [12] The company's organizational structure is also trim and lean. With only 67 employees, the company outsources almost every other organizational function including manufacturing, product distribution, and sales. Smart Balance's structural approach is one that also eliminates organizational boundaries and can be described as a **network organization**, which uses its own employees to do some work activities and networks of outside suppliers to provide other needed product components or work processes. [13] This organizational form is sometimes called a modular organization by manufacturing firms. [14] Such an approach allows organizations to concentrate on what they

---

matrix structure
An organizational structure that assigns specialists from different functional departments to work on one or more projects

project structure
An organizational structure in which employees continuously work on projects

boundaryless organization
An organization whose design is not defined by, or limited to, the horizontal, vertical, or external boundaries imposed by a predefined structure

virtual organization
An organization that consists of a small core of full-time employees and outside specialists temporarily hired as needed to work on projects

network organization
An organization that uses its own employees to do some work activities and networks of outside suppliers to provide other needed product components or work processes

FUTURE VISION

The Working World in 2020

Flexible Organizations

By 2020, a considerably smaller proportion of the labor force will hold full-time jobs. Organizations will increasingly rely on contract employees and part-timers to get the work done, giving the organization greater flexibility. From the employee's standpoint, it will mean greater individual control of the employee's future rather than being dependent on a single employer.

Future workers will be more like outside consultants than full-time employees. Assignments will be temporary. They might last a few weeks or a few years, but the presumption is—on the part of both workers and employers—that the relationship will not become permanent. As such, you will find yourself consistently working on new projects with a different group of coworkers.

Additionally, expect to see fewer large corporate headquarter buildings and centralized corporate centers. Work demands will not require organizations to house large numbers of workers in one place. "Headquarter" cities such as New York, Toronto, or London will find themselves with lots of empty office space. Conversely, job opportunities will be geographically dispersed, and in many cases, not dependent at all on where employees reside. An increasing proportion of the labor force will work from home. And many organizations will create regional satellite centers where employees meet or work. These centers will be less costly to operate than centralized offices and will cut down on commuting distances for workers.

do best by contracting out other activities to companies that do those activities best. For instance, the strategy of British company ARM, a microchip designer, is to find a lot of partners. It contracts with those partners for manufacturing and sales. Because ARM doesn't manufacture, it can encourage its customers (ARM's chip designs serve as the brains of 98% of the world's cell phones) to request whatever they like. Such flexibility is particularly valuable in the cell phone market where having custom chips and software can provide an edge.[15] At Boeing, the company's head of development for the 787 Dreamliner manages thousands of employees and some 100 suppliers at more than 100 sites in different countries.[16] Sweden's Ericsson contracts its manufacturing and even some of its research and development to more cost-effective contractors in New Delhi, Singapore, California, and other global locations.[17] And at Penske Truck Leasing, dozens of business processes, such as securing permits and titles, entering data from drivers' logs, and processing data for tax filings and accounting, have been outsourced to Mexico and India.[18]

Learning Organizations

Let's Get Real

F 2 F

Being a learning organization means *being open to resources, technologies, and ideas that may be outside the box.*

Doing business in an intensely competitive global environment, British retailer Tesco realizes how important it is for its stores to run well behind the scenes.[19] And it does so using a proven "tool" called Tesco in a Box, which is a self-contained complete IT system and matching set of business processes that provides the model for all of Tesco's international business operations. This approach promotes consistency in operations as well as being a way to share innovations. Tesco is an example of a **learning organization**, an organization that has developed the capacity to continuously learn, adapt, and change. "Today's managerial challenge is to inspire and enable knowledge workers to solve, day in and day out, problems that cannot be anticipated."[20] In a learning organization, employees continually acquire and share new knowledge and apply that knowledge in making decisions or doing their work. Some organizational theorists even go so far as to say that an organization's ability to do this—that is, to learn and to apply that learning—may be the only sustainable source of competitive advantage.[21] What structural characteristics does a learning organization need?

Employees throughout the entire organization—across different functional specialties and even at different organizational levels—must share information and collaborate on work activities. Such an environment requires minimal structural and physical barriers, which allows employees to work together in doing the organization's work the best way they can and, in the process, learn from each other. Finally, empowered work teams tend to be an important feature of a learning organization's structural design. These teams make decisions about doing whatever work needs to be done or resolving issues. With empowered employees and teams, there's little need for "bosses" to direct and control. Instead, managers serve as facilitators, supporters, and advocates.

Organizing for Collaboration

11.2

LEARNING OUTCOME
Discuss how organizations organize for collaboration.

In 3M's dental products division, Sumita Mitra, a research scientist, helped develop coatings that prevent tooth plaque and innovative cement bonding materials that could be set by light.[22] However, as cosmetic dentistry's popularity increased, she sensed an opportunity for developing a product that had both the strength and the natural appearance that dentists wanted. Finding that product meant venturing outside the realm of traditional dental materials. Mitra first turned to 3M's database of technical reports written by the company's some 7,000 scientists. Although this database is invaluable for spreading knowledge throughout the company, "the real work of collaboration happens face-to-face, often at events sponsored by TechForum, an employee-run organization designed to foster communications between scientists in different labs or division." There, Mitra found valuable information and guidance from other scientists in different divisions of the company. 3M also has an R&D Workcenter networking Web site, which Mitra describes as "a LinkedIn for 3M scientists." It also proved to be a valuable collaborative tool. Both the TechForum and the R&D Workcenter proved beneficial for Mitra's research efforts. Three years after starting her research, 3M introduced Filtek Supreme Plus, a strong, polishable dental material and the first to include nanoparticles. At 3M, employees are expected to collaborate and are evaluated on their success. Such collaborations among the company's scientists have led to several breakthroughs in product technology.

It's fair to say that the world of work has changed. Organizations need to be more flexible in how work gets done, although it still needs to get done efficiently and effectively. Throw in the fact that innovation and the ability to bring innovations to market quickly is critical and you can begin to appreciate how traditional top-down decision making that strictly follows the chain of command and narrowly defined functional arrangements might not be the best structural mechanisms to do this. Many organizations, like 3M, are encouraging collaborative work among employees. Exhibit 11-3 lists some of the benefits and drawbacks of working collaboratively. An organization's collaboration efforts can be internal—that is, among employees within the organization. Or those efforts can be external collaborations with any stakeholders. In both types, it's important that managers recognize how such collaborative efforts "fit" with the organization's structure and the challenges of making all the pieces work together successfully. Let's take a look at each of these types of collaboration.

Benefits	Drawbacks
• Increased communication and coordination	• Potential interpersonal conflict
• Greater innovative output	• Different views and competing goals
• Enhanced ability to address complex problems	• Logistics of coordinating
• Sharing of information and best practices	

EXHIBIT 11-3

Benefits and Drawbacks of Collaborative Work

Sources: Based on R. Wagner and G. Muller, "The Pinnacle of Partnership: Unselfishness," *Gallup Management Journal Online* [http://gmj.gallup.com], February 18, 2010; M. T. Hansen, "When Internal Collaboration Is Bad for Your Company," *Harvard Business Review*, April 2009, pp. 83–88; G. Ahuja, "Collaboration Networks, Structural Holes and Innovation: A Longitudinal Study," *Academy of Management Proceedings Online*, 1998; and M. Pincher, "Collaboration: Find a New Strength in Unity," *Computer Weekly*, November 27, 2007, p. 18.

learning organization
An organization that has developed the capacity to continuously learn, adapt, and change

Internal Collaboration

When managers believe that collaboration among employees is needed for more coordinated and integrated work efforts, they can use several different structural options. Some of the more popular include cross-functional teams, task forces, and communities of practice.

CROSS-FUNCTIONAL TEAMS.   Organizations are using team-based structures because they've found that teams are more flexible and responsive to changing events than are traditional departments or other permanent work groups. Teams have the ability to quickly assemble, deploy, refocus, and disband. In Chapter 10, we introduced the concept of a **cross-functional team** in our discussion of the various forms of departmentalization. Remember that it's a work team composed of individuals from various functional specialties. When a cross-functional team is formed, team members are brought together to collaborate on resolving mutual problems that affect the respective functional areas. Ideally, the artificial boundaries that separate functions disappear and the team focuses on working together to achieve organizational goals. For instance, at ArcelorMittal, the world's biggest steel company, cross-functional teams of scientists, plant managers, and salespeople review and monitor product innovations.[23] The concept of cross-functional teams is even being applied in health care. For instance, at Suburban Hospital in Bethesda, Maryland, intensive care unit (ICU) teams composed of a doctor trained in intensive care medicine, a pharmacist, a social worker, a nutritionist, the chief ICU nurse, a respiratory therapist, and a chaplain meet daily with every patient's bedside nurse to discuss and debate the best course of treatment. The hospital credits this team care approach with reducing errors, shortening the amount of time patients spent in ICU, and improving communication between families and the medical staff.[24] We'll discuss teams in more detail in Chapter 13.

TASK FORCES.   Another structural option organizations might use is a **task force** (also called an **ad hoc committee**), which is a temporary committee or team formed to tackle a specific short-term problem affecting several departments. The temporary nature of a task force is what differentiates it from a cross-functional team. Task force members usually perform many of their normal work tasks while serving on the task force. However, the members of a task force must collaborate to resolve the issue that's been assigned to them. When the issue or problem is solved, the task force is no longer needed and members return to their regular assignments. Many organizations, from government agencies to

South Korea's Samsung Electronics Company became the world's first electronics maker to release three-dimensional LED televisions. Because innovation and speed to market are critical to Samsung's success, the company encourages collaboration and cooperation among employees within the organization and among its business partners all along the supply chain. At 42 research facilities throughout the world, teams of researchers and engineers collaborate on emerging core technologies. Within its divisions, Samsung uses cross-functional product development teams to commercialize products scheduled for release within one or two years.

universities to businesses, use task forces. For instance, at San Francisco–based accounting firm Eichstaedt & Devereaux, employee task forces have helped develop formal recruiting, mentoring, and training programs. And at Frito-Lay, a subsidiary of PepsiCo, Inc., a task force that included members of the company's Hispanic employees' resource group helped in the development of two new products: Lay's Cool Guacamole potato chips and Doritos Guacamole tortilla chips.[25]

COMMUNITIES OF PRACTICE.   Early in 2008, American soldiers training Afghan and Iraqi armies were having problems using a rocket-propelled grenade launcher. The frustrated unit commander posted a question to one of the U.S. Army's online forums where soldiers ask questions and share ideas with peers around the world. Within a few days, someone who had had a similar experience with the launcher posted a simple solution on the Web site on how to safely prevent misfiring. Problem solved![26] Such types of internal collaborations are called **communities of practice**, which are "groups of people who share a concern, a set of problems, or a passion about a topic, and who deepen their knowledge and expertise in that area by interacting on an ongoing basis."[27] For example, repair technicians at Xerox share "war stories" to communicate their experiences and to help others solve difficult problems with repairing machines.[28] At pharmaceutical firm Pfizer, communities of practice are integrated into the company's formal structure. Called employee councils and networks, these communities share knowledge and help product development teams on difficult issues such as safety.[29] Pfizer's more structured approach to recognizing the value of such collaboration is becoming more common. But how effective are these communities of practice? A recent research study found that communities of practice can "create value by contributing to increased effectiveness in employees' job performance through greater access that they provide to the ideas, knowledge, and best practices shared among community members."[30] Exhibit 11-4 lists some suggestions for making such communities work.

External Collaboration

Like our chapter-opening story about Verizon, Intuit has figured out a way to get its customers involved. Diehard users of QuickBooks have access to a site—QuickBooks Live Community—where they can exchange helpful information with others. For customers, that often means faster answers to problems. And for the company, this "volunteer army"

EXHIBIT 11-4

Making Communities of Practice Work

- Have top management support and set clear expectations.
- Create an environment that will attract people and make them want to return for advice, conversation, and knowledge sharing.
- Encourage regular meetings of the community, whether in person or online.
- Establish regular communication among community members.
- Focus on real problems and issues important to the organization.
- Have clear accountability and managerial oversight.

Sources: Based on R. McDermott and D. Archibald, "Harnessing Your Staff's Informal Networks," *Harvard Business Review,* March 2010, pp. 82–89; S. F. Gale, "The Power of Community, *Workforce Management Online,* March 2009; and E. Wenger, R. McDermott, and W. Snyder, *Cultivating Communities of Practice: A Guide to Managing Knowledge* (Boston: Harvard Business School Press, 2002).

cross-functional team
A work team composed of individuals from various functional specialties

task force (or ad hoc committee)
A temporary committee or team formed to tackle a specific short-term problem affecting several departments

communities of practice
Groups of people who share a concern, a set of problems, or a passion about a topic, and who deepen their knowledge and expertise in that area by interacting on an ongoing basis

means less investment in paid technicians.[31] External collaboration efforts have become quite popular for organizations, especially in the area of product innovation. We're going to look at two forms of external collaboration: open innovation and strategic partnerships. Each of these can provide organizations with needed information, support, and contributions to getting work done and achieving organizational goals. But it's important that managers understand the challenges of how each might fit into the organization's structural design.

OPEN INNOVATION. Pharmaceutical giant GlaxoSmithKline PLC opened to the public the designs behind 13,500 chemical compounds associated with the parasite that causes malaria. Glaxo "hopes that sharing information and working together will lead scientists to come up with a drug for treating the mosquito-borne disease faster than the company could do on its own."[32]

The days when businesses generate their own product development ideas in house and develop, manufacture, market, and deliver those products to customers may be numbered. Today, many companies are trying open innovation, which is opening up the search for new ideas beyond the organization's boundaries and allowing innovations to easily transfer inward and outward. For instance, Procter & Gamble, Starbucks, Dell, Best Buy, and Nike have all created digital platforms that allow customers to help them create new products and messages.[33] As you can see, many of today's successful companies are collaborating directly with customers in the product development process. Others are partnering with suppliers, other outsiders, and even competitors. Exhibit 11-5 describes some of the benefits and drawbacks of open innovation.

STRATEGIC PARTNERSHIPS. Companies worldwide are finding ways to connect to each other. Once bitter rivals, Nokia and Qualcomm formed a cooperative agreement to develop next-generation cell phones for North America. Nokia also collaborated with Yahoo! in a partnership where Yahoo's software powers e-mail and chat services on most Nokia phones.[34]

In today's environment, organizations are looking for advantages wherever they can get them. One way they can do this is with strategic partnerships, which are collaborative relationships between two or more organizations in which they combine their resources and capabilities for some business purpose. Here are some reasons why such partnerships make sense: flexibility and informality of arrangements promote efficiencies, provide access to new markets and technologies, and entail less paperwork when creating and disbanding projects; risks and expenses are shared by multiple parties; independent brand identification is kept and can be exploited; working with partners possessing multiple skills can create major synergies; rivals can often work together harmoniously; partnerships can take on varied forms from simple to complex; dozens of participants can be accommodated in

EXHIBIT 11-5 **Benefits and Drawbacks of Open Innovation**	**Benefits**	**Drawbacks**
	• Gives customers what they want—a voice	• High demands of managing the process
	• Allows organizations to respond to complex problems	• Extensive support needed
	• Nurtures internal and external relationships	• Cultural challenges
	• Brings focus back to marketplace	• Greater need for flexibility
	• Provides way to cope with rising costs and uncertainties of product development	• Crucial changes required in how knowledge is controlled and shared

Sources: Based on S. Lindegaard, "The Side Effects of Open Innovation," *Bloomberg BusinessWeek Online,* June 7, 2010; H. W. Chesbrough and A. R. Garman, "How Open Innovation Can Help You Cope in Lean Times," *Harvard Business Review,* December 2009, pp. 68–76; A. Gabor, "The Promise [and Perils] of Open Collaboration," *Strategy & Business Online,* Autumn 2009; and J. Winsor, "Crowdsourcing: What It Means for Innovation," *BusinessWeek Online,* June 15, 2009.

partnership arrangements; and antitrust laws can protect R&D activities.[35] Strategic partnerships are growing in popularity. However, as with all the collaborative arrangements we've described—external and internal—the challenge for managers is finding ways to exploit the benefits of such collaboration while incorporating the collaborative efforts seamlessly into the organization's structural design.

Flexible Work Arrangements

11.3

LEARNING OUTCOME
Explain flexible work arrangements used by organizations.

Accenture consultant Keyur Patel's job arrangement is becoming the norm, rather than the exception.[36] During his recent consulting assignment, he had three clocks on his desk: one set to Manila time (where his software programmers were), one to Bangalore (where another programming support team worked), and the third for San Francisco, where he was spending four days a week helping a major retailer implement IT systems to track and improve sales. And his cell phone kept track of the time in Atlanta, his home, where he headed on Thursday evenings.

For this new breed of professionals, life is a blend of home and office, work and leisure. Thanks to technology, work can now be done anywhere, anytime. As organizations adapt their structural designs to these new realities, we see more of them adopting flexible working arrangements. Such arrangements not only exploit the power of technology, but give organizations the flexibility to deploy employees when and where needed. In this section, we're going to take a look at some different types of flexible work arrangements including telecommuting and compressed workweeks, flextime, and job sharing. As with the other structural options we've looked at, managers must evaluate these types in light of the implications for decision making, communication, authority relationships, work task accomplishment, and so forth.

Telecommuting

Eve Gelb used to endure hour-and-a-half commutes morning and evening on the 405 Freeway in Los Angeles to her job as a project manager at SCAN Health Plan.[38] Now, she's turned her garage into an office and works from home as a telecommuter. On the days when she does have to go in to the corporate office, she shares a space with her three subordinates who also work flexibly. Information technology has made telecommuting possible, and external environmental changes have made it necessary for many organizations. **Telecommuting** is a work arrangement in which employees work at home and are linked to the workplace by computer. Needless to say, not every job is a candidate for telecommuting, but many are.

Working from home used to be considered a "cushy perk" for a few lucky employees and such an arrangement wasn't allowed very often. Now, many businesses view telecommuting as a business necessity. For instance, at SCAN Health Plan, the company's chief financial officer said that getting more employees to telecommute provided the company a way to grow without having to incur any additional fixed costs such as office buildings, equipment, or parking lots. In addition, some companies view the arrangement as a way to combat high gas prices and to attract talented employees who want more freedom and control over their work.

Despite its apparent appeal, many managers are reluctant to have their employees become "laptop hobos."[39] They argue that employees will waste time surfing the Internet or playing online games instead of working, that they'll ignore clients, and that they'll desperately miss

by the numbers[37]

8 percent of companies surveyed have more than 40 percent of their employees working virtually.

44 percent of employees say their top gripe about working from home is not having face-to-face interaction.

40 percent of respondents view collaborating with customers and suppliers as the most significant impact on the amount of time it took to get new products to market.

20 percent of Americans have "nonstandard" jobs (work fewer than 35 hours a week, independent contractors, day laborers, etc.).

12 percent of respondents to a global workforce survey say that telecommuting is extremely important to them.

81 percent of employers offer some form of flexible work arrangements.

70 percent of the U.S. workforce qualifies as "mobile" at least part of the time.

open innovation
Opening up the search for new ideas beyond the organization's boundaries and allowing innovations to easily transfer inward and outward

strategic partnerships
Collaborative relationships between two or more organizations in which they combine their resources and capabilities for some business purpose

telecommuting
A work arrangement in which employees work at home and are linked to the workplace by computer

Let's Get Real

F2F

Telecommuting can be beneficial because *it allows employee flexibility in work schedules, a reduction in company overhead, and convenience for companies with large geographical footprints.*

the camaraderie and social exchanges of the workplace. In addition, managers wonder how they'll "manage" these employees. How do you interact with an employee and gain his or her trust when they're not physically present? And what if their work performance isn't up to par? How do you make suggestions for improvement? Another significant challenge is making sure that company information is kept safe and secure when employees are working from home. (We'll discuss this particular issue more fully in Chapter 18 when we look at the control process.)

Employees often express the same concerns about working remotely, especially when it comes to the isolation of not being "at work." At Accenture, where employees are scattered around the world, the chief human resources officer says that it isn't easy to maintain that esprit de corps.[40] However, the company has put in place a number of programs and processes to create that sense of belonging for its workforce, including Web-conferencing tools, assigning each employee to a career counselor, and holding quarterly community events at its offices. In addition, the telecommuter employee may find that the line between work and home becomes even more blurred, which can be stressful.[41] Managers and organizations must address these important organizing issues as they move toward having employees telecommute.

So, once an organization decides that it wants to establish telecommuting opportunities for employees, what needs to happen next? One of the first issues to address is encouraging employees to make that decision to become remote workers. For instance, at SCAN Health Plan, the company offered free high-speed Internet access and free office furniture, along with help in setting it up to encourage more of its workforce to work from home. Other companies have encouraged employees to work anywhere but at the office by pointing to the pay "increase" employees would receive from money saved on gas, dry cleaning, and eating out at lunch. Other companies have used the "green" angle . . . emphasizing the carbon-free aspect of not driving long distances to and from the workplace. Managing the telecommuters then becomes a matter of keeping employees feeling like they're connected and engaged, a topic we delve into at the end of the chapter as we look at today's organizational design challenges.

Compressed Workweeks, Flextime, and Job Sharing

During the recent economic crisis in the United Kingdom, accounting firm KPMG needed to reduce costs.[42] It decided to use flexible work options as a way of doing so. The company's program, called Flexible Futures, offered employees four options to choose from: a four-day workweek with a 20 percent salary reduction; a two- to twelve-week sabbatical at

KPMG has created a culture of flexibility throughout its global network of professional firms that provide audit, tax, and advisory services. Employees of KPMG offices in the United Kingdom, shown here, appreciate flexible working options that include shorter work weeks, working from home, job sharing, and "glide time," where the start and finish times of the work day can be adjusted. From research and employee surveys, KPMG has learned that flexible work arrangements are becoming increasingly important to all employees as they strive to balance their work–life commitments. Giving employees freedom in scheduling their work helps KPMG attract and retain the best workforce.

30 percent of pay; both options; or continue with their regular schedule. Some 85 percent of the U.K. employees agreed to the reduced-workweek plan. "Since so many people agreed to the flexible work plans, KPMG was able to cap the salary cut at about 10 percent for the year in most cases." The best thing, though, was that as a result of the plan, KPMG didn't have to do large-scale employee layoffs.

As this example shows, organizations may sometimes find they need to restructure work using forms of flexible work arrangements. One approach is a **compressed workweek**, which is a workweek where employees work longer hours per day but fewer days per week. The most common arrangement is four 10-hour days (a 4-40 program). For example, in Utah, state employees have a mandated (by law) four-day workweek, with offices closed on Fridays in an effort to reduce energy costs. After a year's time, the state found that its compressed workweek resulted in a 13 percent reduction in energy use and estimated that state employees saved as much as $6 million in gasoline costs.[43] Another alternative is **flextime** (also known as **flexible work hours**), which is a scheduling system in which employees are required to work a specific number of hours a week but are free to vary those hours within certain limits. A flextime schedule typically designates certain common core hours when all employees are required to be on the job, but allows starting, ending, and lunch-hour times to be flexible. According to a survey of companies by the Families and Work Institute, 81 percent of the respondents now offer flextime benefits. Another survey by Watson Wyatt of mid- and large-sized companies found that flexible work schedules was the most commonly offered benefit.[44]

In Great Britain, McDonald's is experimenting with an unusual program—dubbed the Family Contract—to reduce absenteeism and turnover at some of its restaurants. Under this Family Contract, employees from the same immediate family can fill in for one another for any work shift without having to clear it first with their manager.[45] This type of job scheduling is called **job sharing**—the practice of having two or more people split a full-time job. Although something like McDonald's Family Contract may be appropriate for a low-skilled job, other organizations might offer job sharing to professionals who want to work but don't want the demands and hassles of a full-time position. For instance, at Ernst & Young, employees in many of the company's locations can choose from a variety of flexible work arrangements including job sharing. Also, many companies have used job sharing during the economic downturn to avoid employee layoffs.[46]

Contingent Workforce

11.4

LEARNING OUTCOME
Discuss organizing issues associated with a contingent workforce.

At Conrad & Co., a small private accounting firm in Spartanburg, South Carolina, Diana Galvin started as a temporary, part-time employee before moving into a full-time staff accountant position. She got her full-time job by learning how to do and then doing her assignments well and offering suggestions on how the company could improve.[47] But not every temporary worker gets offered a full-time job (or wants to be offered one). Prior to her full-time employment, Diana was part of what has been called the contingent workforce. **Contingent workers** are temporary, freelance, or contract workers whose employment is *contingent* upon demand for their services.

"Stung by massive and disruptive layoffs that accompanied the latest recession, companies are starting to rethink the way they get work done."[48] As organizations eliminate full-time jobs through downsizing and other organizational restructurings, they often rely on a contingent workforce to fill in as needed. Also, one of the top-ranking forecasts in a survey that asked HR experts to look ahead 10 years to 2018 was that "Firms will become adept at sourcing and engaging transient talent around short-term needs, and will focus considerable energy

compressed workweek
A workweek where employees work longer hours per day but fewer days per week

flextime (or flexible work hours)
A scheduling system in which employees are required to work a specific number of hours a week but are free to vary those hours within certain limits

job sharing
The practice of having two or more people split a full-time job

contingent workers
Temporary, freelance, or contract workers whose employment is contingent upon demand for their services

Recognizing a shortage of workers in the Netherlands and a shortage of jobs in Poland, two young Dutch entrepreneurs founded Otto Work Force in 2000 as an agency for temporary workers whose employment is contingent on the demand for their services. At the company's office in Opole, Poland, shown here, Otto recruits employees to fill requests from Dutch firms for temporary workers for a limited time, usually from one to six months, for a wide range of jobs ranging from cleaning to construction. Otto recruiters provide the workers with travel to the Netherlands, living accommodations, and transportation to and from work. Otto has expanded its business to other countries as more and more firms rely on the contingent workforce.

on the long-term retention of smaller core talent groups."[49] The model for the contingent worker structural approach can be seen in the film industry. There, people are essentially "free agents" who move from project to project applying their skills—directing, talent casting, costuming, makeup, set design, and so forth—as needed. They assemble for a movie, then disband once it's finished and move on to the next project. This type of contingent worker is common in project organizations. But contingent workers can also be temporary employees brought in to help with special needs such as seasonal work. Let's look at some of the organizational issues associated with contingent workers.

One of the main issues businesses face with their contingent workers, especially those who are independent contractors or freelancers, is classifying who actually qualifies as one.[50] The decision on who is and who isn't an independent contractor isn't as easy or as unimportant as it may seem. Companies don't have to pay Social Security, Medicare, or unemployment insurance taxes on workers classified as independent contractors. And those individuals also aren't covered by most workplace laws. So it's an important decision. For instance, FedEx treats some 12,000 of its package deliverers in its FedEx Ground Division as contractors. Their classification of these workers as independent contractors has caused battles with the Internal Revenue Service and state governments and riled competitor UPS, whose drivers are unionized employees and argues that FedEx's policy is "unfair to taxpayers, competitors, and the workers themselves."[51] The federal government is also looking at increased power to penalize employers that misclassify workers. So, there is an incentive to be totally above-board in classifying who is and is not an independent contractor. The legal definition of a contract worker depends on how much control a company has over the person; that is, does the company control what the worker does and how the worker does his or her job? The more control the company has, "the more likely the individual will be considered an employee rather than an independent contractor."[52] And it isn't just the legal/tax issues that are important in how workers are classified. The structural implications, especially in terms of getting work done and how performance problems are resolved, are important, as well.

Another issue with contingent workers is the process for recruiting, screening, and placing these contingent workers where their work skills and efforts are needed.[53] As we'll discuss in the next chapter on human resource management, these important steps help ensure that the right people are in the right places at the right times in order to get work done efficiently and effectively. Any organization that wants to minimize potential problems with its contingent workers needs to pay attention to hiring.

The final issue we want to look at is the importance of a contingent employee's performance. Just like a regular employee, a contingent employee is brought on board to do some specific work task(s). It's important that managers have a method of establishing goals, schedules, and deadlines with the contingent employees.[54] And it's also important that mechanisms be in place to monitor work performance and goal achievement, especially if the contingent employee is working off-site.

LEARNING OUTCOME 11.5
Describe today's organizational design challenges.

Today's Organizational Design Challenges

As managers look for organizational designs that will best support and facilitate employees doing their work efficiently and effectively, they must contend with certain challenges. These challenges include keeping employees connected and managing global structural issues.

Keeping Employees Connected

Many organizational design concepts were developed during the twentieth century when work was done at an employer's place of business under a manager's supervision, work tasks were fairly predictable and constant, and most jobs were full-time and continued indefinitely.[55] But that's not the way it is today at many companies. For instance, thousands of Cisco Systems employees sit at unassigned desks in team rooms interspersed with communal break areas. At some IBM divisions, only a small percentage of employees—mostly top managers and their assistants—have fixed desks or offices. All others are either mobile employees or they share desks when they need to be at work. At Sabre Holdings, teams are assigned to neighborhoods of workspaces and employees find places for themselves when they arrive.[56]

As these examples show, a major structural design challenge for managers is finding a way to offer flexibility but also keeping widely dispersed and mobile employees connected to the organization. Mobile computing and communication technology have given organizations and employees ways to stay connected and to be more productive. For instance, handheld devices have e-mail, calendars, and contacts that can be used anywhere there's a wireless network. And these devices can be used to log into corporate databases and company intranets. Employees can videoconference using broadband networks and Webcams. Many companies are giving employees key fobs with constantly changing encryption codes that allow them to log onto the corporate network to access e-mail and company data from any computer hooked up to the Internet. Cell phones switch seamlessly between cellular networks and corporate Wi-Fi connections. The biggest issue in doing work anywhere, anytime, however, is security. Companies must protect their important and sensitive information. Fortunately, software and other disabling devices have minimized security issues considerably. Even insurance providers are more comfortable giving their mobile employees access to information. For instance, Health Net Inc. gave BlackBerry phones to many of its managers so they can tap into customer records from anywhere. As one tech company CEO said, "Companies now can start thinking about innovative apps [applications] they can create and deliver to their workers anywhere."[58]

LEADER who made a difference

One senior vice president at Cisco Systems belongs to more internal company teams than "he can count on both hands." While that may sound like a nightmare to some, that's part of the organizational structure "web" created by CEO John T. Chambers.[57] The structure is so complex that it takes some 15 minutes and a whiteboard to explain it. However, Chambers uses three words to describe its benefits: "speed, skill, and flexibility." His idea for the company's structure originated at the end of the 2001 downturn after Cisco wrote off some $2.2 billion in losses. Chambers realized that the "company's hierarchical structure precluded it from moving quickly into new markets." So he began grouping executives into cross-functional teams figuring that this would help break down traditional silos and lead to faster decision making. At first, the executives didn't like it. Some couldn't handle working with unfamiliar colleagues; others were upset with the new team-based compensation structure. However, the company's decision making has accelerated—it only took executives eight days to figure out that it made sense to acquire Web-conferencing company WebEx.

Managing Global Structural Issues

Are there global differences in organizational structures? Are Australian organizations structured like those in the United States? Are German organizations structured like those in France or Mexico? Given the global nature of today's business environment, managers need to be familiar with this issue. Researchers have concluded that the structures and strategies of organizations worldwide are similar, "while the behavior within them is maintaining its cultural uniqueness."[59] What does this distinction between strategy and culture mean for designing effective and efficient structures? When designing or changing structure, managers may need to think about the cultural implications of certain design elements. For instance, one study showed that formalization—rules and bureaucratic mechanisms—may be more important in less economically developed countries and less important in more economically developed countries where employees may have higher levels of professional education and skills.[60] Another study found that organizations with people from high power-distance countries (such as Greece, France, and most of Latin America) find that their employees are much more accepting of mechanistic structures than are employees from low power-distance countries. Other structural design elements may be affected by cultural differences as well.

No matter what structural design managers choose for their organizations, the design should help employees do their work in the best—most efficient and effective—way they can. The structure should support and facilitate organizational members as they carry out the organization's work. After all, an organization's structure is simply a means to an end.

What Would You Do?

**Richard
"Dickie"
Townley**
Sr. Manager Product
Terminals and
Marketing
**Holly Energy
Partners, L.P.
Artesia, NM**

Let's Get Real:

My Response to *A Manager's Dilemma, page 288*

A volunteer organization structure is not a new concept. We have used the volunteer organization structure for years in the health care system (candy stripers) and in political campaign structures. The difference we find here is the Web-based structure and boundaryless nature of Web forums. Many managers today may not be as technologically savvy as the employees they direct and not comfortable with a boundaryless organizational concept. They see the potential value of a Web-based volunteer organizational structure; however, their working knowledge may be limited. I would take a multiphase approach to setting up a volunteer organizational structure. Web forum utilization would be the key component I would use to design a volunteer structure.

Phase one:

- Assign managers to work with the information technology group to identify potential Web forums that would be resources for customer service.
- Have employees as well as management utilize the Web forums in-house by posing a wide range of user issues.

Phase two: Categorize the results of the utilization phase.

- Most knowledgeable responses/forums
- Most dependable responses/forums
- Most user-friendly forums

Phase three:

- Create a marketing strategy to incorporate these sites into your business model.
- Create an organizational flowchart incorporating both the conventional customer service resources and the nonconventional Web forums.

Phase four:

- Continue to utilize the Web forums in-house to assure quality control and customer satisfaction.

CHAPTER SUMMARY
by Learning Outcomes

Describe contemporary organizational designs.

In a team structure, the entire organization is made up of work teams. The matrix structure assigns specialists from different functional departments to work on one or more projects being led by project managers. A project structure is one in which employees continuously work on projects. A virtual organization consists of a small core of full-time employees and outside specialists temporarily hired as needed to work on projects. A network organization is an organization that uses its own employees to do some work activities and networks of outside suppliers to provide other needed product components or work processes. A learning organization is one that has developed the capacity to continuously learn, adapt, and change. It has certain structural characteristics including an emphasis on sharing information and collaborating on work activities, minimal structural and physical barriers, and empowered work team.

Discuss how organizations organize for collaboration.

An organization's collaboration efforts can be internal or external. Internal collaborative structural options include cross-functional teams, task forces, and communities of practice. A cross-functional team is a work team composed of individuals from various functional specialties. A task force is a temporary committee or team formed to tackle a specific short-term problem affecting several departments. Communities of practice are groups of people who share a concern, a set of problems, or a passion about a topic, and who deepen their knowledge and expertise in that area by interacting on an ongoing basis. External collaborative options include open innovation and strategic partnerships. Open innovation expands the search for new ideas beyond the organization's boundaries and allows innovations to easily transfer inward and outward. Strategic partnerships are collaborative relationships between two or more organizations in which they combine resources and capabilities for some business purpose.

Explain flexible work arrangements used by organizations.

Flexible work arrangements give organizations the flexibility to deploy employees when and where they're needed. Structural options include telecommuting, compressed workweeks, flextime, and job sharing. Telecommuting is a work arrangement in which employees work at home and are linked to the workplace by computer. A compressed workweek is one in which employees work longer hours per day but fewer days per week. Flextime is a scheduling system in which employees are required to work a specific number of hours a week but are free to vary those hours within certain limits. Job sharing is when two or more people split a full-time job.

Discuss organizing issues associated with a contingent workforce.

Contingent workers are temporary, freelance, or contract workers whose employment is contingent upon demand for their services. Organizing issues include classifying who actually qualifies as an independent contractor; setting up a process for recruiting, screening, and placing contingent workers; and having a method in place for establishing goals, schedules, and deadlines and for monitoring work performance.

Describe today's organizational design challenges.

The two main organizational design challenges for today include keeping employees connected and managing global structural issues.

mymanagementlab To check your understanding of learning outcomes 11.1 – 11.5 go to **mymanagementlab.com** and try the chapter questions.

REVIEW AND DISCUSSION QUESTIONS

1. Describe the four contemporary organizational designs. How are they similar? Different?
2. Differentiate between matrix and project structures.
3. How can an organization operate without boundaries?
4. The boundaryless organization has the potential to create a major shift in the way we work. Do you agree or disagree? Explain.
5. What types of skills would a manager need to effectively work in a project structure? In a boundaryless organization? In a learning organization?
6. How does each of the different types of collaboration (both internal and external) contribute to more coordinated and integrated work efforts?

7. What structural issues might arise in managing employees' flexible work arrangements? Think about what you've learned about organizational design. How might that information help a manager address those issues?
8. Does the idea of a flexible work arrangement appeal to you? Why or why not?
9. What structural issues might arise in managing contingent workers? Again, think about what you've learned about organizational design. How might that information help a manager address those issues?
10. Why is it a challenge to "keep employees connected" in today's organizations?

PREPARING FOR: My Career

ETHICS DILEMMA

"Ethical hacking." It's probably an understatement to say that people were excited about the introduction of Apple's iPad.[61] Then the news broke that a small group of computer experts calling themselves Goatse Security had hacked into AT&T's Web site and found numbers that identified iPads connected to AT&T's mobile network. Those numbers allowed the group to uncover 114,000 e-mail addresses of thousands of first-adopter iPad customers including prominent officials in companies, politics, and the military. AT&T called it an act of malice, condemned the hackers, and apologized to its affected customers. The group that exposed the flaw said that it did a "public service."

One analyst for CNET also said that the group did a good thing. "Security researchers often disclose holes to keep vendors honest. Many sources complain that they notify companies of security vulnerabilities and that the companies take months, or even years, to provide a fix to customers. In the meantime, malicious hackers may have discovered the same hole and may be using it to steal data, infect computers, or attack systems without the computer owner knowing there is even a risk." What do you think? Is there such a thing as "ethical hacking?" What ethical issues do you see here? What are the implications for various stakeholders in this situation?

SKILLS EXERCISE

Developing Your
Acquiring Power Skill

About the Skill

Power is a natural process in any group or organization, and to perform their jobs effectively, managers need to know how to acquire and use power.[62] Why is having power important? Because power makes you less dependent on others. When a manager has power, he or she is not as

dependent on others for critical resources. And if the resources a manager controls are important, scarce, and nonsubstitutable, her power will increase because others will be more dependent on her for those resources. (See Chapter 17 for more information on leader power.)

Steps in Practicing the Skill

You can be more effective at acquiring and using power if you use the following eight behaviors.

1. *Frame arguments in terms of organizational goals.* To be effective at acquiring power means camouflaging

your self-interests. Discussions over who controls what resources should be framed in terms of the benefits that will accrue to the organization; do not point out how you personally will benefit.

2. *Develop the right image.* If you know your organization's culture, you already understand what the organization wants and values from its employees in terms of dress, associates to cultivate and those to avoid, whether to appear risk taking or risk aversive, the preferred leadership style, the importance placed on getting along well with others, and so forth. With this knowledge, you're equipped to project the appropriate image. Because the assessment of your performance isn't always a fully objective process, you need to pay attention to style as well as substance.

3. *Gain control of organizational resources.* Controlling organizational resources that are scarce *and* important is a source of power. Knowledge and expertise are particularly effective resources to control. They make you more valuable to the organization and, therefore, more likely to have job security, chances for advancement, and a receptive audience for your ideas.

4. *Make yourself appear indispensable.* Because we're dealing with appearances rather than objective facts, you can enhance your power by appearing to be indispensable. You don't really have *to be* indispensable as long as key people in the organization believe that you are.

5. *Be visible.* If you have a job that brings your accomplishments to the attention of others, that's great. However, if you don't have such a job, you'll want to find ways to let others in the organization know what you're doing by highlighting successes in routine reports, having satisfied customers relay their appreciation to senior executives, being seen at social functions, being active in your professional associations, and developing powerful allies who speak positively about your accomplishments. Of course, you'll want to be on the lookout for those projects that will increase your visibility.

6. *Develop powerful allies.* To get power, it helps to have powerful people on your side. Cultivate contacts with potentially influential people above you, at your own level, and at lower organizational levels. These allies often can provide you with information that's otherwise not readily available. In addition, having allies can provide you with a coalition of support if and when you need it.

7. *Avoid "tainted" members.* In almost every organization, there are fringe members whose status is questionable. Their performance and/or loyalty may be suspect. Keep your distance from such individuals.

8. *Support your boss.* Your immediate future is in the hands of your current boss. Because he or she evaluates your performance, you'll typically want to do whatever is necessary to have your boss on your side. You should make every effort to help your boss succeed, make her look good, support her if she is under siege, and spend the time to find out the criteria she will use to assess your effectiveness. Don't undermine your boss. And don't speak negatively of her to others.

Practicing the Skill

The following suggestions are activities you can do to practice the behaviors associated with acquiring power.

1. Keep a one-week journal of your behavior describing incidences when you tried to influence others around you. Assess each incident by asking: Were you successful at these attempts to influence them? Why or why not? What could you have done differently?

2. Review recent issues of a business periodical (such as *Bloomberg BusinessWeek, Fortune, Forbes, Fast Company, Industry Week,* or the *Wall Street Journal*). Look for articles on reorganizations, promotions, or departures from management positions. Find at least two articles where you believe power issues are involved. Relate the content of the articles to the concepts introduced in this skill module.

WORKING TOGETHER
Team Exercise

A company's future may well depend on how well it's able to learn.

Form small groups of three to four individuals. Your team's "job" is to find some current information on learning organizations. You'll probably be able to find numerous articles about the topic, but limit your report to five of what

you consider to be the best sources of information on the topic. Using this information, write a one-page bulleted list discussing your reactions to the statement set in bold at the beginning of this exercise. Be sure to include bibliographic information for your five chosen articles at the end of your one-page bulleted list.

MY TURN TO BE A MANAGER

- Since you may be a telecommuter some time during your career (or may manage employees who are telecommuters), do some research on tips for making telecommuting work.

- Find the most current list of *Fortune*'s Best Companies to Work For (usually published in early February). Look through the list and tally how many of the top 50 provide some type of flexible work arrangements for their employees and the type of flexible work arrangements they use.

- Using current business periodicals, do some research on open innovation efforts by companies. Choose three examples of businesses using this and describe and evaluate what each is doing.

- Create a chart describing each adaptive organizational design discussed in this chapter along with what you perceive as potential advantages and disadvantages of each.

- Steve's and Mary's suggested readings: Richard Donkin, *The Future of Work* (Palgrave Macmillan, 2010); Philip Kotler and John A. Caslione, *Chaotics: The Business of Managing and Marketing in the Age of Turbulence* (Amacom, 2009); Paul Osterman, *The Truth About Middle Managers* (Harvard Business School Press, 2008); and Gary Hamel, *The Future of Management* (Harvard Business School Press, 2007).

- In your own words, write down three things you learned in this chapter about being a good manager.

- Self-knowledge can be a powerful learning tool. Go to mymanagementlab.com and complete these self-assessment exercises: How Well Do I Handle Ambiguity? Do I Trust Others? Do Others See Me as Trustworthy? How Well Do I Respond to Turbulent Change? Using the results of your assessments, identify personal strengths and weaknesses. What will you do to reinforce your strengths and improve your weaknesses?

CASE APPLICATION 1
In the Driver's Seat

One Ford . . . One Team . . . One Plan . . . One Goal.[63] Tens of thousands of Ford employees carry around these words with them on laminated wallet-sized cards. Why? These words reflect the vision CEO Alan Mulally has for the future of Ford Motor Company. And pursuing that vision has implications for how the company will be structured.

Mulally joined Ford Motor in September 2006 from Boeing, where he had led a successful turnaround effort. And Ford, facing serious challenges, needed someone like him. Between the fierce competition in the global car industry and the realities of its manufacturing and product development deficiencies, the company's financial condition was worsening. Family member Bill Ford "handpicked his successor as CEO, gambling that Alan Mulally's team-building skills and industrial savvy would inspire and embolden employees enough to revive the hard-up automaker."

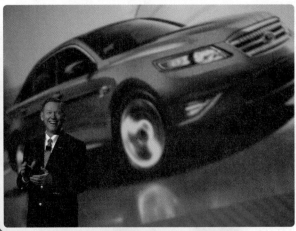

The Ford Focus embodies the vision of CEO Alan Mulally for the automaker to operate as one team throughout the world with one plan and one goal. One of Mulally's key priorities is restructuring the company to achieve profitability in the highly competitive global auto industry.

Mulally's first move was to "immediately dust off his Boeing playbook" as he looked to implement many of the same strategies that had worked in turning around Boeing. Although he recognized the massive problems facing the company in achieving strategic competitiveness and profitability, he was determined to take the dramatic, painful steps and to "plow through gut-wrenching change" to transform the company and return it to global prominence. Guiding his initial efforts was the Way Forward plan that was first announced in January 2006 and the implementation of which was accelerated in September 2006 when Mulally was appointed CEO. This comprehensive plan addressed seven areas where strategic changes would be focused: bold leadership; customer focus; strong brands; bold, innovative products; great quality; clear pricing; and competitive costs and capacity. Mulally also identified four key priorities: (1) aggressively restructure the company to operate profitably at the current real demand and changing model mix; (2) accelerate product development with new products that customers really want and value while achieving manufacturing excellence by reducing complexity and improving quality; (3) obtain financing to do these things and improve the balance sheet; and (4) work together with accountability with all partners. In addition to the Way Forward plan, Mulally fashioned a strategic effort dubbed One Ford in an attempt to "fully leverage the tremendous worldwide resources of Ford." In his remarks to shareholders at the 2008 annual meeting, Mulally had this to say: "We operate in a fiercely competitive global industry. To achieve profitable growth we have to make the best use of our human resources and take advantage of every potential economy of scale and best practice we can find. That means operating as one team around the world, with one plan and one goal . . . One Ford . . . profitable growth for all." These efforts and priorities guided the company over the next few years.

Mulally's vision for Ford culminated at the 2010 Detroit auto show where he unveiled the car that "embodies his strategy for returning Ford to its status as a leader in the global auto industry." That car, the Focus, is Ford's first truly global car—a "single vehicle designed and engineered for customers in every region of the world and sold under one name." Mulally said, "If we were going to be world-class, we needed to pull together and leverage and use our global assets around the world to create a powerhouse 'One Ford'." He also expressed his hope that the vehicle will provide "a rolling blueprint for generations of Ford cars to come."

Discussion Questions

1. Describe and evaluate what Alan Mulally did at Ford Motor Company.

2. What structural implications arise from Mulally's description of Ford being world-class?

3. What types of adaptive organizational designs discussed in this chapter might be needed as Ford continues to pursue its vision of One Ford. . . One Team. . . One Plan. . . One Goal? For each design that you think is appropriate, describe what it is and how the company might use it.

4. What does this case story tell you about how a company's vision and plans affect its structure?

CASE APPLICATION 2
The Virus Hunters

"Imagine what life would be like if your product were never finished, if your work were never done, if your market shifted 30 times a day. The computer-virus hunters at Symantec Corp. don't have to imagine."[64] That's the reality of their daily worklife. At the company's Response Lab in Santa Monica, California, described as the "dirtiest of all our networks at Symantec," software analysts collect viruses and other suspicious code and try to figure out how they work so security updates can be provided to the company's customers. There's even a hazardous materials box by the door to the lab marked DANGER where they put all the disks, tapes, and hard drives with the nasty viruses that need to be completely disposed of. Symantec's situation may seem unique, but the company, which makes content and network security software for both consumers and businesses, reflects the realities facing many organizations today: quickly shifting customer expectations and continuously emerging global competitors that have drastically shortened product life cycles.

The launch of the Blaster-B worm changed the company's approach to dealing with viruses. The domino effect of Blaster-B and other viruses spawned by it meant that frontline software analysts were working around the clock for almost two weeks. The "employee burn-out" potential made the company realize that its virus-hunting team had to be much deeper talent-wise. Now, the response center's team numbers in the hundreds and managers rotate people from the front lines, where they're responsible for responding to new security threats that crop up, into groups where they can help with new-product development. Others write internal research papers. Still others are assigned to develop new tools that will help their colleagues battle the next wave of threats. There's even an individual who tries to figure out what makes the virus writers tick—and the day never ends for these virus hunters. When Santa Monica's team finishes its day, colleagues in Tokyo take over. When the Japanese team finishes its day, it hands off to Dublin, who then hands back to Santa Monica for the new day. It's a frenetic, chaotic, challenging work environment that spans the entire globe.

But the security experts realize that despite their team's best efforts, "they're losing the battle." They plan to add another line of defense and use the power of people to hunt down the cybercriminals by "recruiting victims and other computer users to help them go on the offensive and track down the hackers." Rowan Trollope, senior vice president for consumer products at Symantec, says, "It's time to stop building burglar alarms to keep people out and go after the bad guys." Thus, at the introduction of its new Norton Internet Security system, Symantec is now asking customers to opt in to a program that will collect data about attempted computer intrusions and then forward the information to authorities.

Discussion Questions

1. How might the nature of what the virus hunters do affect the most appropriate structure for getting work done efficiently and effectively?

2. In fighting the onslaught of computer viruses, what will be the challenges of managing a team of professionals and a group of customer "volunteers"?

3. What types of adaptive organizational designs discussed in this chapter might be most appropriate for Symantec to most effectively manage its professionals and its customer volunteers? Explain your choices.

Let's Get Real:

Meet the Manager

Jose Quirarte
HR Manager
D&W Fine Pack, LLC
Fort Calhoun, NE

You'll be hearing more from this real
manager throughout the chapter.

MY JOB:

I am the human resources manager for D&W Fine Pack,
LLC, at the Fort Calhoun, Nebraska, location.

BEST PART OF MY JOB:

The ability to change people's lives by explaining how
they can maximize their group health benefits, mentoring
them to success, or changing the way people live their
lives through continuous education and training that will
allow them to become better individuals personally and
professionally.

Managing Human Resources

LEARNING OUTCOMES

12.1 **Explain** the importance of the human resource management process and the external influences that might affect that process. *page 312*

12.2 **Discuss** the tasks associated with identifying and selecting competent employees. *page 318*

12.3 **Explain** the different types of orientation and training. *page 323*

12.4 **Describe** strategies for retaining competent, high-performing employees. *page 326*

12.5 **Discuss** contemporary issues in managing human resources. *page 328*

WORST PART OF MY JOB:

As a workers' compensation administrator, I find it difficult to interact with employees who have suffered a work-related injury. This is the worst part of my job because I don't like seeing my employees get injured, causing them to change the way they live their lives and interact with their family members. I try to overcome this by always discussing the importance of thinking about safety prior to performing any given task.

BEST MANAGEMENT ADVICE EVER RECEIVED:

"Choose your own battles." I am passionate about my field and love to make a difference in the way people live their lives and to influence them to make the right choices at and away from work. Sometimes I let my passion take over and seek perfection in everything that I do. During a stressful time, a manager told me, "Choose your own battles," meaning, I must pursue the things that will have an overall impact on the organization and those things that will allow the HR department to become a better strategic partner.

It's probably one of the hardest things a manager may have to do.[1] Telling an employee that he or she is being laid off. And some 8 million Americans who have been laid off since the economic recession began in early 2008 have been given that news by someone. In smaller businesses, it's especially difficult because it's often more personal and employees are more like family. In delivering that news, managers may fear that employees will get highly emotional or angry, although those reactions don't happen often. Such reactions are more likely when workers have no notice that layoffs are coming. That's when the situation can become especially raw as those being laid off respond with expressions of shock and disbelief and sometimes crying.

At Ram Tool, a small family-owned manufacturing company in Grafton, Wisconsin, the task fell to Shelly Polum, the company's vice president of administration. After the nine-member management team met to consider which employees would be laid off, Shelly had to inform four workers that they were being let go. "When it was over, trying to maintain her composure, she rushed back to her office and shut the door quickly. Then she sank to the floor and burst into tears." How could this process be made less stressful?

What Would You Do?

With the organization's structure in place, managers have to find people to fill the jobs that have been created or to remove people from jobs if business circumstances require. That's where human resource management (HRM) comes in. It's an important task that involves having the right number of the right people in the right place at the right time. In this chapter, we'll look at the process managers use to do just that. In addition, we'll look at some contemporary HRM issues facing managers.

A major HRM challenge for managers is ensuring that their company has a high-quality workforce. Getting and keeping competent and talented employees is critical to the success of every organization, whether an organization is just starting or has been in business for years. If an organization doesn't take its HRM responsibilities seriously, performance may suffer. Therefore, part of every manager's job when organizing is human resource management. All managers engage in some HRM activities such as interviewing job candidates, orienting new employees, and evaluating their employees' work performance, even if there is a separate HRM department.

LEARNING OUTCOME 12.1
Explain the importance of the human resource management process and the external influences that might affect that process.

The Human Resource Management Process

"At L'Oreal, success starts with people. Our people are our most precious asset. Respect for people, their ideas and differences, is the only path to our sustainable long-term growth."[2] Many organizations profess that their people are their most important asset and acknowledge the important role that employees play in organizational success. However, why is HRM important and what external factors influence the HRM process?

Why Is HRM Important?

HRM is important for three reasons. First, it can be a significant source of competitive advantage as various studies have concluded.[3] And that's true for organizations around the world, not just U.S. firms. The Human Capital Index, a comprehensive study of more than 2,000 global firms, concluded that people-oriented HR gives an organization an edge by creating superior shareholder value.[4]

Second, HRM is an important part of organizational strategies. Achieving competitive success through people means managers must change how they think about their employees and how they view the work relationship. They must work with people and treat them as partners, not just as costs to be minimized or avoided. That's what people-oriented organizations such as Southwest Airlines and W. L. Gore do.

Finally, the way organizations treat their people has been found to significantly impact organizational performance.[5] For instance, one study reported that improving work practices could increase market value by as much as 30 percent.[6] Another study that tracked average annual shareholder returns of companies on *Fortune's* list of 100 Best Companies to Work For found that these companies significantly beat the S&P 500 over 10-year, 5-year, 3-year, and 1-year periods.[7] Work practices that lead to both high individual and high organizational performance are known as **high-performance work practices**. (See some examples in Exhibit 12-1.) The common thread among these practices seems to be a commitment to involving employees; improving the knowledge, skills, and abilities of an organization's employees; increasing their motivation; reducing loafing on the job; and enhancing the retention of quality employees while encouraging low performers to leave.

Even if an organization doesn't use high-performance work practices, other specific HRM activities must be completed in order to ensure that the organization has qualified people to perform the work that needs to be done—activities that comprise the HRM process. Exhibit 12-2 shows the eight activities in this process. The first three activities ensure that competent employees are identified and selected; the next two involve providing employees with up-to-date knowledge and skills; and the final three ensure that the organization retains competent and high-performing employees. Before we discuss those specific activities, we need to look at external factors that affect the HRM process.

External Factors That Affect the HRM Process

The administrative assistant job opening paying $13 an hour at a Burns Harbor, Indiana, truck driver training school for C. R. England, a nationwide trucking company, was posted on a Friday afternoon.[8] By the time the company's head of corporate recruiting arrived at work on Monday morning, there were about 300 applications in the company's e-mail inbox. And an inch-and-a-half stack of résumés was piled up by the now out-of-paper fax machine. Out of those 500 plus applicants, one person, who had lost her job

EXHIBIT 12-1
High-Performance Work Practices

- Self-managed teams
- Decentralized decision making
- Training programs to develop knowledge, skills, and abilities
- Flexible job assignments
- Open communication
- Performance-based compensation
- Staffing based on person–job and person–organization fit
- Extensive employee involvement
- Giving employees more control over decision making
- Increasing employee access to information

Sources: C. H. Chuang and H. Liao, "Strategic Human Resource Management in Service Context: Taking Care of Business by Taking Care of Employees and Customers," *Personnel Psychology,* Spring 2010, pp. 153–196; M. Subramony, "A Meta-Analytic Investigation of the Relationship Between HRM Bundles and Firm Performance," *Human Resource Management,* September–October 2009, pp. 745–768; M. M. Butts et al., "Individual Reactions to High Involvement Work Practices: Investigating the Role of Empowerment and Perceived Organizational Support," *Journal of Occupational Health Psychology,* April 2009, pp. 122–136; and W. R. Evans and W. D. Davis, "High-Performance Work Systems and Organizational Performance: The Mediating Role of Internal Social Structure," *Journal of Management,* October 2005, p. 760.

high-performance work practices
Work practices that lead to both high individual and high organizational performance

External Environment

Human Resource Planning → Recruitment → Selection → Identify and select competent employees

→ Decruitment

Orientation → Training → Provide employees with up-to-date skills and knowledge

Performance Management → Compensation and Benefits → Career Development → Retain competent and high-performing employees

External Environment

EXHIBIT 12-2

HRM Process

four months earlier, impressed the hiring manager so much that the job was hers, leaving the remaining 499 plus people, including a former IBM analyst with 18 years' experience, a former director of human resources, and someone with a master's degree and 12 years' experience at accounting firm Deloitte & Touche, still searching for a job. This is not a unique example. The economic slowdown has made filling a job opening an almost mind-boggling exercise.

Such is the new reality facing HRM. The entire HRM process is influenced by the external environment. Those factors most directly influencing it include the economy, employee labor unions, governmental laws and regulations, and demographic trends.

THE ECONOMY'S EFFECT ON HRM.   The global economic downturn has left what many experts believe to be an enduring mark on HRM practices worldwide. For instance, in Japan, workers used to count on two things: a job for life and a decent pension. Now, lifetime employment is long gone and corporate pension plans are crumbling.[9] In European Union member countries, it's anticipated that the jobless rate will continue to increase, with Spain being hit hardest.[10] And in Thailand, employees in the automotive industry dealt with reduced work hours, which affected their pay and their skill upgrades.[11] In the United States, labor economists say that although jobs may be coming back slowly, they aren't the same ones that employees were used to. Many of these jobs are temporary or contract positions, rather than full-time jobs with benefits. And many of the more than 8.4 million jobs lost during the recession aren't coming back at all, but may be replaced by other types of work in growing industries.[12] All of these changes have affected employers and workers. A Global Workforce Study survey by global professional services company Towers Watson confirmed that the recession has "fundamentally altered the way U.S. employees view their work and leaders. . . . U.S. workers have dramatically lowered their career and retirement expectations for the foreseeable future."[13] Such findings have profound implications for how an organization manages its human resources.

EMPLOYEE LABOR UNIONS.   A planned series of three five-day work stoppages by Unite, the union representing British Airways cabin crews, had the potential for a serious negative effect on Europe's third-largest airline in an industry already struggling from the prolonged economic downturn.[14] If negotiations between management and the union didn't resolve the disputes over work practices, then employees vowed to hit the airline with more strikes during the busy summer period. Then, in China, strikes at Honda and Toyota factories highlighted that country's struggle with income inequality, rising inflation, and soaring property prices. Factory workers, who had been "pushed to work 12-hour days, six days a week on monotonous low-wage assembly line tasks, are pushing back."[15] Work stoppages, labor disputes, and negotiations between management and labor are just a few of the challenges organizations and managers face when their workforce is unionized.

A **labor union** is an organization that represents workers and seeks to protect their interests through collective bargaining. In unionized organizations, many HRM decisions are dictated by collective bargaining agreements, which usually define things such as recruitment sources; criteria for hiring, promotions, and layoffs; training eligibility; and disciplinary practices. Due to information availability, it's difficult to pin down how unionized global workforces are. Current estimates are that about 12.3 percent of the U.S. workforce is unionized.[16] But the percentage of unionized workers tends to be higher in other countries except in France, where some 9.6 percent of workers are unionized. For instance, in Japan, some 19.6 percent of the labor force belongs to a union; in Germany, 27 percent; in Denmark, 75 percent; in Australia, 27.4 percent; in Canada, 30.4 percent; and in Mexico, 19 percent.[17] One union membership trend we're seeing, especially in the more industrialized countries, is that the rate in private enterprise is declining while that in the public sector (which includes teachers, police officers, firefighters, and government workers) is climbing. Although labor unions can affect an organization's HRM practices, the most significant environmental constraint is governmental laws, especially in North America.

LEGAL ENVIRONMENT OF HRM. $250 million. That's the amount a New York City jury awarded in punitive damages to plaintiffs who claim drug company Novartis AG discriminated against women.[18] Billions of dollars. That's the staggering amount that Walmart stores could potentially be liable for in a class-action sex discrimination suit.[19] As you can see, an organization's HRM practices are governed by a country's laws. (See Exhibit 12-3 for some of the important U.S. laws that affect the HRM process.) For example, decisions regarding who will be hired or which employees will be chosen for a training program or what an employee's compensation will be must be made without regard to race, sex, religion, age, color, national origin, or disability. Exceptions can occur only in special circumstances. For instance, a community fire department can deny employment to a firefighter applicant who is confined to a wheelchair; but if that same individual is applying for a desk job, such as a dispatcher, the disability cannot be used as a reason to deny employment. The issues, however, are rarely that clear-cut. For example, employment laws protect most employees whose religious beliefs require a specific style of dress—robes, long shirts, long hair, and the like. However, if the specific style of dress may be hazardous or unsafe in the work setting (such as when operating machinery), a company could refuse to hire a person who won't adopt a safer dress code.

As you can see, a number of important laws and regulations affect what you can and cannot do legally as a manager. Because workplace lawsuits are increasingly targeting supervisors, as well as their organizations, managers must know what they can and cannot do by law.[20] Trying to balance the "shoulds and should-nots" of many laws often falls within the realm of **affirmative action**. Many U.S. organizations have affirmative action programs to ensure that decisions and practices enhance the employment, upgrading, and retention of members from protected groups such as minorities and females. That is, an organization refrains from discrimination and actively seeks to enhance the status of members from protected groups. However, U.S. managers are not completely free to choose whom they hire, promote, or fire, or free to treat employees any way they want. Although laws have helped reduce employment discrimination and unfair work practices, they have, at the same time, reduced managers' discretion over HRM decisions.

labor union
An organization that represents workers and seeks to protect their interests through collective bargaining

affirmative action
Organizational programs that enhance the status of members of protected groups

Laws		
Law or Ruling	**Year**	**Description**
Equal Employment Opportunity and Discrimination		
Equal Pay Act	1963	Prohibits pay differences for equal work based on gender
Civil Rights Act, Title VII	1964 (amended in 1972)	Prohibits discrimination based on race, color, religion, national origin, or gender.
Age Discrimination in Employment Act	1967 (amended in 1978)	Prohibits discrimination against employees 40 years and older
Vocational Rehabilitation Act	1973	Prohibits discrimination on the basis of physical or mental disabilities
Americans with Disabilities Act	1990	Prohibits discrimination against individuals who have disabilities or chronic illnesses; also requires reasonable accommodations for these individuals
Compensation/Benefits		
Worker Adjustment and Retraining Notification Act	1990	Requires employers with more than 100 employees to provide 60 days' notice before a mass layoff or facility closing
Family and Medical Leave Act	1993	Gives employees in organizations with 50 or more employees up to 12 weeks of unpaid leave each year for family or medical reasons
Health Insurance Portability and Accountability Act	1996	Permits portability of employees' insurance from one employer to another
Lilly Ledbetter Fair Pay Act	2009	Changes the statute of limitations on pay discrimination to 180 days from each paycheck
Health/Safety		
Occupational Safety and Health Act (OSHA)	1970	Establishes mandatory and health standards in organizations
Privacy Act	1974	Gives employees the legal right to examine personnel files and letters of reference
Consolidated Omnibus Reconciliation Act (COBRA)	1985	Requires continued health coverage following termination (paid by employee)

EXHIBIT 12-3

Major HRM Laws

We do want to mention three current U.S. laws—one has been signed by the president and the other two are still being debated in Congress—that each have the potential to affect future HRM practices. The first of these, the Patient Protection and Affordable Care Act (commonly called the Health Care Reform Act), was signed into law in March 2010.[21] Employers are beginning to sort through the requirements of the law and the deadlines for compliance. For instance, one employer disclosure requirement says that by 2012, all employers must disclose the value of the benefits they provided in 2011 for each employee's health insurance coverage on the employees' annual Form W-2s. Other parts of the law include compliance deadlines for additional specific information that must be disclosed or provided and protections for employees who provide information or testimony about possible employer violations of Title 1 of the law.[22] Another proposed law—the Work–Life Balance Award Act—is still being debated. This particular piece of legislation would highlight the importance of workplace flexibility issues.[23] The other proposed law stalled in Congressional debates—the Employee Free Choice Act—would amend the National Labor Relations Act and make it easier for workers to form a union.[24]

What about HRM laws globally? It's important that managers in other countries be familiar with the specific laws that apply there. Let's take a look at some of the federal legislation in countries such as Canada, Mexico, Australia, and Germany.

Canadian laws pertaining to HRM practices closely parallel those in the United States. The Canadian Human Rights Act prohibits discrimination on the basis of race, religion, age, marital status, sex, physical or mental disability, or national origin. This act governs practices throughout the country. Canada's HRM environment, however, is somewhat different from that in the United States in that it involves more decentralization of lawmaking to the provincial level. For example, discrimination on the basis of language is not prohibited anywhere in Canada except in Quebec.

In Mexico, employees are more likely to be unionized than they are in the United States. Labor matters in Mexico are governed by the Mexican Federal Labor Law. One hiring law states that an employer has 28 days to evaluate a new employee's work performance. After that period, the employee is granted job security and termination is quite difficult and expensive. Those who violate the Mexican Federal Labor Law are subject to severe penalties, including criminal action that can result in steep fines and even jail sentences for employers who fail to pay, for example, the minimum wage.

Australia's discrimination laws were not enacted until the 1980s, and generally apply to discrimination and affirmative action for women. Yet, gender opportunities for women in Australia appear to lag behind those in the United States. In Australia, however, a significant proportion of the workforce is unionized. The higher percentage of unionized workers has placed increased importance on industrial relations specialists in Australia, and reduced the control of line managers over workplace labor issues. In 1997, Australia overhauled its labor and industrial relations laws with the objective of increasing productivity and reducing union power. The Workplace Relations Bill gives employers greater flexibility to negotiate directly with employees on pay, hours, and benefits. It also simplifies federal regulation of labor–management relations.

Our final example, Germany, is similar to most Western European countries when it comes to HRM practices. Legislation requires companies to practice representative participation, in which the goal is to redistribute power within the organization, putting labor on a more equal footing with the interests of management and stockholders. The two most common forms of representative participation are work councils and board representatives. **Work councils** link employees with management. They are groups of nominated or elected employees who must be consulted when management makes decisions involving personnel. **Board representatives** are employees who sit on a company's board of directors and represent the interests of the firm's employees.

DEMOGRAPHIC TRENDS. Back in 2007, the head of BMW's 2,500-employee power train plant in Dingolfing, Lower Bavaria, was worried about the potential inevitable future decline in productivity due to an aging workforce.[26] That's when company executives decided to redesign its factory for older workers. With input from employees, they implemented physical changes to the workplace—for instance, new wooden floors to reduce joint strain and special chairs for sitting down or relaxing for short periods—that would reduce wear and tear on workers' bodies. As this example shows, demographic trends are impacting HRM practices, worldwide and in the United States.

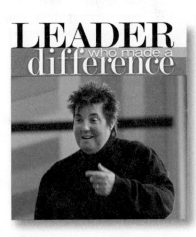

Lisa Brummel, a successful Microsoft product development manager with no HR experience, was named HR chief in 2005. Her mandate: improve the mood around here.[25] Lisa, who had always been a strong people leader, stepped up to do just that and looked for ways that the company could reshape HR at Microsoft. With any HR issue that arose, Lisa used her people skills to find a solution. For instance, one thing she did was to introduce innovative office designs that allowed employees to reconfigure their workspaces for the task they were working on. The customized workspaces included options such as sliding doors, movable walls, and features that made the space seem more like an urban loft than an office. When beginning a workspace redesign, "employees are first divided into four worker types: providers (the godfathers of work groups), travelers (the types who work anywhere but work), concentrators (head-down, always-at-work types), and orchestrators (the company's natural diplomats)." Based on their "type," employees then pick the kind of workspace that works best for them. By allowing their creative, quirky, and talented people freedom to design their workspaces, the company was able to give them some control over their chaotic and often hectic environment.

---

work councils
Groups of nominated or elected employees who must be consulted when management makes decisions involving personnel

board representatives
Employees who sit on a company's board of directors and represent the interests of the firm's employees

Much of the change in the U.S. workforce over the last 50 years can be attributed to federal legislation enacted in the 1960s that prohibited employment discrimination. With these laws, avenues opened up for minority and female job applicants. These two groups dramatically changed the workplace in the latter half of the twentieth century. Women, in particular, have changed the composition of the workforce as they now hold some 49.1 percent of jobs. And that percentage may increase as some 82 percent of jobs lost during the economic crisis were ones held by men. Why the disproportion? Because women tend to be employed in education and health care industries, which are less sensitive to economic ups and downs.[27] If this trend continues, women are set to become the majority group in the workforce.

Workforce trends in the first half of the twenty-first century will be notable for three reasons: (1) changes in racial and ethnic composition, (2) an aging baby boom generation, and (3) an expanding cohort of Gen Y workers. By 2050, Hispanics will grow from today's 13 percent of the workforce to 24 percent; blacks will increase from 12 percent to 14 percent, and Asians will increase from 5 percent to 11 percent. Meanwhile, the labor force is aging. The 55-and-older age group, which currently makes up 13 percent of the workforce, will increase to 20 percent by 2014. However, labor force analysts who had predicted a mass exodus of baby boomers into retirement have pulled back somewhat on those forecasts, especially since many baby boomers lost significant personal financial resources as the economy and stock market floundered. Many baby boomers are postponing retirement until they can better afford it. Another group that's having a significant impact on today's workforce is Gen Y, a population group that includes individuals born from about 1978 to 1994. Gen Y has been the fastest-growing segment of the workforce—increasing from 14 percent to over 24 percent. With Gen Y now in the workforce, analysts point to the four generations that are working side-by-side in the workplace[28]:

▶ The oldest, most experienced workers (those born before 1946) make up 6 percent of the workforce.
▶ The baby boomers (those born between 1946 and 1964) make up 41.5 percent of the workforce.
▶ Gen Xers (those born 1965 to 1977) make up almost 29 percent of the workforce.
▶ Gen Yers (those born 1978 to 1994) make up almost 24 percent of the workforce.

These and other demographic trends are important because of the impact they're having on current and future HRM practices.

Let's Get Real

F2F

HRM responsibilities I have include:
- Promote the company's safety program.
- Oversee the hiring process.
- Oversee and assist in the execution of the plant's affirmative action plan.
- Ensure compliance with state and federal laws and regulations.
- Develop and conduct employee training to minimize skill gaps.
- Address employee concerns and resolve complaints.
- Implement ideas that will allow the HR department become a better strategic partner within the organization.

LEARNING OUTCOME 12.2
Discuss the tasks associated with identifying and selecting competent employees.

Identifying and Selecting Competent Employees

Is a job in the insurance industry on your list of jobs you'll apply for after graduation? Unfortunately for the insurance industry, it's not for many college graduates. Like many other nonglamorous industries including transportation, utilities, and manufacturing, the insurance industry is not "particularly attractive to the so-called 'millennials'—people who turned 21 in 2000 or later." In all these industries, the number of skilled jobs is already starting to overtake the number of qualified people available to fill them.[29]

Every organization needs people to do whatever work is necessary for doing what the organization is in business to do. How do they get those people? And more importantly, what can they do to ensure they get competent, talented people? This first phase of the HRM process involves three tasks: human resource planning, recruitment and decruitment, and selection.

Human Resource Planning

Human resource planning is the process by which managers ensure that they have the right number and kinds of capable people in the right places and at the right times. Through planning, organizations avoid sudden people shortages and surpluses.[30] HR planning entails two steps: (1) assessing current human resources, and (2) meeting future HR needs.

CURRENT ASSESSMENT.   Managers begin HR planning by inventorying current employees. This inventory usually includes information on employees such as name, education, training, prior employment, languages spoken, special capabilities, and specialized skills. Sophisticated databases make getting and keeping this information quite easy. For example, Stephanie Cox, Schlumberger's director of personnel for North and South America, uses a company planning program called PeopleMatch to help pinpoint managerial talent. Suppose that she needs a manager for Brazil. She types in the qualifications: someone who can relocate, speak Portuguese, and is a "high potential" employee. Within a minute, 31 names of possible candidates pop up.[31] That's what good HR planning should do—help managers identify the people they need.

An important part of a current assessment is **job analysis**, an assessment that defines a job and the behaviors necessary to perform it. For instance, what are the duties of a level 3 accountant who works for Kodak? What minimal knowledge, skills, and abilities are necessary to adequately perform this job? How do these requirements compare with those for a level 2 accountant or for an accounting manager? Information for a job analysis is gathered by directly observing individuals on the job, interviewing employees individually or in a group, having employees complete a questionnaire or record daily activities in a diary, or having job "experts" (usually managers) identify a job's specific characteristics.

Using this information from the job analysis, managers develop or revise job descriptions and job specifications. A **job description** is a written statement describing a job—typically job content, environment, and conditions of employment. A **job specification** states the minimum qualifications that a person must possess to successfully perform a given job. It identifies the knowledge, skills, and attitudes needed to do the job effectively. Both the job description and job specification are important documents when managers begin recruiting and selecting.

MEETING FUTURE HR NEEDS.   Future HR needs are determined by the organization's mission, goals, and strategies. Demand for employees results from demand for the organization's products or services. For instance, Corning's expansion into developing countries was slowed by the lack of qualified employees. To continue its growth strategy, it had to plan how to find those qualified employees.[32]

After assessing both current capabilities and future needs, managers can estimate areas in which the organization will be understaffed or overstaffed. Then they're ready to proceed to the next step in the HRM process.

Let's Get Real

Best ways to find the best job candidates are *networking with local community organizations and also being descriptive about the job requirements and qualifications in a job ad.*

Recruitment and Decruitment

Competition for talent by India's two largest technology outsourcing companies has led to an all-out recruiting war. In the United States, the tech sector is also in a hiring push pitting start-up companies against giants such as Google and Intel in the hunt for employees.[33]

If employee vacancies exist, managers should use the information gathered through job analysis to guide them in **recruitment**—that is, locating, identifying, and attracting capable applicants.[34] On the other hand, if HR planning shows a surplus of employees, managers may want to reduce the organization's workforce through **decruitment**.[35]

human resource planning
Ensuring that the organization has the right number and kinds of capable people in the right places and at the right times

job analysis
An assessment that defines jobs and the behaviors necessary to perform them

job description
A written statement that describes a job

job specification
A written statement of the minimum qualifications that a person must possess to perform a given job successfully

recruitment
Locating, identifying, and attracting capable applicants

decruitment
Reducing an organization's workforce

EXHIBIT 12-4

Recruiting Sources

Source	Advantages	Disadvantages
Internet	Reaches large numbers of people; can get immediate feedback	Generates many unqualified candidates
Employee referrals	Knowledge about the organization provided by current employee; can generate strong candidates because a good referral reflects on the recommender	May not increase the diversity and mix of employees
Company Web site	Wide distribution; can be targeted to specific groups	Generates many unqualified candidates
College recruiting	Large centralized body of candidates	Limited to entry-level positions
Professional recruiting organizations	Good knowledge of industry challenges and requirements	Little commitment to specific organization

RECRUITMENT.   Some organizations have interesting approaches to finding employees. For instance, Microsoft launched a new Web site that integrated 103 country sites into one career-related site. There, potential applicants find employee blogs on everything from interview tips to whether a failed start-up on a résumé hurts in applying for a job at the company.[36] Even though Google receives 3,000 applications a day and can afford to be picky about whom it hires, it still needs qualified computer science and engineering candidates. One fun thing the company does is Google Games, a day devoted to student team competitions on the company's campus.[37] Accounting firm Deloitte & Touche created its Deloitte Film Festival to get employee team-produced films about "life" at Deloitte to use in college recruiting.[38] Exhibit 12-4 explains different recruitment sources managers can use to find potential job candidates.[39]

Although online recruiting is popular and allows organizations to identify applicants cheaply and quickly, applicant quality may not be as good as other sources. Research has found that employee referrals generally produce the best candidates.[40] Why? Because current employees know both the job and the person being recommended, they tend to refer applicants who are well qualified. Also, current employees often feel their reputation is at stake and refer others only when they're confident that the person will not make them look bad.

DECRUITMENT.   The other approach to controlling labor supply is decruitment, which is not a pleasant task for any manager. Decruitment options are shown in Exhibit 12-5. Although employees can be fired, other choices may be better. However, no matter how you do it, it's never easy to reduce an organization's workforce.

EXHIBIT 12-5

Decruitment Options

Option	Description
Firing	Permanent involuntary termination
Layoffs	Temporary involuntary termination; may last only a few days or extend to years
Attrition	Not filling openings created by voluntary resignations or normal retirements
Transfers	Moving employees either laterally or downward; usually does not reduce costs but can reduce intraorganizational supply–demand imbalances
Reduced workweeks	Having employees work fewer hours per week, share jobs, or perform their jobs on a part-time basis
Early retirements	Providing incentives to older and more senior employees for retiring before their normal retirement date
Job sharing	Having employees share one full-time position

Selection

Once you have a pool of candidates, the next step in the HRM process is **selection**, screening job applicants to determine who is best qualified for the job. Managers need to "select" carefully since hiring errors can have significant implications. For instance, a driver at Fresh Direct, an online grocer that delivers food to masses of apartment-dwelling New Yorkers, was charged with, and later pled guilty to, stalking and harassing female customers.[41] At T-Mobile, lousy customer service led to its last-place ranking in the J.D. Power's customer-satisfaction survey. The first step in a total overhaul of the customer service area was revamping the company's hiring practices to increase the odds of hiring employees who would be good at customer service.[42]

WHAT IS SELECTION? Selection involves predicting which applicants will be successful if hired. For example, in hiring for a sales position, the selection process should predict which applicants will generate a high volume of sales. As shown in Exhibit 12-6, any selection decision can result in four possible outcomes—two correct and two errors.

A decision is correct when the applicant was predicted to be successful and proved to be successful on the job, or when the applicant was predicted to be unsuccessful and was not hired. In the first instance, we have successfully accepted; in the second, we have successfully rejected.

Problems arise when errors are made in rejecting candidates who would have performed successfully on the job (reject errors) or accepting those who ultimately perform poorly (accept errors). These problems can be significant. Given today's HR laws and regulations, reject errors can cost more than the additional screening needed to find acceptable candidates. Why? Because they can expose the organization to discrimination charges, especially if applicants from protected groups are disproportionately rejected. For instance, two written firefighter exams used by the New York City Fire Department were found to have had a disparate impact on black and Hispanic candidates.[43] On the other hand, the costs of accept errors include the cost of training the employee, the profits lost because of the employee's incompetence, the cost of severance, and the subsequent costs of further recruiting and screening. The major emphasis of any selection activity should be reducing the probability of reject errors or accept errors while increasing the probability of making correct decisions. Managers do this by using selection procedures that are both valid and reliable.

EXHIBIT 12-6

Selection Decision Outcomes

	Selection Decision	
	Accept	**Reject**
Successful	Correct Decision	Reject Error
Unsuccessful	Accept Error	Correct Decision

Later Job Performance

selection
Screening job applicants to ensure that the most appropriate candidates are hired

VALIDITY AND RELIABILITY. A valid selection device is characterized by a proven relationship between the selection device and some relevant criterion. Federal employment laws prohibit managers from using a test score to select employees unless clear evidence shows that, once on the job, individuals with high scores on this test outperform individuals with low test scores. The burden is on managers to support that any selection device they use to differentiate applicants is validly related to job performance.

A reliable selection device indicates that it measures the same thing consistently. On a test that's reliable, any single individual's score should remain fairly consistent over time, assuming that the characteristics being measured are also stable. No selection device can be effective if it's not reliable. Using such a device would be like weighing yourself every day on an erratic scale. If the scale is unreliable—randomly fluctuating, say 5 to 10 pounds every time you step on it—the results don't mean much.

A growing number of companies are adopting a new measure of recruitment effectiveness called "quality of fill."[44] This measure looks at the contributions of good hires versus those of hires who have failed to live up to their potential. Five key factors are considered in defining this quality measure: employee retention, performance evaluations, number of first-year hires who make it into high-potential training programs, number of employees who are promoted, and what surveys of new hires indicate. Such measures help an organization assess whether its selection process is working well.

TYPES OF SELECTION TOOLS. The best-known selection tools include application forms, written and performance-simulation tests, interviews, background investigations, and in some cases, physical exams. Exhibit 12-7 lists the strengths and weaknesses of each.[45] Because many selection tools have limited value for making selection decisions, managers should use ones that effectively predict performance for a given job.

EXHIBIT 12-7

Selection Tools

Application Forms
- Almost universally used
- Most useful for gathering information
- Can predict job performance but not easy to create one that does

Written Tests
- Must be job related
- Include intelligence, aptitude, ability, personality, and interest tests
- Are popular (e.g., personality tests; aptitude tests)
- Relatively good predictor for supervisory positions

Performance-Simulation Tests
- Use actual job behaviors
- Work sampling—test applicants on tasks associated with that job; appropriate for routine or standardized work
- Assessment center—simulate jobs; appropriate for evaluating managerial potential

Interviews
- Almost universally used
- Must know what can and cannot be asked
- Can be useful for managerial positions

Background Investigations
- Used for verifying application data—valuable source of information
- Used for verifying reference checks—not a valuable source of information

Physical Examinations
- Are for jobs that have certain physical requirements
- Mostly used for insurance purposes

REALISTIC JOB PREVIEWS.   One thing managers need to carefully watch is how they portray the organization and the work that an applicant will be doing. If they tell applicants only the good aspects, they're likely to have a workforce that's dissatisfied and prone to high turnover.[46] Negative things can happen when the information an applicant receives is excessively inflated. First, mismatched applicants probably won't withdraw from the selection process. Second, inflated information builds unrealistic expectations so new employees may quickly become dissatisfied and leave the organization. Third, new hires become disillusioned and less committed to the organization when they face the unexpected harsh realities of the job. In addition, these individuals may feel that they were misled during the hiring process and then become problem employees.

To increase employee job satisfaction and reduce turnover, managers should consider a **realistic job preview (RJP)**, which is one that includes both positive and negative information about the job and the company. For instance, in addition to the positive comments typically expressed during an interview, the job applicant might be told that there are limited opportunities to talk to coworkers during work hours, that promotional advancement is unlikely, or that work hours are erratic and they may have to work weekends. Research indicates that applicants who receive an RJP have more realistic expectations about the jobs they'll be performing and are better able to cope with the frustrating elements than are applicants who receive only inflated information.

Providing Employees with Needed Skills and Knowledge

12.3

LEARNING OUTCOME
Explain the different types of
orientation and training.

As one of the nation's busiest airports, Miami International Airport served nearly 34 million passengers in 2009. But Miami International is doing something that no other airport has done. It's "trying to persuade disparate groups of employees to think and act as ambassadors for regional tourism. Airport workers in all jobs are learning the importance of finding solutions to the myriad issues that beset travelers on their way to and from Miami." Accomplishing that means that all employees who work on airport grounds are required to master customer service through a series of tourism training efforts. The required training is tied to renewal of airport ID badges, providing a critical incentive for employees to participate.[47]

If we've done our recruiting and selecting properly, we should have hired competent individuals who can perform successfully on the job. But successful performance requires more than possessing certain skills. New hires must be acclimated to the organization's culture and be trained and given the knowledge to do the job in a manner consistent with the organization's goals. Current employees, like those at Miami International Airport, may have to complete training programs to improve or update their skills. For these acclimation and skill improvement tasks, HRM uses orientation and training.

Orientation

Did you participate in some type of organized "introduction to college life" when you started school? If so, you may have been told about your school's rules and the procedures for activities such as applying for financial aid, cashing a check, or registering for classes; and you were probably introduced to some of the college administrators. A person starting a new job needs the same type of introduction to his or her job and the organization. This introduction is called **orientation**.

There are two types of orientation. *Work unit orientation* familiarizes the employee with the goals of the work unit, clarifies how his or her job contributes to the unit's

---

realistic job preview (RJP)
A preview of a job that provides both positive
and negative information about the job and
the company

orientation
Introducing a new employee to his or her job
and the organization

goals, and includes an introduction to his or her new coworkers. *Organization orienta-tion* informs the new employee about the company's goals, history, philosophy, proce-dures and rules. It should also include relevant HR policies and maybe even a tour of the facilities.

Many organizations have formal orientation programs, while others use a more informal approach in which the manager assigns the new employee to a senior member of the work group who introduces the new hire to immediate coworkers and shows him or her where important things are located. And then there are intense orientation pro-grams like that at Randstad USA, a staffing company based in Atlanta. The company's 16-week program covers everything from the company's culture to on-the-job training. The executive in charge of curriculum development says, "It's a very defined process. It's not just about what new hires have to learn and do, but also about what managers have to do."[48] And managers do have an obligation to effectively and efficiently integrate any new employee into the organization. They should openly discuss mutual obligations of the organization and the employee.[49] It's in the best interests of both the organization and the new employee to get the person up and running in the job as soon as possible. Successful orientation results in an outsider-insider transition that makes the new employee feel comfortable and fairly well adjusted, lowers the likelihood of poor work performance, and reduces the probability of a surprise resignation only a week or two into the job.

by the numbers[50]

36 percent of managers who contact references are most interested in a description of past job duties.

69 percent of employees say they've been asked to do things at work for which they have not received any training.

30 percent of students say that a company's market success was a preferred attribute.

60 percent of employers now offer wellness benefits.

31 percent of HR leaders say that the most important employee characteristic is fitting in with the organization's culture.

40 percent of employees say that their most appealing career model is working for two to three organizations throughout their career.

59 percent of HR recruiters said that the most neglected grooming for job interviews was fingernails.

75 percent of recruiters say that a chronological format is most preferred for a résumé.

Employee Training

On the whole, planes don't cause airline accidents, people do. Most collisions, crashes, and other airline mishaps—nearly three-quarters of them—result from errors by the pilot or air traffic controller, or from inadequate maintenance. Weather and structural failures typically account for the remaining accidents.[51] We cite these statistics to illustrate the importance of training in the airline industry. Such maintenance and human errors could be prevented or significantly reduced by better employee training, as shown by the amaz-ing "landing" of US Airways Flight 1549 in the Hudson River in January 2009 with no loss of life. Pilot Captain Chesley Sullenberger attributed the positive outcome to the extensive and intensive training that all pilots and flight crews undergo.[52] At management and technology consulting firm BearingPoint, the ethics and compliance training pro-gram became a series of fictional films modeled after *The Office*, even with a "Michael Scott-esque leader."[53] The film episodes were an immediate sensation in the company with comments like, "This is the best training I've ever had" or "I think that episode was based on my team." The new episodes became so popular that employees started track-ing them down on the company's staging server, which is pretty amazing considering these training videos covered issues that most employees find boring even though it's critical information. Everything that employees at Ruth's Chris Steak House restaurants need to know can be found on sets of $4 \times 8\frac{1}{2}$-inch cards. Whether it's a recipe for caramelized banana cream pie or how to acknowledge customers, it's on the cards. And since the cards for all jobs are readily available, employees know the behaviors and skills it takes to get promoted. It's a unique approach to employee training, but it seems to work. Since the card system was implemented, employee turnover has decreased, some-thing that's not easy to accomplish in the restaurant industry.[54]

Employee training is an important HRM activity. As job demands change, employee skills have to change. It's been estimated that U.S. business firms spend more than $52.2 billion annually on formal employee training, an amount that has declined during the economic down-turn.[55] Managers, of course, are responsible for deciding what type of training employees need, when they need it, and what form that training should take.

TYPES OF TRAINING. Exhibit 12-8 describes the major types of training that organiza-tions provide. Some of the most popular types include profession/industry-specific train-ing, management/supervisory skills, mandatory/compliance information (such as sexual

Type	Includes
General	Communication skills, computer systems application and programming, customer service, executive development, management skills and development, personal growth, sales, supervisory skills, and technological skills and knowledge
Specific	Basic life/work skills, creativity, customer education, diversity/cultural awareness, remedial writing, managing change, leadership, product knowledge, public speaking/presentation skills, safety, ethics, sexual harassment, team building, wellness, and others

Source: Based on "2005 Industry Report—Types of Training." *Training*, December 2005, p. 22.

EXHIBIT 12-8
Types of Training

harassment, safety, etc.), and customer service training. For many organizations, employee interpersonal skills training—communication, conflict resolution, team building, customer service, and so forth—is a high priority. For example, the director of training and development for Vancouver-based Boston Pizza International said, "Our people know the Boston Pizza concept; they have all the hard skills. It's the soft skills they lack."[56] So the company launched Boston Pizza College, a training program that uses hands-on, scenario-based learning about many interpersonal skills topics. For Canon, Inc., it's the repair personnel's technical skills that are important.[57] As part of their training, repair people play a video game based on the familiar kids' board game Operation in which "lights flashed and buzzers sounded if copier parts were dragged and dropped poorly." The company found that comprehension levels were 5 to 8 percent higher than when traditional training manuals were used.

TRAINING METHODS.   Although employee training can be done in traditional ways, many organizations are relying more on technology-based training methods because of their accessibility, cost, and ability to deliver information. Exhibit 12-9 provides a description of the various traditional and technology-based training methods that managers might use. Of all these training methods, experts believe that organizations will increasingly rely on e-learning applications to deliver important information and to develop employees' skills.

EXHIBIT 12-9
Traditional Training Methods

On-the-job—Employees learn how to do tasks simply by performing them, usually after an initial introduction to the task.

Job rotation—Employees work at different jobs in a particular area, getting exposure to a variety of tasks.

Mentoring and coaching—Employees work with an experienced worker who provides information, support, and encouragement; also called apprenticeships in certain industries.

Experiential exercises—Employees participate in role playing, simulations, or other face-to-face types of training.

Workbooks/manuals—Employees refer to training workbooks and manuals for information.

Classroom lectures—Employees attend lectures designed to convey specific information.

Technology-Based Training Methods

CD-ROM/DVD/videotapes/audiotapes/podcasts—Employees listen to or watch selected media that convey information or demonstrate certain techniques.

Videoconferencing/teleconferencing/satellite TV—Employees listen to or participate as information is conveyed or techniques demonstrated.

E-learning—Internet-based learning where employees participate in multimedia simulations or other interactive modules.

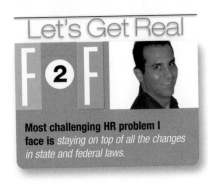
Retaining Competent, High-Performing Employees

At Procter & Gamble, mid-year employee evaluations were used to adjust work goals to reflect more accurately what could be achieved in such a challenging economic environment. The company has directed managers to focus on employees' achievements rather than just to point out areas that need improvement. P&G's director of human resources said that, "Particularly in this economy, people are living in the survival zone. Setting attainable targets was important to keeping up morale."[58]

Once an organization has invested significant dollars in recruiting, selecting, orienting, and training employees, it wants to keep them, especially the competent, high-performing ones! Two HRM activities that play a role in this area are managing employee performance and developing an appropriate compensation and benefits program.

Employee Performance Management

Managers need to know whether their employees are performing their jobs efficiently and effectively. That's what a **performance management system** does—establishes performance standards that are used to evaluate employee performance. How do managers evaluate employees' performance? That's where the different performance appraisal methods come in.

PERFORMANCE APPRAISAL METHODS. More than 70 percent of managers admit they have trouble giving a critical performance review to an underachieving employee.[59] It's particularly challenging when managers and employees alike sense that they're not beneficial.[60] Although appraising someone's performance is never easy, especially with employees who aren't doing their jobs well, managers can be better at it by using any of the seven different performance appraisal methods. A description of each of these methods, including advantages and disadvantages, is shown in Exhibit 12-10.

Compensation and Benefits

Executives at Discovery Communications Inc. had an employee morale problem on their hands. Many of the company's top performers were making the same salaries as the poorer performers and the company's compensation program didn't allow for giving raises to people who stayed in the same position. The only way for managers to reward the top performers was to give them a bonus or promote them to another position. Executives were discovering that not only was that unfair, it was counterproductive. So they overhauled the program.[61]

Most of us expect to receive appropriate compensation from our employer. Developing an effective and appropriate compensation system is an important part of the HRM process.[62] It can help attract and retain competent and talented individuals who help the organization accomplish its mission and goals. In addition, an organization's compensation system has been shown to have an impact on its strategic performance.[63]

Managers must develop a compensation system that reflects the changing nature of work and the workplace in order to keep people motivated. Organizational compensation can include many different types of rewards and benefits such as base wages and salaries, wage and salary add-ons, incentive payments, and other benefits and services. Some organizations offer employees some unusual, but popular, benefits. For instance, at Qualcomm, employees can receive surfing lessons, kayaking tours, and baseball game tickets. Employees at CHG Healthcare Services enjoy an on-site fitness center, fresh fruit baskets every morning, and an annual wellness fair. And at J. M. Smucker, new hires get a gift basket sent to their homes and all employees enjoy softball games and bowling nights.[64]

EXHIBIT **12-10**

Performance Appraisal Methods

Written Essay

Evaluator writes a description of employee's strengths and weaknesses, past performance, and potential; provides suggestions for improvement.

+ Simple to use

− May be better measure of evaluator's writing ability than of employee's actual performance

Critical Incident

Evaluator focuses on critical behaviors that separate effective and ineffective performance.

+ Rich examples, behaviorally based

− Time-consuming, lacks quantification

Graphic Rating Scale

Popular method that lists a set of performance factors and an incremental scale; evaluator goes down the list and rates employee on each factor.

+ Provides quantitative data; not time-consuming

− Doesn't provide in-depth information on job behavior

BARS (Behaviorally Anchored Rating Scale)

Popular approach that combines elements from critical incident and graphic rating scale; evaluator uses a rating scale, but items are examples of actual job behaviors.

+ Focuses on specific and measurable job behaviors

− Time-consuming; difficult to develop

Multiperson Comparison

Employees are rated in comparison to others in work group.

+ Compares employees with one another

− Difficult with large number of employees; legal concerns

MBO

Employees are evaluated on how well they accomplish specific goals.

+ Focuses on goals; results oriented

− Time-consuming

360-Degree Appraisal

Utilizes feedback from supervisors, employees, and coworkers.

+ Thorough

− Time-consuming

How do managers determine who gets paid what? Several factors influence the compensation and benefit packages that different employees receive. Exhibit 12-11 summarizes these factors, which are job-based and business- or industry-based. Many organizations, however, are using alternative approaches to determining compensation: skill-based pay and variable pay.

Skill-based pay systems reward employees for the job skills and competencies they can demonstrate. Under this type of pay system, an employee's job title doesn't define his or her pay category, skills do.[65] Research shows that these types of pay systems tend to be more successful in manufacturing organizations than in service organizations and organizations pursuing technical innovations.[66] On the other hand, many organizations use **variable pay** systems, in which an individual's compensation is contingent on

performance management system
Establishes performance standards that are used to evaluate employee performance

skill-based pay
A pay system that rewards employees for the job skills they can demonstrate

variable pay
A pay system in which an individual's compensation is contingent on performance

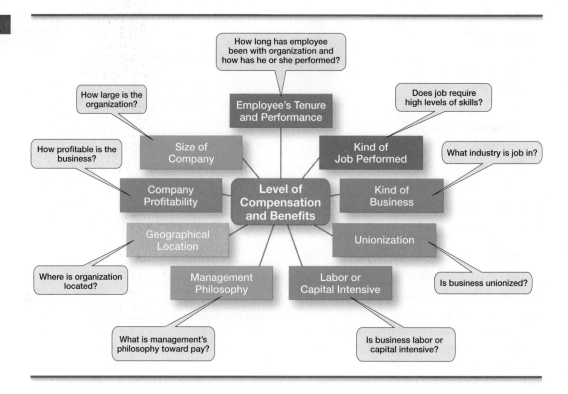

performance—90 percent of U.S. organizations use some type of variable pay plans, and 81 percent of Canadian and Taiwanese organizations do.[67] In Chapter 16, we'll discuss variable pay systems further as they relate to employee motivation.

Although many factors influence the design of an organization's compensation system, flexibility is a key consideration. The traditional approach to paying people reflected a more stable time when an employee's pay was largely determined by seniority and job level. Given the dynamic environments that many organizations face, the trend is to make pay systems more flexible and to reduce the number of pay levels. However, whatever approach managers use, they must establish a fair, equitable, and motivating compensation system that allows the organization to recruit and keep a talented and productive workforce.

LEARNING OUTCOME
Discuss contemporary issues in managing human resources.

12.5

Contemporary Issues in Managing Human Resources

We'll conclude this chapter by looking at some contemporary HR issues facing today's managers. These concerns include managing downsizing, sexual harassment, work–life balance, and controlling HR costs.

Managing Downsizing

"Before 1981, the word 'layoff' in the sense of permanent separation from a job with no prospects for recall, was so uncommon that the U.S. Bureau of Labor Statistics didn't even keep track of such cuts."[68] How things have changed!

Downsizing (or layoffs) is the planned elimination of jobs in an organization. When an organization has too many employees—which can happen when it's faced with an economic recession, declining market share, too aggressive growth, or poorly managed operations—one option for improving profits is to eliminate some of those excess workers. During the most current economic recession, many well-known companies downsized—including, among others, Boeing, Volkswagen, McDonald's, Dell, General Motors, Unisys, Siemens, Merck, Honeywell, and eBay. Now, some HR experts are suggesting that a "cost" associated with mass layoffs is the damage they can cause to long-term growth prospects.[69]

CASE APPLICATION 2
Social Connections

4 00 million users served. That's the traffic milestone achieved by Facebook in early 2010. One of those users is Big Four accounting firm Ernst & Young (E&Y), which has had a Facebook page since the summer of 2006.[115] According to the company's Recruiting Director, E&Y uses its Facebook page to reach out to potential new employees. "Our goal was to find a medium Generation Y commonly goes to, so we could communicate with them in a way that's relevant to their day-to-day activities." The company also hoped to promote its brand and culture and show students (future employees) what E&Y was all about and what it would be like to work there.

A quick look at E&Y's Facebook page confirms that the focus is on what the company most values including the learning and development resources available to its employees, its commitment to social responsibility, its focus on inclusiveness, and its internships. Videos show interns and workers in the workplace describing their experiences with the company. The company's 46,000 plus "fans" can use the company's message board to write questions and comments. And those questions and comments aren't ignored. A response is given quickly in an attempt to create an interactive relationship with students. Again, the purpose is to serve as a recruitment tool for future talent. And Facebook isn't the only social media E&Y is using. Company interns Tweet about their experiences—what their first day was like, work experiences, and experiences with E&Y community events.

The practice of using social networking sites to source applicants isn't without its critics. One law firm partner said, "Social networking sites are problematic because the population is limited and highly selective. I anticipate more race and age claims over the next couple of years, and a significant portion will be from sourcing through social networking sites. . . . We'll see lawsuits." Then, there's the possibility that a company using social media to recruit also could use that same method to check out candidate's personal pages. E&Y has promised not to look at candidates' personal pages.

Discussion Questions

1. What are advantages and drawbacks of using social media in the recruiting process for (a) an applicant and (b) a company?

2. Is the use of social media in recruiting applicants a way to hire smarter or a lawsuit waiting to happen? Explain your position.

3. Go to Facebook and check out Ernst & Young's page. What's your impression? Is it an attractive recruiting tool? Why or why not?

Managing Your Career Module

Jeffrey Hollender is chief inspired protagonist, cofounder, and executive chairperson of Seventh Generation Inc., the country's largest distributor of nontoxic, all-natural cleaning, paper, and personal products. He would undoubtedly be considered a successful businessperson. However, every time Hollender visits Canada, he is detained for extra security screening "because of an incident where authorities arrested and deported the then-23-year-old American for operating an adult-education school in Toronto without a work permit."[1] Other prominent businesspeople also had setbacks early in their career but went on to be successful.

If you want to be successful in your career, maybe you'll face setbacks, but maybe you won't. The main thing to keep in mind is that you are the one responsible for your career.[2] No one else is going to do it for you, including the organization where you're employed. That's why we've included this module in the textbook—to help you better manage your career. The information in this module is set up by topic area so you can pick and choose what you're most interested in. Have fun reading it and good luck in your future career!

Career Opportunities in Management

If you've paid any attention to news reports over the last few years, you know about the widespread layoffs both in the United States and worldwide: Merck cut about 11 percent of its workforce. Unisys reduced its workforce by 10 percent. Pfizer Japan Inc. cut its workforce by 5 percent. Kodak eliminated up to 25,000 jobs. So are management jobs disappearing? You might think so based on these reports. The truth is: The future looks bright! Business administration and management continues to be one of the top 10 most popular college majors, and jobs are likely to be waiting for those graduates!

Almost 2 million individuals in the United States are employed as managers.[3] The U.S. Bureau of Labor Statistics estimates a 5 to 28 percent growth in executive, administrative, and managerial jobs through the year 2018.[4] These jobs, however, may not be in the organizations or fields that you'd expect. The demand for managers in traditional *Fortune* 500 organizations, and particularly in the area of traditional manufacturing, is not going to be as strong as the demand for managers in small and medium-sized organizations in the services field, particularly information and health care services. Keep in mind that a good place to land a management position can be a smaller organization.

Finding a Culture That Fits

Richard D'Ambrosio thought he had found the perfect job at an accounting firm. It had all the outward appearances of a good workplace—employee recognition awards and managers with "politically correct" answers to work–life questions. Yet, as soon as he signed on, he found himself in a culture that prized working long hours just for the sake of working long hours and where junior accountants were expected to be at the beck and call of the partners. If it was your wedding anniversary, too bad. If it was a holiday, too bad. It only took a few months before he quit. How can you avoid the same problem? How can you find a culture that fits?[5] Here are some suggestions.

First, *figure out what suits you*. For instance, do you like working in teams or on your own? Do you like to go out after work with colleagues or go straight home? Are you comfortable in a more formal or a more casual environment? Then, narrow your job search to those kinds of employers.

Once you've gotten through the initial job screening process and begin interviewing, the real detective work begins, which involves more than investigating the "official" information provided by the employer. *Try to uncover the values that drive the organization.* Ask questions such as the proudest accomplishments or how it responded to past emergencies and crises. Ask, "If I have an idea, how do I make it happen?" Ask if you can talk to someone who's on the "fast track" to promotions and find out what they're doing and why they're being rewarded. Ask how you'll be evaluated—after all, if you're going to be in the game, shouldn't you know how the score is kept? Also, look for nonverbal clues. What do people have at their desks—family pictures or only work stuff? Are office doors closed or open? Are there doors? How does the physical climate feel? Is it relaxed and casual or more formal? Do people seem to be helping each other as they work? Are the bathrooms dirty, which might indicate a low value placed on anything to do with employees? Look at the material symbols and who seems to have access to them. And finally, during your investigation, *pay particular attention to the specific department or unit where you'd work.* After all, it is the place where you'd spend the majority of your working hours. Can you see yourself being happy there?

Taking Risks

"IYAD-WYAD-YAG-WYAG: If you always do what you've always done, you'll always get what you've always got! So if your life is ever going to improve, you'll have to take chances." —Anonymous[6]

How will you approach your various career moves over the course of your lifetime? Will you want to do what you've always done? Or will you want to take chances, and how comfortable will you be taking chances? Taking career risks doesn't have to be a gamble. Responsible risk taking can make outcomes more predictable. Here are some suggestions for being a responsible, effective risk taker in career decisions. It's important to thoroughly evaluate the risk. Before committing to a career risk, consider what you could lose or who might be hurt. How important are those things or those people to you? Explore whether you can reach your goal in another way, thus making the risk unnecessary. Find out everything you can about what's involved with taking this career risk—the timing; the people involved; the changes it

will entail; and the potential gains and losses, both in the short run and the long run. Examine closely your feelings about taking this risk: Are you afraid? Are you ready to act now? Will you know if you have risked more than you can afford to lose? Finally, ensure your employability. The most important thing you can do is ensuring that you have choices by keeping your skills current and continually learning new skills.

As with any decision involving risk, the more information you have available, the better able you are to assess the risk. Then, armed with this information, you can make a more informed decision. Even though you won't be able to eliminate all the negatives associated with taking the risk, you can, at least, know about them.

Reinventing Yourself

Face it. The only constant thing about change is that it is constant. These days you don't have the luxury of dealing with change only once in a while. No, the workplace seems to change almost continuously. How can you reinvent yourself to deal with the demands of a constantly changing workplace?[7]

Being prepared isn't a credo just for the Boy Scouts; it should be your motto for dealing with a workplace that is constantly changing. Being prepared means taking the initiative and being responsible for your own personal career development. Rather than depending on your organization to provide you with career development and training opportunities, do it yourself. Take advantage of continuing education or graduate courses at local colleges. Sign up for workshops and seminars that can help you enhance your skills. Upgrading your skills to keep them current is one of the most important things you can do to reinvent yourself.

It's also important for you to be a positive force when faced with workplace changes. We don't mean that you should routinely accept any change that's being implemented. If you think that a proposed change won't work, speak up. Voice your concerns in a constructive manner. Being constructive may mean suggesting an alternative. However, if you feel that the change is beneficial, support it wholeheartedly and enthusiastically.

The changes that organizations make in response to a dynamic environment can be overwhelming and stressful. However, you can take advantage of these changes by reinventing yourself.

Learning to Get Along with Difficult People

We've all been around people who, to put it nicely, are difficult to get along with. These people might be chronic complainers, they might be meddlers who think they know everything about everyone else's job and don't hesitate to tell you so, or they might exhibit any number of other unpleasant interpersonal characteristics. They can make your job as a manager extremely hard and your work day very stressful if you don't know how to deal with them. Being around difficult people tends to bring out the worst in all of us. What can you do? How do you learn to get along with these difficult people?[8]

Getting along with difficult people takes a little bit of patience, planning, and preparation. What you need is an approach that helps you diffuse a lot of the negative aspects of dealing with these individuals. For instance, it helps to write down a detailed description of the person's behavior. Describe what this person does that bothers you. Then, try to understand that behavior. Put yourself in that person's shoes and attempt to see things from his or her perspective. Doing these things initially might help you better understand, predict, and influence behavior.

Unfortunately, trying to understand the person usually isn't enough for getting along. You'll also need some specific strategies for coping with different types of difficult personalities. Here are some of the most common types of difficult people you'll meet and some strategies for dealing with them.

THE HOSTILE, AGGRESSIVE TYPES. With this type, you need to stand up for yourself; give them time to run down; don't worry about being polite, just jump in if you need to; get their attention carefully; get them to sit down; speak from your own point of view; avoid a head-on fight; and be ready to be friendly.

THE COMPLAINERS. With the complainers you need to listen attentively; acknowledge their concerns; be prepared to interrupt their litany of complaints; don't agree, but do acknowledge what they're saying; state facts without comment or apology; and switch them to problem solving.

THE SILENT OR NONRESPONSIVE TYPES. With this type, you need to ask open-ended questions; use the friendly, silent stare; don't fill the silent pauses for them in conversations; comment on what's happening; and help break the tension by making them feel more at ease.

THE KNOW-IT-ALL EXPERTS. The keys to dealing with this type are to be on top of things; listen and acknowledge their comments; question firmly, but don't confront; avoid being a counterexpert; and work with them to channel their energy in positive directions.

What Do I Want from My Job?

If you're reading this textbook, you're likely enrolled in a class that's helping you earn credit toward a college degree. You're also likely taking the courses you need to earn a college degree because you hope to get a good job (or a better

job, if you're already working) upon graduating. With all this effort you're putting forth, have you ever stopped to think about what you really want from your job?[9] A high salary? Work that challenges you? Autonomy and flexibility? Perhaps the results of surveys of workers will give you some insights into what you might want from your job. The top reasons that employees took their jobs and stay with their jobs are as follows:

Work–life balance and flexibility	29%
The work itself	27
Compensation offered	26
Coworkers	25
Work culture	13
Training opportunities	5
Advancement opportunities	5

(Total adds up to more than 100% because individuals indicated more than one factor.)

Do any of these characteristics describe what you want from your job? Whether they do or don't, you should spend some time reflecting on what you want your job to provide you. Then, when it's time to do that all-important job search, look for situations that will provide you what you're looking for.

How Can I Have a Successful Career?

Leaving college after graduation to enter the workforce is always a scary step. However, you can make that transition much easier through one "undeniable element: personal accountability."[10] And because you're likely to be the youngest team member, it's especially important that you take responsibility for your actions and behaviors. By taking an active role in managing your career, your work life can be more exciting, enjoyable, satisfying, and rewarding. So, here are some suggestions that will help you on the path to a successful career:

▶ Understand yourself—your abilities and disabilities; your strengths and weaknesses

▶ Protect your personal brand—watch what you share online and in interactions with others, and watch your e-mails[11]

▶ Be a team player—focus on knowing your peer group and your organization and on the best ways to work within them

▶ Dress appropriately—first impressions count, but so do other impressions that you make every day

▶ Network—develop and keep your links to other professionals open and active by participating in professional organizations, staying in touch with classmates and friends, using online networking sites, and so forth[12]

▶ Ask for help—if you find yourself facing an issue you're not sure how to handle, ask someone for advice or guidance; seek out a mentor

▶ Keep your skills updated—although you might think you know it all, you don't; keep learning about your profession and your industry

▶ Set goals and then work hard to achieve them—showing your boss that you're able to set goals and reach them is always impressive

▶ Do good work—above all, having a successful career means doing your job well, whatever that job might be

Let's Get Real:

Meet the Manager

Tracy K. Tunwall
Assistant Professor of Business
Mount Mercy University
Cedar Rapids, IA

You'll be hearing more from this real manager throughout the chapter.

MY JOB:
I am currently an assistant professor of business at Mount Mercy University, and most recently was the vice president of human resources at Frontier Natural Products. I still play bass guitar with Aeroroot, which is Frontier's corporate band.

BEST PART OF MY JOB:
Working with people. I really believe in the opportunity for managers to have a positive impact on people's work and personal lives. One person can make a difference.

Managing Teams

LEARNING OUTCOMES

WORST PART OF MY JOB:

The hardest part of a manager's job is keeping focus on what really matters. It is easy to get caught up in the day-to-day fire fighting and not make time for the long-term initiatives.

BEST MANAGEMENT ADVICE EVER RECEIVED:

To get where you want to be, do something you are afraid to do. Don't let your fears get in the way of your potential.

Just like the Olympics, the World Cup comes around only every four years.[1] And just like the Olympics, the athletes prepare as only elite athletes know how to do. France's highly regarded national team, Les Bleus, went to the South African World Cup with a motto, "All together for a new dream." However, from its first competitive match through its final defeat, the team lived more of a nightmare.

On paper, France's team was considered one of the world's best. It should have been in prime position to walk away with the World Cup championship. However, the team performed badly on the field, and its behavior was even worse off the field. A top player was sent home for insulting the coach. The team captain hinted that there was a traitor in the team's midst after the coach/player dispute was leaked to the press. And after its first match ended in a draw and its second match in a loss to Mexico, team players refused to participate in a training session in a protest against their bosses. The final straw was the team's defeat in its last match by the host country team. So much for the dream. What went wrong with this team?

You've probably had a lot of experience working in groups—class project teams, maybe an athletic team, a fundraising committee, or even a sales team at work. Work teams are one of the realities—and challenges—of managing in today's dynamic global environment. Many organizations have made the move to restructure work around teams rather than individuals. Why? What do these teams look like? And, like the challenge facing France's national soccer team (or football team as the non-American world refers to it), how can managers build effective teams? We will look at answers to these questions throughout this chapter. Before we can understand teams, however, we first need to understand some basics about groups and group behavior.

LEARNING OUTCOME 13.1
Define groups and the stages of group development.

Groups and Group Development

Each person in the group had his or her assigned role: The Spotter, The Back Spotter, The Gorilla, and the Big Player. For over 10 years, this group—former MIT students who were members of a secret Black Jack Club—used their extraordinary mathematical abilities, expert training, teamwork, and interpersonal skills to take millions of dollars from some of the major casinos in the United States.[2] Although most groups aren't formed for such dishonest purposes, the success of this group at its task was impressive. Managers would like their groups to be successful at their tasks also. The first step is understanding what a group is and how groups develop.

What Is a Group?

A **group** is defined as two or more interacting and interdependent individuals who come together to achieve specific goals. *Formal groups* are work groups that are defined by the organization's structure and have designated work assignments and specific tasks directed at accomplishing organizational goals. Exhibit 13-1 provides some examples. *Informal groups* are social groups. These groups occur naturally in the workplace and tend to form around friendships and common interests. For example, five employees from different departments who regularly eat lunch together are an informal group.

Stages of Group Development

Research shows that groups develop through five stages.[3] As shown in Exhibit 13-2, these five stages are *forming, storming, norming, performing,* and *adjourning.*

- *Command groups*—Groups that are determined by the organization chart and composed of individuals who report directly to a given manager.
- *Task groups*—Groups composed of individuals brought together to complete a specific job task; their existence is often temporary because when the task is completed, the group disbands.
- *Cross-functional teams*—Groups that bring together the knowledge and skills of individuals from various work areas or groups whose members have been trained to do each others' jobs.
- *Self-managed teams*—Groups that are essentially independent and that, in addition to their own tasks, take on traditional managerial responsibilities, such as hiring, planning and scheduling, and evaluating performance.

EXHIBIT 13-1

Examples of Formal Work Groups

The **forming stage** has two phases. The first occurs as people join the group. In a formal group, people join because of some work assignment. Once they've joined, the second phase begins: defining the group's purpose, structure, and leadership. This phase involves a great deal of uncertainty as members "test the waters" to determine what types of behavior are acceptable. This stage is complete when members begin to think of themselves as part of a group.

The **storming stage** is appropriately named because of the intragroup conflict. There's conflict over who will control the group and what the group needs to be doing. During this stage, a relatively clear hierarchy of leadership and agreement on the group's direction emerge.

The **norming stage** is one in which close relationships develop and the group becomes cohesive. There's now a strong sense of group identity and camaraderie. This stage is complete

EXHIBIT 13-2

Stages of Group Development

Stage 1
Forming

Stage 2
Storming

Stage 3
Norming

Stage 4
Performing

Stage 5
Adjourning

group
Two or more interacting and interdependent individuals who come together to achieve specific goals

forming stage
The first stage of group development in which people join the group and then define the group's purpose, structure, and leadership

storming stage
The second stage of group development, characterized by intragroup conflict

norming stage
The third stage of group development, characterized by close relationships and cohesiveness

when the group structure solidifies, and the group has assimilated a common set of expectations (or norms) regarding member behavior.

The fourth stage is the **performing stage**. The group structure is in place and accepted by group members. Their energies have moved from getting to know and understand each other to working on the group's task. This is the last stage of development for permanent work groups. However, for temporary groups—project teams, task forces, or similar groups that have a limited task to do—the final stage is **adjourning**. In this stage, the group prepares to disband. The group focuses its attention on wrapping up activities instead of task performance. Group members react in different ways. Some are upbeat, thrilled about the group's accomplishments. Others may be sad over the loss of camaraderie and friendships.

Many of you have probably experienced these stages as you've worked on a group project for a class. Group members are selected or assigned and then meet for the first time. There's a "feeling out" period to assess what the group is going to do and how it's going to be done. What usually follows is a battle for control: Who's going to be in charge? Once this issue is resolved and a "hierarchy" agreed on, the group identifies specific work that needs to be done, who's going to do each part, and dates by which the assigned work needs to be completed. General expectations are established. These decisions form the foundation for what you hope will be a coordinated group effort culminating in a project that's been done well. Once the project is complete and turned in, the group breaks up. Of course, some groups don't get much beyond the forming or storming stages. These groups may have serious interpersonal conflicts, turn in disappointing work, and get lower grades.

Does a group become more effective as it progresses through the first four stages? Some researchers say yes, but it's not that simple.[4] That assumption may be generally true, but what makes a group effective is a complex issue. Under some conditions, high levels of conflict are conducive to high levels of group performance. In some situations, groups in the storming stage outperform those in the norming or performing stages. Also, groups don't always proceed sequentially from one stage to the next. Sometimes, groups are storming and performing at the same time. Groups even occasionally regress to previous stages. Therefore, don't assume that all groups precisely follow this process or that performing is always the most preferable stage. Think of this model as a general framework that underscores the fact that groups are dynamic entities and managers need to know the stage a group is in so they can understand the problems and issues that are most likely to surface.

13.2 **Work** Group Performance and Satisfaction

Many people consider them the most successful "group" of our times. Who? The Beatles. "The Beatles were great artists and entertainers, but in many respects they were four ordinary guys who, as a group, found a way to achieve extraordinary artistic and financial success and have a great time together while doing it. Every business team can learn from their story."[5]

Why *are* some groups more successful than others? Why do some groups achieve high levels of performance and high levels of member satisfaction and others do not? The answers are complex, but include variables such as the abilities of the group's members, the size of the group, the level of conflict, and the internal pressures on members to conform to the group's norms. Exhibit 13-3 presents the major factors that determine group performance and satisfaction.[6] Let's look at each.

External Conditions Imposed on the Group

Work groups are affected by the external conditions imposed on it, such as the organization's strategy, authority relationships, formal rules and regulations, availability of resources, employee selection criteria, the performance management system and culture, and the general physical layout of the group's work space. For instance, some groups have

EXHIBIT 13-3
Group Performance/Satisfaction Model

modern, high-quality tools and equipment to do their jobs while other groups don't. Or the organization might be pursuing a strategy of lowering costs or improving quality, which will affect what a group does and how it does it.

Group Member Resources

A group's performance potential depends to a large extent on the resources each individual brings to the group. These resources include knowledge, abilities, skills, and personality traits, and they determine what members can do and how effectively they will perform in a group. Interpersonal skills—especially conflict management and resolution, collaborative problem solving, and communication—consistently emerge as important for high performance by work groups.[7]

Personality traits also affect group performance because they strongly influence how the individual will interact with other group members. Research has shown that traits that are viewed as positive in our culture (such as sociability, self-reliance, and independence) tend to be positively related to group productivity and morale. In contrast, negative personality characteristics such as authoritarianism, dominance, and unconventionality tend to be negatively related to group productivity and morale.[8]

Group Structure

Work groups aren't unorganized crowds. They have an internal structure that shapes members' behavior and influences group performance. The structure defines roles, norms, conformity, status systems, group size, group cohesiveness, and leadership. Let's look at the first six of these aspects of structure. Leadership is discussed in Chapter 17.

ROLES. We introduced the concept of roles in Chapter 1 when we discussed what managers do. (Remember Mintzberg's managerial roles?) Of course, managers aren't the only individuals in an organization who play various roles. The concept of roles applies to all employees and to their life outside an organization as well. (Think of the various roles you play: student, sibling, employee, spouse or significant other, etc.)

A **role** refers to behavior patterns expected of someone occupying a given position in a social unit. In a group, individuals are expected to do certain things because of their position (role) in the group. These roles are generally oriented toward either getting work done or keeping group members happy.[10] Think about groups that you've been in and the roles that you played in those groups. Were you continually trying to keep the group focused on getting its work done? If so, you were performing a task accomplishment role. Or were you more concerned that group members had the opportunity to offer ideas and

by the numbers[9]

70 percent of employees say that the biggest benefit of workplace friendships is that it creates a more supportive workplace.

85 percent of *Fortune* 1000 companies use team- or group-based pay.

69 percent of workers say their teams are not given enough resources.

83 percent of respondents to a survey identify teams as a key ingredient to organizational success.

33 percent of females want more face-to-face group meetings.

27 percent of males want more face-to-face group meetings.

40 percent of senior executives say that meeting deadlines is the most important characteristic of a good team player.

performing stage
The fourth stage of group development when the group is fully functional and works on group task

adjourning
The final stage of group development for temporary groups during which group members are concerned with wrapping up activities rather than task performance

role
Behavior patterns expected of someone occupying a given position in a social unit

that they were satisfied with the experience? If so, you were performing a group member satisfaction role. Both roles are important to the group's ability to function effectively and efficiently.

A problem that arises is that individuals play multiple roles and adjust their roles to the group to which they belong at the time. However, the differing expectations of these roles often mean that employees face *role conflicts*.

NORMS. All groups have **norms**—standards or expectations that are accepted and shared by a group's members. Norms dictate things such as work output levels, absenteeism, promptness, and the amount of socializing on the job.

For example, norms dictate the "arrival ritual" among office assistants at Coleman Trust Inc. where the workday begins at 8 A.M. Most employees typically arrive a few minutes before and hang up their coats and put their purses and other personal items on their desk so everyone knows they're "at work." They then go to the break room to get coffee and chat. Anyone who violates this norm by starting work at 8 A.M. is pressured to behave in a way that conforms to the group's standard.

Although a group has its own unique set of norms, common organizational norms focus on effort and performance, dress, and loyalty. The most widespread norms are those related to work effort and performance. Work groups typically provide their members with explicit cues on how hard to work, level of output, when to look busy, when it's acceptable to goof off, and the like. These norms are powerful influences on an individual employee's performance. They're so powerful that you can't predict someone's performance based solely on his or her ability and personal motivation. Dress norms frequently dictate what's acceptable to wear to work. If the norm is more formal dress, anyone who dresses casually may face subtle pressure to conform. Finally, loyalty norms will influence whether individuals work late, work on weekends, or move to locations they might not prefer to live.

One negative thing about group norms is that being part of a group can increase an individual's antisocial actions. If the norms of the group include tolerating deviant behavior, someone who normally wouldn't engage in such behavior might be more likely to do so. For instance, one study found that those working in a group were more likely to lie, cheat, and steal than were individuals working alone.[11] Why? Because groups provide anonymity, thus giving individuals—who might otherwise be afraid of getting caught—a false sense of security.

CONFORMITY. Because individuals want to be accepted by groups to which they belong, they're susceptible to pressures to conform. Early experiments done by Solomon

From food servers to hostesses and supervisors, all employees at Johnny Rockets restaurants are expected to join in to sing "Happy Birthday" when a customer is celebrating his or her special day. Employees are also expected to be friendly and fun-loving as they serve and interact with their guests. As part of Johnny Rockets' nostalgic ambience, waiters and waitresses are expected to wear bow ties, bib aprons, and hats to project an all-American look that matches the restaurant's décor. Common organizational norms related to work effort and dress are powerful influences on individual employees' performance.

EXHIBIT 13-4

Examples of Asch's Cards

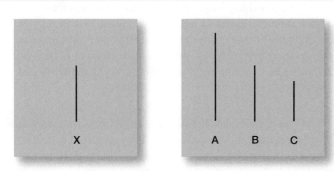

Asch demonstrated the impact that conformity has on an individual's judgment and attitudes.[12] In these experiments, groups of seven or eight people were asked to compare two cards held up by the experimenter. One card had three lines of different lengths and the other had one line which was equal in length to one of the three lines on the other card (see Exhibit 13-4). Each group member was to announce aloud which of the three lines matched the single line. Asch wanted to see what would happen if members began to give incorrect answers. Would pressures to conform cause individuals to give wrong answers just to be consistent with the others? The experiment was "fixed" so that all but one of the members (the unsuspecting subject) were told ahead of time to start giving obviously incorrect answers after one or two rounds. Over many experiments and trials, the unsuspecting subject conformed over a third of the time.

Are these conclusions still valid? Research suggests that conformity levels have declined since Asch's studies. However, managers can't ignore conformity because it can still be a powerful force in groups.[13] Group members often want to be seen as one of the group and avoid being visibly different. We find it more pleasant to agree than to be disruptive, even if being disruptive may improve the group's effectiveness. So we conform. But conformity can go too far, especially when an individual's opinion differs significantly from that of others in the group. In such a case, the group often exerts intense pressure on the individual to align his or her opinion to conform to others' opinions, a phenomenon known as **groupthink**. Groupthink seems to occur when group members hold a positive group image that they want to protect and when the group perceives a collective threat to this positive image.[14]

STATUS SYSTEMS.   Status systems are an important factor in understanding groups. **Status** is a prestige grading, position, or rank within a group. As far back as researchers have been able to trace groups, they have found status hierarchies. Status can be a significant motivator with behavioral consequences especially when individuals see a disparity between what they perceive their status to be and what others perceive it to be.

Status may be informally conferred by characteristics such as education, age, skill, or experience. Anything can have status value if others in the group evaluate it that way. Of course, just because status is informal doesn't mean that it's unimportant or that it's hard to determine who has it or who does not. Group members have no problem placing people into status categories and usually agree about who has high or low status.

Status is also formally conferred, and it's important for employees to believe that the organization's formal status system is congruent—that is, the system shows consistency

---

norms
Standards or expectations that are accepted and shared by a group's members

groupthink
When a group exerts extensive pressure on an individual to align his or her opinion with others' opinions

status
A prestige grading, position, or rank within a group

between the perceived ranking of an individual and the status symbols he or she is given by the organization. For instance, status incongruence would occur when a supervisor earns less than his or her subordinates, a desirable office is occupied by a person in a low-ranking position, or paid country club memberships are provided to division managers but not to vice presidents. Employees expect the "things" an individual receives to be congruent with his or her status. When they're not, employees may question the authority of their managers and may not be motivated by job promotion opportunities.

GROUP SIZE. What's an appropriate size for a group? At Amazon, work teams have considerable autonomy to innovate and to investigate their ideas. And Jeff Bezos, founder and CEO, uses a "two-pizza" philosophy; that is, a team should be small enough that it can be fed with two pizzas. This "two-pizza" philosophy usually limits groups to five to seven people depending, of course, on team member appetites.[15]

Group size affects performance and satisfaction, but the effect depends on what the group is supposed to accomplish.[16] Research indicates, for instance, that small groups are faster at completing tasks than are larger ones. However, for groups engaged in problem solving, large groups consistently get better results than smaller ones. What do these findings mean in terms of specific numbers? Large groups—those with a dozen or more members—are good for getting diverse input. Thus, if the goal of the group is to find facts, a larger group should be more effective. On the other hand, smaller groups—from five to seven members—are better at doing something productive with those facts.

One important research finding related to group size concerns **social loafing**, which is the tendency for an individual to expend less effort when working collectively than when working individually.[17] Social loafing may occur because people believe that others in the group aren't doing their fair share. Thus, they reduce their work efforts in an attempt to make the workload more equivalent. Also, the relationship between an individual's input and the group's output is often unclear. Thus, individuals may become "free riders" and coast on the group's efforts because individuals believe that their contribution can't be measured.

The implications of social loafing are significant. When managers use groups, they must find a way to identify individual efforts. If not, group productivity and individual satisfaction may decline.[18]

GROUP COHESIVENESS. Cohesiveness is important because it has been found to be related to a group's productivity. Groups in which there's a lot of internal disagreement and lack of cooperation are less effective in completing their tasks than are groups in which members generally agree, cooperate, and like each other. Research in this area has focused on **group cohesiveness**, or the degree to which members are attracted to a group and share the group's goals.[19]

Research has generally shown that highly cohesive groups are more effective than are less cohesive ones.[20] However, the relationship between cohesiveness and effectiveness is complex. A key moderating variable is the degree to which the group's attitude aligns with its goals or with the goals of the organization.[21] (See Exhibit 13-5.) The more cohesive the group, the more its members will follow its goals. If the goals are desirable (for instance, high output, quality work, cooperation with individuals outside the group), a cohesive group is more productive than a less cohesive group. But if cohesiveness is high and attitudes are unfavorable, productivity decreases. If cohesiveness is low but goals are supported, productivity increases but not as much as when both cohesiveness and support are high. When cohesiveness is low and goals are not supported, productivity is not significantly affected.

GROUP PROCESSES. The next factor that determines group performance and satisfaction concerns the processes that go on within a work group such as communication, decision making, conflict management, and the like. These processes are important to understanding work groups because they influence group performance and satisfaction positively or negatively. An example of a positive process factor is the synergy of four

EXHIBIT 13-5

Group Cohesiveness and
Productivity

	Cohesiveness	
	High	**Low**
High (Alignment of Group and Organizational Goals)	Strong Increase in Productivity	Moderate Increase in Productivity
Low	Decrease in Productivity	No Significant Effect on Productivity

people on a marketing research team who are able to generate far more ideas as a group than the members could produce individually. However, the group also may have negative process factors such as social loafing, high levels of conflict, or poor communication, which may hinder group effectiveness. We'll look at two important group processes: group decision making and conflict management.

GROUP DECISION MAKING.   It's a rare organization that doesn't use committees, task forces, review panels, study teams, or other similar groups to make decisions. Studies show that managers may spend up to 30 hours a week in group meetings.[22] Undoubtedly, a large portion of that time is spent formulating problems, developing solutions, and determining how to implement the solutions. It's possible, in fact, for groups to be assigned any of the eight steps in the decision-making process. (Refer to Chapter 7 to review these steps.)

What advantages do group decisions have over individual decisions? One is that groups generate more complete information and knowledge. They bring a diversity of experience and perspectives to the decision process that an individual cannot. In addition, groups generate more diverse alternatives because they have a greater amount and diversity of information. Next, groups increase acceptance of a solution. Group members are reluctant to fight or undermine a decision that they helped develop. Finally, groups increase legitimacy. Decisions made by groups may be perceived as more legitimate than decisions made by one person.

Group decisions also have disadvantages. One is that groups almost always take more time to reach a solution than it would take an individual. Another is that a dominant and vocal minority can heavily influence the final decision. In addition, groupthink can undermine critical thinking in the group and harm the quality of the final decision.[23] Finally, in a group, members share responsibility, but the responsibility of any single member is ambiguous.

Determining whether groups are effective at making decisions depends on the criteria used to assess effectiveness.[24] If accuracy, creativity, and degree of acceptance are important, then a group decision may work best. However, if speed and efficiency are important, then an individual decision may be the best. In addition, decision effectiveness is influenced by group size. Although a larger group provides more diverse representation, it also requires more coordination and time for members to contribute their ideas. Evidence indicates that groups of five, and to a lesser extent seven, are the most effective for making decisions.[25]

Let's Get Real

Are decisions made by groups or individuals? *Individual decisions still need to take the group into consideration. You always need the group to feel considered in order to be successful.*

social loafing
The tendency for individuals to expend less effort when working collectively than when working individually

group cohesiveness
The degree to which group members are attracted to one another and share the group's goals

EXHIBIT 13-6
Creative Group Decision Making

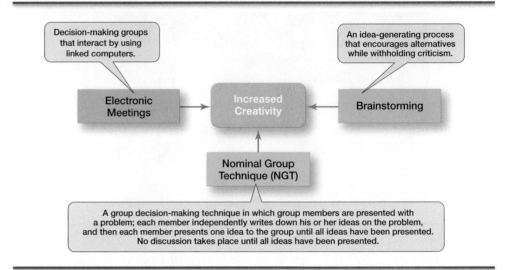

Exhibit 13-6 Creative Group Decision Making

Decision-making groups that interact by using linked computers.

An idea-generating process that encourages alternatives while withholding criticism.

Electronic Meetings → Increased Creativity ← Brainstorming

Nominal Group Technique (NGT)

A group decision-making technique in which group members are presented with a problem; each member independently writes down his or her ideas on the problem, and then each member presents one idea to the group until all ideas have been presented. No discussion takes place until all ideas have been presented.

Having an odd number in the group helps avoid decision deadlocks. Also, these groups are large enough for members to shift roles and withdraw from unfavorable positions but still small enough for quieter members to participate actively in discussions.

What techniques can managers use to help groups make more creative decisions? Exhibit 13-6 describes three possibilities.

CONFLICT MANAGEMENT. Another important group process is how a group manages conflict. As a group performs its assigned tasks, disagreements inevitably arise. **Conflict** is *perceived* incompatible differences resulting in some form of interference or opposition. Whether the differences are real is irrelevant. If people in a group perceive that differences exist, then there is conflict.

Three different views have evolved regarding conflict.[26] The **traditional view of conflict** argues that conflict must be avoided—that it indicates a problem within the group. Another view, the **human relations view of conflict**, argues that conflict is a natural and inevitable outcome in any group and need not be negative, but has potential to be a positive force in contributing to a group's performance. The third and most recent view, the **interactionist view of conflict**, proposes that not only can conflict be a positive force in a group but that some conflict is *absolutely necessary* for a group to perform effectively.

The interactionist view doesn't suggest that all conflicts are good. Some conflicts—**functional conflicts**—are constructive and support the goals of the work group and improve its performance. Other conflicts—**dysfunctional conflicts**—are destructive and prevent a group from achieving its goals. Exhibit 13-7 illustrates the challenge facing managers.

When is conflict functional and when is it dysfunctional? Research indicates that you need to look at the *type* of conflict.[27] **Task conflict** relates to the content and goals of the work. **Relationship conflict** focuses on interpersonal relationships. **Process conflict** refers to how the work gets done. Research shows that *relationship* conflicts are almost always dysfunctional because the interpersonal hostilities increase personality clashes and decrease mutual understanding and the tasks don't get done. On the other hand, low levels of process conflict and low-to-moderate levels of task conflict are functional. For *process* conflict to be productive, it must be minimal. Otherwise, intense arguments over who should do what may become dysfunctional and can lead to uncertainty about task assignments, increase the time to complete tasks, and result in members working at cross-purposes. However, a low-to-moderate level of *task* conflict consistently has a positive effect on group performance because it stimulates discussion of ideas that help groups be

EXHIBIT 13-7

Conflict and Group
Performance

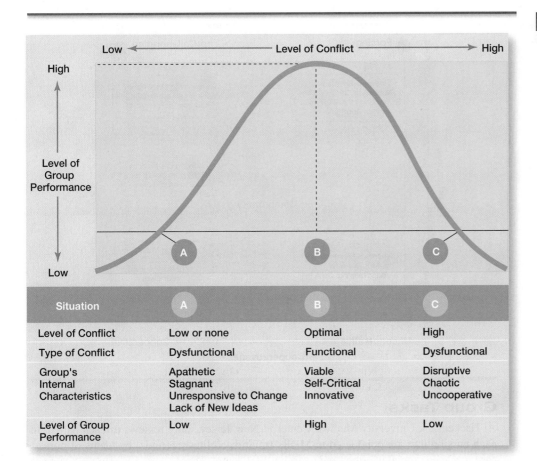

Situation	A	B	C
Level of Conflict	Low or none	Optimal	High
Type of Conflict	Dysfunctional	Functional	Dysfunctional
Group's Internal Characteristics	Apathetic Stagnant Unresponsive to Change Lack of New Ideas	Viable Self-Critical Innovative	Disruptive Chaotic Uncooperative
Level of Group Performance	Low	High	Low

more innovative.[28] Because we don't yet have a sophisticated measuring instrument for assessing whether conflict levels are optimal, too high, or too low, the manager must try to judge that intelligently.

When group conflict levels are too high, managers can select from five conflict management options: avoidance, accommodation, forcing, compromise, and collaboration.[29] (See Exhibit 13-8 for a description of these techniques.) Keep in mind that no one option is ideal for every situation. Which approach to use depends upon the circumstances.

Have you ever been part of a class group in which all teammates received the same grade even though some team members didn't fulfill their responsibilities? How did that make you feel? Did it create conflict within the group and did you feel that the process and outcome were unfair? Recent research also has shown that organizational justice or fairness is an important aspect of managing group conflict.[30] How group members feel about how they're being treated both by each other within the group and by outsiders can affect their work attitudes and behaviors. To promote the sense of fairness, it's important that group leaders build a strong sense of community based on fair and just treatment.

conflict
Perceived incompatible differences that result in interference or opposition

traditional view of conflict
The view that all conflict is bad and must be avoided

human relations view of conflict
The view that conflict is a natural and inevitable outcome in any group

interactionist view of conflict
The view that some conflict is necessary for a group to perform effectively

functional conflicts
Conflicts that support a group's goals and improve its performance

dysfunctional conflicts
Conflicts that prevent a group from achieving its goals

task conflict
Conflicts over content and goals of the work

relationship conflict
Conflict based on interpersonal relationships

process conflict
Conflict over how work gets done

EXHIBIT 13-8

Conflict-Management Techniques

Source: K. Thomas, "Conflict and Negotiation Process in Organizations," in M. D. Dunnette and L. J. Hough (eds.), *Handbook of Industrial and Organizational Psychology*, 2 ed. vol. 3 (Palo Alto, CA: Consulting Psychologists Press, 1992), p. 668. Used with permission by Leaetta Hough-Dunnette.

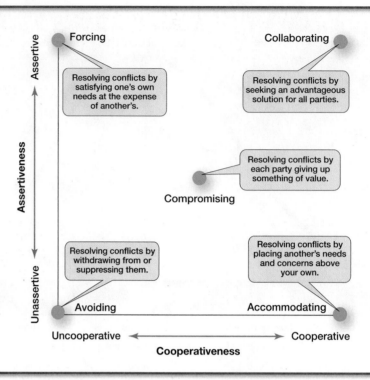

Group Tasks

At Hackensack University Medical Center in New Jersey, daily reviews of each patient in each nursing unit are conducted in MDRs (multidisciplinary rounds) by teams of nurses, case managers, social workers, and an in-hospital doctor. These teams perform tasks such as prescribing drugs or even recommending a patient be discharged. Employee teams at Lockheed Martin's New York facility custom build complex products such as ground-based radar systems using continuous quality improvement techniques. The six people in the Skinny Improv group in Springfield, Missouri, perform their unique brand of comedy every weekend in a downtown venue.[31] Each of these groups has a different type of task to accomplish.

As the group performance/satisfaction model shows, the impact that group processes have on group performance and member satisfaction is modified by the task the group is doing. More specifically, it's the *complexity* and *interdependence* of tasks that influence a group's effectiveness.[32]

Tasks are either simple or complex. Simple tasks are routine and standardized. Complex tasks tend to be novel or nonroutine. It appears that the more complex the task, the more a group benefits from group discussion about alternative work methods. Group members don't need to discuss such alternatives for a simple task, but can rely on standard operating procedures. Similarly, a high degree of interdependence among the tasks that group members must

---

FUTURE VISION | **The Working World in 2020**

Successful organizations will come to recognize that functional conflict—in the form of tolerating dissent—makes an organization stronger, not weaker. Tomorrow's organizations will use blogs, social networking sites, and other vehicles to allow employees to question practices, criticize decisions, and offer improvement suggestions.

The historical practice of minimizing conflict and seeking "peace at any price" didn't produce harmony and loyalty. It merely masked employee concerns and frustrations. To maintain competitiveness, organizations will see conflict in a positive light. And the result will be organizations that adapt faster, generate more and better ideas, and have employees who aren't threatened by saying what's on their minds.

perform means they'll need to interact more. Thus, effective communication and controlled conflict are most relevant to group performance when tasks are complex and interdependent.

Turning Groups into Effective Teams

When companies like W. L. Gore, Volvo, and Kraft Foods introduced teams into their production processes, it made news because no one else was doing it. Today, it's just the opposite— the organization that *doesn't* use teams would be newsworthy. It's estimated that some 80 percent of *Fortune* 500 companies have at least half of their employees on teams. And 83 percent of respondents in a Center for Creative Leadership study said that teams are a key ingredient to organizational success.[33] Without a doubt, team-based work is a core feature of today's organizations. And teams are likely to continue to be popular. Why? Research suggests that teams typically outperform individuals when the tasks being done require multiple skills, judgment, and experience.[34] Organizations are using team-based structures because they've found that teams are more flexible and responsive to changing events than are traditional departments or other permanent work groups. Teams have the ability to quickly assemble, deploy, refocus, and disband. In this section, we'll discuss what a work team is, the different types of teams that organizations might use, and how to develop and manage work teams.

What Is a Work Team?

Most of you are probably familiar with teams especially if you've watched or participated in organized sports events. Work *teams* differ from work *groups* and have their own unique traits (see Exhibit 13-9). Work groups interact primarily to share information and to make decisions to help each member do his or her job more efficiently and effectively. There's no need or opportunity for work groups to engage in collective work that requires joint effort. On the other hand, **work teams** are groups whose members work intensely on a specific, common goal using their positive synergy, individual and mutual accountability, and complementary skills. For instance, at the Sparta, Tennessee, facility of Philips Professional Luminaires, a work team came up with a startling innovation. One team member was commenting on the efficient way that Subway restaurants make their sandwiches

Team-based work is a key ingredient to the success of IBM Corporation. Michael Karasick (center) is the director of Lotus Development at IBM China Software Development Laboratory who leads a team of 800 developers and support staff in Beijing. The China laboratory is one of eight research centers IBM operates throughout the world where large teams benefit from the cross pollination of employees' ideas, experience, and expertise in a broad range of disciplines. Team members work together to find solutions to complicated business problems and to achieve scientific and engineering breakthroughs that lead to innovative IBM products and services.

work teams
Groups whose members work intensely on a specific, common goal using their positive synergy, individual and mutual accountability, and complementary skills

Work Teams	Work Groups
• Leadership role is shared	• One leader clearly in charge
• Accountable to self and team	• Accountable only to self
• Team creates specific purpose	• Purpose is same as broader organizational purpose
• Work is done collectively	• Work is done individually
• Meetings characterized by open-ended discussion and collaborative problem-solving	• Meetings characterized by efficiency; no collaboration or open-ended discussion
• Performance is measured directly by evaluating collective work output	• Performance is measured indirectly according to its influence on others
• Work is decided upon and done together	• Work is decided upon by group leader and delegated to individual group members
• Can be quickly assembled, deployed, refocused, and disbanded	

Sources: J. R. Katzenbach and D. K. Smith, "The Wisdom of Teams," *Harvard Business Review*, July–August 2005, p. 161; A. J. Fazzari and J. B. Mosca, "Partners in Perfection: Human Resources Facilitating Creation and Ongoing Implementation of Self-Managed Manufacturing Teams in a Small Medium Enterprise," *Human Resource Development Quarterly*, Fall 2009, pp. 353–376.

with workers lining up all their ingredients in an easy-to-reach, highly adaptable format. The team decided to apply that same flexible principle to their work of producing lighting fixtures and together figured out a way to make that happen.[35]

Types of Work Teams

Teams can do a variety of things. They can design products, provide services, negotiate deals, coordinate projects, offer advice, and make decisions.[36] For instance, at Rockwell Automation's facility in North Carolina, teams are used in work process optimization projects. At Sylvania, the New Ventures Group creates cool LED-based products. At Arkansas-based Acxiom Corporation, a team of human resource professionals planned and implemented a cultural change. And every summer weekend at any NASCAR race, you can see work teams in action during drivers' pit stops.[37] The four most common types of work teams are problem-solving teams, self-managed work teams, cross-functional teams, and virtual teams.

When work teams first became popular, most were **problem-solving teams**, which are teams from the same department or functional area involved in efforts to improve work activities or to solve specific problems. Members share ideas or offer suggestions on how work processes and methods can be improved. However, these teams are rarely given the authority to implement any of their suggested actions.

Although problem-solving teams were helpful, they didn't go far enough in getting employees involved in work-related decisions and processes. This shortcoming led to another type of team, a **self-managed work team**, which is a formal group of employees who operate without a manager and are responsible for a complete work process or segment. A self-managed team is responsible for getting the work done *and* for managing themselves, which usually includes planning and scheduling of work, assigning tasks to members, collective control over the pace of work, making operating decisions, and taking action on problems. For instance, teams at Corning have no shift supervisors and work closely with other manufacturing divisions to solve production-line problems and coordinate deadlines and deliveries. The teams have the authority to make and implement decisions, finish projects, and address problems.[38] Other organizations such as Xerox, Boeing, PepsiCo, and Hewlett-Packard also use self-managed teams. An estimated 30 percent of U.S. employers now use this form of team; among large firms, the number is probably closer to 50 percent.[39] Most organizations that use self-managed teams find them to be effective.[40]

The third type of team is the **cross-functional team**, which we introduced in Chapters 10 and 11 and defined as a work team composed of individuals from various functional specialties. Many organizations use cross-functional teams. For example, ArcelorMittal, the world's biggest steel company, uses cross-functional teams of scientists, plant managers, and salespeople to review and monitor product innovations.[41] The concept of cross-functional teams is even being applied in health care. For instance, at Suburban Hospital in Bethesda, Maryland, intensive care unit (ICU) teams composed of a doctor trained in intensive care medicine, a pharmacist, a social worker, a nutritionist, the chief ICU nurse, a respiratory therapist, and a chaplain meet daily with every patient's bedside nurse to discuss and debate the best course of treatment. The hospital credits this team care approach with reducing errors, shortening the amount of time patients spent in ICU, and improving communication between families and the medical staff.[42]

The final type of team is the **virtual team**, which is a team that uses technology to link physically dispersed members in order to achieve a common goal. For instance, a virtual team at Boeing-Rocketdyne played a pivotal role in developing a radically new product.[43] Another company, Decision Lens, uses a virtual team environment to generate and evaluate creative ideas.[44] In a virtual team, members collaborate online with tools such as wide-area networks, videoconferencing, fax, e-mail, or Web sites where the team can hold online conferences.[45] Virtual teams can do all the things that other teams can—share information, make decisions, and complete tasks; however, they lack the normal give-and-take of face-to-face discussions. That's why virtual teams tend to be more task-oriented especially if the team members have never met in person.

Creating Effective Work Teams

As our chapter opener illustrated, teams are not always effective. They don't always achieve high levels of performance. However, research on teams provides insights into the characteristics typically associated with effective teams.[46] These characteristics are listed in Exhibit 13-10. One element that you might notice is missing but think is important to being an effective team is that a team be harmonious and friendly.[47] In fact, friendliness is not a necessary ingredient. Even a grumpy team can be effective if these other team characteristics are present. When a team is productive, has done something good together, and is recognized for its efforts, team members can feel good about their effectiveness.

CLEAR GOALS. High-performance teams have a clear understanding of the goal to be achieved. Members are committed to the team's goals, know what they're expected to accomplish, and understand how they will work together to achieve these goals.

RELEVANT SKILLS. Effective teams are composed of competent individuals who have the necessary technical and interpersonal skills to achieve the desired goals while working well together. This last point is important because not everyone who is technically competent has the interpersonal skills to work well as a team member.

Let's Get Real

F2F

The top three characteristics of effective teams are trust, individual accountability, and respected leadership.

---

problem-solving team
A team from the same department or functional area that's involved in efforts to improve work activities or to solve specific problems

self-managed work team
A type of work team that operates without a manager and is responsible for a complete work process or segment

cross-functional team
A work team composed of individuals from various functional specialties

virtual team
A type of work team that uses technology to link physically dispersed members in order to achieve a common goal

EXHIBIT 13-10
Characteristics of
Effective Teams

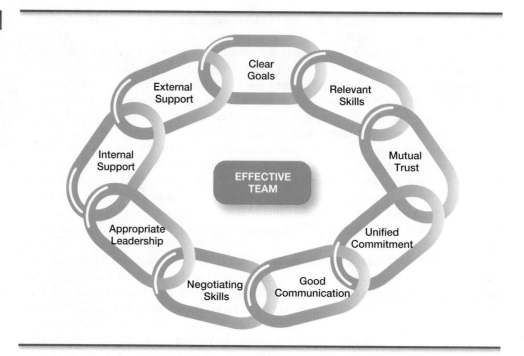

MUTUAL TRUST. Effective teams are characterized by high mutual trust among members. That is, members believe in each other's ability, character, and integrity. But as you probably know from personal relationships, trust is fragile. Maintaining this trust requires careful attention by managers.

UNIFIED COMMITMENT. Unified commitment is characterized by dedication to the team's goals and a willingness to expend extraordinary amounts of energy to achieve them. Members of an effective team exhibit intense loyalty and dedication to the team and are willing to do whatever it takes to help their team succeed.

GOOD COMMUNICATION. Not surprisingly, effective teams are characterized by good communication. Members convey messages, verbally and nonverbally, between each other in ways that are readily and clearly understood. Also, feedback helps guide team members and correct misunderstandings. Like a couple who has been together for many years, members of high-performing teams are able to quickly and efficiently share ideas and feelings.

NEGOTIATING SKILLS. Effective teams are continually making adjustments to whom does what. This flexibility requires team members to possess negotiating skills. Because problems and relationships regularly change within teams, members need to be able to confront and reconcile differences.

APPROPRIATE LEADERSHIP. Effective leaders are important. They can motivate a team to follow them through the most difficult situations. How? By clarifying goals, demonstrating that change is possible by overcoming inertia, increasing the self-confidence of team members, and helping members to more fully realize their potential. Increasingly, effective team leaders act as coaches and facilitators. They help guide and support the team, but don't control it. Studies have shown that when a team leader's emotional displays—positive *and* negative—are used at appropriate times, the team's functioning and performance can be enhanced.[48]

INTERNAL AND EXTERNAL SUPPORT. The final condition necessary for an effective team is a supportive climate. Internally, the team should have a sound infrastructure which means proper training, a clear and reasonable measurement system that team members can use to evaluate their overall performance, an incentive program that recognizes and rewards team activities, and a supportive human resource system. The right infrastructure should support members and reinforce behaviors that lead to high levels of performance. Externally, managers should provide the team with the resources needed to get the job done.

Current Challenges in Managing Teams

13.4
LEARNING OUTCOME
Discuss contemporary issues in managing teams.

Few trends have influenced how work gets done in organizations as much as the use of work teams. The shift from working alone to working on teams requires employees to cooperate with others, share information, confront differences, and sublimate personal interests for the greater good of the team. Managers can build effective teams by understanding what influences performance and satisfaction. However, managers also face some current challenges in managing teams, primarily those associated with managing global teams, building team skills, and understanding organizational social networks.

Managing Global Teams

Two characteristics of today's organizations are obvious: They're global and work is increasingly done by teams. These two aspects mean that any manager is likely to have to manage a global team. What do we know about managing global teams? We know there are both drawbacks and benefits in using global teams (see Exhibit 13-11). Using our group model as a framework, we can see some of the issues associated with managing global teams.

GROUP MEMBER RESOURCES IN GLOBAL TEAMS. In global organizations, understanding the relationship between group performance and group member resources is more challenging because of the unique cultural characteristics represented by members of a global team. In addition to recognizing team members' abilities, skills, knowledge, and personality, managers need to be familiar with and clearly understand the cultural characteristics of the groups and the group members they manage.[50] For instance, is the global team from a culture in which uncertainty avoidance is high? If so, members will not be comfortable dealing with unpredictable and ambiguous tasks.

LEADER who made a difference

Do you know what one of the most important pieces of real estate is on the Internet? Yes, it's Google's search results page.[49] And Marissa Mayer, vice president of search products and user experience, recognizes how important that page's design is. For the eighth iteration, which she called "particularly large and particularly important," the task was turned over to a core design team of 16 staffers from engineering, design, and five other departments. A lot was riding on the redesign, meaning the cross-functional team's efforts were particularly important. However, with Mayer's confidence in their combined abilities, the team collaborated in a process marked by wild illustrations and precise mathematical code to create the page design.

Drawbacks	Benefits
• Dislike of team members	• Greater diversity of ideas
• Mistrust of team members	• Limited groupthink
• Stereotyping	• Increased attention on understanding others' ideas, perspectives, etc.
• Communication problems	
• Stress and tension	

EXHIBIT 13-11

Global Teams

Source: Based on N. Adler, *International Dimensions in Organizational Behavior*, 4th ed. (Cincinnati, OH: South-Western Publishing, 2002), pp. 141–147.

Also, as managers work with global teams, they need to be aware of the potential for stereotyping, which can lead to problems.

GROUP STRUCTURE. Some of the structural areas where we see differences in managing global teams include conformity, status, social loafing, and cohesiveness.

Are conformity findings generalizable across cultures? Research suggests that Asch's findings are culture-bound.[51] For instance, as might be expected, conformity to social norms tends to be higher in collectivistic cultures than in individualistic cultures. Despite this tendency, however, groupthink tends to be less of a problem in global teams because members are less likely to feel pressured to conform to the ideas, conclusions, and decisions of the group.[52]

Also, the importance of status varies between cultures. The French, for example, are extremely status conscious. Also, countries differ on the criteria that confer status. For instance, in Latin America and Asia, status tends to come from family position and formal roles held in organizations. In contrast, while status is important in countries like the United States and Australia, it tends to be less "in your face." And it tends to be given based on accomplishments rather than on titles and family history. Managers must understand who and what holds status when interacting with people from a culture different from their own. An American manager who doesn't understand that office size isn't a measure of a Japanese executive's position or who fails to grasp the importance the British place on family genealogy and social class is likely to unintentionally offend others and lessen his or her interpersonal effectiveness.

Social loafing has a Western bias. It's consistent with individualistic cultures, like the United States and Canada, which are dominated by self-interest. It's not consistent with collectivistic societies, in which individuals are motivated by group goals. For instance, in studies comparing employees from the United States with employees from the People's Republic of China and Israel (both collectivistic societies), the Chinese and Israelis showed no propensity to engage in social loafing. In fact, they actually performed better in a group than when working alone.[53]

Cohesiveness is another group structural element where managers may face special challenges. In a cohesive group, members are unified and "act as one." These groups exhibit a great deal of camaraderie, and group identity is high. In global teams, however, cohesiveness is often more difficult to achieve because of higher levels of "mistrust, miscommunication, and stress."[54]

GROUP PROCESSES. The processes that global teams use to do their work can be particularly challenging for managers. For one thing, communication issues often arise because not all team members may be fluent in the team's working language. This can lead to inaccuracies, misunderstandings, and inefficiencies.[55] However, research also has shown that a multicultural global team is better able to capitalize on the diversity of ideas represented if a wide range of information is used.[56]

Managing conflict in global teams isn't easy, especially when those teams are virtual teams. Conflict can interfere with how information is used by the team. However, research shows that in collectivistic cultures, a collaborative conflict management style can be most effective.[57]

MANAGER'S ROLE. Despite the challenges associated with managing global teams, managers can provide the group with an environment in which efficiency and effectiveness are enhanced.[58] First, because communication skills are vital, managers should focus on developing those skills. Also, as we've said earlier, managers must consider cultural differences when deciding what type of global team to use. For instance, evidence suggests that self-managed teams have not fared well in Mexico largely due to that culture's low tolerance of ambiguity and uncertainty and employees' strong respect for hierarchical authority.[59] Finally, it's vital that managers be sensitive to the unique differences of each member of the global team, but it's also important that team members be sensitive to each other.

Building Team Skills

Have you ever participated in a team-building exercise? Such exercises are commonly used to illustrate and develop specific aspects or skills of being on a team. For instance, maybe you've completed *Lost on the Moon* or *Stranded at Sea* or some other written exercise in which you rank-order what items are most important to your survival. Then, you do the same thing with a group—rank-order the most important items. The rank-ordered items are compared against some expert ranking to see how many you got "right." The intent of the exercise is to illustrate how much more effective decisions can be when made as a team. Or maybe you've been part of a trust-building exercise in which you fall back and team members catch you or an exercise in which your team had to figure out how to get all members across an imaginary river or up a rock wall. Such exercises help teams bond or connect and learn to rely on one another. One of the important tasks managers have is building effective teams.[60] These types of team-building exercises can be an important part of that process. And team building efforts can work. For example, a research project that looked at star performers with poor team skills who went through two cycles of team-building exercises found that those individuals learned how to collaborate better.[61]

Participating in team-building exercises helps Verizon Wireless employees who work from different locations throughout the country learn how to collaborate and cooperate better. Verizon's technical specialists in this photo communicate mostly by electronics from their geographically dispersed workplaces. Periodically they meet face-to-face to learn skills that help them bond, rely on each other, and function as committed team members. Equipped with GPS systems, the technicians are shown here during a scavenger hunt team-building exercise in which they work together to find clues for answering a list of questions.

With the emphasis on teams in today's organizations, managers need to recognize that people don't automatically know how to be part of a team or to be an effective team member. Like any behavior, sometimes you have to learn about the skill and then keep practicing and reinforcing it. In building team skills, managers must view their role as more of being a coach and developing team members in order to create more committed, collaborative, and inclusive teams.[62] It's important to recognize that not everyone is a team player or can learn to be a team player. If attempts at team building aren't working, then maybe it's better to put those people in positions where their work is done individually.

Understanding Social Networks

We can't leave this chapter on managing teams without looking at the patterns of informal connections among individuals within groups—that is, at the **social network structure**.[63] What actually happens *within* groups? How *do* group members relate to each other and how does work get done?

Managers need to understand the social networks and social relationships of work groups. Why? Because a group's informal social relationships can help or hinder its effectiveness. For instance, research on social networks has shown that when people need help getting a job done, they'll choose a friendly colleague over someone who may be more capable.[64] Another recent review of team studies showed that teams with high levels of interpersonal interconnectedness actually attained their goals better and were more committed to staying together.[65] Organizations are recognizing the practical benefits of knowing the social networks within teams. For instance, when Ken Loughridge, an IT manager with MWH Global, was transferred from Cheshire, England, to New Zealand, he had a "map" of the informal relationships and connections among company IT employees. This map had been created a few months before using the results of a survey that asked employees who they "consulted most frequently, who they turned to for expertise, and who either boosted or drained their energy levels." Not only did this map help him

---

social network structure
The patterns of informal connections among individuals within a group

identify well-connected technical experts, it helped him minimize potential problems when a key manager in the Asia region left the company because Loughridge knew who this person's closest contacts were. Loughridge said, "It's as if you took the top off an ant hill and could see where there's a hive of activity. It really helped me understand who the players were."[66]

What Would You Do?

Tracy K. Tunwall
Assistant Professor of Business
**Mount Mercy University
Cedar Rapids, IA**

Let's Get Real:
My Response *to A Manager's Dilemma, page 346*

When teams fail, it is typically due to a lack of ability or a failure of motivation. This team clearly had the ability, and they were expected to win. It sounds like there was failure in leadership to get everyone rowing in the same direction. Top athletes can be difficult to manage, but that is what great coaches are able to do. A lot of conflict between the players and the coaches was evident, including players being removed from the team, press leaks, and a public protest of the training session. Players may have felt anonymous, or that the coaches did not do enough to get to know the players and tap into their individual motivations. The coaches may have done a poor job in helping players draw the line of sight from their individual contributions and actions to the overall outcomes for the team. Other than winning a game, maybe they didn't receive good measurements of what success means, or receive rewards for positive contributions.

The most fundamental problem outlined in the case was the lack of trust. Trust is a necessity for any successful team. If you do not trust people you will not resolve problems because you cannot share information. When problems arise, members will not work with each other because they don't know how the information will be used. If you don't think someone has your best interests in mind, or feel they may use information against you, you don't build the relationships necessary for success.

CHAPTER SUMMARY
by Learning Outcomes

LEARNING OUTCOME 13.1

Define groups and the stages of group development.

A group is two or more interacting and interdependent individuals who come together to achieve specific goals. Formal groups are work groups that are defined by the organization's structure and have designated work assignments and specific tasks directed at accomplishing organizational goals. Informal groups are social groups.

The forming stage consists of two phases: joining the group and defining the group's purpose, structure, and leadership. The storming stage is one of intragroup conflict over who will control the group and what the group will be doing. The norming stage is when close relationships and cohesiveness develop as norms are determined. The performing stage is when group members began to work on the group's task. The adjourning stage is when the group prepares to disband.

LEARNING OUTCOME 13.2

Describe the major components that determine group performance and satisfaction.

The major components that determine group performance and satisfaction include external conditions, group member resources, group structure, group processes, and group tasks.

External conditions, such as availability of resources, organizational goals, and other factors, affect work groups. Group member resources (knowledge, skills, abilities, personality traits) can influence what members can do and how effectively they will perform in a group.

Group roles generally involve getting the work done or keeping group members happy. Group norms are powerful influences on a person's performance and dictate things such as work output levels, absenteeism, and promptness. Pressures to conform can heavily influence a person's judgment and attitudes. If carried to extremes, group-think can be a problem. Status systems can be a significant motivator with individual behavioral consequences, especially if incongruence is a factor. What size group is most effective and efficient depends on the task the group is supposed to accomplish. Cohesiveness is related to a group's productivity.

Group decision making and conflict management are important group processes that play a role in performance and satisfaction. If accuracy, creativity, and degree of acceptance are important, a group decision may work best. Relationship conflicts are almost always dysfunctional. Low levels of process conflicts and low-to-moderate levels of task conflicts are functional. Effective communication and controlled conflict are most relevant to group performance when tasks are complex and interdependent.

LEARNING OUTCOME 13.3

Define teams and best practices influencing team performance.

Characteristics of work groups include a strong, clearly focused leader; individual accountability; purpose that's the same as the broader organizational mission; individual work product; efficient meetings; effectiveness measured by influence on others; and discusses, decides, and delegates together. Characteristics of teams include shared leadership roles; individual and mutual accountability; specific team purpose; collective work products; meetings with open-ended discussion and active problem solving; performance measured directly on collective work products; and discusses, decides, and does real work.

A problem-solving team is one that's focused on improving work activities or solving specific problems. A self-managed work team is responsible for a complete work process or segment and manages itself. A cross-functional team is composed of individuals from various specialties. A virtual team uses technology to link physically dispersed members in order to achieve a common goal.

The characteristics of an effective team include clear goals, relevant skills, mutual trust, unified commitment, good communication, negotiating skills, appropriate leadership, and internal and external support.

LEARNING OUTCOME **13.4** **Discuss** contemporary issues in managing teams.

The challenges of managing global teams can be seen in the group member resources, especially the diverse cultural characteristics; group structure, especially conformity, status, social loafing, and cohesiveness; group processes, especially with communication and managing conflict; and the manager's role in making it all work.

With the emphasis on teams in today's organizations, managers need to recognize that people don't automatically know how to be part of a team or to be an effective team member. Like any behavior, team members have to learn about the skill and then keep practicing and reinforcing it. In building team skills, managers must view their role as more of being a coach and developing others in order to create more committed, collaborative, and inclusive teams.

Managers need to understand the patterns of informal connections among individuals within groups because those informal social relationships can help or hinder the group's effectiveness.

PEARSON **mymanagementlab** To check your understanding of learning outcomes **13.1** – **13.4** go to **mymanagementlab.com** and try the chapter questions.

REVIEW AND DISCUSSION QUESTIONS

1. Describe the different types of groups and the five stages of group development.

2. Explain how external conditions and group member resources affect group performance and satisfaction.

3. Discuss how group structure, group processes, and group tasks influence group performance and satisfaction.

4. Compare groups and teams.

5. Describe the four most common types of teams.

6. List the characteristics of effective teams.

7. What challenges do managers face in managing global teams? How should those challenges be handled?

8. Explain the role of informal (social) networks in managing teams.

9. How do you think scientific management theorists would react to the increased reliance on teams in organizations? How would behavioral science theorists react?

10. Why might a manager want to stimulate conflict in a group or team? How could conflict be stimulated?

PREPARING FOR: My Career

ETHICS DILEMMA

When coworkers work closely on a team project, is there such a thing as TMI (too much information)?[67] At one company, a team that had just finished a major project went out to lunch to celebrate. During lunch, one colleague mentioned that he was training for a 20-mile bike race. In addition to a discussion of his new helmet and Lycra shorts, the person also described shaving his whole body to reduce aerodynamic drag. Later, another team member said, "Why, why, why do we need to go there? This is information about a coworker, not someone I really consider a friend, and now it's forever burned in my brain." What do you think? Why are work colleagues sharing increasingly personal information? How have social media and technology contributed to this type of information disclosure? What are the ethical implications of sharing such personal information in the workplace?

Developing Your Coaching Skill

About the Skill

Effective managers are increasingly being described as coaches rather than bosses. Just like coaches, they're expected to provide instruction, guidance, advice, and encouragement to help team members improve their job performance.

Steps in Practicing the Skill

1. **Analyze ways to improve the team's performance and capabilities.** A coach looks for opportunities for team members to expand their capabilities and improve performance. How? You can use the following behaviors. Observe your team members' behaviors on a day-to-day basis. Ask questions of them: Why do you do a task this way? Can it be improved? What other approaches might be used? Show genuine interest in team members as individuals, not merely as employees. Respect them individually. Listen to each employee.

2. **Create a supportive climate.** It's the coach's responsibility to reduce barriers to development and to facilitate a climate that encourages personal performance improvement. How? You can use the following behaviors. Create a climate that contributes to a free and open exchange of ideas. Offer help and assistance. Give guidance and advice when asked. Encourage your team. Be positive and upbeat. Don't use threats. Ask, "What did we learn from this that can help us in the future?" Reduce obstacles. Assure team members that you value their contribution to the team's goals.

Take personal responsibility for the outcome, but don't rob team members of their full responsibility. Validate team members' efforts when they succeed. Point to what was missing when they fail. Never blame team members for poor results.

3. **Influence team members to change their behavior.** The ultimate test of coaching effectiveness is whether an employee's performance improves. You must encourage ongoing growth and development. How can you do this? Try the following behaviors. Recognize and reward small improvements and treat coaching as a way of helping employees to continually work toward improvement. Use a collaborative style by allowing team members to participate in identifying and choosing among improvement ideas. Break difficult tasks down into simpler ones. Model the qualities that you expect from your team. If you want openness, dedication, commitment, and responsibility from your team members, demonstrate these qualities yourself.

Practicing the Skill

Collaborative efforts are more successful when every member of the group or team contributes a specific role or task toward the completion of the goal. To improve your skill at nurturing team effort, choose two of the following activities and break each one into at least six to eight separate tasks or steps. Be sure to indicate which steps are sequential, and which can be done simultaneously with others. What do you think is the ideal team size for each activity you choose?

a. Making an omelet
b. Washing the car
c. Creating a computerized mailing list
d. Designing an advertising poster
e. Planning a ski trip
f. Restocking a supermarket's produce department

WORKING TOGETHER
Team Exercise

Derek Yach, senior vice president for global health policy at PepsiCo, is assembling a team of "idealistic scientists to find alternatives to Doritos."[68] These physicians and researchers with doctorate degrees, many of whom have built their reputations at places like the Mayo Clinic, the World Health Organization, and like-minded organizations, are tasked with creating healthier options by "making the bad stuff less bad." Suppose that you were put in charge of this elite team. How would you lead it?

Form small groups of three to four individuals. Your team's task is to come up with some suggestions for leading this team. (Hint: Look at Exhibit 13-10.) Come up with a bulleted list of your ideas. Be prepared to share your ideas with the class.

MY TURN TO BE A MANAGER

- Think of a group to which you belong (or have belonged). Trace its development through the stages of group development as shown in Exhibit 13-2. How closely did its development parallel the group development model? How might the group development model be used to improve this group's effectiveness?

- Using this same group, write a report describing the following things about this group: types of roles played by whom, group norms, group conformity issues, status system, size of group and how effective/efficient it is, and group cohesiveness.

- Using the same group, describe how decisions are made. Is the process effective? Efficient? Describe what types of conflicts seem to arise most often (relationship, process, or task) and how those conflicts are handled. Add this information to your report on the group's development and structure.

- What traits do you think good team players have? Do some research to answer this question and write up a report detailing your findings using a bulleted list format.

- Select two of the characteristics of effective teams listed in Exhibit 13-10 and develop a team-building exercise for each characteristic that will help a group improve that characteristic. Be creative. Write a report describing your exercises and be sure to explain how your exercise will help a group improve or develop that characteristic.

- When working in a group (any group to which you're assigned or to which you belong), pay careful attention to what happens in the group as tasks are completed. How does the group's structure or its processes affect how successful the group is at completing its task?

- Steve's and Mary's suggested readings: Tom Rath, *Vital Friends* (Gallup Press, 2006); Jon R. Katzenbach and Douglas K. Smith, *The Wisdom of Teams: Creating the High Performance Organization* (McGraw-Hill, 2005); Patrick Lencioni, *Overcoming the 5 Dysfunctions of a Team* (Jossey-Bass, 2005); Ben Mezrich, *Bringing Down the House: The Inside Story of Six MIT Students Who Took Vegas for Millions* (Free Press, 2002); Jon R. Katzenbach and Douglas K. Smith, *The Discipline of Teams* (Wiley, 2001); and Jean Lipman-Blumen and Harold J. Leavitt, *Hot Groups* (Oxford, 1999).

- Research brainstorming and write a report to your professor explaining what it is and listing suggestions for making it an effective group decision-making tool.

- In your own words, write down three things you learned in this chapter about being a good manager.

- Self-knowledge can be a powerful learning tool. Go to mymanagementlab.com and complete these self-assessment exercises: What's My Attitude Toward Working in Groups? Do I Trust Others? Do Others See Me As Trusting? How Good Am I at Building and Leading a Team? What's My Preferred Conflict-Handing Style? Using the results of your assessments, identify personal strengths and weaknesses. What will you do to reinforce your strengths and improve your weaknesses?

CASE APPLICATION 1
Aiming Higher

Bancolombia is Colombia's biggest bank.[69] At its sleek new headquarters in Medellin, there are no plush executive chairs. Instead, everyone from the bank president to assistants use identical leather and steel ergonomic chairs. The subtle message: no one here has special privileges. The chairs, the open-space offices, and a contemporary design reflect the company's organizational culture that recognizes individual contributions but heavily emphasizes teamwork. González Bacci, Bancolombia's director of human resources, says that this culture developed out of the need to integrate employees from the bank's many acquisitions and forge a single identity among employees and in the eyes of customers. "We want to reinforce the idea with our workers that achieving the group vision depends on everyone, not just on management, and we want to give

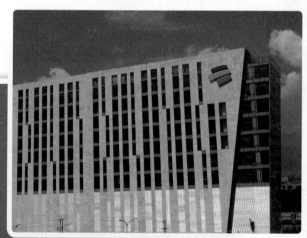

Following the acquisition of many different banks, Bancolombia built new headquarters where all design elements, from open-space offices to furniture, reflect the bank's emphasis on teamwork for the purpose of projecting a single corporate identity for employees and customers.

Cognitive Dissonance Theory

Can we assume from this consistency principle that an individual's behavior can always be predicted if we know his or her attitude on a subject? The answer isn't a simple "yes" or "no." Why? Cognitive dissonance theory.

Cognitive dissonance theory sought to explain the relationship between attitudes and behavior.[40] **Cognitive dissonance** is any incompatibility or inconsistency between attitudes or between behavior and attitudes. The theory argued that inconsistency is uncomfortable and that individuals will try to reduce the discomfort and thus, the dissonance.

Of course, no one can avoid dissonance. You know you should floss your teeth every day, but don't do it. There's an inconsistency between attitude and behavior. How do people cope with cognitive dissonance? The theory proposed that how hard we'll try to reduce dissonance is determined by three things: (1) the *importance* of the factors creating the dissonance, (2) the degree of *influence* the individual believes he or she has over those factors, and (3) the *rewards* that may be involved in dissonance.

If the factors creating the dissonance are relatively unimportant, the pressure to correct the inconsistency will be low. However, if those factors are important, individuals may change their behavior, conclude that the dissonant behavior isn't so important, change their attitude, or identify compatible factors that outweigh the dissonant ones.

How much influence individuals believe they have over the factors also affects their reaction to the dissonance. If they perceive the dissonance is something about which they have no choice, they're won't be receptive to attitude change or feel a need to do so. If, for example, the dissonance-producing behavior was required as a result of a manager's order, the pressure to reduce dissonance would be less than if the behavior had been performed voluntarily. Although dissonance exists, it can be rationalized and justified by the need to follow the manager's orders—that is, the person had no choice or control.

Finally, rewards also influence the degree to which individuals are motivated to reduce dissonance. Coupling high dissonance with high rewards tends to reduce the discomfort by motivating the individual to believe that there is consistency.

Attitude Surveys

Many organizations regularly survey their employees about their attitudes.[41] Exhibit 14-3 shows an example of an actual attitude survey. Typically, **attitude surveys** present the employee with a set of statements or questions eliciting how they feel about their jobs, work groups, supervisors, or the organization. Ideally, the items will be designed to obtain the specific information that managers desire. An attitude score is achieved by summing up responses to individual questionnaire items. These scores can then be averaged for work groups, departments, divisions, or the organization as a whole. For instance, the Tennessee Valley Authority, the largest U.S. government-run energy company, came up with a "Cultural Health Index" to measure employee attitudes. The organization found that business

Let's Get Real

Employee attitude surveys are helpful because *they allow a manager to "listen" through a nonjudgmental avenue, which can foster honest feedback.*

EXHIBIT 14-3

Sample Employee Attitude Survey

Here are some sample statements from an employee attitude survey:

- I have ample opportunities to use my skills/abilities in my job.
- My manager has a good relationship with my work group.
- My organization provides me professional development opportunities.
- I am told if I'm doing good work or not.
- I feel safe in my work environment.
- My organization is a great place to work.

employee engagement
When employees are connected to, satisfied with, and enthusiastic about their jobs

cognitive dissonance
Any incompatibility or inconsistency between attitudes or between behavior and attitudes

attitude surveys
Surveys that elicit responses from employees through questions about how they feel about their jobs, work groups, supervisors, or the organization

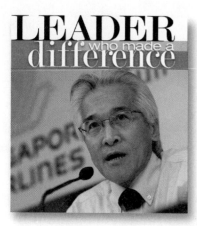

LEADER who made a difference

As one of the top-ranked airlines for customer service, Singapore Airlines (SIA) has a stellar reputation in the fiercely competitive commercial aviation business.[46] The company's top leader, Chew Choon Seng, has created a culture in which employees excel at what they do and enjoy what they do. Passengers appreciate the outstanding customer service provided by the airline's satisfied frontline employees who have earned a reputation as friendly, upbeat, and responsive. In recruiting flight attendants, the company carefully selects people who are warm, hospitable, and happy to serve others. All employees—from bottom to top—are very proud to be part of the SIA family.

units that scored high on the attitude surveys also were the ones whose performance was high. For poorly performing business units, early signs of potential trouble had shown up in the attitude surveys.[42]

Regularly surveying employee attitudes provides managers with valuable feedback on how employees perceive their working conditions. Policies and practices that managers view as objective and fair may not be seen that way by employees. The use of regular attitude surveys can alert managers to potential problems and employees' intentions early so that action can be taken to prevent repercussions.[43]

Implications for Managers

Managers should be interested in their employees' attitudes because they influence behavior. Satisfied and committed employees, for instance, have lower rates of turnover and absenteeism. If managers want to keep resignations and absences down—especially among their more productive employees—they'll want to do things that generate positive job attitudes.

Satisfied employees also perform better on the job. So managers should focus on those factors that have been shown to be conducive to high levels of employee job satisfaction: making work challenging and interesting, providing equitable rewards, creating supportive working conditions, and encouraging supportive colleagues.[44] These factors are likely to help employees be more productive.

Managers should also survey employees about their attitudes. As one study put it, "A sound measurement of overall job attitude is one of the most useful pieces of information an organization can have about its employees."[45]

Finally, managers should know that employees will try to reduce dissonance. If employees are required to do things that appear inconsistent to them or that are at odds with their attitudes, managers should remember that pressure to reduce the dissonance is not as strong when the employee perceives that the dissonance is externally imposed and uncontrollable. It's also decreased if rewards are significant enough to offset the dissonance. So the manager might point to external forces such as competitors, customers, or other factors when explaining the need to perform some work that the individual may have some dissonance about. Or the manager can provide rewards that an individual desires.

LEARNING OUTCOME 14.3
Describe different personality theories.

Personality

"Let's face it, dating is a drag. There was a time when we thought the computer was going to make it all better. . . . But most of us learned the hard way that finding someone who shares our love of film noir and obscure garage bands does not a perfect match make."[47] Using in-depth personality assessment and profiling, Chemistry.com is trying to do something about making the whole dating process better.

Personality. We all have one. Some of us are quiet and passive; others are loud and aggressive. When we describe people using terms such as *quiet, passive, loud, aggressive, ambitious, extroverted, loyal, tense,* or *sociable,* we're describing their personalities. An individual's **personality** is a unique combination of emotional, thought, and behavioral patterns that affect how a person reacts to situations and interacts with others. Personality is most often described in terms of measurable traits that a person exhibits. We're interested in looking at personality because just like attitudes, it too, affects how and why people behave the way they do.

Over the years, researchers have attempted to identify those traits that best describe personality. The two most well-known approaches are: the Myers Briggs Type Indicator® (MBTI) and the Big Five model.

MBTI®

One popular approach to classifying personality traits is the personality-assessment instrument known as the MBTI®. This 100-question assessment asks people how they usually act or feel in different situations.[48] On the basis of their answers, individuals are classified as exhibiting a preference in four categories: extraversion or introversion (E or I), sensing or intuition (S or N), thinking or feeling (T or F), and judging or perceiving (J or P). These terms are defined as follows:

▶ *Extraversion (E) versus Introversion (I).* Individuals showing a preference for extraversion are outgoing, social, and assertive. They need a work environment that's varied and action oriented, that lets them be with others, and that gives them a variety of experiences. Individuals showing a preference for introversion are quiet and shy. They focus on understanding and prefer a work environment that is quiet and concentrated, that lets them be alone, and that gives them a chance to explore in depth a limited set of experiences.

▶ *Sensing (S) versus Intuition (N).* Sensing types are practical and prefer routine and order. They dislike new problems unless there are standard ways to solve them, have a high need for closure, show patience with routine details, and tend to be good at precise work. On the other hand, intuition types rely on unconscious processes and look at the "big picture." They're individuals who like solving new problems, dislike doing the same thing over and over again, jump to conclusions, are impatient with routine details, and dislike taking time for precision.

▶ *Thinking (T) versus Feeling (F).* Thinking types use reason and logic to handle problems. They're unemotional and uninterested in people's feelings, like analysis and putting things into logical order, are able to reprimand people and fire them when necessary, may seem hard-hearted, and tend to relate well only to other thinking types. Feeling types rely on their personal values and emotions. They're aware of other people and their feelings, like harmony, need occasional praise, dislike telling people unpleasant things, tend to be sympathetic, and relate well to most people.

▶ *Judging (J) versus Perceiving (P).* Judging types want control and prefer their world to be ordered and structured. They're good planners, decisive, purposeful, and exacting. They focus on completing a task, make decisions quickly, and want only the information necessary to get a task done. Perceiving types are flexible and spontaneous. They're curious, adaptable, and tolerant. They focus on starting a task, postpone decisions, and want to find out all about the task before starting it.

Combining these preferences provides descriptions of 16 personality types, with every person identified with one of the items in each of the four pairs. Exhibit 14-4 summarizes two of them. As you can see from these descriptions, each personality type would approach work and relationships differently—neither one better than the other, just different.

More than 2 million people a year take the MBTI® in the United States alone. Some organizations that have used the MBTI® include Apple, AT&T, GE, 3M, hospitals, educational

Type	Description
I–S–F–P (introversion, sensing, feeling, perceiving)	Sensitive, kind, modest, shy, and quietly friendly. Such people strongly dislike disagreements and will avoid them. They are loyal followers and quite often are relaxed about getting things done.
E–N–T–J (extraversion, intuition, thinking, judging)	Warm, friendly, candid, and decisive; also skilled in anything that requires reasoning and intelligent talk, but may sometimes overestimate what they are capable of doing.

EXHIBIT 14-4

Examples of MBTI® Personality Types

Source: Based on I. Briggs-Myers, *Introduction to Type* (Palo Alto, CA: Consulting Psychologists Press, 1980), pp. 7–8.

personality
The unique combination of emotional, thought, and behavioral patterns that affect how a person reacts to situations and interacts with others

institutions, and even the U.S. Armed Forces. No hard evidence shows that the MBTI® is a valid measure of personality, but that doesn't seem to deter its widespread use.

How could the MBTI® help managers? Proponents believe that it's important to know these personality types because they influence the way people interact and solve problems. For instance, if your boss is an intuition type and you're a sensing type, you'll gather information in different ways. An intuitive type prefers gut reactions, whereas a sensor prefers facts. To work well with your boss, you would have to present more than just facts about a situation and bring out how you feel about it. Also, the MBTI® has been used to help managers better match employees to certain types of jobs.

The Big Five Model

In recent years, research has shown that five basic personality dimensions underlie all others and encompass most of the significant variation in human personality.[49] The five personality traits in the **Big Five Model** are:

1. *Extraversion:* The degree to which someone is sociable, talkative, assertive, and comfortable in relationships with others.
2. *Agreeableness:* The degree to which someone is good-natured, cooperative, and trusting.
3. *Conscientiousness:* The degree to which someone is reliable, responsible, dependable, persistent, and achievement oriented.
4. *Emotional stability:* The degree to which someone is calm, enthusiastic, and secure (positive) or tense, nervous, depressed, and insecure (negative).
5. *Openness to experience:* The degree to which someone has a wide range of interests and is imaginative, fascinated with novelty, artistically sensitive, and intellectual.

The Big Five Model provides more than just a personality framework. Research has shown that important relationships exist between these personality dimensions and job performance. For example, one study examined five categories of occupations: *professionals* (such as engineers, architects, and attorneys), *police, managers, salespeople,* and *semiskilled and skilled employees.*[50] The results showed that conscientiousness predicted job performance for all five occupational groups. Predictions for the other personality dimensions depended on the situation and on the occupational group. For example, extraversion predicted performance in managerial and sales positions—occupations in which high social interaction is necessary. Openness to experience was found to be important in predicting training competency. Ironically, emotional security wasn't positively related to job performance in any of the occupations. Another study that looked at whether the five-factor model could predict managerial performance found that it could if 360 degree performance ratings (that is, performance ratings from supervisors, peers, and subordinates) were used.[51] Other studies have shown that employees who score higher in conscientiousness develop higher levels of job knowledge, probably because highly conscientious people learn more. In fact, a review of 138 studies revealed that conscientiousness was rather strongly related to GPA.[52]

Let's Get Real
F2F

Personality "problems" I've dealt with
often stem from distractions that cause the employee to lose focus. It is critical to be engaged with your team.

Additional Personality Insights

Although the traits in the Big Five are highly relevant to understanding behavior, they aren't the only personality traits that can describe someone's personality. Five other personality traits are powerful predictors of behavior in organizations.

1. *Locus of Control.* Some people believe that they control their own fate. Others see themselves as pawns, believing that what happens to them in their lives is due to luck or chance. The **locus of control** in the first case is *internal*; these people believe that they control their own destiny. The locus of control in the second case is *external*; these people believe that their lives are controlled by outside forces.[53] Research indicates that employees who are externals are less satisfied with their jobs, more alienated from the work setting, and less involved in their jobs than are those who rate high on internality.[54] A manager might also expect externals to blame a poor performance evaluation on their boss's prejudice, their coworkers, or other events outside their control; internals would explain the same evaluation in terms of their own actions.

2. *Machiavellianism.* The second characteristic is called **Machiavellianism** (Mach), named after Niccolo Machiavelli, who wrote in the sixteenth century on how to gain and manipulate power. An individual who is high in Machiavellianism is pragmatic, maintains emotional distance, and believes that ends can justify means.[55] "If it works, use it" is consistent with a high Mach perspective. Do high Machs make good employees? That depends on the type of job and whether you consider ethical factors in evaluating performance. In jobs that require bargaining skills (such as a purchasing manager) or that have substantial rewards for excelling (such as a salesperson working on commission), high Machs are productive.

3. *Self-Esteem.* People differ in the degree to which they like or dislike themselves, a trait called **self-esteem**.[56] Research on self-esteem (SE) offers some interesting behavioral insights. For example, self-esteem is directly related to expectations for success. High SEs believe that they possess the ability they need in order to succeed at work. Individuals with high SEs will take more risks in job selection and are more likely to choose unconventional jobs than are people with low SEs.

   The most common finding on self-esteem is that low SEs are more susceptible to external influence than are high SEs. Low SEs are dependent on receiving positive evaluations from others. As a result, they're more likely to seek approval from others and are more prone to conform to the beliefs and behaviors of those they respect than are high SEs. In managerial positions, low SEs will tend to be concerned with pleasing others and, therefore, will be less likely to take unpopular stands than are high SEs. Finally, self-esteem has also been found to be related to job satisfaction. A number of studies confirm that high SEs are more satisfied with their jobs than are low SEs.

4. *Self-Monitoring.* Have you ever had the experience of meeting someone new and feeling a natural connection and hitting it off right away? At some time or another, we've all had that experience. That natural ability to "click" with other people may play a significant role in determining career success[57] and is another personality trait called **self-monitoring**, which refers to the ability to adjust behavior to external, situational factors.[58] Individuals high in self-monitoring show considerable adaptability in adjusting their behavior. They're highly sensitive to external cues and can behave differently in different situations. High self-monitors are capable of presenting striking contradictions between their public persona and their private selves. Low self-monitors can't adjust their behavior. They tend to display their true dispositions and attitudes in every situation, and there's high behavioral consistency between who they are and what they do.

   Research on self-monitoring suggests that high self-monitors pay closer attention to the behavior of others and are more flexible than are low self-monitors.[59] In addition, high self-monitoring managers tend to be more mobile in their careers, receive more promotions (both internal and cross-organizational), and are more likely to occupy central positions in an organization.[60] The high self-monitor is capable of putting on different "faces" for different audiences, an important trait for managers who must play multiple, or even contradicting roles.

5. *Risk-Taking.* People differ in their willingness to take chances. Differences in the propensity to assume or to avoid risk have been shown to affect how long it takes managers to make a decision and how much information they require before making their choice. For instance, in one study where managers worked on simulated exercises that required them to make hiring decisions, high risk-taking managers took less time to make decisions and used less information in making their choices than did low-risk taking managers.[61] Interestingly, the decision accuracy was the same for the two groups. To maximize organizational effectiveness, managers should try to align employee risk-taking propensity with specific job demands.

by the numbers[62]

99 percent of people polled say they have been bullied or have witnessed bullying at work.

80 percent of employees attribute their ability to stay motivated and focused on a positive attitude.

15 percent of Millennials say that having a high-paying career is a top priority.

44 percent of Gen Y rank job security as more important than personal job satisfaction.

51 percent of employees say they did nothing when a coworker took credit for an idea that was theirs.

70 percent of executives surveyed say they are satisfied with their job.

24 percent of workers say that what makes them happy is just having a job.

Big Five Model
Personality trait model that includes extraversion, agreeableness, conscientiousness, emotional stability, and openness to experience

locus of control
The degree to which people believe they are masters of their own fate

Machiavellianism
A measure of the degree to which people are pragmatic, maintain emotional distance, and believe that ends justify means

self-esteem
An individual's degree of like or dislike for himself or herself

self-monitoring
A personality trait that measures the ability to adjust behavior to external situational factors

OTHER PERSONALITY TRAITS.   A couple of other personality traits deserve mention. In Chapter 6, we introduced the Type A personality, which describes someone who is continually and aggressively struggling to achieve more and more in less and less time.[63] In the North American culture, the Type A personality is highly valued. Type A individuals subject themselves to continual time pressure and deadlines and have moderate to high levels of stress. They emphasize quantity over quality. On the other hand, a Type B person isn't harried by the desire to achieve more and more. Type Bs don't suffer from a sense of time urgency and are able to relax without guilt.

Another interesting trait that's been studied extensively is the **proactive personality**, which describes people who identify opportunities, show initiative, take action, and persevere until meaningful change occurs. Not surprisingly, research has shown that proactives have many desirable behaviors that organizations want.[64] For instance, they are more likely to be seen as leaders and more likely to act as change agents in organizations; they're more likely to challenge the status quo; they have entrepreneurial abilities; and they're more likely to achieve career success.

Finally, the economic recession has prompted a reexamination of **resilience**, which is an individual's ability to overcome challenges and turn them into opportunities.[65] A recent study by a global consulting firm showed that it is a key factor in keeping a job: A resilient person is likely to be more adaptable, flexible, and goal-focused. OB researchers also have looked at resilience and other individual characteristics including efficacy, hope, and optimism in a concept called positive psychological capital.[66] These characteristics have been found to be related to higher feelings of well-being and less work stress, which ultimately affect how and why people behave the way they do at work.

Personality Types in Different Cultures

Do personality frameworks, like the Big Five model, transfer across cultures? Are dimensions like locus of control relevant in all cultures? Let's try to answer these questions.

The five personality factors studied in the Big Five model appear in almost all cross-cultural studies.[67] These studies include a wide variety of diverse cultures such as China, Israel, Germany, Japan, Spain, Nigeria, Norway, Pakistan, and the United States. Differences are found in the emphasis on dimensions. Chinese, for example, use the category of conscientiousness more often and use the category of agreeableness less often than do Americans. But a surprisingly high amount of agreement is found, especially among individuals from developed countries. As a case in point, a comprehensive review of studies covering people from the European Community found that conscientiousness was a valid predictor of performance across jobs and occupational groups.[68] Studies in the United States found the same thing.

We know that no personality type is common for a given country. You can, for instance, find high risk takers and low risk takers in almost any culture. Yet a country's culture influences the *dominant* personality characteristics of its people. We can see this effect of national culture by looking at one of the personality traits we just discussed: locus of control.

National cultures differ in terms of the degree to which people believe they control their environment. For instance, North Americans believe that they can dominate their environment; other societies, such as those in Middle Eastern countries, believe that life is essentially predetermined. Notice how closely this distinction parallels the concept of internal and external locus of control. On the basis of this particular cultural characteristic, we should expect a larger proportion of internals in the U.S. and Canadian workforces than in the workforces of Saudi Arabia or Iran.

As we have seen throughout this section, personality traits influence employees' behavior. For global managers, understanding how personality traits differ takes on added significance when looking at it from the perspective of national culture.

Emotions and Emotional Intelligence

"Trying to sell wedding gowns to anxious brides-to-be" can be quite a stressful experience for the salesperson, needless to say. To help its employees stay "cheery," David's Bridal, a chain of more than 270 stores, relied on research into joyful emotions. Now, when "faced with an indecisive bride," salespeople have been taught emotional coping techniques and know how to focus on "things that bring them joy."[69]

We can't leave the topic of personality without looking at the important behavioral aspect of emotions. How we respond emotionally and how we deal with our emotions are typically functions of our personality. **Emotions** are intense feelings that are directed at someone or something. They're object-specific; that is, emotions are reactions to an object.[70] For instance, when a work colleague criticizes you for the way you spoke to a client, you might become angry at him. That is, you show emotion (anger) toward a specific object (your colleague). Because employees bring an emotional component with them to work every day, managers need to understand the role that emotions play in employee behavior.[71]

How many emotions are there? Although you could probably name several dozen, research has identified six universal emotions: anger, fear, sadness, happiness, disgust, and surprise.[72] Do these emotions surface in the workplace? Absolutely! I get *angry* after receiving a poor performance appraisal. I *fear* that I could be laid off as a result of a company cutback. I'm *sad* about one of my coworkers leaving to take a new job in another city. I'm *happy* after being selected as employee-of-the-month. I'm *disgusted* with the way my supervisor treats women on our team. And I'm *surprised* to find out that management plans a complete restructuring of the company's retirement program.

People respond differently to identical emotion-provoking stimuli. In some cases, differences can be attributed to a person's personality and because people vary in their ability to express emotions. For instance, you undoubtedly know people who almost never show their feelings. They rarely get angry or show rage. In contrast, you probably also know people who seem to be on an emotional roller coaster. When they're happy, they're ecstatic. When they're sad, they're deeply depressed. And two people can be in the exact same situation—one showing excitement and joy, the other remaining calm.

However, at other times how people respond emotionally is a result of job requirements. Jobs make different demands in terms of what types and how much emotion needs to be displayed. For instance, air traffic controllers, ER nurses, and trial judges are expected to be calm and controlled, even in stressful situations. On the other hand, public-address announcers at sporting events and lawyers in a courtroom must be able to alter their emotional intensity as the need arises.

FUTURE VISION   **The Working World in 2020**

Increased Reliance on Emotional Intelligence

Whether it goes by the name of emotional intelligence, social intelligence, or something else, the ability to understand yourself and others will be a skill that organizations will seek when hiring employees. The ability to get along with others—coworkers, colleagues, team members, bosses, and customers—will be critical to success in most jobs. While more employees are likely to work from off-site, there will still be ongoing contact with others. Those employees who have strong technical skills but are weak on emotional intelligence will find it increasingly difficult to find and hold a job.

proactive personality
People who identify opportunities, show initiative, take action, and persevere until meaningful change occurs.

resilience
An individual's ability to overcome challenges and turn them into opportunities

emotions
Intense feelings that are directed at someone or something

One area of emotions research with interesting insights into personality is **emotional intelligence (EI)**, which is the ability to notice and to manage emotional cues and information.[73] It's composed of five dimensions:

Self-awareness: The ability to be aware of what you're feeling.
Self-management: The ability to manage one's own emotions and impulses.
Self-motivation: The ability to persist in the face of setbacks and failures.
Empathy: The ability to sense how others are feeling.
Social skills: The ability to handle the emotions of others.

EI has been shown to be positively related to job performance at all levels. For instance, one study looked at the characteristics of Lucent Technologies' engineers who were rated as stars by their peers. The researchers concluded that stars were better at relating to others. That is, it was EI, not academic intelligence that characterized high performers. A study of Air Force recruiters generated similar findings. Top-performing recruiters exhibited high levels of EI. Despite these findings, EI has been a controversial topic in OB. Supporters say that EI has intuitive appeal and predicts important behavior.[74] Critics say that EI is vague, can't be measured, and has questionable validity.[75] One thing we can conclude is that EI appears to be relevant to success in jobs that demand a high degree of social interaction.

Implications for Managers

More than 62 percent of companies are using personality tests when recruiting and hiring.[76] Perhaps the major value in understanding personality differences lies in this area. Managers are likely to have higher-performing and more-satisfied employees if consideration is given to matching personalities with jobs. The best-documented personality-job fit theory was developed by psychologist John Holland who identified six basic personality types.[77] His theory states that an employee's satisfaction with his or her job, as well as his or her likelihood of leaving that job, depends on the degree to which the individual's personality matches the job environment. Exhibit 14-5 describes the six types, their personality characteristics, and examples of suitable occupations for each.

Holland's theory proposes that satisfaction is highest and turnover lowest when personality and occupation are compatible. Social individuals should be in "people" type jobs, and so forth. The key points of this theory are that (1) intrinsic differences in personality are apparent among individuals; (2) the types of jobs vary; and (3) people in job environments compatible with their personality types should be more satisfied and less likely to resign voluntarily than should people in incongruent jobs.

In addition, other benefits arise from understanding personality. By recognizing that people approach problem solving, decision making, and job interactions differently, a

EXHIBIT **14-5**	Type	Personality Characteristics	Sample Occupations
Holland's Personality–Job Fit Source: Based on J. L. Holland, *Making Vocational Choices: A Theory of Vocational Personalities and Work Environments* (Odessa, FL: Psychological Assessment Resources, 1997).	*Realistic.* Prefers physical activities that require skill, strength, and coordination.	Shy, genuine, persistent, stable, conforming, practical	Mechanic, drill press operator, assembly-line worker, farmer
	Investigative. Prefers activities involving thinking, organizing, and understanding.	Analytical, original, curious, independent	Biologist, economist, mathematician, news reporter
	Social. Prefers activities that involve helping and developing others.	Sociable, friendly, cooperative, understanding	Social worker, teacher, counselor, clinical psychologist
	Conventional. Prefers rule-regulated, orderly, and unambiguous activities.	Conforming, efficient, practical, unimaginative, inflexible	Accountant, corporate manager, bank teller, file clerk
	Enterprising. Prefers verbal activities that offer opportunities to influence others and attain power.	Self-confident, ambitious, energetic, domineering	Lawyer, real estate agent, public relations specialist, small business manager
	Artistic. Prefers ambiguous and unsystematic activities that allow creative expression.	Imaginative, disorderly, idealistic, emotional, impractical	Painter, musician, writer, interior decorator

manager can better understand why an employee is uncomfortable with making quick decisions or why another employee insists on gathering as much information as possible before addressing a problem. Or, for instance, managers can expect that individuals with an external locus of control may be less satisfied with their jobs than internals and also that they may be less willing to accept responsibility for their actions.

Finally, being a successful manager and accomplishing goals means working well together with others both inside and outside the organization. In order to work effectively together, you need to understand each other. This understanding comes, at least in part, from an appreciation of personality traits and emotions. Also, one of the skills you have to develop as a manager is learning to fine-tune your emotional reactions according to the situation. In other words, you have to learn to recognize when "you have to smile and when you have to bark."[78]

Perception

"Jin knows better than most that your success as a rapper depends almost entirely on your delivery—even when people expect that delivery to be lemon chicken with a side of rice."[79] Most people think Asian Americans are studious geeks and that people who "look" Asian must be foreigners and not U.S. citizens. Although Chinese-American rapper Jin may not fit the stereotype, he has found success as an American rap musician.

14.4

LEARNING OUTCOME
Describe perception and factors that influence it.

Stereotyping is one aspect of **perception**, which is a process by which we give meaning to our environment by organizing and interpreting sensory impressions. Research on perception consistently demonstrates that individuals may look at the same thing yet perceive it differently. One manager, for instance, can interpret the fact that her assistant regularly takes several days to make important decisions as evidence that the assistant is slow, disorganized, and afraid to make decisions. Another manager with the same assistant might interpret the same tendency as evidence that the assistant is thoughtful, thorough, and deliberate. The first manager would probably evaluate her assistant negatively; the second manager would probably evaluate the person positively. The point is that none of us sees reality. We interpret what we see and call it reality. And, of course, as the example shows, we behave according to our perceptions.

Factors That Influence Perception

How do we explain the fact that people can perceive the same thing differently? A number of factors act to shape and sometimes distort perception. These factors are in the *perceiver*, in the *target* being perceived, or in the *situation* in which the perception occurs.

When a person looks at a target and attempts to interpret what he or she sees, the individual's personal characteristics will heavily influence the interpretation. These personal characteristics include attitudes, personality, motives, interests, experiences, or expectations.

The characteristics of the target being observed can also affect what's perceived. Loud people are more likely than quiet people to be noticed in a group as are extremely attractive or unattractive individuals. The relationship of a target to its background also influences perception, as does our tendency to group close things and similar things together. You can experience these tendencies by looking at the visual perception examples shown in Exhibit 14-6. Notice how what you see changes as you look differently at each one.

Finally, the context in which we see objects or events is also important. The time at which an object or event is seen can influence perception, as can location, light, heat, color, and any number of other situational factors.

---

emotional intelligence (EI)
The ability to notice and to manage emotional cues and information

perception
A process by which we give meaning to our environment by organizing and interpreting sensory impressions

EXHIBIT 14-6

What do you see?

Old woman or young woman?   A knight on a horse?

Attribution Theory

Much of the research on perception is directed at inanimate objects. Managers, however, are concerned with people. Our perceptions of people differ from our perception of inanimate objects because we make inferences about the behaviors of people that we don't make about objects. Objects don't have beliefs, motives, or intentions; people do. The result is that when we observe an individual's behavior, we try to develop explanations of why they behave in certain ways. Our perception and judgment of a person's actions are significantly influenced by the assumptions we make about the person.

Attribution theory was developed to explain how we judge people differently depending on what meaning we attribute to a given behavior.[80] Basically, the theory suggests that when we observe an individual's behavior, we attempt to determine whether it was internally or externally caused. Internally caused behaviors are those that are believed to be under the personal control of the individual. Externally caused behavior results from outside factors; that is, the person is forced into the behavior by the situation. That determination, however, depends on three factors: distinctiveness, consensus, and consistency.

Distinctiveness refers to whether an individual displays different behaviors in different situations. Is the employee who arrived late today the same person who some employees complain of as being a "goof-off"? What we want to know is whether this behavior is unusual. If it's unusual, the observer is likely to attribute the behavior to external forces, something beyond the control of the person. However, if the behavior isn't unusual, it will probably be judged as internal.

If everyone who's faced with a similar situation responds in the same way, we can say the behavior shows *consensus*. A tardy employee's behavior would meet this criterion if all employees who took the same route to work were also late. From an attribution perspective, if consensus is high, you're likely to give an external attribution to the employee's tardiness; that is, some outside factor—maybe road construction or a traffic accident—caused the behavior. However, if other employees who come the same way to work made it on time, you would conclude that the cause of the late behavior was internal.

Finally, an observer looks for *consistency* in a person's actions. Does the person engage in the behaviors regularly and consistently? Does the person respond the same way over time? Coming in 10 minutes late for work isn't perceived in the same way if, for one employee, it represents an unusual case (she hasn't been late in months), while for another employee, it's part of a routine pattern (she's late two or three times every week). The more consistent the behavior, the more the observer is inclined to attribute it to internal causes. Exhibit 14-7 summarizes the key elements of attribution theory.

One interesting finding from attribution theory is that errors or biases distort our attributions. For instance, substantial evidence supports the fact that when we make judgments about the behavior of other people, we have a tendency to *under*estimate the influence of external factors and to *over*estimate the influence of internal or personal factors.[81] This

Observation	Interpretation	Attribution of Cause
Does person behave this way in other situations?	Yes: Low distinctiveness No: High distinctiveness	Internal attribution External attribution
Do other people behave the same way in similar situations?	Yes: High consensus No: Low consensus	External attribution Internal attribution
Does person behave this way consistently?	Yes: High consistency No: Low consistency	Internal attribution External attribution

EXHIBIT 14-7

Attribution Theory

tendency is called the **fundamental attribution error** and can explain why a sales manager may attribute the poor performance of her sales representative to laziness rather than to the innovative product line introduced by a competitor. Another tendency is to attribute our own successes to internal factors, such as ability or effort, while putting the blame for personal failure on external factors, such as luck. This tendency is called the **self-serving bias** and suggests that feedback provided to employees in performance reviews will be distorted by them depending on whether it's positive or negative.

Are these errors or biases that distort attributions universal across different cultures? We can't say for sure, but preliminary evidence indicates cultural differences.[82] For instance, a study of Korean managers found that, contrary to the self-serving bias, they tended to accept responsibility for group failure "because I was not a capable leader" instead of attributing it to group members.[83] Attribution theory was developed largely based on experiments with Americans and Western Europeans. But the Korean study suggests caution in making attribution theory predictions in non-Western societies, especially in countries with strong collectivist traditions.

Shortcuts Used in Judging Others

Perceiving and interpreting people's behavior is a lot of work, so we use shortcuts to make the task more manageable. These techniques can be valuable when they let us make accurate interpretations quickly and provide valid data for making predictions. However, they aren't perfect. They can and do get us into trouble.

It's easy to judge others if we assume that they're similar to us. In **assumed similarity**, or the "like me" effect, the observer's perception of others is influenced more by the observer's own characteristics than by those of the person observed. For example, if you want challenges and responsibility in your job, you'll assume that others want the same. People who assume that others are like them can, of course, be right, but not always.

When we judge someone on the basis of our perception of a group he or she is part of, we're using the shortcut called **stereotyping**. For instance, "Married people are more stable employees than single persons" is an example of stereotyping. To the degree that a stereotype is based on fact, it may produce accurate judgments. However, many stereotypes aren't factual and distort our judgment.[84]

When we form a general impression about a person on the basis of a single characteristic, such as intelligence, sociability, or appearance, we're being influenced by the **halo effect**. This effect frequently occurs when students evaluate their classroom instructor. Students may

attribution theory
A theory used to explain how we judge people differently depending on what meaning we attribute to a given behavior

fundamental attribution error
The tendency to underestimate the influence of external factors and overestimate the influence of internal factors when making judgments about the behavior of others

self-serving bias
The tendency for individuals to attribute their own successes to internal factors while putting the blame for failures on external factors

assumed similarity
The assumption that others are like oneself

stereotyping
Judging a person on the basis of one's perception of a group to which he or she belongs

halo effect
A general impression of an individual based on a single characteristic

isolate a single trait such as enthusiasm and allow their entire evaluation to be slanted by the perception of this one trait. An instructor may be quiet, assured, knowledgeable, and highly qualified, but if his classroom teaching style lacks enthusiasm, he might be rated lower on a number of other characteristics.

Implications for Managers

Managers need to recognize that their employees react to perceptions, not to reality. So whether a manager's appraisal of an employee's performance is actually objective and unbiased or whether the organization's wage levels are among the highest in the community is less relevant than what employees perceive them to be. If individuals perceive appraisals to be biased or wage levels as low, they'll behave as if those conditions actually exist. Employees organize and interpret what they see, so the potential for perceptual distortion is always present. The message is clear: Pay close attention to how employees perceive both their jobs and management actions.

LEARNING OUTCOME **14.5**
Discuss learning theories and their relevance in shaping behavior.

Learning

When 20-year-old Elvis Andrus was signed by the Texas Rangers in 2009, he was excited to find out that the Rangers had signed another shortstop—11-time Gold Glove winner and fellow Venezuelan Omar Vizquel. Vizquel's role was clear: to be a mentor to the talented young player. Managers of major league baseball teams "regularly mix savvy veterans with talented young players, hoping tricks of the trade and advice on everything from how to turn a double play to how to avoid trouble in night spots on the road will rub off."[85]

Mentoring is a good example of the last individual behavior concept we're going to look at—learning. Learning is included in our discussion of individual behavior for the obvious reason that almost all behavior is learned. If we want to explain, predict, and influence behavior, we need to understand how people learn.

The psychologists' definition of learning is considerably broader than the average person's view that "it's what we do in school." Learning occurs all the time as we continuously learn from our experiences. A workable definition of **learning** is any relatively permanent change in behavior that occurs as a result of experience. Two learning theories help us understand how and why individual behavior occurs.

Operant Conditioning

Operant conditioning argues that behavior is a function of its consequences. People learn to behave to get something they want or to avoid something they don't want. Operant behavior is voluntary or learned behavior, not reflexive or unlearned behavior. The tendency to repeat learned behavior is influenced by reinforcement or lack of reinforcement that happens as a result of the behavior. Reinforcement strengthens a behavior and increases the likelihood that it will be repeated. Lack of reinforcement weakens a behavior and lessens the likelihood that it will be repeated.

B. F. Skinner's research widely expanded our knowledge of operant conditioning.[86] Behavior is assumed to be determined from without—that is, *learned*—rather than from within—reflexive or unlearned. Skinner argued that people will most likely engage in desired behaviors if they are positively reinforced for doing so, and rewards are most effective if they immediately follow the desired response. In addition, behavior that isn't rewarded or is punished is less likely to be repeated.

You see examples of operant conditioning everywhere. Any situation in which it's either explicitly stated or implicitly suggested that reinforcement (rewards) are contingent on some action on your part is an example of operant conditioning. Your instructor says that if you want a high grade in this course, you must perform well on tests by giving correct answers. A salesperson working on commission knows that earning a sizeable income is contingent upon generating high sales in his or her territory. Of course, the linkage between behavior and reinforcement can also work to teach the individual to behave in ways that work against the best interests of the organization. Assume that your boss tells you that if you'll work overtime during the next three-week busy season, you'll be compensated for it at the next performance appraisal. Then, when performance appraisal time comes, you are given no positive reinforcements (such as being praised for pitching in and helping out when needed). What will you do the next time your boss asks you to work overtime? You'll probably refuse. Your behavior can be explained by operant conditioning: If a behavior isn't positively reinforced, the probability that the behavior will be repeated declines.

Social Learning

Some 60 percent of the Radio City Rockettes have danced in prior seasons. The veterans help newcomers with "Rockette style"—where to place their hands, how to hold their hands, how to keep up stamina, and so forth.[87]

As the Rockettes are well aware, individuals can also learn by observing what happens to other people and just by being told about something as well as by direct experiences. Much of what we have learned comes from watching others (models)—parents, teachers, peers, television and movie actors, managers, and so forth. This view that we can learn both through observation and direct experience is called **social learning theory**.

The influence of others is central to the social learning viewpoint. The amount of influence that these models have on an individual is determined by four processes:

1. *Attentional processes.* People learn from a model when they recognize and pay attention to its critical features. We're most influenced by models who are attractive, repeatedly available, thought to be important, or seen as similar to us.
2. *Retention processes.* A model's influence will depend on how well the individual remembers the model's action, even after the model is no longer readily available.
3. *Motor reproduction processes.* After a person has seen a new behavior by observing the model, the watching must become doing. This process then demonstrates that the individual can actually do the modeled activities.
4. *Reinforcement processes.* Individuals will be motivated to exhibit the modeled behavior if positive incentives or rewards are provided. Behaviors that are reinforced will be given more attention, learned better, and performed more often.

Shaping: A Managerial Tool

Because learning takes place on the job as well as prior to it, managers are concerned with how they can teach employees to behave in ways that most benefit the organization. Thus, managers will often attempt to "mold" individuals by guiding their learning in graduated steps, through a method called **shaping behavior**.

Consider the situation in which an employee's behavior is significantly different from that sought by a manager. If the manager reinforced the individual only when he or she showed desirable responses, the opportunity for reinforcement might occur too infrequently. Shaping offers a logical approach toward achieving the desired behavior. We shape behavior by systematically reinforcing each successive step that moves the individual closer to the desired behavior. If an employee who has chronically been a half-hour late for work comes in only 20 minutes late, we can reinforce the improvement. Reinforcement would increase as an employee gets closer to the desired behavior.

Four ways to shape behavior include positive reinforcement, negative reinforcement, punishment, and extinction. When a behavior is followed by something pleasant, such as praising an employee for a job well done, it's called *positive reinforcement*. Positive reinforcement

learning
Any relatively permanent change in behavior that occurs as a result of experience

operant conditioning
A theory of learning that says behavior is a function of its consequences

social learning theory
A theory of learning that says people can learn through observation and direct experience

shaping behavior
The process of guiding learning in graduated steps using reinforcement or lack of reinforcement

increases the likelihood that the desired behavior will be repeated. Rewarding a response by eliminating or withdrawing something unpleasant is *negative reinforcement*. A manager who says "I won't dock your pay if you start getting to work on time" is using negative reinforcement. The desired behavior (getting to work on time) is being encouraged by the withdrawal of something unpleasant (the employee's pay being docked). On the other hand, *punishment* penalizes undesirable behavior and will eliminate it. Suspending an employee for two days without pay for habitually coming to work late is an example of punishment. Finally, eliminating any reinforcement that's maintaining a behavior is called *extinction*. When a behavior isn't reinforced, it gradually disappears. In meetings, managers who wish to discourage employees from continually asking irrelevant or distracting questions can eliminate this behavior by ignoring those employees when they raise their hands to speak. Soon this behavior should disappear.

Both positive and negative reinforcement result in learning. They strengthen a desired behavior and increase the probability that the desired behavior will be repeated. Both punishment and extinction also result in learning but do so by weakening an undesired behavior and decreasing its frequency.

Let's Get Real

F2F

I shape my employees' behavior by
earning their trust, truly listening to what they say, understanding their perspective on things, and empowering them to be successful.

Implications for Managers

Employees are going to learn on the job. The only issue is whether managers are going to manage their learning through the rewards they allocate and the examples they set, or allow it to occur haphazardly. If marginal employees are rewarded with pay raises and promotions, they will have little reason to change their behavior. In fact, productive employees, who see marginal performance rewarded, might change their behavior. If managers want behavior A, but reward behavior B, they shouldn't be surprised to find employees' learning to engage in behavior B. Similarly, managers should expect that employees will look to them as models. Managers who are consistently late to work, or take two hours for lunch, or help themselves to company office supplies for personal use should expect employees to read the message they are sending and model their behavior accordingly.

LEARNING OUTCOME 14.6
Discuss contemporary issues in organizational behavior.

Contemporary Issues in Organizational Behavior

By this point, you're probably well aware of the reasons managers need to understand how and why employees behave the way they do. We conclude this chapter by looking at two OB issues with a major influence on managers' jobs today.

Managing Generational Differences

Every year since 1998, Beloit College in Wisconsin has assembled a Mindset List that helps identify the experiences that have shaped the lives of incoming freshmen.[88] The authors of the list state that it is an effort to better understand the "experiences that have shaped the lives and formed the mindset of students." Here are some of the observations from the 2014 list (generated in 2010):

► Few in the class know how to write in cursive.
► E-mail is just too slow, and they seldom, if ever, use snail mail.
► Al Gore has always been animated.
► Colorful lapel ribbons have always been worn to indicate support for a cause.
► Korean cars have always been a staple on American highways.
► Computers have always had a CD-ROM disk drive.

What will *this* group of young employees be like when they enter the workforce after graduation? Will they share the characteristics of the earlier members of Gen Y? Let's take a look at how Gen Y is changing the workplace.

By observing Generation Y employees at work, Alicia Blain, vice president of information systems for Visa International, learned a lot from young workers like Julio Delgado, shown here with Blain. Recognizing what motivates Gen Y employees, such as flexibility and work–life balance, and valuing the contributions they bring to the multigenerational workplace help managers capitalize on the talents of this group. Of special value is Gen Y's knowledge and application of computer technology in solving problems, detecting emerging trends, and locating relevant and difficult-to-find information quickly.

They're young, smart, and brash. They wear flip-flops to the office and listen to iPods at their desk. They want to work, but don't want work to be their life. This is Generation Y, some 70 million of them, many of whom are embarking on their careers, taking their place in an increasingly multigenerational workplace.[89]

JUST WHO IS GEN Y?   There's no consensus about the exact time span that Gen Y comprises, but most definitions include those individuals born from about 1982 to 1997. One thing is for sure—they're bringing new attitudes with them to the workplace. Gen Ys have grown up with an amazing array of experiences and opportunities. And they want their work life to provide that as well, as shown in Exhibit 14-8. For instance, Stella Kenyi, who

---

Gen Y Workers

High Expectations of Self
They aim to work faster and better than other workers.

High Expectations of Employers
They want fair and direct managers who are highly engaged in their professional development.

Ongoing Learning
They seek out creative challenges and view colleagues as vast resources from whom to gain knowledge.

Immediate Responsibility
They want to make an important impact on Day 1.

Goal Oriented
They want small goals with tight deadlines so they can build up ownership of tasks.

EXHIBIT 14-8

Gen Y Workers

Source: Bruce Tulgan (New Haven, CT) is the author or coauthor of numerous books, including *Not Everyone Gets a Trophy: How to Manage Generation Y* (2009) and the classic *Managing Generation X* (1995). Since founding the management training firm RainmakerThinking in 1993, he has been a sought-after keynote speaker and seminar leader. Tulgan's weekly video newsletter is available for free at www.rainmakerthinking.com.

is passionately interested in international development, was sent by her employer, the National Rural Electric Cooperative Association, to Yai, Sudan, to survey energy use.[90] At Best Buy's corporate offices Beth Trippie, a senior scheduling specialist, feels that as long as the results are there, why should it matter how it gets done. She says, "I'm constantly playing video games, on a call, doing work, and the thing is, all of it gets done, and it gets done well."[91] And Katie Patterson, an assistant account executive in Atlanta, says, "We are willing and not afraid to challenge the status quo. An environment where creativity and independent thinking are looked upon as a positive is appealing to people my age. We're very independent and tech savvy."[92]

DEALING WITH THE MANAGERIAL CHALLENGES. Managing Gen Y workers presents some unique challenges. Conflicts and resentment can arise over issues such as appearance, technology, and management style.

How flexible must an organization be in terms of "appropriate" office attire? It may depend on the type of work being done and the size of the organization. In many organizations, jeans, t-shirts, and flip-flops are acceptable. However, in other settings, employees are expected to dress more conventionally. But even in those more conservative organizations, one possible solution to accommodate the more casual attire preferred by Gen Y is to be more flexible in what's acceptable. For instance, the guideline might be that when the person is not interacting with someone outside the organizations, more casual wear (with some restrictions) can be worn.

What about technology? This generation has lived much of their lives with ATMs, DVDs, cell phones, e-mail, texting, laptops, and the Internet. When they don't have information they need, they just simply enter a few keystrokes to get it. Having grown up with technology, Gen Ys tend to be totally comfortable with it. They're quite content to meet virtually to solve problems, while bewildered baby boomers expect important problems to be solved with an in-person meeting. Baby boomers complain about Gen Y's inability to focus on one task, while Gen Ys see nothing wrong with multitasking. Again, flexibility from both is the key.

Finally, what about managing Gen Ys? Like the old car advertisement that used to say, "This isn't your father's car," we can say that "this isn't your father's or mother's way of managing." Gen Y employees want bosses who are open minded; experts in their field, even if they aren't tech-savvy; organized; teachers, trainers, and mentors; not authoritarian or paternalistic; respectful of their generation; understanding of their need for work–life balance; providing constant feedback; communicating in vivid and compelling ways; and providing stimulating and novel learning experiences.[93]

Gen Y employees have a lot to offer organizations in terms of their knowledge, passion, and abilities. Mangers, however, have to recognize and understand the behaviors of this group in order to create an environment in which work can be accomplished efficiently, effectively, and without disruptive conflict.

Managing Negative Behavior in the Workplace

Jerry notices the oil is low in his forklift but continues to drive it until it overheats and can't be used. After enduring 11 months of repeated insults and mistreatment from her supervisor, Maria quits her job. An office clerk slams her keyboard and then shouts profanity whenever her computer freezes up. Rudeness, hostility, aggression, and other forms of workplace negativity have become all too common in today's organizations. In a survey of U.S. employees, 10 percent said they witnessed rudeness daily within their workplaces and 20 percent said that they personally were direct targets of incivility at work at least once a week. In a survey of Canadian workers, 25 percent reported seeing incivility daily and 50 percent said they were the direct targets at least once per week.[94] Some estimates put the costs of negativity to the U.S. economy at $300 billion a year.[95] What can managers do to manage negative behavior in the workplace?

The main thing is to recognize that it's there. Pretending that negative behavior doesn't exist or ignoring such misbehaviors will only confuse employees about what is expected and acceptable behavior. Although some debate among researchers questions whether preventive or responsive actions to negative behaviors are more effective, in reality, both are needed.[96] Preventing negative behaviors by carefully screening potential employees for certain personality traits and responding immediately and decisively to unacceptable negative behaviors can go a long way toward managing negative workplace behaviors. But it's also important to pay attention to employee attitudes, because negativity will show up there as well. As we said earlier, when employees are dissatisfied with their jobs, they *will* respond somehow.

Let's Get Real:

My Response *to A Manager's Dilemma, page 372*

Maintaining an "employees first" philosophy can be a cornerstone on which a company can build success. At Integrity Home Care our mission statement articulates that approach: "Our mission is to cultivate a Christian-based environment in which we can identify and meet the home care needs of our clients and the career needs of our employees with unmatched skill, compassion, and integrity."

The key to identifying the career needs of your employees begins in the relationship that you have with those individuals. When you invest your time, energy, and compassion in your employees, they will respond by reinvesting themselves in the company. If you can motivate team members within your department, then the performance of each individual will often surpass what you think he or she is capable of.

What Would You Do?

Jake Martin
Marketing Manager
Integrity Home Care
Springfield, MO

CHAPTER SUMMARY
by Learning Outcomes

LEARNING
OUTCOME **Identify** the focus and goals of individual behavior within organizations.

Just like an iceberg, it's the hidden organizational elements (attitudes, perceptions, norms, etc.) that make understanding individual behavior so challenging.

Organization behavior (OB) focuses on three areas: individual behavior, group behavior, and organizational aspects. The goals of OB are to explain, predict, and influence behavior.

Employee productivity is a performance measure of both efficiency and effectiveness. Absenteeism is the failure to report to work. Turnover is the voluntary and involuntary permanent withdrawal from an organization. Organizational citizenship behavior (OCB) is discretionary behavior that's not part of an employee's formal job requirements but it promotes the effective functioning of an organization. Job satisfaction is an individual's general attitude toward his or her job. Workplace misbehavior is any intentional employee behavior that is potentially harmful to the organization or individuals within the organization.

LEARNING
OUTCOME **Explain** the role that attitudes play in job performance.

The cognitive component refers to the beliefs, opinions, knowledge, or information held by a person. The affective component is the emotional or feeling part of an attitude. The behavioral component refers to an intention to behave in a certain way toward someone or something.

Job satisfaction refers to a person's general attitude toward his or her job. Job involvement is the degree to which an employee identifies with his or her job, actively participates in it, and considers his or her job performance to be important to his or her self-worth. Organizational commitment is the degree to which an employee identifies with a particular organization and its goals and wishes to maintain membership in that organization. Employee engagement is when employees are connected to, satisfied with, and enthusiastic about their jobs.

Job satisfaction positively influences productivity, lowers absenteeism levels, lowers turnover rates, promotes positive customer satisfaction, moderately promotes OCB, and helps minimize workplace misbehavior.

Individuals try to reconcile attitude and behavior inconsistencies by altering their attitudes, altering their behavior, or rationalizing the inconsistency.

LEARNING
OUTCOME **Describe** different personality theories.

The MBTI measures four dimensions: social interaction, preference for gathering data, preference for decision making, and style of making decisions. The Big Five Model consists of five personality traits: extraversion, agreeableness, conscientiousness, emotional stability, and openness to experience.

The five personality traits that help explain individual behavior in organizations are locus of control, Machiavellianism, self-esteem, self-monitoring, and risk-taking. Other personality traits include Type A/Type B personalities, proactive personality, and resilience.

How a person responds emotionally and how they deal with their emotions is a function of personality. A person who is emotionally intelligent has the ability to notice and to manage emotional cues and information.

Describe perception and factors that influence it.

Perception is how we give meaning to our environment by organizing and interpreting sensory impressions. Because people behave according to their perceptions, managers need to understand it.

Attribution theory depends on three factors. Distinctiveness is whether an individual displays different behaviors in different situations (that is, is the behavior unusual). Consensus is whether others facing a similar situation respond in the same way. Consistency is when a person engages in behaviors regularly and consistently. Whether these three factors are high or low helps managers determine whether employee behavior is attributed to external or internal causes.

The fundamental attribution error is the tendency to underestimate the influence of external factors and overestimate the influence of internal factors. The self-serving bias is the tendency to attribute our own successes to internal factors and to put the blame for personal failure on external factors.

Three shortcuts used in judging others are assumed similarity, stereotyping, and the halo effect.

Discuss learning theories and their relevance in shaping behavior.

Operant conditioning argues that behavior is a function of its consequences. Managers can use it to explain, predict, and influence behavior.

Social learning theory says that individuals learn by observing what happens to other people and by directly experiencing something.

Managers can shape behavior by using positive reinforcement (reinforcing a desired behavior by giving something pleasant), negative reinforcement (reinforcing a desired response by withdrawing something unpleasant), punishment (eliminating undesirable behavior by applying penalties), or extinction (not reinforcing a behavior to eliminate it).

Discuss contemporary issues in organizational behavior.

The challenge of managing Gen Y workers is that they bring new attitudes to the workplace. The main challenges are over issues such as appearance, technology, and management style.

Workplace misbehavior can be dealt with by recognizing that it's there; carefully screening potential employees for possible negative tendencies; and most importantly, by paying attention to employee attitudes through surveys about job satisfaction and dissatisfaction.

---

^{PEARSON} **mymanagementlab** To check your understanding of learning outcomes **14.1** – **14.6** go to **mymanagementlab.com** and try the chapter questions.

REVIEW AND DISCUSSION QUESTIONS

1. Does the importance of knowledge of OB differ based on a manager's levels in the organization? If so, how? If not, why not? Be specific.
2. Explain why the concept of an organization as an iceberg is important.
3. Describe the focus and goals of OB.
4. Define the six important employee behaviors.
5. Describe the three components of an attitude and explain the four job-related attitudes.
6. Contrast the MBTI and the Big Five model. Describe five other personality traits that help explain individual behavior in organizations.

7. Explain how an understanding of perception can help managers better understand individual behavior. Name three shortcuts used in judging others.

8. Describe the key elements of attribution theory. Discuss the fundamental attribution error and self-serving bias.

9. Describe operant conditioning and how managers can shape behavior.

10. Explain the challenges facing managers in managing generational differences and negative behavior in the workplace.

PREPARING FOR: My Career

ETHICS DILEMMA

It's been called the "desperation hustle."[97] Employees who are "anxious about layoffs want to look irreplaceable." So they clean up their act. Those who might not have paid much attention to their manner of dress now do. Those who were mouthy and argumentative are now quiet and compliant. Those who used to "watch the clock" are now the last to leave. The fear is there and it's noticeable. "Managing that fear can be challenging." What ethical issues might arise for both employees and for managers? How could managers approach these circumstances ethically?

SKILLS EXERCISE

Developing Your Shaping Behavior Skill

About the Skill

In today's dynamic work environments, learning is continual. But this learning shouldn't be done in isolation or without any guidance. Most employees need to be shown what's expected of them on the job. As a manager, you must teach your employees the behaviors that are most critical to their, and the organization's, success.

Steps in Practicing the Skill

1. **Identify the critical behaviors that have a significant impact on an employee's performance.** Not everything employees do on the job is equally important in terms of performance outcomes. A few critical behaviors may, in fact, account for the majority of one's results. These high impact behaviors need to be identified.

2. **Establish a baseline of performance.** A baseline is obtained by determining the number of times the identified behaviors occur under the employee's present job conditions.

3. **Analyze the contributing factors to performance and their consequences.** A number of factors, such as the norms of a group, may be contributing to the baseline performance. Identify these factors and their effect on performance.

4. **Develop a shaping strategy.** The change that may occur will entail changing some element of performance—structure, processes, technology, groups, or the task. The purpose of the strategy is to strengthen the desirable behaviors and weaken the undesirable ones.

5. **Apply the appropriate strategy.** Once the strategy has been developed, it needs to be implemented. In this step, an intervention occurs.

6. **Measure the change that has occurred.** An intervention should produce the desired results in performance behaviors. Evaluate the number of times the identified behaviors now occur. Compare these with the baseline evaluation in step 2.

7. **Reinforce desired behaviors.** If an intervention has been successful and the new behaviors are producing the desired results, maintain these behaviors through reinforcement mechanisms.

Practicing the Skill

a. Imagine that your assistant is ideal in all respects but one—he or she is hopeless at taking phone messages for you when you're not in the office. You're often in training sessions and the calls are sales leads you want to follow up, so you have identified taking accurate messages as a high impact behavior for your assistant.

b. Focus on steps 3 and 4, and devise a way to shape your assistant's behavior. Identify some factors that might contribute to his or her failure to take messages—these could range from a heavy workload to a poor understanding of the task's importance (you can rule out insubordination). Then develop a shaping strategy by determining what you can change—the available technology, the task itself, the structure of the job, or some other element of performance.

c. Now plan your intervention and take a brief meeting with your assistant in which you explain the change you expect. Recruit a friend to help you role-play your intervention. Do you think you would succeed in a real situation?

WORKING TOGETHER
Team Exercise

You may not like it or want to believe it, but unprofessional dress can be a career-killer.[98] Pretend that you're a manager in a large, multinational company. Your company has a dress code policy, but men and women alike "cross the line." One of your female subordinates is the worst offender. Several times, she has come to work dressed in sheer, low-cut, sleeveless blouses with a micro-mini skirt and strappy sandals. How would you change her behavior?

Form small groups of three to four individuals. Your team's task is to come up with a specific plan for changing (shaping) the behavior of any employee who violates the dress code policy. Write this up and be prepared to share your ideas with the class.

MY TURN TO BE A MANAGER

- For one week, pay close attention to how people around you behave, especially those people who are close to you (roommates, siblings, significant others, coworkers, etc.). Use what you've learned about attitudes, personality, perception, and learning to understand and explain how and why they're behaving the way they do. Write your observations and your explanations in a journal.

- Write down three attitudes you have. Identify the cognitive, affective, and behavioral components of those attitudes.

- Survey 15 employees (at your place of work or at some campus office). Be sure to obtain permission before doing this anonymous survey. Ask them what rude or negative behaviors they've seen at work. Compile your findings in a report and be prepared to discuss this in class. If you were the manager in this workplace, how would you handle this behavior?

- If you've never taken a personality or career compatibility test, contact your school's testing center to see if you can take one. Once you get your results, evaluate what they mean for your career choice. Have you chosen a career that "fits" your personality? What are the implications?

- Have you ever heard of the "waiter rule"? A lot of business people think that how you treat service workers says a lot about your character and attitudes. What do you think this means? Do you agree with this idea? Why or why not? How would you be evaluated on the "waiter rule"?

- Like it or not, each of us is continually shaping the behavior of those around us. For one week, keep track of how many times you use positive reinforcement, negative reinforcement, punishment, or extinction to shape behaviors. At the end of the week, which one did you tend to use most? What were you trying to do; that is, what behaviors were you trying to shape? Were your attempts successful? Evaluate. What could you have done differently if you were trying to change someone's behavior?

- Create a job satisfaction survey for a business you're familiar with.

- Now, do a Web search for sample job satisfaction surveys. Find one or two samples. Write a report describing, comparing, and evaluating the examples you found and the survey you created.

- Steve's and Mary's recommended readings: Jonathan Littman and Mark Herson, *I Hate People!* (Little-Brown, 2009); Yoav Vardi and Ely Weitz, *Misbehavior in Organizations* (Lawrence Erlbaum Associates, 2004); Murray R. Barrick and A. M. Ryan, eds., *Personality and Work* (Jossey-Bass, 2003); Daniel Goleman, *Destructive Emotions: How Can We Overcome Them?* (Bantam, 2003); L. Thomson, *Personality Type: An Owner's Manual* (Shambhala, 1998); and Daniel Goleman, *Working with Emotional Intelligence* (Bantam, 1998).

- Survey 10 Gen Yers. Ask them three questions: (1) What do you think appropriate office attire is? (2) How comfortable are you with using technology and what types of technology do you rely on most? (3) What do you think the "ideal" boss would be like? Compile your results into a paper that reports your data and summarizes your findings in a bulleted list format.

- In your own words, write down three things you learned in this chapter about being a good manager.

- Self-knowledge can be a powerful learning tool. Go to mymanagementlab.com and complete these self-assessment exercises: What's My Basic Personality? What's My Jungian 16-Type Personality? (Note that this is a miniature version of the MBTI.) Am I a Type A? What Do I Value? How Involved Am I in My Job? How Satisfied Am I With My Job? Am I Engaged? How Are You Feeling Right Now? What's My Affect Intensity? What's My Emotional Intelligence Score? How Committed Am I to My Organization? Using the results of your assessments, identify personal strengths and weaknesses. What will you do to reinforce your strengths and improve your weaknesses?

CASE APPLICATION 1
Understanding HCLites: Part 2

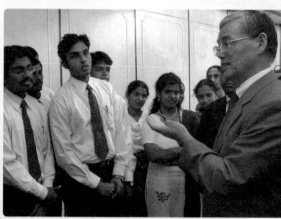

These new engineers at HCL Technologies received certificates for becoming proficient in the Japanese language. As part of its "employees first" culture, the company invests in language training and other development programs that help satisfy HCLites' high need for achievement.

HCL Technologies is headquartered in the world's largest democracy, so it's quite fitting that the New Delhi-based company is attempting a radical experiment in workplace democracy. CEO Vineet Nayar is committed to creating a company where the job of company leaders is to enable people to find their own destiny by gravitating to their strengths.[99] As we discussed in the chapter opener, one thing that Nayar has done is to pioneer a culture in which employees are first. What has he done to put employees first? Part of the cultural initiative dealt with the organization's structure. HCL inverted its organizational structure and placed more power in the hands of frontline employees, especially those in direct contact with customers and clients. It increased its investment in employee development and improved communication through greater transparency. Employees were encouraged to communicate directly with Nayar. Through a forum called U&I (You and I), Nayar fielded more than 100 questions from employees every week. "I threw open the door and invited criticism," he said. However, the signature piece of the company's cultural mission is probably what HCL called "trust pay." In contrast to the industry standard in which the average employee's pay is 30 percent variable, HCL decided to pay higher fixed salaries and reduce the variable component.

Does the unique "employees first" culture at HCL Technologies attract unique employees? Rajeev Sawhney, HCL's European president, would say it does. He uses *Slumdog Millionaire*, the movie that won the Academy Award for Best Picture in 2009, as a parallel. "It (the movie) is a reflection of the Indian race. It shows the adversity that creates the desire in people to reach out and create.... With each adversity they face, there is a greater desire to reach out and do something more." Sawhney says that entrepreneurialism is a key value of the HCL culture. "You can still tell an HCL person from a mile off. I think there is a particular DNA for an HCL person. It includes a very high need for achievement and very persuasive skills. HCL people are very energetic; they want to do lots of things and to take risks on behalf of the company."

Discussion Questions

1. What is your impression of an "employee first" culture? Would this work in other organizations? Why or why not? What would it take to make it work?

2. How might an understanding of organizational behavior help CEO Vineet Nayar lead his company? Be specific. How about first-line company supervisors? Again, be specific.

3. What aspects of personality do you see in this story about HCL? How have the personality traits of HCL employees contributed to make what HCL what it is?

4. Design an employee attitude survey for HCL's employees. Compare your ideas with what our "real" manager suggested.

CASE APPLICATION

Odd Couples

A 29-year-old and a 68-year-old. How much could they possibly have in common? And what could they learn from each other? At Randstad USA's Manhattan office, such employee pairings are common.[100] One such pair of colleagues sits inches apart facing each other. "They hear every call the other makes. They read every e-mail the other sends or receives. Sometimes they finish each other's sentences."

Randstad Holding NV, a Dutch company, has been using this pairing idea since its founding more than 40 years ago. The founder's motto was "Nobody should be alone." The original intent was to boost productivity by having sales agents share one job and trade off job responsibilities. Today, these partners in the home office have an arrangement where one is in the office one week while the other one is out making sales calls, then the next week, they switch. The company brought its partner arrangement to the United States in the late 1990s. But when it began recruiting new employees, the vast majority of whom were in their twenties, it realized the challenges and the potential of pairing different generations together. "Knowing that these Gen Yers need lots of attention in the workplace, Randstad executives figured that if they shared a job with someone whose own success depended on theirs, they were certain to get all the nurturing they required."

Randstad doesn't simply pair up people and hope it works. There's more to it than that! The company looks for people who will work well with others by conducting extensive interviews and requiring job applicants to shadow a sales agent for half a day. "One question Randstad asks is: What's your most memorable moment while being on a team? If they respond: When I scored the winning touchdown, that's a deal killer. Everything about our organization is based on the team and group." When a new hire is paired with an experienced agent, both individuals have some adjusting. One of the most interesting elements of Randstad's program is that neither person is "the boss." And both are expected to teach the other.

Discussion Questions

1. What topics of individual behavior do you see in this story? Explain.

2. What do you think about this pairing-up idea? Would you be comfortable with such an arrangement? Why or why not?

3. What personality traits would be most needed for this type of work arrangement? Why?

4. What types of issues might a Gen Y employee and an older, more-experienced employee face? How could two people in such a close-knit work arrangement deal with those issues? That is, how could both make the adjustment easier?

5. Design an employee attitude survey for Randstad's employees.

Let's Get Real:

Meet the Manager

Glenn A. Jones
Oral Care Consultant/Technology Trainer
Colgate Oral Pharmaceuticals
New York, NY

You'll be hearing more from this real manager throughout the chapter.

MY JOB:

I'm an oral care consultant for Colgate Oral Pharmaceuticals in northern New Jersey. My primary job duties involve selling, advising, and educating dental professionals regarding prescription-strength oral care products for their patients. In addition to this, I serve as a technology trainer for Colgate. In this capacity I provide training and support to our sales team as it relates to the various technologies required to do our jobs.

BEST PART OF MY JOB:

What I love most about my job is advising dental professionals on the products and courses of action that will deliver the best outcomes for their patient's oral health. In addition, I love the fact that I can help dental professionals maximize their success from an efficiency standpoint, which will in turn help grow their business.

Managers *and* Communication

15.1
Define the nature and function of communication. *page 404*

15.2
Compare and contrast methods of interpersonal communication. *page 406*

15.3
Identify barriers to effective interpersonal communication and how to overcome them. *page 409*

15.4
Explain how communication can flow most effectively in organizations. *page 412*

15.5
Describe how technology affects managerial communication and organizations. *page 416*

15.6
Discuss contemporary issues in communication. *page 417*

LEARNING OUTCOMES

WORST PART OF MY JOB:

Something I would like to change about my job is how we manage relationships. Often because of the size of a given territory it is not possible to see dental professionals on regular basis. This makes it hard to build up a trust and comfort level with those I am advising. Every day I seek to find ways to better foster these client relationships. It is the key to long-term success.

BEST MANAGEMENT ADVICE EVER RECEIVED:

You are only as strong as your weakest link. This really resonated with me because no matter how successful you or your organization becomes, it is always vulnerable if strength is not developed through and through. If one employee or aspect of your organization is not strong enough because of inadequate training, disillusionment, or other negative practices, it can cause a domino effect that leads to more and more problems and failures. In this respect, individuals and organizations should seek continuous improvement to shore up weak points and to foster continued success and longevity.

Tweets. Twittering. Five years ago, the only definition we would have known for these words would have involved birds and the sounds they make. Now, practically everyone knows that Twitter is also an online service used by millions of people to trade short messages of 140 characters or less via the Web, cell phones, and other devices.[1] According to its founders (Jack Dorsey, Biz Stone, and Evan Williams), Twitter is many things: a messaging service, a customer-service tool to reach customers, real-time search, and microblogging. And as the numbers show, it's become quite popular!

One place where Twitter has caught on is college sports. For instance, Les Miles, head football coach at Louisiana State University calls himself "a Twittering kind of guy." He understands the power of instant communication. Miles wants to stay ahead of the competition, especially when it comes to recruiting and keeping fans informed. He said, "It (Twittering) allows us to communicate blasts of information to those people that subscribe. And it's also an opportunity for those recruiting prospects that subscribe to communicate to us." During the fall 2009 season, he Twittered (via a

staff assistant) before games, at halftime, and after games. The challenge for organizations is how to control the information flow.

What Would You Do?

Welcome to the new world of communication! In this "world," managers are going to have to understand both the importance and the drawbacks of communication—all forms of communication. Communication between managers and employees is important because it provides the information necessary to get work done in organizations. Thus, there's no doubt that communication is fundamentally linked to managerial performance.[2]

The Nature and Function of Communication

On a recent summer day, Chevrolet employees at General Motors' Detroit headquarters got an internal memo requesting that they stop using the word "Chevy" when referring to their car brand.[3] Despite the fact that "Chevy" has been one of the world's best-known, longest-lived product nicknames for a best-selling line of cars and trucks and was immortalized in a song about Miss American Pie driving to the levee, the memo was signed by two top corporate Chevrolet division executives who cited the need for brand consistency. After the memo made its way into the media and invoked a strong public reaction, GM backtracked. It posted a video interview with one of the executives who had signed the memo on Chevrolet's YouTube channel. During the video, the executive used the word Chevy no fewer than six times in less than two minutes. He also called the memo a "rough draft" and "a bit of fun" and explained that "there would be no massive change of direction." This example shows why it's important for managers to understand the impact of communication.

The importance of effective communication for managers can't be overemphasized for one specific reason: Everything a manager does involves communicating. Not *some* things, but everything! A manager can't make a decision without information. That information has to be communicated. Once a decision is made, communication must again take place. Otherwise, no one would know that a decision was made. The best idea, the most creative suggestion, the best plan, or the most effective job redesign can't take shape without communication.

What Is Communication?

Communication is the transfer and understanding of meaning. Note the emphasis on the *transfer* of meaning: If information or ideas have not been conveyed, communication hasn't taken place. The speaker who isn't heard or the writer whose materials aren't read

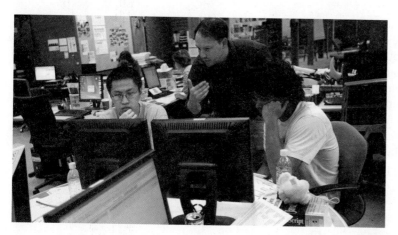

Menlo Innovations is a noisy, high-energy workplace where communication provides the information employees need to accomplish their work and the motivation to improve their performance. All employees at this software design firm work side by side in pairs and share a computer in one large work room. At the end of each week, the pairs switch partners. When a veteran employee and intern work together, the veteran can pass along experience and knowledge and the intern can share what's new in college computer classes. Menlo's CEO Richard Sheridan believes that continual information-sharing among employees results in higher-quality work and greater productivity and also boosts employee morale.

hasn't communicated. More importantly, however, communication involves the *understanding* of meaning. For communication to be successful, the meaning must be imparted and understood. A letter written in Spanish addressed to a person who doesn't read Spanish can't be considered communication until it's translated into a language the person does read and understand. Perfect communication, if such a thing existed, would be when a transmitted thought or idea was received and understood by the receiver exactly as it was envisioned by the sender.

Another point to keep in mind is that *good* communication is often erroneously defined by the communicator as *agreement* with the message instead of clear understanding of the message.[4] If someone disagrees with us, we assume that the person just didn't fully understand our position. In other words, many of us define good communication as having someone accept our views. But I can clearly understand what you mean and just *not* agree with what you say.

The final point we want to make about communication is that it encompasses both **interpersonal communication**—communication between two or more people—and **organizational communication**, which is all the patterns, networks, and systems of communication within an organization. Both types are important to managers.

Functions of Communication

Kevin M. Warren, chairman of the board, president, and CEO of Xerox Canada, Ltd. was awarded the 2010 Excellence in Communication Leadership (EXCEL) Award by the International Association of Business Communicators. This award recognizes leaders who foster excellence in communication and contribute to the development and support of organizational communication. His award nomination stated, "Kevin has been an advocate of communication from the start. He is its biggest supporter and a role model for others. Kevin clearly understands the relationship of employee communication and engagement, and ultimately business success. The positive impact of his commitment is far-reaching, and extends beyond employees to all his constituencies."[5]

Throughout Xerox Canada and many other organizations, communication serves four major functions: control, motivation, emotional expression, and information.[6] Each function is equally important.

Communication acts to *control* employee behavior in several ways. As we know from Chapter 10, organizations have authority hierarchies and formal guidelines that employees are expected to follow. For instance, when employees are required to communicate any job-related grievance to their immediate manager, to follow their job description, or to comply with company policies, communication is being used to control. Informal communication also controls behavior. When a work group teases a member who's ignoring the norms by working too hard, they're informally controlling the member's behavior.

communication
The transfer and understanding of meaning

interpersonal communication
Communication between two or more people

organizational communication
All the patterns, networks, and systems of communication within an organization

Next, communication acts to *motivate* by clarifying to employees what is to be done, how well they're doing, and what can be done to improve performance if it's not up to par. As employees set specific goals, work toward those goals, and receive feedback on progress toward goals, communication is required.

For many employees, their work group is a primary source of social interaction. The communication that takes place within the group is a fundamental mechanism by which members share frustrations and feelings of satisfaction. Communication, therefore, provides a release for *emotional expression* of feelings and for fulfillment of social needs.

Finally, individuals and groups need information to get things done in organizations. Communication provides that *information*.

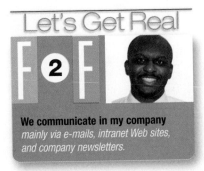

Methods of Interpersonal Communication

Before communication can take place, a purpose, expressed as a **message** to be conveyed, must exist. It passes between a source (the sender) and a receiver. The message is converted to symbolic form (called **encoding**) and passed by way of some medium (**channel**) to the receiver, who retranslates the sender's message (called **decoding**). The result is the transfer of meaning from one person to another.[7]

Exhibit 15-1 illustrates the elements of the **communication process**. Note that the entire process is susceptible to **noise**—disturbances that interfere with the transmission, receipt, or feedback of a message. Typical examples of noise include illegible print, phone static, inattention by the receiver, or background sounds of machinery or coworkers. However, anything that interferes with understanding can be noise, and noise can create distortion at any point in the communication process.

A personal written letter from a U.S. Army commander in Afghanistan to his troops assured them that they are "contributing to the overall success of the mission" here. Colonel David Haight, of the 10th Mountain Division's 3rd Brigade Combat team, sent the letter to each of the 3,500 men and women after two of their fellow soldiers were killed in combat and his chaplains reported that many were disillusioned about the war. Haight said, "I can tell a soldier to do anything, and he may or may not in his mind question why. But if you explain the why very, very clearly, he will not only accomplish the mission, but he will do the mission to a much higher standard."[8] Here's a manager who understands the role of communication and how best to communicate to his subordinates.

You need to communicate to your employees the organization's new policy on sexual harassment; you want to compliment one of your workers on the extra hours she's put in to help your team complete a customer's order; you must tell one of your employees about changes to his job; or you would like to get employees' feedback on your proposed budget for next year. In each of these instances, how would you communicate? Managers have a wide variety of communication methods from which to choose and can use 12 questions to help them evaluate these methods.[9]

1. *Feedback*: How quickly can the receiver respond to the message?
2. *Complexity capacity*: Can the method effectively process complex messages?
3. *Breadth potential*: How many different messages can be transmitted using this method?

4. *Confidentiality*: Can communicators be reasonably sure their messages are received only by those intended?
5. *Encoding ease*: Can sender easily and quickly use this channel?
6. *Decoding ease*: Can receiver easily and quickly decode messages?
7. *Time-space constraint*: Do senders and receivers need to communicate at the same time and in the same space?
8. *Cost*: How much does it cost to use this method?
9. *Interpersonal warmth*: How well does this method convey interpersonal warmth?
10. *Formality*: Does this method have the needed amount of formality?
11. *Scanability*: Does this method allow the message to be easily browsed or scanned for relevant information?
12. *Time of consumption*: Does the sender or receiver exercise the most control over when the message is dealt with?

Exhibit 15-2 provides a comparison of various communication methods. Which method a manager ultimately chooses should reflect the needs of the sender, the attributes of the message, the attributes of the channel, and the needs of the receiver. For instance, if you need to communicate to an employee about the changes being made in her job, face-to-face communication would be a better choice than a memo because you want to be able to address immediately any questions and concerns she might have.

An important part of interpersonal communication is **nonverbal communication**—that is, communication transmitted without words. Some of the most meaningful communications are neither spoken nor written. When a college instructor is teaching a class, she doesn't need words to tell her that students are tuned out when they begin to read a newspaper in the middle of class. Similarly, when students start putting their book, papers, and notebooks away, the message is clear: Class time is about over. The size of a person's office or the clothes he or she wears also convey messages to others. Among these various forms of nonverbal communication, the best-known types are body language and verbal intonation.

Body language refers to gestures, facial expressions, and other body movements that convey meaning. A person frowning "says" something different from one who's smiling. Hand motions, facial expressions, and other gestures can communicate emotions or temperaments such as aggression, fear, shyness, arrogance, joy, and anger. Knowing the meaning behind someone's body moves and learning how to put forth your best body language can help you personally and professionally.[10]

Verbal intonation refers to the emphasis someone gives to words or phrases in order to convey meaning. To illustrate how intonations can change the meaning of a message, consider the student who asks the instructor a question. The instructor replies, "What do you mean by that?" The student's reaction will vary, depending on the tone of the instructor's response. A soft, smooth vocal tone conveys interest and creates a different meaning from one that is abrasive and puts a strong emphasis on saying the last word. Most of us would

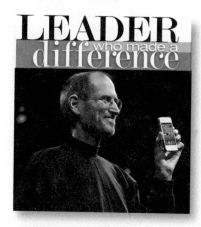

Steve Jobs is known as the cofounder of Apple and purveyor of cool tech products.[11] When he takes the stage at MacWorld, the annual conference/expo of everything Mac where he introduces Apple's new products, you won't see him in a suit and tie like most CEOs at their most important annual event. Jobs has fashioned a distinctive image for himself with his consistent choice of black polo shirt and black or blue jeans . . . an image that portrays Apple as being alternative, savvy, and hip. And some say, it's a smart way of communicating with Gen X and Gen Y consumers who thrive on transparency, creativity, and personal choice. And Jobs has a sense of humor. At his recent MacWorld introduction of the new iPhone 4, Jobs made a humorous reference to the prototype found in a coffee shop by a tech magazine writer, by saying, "Stop me if you have already seen this," when he first showed the device. Here's a leader who understands and exploits the power of nonverbal communication and connecting with his audience.

message
A purpose to be conveyed
encoding
Converting a message into symbols
channel
The medium a message travels along

decoding
Retranslating a sender's message
communication process
The seven elements involved in transferring meaning from one person to another
noise
Any disturbances that interfere with the transmission, receipt, or feedback of a message

nonverbal communication
Communication transmitted without words
body language
Gestures, facial configurations, and other body movements that convey meaning
verbal intonation
An emphasis given to words or phrases that conveys meaning

EXHIBIT 15-2

Comparison of Communication Methods

High Feedback Potential
- Face-to-face
- Telephone
- Computer conference

High Complexity Capacity
- Face-to-face

High Breadth Potential
- Face-to-face
- Bulletin boards
- E-mail

High Confidentiality
- Face-to-face
- Voice mail

High Encoding Ease
- Face-to-face
- Telephone

High Time-Decoding Ease
- Face-to-face
- Telephone
- Hotlines
- Voice mail

High Space Constraint
- Face-to-face
- Group meetings
- Formal presentations

High Cost
- Group meetings
- Formal presentations
- Videoconference

High Personal Warmth
- Face-to-face

High Formality
- Postal mail
- Publications

High Scanability
- Memos
- Postal mail
- Fax
- Publications
- Bulletin boards

Low Feedback Potential
- Publications

Low Complexity Capacity
- Bulletin boards

Low Breadth Potential
- Postal mail
- Audio-videotapes

Low Confidentiality
- Publications
- Bulletin boards
- Audio-videotapes
- Teleconference

Low Encoding Ease
- Publications

Low Time-Decoding Ease
- Memos
- Postal mail
- Fax
- Publications

Low Space Constraint
- Memos
- Postal mail
- Fax
- Publications
- Voice mail

Low Cost
- Bulletin boards

Low Personal Warmth
- Memos
- Bulletin boards

Low Formality
- Face-to-face
- Telephone
- Voice mail

Low Scanability
- Formal presentations
- Face-to-face
- Telephone
- Group meetings
- Audio-videotapes
- Hotlines
- E-mail
- Computer conference
- Voice mail
- Teleconference
- Videoconference

Source: Based on P. G. Clampitt, *Communicating for Managerial Effectiveness* (Newbury Park, CA: Sage Publications, 1991), p. 136.

view the first intonation as coming from someone sincerely interested in clarifying the student's concern, whereas the second suggests that the person resents the question.

Managers need to remember that as they communicate, the nonverbal component usually carries the greatest impact. It's not *what* you say, but *how* you say it.

Effective Interpersonal Communication

15.3

LEARNING OUTCOME
Identify barriers to effective interpersonal communication and how to overcome them.

A company with 100 employees can expect to lose approximately $450,000 a year, or more, because of e-mail blunders, inefficiencies, and misunderstandings.[12] The chief executive of a marketing firm in New York was in a meeting with a potential client. For the entire hour-and-a-half meeting, the client was fiddling with his iPhone. Doing what? Playing a racing game, although he did glance up occasionally and ask questions.[13] Research done by an HR consulting firm found that U.S. and U.K. employees cost their businesses $37 billion every year because they don't really understand their jobs.[14]

Somewhere, somehow communication isn't being as effective as it needs to be. One reason is that managers face barriers that can distort the interpersonal communication process. Let's look at these barriers to effective communication.

Barriers to Communication

FILTERING. **Filtering** is the deliberate manipulation of information to make it appear more favorable to the receiver. For example, when a person tells his or her manager what the manager wants to hear, information is being filtered. Or if information being communicated up through organizational levels is condensed by senders, that's filtering.

How much filtering takes place tends to be a function of the number of vertical levels in the organization and the organizational culture. The more vertical levels in an organization, the more opportunities there are for filtering. As organizations use more collaborative, cooperative work arrangements, information filtering may become less of a problem. In addition, e-mail reduces filtering because communication is more direct. Finally, the organizational culture encourages or discourages filtering by the type of behavior it rewards. The more that organizational rewards emphasize style and appearance, the more managers may be motivated to filter communications in their favor.

EMOTIONS. How a receiver feels when a message is received influences how he or she interprets it. Extreme emotions are most likely to hinder effective communication. In such instances, we often disregard our rational and objective thinking processes and substitute emotional judgments.

INFORMATION OVERLOAD. A marketing manager goes on a week-long sales trip to Spain where he doesn't have access to his e-mail, and he faces 1,000 messages on his return. It's not possible to fully read and respond to each message without facing **information overload**, which is when information exceeds our processing capacity. Today's employees frequently complain of information overload. Statistics show that 87 percent of employees use e-mail and that the average business e-mail user devotes 107 minutes a day to e-mail—about 25 percent of the workday. Other statistics show that employees send and receive an average of 150 e-mail messages every day. And the number of worldwide e-mail messages sent daily is a staggering 97.3 billion.[15] The demands of keeping up with e-mail, text messages, phone calls, faxes, meetings, and professional reading create an onslaught of data. What happens when individuals have more information than they can process? They tend to ignore, pass over, forget, or selectively choose information. Or they may stop communicating. Regardless, the result is lost information and ineffective communication.

DEFENSIVENESS. When people feel they're being threatened, they tend to react in ways that hinder effective communication and reduce their ability to achieve mutual understanding. They become defensive—verbally attacking others, making sarcastic remarks, being overly judgmental, or questioning others' motives.[16]

LANGUAGE. Conservative author/journalist Ann Coulter and rapper Nelly both speak English, but the language each uses is vastly different. Words mean different things to different people. Age, education, and cultural background are three of the more obvious variables that influence the language a person uses and the definitions he or she gives to words.

In an organization, employees come from diverse backgrounds and have different patterns of speech. Even employees who work for the same organization but in different departments often have different **jargon**—specialized terminology or technical language that members of a group use to communicate among themselves.

Let's Get Real

F2F

The most frequent communication problem *that I deal with is deciphering what is important and what is not among the large volume of communications circulated.*

NATIONAL CULTURE. For technological and cultural reasons, the Chinese people dislike voice mail.[17] This general tendency illustrates how communication differences can arise from national culture as well as different languages. For example, let's compare countries that value individualism (such as the United States) with countries that emphasize collectivism (such as Japan).[18]

In an individualistic country like the United States, communication is more formal and is clearly spelled out. Managers rely heavily on reports, memos, and other formal forms of communication. In a collectivist country like Japan, more interpersonal contact takes place, and face-to-face communication is encouraged. A Japanese manager extensively consults with subordinates over an issue first and draws up a formal document later to outline the agreement that was made.

Overcoming the Barriers

On average, an individual must hear new information seven times before he or she truly understands.[19] In light of this fact and the communication barriers just described, what can managers do to be more effective communicators?

USE FEEDBACK. Many communication problems are directly attributed to misunderstanding and inaccuracies. These problems are less likely to occur if the manager gets feedback, both verbal and nonverbal.

A manager can ask questions about a message to determine whether it was received and understood as intended. Or the manager can ask the receiver to restate the message in his or her own words. If the manager hears what was intended, understanding and accuracy should improve. Feedback can also be more subtle, and general comments can give a manager a sense of the receiver's reaction to a message.

Feedback also doesn't have to be verbal. If a sales manager e-mails information about a new monthly sales report that all sales representatives will need to complete and some of them don't turn it in, the sales manager has received feedback. This feedback suggests that the sales manager needs to clarify the initial communication. Similarly, managers can look for nonverbal cues to tell whether someone's getting the message.

SIMPLIFY LANGUAGE. Because language can be a barrier, managers should consider the audience to whom the message is directed and tailor the language to them.[20] Remember, effective communication is achieved when a message is both received and *understood*. For example, a hospital administrator should always try to communicate in clear, easily understood terms and to use language tailored to different employee groups. Messages to the surgical staff should be purposefully different from those used with office employees.

Jargon can facilitate understanding if it's used within a group that knows what it means, but can cause problems when used outside that group.

LISTEN ACTIVELY. When someone talks, we hear, but too often we don't listen. Listening is an active search for meaning, whereas hearing is passive. In listening, the receiver is also putting effort into the communication.

Many of us are poor listeners. Why? Because it's difficult, and most of us would rather do the talking. Listening, in fact, is often more tiring than talking. Unlike hearing, **active listening**, which is listening for full meaning without making premature judgments or interpretations, demands total concentration. The average person normally speaks at a rate of about 125 to 200 words per minute. However, the average listener can comprehend up to 400 words per minute.[21] The difference leaves lots of idle brain time and opportunities for the mind to wander.

Active listening is enhanced by developing empathy with the sender—that is, by putting yourself in the sender's position. Because senders differ in attitudes, interests, needs, and expectations, empathy makes it easier to understand the actual content of a message. An empathetic listener reserves judgment on the message's content and carefully listens to what is being said. The goal is to improve one's ability to get the full meaning of a communication without distorting it by premature judgments or interpretations. Other specific behaviors that active listeners demonstrate are listed in Exhibit 15-3. As you can see, active listening takes effort, but it can help make communication much more effective.

CONSTRAIN EMOTIONS. It would be naïve to assume that managers always communicate in a rational manner. We know that emotions can cloud and distort communication. A manager who's upset over an issue is more likely to misconstrue incoming messages and fail to communicate his or her outgoing messages clearly and accurately. What to do? The simplest answer is to calm down and get emotions under control before communicating.

WATCH NONVERBAL CUES. If actions speak louder than words, then it's important to make sure your actions align with and reinforce the words that go along with them. An effective communicator watches his or her nonverbal cues to ensure that they convey the desired message.

EXHIBIT 15-3

Active Listening Behaviors

Sources: Based on J. V. Thill and C. L. Bovee, *Excellence in Business Communication*, 9th ed. (Upper Saddle River, NJ: Prentice Hall, 2011), pp. 48–49; and S. P. Robbins and P. L. Hunsaker, *Training in Interpersonal Skills*, 5th ed. (Upper Saddle River, NJ: Prentice Hall, 2009), pp. 90–92.

jargon
Specialized terminology or technical language that members of a group use to communicate among themselves

active listening
Listening for full meaning without making premature judgments or interpretations

LEARNING OUTCOME
Explain how communication
can flow most effectively
in organizations.

15.4

Organizational Communication

Maybe you've had the experience of sitting in an employee meeting with managers when they ask if anyone has any questions—only to be met with deafening silence.[22] Communication can be an interesting thing, especially in organizations. As we've seen, managerial communication is important, but it is a two-way street. An understanding of managerial communication isn't possible without looking at organizational communication. In this section, we look at several important aspects of organizational communication, including formal versus informal communication, the flow patterns of communication, formal and informal communication networks, and workplace design.

Formal Versus Informal Communication

Communication within an organization is described as formal or informal. **Formal communication** refers to communication that takes place within prescribed organizational work arrangements. For example, when a manager asks an employee to complete a task, that's formal communication. Another example of formal communication occurs when an employee communicates a problem to his or her manager.

    Informal communication is organizational communication not defined by the organization's structural hierarchy. When employees talk with each other in the lunch room, as they pass in hallways, or as they're working out at the company wellness facility, they engage in informal communication. Employees form friendships and communicate with each other. The informal communication system fulfills two purposes in organizations: (1) it permits employees to satisfy their need for social interaction, and (2) it can improve an organization's performance by creating alternative, and frequently faster and more efficient, channels of communication.

Direction of Communication Flow

Let's look at the ways that organizational communication can flow: downward, upward, laterally, or diagonally.

DOWNWARD.   Every morning and often several times a day, managers at UPS package delivery facilities gather workers for mandatory meetings that last precisely three minutes. During those 180 seconds, managers relay company announcements and go over local information like traffic conditions or customer complaints. Then, each meeting ends with a safety tip. The three-minute meetings have proved so successful that many of the company's office workers are using the idea.[23] This **downward communication** is communication that flows from a manager to employees. It's used to inform, direct, coordinate, and evaluate employees. When managers assign goals to their employees, they're using downward communication. They're also using downward communication when providing employees with job descriptions, informing them of organizational policies and procedures, pointing out problems that need attention, or evaluating their performance. Downward communication can take place through any of the communication methods we described earlier.

UPWARD COMMUNICATION.   Managers rely on their employees for information. For instance, reports are given to managers to inform them of progress toward goals or to report any problems. **Upward communication** is communication that flows from employees to managers. It keeps managers aware of how employees feel about their jobs, their coworkers, and the organization in general. Managers also rely on upward communication for ideas on how things can be improved. Some examples of upward communication include performance reports prepared by employees, suggestion boxes, employee attitude surveys, grievance procedures, manager-employee discussions, and informal group sessions in which employees have the opportunity to discuss problems with their manager or representatives of top-level management.

    How much upward communication is used depends on the organizational culture. If managers have created a climate of trust and respect and use participative decision making or empowerment, considerable upward communication will occur as employees provide input to decisions. In a more highly structured and authoritarian environment, upward communication still takes place, but is limited.

LATERAL COMMUNICATION. Communication that takes place among employees on the same organizational level is called **lateral communication**. In today's dynamic environment, horizontal communications are frequently needed to save time and facilitate coordination. Cross-functional teams, for instance, rely heavily on this form of communication interaction. However, conflicts can arise if employees don't keep their managers informed about decisions they've made or actions they've taken.

DIAGONAL COMMUNICATION. **Diagonal communication** is communication that crosses both work areas *and* organizational levels. A credit analyst who communicates directly with a regional marketing manager about a customer's problem—note the different department and different organizational level—uses diagonal communication. Because of its efficiency and speed, diagonal communication can be beneficial. Increased e-mail use facilitates diagonal communication. In many organizations, any employee can communicate by e-mail with any other employee, regardless of organizational work area or level, even with upper-level managers. In many organizations, CEOs have adopted an "open inbox" e-mail policy. For example, William H. Swanson, head of defense contractor Raytheon Company, figures that he has received and answered more than 150,000 employee e-mails. And Henry McKinnell Jr., former CEO of Pfizer, says that the approximately 75 internal e-mails he received every day were "an avenue of communication I didn't otherwise have."[24] However, diagonal communication also has the potential to create problems if employees don't keep their managers informed.

Organizational Communication Networks

The vertical and horizontal flows of organizational communication can be combined into a variety of patterns called **communication networks**. Exhibit 15-4 illustrates three common communication networks.

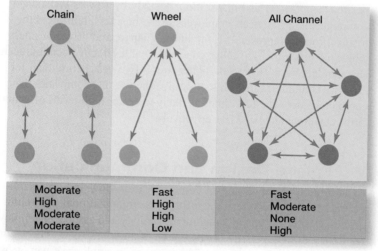

CRITERIA	Chain	Wheel	All Channel
Speed	Moderate	Fast	Fast
Accuracy	High	High	Moderate
Emergence of leader	Moderate	High	None
Member satisfaction	Moderate	Low	High

EXHIBIT 15-4

Organizational Communication Networks

formal communication
Communication that takes place within prescribed organizational work arrangements

informal communication
Communication that is not defined by the organization's structural hierarchy

downward communication
Communication that flows downward from a manager to employees

upward communication
Communication that flows upward from employees to managers

lateral communication
Communication that takes place among any employees on the same organizational level

diagonal communication
Communication that cuts across work areas and organizational levels

communication networks
The variety of patterns of vertical and horizontal flows of organizational communication

TYPES OF COMMUNICATION NETWORKS. In the *chain* network, communication flows according to the formal chain of command, both downward and upward. The *wheel* network represents communication flowing between a clearly identifiable and strong leader and others in a work group or team. The leader serves as the hub through whom all communication passes. Finally, in the *all-channel* network, communication flows freely among all members of a work team.

Which form of network you should use depends on your goal. Exhibit 15-4 also summarizes each network's effectiveness according to four criteria: speed, accuracy, the probability that a leader will emerge, and the importance of member satisfaction. One observation is immediately apparent: No single network is best for all situations.

THE GRAPEVINE. We can't leave our discussion of communication networks without discussing the **grapevine**—the informal organizational communication network. The grapevine is active in almost every organization. Is it an important source of information? You bet! One survey reported that 63 percent of employees say that they hear about important matters first through rumors or gossip on the grapevine.[25]

Certainly, the grapevine is an important part of any communication network and well worth understanding.[26] Acting as both a filter and a feedback mechanism, it pinpoints those bewildering issues that employees consider important. More importantly, from a managerial point of view, it *is* possible to analyze what is happening on the grapevine—what information is being passed, how information seems to flow, and what individuals seem to be key information conduits. By staying aware of the grapevine's flow and patterns, managers can identify issues that concern employees, and, in turn, use the grapevine to disseminate important information. Because the grapevine can't be eliminated, managers should "manage" it as an important information network.

Rumors that flow along the grapevine also can never be eliminated entirely. However, managers can minimize the negative consequences of rumors. How? By communicating openly, fully, and honestly with employees, particularly in situations where employees may not like proposed or actual managerial decisions. Open and honest communication has positive benefits for an organization. A study by Towers Watson concluded that effective communication "connects employees to the business, reinforces the organization's vision, fosters process improvement, facilitates change, and drives business results by changing employee behavior." For those companies with effective communication, total returns to shareholders were 91 percent higher over a five-year period than for companies with less effective communication. This study also showed that companies that were highly effective communicators were four times as likely to report high levels of employee engagement as firms that communicated less effectively.[27]

Workplace Design and Communication

In addition to the direction of communication flow and organizational communication networks, another factor that influences organizational communication is workplace design. Despite all the information technology and associated employee mobility (which we'll discuss in the next section), much of an organization's communication still occurs in the workplace. In fact, some 74 percent of an employee's average workweek is spent in an office.[28] How that office workspace is designed and configured can affect the communication that occurs as well as influence an organization's overall performance. In fact, in a survey of American workers, 90 percent believed that better workplace design and layout result in better overall employee performance.[29]

Research shows that a workplace design should successfully support four types of employee work: focused work, collaboration, learning, and socialization.[30] Focused work is when an employee needs to concentrate on completing a task. In collaboration, employees need to work together to complete a task. Learning is when employees are engaged in training or doing something new and could involve both focused work and

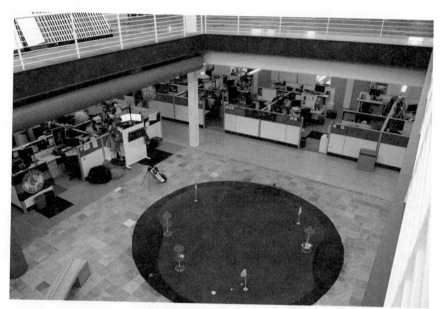

The workplace design at YouTube headquarters is flexible to support the flexibility employees have in doing their work. They are given the freedom to learn how to do something and complete a task on their own or to collaborate with coworkers, and the workplace design accommodates both situations. In open cubicles adjacent to an atrium and in small work rooms employees can concentrate on a job and learn new skills. Several different meeting rooms and informal areas enable small work teams to collaborate on completing a project and learn from members with different areas of expertise. YouTube also provides employees with many places to socialize, including a café, indoor garden, fitness center, and putting green.

collaboration. And socialization happens when employees informally gather to chat or to exchange ideas. A survey found that when workers had these types of "oases" or informal meeting places nearby, they had 102 percent more face-to-face communication than people who had only minimal access to such spots.[31] Because communication can and does take place in each of these settings, the workplace design needs to accommodate these organizational and interpersonal communications—all directions and all types—in order to be most effective.

As managers design the physical work environment, two common design elements have the greatest impact on communication.[32] First, the enclosures and barriers used in the workspace. Many organizational workplaces today are **open workplaces**; that is, they include few physical barriers and enclosures. Research has shown both the merits and the drawbacks of an open workplace.[33] One of the things we know for sure about this type of arrangement and its effect on communication is *visibility*. People in open cubicles placed along main routes of circulation or adjacent to atria reported almost 60 percent more face-to-face communication with team members than did those in lower-visibility locations. Another thing is *density*. More people populating an immediate work area meant that more face-to-face interactions took place. Workspaces with a high density yielded 84 percent more team-member communication than did workspace arrangements with a low density. If it's important that employees communicate and collaborate, managers need to consider visibility and density in workplace design.

Another workplace design element is the availability of adjustable work arrangements, equipment, and furnishings. As organizations have moved toward nontraditional work arrangements, the adjustability and customizability of employee workspace have become essential and influence organizational communication. For instance, one study found that adjustable partitions were associated with both greater perceived privacy and better communication.

As companies shrink workspaces to save money, managers need to ensure that the smaller and generally more open workspaces are useful and contribute to efficient and effective work.[34] By providing workspaces where employees can have some privacy and still have opportunities for collaborative efforts, both interpersonal and organizational communication can flourish and contribute to the organization's overall performance.

grapevine
The informal organizational communication network

open workplaces
Workplaces with few physical barriers and enclosures

15.5 Information Technology and Communication

Technology is changing the way we live and work. Take the following four examples: A Nielsen survey done in August 2009 showed that 276.9 million people used e-mail across the United States, several European countries, Australia, and Brazil, up 21 percent from 2008. Japanese employees, managers, housewives, and teens use wireless interactive Web phones to send e-mail, surf the Web, swap photos, and play computer games. At Dream-Works Animation, a sophisticated videoconferencing system allows animators in three different locations to collaboratively edit films. Several thousand employees at Ford use cell phones exclusively at work. A recent survey of employees showed that 93 percent of those polled use the Internet at work. Employees at Lockheed Martin Corporation can access an internal social media site called Unity, which includes tools such as blogs, wikis, file-sharing, discussion forums, and social bookmarking.[35]

The world of communication isn't what it used to be! Although changing technology has been a significant source of the environmental uncertainty facing organizations, these same technological changes have enabled managers to coordinate employees' work efforts in more efficient and effective ways. Information technology (IT) now touches every aspect of almost every company's business. The implications for the ways managers communicate are profound.

How Technology Affects Managerial Communication

IT has radically changed the way organizational members communicate. For example, it has significantly improved a manager's ability to monitor individual and team performance, has allowed employees to have more complete information to make faster decisions, and has provided employees more opportunities to collaborate and share information. In addition, IT has made it possible for people in organizations to be fully accessible, any time, regardless of where they are. Employees don't have to be at their desk with their computer running to communicate with others in the organization. Two IT developments that are most significant for managerial communication are networked systems and wireless capabilities.

NETWORKED SYSTEMS. In a networked system, an organization's computers are linked. Organizational members can communicate with each other and tap into information whether they're down the hall, across town, or halfway across the world. We're not looking at the mechanics of how a network system works, but some of its communication applications include e-mail; instant messaging; social media such as blogs, wikis, and Twitter; webinars; voice-mail; fax; teleconferencing and videoconferencing; and intranets.

FUTURE VISION **The Working World In 2020**

"Google's latest product combines communication, collaboration, and media-sharing into one insanely useful app. Is this the new e-mail?"[36]

In no area is the future more likely to change than in communication. Employees will rely on multiple channels of communication with heavy reliance on social networks, text messaging, and instant messaging. E-mail is likely to decline in popularity, largely because other channels are faster, more fluid, and more immediate.

Accurately forecasting tomorrow's technology is impossible. But several patterns seem to be evolving. For instance, the combining of functions in a single device is likely to result in employees having a single product that will combine phone, text messaging, Internet access, video camera, teleconferencing, and language translator. It will allow people to read proposals, legal papers, news, or almost any document digitally. It won't need a keyboard and will operate via voice commands. It's also likely not to be

handheld but rather something akin to combining reading glasses and an earpiece. You'll read documents through the lenses of what look like normal reading glasses and the earpiece/microphone will make it hands-free.

Another outcome made possible by technology will be a significant decrease in business travel. Improvements in computer-mediated groupware will allow individuals to conduct meetings in environments that closely simulate face-to-face interactions.

WIRELESS CAPABILITIES. At Seattle-based Starbucks Corporation, district managers use mobile technology, giving them more time to spend in the company's stores. A company executive says, "These are the most important people in the company. Each has between 8 to 10 stores that he or she services. And while their primary job is outside of the office—and in those stores—they still need to be connected."[37] As this example shows, wireless communication technology has the ability to improve work for managers and employees. Even Internet access is available through Wi-Fi and WiMax hot spots, which are locations where users gain wireless access. The number of these hot spot locations continues to grow. With more than 50 million "mobile" workers in the United States, smartphones, notebook computers, computing devices such as iPad, and other pocket communication devices have generated whole new ways for managers to "keep in touch." And the number of mobile communication users keeps increasing.[38] Employees don't have to be at their desks to communicate with others in the organization. As wireless technology continues to improve, we'll see more organizational members using it as a way to collaborate and share information.

How Information Technology Affects Organizations

Monsanto Company wanted to raise the visibility of some projects and to make a stronger argument for bioengineered crops. Using a YouTube approach, the company sent camera crews to the Philippines, Australia, and other countries to film testimonials from farmers using Monsanto products to grow these crops. The clips were posted on a company Web site, which now attracts more than 15,000 visitors a month. The PR manager in charge of the project said, "When the people involved relate how their life has changed and you actually see it, it's more compelling."[39] That's the power of IT at work. Employees—working in teams or as individuals—need information to make decisions and to do their work. It's clear that technology *can* significantly affect the way that organizational members communicate, share information, and do their work.

Communication and the exchange of information among organizational members are no longer constrained by geography or time. Collaborative work efforts among widely dispersed individuals and teams, sharing of information, and integration of decisions and work throughout an entire organization have the potential to increase organizational efficiency and effectiveness. And while the economic benefits of IT are obvious, managers must not forget the psychological drawbacks.[40] For instance, what is the psychological cost of an employee always being accessible? Will it lead to increased pressure for employees to "check in" even during their off hours? How important is it for employees to separate their work and personal lives? These questions don't come with easy answers, and managers will have to face these and similar issues.

Communication Issues in Today's Organizations

(15.6)

LEARNING OUTCOME
Discuss contemporary
issues in communication.

"Pulse lunches." That's what managers at Citibank's offices throughout Malaysia used to address pressing problems of declining customer loyalty and staff morale and increased employee turnover. By connecting with employees and listening to their concerns—that is, taking their "pulse"—during informal lunch settings, managers were able to make changes that boosted both customer loyalty and employee morale by more than 50 percent and reduced employee turnover to nearly zero.[41]

Being an effective communicator in today's organizations means being connected—not only to employees and customers, but to any of the organization's stakeholders. In this section, we examine five communication issues of particular significance to today's managers: managing communication in an Internet world, managing the organization's knowledge resources, communicating with customers, getting employee input, and communicating ethically.

Managing Communication in an Internet World

Lars Dalgaard, founder and chief executive of SuccessFactors, a human resource management software company, recently sent an e-mail to his employees banning in-house e-mail for a week. His goal? Getting employees to "authentically address issues amongst each

Let's Get Real

A major communication issue facing managers is *cutting through the clutter. Reducing the communication to what is most basic and essential in an effort to keep employees from being overwhelmed.*

other."[42] And he's not alone. Other companies including U.S. Cellular have tried the same thing. As we discussed earlier, e-mail can consume employees, but it's not always easy for them to let go of it, even when they know it can be "intexticating." But e-mail is only one communication challenge in this Internet world. A recent survey found that 20 percent of employees at large companies say they contribute regularly to blogs, social networks, wikis, and other Web services.[43] Managers are learning, the hard way sometimes, that all this new technology has created special communication challenges. The two main ones are (1) legal and security issues, and (2) lack of personal interaction.

LEGAL AND SECURITY ISSUES.   Chevron paid $2.2 million to settle a sexual-harassment lawsuit stemming from inappropriate jokes being sent by employees over company e-mail. U.K. firm Norwich Union had to pay £450,000 in an out-of-court settlement after an employee sent an e-mail stating that their competitor Western Provident Association was experiencing financial difficulties. Whole Foods Market was investigated by federal regulators and its board after CEO John P. Mackey used a pseudonym to post comments on a blog attacking the company's rival Wild Oats Markets.[44]

Although e-mail, blogs, tweets, and other forms of online communication are quick and easy ways to communicate, managers need to be aware of potential legal problems from inappropriate usage. Electronic information is potentially admissible in court. For instance, during the Enron trial, prosecutors entered into evidence e-mails and other documents they say showed that the defendants defrauded investors. Says one expert, "Today, e-mail and instant messaging are the electronic equivalent of DNA evidence."[45] But legal problems aren't the only issue, security concerns are as well.

A survey addressing outbound e-mail and content security found that 26 percent of the companies surveyed saw their businesses affected by the exposure of sensitive or embarrassing information.[46] Managers need to insure that confidential information is kept confidential. Employee e-mails and blogs should not communicate—inadvertently or purposely—proprietary information. Corporate computer and e-mail systems should be protected against hackers (people who try to gain unauthorized access) and spam (electronic junk mail). These serious issues must be addressed if the benefits of communication technology are to be realized.

PERSONAL INTERACTION.   It may be called social media, but another communication challenge posed by the Internet age we live and work in is the lack of personal interaction.[47] Even when two people are communicating face-to-face, understanding is not always achieved. However, it can be especially challenging to achieve understanding and collaborate on getting work done when communication takes place in a virtual environment. In response, some companies have banned e-mail on certain days, as we saw earlier. Others have simply encouraged employees to collaborate more in-person. Yet, in some situations and at certain times, personal interaction isn't physically possible—your colleagues work across the continent or even across the globe. In those instances, real-time collaboration software (such as private workplace wikis, blogs, instant messengers, and other types of groupware) may be a better communication choice than sending an e-mail and waiting for a response.[48] Instead of fighting it, other companies are encouraging employees to utilize the power of social networks to collaborate on work and to build strong connections. This form of interaction is especially appealing to younger workers who are comfortable with this communication medium. Some companies have gone as far as creating their own in-house social networks. For instance, employees at Starcom MediaVest Group tap into SMG Connected to find colleague profiles that outline their jobs, list the brands they admire, and describe their values. A company vice president says, "Giving our employees a way to connect over the Internet around the world made sense because they were doing it anyway."[49]

Managing the Organization's Knowledge Resources

Kara Johnson is a materials expert at product design firm IDEO. To make finding the right materials easier, she's building a master library of samples linked to a database that explains their properties and manufacturing processes.[51] What Johnson is doing is managing knowledge and

by the numbers[50]

25 percent of employees say they withhold feedback on routine problems to avoid wasting their time.

47 percent of Wi-Fi users say they can wait one hour or less before getting "antsy" about checking e-mail, instant messaging, and social networking sites.

64 seconds is how long it takes to retrieve your train of thought after an e-mail interruption.

69 percent of executives say they're sending out more messages than ever to employees.

37 percent of employees say they're receiving more messages from executives.

54 percent of employees say their company prohibits employees from visiting social networking sites while at work.

42 percent of employees who have received employer-provided wireless devices feel they are expected to always be available.

28 percent of a day is how much the average worker loses to interruptions.

making it easier for others at IDEO to learn and benefit from her knowledge. That's what today's managers need to do with the organization's knowledge resources—make it easy for employees to communicate and share their knowledge so they can learn from each other ways to do their jobs more effectively and efficiently. One way organizations can do this is to build online information databases that employees can access. For example, William Wrigley Jr. Co. launched an interactive Web site that allows sales agents to access marketing data and other product information. The sales agents can question company experts about products or search an online knowledge bank. In its first year, Wrigley estimates that the site cut research time of the sales force by 15,000 hours, making them more efficient and effective.[52]

In addition to online information databases for sharing knowledge, companies could create communities of practice, a concept that we introduced in Chapter 11 as a type of internal collaboration. To make these communities of practice work, however, it's important to maintain strong human interactions through communication using such essential tools as interactive Web sites, e-mail, and videoconferencing. In addition, these groups face the same communication problems that individuals face—filtering, emotions, defensiveness, over-documentation, and so forth. However, groups can resolve these issues by focusing on the same suggestions we discussed earlier.

The Role of Communication in Customer Service

You've been a customer many times; in fact, you probably find yourself in a customer service encounter several times a day. So what does this have to do with communication? As it turns out, a lot! *What* communication takes place and *how* it takes place can have a significant impact on a customer's satisfaction with the service and the likelihood of being a repeat customer. Managers in service organizations need to make sure that employees who interact with customers are communicating appropriately and effectively with those customers. How? By first recognizing the three components in any service delivery process: the customer, the service organization, and the individual service provider.[53] Each plays a role in whether communication is working. Obviously, managers don't have a lot of control over what or how the customer communicates, but they can influence the other two.

An organization with a strong service culture already values taking care of customers—finding out what their needs are, meeting those needs, and following up to make sure that their needs were met satisfactorily. Each of these activities involves communication, whether face-to-face, by phone or e-mail, or through other channels. In addition, communication is part of the specific customer service strategies the organization pursues. One strategy that many service organizations use is personalization. For instance, at Ritz-Carlton Hotels, customers are provided with more than a clean bed and room. Customers who have stayed at a location previously and indicated that certain items are important to them—such as extra pillows, hot chocolate, or a certain brand of shampoo—will find those items waiting in their room at arrival. The hotel's database allows service to be personalized to customers' expectations. In addition, all employees are asked to communicate information related to service provision. For instance, if a room attendant overhears guests talking about celebrating an anniversary,

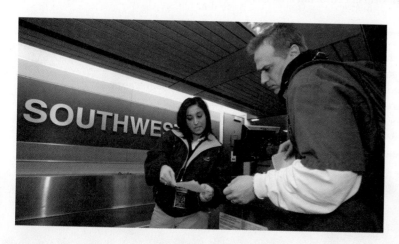

Communication is an important part of customer service strategy at Southwest Airlines. With a strong service culture that values taking care of passengers, the airline trains its service providers to communicate appropriately and effectively with customers. In helping a passenger rebook a flight after his was cancelled due to bad weather, the Southwest customer service agent shown here finds out what the customer's needs are, how she can meet those needs, and then follows through to make sure his needs were met satisfactorily. Her ability to listen actively and communicate effectively greatly influences the customer's satisfaction with Southwest Airlines and the likelihood of being a repeat customer.

he or she is supposed to relay the information so something special can be done.[54] Communication plays an important role in the hotel's customer personalization strategy.

Communication also is important to the individual service provider or contact employee. The quality of the interpersonal interaction between the customer and that contact employee does influence customer satisfaction, especially when the service encounter isn't up to expectations.[55] People on the front line involved with those "critical service encounters" are often the first to hear about or notice service failures or breakdowns. They must decide *how* and *what* to communicate during these instances. Their ability to listen actively and communicate appropriately with the customer goes a long way in whether the situation is resolved to the customer's satisfaction or spirals out of control. Another important communication concern for the individual service provider is making sure that he or she has the information needed to deal with customers efficiently and effectively. If the service provider doesn't personally have the information, some way needs to be devised to get the information easily and promptly.[56]

Getting Employee Input

Nokia recently set up an intranet soapbox known as Blog-Hub, opening it up to employee bloggers around the world. There, employees have griped about their employer, but rather than shutting it down, Nokia managers want them to "fire away." They feel that Nokia's growth and success can be attributed to a "history of encouraging employees to say whatever's on their minds, with faith that smarter ideas will result."[57]

In today's challenging environment, companies need to get input from their employees. Have you ever worked somewhere that had an employee suggestion box? When an employee had an idea about a new way of doing something—such as reducing costs, improving delivery time, and so forth—it went into the suggestion box where it usually sat until someone decided to empty the box. Businesspeople frequently joked about the suggestion box and cartoonists lambasted the futility of putting ideas in the employee suggestion box. And unfortunately, this attitude about suggestion boxes still persists in many organizations, and it shouldn't. Managers do business in a world today where you can't afford to ignore such potentially valuable information. Exhibit 15-5 lists some suggestions for letting employees know that their opinions matter.

Communicating Ethically

It's particularly important today that a company's communication efforts be ethical. **Ethical communication** "includes all relevant information, is true in every sense, and is not deceptive in any way."[58] On the other hand, unethical communication often distorts the truth or manipulates audiences. What are some ways that companies communicate unethically? It could be by omitting essential information. For instance, not telling employees that an impending merger is going to mean some of them will lose their jobs is unethical. It's unethical to plagiarize, which is "presenting someone else's words or other creative product as your own."[59] It would also be unethical communication to selectively misquote, misrepresent numbers, distort visuals, and fail to respect privacy or information security needs. For instance, although British Petroleum attempted to communicate openly and truthfully about

---

EXHIBIT 15-5

How to Let Employees Know Their Input Matters

- *Hold town-hall meetings* where information is shared and input solicited.
- *Provide information* about what's going on, good and bad.
- *Invest in training* so that employees see how they impact the customer experience.
- *Analyze problems together*—managers and employees.
- *Make it easy* for employees to give input by setting up different ways for them to do so (online, suggestion box, preprinted cards, and so forth).

ethical communication
Communication that includes all relevant information, is true in every sense, and is not deceptive in any way

the Gulf Coast oil spill in the summer of 2010, the public still felt that much of the company's communication contained some unethical elements.

So how can managers encourage ethical communications? One thing is to "establish clear guidelines for ethical behavior, including ethical business communication.[60] In a global survey by the International Association of Business Communicators, 70 percent of communication professionals said their companies clearly define what is considered ethical and unethical behavior."[61] If no clear guidelines exist, it's important to answer the following questions:

► Has the situation been defined fairly and accurately?
► Why is the message being communicated?
► How will the people who may be affected by the message or who receive the message be impacted?
► Does the message help achieve the greatest possible good while minimizing possible harm?
► Will this decision that appears to be ethical now seem so in the future?
► How comfortable are you with your communication effort? What would a person you admire think of it?[62]

Remember that as a manager, you have a responsibility to think through your communication choices and the consequences of those choices. If you always operate with these two things in mind, you're likely to have ethical communication.

Let's Get Real:

My Response *to A Manager's Dilemma, page 404*

to A Manager's Dilemma, page 404

Twitter has become a revolutionary tool for communication. It allows individuals and organizations to foster connections and an intimacy with others on a scale that would have not been possible just a few years ago. It also allows for an unparalleled immediacy in sharing information. In this example, Twitter allows fans and potential recruits to have unfettered access to their college team. The closeness Twitter develops between the organizations its recruits and its fans will lead to increased loyalty and excitement. These developments are all positive; however, these kinds of technologies can be a double-edged sword. In most cases, before organizations share information, information needs to be scrutinized and peer reviewed as to its suitability. The immediacy Twitter provides does not allow for this level of scrutiny, thus increasing the possibility that incorrect or potentially detrimental information will be shared, causing negative repercussions for an organization. In the case of Les Miles he might share sensitive information or commit recruiting violations if his "tweets" are not adequately censored.

In this example my advice would be to create a holding period for Les Miles's tweets. This holding period could be a short time frame in which the content could be reviewed by someone in the organization as to its appropriateness before it is shared. Although some immediacy would be lost, it would allow the organization to continue to give its fans and recruits increased access while insulating the organization from potentially embarrassing and otherwise negative situations.

What Would You Do?

Glenn A. Jones
Oral Care Consultant/
Technology Trainer
**Colgate Oral
Pharmaceuticals
New York, NY**

CHAPTER SUMMARY
by Learning Outcomes

LEARNING OUTCOME **15.1** **Define** the nature and function of communication.

Communication is the transfer and understanding of meaning. Interpersonal communication is communication between two or more people. Organizational communication includes all the patterns, networks, and systems of communication within an organization.

The functions of communication include controlling employee behavior, motivating employees, providing a release for emotional expression of feelings and fulfillment of social needs, and providing information.

LEARNING OUTCOME **15.2** **Compare** and contrast methods of interpersonal communication.

The communication process contains seven elements. First, a *sender* has a message. A *message* is a purpose to be conveyed. *Encoding* converts a message into symbols. A *channel* is the medium a message travels along. *Decoding* happens when the *receiver* retranslates a sender's message. Finally, *feedback* occurs.

Managers can evaluate the various communication methods according to their feedback, complexity capacity, breadth potential, confidentiality, encoding ease, decoding ease, time-space constraint, cost, interpersonal warmth, formality, scanability, and time of consumption.

The communication methods include face-to-face, telephone, group meetings, formal presentations, memos, traditional mail, fax, employee publications, bulletin boards, other company publications, audio- and videotapes, hotlines, e-mail, computer conferencing, voice mail, teleconferences, and videoconferences.

LEARNING OUTCOME **15.3** **Identify** barriers to effective interpersonal communication and how to overcome them.

The barriers to effective communication include filtering, emotions, information overload, defensiveness, language, and national culture.

Managers can overcome these barriers by using feedback, simplifying language, listening actively, constraining emotions, and watching for nonverbal clues.

LEARNING OUTCOME **15.4** **Explain** how communication can flow most effectively in organizations.

Formal communication is communication that takes place within prescribed organizational work arrangements. Informal communication is not defined by the organization's structural hierarchy.

Communication in an organization can flow downward, upward, laterally, and diagonally.

The three communication networks include the chain, in which communication flows according to the formal chain of command; the wheel, in which communication flows between a clearly identifiable and strong leader and others in a work team; and the all-channel, in which communication flows freely among all members of a work team.

Managers should manage the grapevine as an important information network. The negative consequences of rumors can be minimized by communicating openly, fully, and honestly with employees.

Workplace design also influences organizational communication. That design should support four types of employee work: focused work, collaboration, learning, and socialization. In each of these circumstances, communication must be considered.

Describe how technology affects managerial communication and organizations.

Technology has radically changed the way organizational members communicate. It improves a manager's ability to monitor performance; it gives employees more complete information to make faster decisions; it has provided employees more opportunities to collaborate and share information; and it has made it possible for people to be fully accessible, anytime anywhere.

IT affects organizations by influencing the way that organizational members communicate, share information, and do their work.

Discuss contemporary issues in communication.

The two main challenges of managing communication in an Internet world are the legal and security issues and the lack of personal interaction.

Organizations can manage knowledge by making it easy for employees to communicate and share their knowledge, which can help them learn from each other ways to do their jobs more effectively and efficiently. One way is through online information databases and another way is through creating communities of practice.

Communicating with customers is an important managerial issue since *what* communication takes place and *how* it takes place can significantly affect a customer's satisfaction with the service and the likelihood of being a repeat customer.

It's important for organizations to get input from their employees. Such potentially valuable information should not be ignored.

Finally, a company's communication efforts need to be ethical. Ethical communication can be encouraged through clear guidelines and through answering questions that force a communicator to think through the communication choices made and the consequences of those choices.

 To check your understanding of learning outcomes 15.1 – 15.6 go to **mymanagementlab.com** and try the chapter questions.

REVIEW AND DISCUSSION QUESTIONS

1. Define communication, interpersonal communication, and organizational communication. Why isn't effective communication synonymous with *agreement?*

2. What are the functions of communication?

3. Explain the components in the communication process.

4. What are the various communication methods managers can use? What criteria can managers use to evaluate those communication methods?

5. What are the barriers to effective communication? How can those barriers be overcome?

6. Contrast formal and informal communication.

7. Explain communication flow, the three common communication networks, and how managers should handle the grapevine.

8. How does technology affect managerial communication? How does it affect organizations?

9. Discuss the five contemporary communication issues facing managers.

10. Which do you think is more important for a manager: speaking accurately or listening actively? Why?

ETHICS DILEMMA

Social networking Web sites can be fun. Staying in touch with old friends or even family is one of the pleasures of joining. However, what happens when colleagues or even your boss want to "friend" you? Experts say that you should proceed with caution.[63] What do you think? Is it okay to provide people you know in a professional sense a "window into your personal life?" What ethical issues might arise in such a situation?

SKILLS EXERCISE

Developing Your Active Listening Skill

About the Skill

Active listening requires you to concentrate on what is being said. It's more than just hearing the words. It involves a concerted effort to understand and interpret the speaker's message.

Steps in Practicing the Skill

1. **Make eye contact.** How do you feel when somebody doesn't look at you when you're speaking? If you're like most people, you're likely to interpret this behavior as aloofness or disinterest. Making eye contact with the speaker focuses your attention, reduces the likelihood that you will become distracted, and encourages the speaker.

2. **Exhibit affirmative nods and appropriate facial expressions.** The effective listener shows interest in what is being said through nonverbal signals. Affirmative nods and appropriate facial expressions, when added to good eye contact, convey to the speaker that you're listening.

3. **Avoid distracting actions or gestures that suggest boredom.** In addition to showing interest, you must avoid actions that suggest that your mind is somewhere else. When listening, don't look at your watch, shuffle papers, play with your pencil, or engage in similar distractions. They make the speaker feel that you're bored or disinterested, or indicate that you aren't fully attentive.

4. **Ask questions.** The critical listener analyzes what he or she hears and asks questions. This behavior provides clarification, ensures understanding, and assures the speaker that you're listening.

5. **Paraphrase what's been said.** The effective listener uses phrases such as "What I hear you saying is ..." or "Do you mean ...?" Paraphrasing is an excellent control device to check on whether you're listening carefully and to verify that what you heard is accurate.

6. **Avoid interrupting the speaker.** Let the speaker complete his or her thought before you try to respond. Don't try to second-guess where the speaker's thoughts are going. When the speaker is finished, you'll know it.

7. **Stay motivated to listen.** Most of us would rather express our own ideas than listen to what someone else says. Talking might be more fun and silence might be uncomfortable, but you can't talk and listen at the same time. The good listener recognizes this fact and doesn't overtalk.

8. **Make smooth transitions between the roles of speaker and listener.** The effective listener makes transitions smoothly from speaker to listener and back to speaker. From a listening perspective, this means concentrating on what a speaker has to say and practicing not thinking about what you're going to say as soon as you get your chance.

Practicing the Skill

Ask a friend to tell you about his or her day and listen without interrupting. When your friend has finished speaking, ask two or three questions if needed to obtain more clarity and detail. Listen carefully to the answers. Now summarize your friend's day in no more than five sentences.

How well did you do? Let your friend rate the accuracy of your paraphrase (and try not to interrupt).

WORKING TOGETHER
Team Exercise

We've all watched and laughed at the oddball videos on YouTube and other online video sites. But what about using online video for work purposes?[64] What uses do you see for online video at work? What would be the advantages and drawbacks of using online video?

Form small groups of three to four individuals. Your team's task is to look at these issues. Answer the questions and be prepared to share your answers with the class.

MY TURN TO BE A MANAGER

- Research the characteristics of a good communicator. Keeping these characteristics in mind, practice being a good communicator—both as a sender and a listener.

- For one day, keep track of the types of communication you use (see Exhibit 15-2 for a list of various types). Which do you use most? Least? Were your choices of communication methods effective? Why or why not? Could they have been improved? How?

- For one day, track nonverbal communication that you notice in others. What types did you observe? Was the nonverbal communication always consistent with the verbal communication taking place? Describe.

- Research new types of IT devices. Write a report describing these devices (at least three) and their applicability to employees and organizations. Be sure to look at both the positive and negative aspects.

- Survey five different managers for their advice on being a good communicator. Put this information in a bulleted list format and be prepared to present it in class.

- Steve's and Mary's recommended readings: Phillip G. Clampitt, *Communicating for Managerial Effectiveness,* 4th ed. (Sage Publications, 2009); John Baldoni, *Great Communication Secrets of Great Leaders* (McGraw-Hill, 2003); Robert Mai and Alan Akerson, *The Leader as Communicator* (AMACOM, 2003); Boyd Clarke,

The Leader's Voice: How Communication Can Inspire Action and Get Results! (Select Books, 2002); Jo-Ellan Dimitrius and Mark Mazzarella, *Reading People* (Random House, 1998).

- Survey 10 office workers. Ask them: (1) the number of e-mail messages they receive daily, on average; (2) how many times in one day they check their e-mail; and (3) if they think a ban on e-mail messages one day a week would be a good idea and why or why not. Compile this information into a report.

- Pick one of the five topics addressed in the section on Communication Issues in Today's Organizations and do some additional research. Put your findings in a bulleted list and be prepared to discuss in class. Be sure to cite your sources!

- In your own words, write down three things you learned in this chapter about being a good manager.

- Self-knowledge can be a powerful learning tool. Go to mymanagementlab.com and complete these self-assessment exercises: What's My Face-to-Face Communication Style? How Good Are My Listening Skills? How Good Am I at Giving Performance Feedback? Am I a Gossip? Using the results of your assessments, identify personal strengths and weaknesses. What will you do to reinforce your strengths and improve your weaknesses?

CASE APPLICATION 1
Gossip Girls

Sixty percent. That's the percentage of respondents in a recent employee survey who said that gossip was their biggest pet peeve about their jobs.[65] Most gossip centers around the workplace and the personal lives of coworkers. How often have you gossiped at work … either as a sender or a receiver? Although you may think workplace gossip is harmless, it can have some pretty serious consequences. First, spreading rumors can damage morale and increase anxiety. Secondly, it can hamper productivity and affect performance. And it can lead to something you might not even have considered, as it did for four former employees of the town of Hooksett, New Hampshire. Fired by the city council for gossiping about their boss, they learned the hard way that gossip can cost you your job.

The longtime employees were fired because one of the women had used derogatory terms to describe the town administrator and because

Gossiping at work isn't as harmless as some may think and can result in serious consequences, such as damaged morale, increased anxiety, lost productivity, and poor performance. As the women shown here learned, it can cost you your job.

all of them had discussed a rumor that he was having an affair with a female subordinate. All four of the women acknowledged feeling resentment toward the woman, who worked in a specially created position and was paid more than two of the employees, despite having less experience and seniority.

Despite an appeal of their dismissal by the four employees, the Hooksett council didn't budge and stated, "These employees do not represent the best interests of the town of Hooksett and the false rumors, gossip and derogatory statements have contributed to a negative working environment and malcontent among their fellow employees." Despite national media attention and a petition signed by 419 residents asking for the women to be reinstated, the city council didn't waver on its decision. An attorney for the four women said that his clients were "legitimately questioning the conduct of their supervisor, and whether the female subordinate was getting preferential treatment. It almost cheapens it to call it gossip. It might have been idle, not particularly thoughtful, talk. But there was no harm intended."

Although the four women represented nearly 50 years of combined service to the city and all had positive performance reviews, the town council believed that the women's actions were "insubordinate" and "dishonest." All four received a settlement for being fired, which cost the town a total of $330,000. The settlement agreement also stipulated, however, that two of the women can never apply for a job with the town again.

Discussion Questions

1. What do you think of this situation? Do you agree with the town council's decision about the firing and refusal to reinstate the employees?

2. As was stated in the case, a recent survey showed that 60 percent of the respondents indicated that the biggest pet peeve they have about their jobs is workplace gossip. Research the topic of office gossip/office rumors. Is office gossip always harmful? Discuss. Could it ever be useful to managers?

3. In retrospect, what could these four women have done differently?

4. What implications can you see for managers and communication from this story?

CASE APPLICATION 2
Delivery Disaster

When two Domino's Pizza employees filmed a gross prank in the kitchen of the restaurant in Conover, North Carolina, the company suddenly had a major public relations crisis on its hands.[66] The video ended up posted on YouTube and other sites and showed a Domino's employee preparing "sandwiches for delivery while putting cheese up his nose, nasal mucus on the sandwiches, and violating other health-code standards," with another employee providing narration. By the next day, over a million disgusted people had viewed the video and discussion about Domino's had spread throughout Twitter and Google.

As Domino's quickly realized, social media has the power to take tiny incidents and turn them into marketing crises. A company spokesperson said, "We got blindsided by two idiots with a video camera and an awful idea." When the company first learned about the video, executives decided not to respond aggressively, hoping the controversy would quiet down. What they missed, though, was the "perpetual mushroom effect of viral sensations." The chief marketing officer of a social media marketing firm said, "If you think it's not going to spread, that's when it gets bigger." And as Domino's discovered, it did. In just a matter of days, Domino's reputation was damaged. Customers' perception of its quality went from positive to negative. One brand expert said, "It's graphic enough in the video, and it's created enough of a stir, that it gives people a little pause."

So what happened to the two employees? Although they told Domino's executives they never actually delivered the tainted food, they were fired and charged with a felony. And Domino's posted its own video featuring its top manager addressing the incident on YouTube not long after it occurred.

Discussion Questions

1. Beyond its being vulgar and disgusting, what do you think of this situation from the perspective of managing communications?

2. Why do you think Domino's executives took a wait-and-see attitude? Why was this response a problem?

3. How could this type of communication problem be prevented at other Domino's Pizza restaurants?

4. Do incidents like this one and the possibility of them happening anywhere, anytime, mean that all forms of social media should be banned from workplaces? What are the implications for policies regarding communication technology? Discuss.

Let's Get Real:

Meet the Manager

Aisha Warren
Retail Store Manager
Dots, LLC
Warren, MI

You'll be hearing more from this real manager throughout the chapter.

MY JOB:

I am a retail clothing store manager for Dots, LLC. I am responsible for leading, motivating, and coaching a team of approximately 10 employees. I am focused on customer service and sales results.

BEST PART OF MY JOB:

The relationships that I have built with customers and staff members. I am amazed by the many follow-up visits and phone calls I receive from past staff members and customers. Many have expressed their gratitude for what I have taught them about management, sales, and fashion.

Motivating Employees

LEARNING OUTCOMES

WORST PART OF MY JOB:

The feeling of defeat when my team and I do not meet our sales goal. Achieving our sales goal can be difficult. The key is to motivate team members with incentives that keep them pushing to achieve the goal.

BEST MANAGEMENT ADVICE EVER RECEIVED:

Be a leader and not a boss. It is important to set the tone for your expectations and lead by example. This advice has made me successful.

A Manager's Dilemma

Ministers. Customers. Embassies. These are the interesting "names" given to employees, customers, and retailers at gourmet tea company Republic of Tea.[1] Like many companies, big and small, Republic of Tea struggled through the economic recession. As the crisis intensified, "CEO Ron Rubin sat in his office and asked himself, What more can we do to help our ministers?" The answer was as unexpected as the question that prompted it.

Within weeks, the company rolled out a program called "Healthy Ministry, dedicated to improving the health, physical fitness and well-being of its 100 employees." At the company's Novato, California, headquarters and its Nashville, Illinois, warehouse, employees now have access to a full-time nutritionist, on-site health screenings, and a $500 credit that can be used for gym memberships or health plans such as Weight Watchers. With a workday walking program, employees are encouraged to take 10- to 15-minute walks. Some might consider Rubin's ideas silly, but he believes that if you take care of your employees, they will take care of your business. Although Ron Rubin has tried to make Republic of Tea a better place to work for his employees during a challenging period, what other things could he do?

What Would You Do?

Successful managers, like Ron Rubin, understand that what motivates them personally may have little or no effect on others. Just because *you're* motivated by being part of a cohesive work team, don't assume everyone is. Or just because *you're* motivated by your job doesn't mean that everyone is. Effective managers who get employees to put forth maximum effort know how and why those employees are motivated and tailor motivational practices to satisfy their needs and wants.

LEARNING OUTCOME
Define motivation.

16.1

What Is Motivation?

According to LinkedIn Corporation, a Web site that provides networking for more than 65 million professionals, "ninja" has far outpaced the growth of other trendy job titles.[2] Although most individuals using that title are computer programmers—who attack writing code like a ninja, with tons of tools available to do battle—the term also has been used to describe expertise in everything from customer service to furniture movers. For instance, in Salt Lake City, one business owner sells the services of "ninja workers" who will do everything from hauling junk to personal security to house-sitting. And at Bonobos, Inc., a New York City start-up that makes and sells men's apparel online, customer-service employees are also called ninjas. Why would a job title matter to employees? Many people, especially the young and young-at-heart, like vivid and unusual titles that celebrate their hard work. And ninja, like other popular job titles before it (guru, evangelist, or even sandwich artist) shows employees that their efforts aren't plain and ordinary, but are appreciated.

Would you ever have thought that a job title might be motivating? Have you ever thought about to how to motivate someone? It's an important topic in management and researchers have long been interested in it.[3] All managers need to be able to motivate their employees, which first requires understanding what motivation is. Let's begin by pointing out what motivation is not. Why? Because many people incorrectly view motivation as a personal trait; that is, they think some people are motivated and others aren't. Our knowledge of motivation tells us that we can't label people that way because individuals differ in motivational drive and their overall motivation varies from situation to situation. For instance, you're probably more motivated in some classes than in others.

Motivation refers to the process by which a person's efforts are energized, directed, and sustained toward attaining a goal.[4] This definition has three key elements: energy, direction, and persistence.[5]

430

The *energy* element is a measure of intensity, drive, and vigor. A motivated person puts forth effort and works hard. However, the quality of the effort must be considered as well as its intensity. High levels of effort don't necessarily lead to favorable job performance unless the effort is channeled in a *direction* that benefits the organization. Effort that's directed toward, and consistent with, organizational goals is the kind of effort we want from employees. Finally, motivation includes a *persistence* dimension. We want employees to persist in putting forth effort to achieve those goals.

Motivating high levels of employee performance is an important organizational concern and managers keep looking for answers. For instance, a Gallup poll found that a large majority of U.S. employees—some 73 percent—are not excited about their work. As the researchers stated, "These employees have essentially 'checked out.' They're sleepwalking through their workday, putting time, but not energy or passion, into their work."[6] It's no wonder then that both managers and academics want to understand and explain employee motivation.

Let's Get Real

Motivating employees is important because *it contributes to positive team morale.*

Early Theories of Motivation

We begin by looking at four early motivation theories: *Maslow's hierarchy of needs*, *McGregor's theories X and Y*, *Herzberg's two-factor theory*, and *McClelland's three-needs theory*. Although more valid explanations of motivation have been developed, these early theories are important because they represent the foundation from which contemporary motivation theories were developed and because many practicing managers still use them.

16.2

LEARNING OUTCOME
Compare and contrast early
theories of motivation.

Maslow's Hierarchy of Needs Theory

Having a car to get to work is a necessity for many workers. When two crucial employees of Vurv Technology in Jacksonville, Florida, had trouble getting to work, owner Derek Mercer decided to buy two inexpensive used cars for the employees. He said, "I felt that they were good employees and a valuable asset to the company." One of the employees who got

Intel managers understand employee needs and their impact on motivation. The company helps satisfy the social needs of its young workforce in Vietnam, where more than half of the population is under the age of 25. Intel provides opportunities for its young employees, who love American culture, to have fun with their coworkers during work breaks as ways to satisfy their needs for belongingness and friendship. Recognizing that its employees are eager to learn western ways of doing business and have a strong drive for self-development and achievement, Intel offers them training programs for personal growth and career development to satisfy their esteem and self-actualization needs.

motivation
The process by which a person's efforts are energized, directed, and sustained toward attaining a goal

one of the cars said, "It wasn't the nicest car. It wasn't the prettiest car. But boy did my overwhelming feeling of dread go from that to enlightenment. The 80-hour weeks we worked after that never meant anything. It was give and take. I was giving and the company was definitely giving back."[7] Derek Mercer understands employee needs and their impact on motivation. The first motivation theory we're going to look at addresses employee needs.

The best-known theory of motivation is probably Abraham Maslow's **hierarchy of needs theory**.[8] Maslow was a psychologist who proposed that within every person is a hierarchy of five needs:

1. **Physiological needs**: A person's needs for food, drink, shelter, sex, and other physical requirements.
2. **Safety needs**: A person's needs for security and protection from physical and emotional harm, as well as assurance that physical needs will continue to be met.
3. **Social needs**: A person's needs for affection, belongingness, acceptance, and friendship.
4. **Esteem needs**: A person's needs for internal esteem factors such as self-respect, autonomy, and achievement and external esteem factors such as status, recognition, and attention.
5. **Self-actualization needs**: A person's needs for growth, achieving one's potential, and self-fulfillment; the drive to become what one is capable of becoming.

Maslow argued that each level in the needs hierarchy must be substantially satisfied before the next need becomes dominant. An individual moves up the needs hierarchy from one level to the next. (See Exhibit 16-1.) In addition, Maslow separated the five needs into higher and lower levels. Physiological and safety needs were considered *lower-order needs*; social, esteem, and self-actualization needs were considered *higher-order needs*. Lower-order needs are predominantly satisfied externally while higher-order needs are satisfied internally.

How does Maslow's theory explain motivation? Managers using Maslow's hierarchy to motivate employees do things to satisfy employees' needs. But the theory also says that once a need is substantially satisfied, an individual is no longer motivated to satisfy that need. Therefore, to motivate someone, you need to understand what need level that person is on in the hierarchy and focus on satisfying needs at or above that level.

Maslow's need theory was widely recognized during the 1960s and 1970s, especially among practicing managers, probably because it was intuitively logical and easy to understand. But Maslow provided no empirical support for his theory, and several studies that sought to validate it could not.[9]

McGregor's Theory X and Theory Y

Andy Grove, cofounder of Intel Corporation and now a senior advisor to the company, was known for being open with his employees. However, he was also known for his tendency to yell. Intel's current CEO, Paul Otellini said, "When Andy was yelling at you, it wasn't because he didn't care about you. He was yelling at you because he wanted you to do better."[10] Although managers like Andy Grove want their employees to do better, that approach might not have been the best way to motivate employees as McGregor's Theory X and Theory Y suggest.

EXHIBIT 16-1

Maslow's Hierarchy of Needs

Source: Abraham H. Maslow, Robert D. Frager, Robert D., and James Fadiman, *Motivation and Personality*, 3rd Edition, © 1987. Adapted by permission of Pearson Education, Inc., Upper Saddle River, NJ.

Self-Actualization
Esteem
Social
Safety
Physiological

Douglas McGregor is best known for proposing two assumptions about human nature: Theory X and Theory Y.[11] Very simply, **Theory X** is a negative view of people that assumes workers have little ambition, dislike work, want to avoid responsibility, and need to be closely controlled to work effectively. **Theory Y** is a positive view that assumes employees enjoy work, seek out and accept responsibility, and exercise self-direction. McGregor believed that Theory Y assumptions should guide management practice and proposed that participation in decision making, responsible and challenging jobs, and good group relations would maximize employee motivation.

Unfortunately, no evidence confirms that either set of assumptions is valid or that being a Theory Y manager is the only way to motivate employees. For instance, Jen-Hsun Huang, founder of Nvidia Corporation, an innovative and successful microchip manufacturer, has been known to use both reassuring hugs and tough love in motivating employees. But he has little tolerance for screw-ups. "In one legendary meeting, he's said to have ripped into a project team for its tendency to repeat mistakes. 'Do you suck?' he asked the stunned employees. 'Because if you suck, just get up and say you suck.'"[12] His message, delivered in classic Theory X style, was that if you need help, ask for it. It's a harsh approach, but in this case, it worked.

Herzberg's Two-Factor Theory

Frederick Herzberg's **two-factor theory** (also called motivation-hygiene theory) proposes that intrinsic factors are related to job satisfaction, while extrinsic factors are associated with job dissatisfaction.[13] Herzberg wanted to know when people felt exceptionally good (satisfied) or bad (dissatisfied) about their jobs. (These findings are shown in Exhibit 16-2.) He concluded that the replies people gave when they felt good about their jobs were significantly different from the replies they gave when they felt badly. Certain characteristics were consistently related to job satisfaction (factors on the left side of the exhibit), and others to job

EXHIBIT 16-2

Herzberg's Two Factor Theory

Source: Based on F. Herzberg, B. Mausner, and B. B. Snyderman, *The Motivation to Work* (New York: John Wiley, 1959).

hierarchy of needs theory
Maslow's theory that human needs—physiological, safety, social, esteem, and self-actualization—form a sort of hierarchy

physiological needs
A person's needs for food, drink, shelter, sexual satisfaction, and other physical needs

safety needs
A person's needs for security and protection from physical and emotional harm

social needs
A person's needs for affection, belongingness, acceptance, and friendship

esteem needs
A person's needs for internal factors such as self-respect, autonomy, and achievement, and external factors such as status, recognition, and attention

self-actualization needs
A person's need to become what he or she is capable of becoming.

Theory X
The assumption that employees dislike work, are lazy, avoid responsibility, and must be coerced to perform

Theory Y
The assumption that employees are creative, enjoy work, seek responsibility, and can exercise self-direction

two-factor theory (motivation-hygiene theory)
The motivation theory that intrinsic factors are related to job satisfaction and motivation, whereas extrinsic factors are associated with job dissatisfaction

EXHIBIT 16-3

Contrasting Views of
Satisfaction–Dissatisfaction

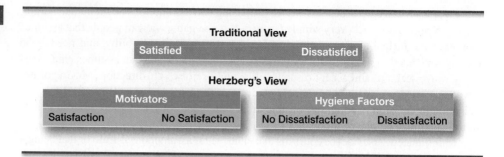

dissatisfaction (factors on the right side). When people felt good about their work, they tended to cite intrinsic factors arising from the job itself such as achievement, recognition, and responsibility. On the other hand, when they were dissatisfied, they tended to cite extrinsic factors arising from the job context such as company policy and administration, supervision, interpersonal relationships, and working conditions.

In addition, Herzberg believed that the data suggested that the opposite of satisfaction was not dissatisfaction, as traditionally had been believed. Removing dissatisfying characteristics from a job would not necessarily make that job more satisfying (or motivating). As shown in Exhibit 16-3, Herzberg proposed that a dual continuum existed: The opposite of "satisfaction" is "no satisfaction," and the opposite of "dissatisfaction" is "no dissatisfaction."

Again, Herzberg believed that the factors that led to job satisfaction were separate and distinct from those that led to job dissatisfaction. Therefore, managers who sought to eliminate factors that created job dissatisfaction could keep people from being dissatisfied but not necessarily motivate them. The extrinsic factors that create job dissatisfaction were called **hygiene factors**. When these factors are adequate, people won't be dissatisfied, but they won't be satisfied (or motivated) either. To motivate people, Herzberg suggested emphasizing **motivators**, the intrinsic factors having to do with the job itself.

Herzberg's theory enjoyed wide popularity from the mid-1960s to the early 1980s, despite criticisms of his procedures and methodology. Although some critics said his theory was too simplistic, it has influenced how we currently design jobs, especially when it comes to job enrichment, which we'll discuss at a later point in this chapter.

Three-Needs Theory

David McClelland and his associates proposed the **three-needs theory**, which says there are three acquired (not innate) needs that are major motives in work.[14] These three needs include the **need for achievement (nAch)**, which is the drive to succeed and excel in relation to a set of standards; the **need for power (nPow)**, which is the need to make others behave in a way that they would not have behaved otherwise; and the **need for affiliation (nAff)**, which is the desire for friendly and close interpersonal relationships. Of these three needs, the need for achievement has been researched the most.

People with a high need for achievement are striving for personal achievement rather than for the trappings and rewards of success. They have a desire to do something better or more efficiently than it's been done before.[15] They prefer jobs that offer personal responsibility for finding solutions to problems, in which they can receive rapid and unambiguous feedback on their performance in order to tell whether they're improving, and in which they can set moderately challenging goals. High achievers avoid what they perceive to be very easy or very difficult tasks. Also, a high need to achieve doesn't necessarily lead to being a good manager, especially in large organizations. That's because high achievers focus on their *own* accomplishments, while good managers emphasize helping *others* accomplish their goals.[16] McClelland showed that employees can be trained to stimulate their achievement need by being in situations where they have personal responsibility, feedback, and moderate risks.[17]

The other two needs in this theory haven't been researched as extensively as the need for achievement. However, we do know that the best managers tend to be high in the need for power and low in the need for affiliation.[18]

nAch: Indicated by someone in the story wanting to perform or do something better.
nAff: Indicated by someone in the story wanting to be with someone else and enjoy mutual friendship.
nPow: Indicated by someone in the story desiring to have an impact or make an impression on others in the story.

EXHIBIT 16-4

TAT Pictures

All three of these needs can be measured by using a projective test (known as the Thematic Apperception Test or TAT) in which respondents react to a set of pictures. Each picture is briefly shown to a person who writes a story based on the picture. (See Exhibit 16-4 for some examples.) Trained interpreters then determine the individual's levels of nAch, nPow, and nAff from the stories written.

Contemporary Theories of Motivation

16.3

LEARNING OUTCOME
Compare and contrast contemporary theories of motivation.

The theories we look at in this section represent current explanations of employee motivation. Although these theories may not be as well known as those we just discussed, they are supported by research.[19] These contemporary motivation approaches include goal-setting theory, reinforcement theory, job design theory, equity theory, expectancy theory, and high-involvement work practices.

Goal-Setting Theory

At Wyeth's research division, executive vice president Robert Ruffolo established challenging new product quotas for the company's scientists in an attempt to bring more efficiency to the innovation process. And he made bonuses contingent on meeting those goals.[20] Before a big assignment or major class project presentation, has a teacher ever encouraged you to "Just do your best"? What does that vague statement, "do your best," mean? Would your performance on a class project have been higher had that teacher said you needed to score a

hygiene factors
Factors that eliminate job dissatisfaction, but don't motivate

motivators
Factors that increase job satisfaction and motivation

three-needs theory
The motivation theory that says three acquired (not innate) needs—achievement, power, and affiliation—are major motives in work

need for achievement (nAch)
The drive to succeed and excel in relation to a set of standards

need for power (nPow)
The need to make others behave in a way that they would not have behaved otherwise

need for affiliation (nAff)
The desire for friendly and close interpersonal relationships

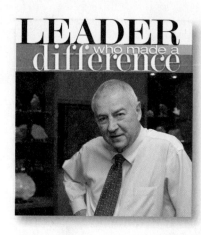

LEADER who made a difference

His privately held software company (the world's largest) has made *Fortune* magazine's list of "Best Companies to Work For" for all 13 years that it's been published.[21] "He" is John Goodnight, CEO and co-founder of Cary, North Carolina–based SAS. Goodnight has always believed in taking care of his employees. His company's approach to giving employees flexibility and perks is "so legendary that even Google uses SAS as a model." Goodnight fashioned SAS's culture around the idea of "trust between our employees and the company." And employees love it! Annual turnover is a low 2 percent and the company is highly profitable. There's something to be said for recognizing that your employees are your most important asset!

93 percent to keep your A in the class? Research on goal-setting theory addresses these issues, and the findings, as you'll see, are impressive in terms of the effect that goal specificity, challenge, and feedback have on performance.[22]

Research provides substantial support for **goal-setting theory**, which says that specific goals increase performance and that difficult goals, when accepted, result in higher performance than do easy goals. What does goal-setting theory tell us?

First, working toward a goal is a major source of job motivation. Studies on goal setting have demonstrated that specific and challenging goals are superior motivating forces.[23] Such goals produce a higher output than does the generalized goal of "do your best." The specificity of the goal itself acts as an internal stimulus. For instance, when a sales rep commits to making eight sales calls daily, this intention gives him a specific goal to try to attain.

It's not a contradiction that goal-setting theory says that motivation is maximized by *difficult* goals, whereas achievement motivation (from three-needs theory) is stimulated by *moderately challenging* goals.[24] First, goal-setting theory deals with people in general, whereas the conclusions on achievement motivation are based on people who have a high nAch. Given that no more than 10 to 20 percent of North Americans are high achievers (a proportion that's likely lower in underdeveloped countries), difficult goals are still recommended for the majority of employees. Second, the conclusions of goal-setting theory apply to those who accept and are committed to the goals. Difficult goals will lead to higher performance *only* if they are accepted.

Next, will employees try harder if they have the opportunity to participate in the setting of goals? Not always. In some cases, participatively set goals elicit superior performance; in other cases, individuals performed best when their manager assigned goals. However, participation is probably preferable to assigning goals when employees might resist accepting difficult challenges.[25]

Finally, we know that people will do better if they get feedback on how well they're progressing toward their goals because feedback helps identify discrepancies between what they have done and what they want to do. But all feedback isn't equally effective. Self-generated feedback—where an employee monitors his or her own progress—has been shown to be a more powerful motivator than feedback coming from someone else.[26]

Three other contingencies besides feedback influence the goal-performance relationship: goal commitment, adequate self-efficacy, and national culture.

First, goal-setting theory assumes that an individual is committed to the goal. Commitment is most likely when goals are made public, when the individual has an internal locus of control, and when the goals are self-set rather than assigned.[27]

Next, **self-efficacy** refers to an individual's belief that he or she is capable of performing a task.[28] The higher your self-efficacy, the more confidence you have in your ability to succeed in a task. So, in difficult situations, we find that people with low self-efficacy are likely to reduce their effort or give up altogether, whereas those with high self-efficacy will try harder to master the challenge.[29] In addition, individuals with high self-efficacy seem to respond to negative feedback with increased effort and motivation, whereas those with low self-efficacy are likely to reduce their effort when given negative feedback.[30]

Finally, the value of goal-setting theory depends on the national culture. It's well adapted to North American countries because its main ideas align reasonably well with those cultures. It assumes that subordinates will be reasonably independent (not a high score on power distance), that people will seek challenging goals (low in uncertainty avoidance), and that performance is considered important by both managers and subordinates (high in assertiveness). Don't expect goal setting to lead to higher employee performance in countries where the cultural characteristics aren't like this.

EXHIBIT 16-5
Goal-Setting Theory

Exhibit 16-5 summarizes the relationships among goals, motivation, and performance. Our overall conclusion is that the intention to work toward hard and specific goals is a powerful motivating force. Under the proper conditions, it can lead to higher performance. However, no evidence indicates that such goals are associated with increased job satisfaction.[31]

Reinforcement Theory

Reinforcement theory says that behavior is a function of its consequences. Those consequences that immediately follow a behavior and increase the probability that the behavior will be repeated are called **reinforcers**.

Reinforcement theory ignores factors such as goals, expectations, and needs. Instead, it focuses solely on what happens to a person when he or she does something. For instance, Walmart improved its bonus program for hourly employees. Employees who provide outstanding customer service get a cash bonus. And all Walmart hourly full- and part-time store employees are eligible for annual "My$hare" bonuses, which are allocated on store performance and distributed quarterly so that workers are rewarded more frequently.[32] The company's intent: keep the workforce motivated to meet goals by rewarding them when they did, thus reinforcing the behaviors.

In Chapter 14 we showed how managers use reinforcers to shape behavior, but the concept is also widely believed to explain motivation. According to B. F. Skinner, people will most likely engage in desired behaviors if they are rewarded for doing so. These rewards are most effective if they immediately follow a desired behavior; and behavior that isn't rewarded, or is punished, is less likely to be repeated.[33]

Using reinforcement theory, managers can influence employees' behavior by using positive reinforcers for actions that help the organization achieve its goals. And managers should ignore, not punish, undesirable behavior. Although punishment eliminates undesired behavior faster than nonreinforcement does, its effect is often temporary and may have unpleasant side effects including dysfunctional behavior such as workplace conflicts, absenteeism, and turnover. Although reinforcement is an important influence on work behavior, it isn't the only explanation for differences in employee motivation.[34]

goal-setting theory
The proposition that specific goals increase performance and that difficult goals, when accepted, result in higher performance than do easy goals

self-efficacy
An individual's belief that he or she is capable of performing a task

reinforcement theory
The theory that behavior is a function of its consequences

reinforcers
Consequences immediately following a behavior, which increase the probability that the behavior will be repeated

Designing Motivating Jobs

It's not unusual to find shop-floor workers at Cordis LLC's San German, Puerto Rico, facility interacting directly with customers, especially if that employee has special skills or knowledge that could help come up with a solution to a customer's problem.[35] One company executive said, "Our sales guys often encourage this in specific situations because they don't always have all the answers. If by doing this, we can better serve the customers, then we do it." As this example shows, the tasks an employee performs in his or her job are often determined by different factors, such as providing customers what they need when they need it.

Because managers want to motivate individuals on the job, we need to look at ways to design motivating jobs. If you look closely at what an organization is and how it works, you'll find that it's composed of thousands of tasks. These tasks are, in turn, aggregated into jobs. We use the term **job design** to refer to the way tasks are combined to form complete jobs. The jobs that people perform in an organization should not evolve by chance. Managers should design jobs deliberately and thoughtfully to reflect the demands of the changing environment, the organization's technology, and employees' skills, abilities, and preferences.[36] When jobs are designed like that, employees are motivated to work hard. Let's look at some ways that managers can design motivating jobs.[37]

JOB ENLARGEMENT.   As we saw in the Management History Module and Chapter 10, job design historically has been to make jobs smaller and more specialized. It's difficult to motivate employees when jobs are like this. An early effort at overcoming the drawbacks of job specialization involved horizontally expanding a job through increasing **job scope**— the number of different tasks required in a job and the frequency with which these tasks are repeated. For instance, a dental hygienist's job could be enlarged so that in addition to cleaning teeth, he or she is pulling patients' files, refiling them when finished, and sanitizing and storing instruments. This type of job design option is called **job enlargement**.

Most job enlargement efforts that focused solely on increasing the number of tasks don't seem to work. As one employee who experienced such a job redesign said, "Before, I had one lousy job. Now, thanks to job enlargement, I have three lousy jobs!" However, research has shown that *knowledge* enlargement activities (expanding the scope of knowledge used in a job) lead to more job satisfaction, enhanced customer service, and fewer errors.[38]

JOB ENRICHMENT.   Another approach to job design is the vertical expansion of a job by adding planning and evaluating responsibilities—**job enrichment**. Job enrichment increases **job depth**, which is the degree of control employees have over their work. In other words, employees are empowered to assume some of the tasks typically done by their managers. Thus, an enriched job allows workers to do an entire activity with increased freedom, independence, and responsibility. In addition, workers get feedback so they can assess and correct their own performance. For instance, if our dental hygienist had an enriched job, he or she could, in addition to cleaning teeth, schedule appointments (planning) and follow up with clients (evaluating). Although job enrichment may improve the quality of work, employee motivation, and satisfaction, research evidence has been inconclusive as to its usefulness.[39]

JOB CHARACTERISTICS MODEL.   Even though many organizations implemented job enlargement and job enrichment programs and experienced mixed results, neither approach provided an effective framework for managers to design motivating jobs. But the **job characteristics model (JCM)** does.[40] It identifies five core job dimensions, their interrelationships, and their impact on employee productivity, motivation, and satisfaction. These five core job dimensions are:

1. **Skill variety**, the degree to which a job requires a variety of activities so that an employee can use a number of different skills and talents.
2. **Task identity**, the degree to which a job requires completion of a whole and identifiable piece of work.

Let's Get Real

The hardest part of motivating employees is *when an employee is dealing with a situation outside of work.*

3. **Task significance**, the degree to which a job has a substantial impact on the lives or work of other people.
4. **Autonomy**, the degree to which a job provides substantial freedom, independence, and discretion to the individual in scheduling the work and determining the procedures to be used in carrying it out.
5. **Feedback**, the degree to which doing work activities required by a job results in an individual obtaining direct and clear information about the effectiveness of his or her performance.

The JCM is shown in Exhibit 16-6. Notice how the first three dimensions—skill variety, task identity, and task significance—combine to create meaningful work. In other words, if these three characteristics exist in a job, we can predict that the person will view his or her job as being important, valuable, and worthwhile. Notice, too, that jobs that possess autonomy give the jobholder a feeling of personal responsibility for the results and that if a job provides feedback, the employee will know how effectively he or she is performing.

The JCM suggests that employees are likely to be motivated when they *learn* (knowledge of results through feedback) that they *personally* (experienced responsibility through autonomy of work) performed well on tasks that they *care about* (experienced meaningfulness through skill variety, task identity, or task significance).[41] The more a job is designed around these three elements, the greater the employee's motivation, performance, and satisfaction and the lower his or her absenteeism and likelihood of resigning. As the model shows, the links between the job dimensions and the outcomes are moderated by the strength of the individual's growth need (the person's desire for self-esteem and self-actualization). Individuals with a high growth need are more likely to experience the critical psychological states and

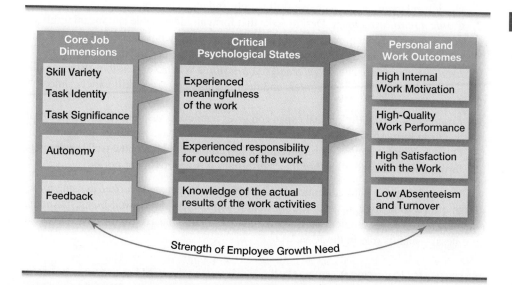

EXHIBIT 16-6

Job Characteristics Model

Source: J. R. Hackman and J. L. Suttle (eds.), *Improving Life at Work* (Glenview, IL: Scott, Foresman, 1977). With permission of authors.

---

job design
The way tasks are combined to form complete jobs

job scope
The number of different tasks required in a job and the frequency with which those tasks are repeated

job enlargement
The horizontal expansion of a job by increasing job scope

job enrichment
The vertical expansion of a job by adding planning and evaluating responsibilities

job depth
The degree of control employees have over their work

job characteristics model (JCM)
A framework for analyzing and designing jobs that identifies five primary core job dimensions, their interrelationships, and their impact on outcomes

skill variety
The degree to which a job requires a variety of activities so that an employee can use a number of different skills and talents

task identity
The degree to which a job requires completion of a whole and identifiable piece of work

task significance
The degree to which a job has a substantial impact on the lives or work of other people

autonomy
The degree to which a job provides substantial freedom, independence, and discretion to the individual in scheduling work and determining the procedures to be used in carrying it out

feedback
The degree to which carrying out work activities required by a job results in the individual's obtaining direct and clear information about his or her performance effectiveness

EXHIBIT 16-7

Guidelines for Job Redesign

Source: J. R. Hackman and J. L. Suttle
(eds.), *Improving Life at Work*
(Glenview, IL: Scott, Foresman, 1977).
With permission of authors.

respond positively when their jobs include the core dimensions than are low-growth individuals. This distinction may explain the mixed results with job enrichment: Individuals with low growth need aren't likely to achieve high performance or satisfaction by having their jobs enriched.

The JCM provides specific guidance to managers for job design. (See Exhibit 16-7.) These suggestions specify the types of changes that are most likely to lead to improvement in the five core job dimensions. You'll notice that two suggestions incorporate job enlargement and job enrichment, although the other suggestions involve more than vertical and horizontal expansion of jobs.

1. *Combine tasks.* Put fragmented tasks back together to form a new, larger work module (job enlargement) to increase skill variety and task identity.
2. *Create natural work units.* Design tasks that form an identifiable and meaningful whole to increase employee "ownership" of the work. Encourage employees to view their work as meaningful and important rather than as irrelevant and boring.
3. *Establish client (external or internal) relationships.* Whenever possible, establish direct relationships between workers and their clients to increase skill variety, autonomy, and feedback.
4. *Expand jobs vertically.* Vertical expansion gives employees responsibilities and controls that were formerly reserved for managers, which can increase employee autonomy.
5. *Open feedback channels.* Direct feedback lets employees know how well they're performing their jobs and whether their performance is improving or not.

Research into the JCM continues. For instance, one recent study looked at using job redesign efforts to change job characteristics and improve employee well-being.[42] Another study examined psychological ownership—that is, a personal feeling of "mine-ness" or "our-ness"—and its role in the JCM.[43]

REDESIGNING JOB DESIGN APPROACHES.[44] Although the JCM has proven to be useful, it may not be totally appropriate for today's jobs that are more service and knowledge-oriented. The nature of these jobs has also changed the tasks that employees do in those jobs. Two emerging viewpoints on job design are causing a rethink of the JCM and other standard approaches. Let's take a look at each perspective.

The first perspective, the **relational perspective of work design**, focuses on how people's tasks and jobs are increasingly based on social relationships. In jobs today, employees have more interactions and interdependence with coworkers and others both inside and outside the organization. In doing their job, employees rely more and more on those around them for information, advice, and assistance. So what does this mean for designing motivating jobs? It means that managers need to look at important components of those employee relationships such as access to and level of social support in an organization, types of interactions outside an organization, amount of task interdependence, and interpersonal feedback.

The second perspective, the **proactive perspective of work design**, says that employees are taking the initiative to change how their work is performed. They're much

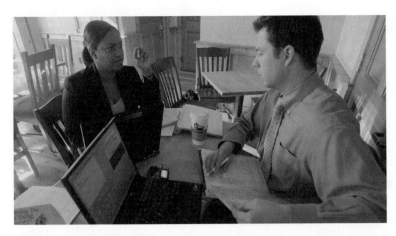

The Pfizer pharmaceutical sales reps shown here use a coffee shop with Internet access as their office to work on scheduling visits with physicians. As more and more physicians are relying on the Internet to find medical information, sales reps are taking a proactive approach to how their work is performed. They are enhancing their traditional face-to-face office meetings with doctors to include teleconferences, webcasts, and social media. By using digital technology, sales reps are able to provide doctors with the accurate, relevant, and timely information they need to make educated decisions that will best help their patients.

more involved in decisions and actions that affect their work. Important job design factors according to this perspective include autonomy (which *is* part of the JCM), amount of ambiguity and accountability, job complexity, level of stressors, and social or relationship context. Each of these has been shown to influence employee proactive behavior.

One stream of research that's relevant to proactive work design is that on **high-involvement work practices**, which are work practices designed to elicit greater input or involvement from workers.[45] The level of employee proactivity is believed to increase as employees become more involved in decisions that affect their work. Another term for this approach, which we discussed in an earlier chapter, is employee empowerment.

Equity Theory

Do you ever wonder what kind of grade the person sitting next to you in class makes on a test or on a major class assignment? Most of us do! Being human, we tend to compare ourselves with others. If someone offered you $50,000 a year on your first job after graduating from college, you'd probably jump at the offer and report to work enthusiastic, ready to tackle whatever needed to be done, and certainly satisfied with your pay. How would you react, though, if you found out a month into the job that a coworker—another recent graduate, your age, with comparable grades from a comparable school, and with comparable work experience—was getting $55,000 a year? You'd probably be upset! Even though in absolute terms, $50,000 is a lot of money for a new graduate to make (and you know it!), that suddenly isn't the issue. Now you see the issue as what you believe is *fair*—what is *equitable*. The term *equity* is related to the concept of fairness and equitable treatment compared with others who behave in similar ways. Evidence indicates that employees compare themselves to others and that inequities influence how much effort employees exert.[46]

Equity theory, developed by J. Stacey Adams, proposes that employees compare what they get from a job (outcomes) in relation to what they put into it (inputs), and then they compare their inputs–outcomes ratio with the inputs–outcomes ratios of relevant others (Exhibit 16-8). If an employee perceives her ratio to be equitable in comparison to those of relevant others, there's no problem. However, if the ratio is inequitable, she views herself as underrewarded or overrewarded. When inequities occur, employees attempt to do something about it.[47] The result might be lower or higher productivity, improved or reduced quality of output, increased absenteeism, or voluntary resignation.

relational perspective of work design
An approach to job design that focuses on how people's tasks and jobs are increasingly based on social relationships

proactive perspective of work design
An approach to job design in which employees take the initiative to change how their work is performed

high-involvement work practices
Work practices designed to elicit greater input or involvement from workers

equity theory
The theory that an employee compares his or her job's input-outcomes ratio with that of relevant others and then corrects any inequity

	Perceived Ratio Comparison[a]	Employee's Assessment
EXHIBIT 16-8 **Equity Theory**	$\dfrac{\text{Outcomes A}}{\text{Inputs A}} < \dfrac{\text{Outcomes B}}{\text{Inputs B}}$	Inequity (underrewarded)
	$\dfrac{\text{Outcomes A}}{\text{Inputs A}} = \dfrac{\text{Outcomes B}}{\text{Inputs B}}$	Equity
	$\dfrac{\text{Outcomes A}}{\text{Inputs A}} > \dfrac{\text{Outcomes B}}{\text{Inputs B}}$	Inequity (overrewarded)

[a]Person A is the employee, and person B is a relevant other or referent.

The **referent**—the other persons, systems, or selves individuals compare themselves against in order to assess equity—is an important variable in equity theory.[48] Each of the three referent categories is important. The "persons" category includes other individuals with similar jobs in the same organization but also includes friends, neighbors, or professional associates. Based on what they hear at work or read about in newspapers or trade journals, employees compare their pay with that of others. The "system" category includes organizational pay policies, procedures, and allocation. The "self" category refers to inputs–outcomes ratios that are unique to the individual. It reflects past personal experiences and contacts and is influenced by criteria such as past jobs or family commitments.

Originally, equity theory focused on **distributive justice**, which is the perceived fairness of the amount and allocation of rewards among individuals. More recent research has focused on looking at issues of **procedural justice**, which is the perceived fairness of the process used to determine the distribution of rewards. This research shows that distributive justice has a greater influence on employee satisfaction than procedural justice, while procedural justice tends to affect an employee's organizational commitment, trust in his or her boss, and intention to quit.[49] What are the implications for managers? They should consider openly sharing information on how allocation decisions are made, follow consistent and unbiased procedures, and engage in similar practices to increase the perception of procedural justice. By increasing the perception of procedural justice, employees are likely to view their bosses and the organization as positive even if they're dissatisfied with pay, promotions, and other personal outcomes.

Expectancy Theory

The most comprehensive explanation of how employees are motivated is Victor Vroom's **expectancy theory**.[50] Although the theory has its critics,[51] most research evidence supports it.[52]

Expectancy theory states that an individual tends to act in a certain way based on the expectation that the act will be followed by a given outcome and on the attractiveness of that outcome to the individual. It includes three variables or relationships (see Exhibit 16-9):

1. *Expectancy* or *effort–performance linkage* is the probability perceived by the individual that exerting a given amount of effort will lead to a certain level of performance.

EXHIBIT 16-9

Expectancy Model

A = Effort–performance linkage
B = Performance–reward linkage
C = Attractiveness of reward

2. *Instrumentality* or *performance–reward linkage* is the degree to which the individual believes that performing at a particular level is instrumental in attaining the desired outcome.

3. *Valence* or *attractiveness of reward* is the importance that the individual places on the potential outcome or reward that can be achieved on the job. Valence considers both the goals and needs of the individual.

This explanation of motivation might sound complicated, but it really isn't. It can be summed up in the questions: How hard do I have to work to achieve a certain level of performance, and can I actually achieve that level? What reward will performing at that level of performance get me? How attractive is the reward to me, and does it help me achieve my own personal goals? Whether you are motivated to put forth effort (that is, to work hard) at any given time depends on your goals and your perception of whether a certain level of performance is necessary to attain those goals. Let's look at an example. Your second author had a student many years ago who went to work for IBM as a sales rep. Her favorite work "reward" was having an IBM corporate jet fly into Springfield, Missouri, to pick up her best customers and her and take them for a weekend of golfing at some fun location. But to get that particular "reward," she had to achieve at a certain level of performance, which involved exceeding her sales goals by a specified percentage. How hard she was willing to work (that is, how motivated she was to put forth effort) was dependent on the level of performance that had to be met and the likelihood that if she achieved at that level of performance she would receive that reward. Because she "valued" that reward, she always worked hard to exceed her sales goals. And the performance–reward linkage was clear because her hard work and performance achievements were always rewarded by the company with the reward she valued (access to the corporate jet).

The key to expectancy theory is understanding an individual's goal and the linkage between effort and performance, between performance and rewards, and finally, between rewards and individual goal satisfaction. It emphasizes payoffs, or rewards. As a result, we have to believe that the rewards an organization is offering align with what the individual wants. Expectancy theory recognizes that no universal principle explains what motivates individuals and thus stresses that managers understand why employees view certain outcomes as attractive or unattractive. After all, we want to reward individuals with those things they value positively. Also, expectancy theory emphasizes expected behaviors. Do employees know what is expected of them and how they'll be evaluated? Finally, the theory is concerned with perceptions. Reality is irrelevant. An individual's own perceptions of performance, reward, and goal outcomes, not the outcomes themselves, will determine his or her motivation (level of effort).

Integrating Contemporary Theories of Motivation

Many of the ideas underlying the contemporary motivation theories are complementary, and you'll understand better how to motivate people if you see how the theories fit together.[53] Exhibit 16-10 presents a model that integrates much of what we know about motivation. Its basic foundation is the expectancy model. Let's work through the model, starting on the left.

The individual effort box has an arrow leading into it. This arrow flows from the individual's goals. Consistent with goal-setting theory, this goals–effort link is meant to illustrate that goals direct behavior. Expectancy theory predicts that an employee will exert a high level of effort if he or she perceives a strong relationship between effort and performance, performance and rewards, and rewards and satisfaction of personal goals. Each of these relationships is, in turn, influenced by certain factors. You can see from the model that the level of individual performance is determined not only by the level of individual effort but also by the

referents
The persons, systems, or selves against which individuals compare themselves to assess equity

distributive justice
Perceived fairness of the amount and allocation of rewards among individuals

procedural justice
Perceived fairness of the process used to determine the distribution of rewards

expectancy theory
The theory that an individual tends to act in a certain way based on the expectation that the act will be followed by a given outcome and on the attractiveness of that outcome to the individual

EXHIBIT 16-10
Integrating Contemporary
Theories of Motivation

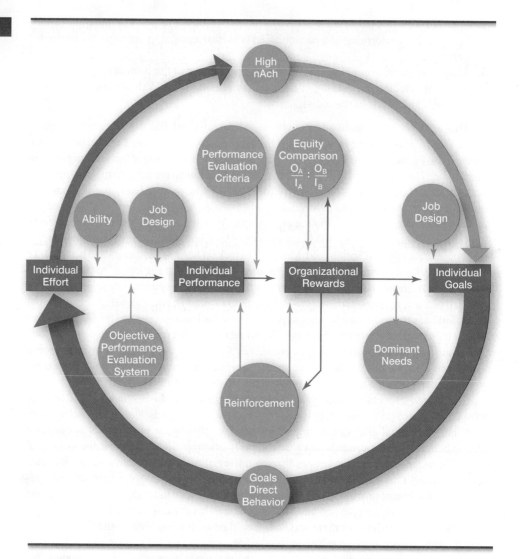

individual's ability to perform and by whether the organization has a fair and objective performance evaluation system. The performance–reward relationship will be strong if the individual perceives that performance (rather than seniority, personal favorites, or some other criterion) is what is rewarded. The final link in expectancy theory is the rewards–goal relationship. The traditional need theories come into play at this point. Motivation would be high to the degree that the rewards an individual received for his or her high performance satisfied the dominant needs consistent with his or her individual goals.

A closer look at the model also shows that it considers the achievement–need, reinforcement, equity, and JCM theories. The high achiever isn't motivated by the organization's assessment of his or her performance or organizational rewards; hence the jump from effort to individual goals for those with a high nAch. Remember that high achievers are internally driven as long as the jobs they're doing provide them with personal responsibility, feedback, and moderate risks. They're not concerned with the effort–performance, performance–reward, or rewards–goals linkages.

Reinforcement theory is seen in the model by recognizing that the organization's rewards reinforce the individual's performance. If managers have designed a reward system that is seen by employees as "paying off" for good performance, the rewards will reinforce and encourage continued good performance. Rewards also play a key part in equity theory. Individuals will compare the rewards (outcomes) they have received from the inputs or efforts they made with the inputs–outcomes ratio of relevant others. If inequities exist, the effort expended may be influenced.

Finally, the JCM is seen in this integrative model. Task characteristics (job design) influence job motivation at two places. First, jobs that are designed around the five job dimensions are likely to lead to higher actual job performance because the individual's motivation will be stimulated by the job itself—that is, they will increase the linkage between effort and performance. Second, jobs that are designed around the five job dimensions also increase an employee's control over key elements in his or her work. Therefore, jobs that offer autonomy, feedback, and similar task characteristics help to satisfy the individual goals of employees who desire greater control over their work.

Current Issues in Motivation

After Vincent Stevens's church ran an experiment in which 10 members were each given $100 to help their communities, some used it as seed capital to raise thousands more. As a partner in a Bellevue, Washington, accounting firm, he wondered what would happen if he tried the same thing with his employees. To find out, his company launched Caring, Serving, and Giving, a program that lets employees apply for grants of up to $500 to fund community service projects. By empowering employees to use the seed money as they saw fit, they were motivated to make the best use of it. Another benefit that was realized was a boost in employee morale.[54]

Understanding and predicting employee motivation is one of the most popular areas in management research. We've introduced you to several motivation theories. However, even the contemporary theories of employee motivation are influenced by some significant workplace issues—motivating in tough economic circumstances, managing cross-cultural challenges, motivating unique groups of workers, and designing appropriate rewards programs.

16.4

LEARNING OUTCOME
Discuss current issues in motivation.

Motivating in Tough Economic Circumstances

Zappos, the quirky Las Vegas–based online shoe retailer (now a part of Amazon.com), has always had a reputation for being a fun place to work.[55] However, during the economic recession, it, like many companies, had to cut staff—124 employees in total. CEO Tony Hsieh wanted to get out the news fast to lessen the stress for his employees. So he announced the layoff in an e-mail, on his blog, and on his Twitter account. Although some might think these are terrible ways to communicate that kind of news, most employees thanked him for being so open and so honest. The company also took good care of those being laid off. Laid-off employees with less than two years of service were paid through the end of the year. Longer-tenured employees got four weeks for every year of service. All got six months of continued paid health coverage and, at the request of the employees, got to keep their 40 percent merchandise discount through the Christmas season. Zappos had always been a model of how to nurture employees in good times, now it showed how to treat employees in bad times.

The economic recession of the last few years was difficult for many organizations, especially when it came to their employees. Layoffs, tight budgets, minimal or no pay raises, benefit cuts, no bonuses, long hours doing the work of those who had been laid off—this was the reality that many employees faced. As conditions deteriorated, employee confidence, optimism, and job engagement plummeted as well. As you can imagine, it wasn't an easy thing for managers to keep employees motivated under such challenging circumstances.

Managers came to realize that in an uncertain economy, they had to be creative in keeping their employees' efforts energized, directed, and sustained toward achieving goals. They were forced to look at ways to motivate employees that didn't involve money or that were relatively inexpensive.[56] So they relied on actions such as holding meetings with employees to keep the lines of communication open and to get their input on issues; establishing a common goal, such as maintaining excellent customer service, to keep everyone focused; creating a community feel so employees could see that managers cared about them and their work; and giving employees opportunities to continue to learn and grow. And, of course, an encouraging word always went a long way.

Managing Cross-Cultural Motivational Challenges

Scores of employees at Denmark's largest brewer, Carlsberg A/S, walked off their jobs in protest after the company tightened rules on workplace drinking and removed beer coolers from work sites.[57] Now that's a motivational challenge you don't often see in U.S. workplaces!

In an uncertain economy and with less money to spend on raises and health benefits, companies are setting up vegetable and herb gardens as a creative, easy, and relatively inexpensive way to motivate employees, improve their health, and help them save money on their food bills. In company gardens, employees can work, take home what they harvest, and share extra produce with their local food bank. Some firms use their gardens for team-building exercises such as constructing tomato trellises together, and others incorporate them into their health and wellness programs. Shown here are employees of Harvard Pilgrim Health Care planting chard starts in raised beds at their company garden.

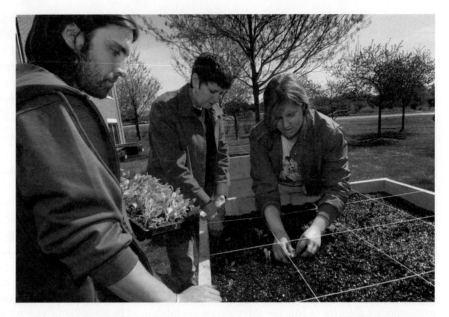

In today's global business environment, managers can't automatically assume that motivational programs that work in one geographic location are going to work in others. Most current motivation theories were developed in the United States by Americans and about Americans.[58] Maybe the most blatant pro-American characteristic in these theories is the strong emphasis on individualism and achievement. For instance, both goal-setting and expectancy theories emphasize goal accomplishment as well as rational and individual thought. Let's look at the motivation theories to see their level of cross-cultural transferability.

Maslow's need hierarchy argues that people start at the physiological level and then move progressively up the hierarchy in order. This hierarchy, if it has any application at all, aligns with American culture. In countries like Japan, Greece, and Mexico, where uncertainty avoidance characteristics are strong, security needs would be the foundational layer of the need hierarchy. Countries that score high on nurturing characteristics—Denmark, Sweden, Norway, the Netherlands, and Finland—would have social needs as their foundational level.[59] We would predict, for instance, that group work will be more motivating when the country's culture scores high on the nurturing criterion.

Another motivation concept that clearly has an American bias is the achievement need. The view that a high achievement need acts as an internal motivator presupposes two cultural characteristics—a willingness to accept a moderate degree of risk (which excludes countries with strong uncertainty avoidance characteristics) and a concern with performance (which applies almost singularly to countries with strong achievement characteristics). This combination is found in Anglo-American countries such as the United States, Canada, and Great Britain.[60] On the other hand, these characteristics are relatively absent in countries such as Chile and Portugal.

Equity theory has a relatively strong following in the United States, which is not surprising given that U.S.-style reward systems are based on the assumption that workers are highly sensitive to equity in reward allocations. In the United States, equity is meant to closely link pay to performance. However, recent evidence suggests that in collectivist cultures, especially in the former socialist countries of Central and Eastern Europe, employees expect rewards to reflect their individual needs as well as their performance.[61] Moreover, consistent with a legacy of communism and centrally planned economies, employees exhibited a greater "entitlement" attitude—that is, they expected outcomes to be greater than their inputs.[62] These findings suggest that U.S.-style pay practices may need to be modified in some countries in order to be perceived as fair by employees.

Another research study of more than 50,000 employees around the world examined two cultural characteristics from the GLOBE framework—individualism and masculinity—(see Chapter 3 for a discussion of these characteristics) in relation to motivation.[63] The researchers found that in individualistic cultures such as the United States and Canada, individual initiative, individual freedom, and individual achievement are highly valued. In more collective cultures such as Iran, Peru, and China, however, employees may be less interested in receiving individual praise but place a greater emphasis on harmony, belonging, and consensus. They also found that in masculine (achievement/assertive) cultures such as Japan and Slovakia, the focus is on material success. Those work environments are designed to push employees hard and then reward top performers with high earnings. However, in more feminine (nurturing) cultures such as Sweden and the Netherlands, smaller wage gaps among employees are common, and employees are likely to have extensive quality-of-life benefits.

Despite these cross-cultural differences in motivation, some cross-cultural consistencies are evident. For instance, the desire for interesting work seems important to almost all workers, regardless of their national culture. In a study of seven countries, employees in Belgium, Britain, Israel, and the United States ranked "interesting work" number one among 11 work goals. It was ranked either second or third in Japan, the Netherlands, and Germany.[64] Similarly, in a study comparing job-preference outcomes among graduate students in the United States, Canada, Australia, and Singapore, growth, achievement, and responsibility were rated the top three and had identical rankings.[65] Both studies suggest some universality to the importance of intrinsic factors identified by Herzberg in his two-factor theory. Another recent study examining workplace motivation trends in Japan also seems to indicate that Herzberg's model is applicable to Japanese employees.[66]

Motivating Unique Groups of Workers

At Deloitte, employees are allowed to "dial up" or "dial down" their job responsibilities to fit their personal and professional goals.[67] The company's program called Mass Career Customization has been a huge hit with its employees! In the first 12 months after it was rolled out, employee satisfaction with "overall career/life fit" rose by 25 percent. Also, the number of high-performing employees staying with Deloitte increased.

Motivating employees has never been easy! Employees come into organizations with different needs, personalities, skills, abilities, interests, and aptitudes. They have different expectations of their employers and different views of what they think their employer has a right to expect of them. And they vary widely in what they want from their jobs. For instance, some employees get more satisfaction out of their personal interests and pursuits and only want a weekly paycheck—nothing more. They're not interested in making their work more challenging or interesting or in "winning" performance contests. Others derive a great deal of satisfaction in their jobs and are motivated to exert high levels of effort. Given these differences, how can managers do an effective job of motivating the unique groups of employees found in today's workforce? One thing is to understand the motivational requirements of these groups including diverse employees, professionals, contingent workers, and low-skilled minimum-wage employees.

FUTURE VISION ⏐ **The Working World in 2020**

Individualized Rewards

Organizations have historically assumed that "one size fits all" when it comes to allocating rewards. Managers typically assumed that everyone wants more money and more vacation time. But as organizations become less bureaucratic and more capable of differentiating rewards, managers will be encouraged to differentiate rewards among employees as well as for individual employees over time.

Organizations control a vast number of potential rewards that employees might find appealing. A partial list would include increased base pay, bonuses, shortened workweeks, extended vacations, paid sabbaticals, flexible work hours, part-time employment, guaranteed job security, increased pension contributions, college tuition reimbursement, personal days off, help in purchasing a home, recognition awards, paid club memberships, and work-from-home options. In the future, most organizations will structure individual reward packages in ways that will maximize employee motivation.

MOTIVATING A DIVERSE WORKFORCE.   To maximize motivation among today's workforce, managers need to think in terms of *flexibility*. For instance, studies tell us that men place more importance on having autonomy in their jobs than do women. In contrast, the opportunity to learn, convenient and flexible work hours, and good interpersonal relations are more important to women.[68] Having the opportunity to be independent and to be exposed to different experiences is important to Gen Y employees whereas older workers may be more interested in highly structured work opportunities.[69] Managers need to recognize that what motivates a single mother with two dependent children who's working full time to support her family may be very different from the needs of a single part-time employee or an older employee who is working only to supplement his or her retirement income. A diverse array of rewards is needed to motivate employees with such diverse needs. Many of the work–life balance programs (see Chapter 12) that organizations have implemented are a response to the varied needs of a diverse workforce. In addition, many organizations have developed flexible work arrangements—such as compressed workweeks, flextime, and job sharing, which we discussed in Chapter 11—that recognize different needs. Another job alternative that we also discussed earlier is telecommuting. However, keep in mind that not all employees embrace the idea of telecommuting. Some workers relish the informal interactions at work that satisfy their social needs as well as being a source of new ideas.

Do flexible work arrangements motivate employees? Although such arrangements might seem highly motivational, both positive and negative relationships have been found. For instance, a recent study that looked at the impact of telecommuting on job satisfaction found that job satisfaction initially increased as the extent of telecommuting increased, but as the number of hours spent telecommuting increased, job satisfaction started to level off, decreased slightly, and then stabilized.[70]

MOTIVATING PROFESSIONALS.   In contrast to a generation ago, the typical employee today is more likely to be a professional with a college degree than a blue-collar factory worker. What special concerns should managers be aware of when trying to motivate a team of engineers at Intel's India Development Center, software designers at SAS Institute in North Carolina, or a group of consultants at Accenture in Singapore?

Professionals are different from nonprofessionals.[71] They have a strong and long-term commitment to their field of expertise. To keep current in their field, they need to regularly update their knowledge, and because of their commitment to their profession they rarely define their workweek as 8 A.M. to 5 P.M. five days a week.

What motivates professionals? Money and promotions typically are low on their priority list. Why? They tend to be well paid and enjoy what they do. In contrast, job challenge tends to be ranked high. They like to tackle problems and find solutions. Their chief reward is the work itself. Professionals also value support. They want others to think that what they are working on is important. That may be true for all employees, but professionals tend to be focused on their work as their central life interest, whereas nonprofessionals typically have other interests outside of work that can compensate for needs not met on the job.

MOTIVATING CONTINGENT WORKERS.   We discussed in Chapter 11 the increased number of contingent workers employed by organizations. There's no simple solution for motivating these employees. For that small set of individuals who prefer the freedom of their temporary status, the lack of stability may not be an issue. In addition, temporariness might be preferred by highly compensated physicians, engineers, accountants, or financial planners who don't want the demands of a full-time job. But these individuals are the exceptions. For the most part, temporary employees are not temporary by choice.

What will motivate involuntarily temporary employees? An obvious answer is the opportunity to become a permanent employee. In cases in which permanent employees are selected from a pool of temps, the temps will often work hard in hopes of becoming permanent. A less obvious answer is the opportunity for training. The ability of a temporary employee to find a new job is largely dependent on his or her skills. If an employee sees that the job he or she is doing can help develop marketable skills, then motivation is increased. From an equity standpoint, when temps work alongside permanent employees who earn more and get benefits too for doing the same job, the performance of temps is likely to suffer. Separating such employees or perhaps minimizing interdependence between them might help managers counteract potential problems.[72]

MOTIVATING LOW-SKILLED, MINIMUM-WAGE EMPLOYEES.   Suppose that in your first managerial position after graduating, you're responsible for managing a work group of low-skilled, minimum-wage employees. Offering more pay to these employees for high levels of performance is out of the question: your company just can't afford it. In addition, these employees have limited education and skills. What are your motivational options at this point?

One trap we often fall into is thinking that people are motivated only by money. Although money is important as a motivator, it's not the only reward that people seek and that managers can use. In motivating minimum-wage employees, managers might look at employee recognition programs. Many managers also recognize the power of praise although these "pats on the back" must be sincere and given for the right reasons.

Let's Get Real

F2F

My biggest motivation challenge is
motivating employees who do not want to be motivated.

Designing Appropriate Rewards Programs

Blue Cross of California, one of the nation's largest health insurers, pays bonuses to doctors serving its health maintenance organization members based on patient satisfaction and other quality standards. FedEx's drivers are motivated by a pay system that rewards them for timeliness and how much they deliver.[73] Employee rewards programs play a powerful role in motivating appropriate employee behavior.

OPEN-BOOK MANAGEMENT.   Within 24 hours after managers of the Heavy Duty Division of Springfield Remanufacturing Company (SRC) gather to discuss a multi-page financial document, every plant employee will have seen the same information. If the employees can meet shipment goals, they'll all share in a large year-end bonus.[74] Many organizations of various sizes involve their employees in workplace decisions by opening up the financial statements (the "books"). They share that information so that employees will be motivated to make better decisions about their work and better able to understand the implications of what they do, how they do it, and the ultimate impact on the bottom line. This approach is called **open-book management** and many organizations are using it.[75] For instance, at Parrish Medical Center in Titusville, Florida, CEO George Mikitarian was struggling with the prospect of massive layoffs, facilities closing, and profits declining. So he turned to "town hall meetings" in which employees received updates on the financial condition of the hospital. He also told his employees that it would require their commitment to help find ways to reduce expenses and cut costs.[76]

The goal of open-book management is to get employees to think like an owner by seeing the impact their decisions have on financial results. Since many employees don't have the knowledge or background to understand the financials, they have to be taught how to read and understand the organization's financial statements. Once employees have this knowledge, however, managers need to regularly share the numbers with them. By sharing this information, employees begin to see the link between their efforts, level of performance, and operational results.

EMPLOYEE RECOGNITION PROGRAMS.   **Employee recognition programs** consist of personal attention and expressing interest, approval, and appreciation for a job well done.[78] They can take numerous forms. For instance, Kelly Services introduced a new version of its points-based incentive system to better promote productivity and retention among its

by the numbers[77]

54 percent of employees say that their colleagues are the ones who appreciate them the most at work.

70 percent of employees say that their relationship with their manager is important to their level of engagement.

47 percent of employees say that their employer doesn't provide any forms of motivation.

50 percent of employees say that the perk they'd most like from their employer is free soda or water.

42 percent of employees say that verbal recognition is their most preferred form of recognition at work.

27 percent of employees say that the work itself is what makes going to work worthwhile.

51 percent of employees say they're underpaid for the work they do.

open-book management
A motivational approach in which an organization's financial statements (the "books") are shared with all employees

employee recognition programs
Personal attention and expressing interest, approval, and appreciation for a job well done

employees. The program, called Kelly Kudos, gives employees more choices of awards and allows them to accumulate points over a longer time period. It's working. Participants generate three times more revenue and hours than employees not receiving points do.[79] Nichols Foods, a British manufacturer, has a comprehensive recognition program. The main hallway in the production department is hung with "bragging boards" on which the accomplishments of employee teams are noted. Monthly awards are presented to people who have been nominated by peers for extraordinary effort on the job. And monthly award winners are eligible for further recognition at an off-site meeting for all employees.[80] Most managers, however, use a far more informal approach. For example, when Julia Stewart, currently the president and CEO of IHOP International, was president of Applebee's Restaurants, she would frequently leave sealed notes on the chairs of employees after everyone had gone home.[81] These notes explained how important Stewart thought the person's work was or how much she appreciated the completion of a project. Stewart also relied heavily on voice mail messages left after office hours to tell employees how appreciative she was for a job well done. And recognition doesn't have to come only from managers. Some 35 percent of companies encourage coworkers to recognize peers for outstanding work efforts.[82] For instance, managers at Yum Brands Inc. (the Kentucky-based parent of food chains Taco Bell, KFC, and Pizza Hut) were looking for ways to reduce employee turnover. They found a successful customer-service program involving peer recognition at KFC restaurants in Australia. Workers there spontaneously rewarded fellow workers with "Champs cards, an acronym for attributes such as cleanliness, hospitality, and accuracy." Yum implemented the program in other restaurants around the world, and credits the peer recognition with reducing hourly employee turnover from 181 percent to 109 percent.[83]

A recent survey of organizations found that 84 percent had some type of program to recognize worker achievements.[84] And do employees think these programs are important? You bet! In a survey conducted a few years ago, a wide range of employees was asked what they considered the most powerful workplace motivator. Their response? Recognition, recognition, and more recognition![85]

Consistent with reinforcement theory, rewarding a behavior with recognition immediately following that behavior is likely to encourage its repetition. And recognition can take many forms. You can personally congratulate an employee in private for a good job. You can send a handwritten note or e-mail message acknowledging something positive that the employee has done. For employees with a strong need for social acceptance, you can publicly recognize accomplishments. To enhance group cohesiveness and motivation, you can celebrate team successes. For instance, you can do something as simple as throw a pizza party to celebrate a team's accomplishments. During the economic recession, managers got quite creative in how they showed employees they were appreciated.[86] For instance, employees at one company got to take home fresh vegetables from the company vegetable garden. In others, managers treated employees who really put forth efforts on a project to a special meal or movie tickets. Also, managers can show employees that no matter what his or her role may be, that their contributions matter. Some of these things may seem simple, but they can go a long way in showing employees they're valued.

PAY-FOR-PERFORMANCE. Here's a survey statistic that may surprise you: 40 percent of employees see no clear link between performance and pay.[87] So what are the companies where these employees work paying for? They're obviously not clearly communicating performance expectations.[88] **Pay-for-performance programs** are variable compensation plans that pay employees on the basis of some performance measure.[89] Piece-rate pay plans, wage incentive plans, profit-sharing, and lump-sum bonuses are examples. What differentiates these forms of pay from more traditional compensation plans is that instead of paying a person for time on the job, pay is adjusted to reflect some performance measure. These

Let's Get Real

F | 2 | F

Guidelines for being a good motivator include:
- Lead by example.
- Have a positive attitude.
- Be able to recognize positive behaviors.
- Allow your team to be a part of the planning and problem-solving process.

pay-for-performance programs
Variable compensation plans that pay employees on the basis of some performance measure

performance measures might include such things as individual productivity, team or work group productivity, departmental productivity, or the overall organization's profit performance.

Pay-for-performance is probably most compatible with expectancy theory. Individuals should perceive a strong relationship between their performance and the rewards they receive for motivation to be maximized. If rewards are allocated only on nonperformance factors—such as seniority, job title, or across-the-board pay raises—then employees are likely to reduce their efforts. From a motivation perspective, making some or all an employee's pay conditional on some performance measure focuses his or her attention and effort toward that measure, then reinforces the continuation of the effort with a reward. If the employee's team's or organization's performance declines, so does the reward. Thus, there's an incentive to keep efforts and motivation strong.

Pay-for-performance programs are popular. Some 80 percent of large U.S. companies have some form of variable pay plan.[90] These types of pay plans have also been tried in other countries such as Canada and Japan. About 30 percent of Canadian companies and 22 percent of Japanese companies have company-wide pay-for-performance plans.[91]

Do pay-for-performance programs work? For the most part, studies seem to indicate that they do. For instance, one study found that companies that used pay-for-performance programs performed better financially than those that did not.[92] Another study showed that pay-for-performance programs with outcome-based incentives had a positive impact on sales, customer satisfaction, and profits.[93] If an organization uses work teams, managers should consider group-based performance incentives that will reinforce team effort and commitment. But whether these programs are individual based or team based, managers need to ensure that they're specific about the relationship between an individual's pay and his or her expected level of appropriate performance. Employees must clearly understand exactly how performance—theirs and the organization's—translates into dollars on their paychecks.[94]

Let's Get Real:
My Response *to A Manager's Dilemma, page 430*

What Would You Do?

I would determine what motivates the employees to perform well by doing a survey. Based upon the survey results, I would create a contest with rewards that motivate the employees. I would also focus on rewarding great behavior. Everyone deserves to be rewarded for their hard work and effort toward achieving the goal. When companies award their employees, it proves to the employees that they are appreciated. Therefore, the employees will work harder and do better. If you take care of your team, the team will take care of you.

Aisha Warren
Retail Store Manager
Dots, LLC
Warren, MI

CHAPTER SUMMARY
by Learning Outcomes

LEARNING OUTCOME **Define** motivation.

Motivation is the process by which a person's efforts are energized, directed, and sustained toward attaining a goal.

The *energy* element is a measure of intensity, drive, or vigor. The high level of effort needs to be *directed* in ways that help the organization achieve its goals. Employees must *persist* in putting forth effort to achieve those goals.

LEARNING OUTCOME **Compare** and contrast early theories of motivation.

In Maslow's hierarchy, individuals move up the hierarchy of five needs (physiological, safety, social, esteem, and self-actualization) as needs are substantially satisfied. A need that's substantially satisfied no longer motivates.

A Theory X manager believes that people don't like to work or won't seek out responsibility so they have to be threatened and coerced to work. A Theory Y manager assumes that people like to work and seek out responsibility, so they will exercise self-motivation and self-direction.

Herzberg's theory proposed that intrinsic factors associated with job satisfaction were what motivated people. Extrinsic factors associated with job dissatisfaction simply kept people from being dissatisfied.

Three-needs theory proposed three acquired needs that are major motives in work: need for achievement, need for affiliation, and need for power.

intrinsic — *satisfy*
Extrinsic — *Dissatisfy*

LEARNING OUTCOME **Compare** and contrast contemporary theories of motivation.

Goal-setting theory says that specific goals increase performance, and difficult goals, when accepted, result in higher performance than do easy goals. Important points in goal-setting theory include intention to work toward a goal as a major source of job motivation; specific hard goals that produce higher levels of output than generalized goals; participation in setting goals as preferable to assigning goals, but not always; feedback that guides and motivates behavior, especially self-generated feedback; and contingencies that affect goal setting—goal commitment, self-efficacy, and national culture. Reinforcement theory says that behavior is a function of its consequences. To motivate, use positive reinforcers to reinforce desirable behaviors. Ignore undesirable behavior rather than punishing it.

Job enlargement involves horizontally expanding job scope by adding more tasks or increasing how many times the tasks are done. Job enrichment vertically expands job depth by giving employees more control over their work. The job characteristics model says five core job dimensions (skill variety, task identity, task significance, autonomy, and feedback) are used to design motivating jobs. Another job design approach proposed looking at relational aspects and proactive aspects of jobs.

Equity theory focuses on how employees compare their inputs–outcomes ratios to relevant others' ratios. A perception of inequity will cause an employee to do something about it. Procedural justice has a greater influence on employee satisfaction than does distributive justice.

Expectancy theory says that an individual tends to act in a certain way based on the expectation that the act will be followed by a desired outcome. Expectancy is the effort–performance linkage (how much effort do I need to exert to achieve a certain level of performance); instrumentality is the performance–reward linkage (achieving at a certain level of performance will get me a specific reward); and valence is the attractiveness of the reward (Is it the reward that I want?).

Discuss current issues in motivation.

Managers must cope with four current motivation issues: motivating in tough economic circumstances, managing cross-cultural challenges, motivating unique groups of workers, and designing appropriate rewards programs.

During tough economic conditions, managers must look for creative ways to keep employees' efforts energized, directed, and sustained toward achieving goals.

Most motivational theories were developed in the United States and have a North American bias. Some theories (Maslow's need hierarchy, achievement need, and equity theory) don't work well for other cultures. However, the desire for interesting work seems important to all workers and Herzberg's motivator (intrinsic) factors may be universal.

Managers face challenges in motivating unique groups of workers. A diverse workforce is looking for flexibility. Professionals want job challenge and support, and are motivated by the work itself. Contingent workers want the opportunity to become permanent or to receive skills training. Recognition programs and sincere appreciation for work done can be used to motivate low-skilled, minimum-wage workers.

Open-book management is when financial statements (the books) are shared with employees who have been taught what they mean. Employee recognition programs consist of personal attention, approval, and appreciation for a job well done. Pay-for-performance programs are variable compensation plans that pay employees on the basis of some performance measure.

 PEARSON mymanagementlab To check your understanding of learning outcomes 16.1 – 16.4 go to **mymanagementlab.com** and try the chapter questions.

REVIEW AND DISCUSSION QUESTIONS

1. What is motivation? Explain the three key elements of motivation.

2. Describe each of the four early theories of motivation.

3. How do goal-setting, reinforcement, and equity theories explain employee motivation?

4. What are the different job design approaches to motivation?

5. Explain the three key linkages in expectancy theory and their role in motivation.

6. What economic and cross-cultural challenges do managers face when motivating employees?

7. What challenges do managers face in motivating today's workforce?

8. Describe open book management, employee recognition, and pay-for-performance programs.

9. Most of us have to work for a living, and a job is a central part of our lives. So why do managers have to worry so much about employee motivation issues?

10. Can an individual be too motivated? Discuss.

PREPARING FOR: My Career

ETHICS DILEMMA

A cashier for a large chain bookstore in Manhattan is tired of the elaborate scripts she's required to recite during every transaction.[95] "It's tedious to blurt out those little phrases and customers just look away." And you've probably heard these scripted appeals if you've gone through a fast-food drive-through—would you like fries or a drink with that or

would you like to make that a large? Retail workers today "get more micromanaging than Noah got from God" . . . all in an attempt to boost sales. What do you think of these techniques? Are they just simply annoying or do they contain some element of ethics? What ethical issues do you see in these attempts at efficiency and productivity? How could organizations ensure that such activities aren't ethically questionable?

SKILLS EXERCISE
Developing Your
Motivating Employees Skill

About the Skill

Because a simple, all-encompassing set of motivational guidelines is not available, the following suggestions draw on the essence of what we know about motivating employees.

Steps in Practicing the Skill

1. **Recognize individual differences.** Almost every contemporary motivation theory recognizes that employees are not homogeneous. They have different needs. They also differ in terms of attitudes, personality, and other important individual variables.

2. **Match people to jobs.** A great deal of evidence shows the motivational benefits of carefully matching people to jobs. People who lack the necessary skills to perform successfully will be at a disadvantage.

3. **Use goals.** You should ensure that employees have hard, specific goals and feedback on how well they're doing in pursuit of those goals. In many cases, these goals should be participatively set.

4. **Ensure that goals are perceived as attainable.** Regardless of whether goals are actually attainable, employees who see goals as unattainable will reduce their effort. Be sure, therefore, that employees feel confident that increased efforts can lead to achieving performance goals.

5. **Individualize rewards.** Because employees have different needs, what acts as a reinforcer for one may not do so for another. Use your knowledge of employee differences to individualize the rewards over which you have control. Some of the more obvious rewards that you can allocate include pay, promotions, autonomy, and the opportunity to participate in goal setting and decision making.

6. **Link rewards to performance.** You need to make rewards contingent on performance. Rewarding factors other than performance will only reinforce the importance of those other factors. Key rewards such as pay increases and promotions should be given for the attainment of employees' specific goals.

7. **Check the system for equity.** Employees should perceive that rewards or outcomes are equal to the inputs given. On a simplistic level, experience, ability, effort, and other obvious inputs should explain differences in pay, responsibility, and other obvious outcomes.

8. **Don't ignore money.** It's easy to get so caught up in setting goals, creating interesting jobs, and providing opportunities for participation that you forget that money is a major reason why most people work. Thus, the allocation of performance-based wage increases, piece-work bonuses, employee stock ownership plans, and other pay incentives are important in determining employee motivation.

WORKING TOGETHER
Team Exercise

List five criteria (for example, pay, recognition, challenging work, friendships, status, the opportunity to do new things, the opportunity to travel, and so forth) that would be most important to you in a job. Rank them by order of importance.

Break into small groups of three or four and compare your responses. What patterns, if any, did you find?

MY TURN TO BE A MANAGER

- A good habit to get into if you don't already do it is goal-setting. Set goals for yourself using the suggestions from goal-setting theory. Write these down and keep them in a notebook. Track your progress toward achieving these goals.

- Describe a task that you've done recently for which you exerted a high level of effort. Explain your behavior, using any three of the motivation approaches described in this chapter.

- Pay attention to times when you're highly motivated and times when you're not as motivated. Write down a description of these. What accounts for the difference in your level of motivation?

- Interview three managers about how they motivate their employees. What have they found that works the best? Write up your findings in a report and be prepared to present it in class.

- Using the job characteristics model, redesign the following jobs to be more motivating: retail store sales associate, utility company meter reader, and checkout cashier at a discount store. In a written report, describe for each job at least two specific actions you would take for each of the five core job dimensions.

- Do some serious thinking about what you want from your job after graduation. Make a list of what's important to you. Are you looking for a pleasant work environment, challenging work, flexible work hours, fun coworkers, or what? Discuss how you will discover whether a particular job will help you get those things.

- Steve's and Mary's recommended readings: Terry R. Bacon, *What People Want* (Davies-Black Publishing, 2006); Dennis W. Bakke, *Joy at Work* (PVG, 2005); Leon Martel, *High Performers* (Jossey-Bass, 2002); Jon R. Katzenbach, *Peak Performance* (Harvard Business School Press, 2000); and Steven Kerr (ed.), *Ultimate Rewards: What Really Motivates People to Achieve* (Harvard Business School Press, 1997).

- Find five different examples of employee recognition programs from organizations with which you're familiar or from articles that you find. Write a report describing your examples and evaluating what you think about the various approaches.

- Find the Web site of Great Place to Work Institute [www.greatplacetowork.com]. What does the Institute say about what makes an organization a great place to work? Next, locate the lists of the Best Companies to Work For. Choose one company from each of the international lists. Now research that company and describe what it does that makes it a great place to work.

- In your own words, write down three things you learned in this chapter about being a good manager.

- Self-knowledge can be a powerful learning tool. Go to mymanagementlab.com and complete these self-assessment exercises: What Motivates Me? What Are My Dominant Needs? What Rewards Do I Value Most? What's My View on the Nature of People? What's My Job's Motivating Potential? Do I Want an Enriched Job? How Confident Am I in My Ability to Succeed? What's My Attitude Toward Achievement? Using the results of your assessments, identify personal strengths and weaknesses. What will you do to reinforce your strengths and improve your weaknesses?

CASE APPLICATION **1**
Searching For?

It gets more than 3,000 applications a day.[96] And it's no wonder! With a massage every other week, onsite laundry, swimming pool and spa, free delicious all-you-can-eat gourmet meals, what more could an employee want? Sounds like an ideal job, doesn't it? However, at Google, many people are demonstrating by their decisions to leave the company that all those perks (and these are just a few) aren't enough to keep them there. As one analyst said, "Yes, Google's making gobs of money. Yes, it's full of smart people. Yes, it's a wonderful place to work. So why are so many people leaving?"

Google has been in the top five list of "best companies to work for" by *Fortune* magazine for four years running and was number one on the list for two of those four years. But make no mistake. Google's executives decided to offer all these fabulous perks for several reasons: to attract the best knowledge workers it can in an intensely competitive, cutthroat market; to help employees work long hours and not have to deal with time-consuming personal chores; to show employees they're

Former Google vice president Adam Bosworth, who headed up the Google Health team, left the company to start his own Web-based consumer health service, Keas, Inc. The vision at Keas is to help people manage their health care online from staying healthy to recovering from an illness.

valued; and to have employees remain Googlers (the name used for employees) for many years. But a number of Googlers have jumped ship and given up these fantastic benefits to go out on their own.

For instance, Sean Knapp and two colleagues, brothers Bismarck and Belsasar Lepe, came up with an idea on how to handle Web video. They left Google, or as one person put it, "expelled themselves from paradise to start their own company." When the threesome left the company, Google really wanted them and their project to stay. Google offered them a "blank check." But the trio realized they would do all the hard work and Google would own the product. So off they went, for the excitement of a start-up.

If this were an isolated occurrence, it would be easy to write off. But it's not. Other talented Google employees have done the same thing. In fact, there are so many of them who have left that they've formed an informal alumni club of ex-Googlers turned entrepreneurs.

Discussion Questions

1. What's it like to work at Google? (Hint: Go to Google's Web site and click on About Google. Find the section on Jobs at Google and go from there.) What's your assessment of the company's work environment?

2. Google is doing a lot for its employees, but not enough to retain some talented employees. Using what you've learned from studying the various motivation theories, what does this situation tell you about employee motivation?

3. What do you think is Google's biggest challenge in keeping employees motivated?

4. If you were managing a team of Google employees, how would you keep them motivated?

CASE APPLICATION

Best Practices at Best Buy

Do traditional workplaces reward long hours instead of efficient hours? Wouldn't it make more sense to have a workplace in which "people can do whatever they want, whenever they want, as long as the work gets done?" Well, that's the approach that Best Buy is taking.[97] And this radical workplace experiment, which obviously has many implications for employee motivation, has been an interesting and enlightening journey for the company.

In 2002, then CEO Brad Anderson (now the company's vice chairman) introduced a carefully crafted program called ROWE—Results-Only Work Environment. ROWE was the inspiration of two HRM managers at Best Buy, Cali Ressler and Jody Thompson, who had been given the task of taking a flexible work program that was in effect at corporate headquarters in Minnesota and developing it for everyone in the company. Ressler and Thompson said, "We realized that the flexible work program was successful as employee engagement was up, productivity was higher, but the problem was the participants were being viewed as 'not working.'" And that was a common reaction from managers who didn't really view flexible work employees as "really working because they aren't in the office working traditional hours." The two women set about to change that by creating a program in which "everyone would be evaluated solely on their results, not on how long they worked."

The first thing to understand about ROWE is that it's not about schedules. Instead, it's about changing the work culture of an organization, which is infinitely more difficult than changing schedules. With Anderson's blessing and support, they embarked on this journey to overhaul the company's corporate workplace.

The first step in implementing ROWE was a culture audit at company headquarters, which helped them establish a baseline for how employees perceived their work environment. After four months, the audit was repeated. During this time, Best Buy executives were being educated about ROWE and what it was all about. Obviously, it was important to have their commitment to the program. The second phase involved explaining the ROWE philosophy to all the corporate employees and training managers on how to maintain control in a ROWE workplace. In the third phase, work unit teams were free to figure out how to implement the changes. Each team found a different way to keep the flexibility from spiraling into chaos. For instance, the public relations team got pagers to make sure someone was always available in an emergency. Some employees in the finance department used software that turns voice mail into e-mail files accessible from anywhere, making it easier for them to work at home. Four months after ROWE was implemented, Ressler and Thompson followed up with another culture check to see how everyone was doing.

So what's the bottom line for Best Buy? Productivity jumped 41 percent and voluntary turnover fell to 8 percent from 12 percent. They also discovered that when employees' engagement with their jobs increased, average annual sales increased 2 percent. And employees said that the freedom changed their lives. "They don't know if they work fewer hours—they've stopped counting—but they are more productive." As Ressler and Thompson stated, "Work isn't a place you go—it's something you do."

Discussion Questions

1. Describe the elements of ROWE. What do you think might be the advantages and drawbacks of this program?
2. Using one or more motivation theories from the chapter, explain why you think ROWE works.
3. What might be the challenges for managers in motivating employees in a program like this?
4. Does this sound like something you would be comfortable with? Why or why not?
5. What's your interpretation of the statement that "Work isn't a place you go—it's something you do"? Do you agree? Why or why not?

Let's Get Real:

Meet the Manager

Keith D. Lynn
Agency Field Executive
State Farm Insurance
Tulsa, OK

You'll be hearing more from this real manager throughout the chapter.

MY JOB:

I am an agency field executive for State Farm Insurance Companies and am responsible for managing 50 State Farm agents and their 125 team members in a geographic area encompassing 28,000 square miles. Because these agents are independent contractors, my management of them is only through persuasion and motivation. I do have a four-person team reporting to me directly to assist in the management and marketing efforts for this agency field office.

BEST PART OF MY JOB:

I have one of the best jobs in the world. I get to work with high-quality individuals who deliver on a promise to protect people from the unexpected and to help them reach their financial goals. What career could be better? More specifically, I have built personal relationships with many of those whom I support. This allows me to, in some ways, be a part of their lives and help them reach their goals and support them when they help others.

Managers *as* Leaders

LEARNING OUTCOMES

WORST PART OF MY JOB:

Balancing priorities. Many supposedly "urgent" tasks steal time every day. Many of these tasks are urgent but not important, yet they take time and keep me from succeeding in the more important functions of my job.

BEST MANAGEMENT ADVICE EVER RECEIVED:

As a second lieutenant in the army, my commanding officer was a lieutenant colonel who had been promoted up the ranks from private. He understood how to motivate people and how to get a group to function at the highest levels. His advice, which I have used in every position I have held, was: Treat everyone as you would want to be treated, be respectful of them no matter what their rank and they will ensure you succeed. Treat them badly, and you and your team will suffer.

Too often, I find young prideful managers who treat those who report to them and even their former peers as inferiors, often insisting on respect. These individuals will never gain the loyalty and respect they demand.

Not every company has a chief leadership officer. But Accenture does and London-based Adrian Lajtha fills that position.[1] So what exactly does a chief leadership officer do? As the world's largest consulting company, Accenture needs to deliberately and systematically develop leaders with the skills and abilities to help it be better prepared for the future. Lajtha is responsible for making that happen.

In his position, Lajtha has four main responsibilities: (1) leadership development and succession planning; (2) human-capital strategy, which entails thinking about the future of the company and what that means for the company's culture, leadership, and people; (3) all inclusion and diversity programs; and (4) corporate citizenship.

To see the importance of these actions, all you have to do is look at Accenture's growth in markets such as China and India, which will need organizational leaders from within those countries. Accenture launched high-potential programs in those countries (and in Russia, Mexico, and Korea) to "identify that group of people who we think are going to be the leaders five years from now." Such programs require a lot of trust between leaders and followers. How can Lajtha continue to build that trust?

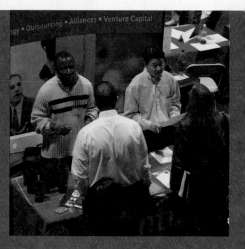

What Would You Do?

Adrian Lajtha of Accenture is a good example of doing what is needed for an organization to have good leaders in place. He has created programs that identify employees with the potential to be leaders. Helping turn that potential into reality requires an environment and culture of trust. Accenture's leadership development programs are so effective that the company was ranked number 5 on the list of top 20 Best Companies for Leadership.[2] Why is leadership so important? Because it's the leaders in organizations who make things happen.

LEARNING OUTCOME 17.1
Define leader and leadership.

Who Are Leaders and What Is Leadership?

Let's begin by clarifying who leaders are and what leadership is. Our definition of a **leader** is someone who can influence others and who has managerial authority. **Leadership** is what leaders do. It's a process of leading a group and influencing that group to achieve its goals.

Are all managers leaders? Because leading is one of the four management functions, yes, ideally, all managers *should* be leaders. Thus, we're going to study leaders and leadership from a managerial perspective.[3] However, even though we're looking at these from a managerial perspective, we're aware that groups often have informal leaders who emerge. Although these informal leaders may be able to influence others, they have not been the focus of most leadership research and are not the types of leaders we're studying in this chapter.

Leaders and leadership, like motivation, are organizational behavior topics that have been researched a lot. Most of that research has been aimed at answering the question: *What is an effective leader?* We'll begin our study of leadership by looking at some early leadership theories that attempted to answer that question.

LEARNING OUTCOME 17.2
Compare and contrast early theories of leadership.

Early Leadership Theories

People have been interested in leadership since they started coming together in groups to accomplish goals. However, it wasn't until the early part of the twentieth century that researchers actually began to study leadership. These early leadership theories focused on the *leader* (leadership trait theories) and how the *leader interacted* with his or her group members (leadership behavior theories).

Leadership Trait Theories

Researchers at the University of Cambridge in England recently reported that men with longer ring fingers, compared to their index fingers, tended to be more successful in the frantic high-frequency trading in the London financial district.[4] What does a study of the finger lengths of financial traders have to do with trait theories of leadership? Well, that's also what leadership trait theories have attempted to do—identify certain traits that all leaders have.

Leadership research in the 1920s and 1930s focused on isolating leader traits—that is, characteristics—that would differentiate leaders from nonleaders. Some of the traits studied included physical stature, appearance, social class, emotional stability, fluency of speech, and sociability. Despite the best efforts of researchers, it proved impossible to identify a set of traits that would *always* differentiate a leader (the person) from a non-leader. Maybe it was a bit optimistic to think that a set of consistent and unique traits would apply universally to all effective leaders, no matter whether they were in charge of Kraft Foods, the Moscow Ballet, the country of France, a local collegiate chapter of Alpha Chi Omega, Ted's Malibu Surf Shop, or Oxford University. However, later attempts to identify traits consistently associated with *leadership* (the process of leading, not the person) were more successful. The seven traits shown to be associated with effective leadership are described briefly in Exhibit 17-1.[5]

Researchers eventually recognized that traits alone were not sufficient for identifying effective leaders since explanations based solely on traits ignored the interactions of leaders and their group members as well as situational factors. Possessing the appropriate traits only made it more likely that an individual would be an effective leader. Therefore, leadership research from the late 1940s to the mid-1960s concentrated on the preferred behavioral styles that leaders demonstrated. Researchers wondered whether something unique in what effective leaders *did*—in other words, in their *behavior*—was the key.

Let's Get Real

F2F

Traits that leaders should have:
- Honesty—if you can't explain something, say so.
- Integrity—100% of the time.
- Vision that goes beyond tomorrow.

---

1. *Drive.* Leaders exhibit a high effort level. They have a relatively high desire for achievement, they are ambitious, they have a lot of energy, they are tirelessly persistent in their activities, and they show initiative.

2. *Desire to lead.* Leaders have a strong desire to influence and lead others. They demonstrate the willingness to take responsibility.

3. *Honesty and integrity.* Leaders build trusting relationships with followers by being truthful or nondeceitful and by showing high consistency between word and deed.

4. *Self-confidence.* Followers look to leaders for an absence of self-doubt. Leaders, therefore, need to show self-confidence in order to convince followers of the rightness of their goals and decisions.

5. *Intelligence.* Leaders need to be intelligent enough to gather, synthesize, and interpret large amounts of information, and they need to be able to create visions, solve problems, and make correct decisions.

6. *Job-relevant knowledge.* Effective leaders have a high degree of knowledge about the company, industry, and technical matters. In-depth knowledge allows leaders to make well-informed decisions and to understand the implications of those decisions.

7. *Extraversion.* Leaders are energetic, lively people. They are sociable, assertive, and rarely silent or withdrawn.

EXHIBIT 17-1

Seven Traits Associated with Leadership

Sources: Based on S. A. Kirkpatrick and E. A. Locke, "Leadership: Do Traits Really Matter?" *Academy of Management Executive*, May 1991, pp. 48–60; and T. A. Judge, J. E. Bono, R. Ilies, and M. W. Gerhardt, "Personality and Leadership: A Qualitative and Quantitative Review," *Journal of Applied Psychology*, August 2002, pp. 765–780.

---

leader
Someone who can influence others and who has managerial authority

leadership
A process of influencing a group to achieve goals

Leadership Behavior Theories

Bill Watkins, former CEO of disk drive manufacturer Seagate Technology, once responded when asked how he handled his board of directors, "You never ask board members what they think. You tell them what you're going to do." In contrast, Joe Lee, CEO of Darden Restaurants during the aftermath of 9/11, was focused on only two things that morning: his Darden people who were traveling and his company's Muslim colleagues.[6] These two leaders of successful companies, as you can see, behaved in two very different ways. What do we know about leader behavior and how can it help us in our understanding of what an effective leader is?

Researchers hoped that the **behavioral theories** approach would provide more definitive answers about the nature of leadership than did the trait theories. The four main leader behavior studies are summarized in Exhibit 17-2.

UNIVERSITY OF IOWA STUDIES.   The University of Iowa studies explored three leadership styles to find which was the most effective.[7] The **autocratic style** described a leader who dictated work methods, made unilateral decisions, and limited employee participation. The **democratic style** described a leader who involved employees in decision making, delegated authority, and used feedback as an opportunity for coaching employees. Finally, the **laissez-faire style** leader let the group make decisions and complete the work in whatever way it saw fit. The researchers' results seemed to indicate that the democratic style contributed to both good quantity and quality of work. Had the answer to the question of the most effective leadership style been found? Unfortunately, it wasn't that simple. Later studies of the autocratic and democratic styles showed mixed results. For instance, the democratic style sometimes produced higher performance levels than the autocratic style, but at other times, it didn't. However, more consistent results were found when a measure of employee satisfaction was used. Group members were more satisfied under a democratic leader than under an autocratic one.[8]

EXHIBIT 17-2		Behavioral Dimension	Conclusion
Behavioral Theories of Leadership	University of Iowa	*Democratic style:* involving subordinates, delegating authority, and encouraging participation *Autocratic style:* dictating work methods, centralizing decision making, and limiting participation *Laissez-faire style:* giving group freedom to make decisions and complete work	Democratic style of leadership was most effective, although later studies showed mixed results.
	Ohio State	*Consideration:* being considerate of followers' ideas and feelings *Initiating structure:* structuring work and work relationships to meet job goals	High–high leader (high in consideration and high in initiating structure) achieved high subordinate performance and satisfaction, but not in all situations
	University of Michigan	*Employee oriented:* emphasized interpersonal relationships and taking care of employees' needs *Production oriented:* emphasized technical or task aspects of job	Employee-oriented leaders were associated with high group productivity and higher job satisfaction.
	Managerial Grid	*Concern for people:* measured leader's concern for subordinates on a scale of 1 to 9 (low to high) *Concern for production:* measured leader's concern for getting job done on a scale 1 to 9 (low to high)	Leaders performed best with a 9,9 style (high concern for production and high concern for people).

Now leaders had a dilemma! Should they focus on achieving higher performance or on achieving higher member satisfaction? This recognition of the dual nature of a leader's behavior—that is, focus on the task and focus on the people—was also a key characteristic of the other behavioral studies.

THE OHIO STATE STUDIES. The Ohio State studies identified two important dimensions of leader behavior.[9] Beginning with a list of more than 1,000 behavioral dimensions, the researchers eventually narrowed it down to just two that accounted for most of the leadership behavior described by group members. The first was called **initiating structure**, which referred to the extent to which a leader defined his or her role and the roles of group members in attaining goals. It included behaviors that involved attempts to organize work, work relationships, and goals. The second was called **consideration**, which was defined as the extent to which a leader had work relationships characterized by mutual trust and respect for group members' ideas and feelings. A leader who was high in consideration helped group members with personal problems, was friendly and approachable, and treated all group members as equals. He or she showed concern for (was considerate of) his or her followers' comfort, well-being, status, and satisfaction. Research found that a leader who was high in both initiating structure and consideration (a **high–high leader**) sometimes achieved high group task performance and high group member satisfaction, but not always.

UNIVERSITY OF MICHIGAN STUDIES. Leadership studies conducted at the University of Michigan at about the same time as those being done at Ohio State also hoped to identify behavioral characteristics of leaders that were related to performance effectiveness. The Michigan group also came up with two dimensions of leadership behavior, which they labeled employee oriented and production oriented.[10] Leaders who were *employee oriented* were described as emphasizing interpersonal relationships. The *production-oriented* leaders, in contrast, tended to emphasize the task aspects of the job. Unlike the other studies, the Michigan researchers concluded that leaders who were employee oriented were able to get high group productivity and high group member satisfaction.

THE MANAGERIAL GRID. The behavioral dimensions from these early leadership studies provided the basis for the development of a two-dimensional grid for appraising leadership styles. This **managerial grid** used the behavioral dimensions "concern for people" (the vertical part of the grid) and "concern for production" (the horizontal part of the grid) and evaluated a leader's use of these behaviors, ranking them on a scale from 1 (low) to 9 (high).[11] Although the grid had 81 potential categories into which a leader's behavioral style might fall, only five styles were named: impoverished management (1,1 or low concern for production, low concern for people), task management (9,1 or high concern for production, low concern for people), middle-of-the-road management (5,5 or medium concern for production, medium concern for people), country club management (1,9 or low concern for production, high concern for people), and team management (9,9 or high concern for production, high concern for people). Of these five styles, the researchers concluded that managers performed best when using a 9,9 style. Unfortunately, the grid offered no answers to the question of what made a manager an effective leader; it only

---

behavioral theories
Leadership theories that identify behaviors that differentiated effective leaders from ineffective leaders

autocratic style
A leader who dictates work methods, makes unilateral decisions, and limits employee participation

democratic style
A leader who involves employees in decision making, delegates authority, and uses feedback as an opportunity for coaching employees

laissez-faire style
A leader who lets the group make decisions and complete the work in whatever way it sees fit

initiating structure
The extent to which a leader defines his or her role and the roles of group members in attaining goals

consideration
The extent to which a leader has work relationships characterized by mutual trust and respect for group members' ideas and feelings

high–high leader
A leader high in both initiating structure and consideration behaviors

managerial grid
A two-dimensional grid for appraising leadership styles

At the U.S. Army's largest overseas medical research laboratory, located in Bangkok, Thailand, a scientist prepares a specimen while working on a vaccine against dengue fever. This scientist and other medical researchers at the laboratory have a high level of follower readiness. As responsible, experienced, and mature employees, they are both able and willing to complete their tasks under leadership that gives them freedom to make and implement decisions. This leader–follower relationship is consistent with Hersey and Blanchard's situational leadership theory in acknowledging the importance of followers in leadership effectiveness.

provided a framework for conceptualizing leadership style. In fact, little substantive evidence supports the conclusion that a 9,9 style is most effective in all situations.[12]

Leadership researchers were discovering that predicting leadership success involved something more complex than isolating a few leader traits or preferable behaviors. They began looking at situational influences. Specifically, which leadership styles might be suitable in different situations and what were these different situations?

LEARNING OUTCOME
Describe the three major contingency theories of leadership.

17.3 Contingency Theories of Leadership

"The corporate world is filled with stories of leaders who failed to achieve greatness because they failed to understand the context they were working in."[13] In this section we examine three contingency theories—Fiedler, Hersey-Blanchard, and path-goal. Each looks at defining leadership style and the situation, and attempts to answer the *if-then* contingencies (that is, *if* this is the context or situation, *then* this is the best leadership style to use).

The Fiedler Model

The first comprehensive contingency model for leadership was developed by Fred Fiedler.[14] The **Fiedler contingency model** proposed that effective group performance depended upon properly matching the leader's style and the amount of control and influence in the situation. The model was based on the premise that a certain leadership style would be most effective in different types of situations. The keys were to (1) define those leadership styles and the different types of situations, and then (2) identify the appropriate combinations of style and situation.

Fiedler proposed that a key factor in leadership success was an individual's basic leadership style, either task oriented or relationship oriented. To measure a leader's style, Fiedler developed the **least-preferred coworker (LPC) questionnaire**. This questionnaire contained 18 pairs of contrasting adjectives—for example, pleasant–unpleasant, cold–warm, boring–interesting, or friendly–unfriendly. Respondents were asked to think of all the coworkers they had ever had and to describe that one person they *least enjoyed* working with by rating him or her on a scale of 1 to 8 for each of the 18 sets of adjectives (the 8 always described the positive adjective out of the pair and the 1 always described the negative adjective out of the pair).

If the leader described the least preferred coworker in relatively positive terms (in other words, a "high" LPC score—a score of 64 or above), then the respondent was primarily interested in good personal relations with coworkers and the style would be described as *relationship oriented*. In contrast, if you saw the least preferred coworker in relatively unfavorable terms (a low LPC score—a score of 57 or below), you were primarily interested in productivity and getting the job done; thus, your style would be labeled as *task oriented*. Fiedler did acknowledge that a small number of people might fall in between these two extremes and not have a cut-and-dried leadership style. One other important point is that Fiedler assumed a person's leadership style was fixed regardless of the situation. In other words, if you were a relationship-oriented leader, you'd always be one, and the same for task-oriented.

After an individual's leadership style had been assessed through the LPC, it was time to evaluate the situation in order to be able to match the leader with the situation. Fiedler's research uncovered three contingency dimensions that defined the key situational factors in leader effectiveness.

▶ **Leader–member relations**: the degree of confidence, trust, and respect employees had for their leader; rated as either good or poor.
▶ **Task structure**: the degree to which job assignments were formalized and structured; rated as either high or low.
▶ **Position power**: the degree of influence a leader had over activities such as hiring, firing, discipline, promotions, and salary increases; rated as either strong or weak.

Each leadership situation was evaluated in terms of these three contingency variables, which when combined produced eight possible situations that were either favorable or unfavorable for the leader. (See the bottom of the chart in Exhibit 17-3.) Situations I, II, and III were classified as highly favorable for the leader. Situations IV, V, and VI were

EXHIBIT 17-3
The Fiedler Model

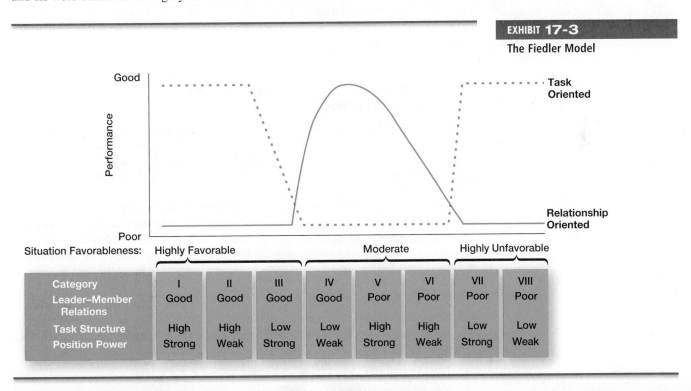

Category	I	II	III	IV	V	VI	VII	VIII
Leader–Member Relations	Good	Good	Good	Good	Poor	Poor	Poor	Poor
Task Structure	High	High	Low	Low	High	High	Low	Low
Position Power	Strong	Weak	Strong	Weak	Strong	Weak	Strong	Weak

Fiedler contingency model
A leadership theory proposing that effective group performance depends upon the proper match between a leader's style and the degree to which the situation allows the leader to control and influence

least-preferred coworker (LPC) questionnaire
A questionnaire that measures whether a leader is task or relationship oriented

leader–member relations
One of Fiedler's situational contingencies that describes the degree of confidence, trust, and respect employees had for their leader

task structure
One of Fiedler's situational contingencies that describes the degree to which job assignments are formalized and structured

position power
One of Fiedler's situational contingencies that describes the degree of influence a leader has over activities such as hiring, firing, discipline, promotions, and salary increases

moderately favorable for the leader. And situations VII and VIII were described as highly unfavorable for the leader.

Once Fiedler had described the leader variables and the situational variables, he had everything he needed to define the specific contingencies for leadership effectiveness. To do so, he studied 1,200 groups where he compared relationship-oriented versus task-oriented leadership styles in each of the eight situational categories. He concluded that task-oriented leaders performed better in very favorable situations and in very unfavorable situations. (See the top of Exhibit 17-3 where performance is shown on the vertical axis and situation favorableness is shown on the horizontal axis.) On the other hand, relationship-oriented leaders performed better in moderately favorable situations.

Because Fiedler treated an individual's leadership style as fixed, only two ways could improve leader effectiveness. First, you could bring in a new leader whose style better fit the situation. For instance, if the group situation was highly unfavorable but was led by a relationship-oriented leader, the group's performance could be improved by replacing that person with a task-oriented leader. The second alternative was to change the situation to fit the leader. This could be done by restructuring tasks; by increasing or decreasing the power that the leader had over factors such as salary increases, promotions, and disciplinary actions; or by improving the leader–member relations.

Research testing the overall validity of Fiedler's model has shown considerable evidence to support the model.[15] However, his theory wasn't without criticisms. The major one is that it's probably unrealistic to assume that a person can't change his or her leadership style to fit the situation. Effective leaders can, and do, change their styles. Another is that the LPC wasn't very practical. Finally, the situation variables were difficult to assess.[16] Despite its shortcomings, the Fiedler model showed that effective leadership style needed to reflect situational factors.

Hersey and Blanchard's Situational Leadership Theory

Paul Hersey and Ken Blanchard developed a leadership theory that has gained a strong following among management development specialists.[17] This model, called **situational leadership theory (SLT)**, is a contingency theory that focuses on followers' readiness. Before we proceed, two points need clarification: Why a leadership theory focuses on the followers, and what is meant by the term *readiness*.

The emphasis on the followers in leadership effectiveness reflects the reality that it *is* the followers who accept or reject the leader. Regardless of what the leader does, the group's effectiveness depends on the actions of the followers. This important dimension has been overlooked or underemphasized in most leadership theories. And **readiness**, as defined by Hersey and Blanchard, refers to the extent to which people have the ability and willingness to accomplish a specific task.

SLT uses the same two leadership dimensions that Fiedler identified: task and relationship behaviors. However, Hersey and Blanchard go a step further by considering each as either high or low and then combining them into four specific leadership styles described as follows:

- ▶ *Telling* (high task–low relationship): The leader defines roles and tells people what, how, when, and where to do various tasks.
- ▶ *Selling* (high task–high relationship): The leader provides both directive and supportive behavior.
- ▶ *Participating* (low task–high relationship): The leader and followers share in decision making; the main role of the leader is facilitating and communicating.
- ▶ *Delegating* (low task–low relationship): The leader provides little direction or support.

The final component in the model is the four stages of follower readiness:

- ▶ *R1:* People are both *unable and unwilling* to take responsibility for doing something. Followers aren't competent or confident.

▶ *R2:* People are *unable but willing* to do the necessary job tasks. Followers are motivated but lack the appropriate skills.

▶ *R3:* People are *able but unwilling* to do what the leader wants. Followers are competent, but don't want to do something.

▶ *R4:* People are both *able and willing* to do what is asked of them.

SLT essentially views the leader–follower relationship as like that of a parent and a child. Just as a parent needs to relinquish control when a child becomes more mature and responsible, so, too, should leaders. As followers reach higher levels of readiness, the leader responds not only by decreasing control over their activities but also decreasing relationship behaviors. The SLT says if followers are at R1 (*unable* and *unwilling* to do a task), the leader needs to use the telling style and give clear and specific directions; if followers are at R2 (*unable* and *willing*), the leader needs to use the selling style and display high task orientation to compensate for the followers' lack of ability and high relationship orientation to get followers to "buy into" the leader's desires; if followers are at R3 (*able* and *unwilling*), the leader needs to use the participating style to gain their support; and if employees are at R4 (both *able* and *willing*), the leader doesn't need to do much and should use the delegating style.

SLT has intuitive appeal. It acknowledges the importance of followers and builds on the logic that leaders can compensate for ability and motivational limitations in their followers. However, research efforts to test and support the theory generally have been disappointing.[18] Possible explanations include internal inconsistencies in the model as well as problems with research methodology. Despite its appeal and wide popularity, we have to be cautious about any enthusiastic endorsement of SLT.

Path-Goal Model

Another approach to understanding leadership is **path-goal theory**, which states that the leader's job is to assist followers in attaining their goals and to provide direction or support needed to ensure that their goals are compatible with the goals of the group or organization. Developed by Robert House, path-goal theory takes key elements from the expectancy theory of motivation.[19] The term *path-goal* is derived from the belief that effective leaders remove the roadblocks and pitfalls so that followers have a clearer path to help them get from where they are to the achievement of their work goals.

House identified four leadership behaviors:

▶ *Directive leader:* Lets subordinates know what's expected of them, schedules work to be done, and gives specific guidance on how to accomplish tasks.

▶ *Supportive leader:* Shows concern for the needs of followers and is friendly.

▶ *Participative leader:* Consults with group members and uses their suggestions before making a decision.

▶ *Achievement oriented leader:* Sets challenging goals and expects followers to perform at their highest level.

In contrast to Fiedler's view that a leader couldn't change his or her behavior, House assumed that leaders are flexible and can display any or all of these leadership styles depending on the situation.

As Exhibit 17-4 illustrates, path-goal theory proposes two situational or contingency variables that moderate the leadership behavior–outcome relationship: those in the *environment* that are outside the control of the follower (factors including task structure, formal authority

---

situational leadership theory (SLT)
A leadership contingency theory that focuses on followers' readiness

readiness
The extent to which people have the ability and willingness to accomplish a specific task

path-goal theory
A leadership theory that says the leader's job is to assist followers in attaining their goals and to provide direction or support needed to ensure that their goals are compatible with the goals of the group or organization

EXHIBIT 17-4

Path-Goal Model

system, and the work group) and those that are part of the personal characteristics of the *follower* (including locus of control, experience, and perceived ability). Environmental factors determine the type of leader behavior required if subordinate outcomes are to be maximized; personal characteristics of the follower determine how the environment and leader behavior are interpreted. The theory proposes that a leader's behavior won't be effective if it's redundant with what the environmental structure is providing or is incongruent with follower characteristics. For example, some predictions from path-goal theory are:

▶ Directive leadership leads to greater satisfaction when tasks are ambiguous or stressful than when they are highly structured and well laid out. The followers aren't sure what to do, so the leader needs to give them some direction.

▶ Supportive leadership results in high employee performance and satisfaction when subordinates are performing structured tasks. In this situation, the leader only needs to support followers, not tell them what to do.

▶ Directive leadership is likely to be perceived as redundant among subordinates with high perceived ability or with considerable experience. These followers are quite capable so they don't need a leader to tell them what to do.

▶ The clearer and more bureaucratic the formal authority relationships, the more leaders should exhibit supportive behavior and deemphasize directive behavior. The organizational situation has provided the structure as far as what is expected of followers, so the leader's role is simply to support.

▶ Directive leadership will lead to higher employee satisfaction when there is substantive conflict within a work group. In this situation, the followers need a leader who will take charge.

▶ Subordinates with an internal locus of control will be more satisfied with a participative style. Because these followers believe that they control what happens to them, they prefer to participate in decisions.

▶ Subordinates with an external locus of control will be more satisfied with a directive style. These followers believe that what happens to them is a result of the external environment so they would prefer a leader that tells them what to do.

▶ Achievement-oriented leadership will increase subordinates' expectancies that effort will lead to high performance when tasks are ambiguously structured. By setting challenging goals, followers know what the expectations are.

Testing path-goal theory has not been easy. A review of the research suggests mixed support.[20] To summarize the model, however, an employee's performance and satisfaction are likely to be positively influenced when the leader chooses a leadership style that compensates for shortcomings in either the employee or the work setting. However, if the leader spends time explaining tasks that are already clear or when the employee has the ability and experience to handle them without interference, the employee is likely to see such directive behavior as redundant or even insulting.

Contemporary Views of Leadership 17.4

What are the latest views of leadership? We want to look at four of these views: leader–member exchange theory, transformational-transactional leadership, charismatic-visionary leadership, and team leadership.

Leader–Member Exchange (LMX) Theory

Have you ever been in a group in which the leader had "favorites" who made up his or her in-group? If so, that's the premise behind leader–member exchange (LMX) theory.[21] **Leader–member exchange theory (LMX)** says that leaders create in-groups and out-groups and those in the in-group will have higher performance ratings, less turnover, and greater job satisfaction.

LMX theory suggests that early on in the relationship between a leader and a given follower, a leader will implicitly categorize a follower as an "in" or as an "out." That relationship tends to remain fairly stable over time. Leaders also encourage LMX by rewarding those employees with whom they want a closer linkage and punishing those with whom they do not.[22] For the LMX relationship to remain intact, however, both the leader and the follower must "invest" in the relationship.

It's not exactly clear how a leader chooses who falls into each category, but evidence shows that in-group members have demographic, attitude, personality, and even gender similarities with the leader or they have a higher level of competence than out-group members.[23] The leader does the choosing, but the follower's characteristics drive the decision.

Research on LMX has been generally supportive. It appears that leaders do differentiate among followers; that these disparities are not random; and followers with in-group status will have higher performance ratings, engage in more helping or "citizenship" behaviors at work, and report greater satisfaction with their boss.[24] This probably shouldn't be surprising since leaders invest their time and other resources in those whom they expect to perform best.

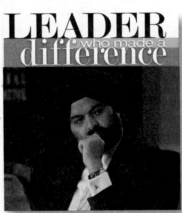

LEADER who made a difference

Ajay Banga, CEO of MasterCard, has had well-rounded leadership experiences.[25] Born in India, Banga honed his leadership skills at Nestlé and PepsiCo before moving to Citigroup to head up its Asia-Pacific division. Citigroup was a challenging situation as he found a vast banking group that "worked fluidly in its product clusters but lacked coordination, synergy, or vision." Banga undertook the painful process of breaking down those "silos and stitching them together again under a single umbrella structure." When he was offered a position at MasterCard as president and chief operating officer, Banga jumped at the chance. Now as CEO, Banga is the company's cheerleader, shaking up the company's low-key corporate culture with hugs and fist bumps in the hallways. One analyst describes him as "energetic, open, and engaging."

Transformational-Transactional Leadership

Many early leadership theories viewed leaders as **transactional leaders**; that is, leaders that lead primarily by using social exchanges (or transactions). Transactional leaders guide or motivate followers to work toward established goals by exchanging rewards for their productivity.[26] But another type of leader—a **transformational leader**—stimulates and inspires (transforms) followers to achieve extraordinary outcomes. Examples include Jim Goodnight of SAS Institute and Andrea Jung of Avon. They pay attention to the concerns and developmental needs of individual followers; they change followers' awareness of issues by helping those followers look at old problems in new ways; and they are able to excite, arouse, and inspire followers to exert extra effort to achieve group goals.

Transactional and transformational leadership shouldn't be viewed as opposing approaches to getting things done.[27] Transformational leadership develops from transactional leadership. Transformational leadership produces levels of employee effort and performance that go beyond what would occur with a transactional approach alone. Moreover, transformational leadership is more than charisma, because the transformational leader attempts to instill in followers the ability to question not only established views but those views held by the leader.[28]

The evidence supporting the superiority of transformational leadership over transactional leadership is overwhelmingly impressive. For instance, studies that looked at managers in different settings, including the military and business, found that transformational leaders were evaluated as more effective, higher performers, more promotable than their transactional counterparts, and more interpersonally sensitive.[29] In addition, evidence indicates that transformational leadership is strongly correlated with lower turnover rates and higher levels of productivity, employee satisfaction, creativity, goal attainment, follower well-being, and corporate entrepreneurship, especially in start-up firms.[30]

Charismatic-Visionary Leadership

Jeff Bezos, founder and CEO of Amazon.com, is a person who exudes energy, enthusiasm, and drive.[31] He's fun-loving (his legendary laugh has been described as a flock of Canadian geese on nitrous oxide), but has pursued his vision for Amazon with serious intensity and has demonstrated an ability to inspire his employees through the ups and downs of a rapidly growing company. Bezos is what we call a **charismatic leader**—that is, an enthusiastic, self-confident leader whose personality and actions influence people to behave in certain ways.

Several authors have attempted to identify personal characteristics of the charismatic leader.[32] The most comprehensive analysis identified five such characteristics: they have a vision, the ability to articulate that vision, a willingness to take risks to achieve that vision, a sensitivity to both environmental constraints and follower needs, and behaviors that are out of the ordinary.[33]

An increasing body of evidence shows impressive correlations between charismatic leadership and high performance and satisfaction among followers.[34] Although one study found that charismatic CEOs had no impact on subsequent organizational performance, charisma is still believed to be a desirable leadership quality.[35]

If charisma is desirable, can people learn to be charismatic leaders? Or are charismatic leaders born with their qualities? Although a small number of experts still think that charisma can't be learned, most believe that individuals can be trained to exhibit charismatic behaviors.[36] For example, researchers have succeeded in teaching undergraduate students to "be" charismatic. How? They were taught to articulate a far-reaching goal, communicate high performance expectations, exhibit confidence in the ability of subordinates to meet those expectations, and empathize with the needs of their subordinates; they learned to project a powerful, confident, and dynamic presence; and they practiced using a captivating and engaging voice tone. The researchers also trained the student leaders to use charismatic nonverbal behaviors, including leaning toward the follower when communicating, maintaining direct eye contact, and having a relaxed posture and animated facial expressions. In groups with these "trained" charismatic leaders, members had higher task performance, higher task adjustment, and better adjustment to the leader and to the group than did group members who worked in groups led by noncharismatic leaders.

One last thing we should say about charismatic leadership is that it may not always be necessary to achieve high levels of employee performance. It may be most appropriate when the follower's task has an ideological purpose or when the environment involves a high degree of stress and uncertainty.[37] This distinction may explain why, when charismatic leaders surface, it's more likely to be in politics, religion, or wartime; or when a business firm is starting up or facing a survival crisis. For example, Martin Luther King Jr. used his charisma to bring about social equality through nonviolent means, and Steve Jobs achieved unwavering loyalty and commitment from Apple's technical staff in the early 1980s by articulating a vision of personal computers that would dramatically change the way people lived.

Although the term *vision* is often linked with charismatic leadership, **visionary leadership** is different; it's the ability to create and articulate a realistic, credible, and attractive vision of the future that improves upon the present situation.[38] This vision, if properly selected and implemented, is so energizing that it "in effect jump-starts the future by calling forth the skills, talents, and resources to make it happen."[39]

An organization's vision should offer clear and compelling imagery that taps into people's emotions and inspires enthusiasm to pursue the organization's goals. It should be able to generate possibilities that are inspirational and unique and offer new ways of doing things that are clearly better for the organization and its members. Visions that are clearly articulated and have powerful imagery are easily grasped and accepted. For instance, Michael Dell (Dell Computer) created a vision of a business that sells and delivers customized PCs directly to customers in less than a week. The late Mary Kay Ash's vision of women as entrepreneurs selling products that improved their self-image gave impetus to her cosmetics company, Mary Kay Cosmetics.

Team Leadership

Because leadership is increasingly taking place within a team context and more organizations are using work teams, the role of the leader in guiding team members has become increasingly important. The role of team leader *is* different from the traditional leadership role, as J. D. Bryant, a supervisor at Texas Instruments' Forest Lane plant in Dallas, discovered.[41] One day he was contentedly overseeing a staff of 15 circuit board assemblers. The next day he was told that the company was going to use employee teams and he was to become a "facilitator." He said, "I'm supposed to teach the teams everything I know and then let them make their own decisions." Confused about his new role, he admitted, "There was no clear plan on what I was supposed to do." What *is* involved in being a team leader?

Many leaders are not equipped to handle the change to employee teams. As one consultant noted, "Even the most capable managers have trouble making the transition because all the command-and-control type things they were encouraged to do before are no longer appropriate. There's no reason to have any skill or sense of this."[42] This same consultant estimated that "probably 15 percent of managers are natural team leaders; another 15 percent could never lead a team because it runs counter to their personality—that is, they're unable to sublimate their dominating style for the good of the team. Then there's that huge group in the middle: Team leadership doesn't come naturally to them, but they can learn it."[43]

The challenge for many managers is learning how to become an effective team leader. They have to learn skills such as patiently sharing information, being able to trust others and to give up authority, and understanding when to intervene. And effective team leaders have mastered the difficult balancing act of knowing when to leave their teams alone and when to get involved. New team leaders may try to retain too much control at a time when team members need more autonomy, or they may abandon their teams at times when the teams need support and help.[44]

by the numbers[40]

59 percent of companies say that what they value in leaders is strategic thinking.

75 percent of companies say that leadership development programs better allow employees to accomplish goals and strategies.

68 percent of companies say that everyone in their company has the opportunity to develop and practice the capabilities needed to lead others.

72 percent of employees want a leader who can create a shared vision.

54 percent of companies say they have a process in place to identify potential leaders.

98 percent of U.S. CEOs say they are spending more time on regulatory issues; only 28 percent say they're spending more time on day-to-day management.

61 percent of Indian leaders said that envisioning and articulating a path to the future is most critical to their exercise of leadership.

transformational leaders
Leaders who stimulate and inspire (transform) followers to achieve extraordinary outcomes

charismatic leader
An enthusiastic, self-confident leader whose personality and actions influence people to behave in certain ways

visionary leadership
The ability to create and articulate a realistic, credible, and attractive vision of the future that improves upon the present situation

One study looking at organizations that reorganized themselves around employee teams found certain common responsibilities of all leaders. These leader responsibilities included coaching, facilitating, handling disciplinary problems, reviewing team and individual performance, training, and communication.[45] However, a more meaningful way to describe the team leader's job is to focus on two priorities: (1) managing the team's external boundary and (2) facilitating the team process.[46] These priorities entail four specific leadership roles. (See Exhibit 17-5.)

LEARNING OUTCOME 17.5
Discuss contemporary issues affecting leadership.

Leadership Issues in the Twenty-First Century

It's not easy being a chief information officer (CIO) today. The person responsible for managing a company's information technology activities will find that the task comes with a lot of external and internal pressures. Technology continues to change rapidly—almost daily, it sometimes seems. Business costs continue to rise. Rob Carter, CIO of FedEx, is on the hot seat facing such challenges.[47] He's responsible for all the computer and communication systems that provide around-the-clock and around-the-globe support for FedEx's products and services. If anything goes wrong, you know who takes the heat. However, Carter has been an effective leader in this seemingly chaotic environment.

Leading effectively in today's environment is likely to involve such challenging circumstances for many leaders. In addition, twenty-first-century leaders do face some important leadership issues. In this section, we look at these issues that include managing power, developing trust, empowering employees, leading across cultures, and becoming an effective leader.

Managing Power

Where do leaders get their power—that is, their right and capacity to influence work actions or decisions? Five sources of leader power have been identified: legitimate, coercive, reward, expert, and referent.[48]

Legitimate power and authority are the same. Legitimate power represents the power a leader has as a result of his or her position in the organization. Although people in positions of authority are also likely to have reward and coercive power, legitimate power is broader than the power to coerce and reward.

Coercive power is the power a leader has to punish or control. Followers react to this power out of fear of the negative results that might occur if they don't comply. Managers typically have some coercive power, such as being able to suspend or demote employees or to assign them work they find unpleasant or undesirable.

Reward power is the power to give positive rewards. A reward can be anything that a person values such as money, favorable performance appraisals, promotions, interesting work assignments, friendly colleagues, and preferred work shifts or sales territories.

Expert power is power that's based on expertise, special skills, or knowledge. If an employee has skills, knowledge, or expertise that's critical to a work group, that person's expert power is enhanced.

Finally, **referent power** is the power that arises because of a person's desirable resources or personal traits. If I admire you and want to be associated with you, you can exercise power over me because I want to please you. Referent power develops out of admiration of another and a desire to be like that person.

Most effective leaders rely on several different forms of power to affect the behavior and performance of their followers. For example, the commanding officer of one of Australia's state-of-the-art submarines, the HMAS *Sheean,* employs different types of power in managing his crew and equipment. He gives orders to the crew (legitimate), praises them (reward), and disciplines those who commit infractions (coercive). As an effective leader, he also strives to have expert power (based on his expertise and knowledge) and referent power (based on his being admired) to influence his crew.

Developing Trust

In today's uncertain environment, an important consideration for leaders is building trust and credibility, both of which can be extremely fragile. Before we can discuss ways leaders can build trust and credibility, we have to know what trust and credibility are and why they're so important.

The main component of credibility is honesty. Surveys show that honesty is consistently singled out as the number one characteristic of admired leaders. "Honesty is absolutely essential to leadership. If people are going to follow someone willingly, whether it be into battle or into the boardroom, they first want to assure themselves that the person is worthy of their trust."[49] In addition to being honest, credible leaders are competent and inspiring. They are personally able to effectively communicate their confidence and enthusiasm. Thus, followers judge a leader's **credibility** in terms of his or her honesty, competence, and ability to inspire.

Trust is closely entwined with the concept of credibility, and, in fact, the terms are often used interchangeably. **Trust** is defined as the belief in the integrity, character, and ability of a leader. Followers who trust a leader are willing to be vulnerable to the leader's actions because they are confident that their rights and interests will not be abused.[50] Research has identified five dimensions that make up the concept of trust:[51]

- ▶ *Integrity:* honesty and truthfulness
- ▶ *Competence:* technical and interpersonal knowledge and skills
- ▶ *Consistency:* reliability, predictability, and good judgment in handling situations
- ▶ *Loyalty:* willingness to protect a person, physically and emotionally
- ▶ *Openness:* willingness to share ideas and information freely

Of these five dimensions, integrity seems to be the most critical when someone assesses another's trustworthiness.[52] Both integrity and competence were seen in our earlier discussion of leadership traits found to be consistently associated with leadership. Workplace changes have reinforced why such leadership qualities are important. For instance, the trends toward empowerment and self-managed work teams have reduced many of the traditional control mechanisms used to monitor employees. If a work team is free to schedule its own work, evaluate its own performance, and even make its own hiring decisions, trust becomes critical. Employees have to trust managers to treat them fairly, and managers have to trust employees to conscientiously fulfill their responsibilities.

Let's Get Real

I build trust with my employees by:
- First and foremost, trusting them.
- Being open and honest always.
- Being respectful of their time.
- Being accessible.
- Using two-way communication.

---

legitimate power
The power a leader has as a result of his or her position in the organization

coercive power
The power a leader has to punish or control

reward power
The power a leader has to give positive rewards

expert power
Power that's based on expertise, special skills, or knowledge

referent power
Power that arises because of a person's desirable resources or personal traits

credibility
The degree to which followers perceive someone as honest, competent, and able to inspire

trust
The belief in the integrity, character, and ability of a leader

EXHIBIT 17-6
Building Trust

> *Practice openness.*
> *Be fair.*
> *Speak your feelings.*
> *Tell the truth.*
> *Show consistency.*
> *Fulfill your promises.*
> *Maintain confidences.*
> *Demonstrate competence.*

Managers at Whole Foods Markets lead by empowering employees like this young man who offers to help an appreciative customer load her Thanksgiving Day dinner into her shopping cart. At Whole Foods, employees have a high degree of autonomy in making key operating decisions that directly affect their work. All employees work in small teams that are empowered to make decisions about product selection, pricing, ordering, staffing, and in-store promotion. Whole Foods management believes that empowering employees creates a respectful working environment where people are treated fairly, are highly motivated to succeed, and can respond quickly to customer needs.

Also, leaders have to increasingly lead others who may not be in their immediate work group or may even be physically separated—members of cross-functional or virtual teams, individuals who work for suppliers or customers, and perhaps even people who represent other organizations through strategic alliances. These situations don't allow leaders the luxury of falling back on their formal positions for influence. Many of these relationships, in fact, are fluid and fleeting. So the ability to quickly develop trust and sustain that trust is crucial to the success of the relationship.

Why is it important that followers trust their leaders? Research has shown that trust in leadership is significantly related to positive job outcomes including job performance, organizational citizenship behavior, job satisfaction, and organizational commitment.[53] Given the importance of trust to effective leadership, how can leaders build trust? Exhibit 17-6 lists some suggestions. (Also, see the Building Your Skill exercise in Chapter 5.)[54]

Now, more than ever, managerial and leadership effectiveness depends on the ability to gain the trust of followers.[55] Downsizing, financial challenges, and the increased use of temporary employees have undermined employees' trust in their leaders and shaken the confidence of investors, suppliers, and customers. A survey found that only 39 percent of U.S. employees and 51 percent of Canadian employees trusted their executive leaders.[56] Today's leaders are faced with the challenge of rebuilding and restoring trust with employees and with other important organizational stakeholders.

Empowering Employees

Employees at DuPont's facility in Uberaba, Brazil, planted trees to commemorate the site's 10th anniversary. Although they had several things to celebrate, one of the most important was the fact that since production began, the facility has had zero environmental incidents and no recordable safety violations. The primary reason for this achievement was the company's STOP (Safety Training Observation Program) program—a program in which empowered employees were responsible for observing one another, correcting improper procedures, and encouraging safe procedures.[57]

As we've described in different places throughout the text, managers are increasingly leading by empowering their employees. As we've said before, empowerment involves increasing the decision-making discretion of workers. Millions of individual employees and employee teams are making the key operating decisions that directly affect their work. They're developing budgets, scheduling workloads, controlling inventories, solving quality problems, and engaging in similar activities that until very recently were viewed exclusively as part of the manager's job.[58] For instance, at The Container Store, any employee who gets a customer request has permission to take care of it. Garret Boone, chairman emeritus, says, "Everybody we hire, we hire as a leader. Anybody in our store can take an action that you might think of typically being a manager's action."[59]

One reason more companies are empowering employees is the need for quick decisions by those people who are most knowledgeable about the issues—often those at lower organizational levels. If organizations want to successfully compete in a dynamic global economy, employees have to be able to make decisions and implement changes quickly. Another reason is that organizational downsizings left many managers with larger spans of control. In order to cope with the increased work demands, managers had to empower their people. Although empowerment is not a universal answer, it can be beneficial when employees have the knowledge, skills, and experience to do their jobs competently.

Leading Across Cultures

"In the United States, leaders are expected to look great, sound great, and be inspiring. In other countries—not so much."[60] In this global economy, how can managers account for cross-cultural differences as they lead?

One general conclusion that surfaces from leadership research is that effective leaders do not use a single style. They adjust their style to the situation. Although not mentioned explicitly, national culture is certainly an important situational variable in determining which leadership style will be most effective. What works in China isn't likely to be effective in France or Canada. For instance, one study of Asian leadership styles revealed that Asian managers preferred leaders who were competent decision makers, effective communicators, and supportive of employees.[61]

National culture affects leadership style because it influences how followers will respond. Leaders can't (and shouldn't) just choose their styles randomly. They're constrained by the cultural conditions their followers have come to expect. Exhibit 17-7 provides some findings from selected examples of cross-cultural leadership studies. Because most leadership theories were developed in the United States, they have an American bias. They emphasize follower responsibilities rather than rights; assume self-gratification rather than commitment to duty or altruistic motivation; assume centrality of work and democratic value orientation; and stress rationality rather than spirituality, religion, or superstition.[62] However, the GLOBE research program, which we first introduced in Chapter 3, is the most extensive and comprehensive cross-cultural study of leadership ever undertaken. The GLOBE study found that leadership has some universal aspects. Specifically, a number of elements of transformational leadership appear to be associated with effective leadership regardless of what country the leader is in.[63] These elements include vision, foresight, providing encouragement, trustworthiness, dynamism, positiveness, and proactiveness. The results led two members of the GLOBE team to conclude that "effective business leaders in any country are expected by their subordinates to provide a

---

EXHIBIT 17-7

Cross-Cultural Leadership

- Korean leaders are expected to be paternalistic toward employees.
- Arab leaders who show kindness or generosity without being asked to do so are seen by other Arabs as weak.
- Japanese leaders are expected to be humble and speak frequently.
- Scandinavian and Dutch leaders who single out individuals with public praise are likely to embarrass, not energize, those individuals.
- Effective leaders in Malaysia are expected to show compassion while using more of an autocratic than a participative style.
- Effective German leaders are characterized by high performance orientation, low compassion, low self-protection, low team orientation, high autonomy, and high participation.

Sources: Based on J. C. Kennedy, "Leadership in Malaysia: Traditional Values, International Outlook," *Academy of Management Executive,* August 2002, pp. 15–17; F. C. Brodbeck, M. Frese, and M. Javidan, "Leadership Made in Germany: Low on Compassion, High on Performance," *Academy of Management Executive,* February 2002, pp. 16–29; M. F. Peterson and J. G. Hunt, "International Perspectives on International Leadership," *Leadership Quarterly,* Fall 1997, pp. 203–231; R. J. House and R. N. Aditya, "The Social Scientific Study of Leadership: Quo Vadis?" *Journal of Management,* vol. 23, no. 3, 1997, p. 463; and R. J. House, "Leadership in the Twenty-First Century," in A. Howard (ed.), *The Changing Nature of Work* (San Francisco: Jossey-Bass, 1995), p. 442.

powerful and proactive vision to guide the company into the future, strong motivational skills to stimulate all employees to fulfill the vision, and excellent planning skills to assist in implementing the vision."[64] Some people suggest that the universal appeal of these transformational leader characteristics is due to the pressures toward common technologies and management practices, as a result of global competitiveness and multinational influences.

Becoming an Effective Leader

Organizations need effective leaders. Two issues pertinent to becoming an effective leader are leader training and recognizing that sometimes being an effective leader means *not* leading. Let's take a look at these issues.

LEADER TRAINING.   Organizations around the globe spend billions of dollars, yen, and euros on leadership training and development.[65] These efforts take many forms—from $50,000 leadership programs offered by universities such as Harvard to sailing experiences at the Outward Bound School. Although much of the money spent on leader training may provide doubtful benefits, our review suggests that managers can do some things to get the maximum effect from such training.[66]

First, let's recognize the obvious. Some people don't have what it takes to be a leader. Period. For instance, evidence indicates that leadership training is more likely to be successful with individuals who are high self-monitors than with low self-monitors. Such individuals have the flexibility to change their behavior as different situations may require. In addition, organizations may find that individuals with higher levels of a trait called motivation to lead are more receptive to leadership development opportunities.[67]

What kinds of things can individuals learn that might be related to being a more effective leader? It may be a bit optimistic to think that "vision-creation" can be taught, but implementation skills can be taught. People can be trained to develop "an understanding about content themes critical to effective visions."[68] We can also teach skills such as trust-building and mentoring. And leaders can be taught situational analysis skills. They can learn how to evaluate situations, how to modify situations to make them fit better with their style, and how to assess which leader behaviors might be most effective in given situations.

SUBSTITUTES FOR LEADERSHIP.   Despite the belief that some leadership style will always be effective regardless of the situation, leadership may not always be important! Research indicates that, in some situations, any behaviors a leader exhibits are irrelevant. In other words, certain individual, job, and organizational variables can act as "substitutes for leadership," negating the influence of the leader.[69]

For instance, follower characteristics such as experience, training, professional orientation, or need for independence can neutralize the effect of leadership. These characteristics can replace the employee's need for a leader's support or ability to create structure and reduce task ambiguity. Similarly, jobs that are inherently unambiguous and routine or that are intrinsically satisfying may place fewer demands on leaders. Finally, such organizational characteristics as explicit formalized goals, rigid rules and procedures, or cohesive work groups can substitute for formal leadership.

Let's Get Real:

My Response *to A Manager's Dilemma, page 460*

Adrian Lajtha has an enviable but high-risk challenge. I believe he must do the following to build trust:

- Be respectful of their culture. This will require him to study each ethnicity to ensure he can be effective in his communication.

- Meet with each individual who has been chosen to take part in this leadership program to assess their understanding of the program.

- Develop a multi-tiered program to challenge each person who has been chosen. Each will be on different levels both in communication and skills, and a program must have the flexibility in it to recognize and manage these differences.

- Identify and train a highly skilled team of educators to assist with the program development and implementation. A cross-cultural team will build a stronger development program.

- Communicate, communicate, communicate. Don't leave anything to chance. Working across cultures, this communication may take different forms. Be concise about expectations, timing, and requirements.

- Develop measurement tools that are as nonsubjective as possible.

Keith D. Lynn
Agency Field Executive
State Farm Insurance
Tulsa, OK

CHAPTER SUMMARY
by Learning Outcomes

LEARNING
OUTCOME   **Define** leader and leadership.

A leader is someone who can influence others and who has managerial authority. Leadership is a process of leading a group and influencing that group to achieve its goals. Managers should be leaders because leading is one of the four management functions.

LEARNING
OUTCOME   **Compare** and contrast early theories of leadership.

Early attempts to define leader traits were unsuccessful although later attempts found seven traits associated with leadership.

The University of Iowa studies explored three leadership styles. The only conclusion was that group members were more satisfied under a democratic leader than under an autocratic one. The Ohio State studies identified two dimensions of leader behavior—initiating structure and consideration. A leader high in both those dimensions at times achieved high group task performance and high group member satisfaction, but not always. The University of Michigan studies looked at employee-oriented leaders and production-oriented leaders. They concluded that leaders who were employee oriented could get high group productivity and high group member satisfaction. The Managerial Grid looked at leaders' concern for production and concern for people and identified five leader styles. Although it suggested that a leader who was high in concern for production and high in concern for people was the best, there was no substantive evidence for that conclusion.

As the behavioral studies showed, a leader's behavior has a dual nature: a focus on the task and a focus on the people.

LEARNING
OUTCOME   **Describe** the three major contingency theories of leadership.

Fiedler's model attempted to define the best style to use in particular situations. He measured leader style—relationship oriented or task oriented—using the least-preferred coworker questionnaire. Fiedler also assumed a leader's style was fixed. He measured three contingency dimensions: leader–member relations, task structure, and position power. The model suggests that task-oriented leaders performed best in very favorable and very unfavorable situations, and relationship-oriented leaders performed best in moderately favorable situations.

Hersey and Blanchard's situational leadership theory focused on followers' readiness. They identified four leadership styles: telling (high task–low relationship), selling (high task–high relationship), participating (low task–high relationship), and delegating (low task–low relationship). They also identified four stages of readiness: unable and unwilling (use telling style), unable but willing (use selling style), able but unwilling (use participative style), and able and willing (use delegating style).

The path-goal model developed by Robert House identified four leadership behaviors: directive, supportive, participative, and achievement-oriented. He assumed that a leader can and should be able to use any of these styles. The two situational contingency variables were found in the environment and in the follower. Essentially the path-goal model says that a leader should provide direction and support as needed; that is, structure the path so the followers can achieve goals.

LEARNING
OUTCOME 17.4 **Describe** contemporary views of leadership.

Leader–member exchange theory (LMX) says that leaders create in-groups and out-groups and those in the in-group will have higher performance ratings, less turnover, and greater job satisfaction.

A transactional leader exchanges rewards for productivity where a transformational leader stimulates and inspires followers to achieve goals.

A charismatic leader is an enthusiastic and self-confident leader whose personality and actions influence people to behave in certain ways. People can learn to be charismatic. A visionary leader is able to create and articulate a realistic, credible, and attractive vision of the future.

A team leader has two priorities: manage the team's external boundary and facilitate the team process. Four leader roles are involved: liaison with external constituencies, troubleshooter, conflict manager, and coach.

Discuss contemporary issues affecting leadership.

LEARNING OUTCOME **17.5**

The five sources of a leader's power are legitimate (authority or position), coercive (punish or control), reward (give positive rewards), expert (special expertise, skills, or knowledge), and referent (desirable resources or traits).

Today's leaders face the issues of managing power, developing trust, empowering employees, leading across cultures, and becoming an effective leader.

 To check your understanding of learning outcomes **17.1** – **17.5** go to **mymanagementlab.com** and try the chapter questions.

REVIEW AND DISCUSSION QUESTIONS

1. Define leader and leadership and explain why managers should be leaders.
2. What does each of the four behavioral leadership theories say about leadership?
3. Explain Fiedler's contingency model of leadership.
4. How do situational leadership theory and path-goal theory each explain leadership?
5. What is leader–member exchange theory and what does it say about leadership?

6. Differentiate between transactional and transformational leaders and between charismatic and visionary leaders.
7. What are the five sources of a leader's power?
8. What issues do today's leader's face?
9. Do you think that most managers in real life use a contingency approach to increase their leadership effectiveness? Explain.
10. Do the followers make a difference in whether a leader is effective? Discuss.

PREPARING FOR: My Career

ETHICS DILEMMA

Many people would agree that public school education isn't as effective as it needs to be. But who's to blame? At Central Falls High School, a struggling school in Central Falls, Rhode Island, it seemed that everyone was to blame. Every teacher, principal, administrator, and assistant at an underperforming Rhode Island school was fired in February 2010 by the superintendent, the district's head leader.[70] The move was part of a turnaround

plan proposed by the superintendent and approved by the state educational commissioner. Advocates of the "fire them all" approach called a turnaround an efficient way to remove bad teachers and clean up a culture that made it difficult for teachers to perform well. Even the U.S. Secretary of Education praised the Central Falls action, saying that the leaders there are "showing courage and doing the right thing for the kids." Critics said that this approach doesn't reflect the complexity of teaching in challenging schools. Union officials said, "This is immoral, illegal, unjust, irresponsible, disgraceful and disrespectful." What's your opinion? What ethical issues do you see in this situation? (Think about all the possible stakeholders and their concerns.) What lessons do you see for ethical leadership?

(Postscript: In early June 2010, the Central Falls' school board approved an agreement to let teachers at the city's troubled high school keep their jobs. However, under a deal approved by the teachers' union, the school day will be lengthened by half an hour, and teachers will be required to spend an hour tutoring students each week and to eat lunch with students once a week. They will also be subject to a more rigorous evaluation system.)

SKILLS EXERCISE

Developing Your Choosing an Effective Leadership Style Skill

About the Skill

Effective leaders are skillful at helping the groups they lead be successful as the group goes through various stages of development. No leadership style is consistently effective. Situational factors, including follower characteristics, must be taken into consideration in the selection of an effective leadership style. The key situational factors that determine leadership effectiveness include stage of group development, task structure, position power, leader–member relations, the work group, employee characteristics, organizational culture, and national culture.

Steps in Practicing the Skill

You can choose an effective leadership style if you use the following six suggestions.

1. *Determine the stage in which your group or team is operating: forming, storming, norming, or performing.* Because each team stage involves specific and different issues and behaviors, it's important to know in which stage your team is. *Forming* is the first stage of group development during which people join a group and then help define the group's purpose, structure, and leadership. *Storming* is the second stage characterized by intragroup conflict. *Norming* is the third stage characterized by close relationships and cohesiveness. *Performing* is the fourth stage when the group is fully functional.

2. *If your team is in the forming stage, you want to exhibit certain leader behaviors.* These include making certain that all team members are introduced to one another, answering member questions, working to establish a foundation of trust and openness, modeling the behaviors you expect from the team members, and clarifying the team's goals, procedures, and expectations.

3. *If your team is in the storming stage, you want to exhibit certain leader behaviors.* These behaviors include identifying sources of conflict and adopting a mediator role, encouraging a win-win philosophy, restating the team's vision and its core values and goals, encouraging open discussion, encouraging an analysis of team processes in order to identify ways to improve, enhancing team cohesion and commitment, and providing recognition to individual team members as well as the team.

4. *If your team is in the norming stage, you want to exhibit certain leader behaviors.* These behaviors include clarifying the team's goals and expectations, providing performance feedback to individual team members and the team, encouraging the team to articulate a vision for the future, and finding ways to publicly and openly communicate the team's vision.

5. *If your team is in the performing stage, you want to exhibit certain leader behaviors.* These behaviors include providing regular and ongoing performance feedback, fostering innovation and innovative behavior, encouraging the team to capitalize on its strengths, celebrating achievements (large and small), and providing the team whatever support it needs to continue doing its work.

6. *Monitor the group for changes in behavior and adjust your leadership style accordingly.* Because a group is not a static entity, it will go through up periods and down periods. You should adjust your leadership style to the needs of the situation. If the group appears to need more direction from you, provide it. If it appears to be functioning at a high level on its own, provide whatever support is necessary to keep it functioning at that level.

Practicing the Skill

The following suggestions are activities you can do to practice the behaviors in choosing an effective leadership style.

1. Think of a group or team to which you currently belong or of which you have been a part. What type of leadership style did the leader of this group appear to

exhibit? Give some specific examples of the types of leadership behaviors he or she used. Evaluate the leadership style. Was it appropriate for the group? Why or why not? What would you have done differently? Why?

2. Observe a sports team (either college or professional) that you consider extremely successful and one that you would consider not successful. What leadership styles appear to be used in these team situations? Give some specific examples of the types of leadership behaviors you observe. How would you evaluate the leadership style? Was it appropriate for the team? Why or why not? To what degree do you think leadership style influenced the team's outcomes?

WORKING TOGETHER
Team Exercise

Everybody's probably had at least one experience with a *bad boss*. But what *is* a bad boss? And more importantly, what can you do in such a situation?

Break into small groups of three to four other class members. Come up with a bulleted list of characteristics and behaviors you believe a bad boss would have or exhibit. Then, come up with another bulleted list of what you can do if you find yourself in a situation with a bad boss. Be realistic about your suggestions; that is, don't suggest tampering with the person's coffee or slashing the person's tires!

MY TURN TO BE A MANAGER

- Think of the different organizations to which you belong. Note the different styles of leadership used by the leaders in these organizations. Write a paper describing these individual's style of leading (no names, please) and evaluate the styles being used.

- Write down three people that you consider to be effective leaders. Make a bulleted list of the characteristics these individuals exhibit that you think make them effective leaders.

- Think about the times that you have had to lead. Describe what you think your own personal leadership style is. What could you do to improve your leadership style? Come up with an action plan of steps that you can take. Put all this information into a brief paper.

- Managers say that increasingly they must use influence to get things done. Do some research on the art of persuasion. Make a bulleted list of suggestions that you find on how to improve your skills at influencing others.

- Here's a list of leadership skills. Choose two and develop a training exercise that will help develop or improve that skill: building employee communities; building teams; coaching and motivating others; communicating with impact, confidence, and energy; leading by example; leading change; making decisions; providing direction and focus; and valuing diversity.

- Steve's and Mary's recommended readings: Stephen M. R. Covey with Rebecca Merrell, *The Speed of Trust: The One Thing That Changes Everything* (Free Press, 2006); Nancy S. Ahlrichs, *Manager of Choice* (Davies-Black Publishing, 2003); John H. Zenger and Joseph Folkman, *The Extraordinary Leader: Turning Good Managers into Great Leaders* (McGraw-Hill, 2002); Robert H. Rosen, *Leading People* (Viking Penguin Publishing, 1996); Margaret J. Wheatley, *Leadership and the New Science* (Berrett-Koehler Publishers, 1994); Max DePree, *Leadership Jazz* (Dell Publishing, 1992); and Max DePree, *Leadership Is an Art* (Dell Publishing, 1989).

- Select one of the topics in the section on leadership issues in the twenty-first century. Do some additional research on the topic and put your findings in a bulleted list that you are prepared to share in class. Be sure to cite your sources.

- Interview three managers about what they think it takes to be a good leader. Write up your findings in a report and be prepared to present it in class.

- In your own words, write down three things you learned in this chapter about being a good manager.

- Self-knowledge can be a powerful learning tool. Go to mymanagementlab.com and complete these self-assessment exercises: What's My Leadership Style? What Is My LPC Score? How Charismatic Am I? Do I Trust Others? Do Others See Me as Trustworthy? How Good Am I at Building and Leading a Team? Am I an Ethical Leader? Using the results of your assessments, identify personal strengths and weaknesses. What will you do to reinforce your strengths and improve your weaknesses?

CASE APPLICATION 1
Growing Leaders

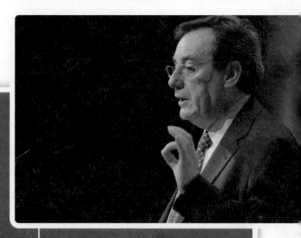

How important are excellent leaders to organizations? If you were to ask 3M CEO George Buckley, he'd say extremely important.[71] But he'd also say that excellent leaders don't just pop up out of nowhere. A company has to cultivate leaders who have the skills and abilities to help it survive and thrive. And like a successful baseball team with strong performance statistics that has a player development plan in place, 3M has its own farm system. Except its farm system is designed to develop company leaders.

3M's leadership development program is so effective that in 2010 it was number three on the list of *BusinessWeek's* "Top 20 Companies for Leadership" and in 2009, *Chief Executive* magazine and Hay Consulting Group named the company the best at developing future leaders. What is 3M's leadership program all about? About 8 years ago, the company's

CEO George Buckley continues to pursue 3M's leadership excellence based on six leadership attributes: the ability to "chart the course; energize and inspire others; demonstrate ethics, integrity, and compliance; deliver results; raise the bar; and innovate resourcefully."

former CEO (Jim McNerney, who is now Boeing's CEO) and his top team spent 18 months developing a new leadership model for the company. After numerous brainstorming sessions and much heated debate, the group finally agreed on six "leadership attributes" that they believed were essential for the company to become skilled at executing strategy and being accountable. Those six attributes included the ability to "chart the course; energize and inspire others; demonstrate ethics, integrity, and compliance; deliver results; raise the bar; and innovate resourcefully." And now under Buckley's guidance, the company is continuing and reinforcing its pursuit of leadership excellence with these six attributes.

When asked about his views on leadership, Buckley said that he believes leaders differ from managers. "A leader is as much about inspiration as anything else. A manager is more about process." He believes that the key to developing leaders is to focus on those things that can be developed—like strategic thinking. Buckley also believes that leaders should not be promoted up and through the organization too quickly. They need time to experience failures and what it takes to rebuild.

Finally, when asked about his own leadership style. Buckley responded, "The absolutely best way for me to be successful is to have people working for me who are better. Having that kind of emotional self-confidence is vital to leaders. You build respect in those people because you admire what they do. Having built respect, you build trust. However hokey it sounds, it works." And it must be working as the company was named the number one most admired company in the medical and other precision equipment division of *Fortune's* most admired ranking for 2009.

Discussion Questions

1. What do you think about Buckley's statement that leaders and managers differ? Do you agree? Why or why not?

2. What leadership models/theories/issues do you see in this case? List and describe.

3. Take each of the six leadership attributes that the company feels is important. Explain what you think each one involves. Then discuss how those attributes might be developed and measured.

4. What did this case teach you about leadership?

CASE APPLICATION 2
Master and Commander

The U.S. military is widely known for its leaders and its leadership training.[72] And rightly so. It's important in the types of situations faced by military units, teams, and squads that they have strong leaders, leaders who can take command and who can understand the situation in deciding what needs to happen. But how and where does leader style factor in? Is it expected and accepted that by the very nature of those types of situations, military leaders have to be hard-nosed, no-nonsense, and tough?

With a father who was a Navy captain, Holly Graf, the first woman to command a Navy cruiser, had long dreamed of doing just that ever since her high school days in Connecticut. Upon graduation from the U.S. Naval Academy in 1985, colleagues sensed that she was on a fast track to leadership. Her assignments were well-rounded—from tours aboard a destroyer tender, a frigate, and a destroyer, to shore assignments at the Pentagon and as a Navy instructor at Villanova University. However, Graf's "darker side began to emerge when she was assigned to the destroyer USS *Curtis Wilbur* as the executive officer (XO) or second in command." One individual (now retired) says his tour on the *Curtis Wilbur* was "the worst time in my life." Graf's constant berating of the crew led him to complain, but nothing was done. A few years later, Graf made U.S. Naval history by becoming the first female commander of a destroyer, the USS *Winston Churchill*. A Navy chaplain recalls his time aboard the *Churchill* as "the strangest of more than 200 such visits to ships in his career. Morale was the lowest he had ever encountered on any vessel." He tried to talk to Graf about what he was hearing from the crew and junior officers, but she cut him off and said she didn't want to talk to him about it. Then, one eventful night began the unraveling of Graf's career.

On the eve of the Iraq war in 2003, the *Churchill* was steaming out of a Sicilian port when, without warning, all 9,000 tons of the vessel shuddered as it cleared the harbor's breakwater. It wasn't long before the 511-foot-long ship was adrift. Commander Graf grabbed the cowering navigator and pulled him aside screaming, "Did you run my x_____x ship aground?" But amid all the chaos and shouting, the Navy chaplain aboard said that "the sound heard next was more startling. Sailors on the *Churchill's* stern, suspecting that their ship had run aground—meaning Graf's career would be instantly over—broke gleefully into song: "Ding Dong, the witch is dead!" He couldn't believe what he was hearing. Even today, the chaplain can't fathom which was worse, that U.S. sailors were openly berating a captain or that the captain seemed to deserve it. But that incident didn't end her career.

Graf's next command as captain of the guided missile-cruiser USS *Cowpens* would be her last, however. She was relieved of duty in January 2010, after nearly two years, for "cruelty and maltreatment" of her crew. The Navy Inspector General's report stated, "Persons in authority are forbidden to injure their subordinates by tyrannical or capricious conduct, or by abusive language." But Graf did so "by demeaning, humiliating, publicly belittling and verbally assaulting . . . subordinates while in command of *Cowpens* with harsh language and profanity . . . rarely followed by any instruction."

Discussion Questions

1. What do you think of this description of Captain Holly Graf's leader style? Do you think that Captain Graf could even be called a leader? Discuss.
2. What kinds of power do you think Graf used as a ship commander? Explain your choices.
3. Not surprisingly, this whole scenario rocked the Navy to its core because it reflected on the way the Navy chooses, promotes, and then monitors its handpicked leaders. What changes, if any, do you think need to take place in its leadership training and development?
4. Some critics of Graf's treatment have said that institutional sexism played a role in her removal. Do you think that could be possible? Discuss. Would that "excuse" the way she led? Explain.

Let's Get Real:

Meet the Manager

Mike Stutzman
Rockwell Collins
Cedar Rapids, IA

You'll be hearing more from this real manager throughout the chapter.

MY JOB:

I am currently leading several initiatives in organizational and leadership development. I am responsible for aligning the learning and development of our leaders to the objectives of the business. I basically am responsible for helping leaders become better leaders so they can demonstrate desired leadership skills and execute their business plans.

BEST PART OF MY JOB:

The single most competitive advantage a company has in any industry today is the ability of its people to continuously learn and grow. Every company has the same access to information and technology. The true differentiator is how learned and engaged an organization's people are in their jobs. I take a lot of pride in and enjoy having a direct impact on a leader's personal and professional development.

Contemporary Issues in Control

LEARNING OUTCOME
Discuss contemporary
issues in control.

The employees of Integrated Information Systems Inc. didn't think twice about exchanging digital music over a dedicated office server they had set up. Like office betting on college and pro sports, it was technically illegal, but harmless, or so they thought. But after the company had to pay a $1 million settlement to the Recording Industry Association of America, managers wished they had controlled the situation better.[29] Control is an important managerial function. We're going to look at four control issues that managers face today: cross-cultural differences, workplace concerns, customer interactions, and corporate governance.

Adjusting Controls for Cross-Cultural Differences

The concepts of control that we've been discussing are appropriate for an organization whose work units are not geographically separated or culturally distinct. But control techniques can be quite different for different countries. The differences are primarily in the measurement and corrective action steps of the control process. In a global corporation, managers of foreign operations tend to be less controlled by the home office, if for no other reason than distance keeps managers from being able to observe work directly. Because distance creates a tendency to formalize controls, such organizations often rely on extensive formal reports for control, most of which are communicated electronically.

Technology's impact on control is also seen when comparing technologically advanced nations with less technologically advanced countries. Managers in countries where technology is more advanced often use indirect control devices such as computer-generated reports and analyses in addition to standardized rules and direct supervision to ensure that work activities are going as planned. In less technologically advanced countries, however, managers tend to use more direct supervision and highly centralized decision making for control.

Managers in foreign countries also need to be aware of constraints on corrective actions they can take. Some countries' laws prohibit closing facilities, laying off employees, taking money out of the country, or bringing in a new management team from outside the country.

Finally, another challenge for global managers in collecting data for measurement and comparison is comparability. For instance, a company that manufactures apparel in Cambodia might produce the same products at a facility in Scotland. However, the Cambodian facility might be more labor intensive than its Scottish counterpart to take advantage of lower labor costs in Cambodia. This difference makes it hard to compare, for instance, labor costs per unit.

Let's Get Real

Control is especially important today because *you get what you measure and consistent measurement of daily expectation of performance is the way to meet organizational goals.*

Workplace Concerns

The month-long World Cup games are a big drain on global productivity. A survey by the Chartered Management Institute says that in the United Kingdom, productivity losses could total just under 1 billion pounds ($1.45 billion). In the United States, March Madness also leads to a drop in productivity—estimated at $1.8 billion during the first week of the tournament—as employees fill out their brackets and survey the message boards and blogs.[30]

Today's workplaces present considerable control challenges for managers. From monitoring employees' computer usage at work to protecting the workplace against disgruntled employees intent on doing harm, managers need controls to ensure that work can be done efficiently and effectively as planned.

benchmarking
The search for the best practices among competitors or noncompetitors that lead to their superior performance

benchmark
The standard of excellence against which to measure and compare

*by the numbers*³⁷

68 percent of workers say they participated in a Super Bowl office pool, and 56 percent participate in a March Madness basketball office pool.

1.7 hours a day is what employees spend doing nothing, costing businesses $4.4 billion a day.

29 percent of fraud cases are in the amount of $100,000 to $499,999.

42 percent of employees who have stolen items from work say it's because they need the items.

88 percent of all data breaches involve insider negligence.

7 percent of revenues is what insider fraud is equal to.

58 percent of employees say they have a boss who plays online games at work.

2 years is the average length of time from fraud start to detection.

WORKPLACE PRIVACY. If you work, do you think you have a right to privacy at your job? What can your employer find out about you and your work? You might be surprised at the answers! Employers can (and do), among other things, read your e-mail (even those marked "personal or confidential"), tap your telephone, monitor your work by computer, store and review computer files, monitor you in an employee bathroom or dressing room, and track your whereabouts in a company vehicle. And these actions aren't that uncommon. In fact, some 26 percent of companies have fired an employee for e-mail misuse; 26 percent have fired workers for misusing the Internet; 6 percent have fired employees for inappropriate cell phone use; 4 percent have fired someone for instant messaging misuse; and 3 percent have fired someone for inappropriate text messaging.[31]

Why do managers feel they need to monitor what employees are doing? A big reason is that employees are hired to work, not to surf the Web checking stock prices, watching online videos, playing fantasy baseball, or shopping for presents for family or friends. Recreational on-the-job Web surfing is thought to cost billions of dollars in lost work productivity annually. In fact, a survey of U.S. employers said that 87 percent of employees look at non-work-related Web sites while at work and more than half engage in personal Web site surfing every day.[32] Watching online video has become an increasingly serious problem not only because of the time being wasted by employees but because it clogs already-strained corporate computer networks.[33] All this nonwork adds up to significant costs to businesses.

Another reason that managers monitor employee e-mail and computer usage is that they don't want to risk being sued for creating a hostile workplace environment because of offensive messages or an inappropriate image displayed on a coworker's computer screen. Concerns about racial or sexual harassment are one reason companies might want to monitor or keep backup copies of all e-mail. Electronic records can help establish what actually happened so managers can react quickly.[34]

Finally, managers want to ensure that company secrets aren't being leaked.[35] In addition to typical e-mail and computer usage, companies are monitoring instant messaging and banning camera phones in the office. Managers need to be certain that employees are not, even inadvertently, passing information on to others who could use that information to harm the company.

Because of the potentially serious costs and given the fact that many jobs now entail computers, many companies have workplace monitoring policies. Such policies should control employee behavior in a nondemeaning way and employees should be informed about those policies.[36]

EMPLOYEE THEFT. At the Saks flagship store in Manhattan, a 23-year-old sales clerk was caught ringing up $130,000 in false merchandise returns and putting the money onto a gift card.[38] And such practices have occurred at other retailers as well.

Would you be surprised to find that up to 85 percent of all organizational theft and fraud is committed by employees, not outsiders?[39] And it's a costly problem—estimated to be around $4,500 per worker per year.[40]

Employee theft is defined as any unauthorized taking of company property by employees for their personal use.[41] It can range from embezzlement to fraudulent filing of expense reports to removing equipment, parts, software, or office supplies from company premises. Although retail businesses have long faced serious potential losses from employee theft, loose financial controls at start-ups and small companies and the ready availability of information technology have made employee stealing an escalating problem in all kinds and sizes of organizations. Managers need to educate themselves about this control issue and be prepared to deal with it.[42]

Why do employees steal? The answer depends on whom you ask.[43] Experts in various fields—industrial security, criminology, clinical psychology—have different perspectives. The industrial security people propose that people steal because the opportunity presents itself through lax controls and favorable circumstances. Criminologists say that it's because people have financial-based pressures (such as personal financial problems) or vice-based pressures (such as gambling debts). And the clinical psychologists suggest that people steal because they can rationalize whatever they're doing as being correct and appropriate behavior ("everyone does it," "they had it coming," "this company makes enough money and they'll never miss anything this small," "I deserve this for all that I put up with," and so forth).[44] Although each approach provides compelling insights into employee theft and has been instrumental in attempts to deter it, unfortunately, employees continue to steal. What can managers do?

The concept of feedforward, concurrent, and feedback control is useful for identifying measures to deter or reduce employee theft.[45] Exhibit 18-11 summarizes several possible managerial actions.

Workplace Violence

In August 2010, a driver about to lose his job at Hartford Distributors in Hartford, Connecticut, opened fire killing eight other employees and himself. In July 2010, a former employee at a solar products manufacturer in Albuquerque, New Mexico, walked into the business and opened fire killing two people and wounding four others. On November 6, 2009, in Orlando, Florida, an engineer who had been dismissed from his job for poor performance returned and shot and killed one person while wounding five others. This incident happened only one day after an Army psychiatrist went on a shooting rampage at Fort Hood Army post killing 13 and wounding 27. On June 25, 2008, in Henderson, Kentucky, an employee at a plastics plant returned hours after arguing with his supervisor over his not wearing safety goggles and for using his cell phone while working on the assembly line. He shot and killed the supervisor, four other coworkers, and himself. On January 30, 2006, a former employee who was once removed from a Santa Barbara, California, postal facility because of "strange behavior"

Feedforward	Concurrent	Feedback
Careful prehiring screening.	Treat employees with respect and dignity.	Make sure employees know when theft or fraud has occurred—not naming names but letting people know this is not acceptable.
Establish specific policies defining theft and fraud and discipline procedures.	Openly communicate the costs of stealing.	Use the services of professional investigators.
Involve employees in writing policies.	Let employees know on a regular basis about their successes in preventing theft and fraud.	Redesign control measures.
Educate and train employees about the policies.	Use video surveillance equipment if conditions warrant.	Evaluate your organization's culture and the relationships of managers and employees.
Have a professional review of your internal security controls.	Install "lock-out" options on computers, telephones, and e-mail.	
	Use corporate hotlines for reporting incidences.	
	Set a good example.	

EXHIBIT 18-11

Controlling Employee Theft

Sources: Based on A. H. Bell and D. M. Smith, "Protecting the Company Against Theft and Fraud," *Workforce Management Online,* December 3, 2000; J. D. Hansen, "To Catch a Thief," *Journal of Accountancy,* March 2000, pp. 43–46; and J. Greenberg, "The Cognitive Geometry of Employee Theft," in S. B. Bacharach, A. O'Leary-Kelly, J. M. Collins, and R. W. Griffin (eds.), *Dysfunctional Behavior in Organizations: Nonviolent and Deviant Behavior* (Stamford, CT: JAI Press, 1998), pp. 147–193.

employee theft
Any unauthorized taking of company property by employees for their personal use

came back and shot five workers to death, critically wounded another, and killed herself. On January 26, 2005, an autoworker at a Jeep plant in Toledo, Ohio, who had met the day before with plant managers about a problem with his work, came in and killed a supervisor and wounded two other employees before killing himself. During April 2003 in Indianapolis, a manager of a Boston Market restaurant was killed by a fellow employee after the restaurant closed because the manager had refused the employee's sexual advances. In July 2003, an employee at an aircraft assembly plant in Meridian, Mississippi, walked out of a mandatory class on ethics and respect in the workplace, returned with firearms and ammunition, shot 14 of his coworkers, killing five and himself.[46] Is workplace violence really an issue for managers? Yes. Despite these examples, thankfully the number of workplace shootings has decreased.[47] However, the U.S. National Institute of Occupational Safety and Health still says that each year, some 2 million American workers are victims of some form of workplace violence. In an average week, one employee is killed and at least 25 are seriously injured in violent assaults by current or former coworkers. And according to a Department of Labor survey, 58 percent of firms reported that managers received verbal threats from workers.[48] Anger, rage, and violence in the workplace are intimidating to coworkers and adversely affect their productivity. The annual cost to U.S. businesses is estimated to be between $20 and $35 billion.[49] And office rage isn't a uniquely American problem. A survey of aggressive behavior in Britain's workplaces found that 18 percent of managers say they have personally experienced harassment or verbal bullying and 9 percent claim to have experienced physical attacks.[50]

What factors are believed to be contributing to workplace violence? Undoubtedly, employee stress caused by an uncertain economic environment, job uncertainties, declining value of retirement accounts, long hours, information overload, other daily interruptions, unrealistic deadlines, and uncaring managers play a role. Even office layout designs with small cubicles where employees work amidst the noise and commotion from those around them have been cited as contributing to the problem.[51] Other experts have described dangerously dysfunctional work environments characterized by the following as primary contributors to the problem:[52]

▶ Employee work driven by TNC (time, numbers, and crises).
▶ Rapid and unpredictable change where instability and uncertainty plague employees.
▶ Destructive communication style where managers communicate in an excessively aggressive, condescending, explosive, or passive-aggressive styles; excessive workplace teasing or scapegoating.
▶ Authoritarian leadership with a rigid, militaristic mind-set of managers versus employees; employees aren't allowed to challenge ideas, participate in decision making, or engage in team-building efforts.
▶ Defensive attitude where little or no performance feedback is given; only numbers count; and yelling, intimidation, or avoidance is the preferred way of handling conflict.
▶ Double standards in terms of policies, procedures, and training opportunities for managers and employees.
▶ Unresolved grievances because the organization provides no mechanisms or only adversarial ones for resolving them; dysfunctional individuals may be protected or ignored because of long-standing rules, union contract provisions, or reluctance to take care of problems.
▶ Emotionally troubled employees and no attempt by managers to get help for these people.
▶ Repetitive, boring work with no chance for doing something else or for new people coming in.
▶ Faulty or unsafe equipment or deficient training, which keeps employees from being able to work efficiently or effectively.
▶ Hazardous work environment in terms of temperature, air quality, repetitive motions, overcrowded spaces, noise levels, excessive overtime, and so forth. To minimize costs,

no additional employees are hired when workload becomes excessive, leading to potentially dangerous work expectations and conditions.

▶ Culture of violence that has a history of individual violence or abuse; violent or explosive role models; or tolerance of on-the-job alcohol or drug abuse.

Reading through this list, you surely hope that workplaces where you'll spend your professional life won't be like this. However, the competitive demands of succeeding in a 24/7 global economy put pressure on organizations and employees in many ways.

What can managers do to deter or reduce possible workplace violence? Once again, the concept of feedforward, concurrent, and feedback control can help identify actions that managers can take.[53] Exhibit 18-12 summarizes several suggestions.

Controlling Customer Interactions

Every month, every local branch of Enterprise Rent-a-Car conducts telephone surveys with customers.[54] Each branch earns a ranking based on the percentage of its customers who say they were "completely satisfied" with their last Enterprise experience—a level of satisfaction referred to as "top box." Top box performance is important to Enterprise because completely satisfied customers are far more likely to be repeat customers. By using this service quality index measure, employees' careers and financial aspirations are linked with the organizational goal of providing consistently superior service to each and every customer. Managers at Enterprise Rent-a-Car understand the connection between employees and customers and the importance of controlling these customer interactions.

There's probably no better area to see the link between planning and controlling than in customer service. If a company proclaims customer service as one of its goals, it quickly and clearly becomes apparent whether that goal is being achieved by seeing how satisfied

Feedforward	Concurrent	Feedback
MBWA (managing by walking around) to identify potential problems; observe how employees treat and interact with each other.	Ensure management commitment to functional, not dysfunctional, work environments.	Communicate openly about incidences and what's being done.
Provide employee assistance programs (EAPs) to help employees with behavioral problems.	Allow employees or work groups to "grieve" during periods of major organizational change.	Investigate incidences and take appropriate action.
Enforce organizational policy that any workplace rage, aggression, or violence will not be tolerated.	Be a good role model in how you treat others.	Review company policies and change, if necessary.
Use careful prehiring screening.	Use corporate hotlines or some other mechanism for reporting and investigating incidences.	
Never ignore threats.	Use quick and decisive intervention.	
Train employees about how to avoid danger if situation arises.	Get expert professional assistance if violence erupts.	
Clearly communicate policies to employees.	Provide necessary equipment or procedures for dealing with violent situations (cell phones, alarm system, code names or phrases, and so forth).	

EXHIBIT 18-12

Controlling Workplace Violence

Sources: Based on M. Gorkin, "Five Strategies and Structures for Reducing Workplace Violence," *Workforce Management Online*, December 3, 2000; "Investigating Workplace Violence: Where Do You Start? *Workforce Management Online*, December 3, 2000; "Ten Tips on Recognizing and Minimizing Violence," *Workforce Management Online*, December 3, 2000; and "Points to Cover in a Workplace Violence Policy," *Workforce Management Online*, December 3, 2000.

customers are with their service! How can managers control the interactions between the goal and the outcome when it comes to customers? The concept of a service profit chain can help.[55]

A **service profit chain** is the service sequence from employees to customers to profit. According to this concept, the company's strategy and service delivery system influence how employees deal with customers; that is, how productive they are in providing service and the quality of that service. The level of employee service productivity and service quality influences customer perceptions of service value. When service value is high, it has a positive impact on customer satisfaction, which leads to customer loyalty. And customer loyalty improves organizational revenue growth and profitability.

What does this concept mean for managers? Managers who want to control customer interactions should work to create long-term and mutually beneficial relationships among the company, employees, and customers. How? By creating a work environment that enables employees to deliver high levels of quality service and which makes them feel they're capable of delivering top-quality service. In such a service climate, employees are motivated to deliver superior service. Employee efforts to satisfy customers, coupled with the service value provided by the organization, improve customer satisfaction. And when customers receive high service value, they're loyal and return, which ultimately improves the company's growth and profitability.

There's no better example of this concept in action than Southwest Airlines, which is the most consistently profitable U.S. airline (the year 2009 marked 37 straight profitable years). Its customers are fiercely loyal because the company's operating strategy (hiring, training, rewards and recognition, teamwork, and so forth) is built around customer service. Employees consistently deliver outstanding service value to customers. And Southwest's customers reward the company by coming back. It's through efficiently and effectively controlling these customer interactions that companies like Southwest and Enterprise have succeeded.

Corporate Governance

Although Andrew Fastow—Enron's former chief financial officer who pled guilty to wire and securities fraud—had an engaging and persuasive personality, that still didn't explain why Enron's board of directors failed to raise even minimal concerns about management's questionable accounting practices. The board even allowed Fastow to set up off-balance-sheet partnerships for his own profit at the expense of Enron's shareholders.

Corporate governance, the system used to govern a corporation so that the interests of corporate owners are protected, failed abysmally at Enron, as it has at many companies caught in financial scandals. In the aftermath of these scandals, corporate governance has been reformed. Two areas where reform has taken place are the role of

Christi Day, public relations coordinator at Southwest Airlines, monitors the airline's social networking sites at company headquarters in Dallas, Texas. Social networking gives customers the opportunity to share their experiences as passengers, and it allows the airline to reach out and respond to customers' comments and concerns. It's a great way for Southwest to develop relationships with customers and to make them feel like the airline appreciates their business and values their input. By efficiently and effectively controlling customer interactions at its social networking sites, Southwest can improve the delivery of quality service that results in satisfied and loyal customers and increased company growth and profitability.

boards of directors and financial reporting. Such reforms aren't limited to U.S. corporations; corporate governance problems are global.[56] Some 75 percent of senior executives at U.S. and Western European corporations expect their boards of directors to take a more active role.[57]

THE ROLE OF BOARDS OF DIRECTORS.   The original purpose of a board of directors was to have a group, independent from management, looking out for the interests of shareholders who were not involved in the day-to-day management of the organization. However, it didn't always work that way. Board members often enjoyed a cozy relationship with managers in which each took care of the other.

This type of "quid pro quo" arrangement has changed. The Sarbanes-Oxley Act puts greater demands on board members of publicly traded companies in the United States to do what they were empowered and expected to do.[58] To help boards do this better, researchers at the Corporate Governance Center at Kennesaw State University developed 13 governance principles for U.S. public companies. (See [www.kennesaw.edu/cgc/21stcentury_2007.pdf] for a list and discussion of these principles.)

FINANCIAL REPORTING AND THE AUDIT COMMITTEE.   In addition to expanding the role of boards of directors, the Sarbanes-Oxley Act also called for more disclosure and transparency of corporate financial information. In fact, senior managers in the United States are now required to certify their companies' financial results. Such changes have led to better information—that is, information that is more accurate and reflective of a company's financial condition. In fulfilling their financial reporting responsibilities, managers might want to follow the principles also developed by the researchers at the Corporate Governance Center at Kennesaw State University. These 15 principles also can be found at [www.kennesaw.edu/cgc/21stcentury_2007.pdf].

service profit chain
The service sequence from employees to customers to profit

corporate governance
The system used to govern a corporation so that the interests of corporate owners are protected

What Would You Do?

**Mike
Stutzman**
Rockwell Collins
Cedar Rapids, IA

Let's Get Real:
My Response *to A Manager's Dilemma, page 486*

I do believe more controls could have helped. However, not in the sense of the *number* of controls, but more along the lines of how the controls were managed. I have found that it's not so much the formality or complexity of the internal controls themselves that have a tendency to fail, it's the behavioral side of how people implement and manage them.

I work in an industry, Aerospace and Aviation Electronics solutions, that demands flawless execution or people's lives are potentially impacted. Our success is not based in the sheer number of controls we have, but rather around how they are managed. In a truly effective controlled environment

- People need to feel safe to speak up when errors occur or to question a process.
- Criticism is given in a way that does not threaten or create a negative stigma.
- Leaders are skilled in holding high-stakes conversations.

I believe in the case of the FIL and Vancouver Organizing Committee that the pressures included time, schedules, and public image, which may have led to a breakdown in the control process.

The eventual solution was to move the starting gate for the luge down the hill to reduce the speed. This outcome suggests a design flaw that may have been discovered through a more thorough analysis and testing of the control processes.

CHAPTER SUMMARY
by Learning Outcomes

Explain the nature and importance of control.

Controlling is the process of monitoring, comparing, and correcting work performance. As the final step in the management process, controlling provides the link back to planning. If managers didn't control, they'd have no way of knowing whether goals were being met.

Control is important because (1) it's the only way to know if goals are being met, and if not, why; (2) it provides information and feedback so managers feel comfortable empowering employees; and (3) it helps protect an organization and its assets.

Describe the three steps in the control process.

The three steps in the control process are measuring, comparing, and taking action. Measuring involves deciding how to measure actual performance and what to measure. Comparing involves looking at the variation between actual performance and the standard (goal). Deviations outside an acceptable range of variation need attention.

Taking action can involve doing nothing, correcting the actual performance, or revising the standards. Doing nothing is self-explanatory. Correcting the actual performance can involve different corrective actions, which can either be immediate or basic. Standards can be revised by either raising or lowering them.

Explain how organizational performance is measured.

Organizational performance is the accumulated results of all the organization's work activities. Three frequently used organizational performance measures include (1) productivity, which is the output of goods or services produced divided by the inputs needed to generate that output; (2) effectiveness, which is a measure of how appropriate organizational goals are and how well those goals are being met; and (3) industry and company rankings compiled by various business publications.

Describe tools used to measure organizational performance.

Feedforward controls take place before a work activity is done. Concurrent controls take place while a work activity is being done. Feedback controls take place after a work activity is done.

Financial controls that managers can use include financial ratios (liquidity, leverage, activity, and profitability) and budgets. One information control managers can use is an MIS, which provides managers with needed information on a regular basis. Others include comprehensive and secure controls such as data encryption, system firewalls, data backups, and so forth that protect the organization's information.

Balanced scorecards provide a way to evaluate an organization's performance in four different areas rather than just from the financial perspective. Benchmarking provides control by finding the best practices among competitors or noncompetitors and from inside the organization itself.

Discuss contemporary issues in control.

Adjusting controls for cross-cultural differences may be needed primarily in the areas of measuring and taking corrective actions.

Workplace concerns include workplace privacy, employee theft, and workplace violence. For each of these issues, managers need to have policies in place to control inappropriate actions and ensure that work is getting done efficiently and effectively.

Control is important to customer interactions because employee service productivity and service quality influences customer perceptions of service value. Organizations want long-term and mutually beneficial relationships among their employees and customers.

Corporate governance is the system used to govern a corporation so that the interests of corporate owners are protected.

mymanagementlab To check your understanding of learning outcomes **18.1** – **18.5** go to **mymanagementlab.com** and try the chapter questions.

REVIEW AND DISCUSSION QUESTIONS

1. What is control and how is control related to planning?
2. What are the three steps in the control process? Describe in detail.
3. What is organizational performance?
4. Contrast feedforward, concurrent, and feedback controls.
5. Discuss the various types of tools used to monitor and measure organizational performance.
6. What workplace concerns do managers have to deal with? How might those concerns be controlled?
7. Why is control important to customer interactions?
8. In Chapter 6 we discussed the white-water rapids view of change. Do you think it's possible to establish and maintain effective standards and controls in this type of environment? Discuss.
9. What are some work activities in which the acceptable range of variation might be higher than average? What about lower than average? (Hint: Think in terms of the output from the work activities, who it might affect, and how it might affect them.)
10. "Every individual employee in an organization plays a role in controlling work activities." Do you agree with this statement, or do you think control is something that only managers are responsible for? Explain.

PREPARING FOR: My Career

ETHICS DILEMMA

The practice is called "sweethearting."[59] It's when cashiers use subtle tricks to pass free goods to friends, doing things such as concealing the bar code, slipping an item behind the scanner, passing two items at a time but only charging for one. It's impossible for even the most watchful human eyes to keep it from happening. So retailers are using technology to block it. Surveillance cameras are used to record and study cashiers staffing checkout lines. What do you think? Is surveillance less invasive when it's a computer watching instead of a human? How could organizations make sure they're monitoring employees' work activities ethically?

SKILLS EXERCISE

Developing Your Performance Feedback Skill

About the Skill

One of the more critical feedback sessions will occur when you, as a manager, are using feedback control to address performance issues.

Steps in Practicing the Skill

1. **Schedule the feedback session in advance and be prepared.** One of the biggest mistakes you can make is to treat feedback control lightly. Simply calling in an employee and giving feedback that's not well organized serves little purpose for you and your employee. For feedback to be effective, you must plan ahead. Identify the issues you wish to address and cite specific examples to reinforce what you are saying. Furthermore, set aside the time for the meeting with the employee. Make sure that what you do is done in private and can be completed without interruptions. That may mean closing your office door (if you have one), not taking phone calls, and the like.

2. **Put the employee at ease.** Regardless of how you feel about the feedback, you must create a supportive climate for the employee. Recognize that giving and getting this feedback can be an emotional event even when the feedback is positive. By putting your employee at ease, you begin to establish a supportive environment in which understanding can take place.

3. **Make sure the employee knows the purpose of this feedback session.** What is the purpose of the meeting? That's something any employee will be wondering. Clarifying what you are going to do sets the appropriate stage for what is to come.

4. **Focus on specific rather than general work behaviors.** Feedback should be specific rather than general.

General statements are vague and provide little useful information—especially if you are attempting to correct a problem.

5. **Keep comments impersonal and job-related.** Feedback should be descriptive rather than judgmental or evaluative, especially when you are giving negative feedback. No matter how upset you are, keep the feedback job-related and never criticize someone personally because of an inappropriate action. You're correcting job-related behavior, not the person.

6. **Support feedback with hard data.** Tell your employee how you came to your conclusion on his or her performance. Hard data help your employees to identify with specific behaviors. Identify the "things" that were done correctly and provide a detailed critique. And if you need to criticize, state the basis of your conclusion that a good job was not completed.

7. **Direct the negative feedback toward work-related behavior that the employee controls.** Negative feedback should be directed toward work-related behavior that the employee can do something about. Indicate what he or she can do to improve the situation. This practice helps take the sting out of the criticism and offers guidance to an individual who understands the problem but doesn't know how to resolve it.

8. **Let the employee speak.** Get the employee's perceptions of what you are saying, especially if you are addressing a problem. Of course, you're not looking for excuses, but you need to be empathetic to the employee. Get his or her side. Maybe something has contributed to the issue. Letting the employee speak involves your employee and just might provide information you were unaware of.

9. **Ensure that the employee has a clear and full understanding of the feedback.** Feedback must be concise and complete enough so that your employee clearly and fully understands what you have said. Consistent with active listening techniques, have your employee rephrase the content of your feedback to check whether it fully captures your meaning.

10. **Detail a future plan of action.** Performing doesn't stop simply because feedback occurred. Good performance must be reinforced, and new performance goals set. However, when performance deficiencies are the issue, time must be devoted to helping your employee develop a detailed, step-by-step plan to correct the situation. This plan includes what has to be done, when, and how you will monitor the activities. Offer whatever assistance you can to help the employee, but make it clear that it is the employee, not you, who has to make the corrections.

Practicing the Skill

Think of a skill you would like to acquire or improve, or a habit you would like to break. Perhaps you would like to learn a foreign language, start exercising, quit smoking, ski better, or spend less. For the purpose of this exercise, assume you have three months to make a start on your project and all the necessary funds. Draft a plan of action that outlines what you need to do, when you need to do it, and how you will know that you have successfully completed each step of your plan. Be realistic, but don't set your sights too low either.

Review your plan. What outside help or resources will you require? How will you get them? Add these to your plan. Could someone else follow the steps you've outlined to achieve the goal you set? What modifications would you have to make, if any?

WORKING TOGETHER
Team Exercise

Research says that up to 80 percent of U.S. teens have worked for pay at some time during high school.[60] As the number of employed teens has risen, so has the likelihood of their getting hurt on the job. How can organizations keep teen workers safe?

Form small groups of three to four students. Come up with some ideas about things an organization could do to keep its teen workers safe. Put your ideas in a bulleted list format and be prepared to share those ideas with the class.

MY TURN TO BE A MANAGER

- You have a major class project due in a month. Identify some performance measures that you could use to help you determine whether the project is going as planned and will be completed efficiently (on time) and effectively (high quality).

- How could you use the concept of control in your personal life? Be specific. (Think in terms of feedforward, concurrent, and feedback controls as well as specific controls for the different aspects of your life—school, work, family relationships, friends, hobbies, etc.)

- Survey 30 people as to whether they have experienced office rage. Ask them specifically whether they have experienced any of the following: yelling or other verbal abuse, yelled at coworkers themselves, cried over work-related issues, seen someone purposely damage machines or furniture, seen physical violence in the workplace, or struck a coworker. Compile your findings in a table. Are you surprised at the results? Be prepared to present these in class.

- Pretend you're the manager of a customer call center for timeshare vacations. What types of control measures would you use to see how efficient and effective an employee is? How about measures for evaluating the entire call center?

- Disciplining employees is one of the least favorite tasks of managers, but is something that all managers have to do. Survey three managers about their experiences with employee discipline. What types of employee actions have caused the need for disciplinary action? What disciplinary actions have they used? What do they think is the most difficult thing to do when disciplining employees? What suggestions do they have for disciplining employees?

- Steve's and Mary's recommended readings: Marcus Buckingham, *Go Put Your Strengths to Work* (Free Press, 2007); W. Steven Brown, *13 Fatal Errors Managers Make and How You Can Avoid Them* (Berkley Business, 1987); and Peter F. Drucker, *Management: Tasks, Responsibilities, Practices* (Harper Business, 1974).

- Research "The Great Package Race." Write a paper describing what it is and how it's a good example of organizational control.

- In your own words, write down three things you learned in this chapter about being a good manager.

- Self-knowledge can be a powerful learning tool. Go to mymanagementlab.com and complete these self-assessment exercises: How Good Am I at Disciplining Others? How Willing Am I to Delegate? What Time of Day Am I Most Productive? How Good Am I at Giving Performance Feedback? Using the results of your assessments, identify personal strengths and weaknesses. What will you do to reinforce your strengths and improve your weaknesses?

CASE APPLICATION 1
Deepwater in Deep Trouble

When all is said and done, which may not be for many years, it's likely to be one of the worst environmental disasters, if not the worst, in U.S. history.[61] When British Petroleum's (BP) Deepwater Horizon off-shore rig in the Gulf of Mexico exploded in a ball of flames on April 20, 2010, killing 11 employees, it set in motion frantic efforts to stop the flow of oil and to initiate the long and arduous cleanup process. Although the impacts of the explosion and oil spill were felt most intensely by businesses and residents along the coast and by coastal wildlife, those of us inland who watched the disaster unfold were also stunned and dismayed by what we saw happening. What led to this disaster and what can BP do to ensure that the likelihood of it ever happening again is minimized?

Strong warning signs indicated serious problems with well equipment and other safety aspects of the Deepwater Horizon oil rig, but a lack of effective controls needed to protect the rig as the employees' workplace resulted in a tragic explosion and oil spill.

One thing that has come to light in the disaster investigation is that it's no surprise that something like this happened. After Hurricane Dennis blew through in July 2005, a passing ship was shocked to see BP's new massive $1 billion Thunder Horse oil platform "listing precariously to one side, looking for all the world as if it were about to sink." Thunder Horse "was meant to be the company's crowning glory, the embodiment of its bold gamble to outpace its competitors in finding and exploiting the vast reserves of oil beneath the waters of the gulf." But the problems with this rig soon became evident. A valve installed backwards caused it to flood during the hurricane even before any oil had been pumped. Other problems included a welding job so shoddy that it left underwater pipelines brittle and full of cracks. "The problems at Thunder Horse were not an anomaly, but a warning that BP was taking too many risks and cutting corners in pursuit of growth and profits."

Then came the tragic explosion on the Deepwater Horizon. Before the rig exploded, strong warning signs indicated that something was terribly wrong with the oil well. Among the red flags were several equipment readings suggesting that gas was bubbling into the well, a potential sign of an impending blowout. Those red flags were ignored. Other decisions made in the 24 hours before the explosion included a critical decision to replace heavy mud in the pipe rising from the seabed with seawater, again possibly increasing the risk of an explosion. Internal BP documents also show serious problems and safety concerns with Deepwater. Those problems involved the well casing and blowout preventer. One BP senior drilling engineer warned, "This would certainly be a worst-case scenario."

The federal panel charged with investigating the spill has been examining 20 "anomalies in the well's behavior and the crew's response." The panel is also investigating in particular why "rig workers missed telltale signs that the well was close to an uncontrolled blowout."

Discussion Questions

1. What type(s) of control—feedforward, concurrent, or feedback—do you think would have been most useful in this situation? Explain your choice(s).
2. Using Exhibit 18-2, explain what BP could have done better.
3. Why do you think company employees ignored the red flags? How could such behavior be changed in the future?
4. What could other organizations learn from BP's mistakes?

CASE APPLICATION
Baggage Blunders

Terminal 5 (T5), built by British Airways for $8.6 billion, is London Heathrow Airport's newest state-of-the-art facility.[62] Made of glass, concrete, and steel, it's the largest free-standing building in the United Kingdom and has more than 10 miles of belts for moving luggage. At the terminal's unveiling in March of 2008, Queen Elizabeth II called it a "twenty-first-century gateway to Britain." Alas . . . the accolades didn't last long! After two decades in planning and 100 million hours in manpower, opening day didn't work out as planned. Endless lines and major baggage handling delays led to numerous flight cancellations stranding many irate passengers. Airport operators said the problems were triggered by glitches in the terminal's high-tech baggage-handling system.

With its massive automation features, T5 was planned to ease congestion at Heathrow and improve the flying experience for the 30 million passengers expected to pass through it annually. With 96 self-service check-in kiosks, more than 90 fast check-in bag drops, 54 standard check-in desks, and miles of suitcase-moving belts estimated to be able to process 12,000 bags per hour, the facility's design seemed to support those goals.

However, within the first few hours of the terminal's operation, problems developed. Presumably understaffed, baggage workers were unable to clear incoming luggage fast enough. Arriving passengers waited more than an hour for their bags. Departing passengers tried in vain to check in for flights. Flights left with empty cargo holds. Sometime on day one, the airline checked in only those passengers with no luggage. And it didn't help that the moving belt system jammed at one point. Lesser problems also became apparent: a few broken escalators, some hand dryers that didn't work, a gate that wouldn't function at the new Underground station, and inexperienced ticket sellers who didn't know the fares between Heathrow and various stations on the Piccadilly line. By the end of the first full day of operation, Britain's Department of Transportation released a statement calling for British Airways and the airport operator BAA to "work hard to resolve these issues and limit disruptions to passengers."

You might be tempted to think that all of this could have been prevented if British Airways had only tested the system. But thorough runs of all systems "from toilets to check in and seating" took place six months before opening, including four full-scale test runs using 16,000 volunteers.

Although T5's debut was far from perfect, things have certainly changed. A recent customer satisfaction survey showed that 80 percent of passengers waited less than five minutes to check in. And those passengers are extremely satisfied with the terminal's lounges, catering, facilities, and ambience. It's a nice ending to the chaotic beginning.

Discussion Questions

1. What type of control—feedforward, concurrent, or feedback—do you think would be most important in this situation? Explain your choice.
2. How might immediate corrective action have been used in this situation? How about basic corrective action?
3. Could British Airways' controls have been more effective? How?
4. What role would information controls play in this situation? Customer interaction controls? Benchmarking?

Let's Get Real:

Meet the Manager

Andy Pothast
Plant Manager
Sargento Foods, Inc.
Hilbert, WI

You'll be hearing more from this real manager throughout the chapter.

MY JOB:

I'm a plant manager for Sargento Foods Inc. and am responsible for the day-to-day operations of a food manufacturing plant that specializes in the production of cheese products sold to large restaurant chains and other food companies.

BEST PART OF MY JOB:

The satisfaction of seeing people succeed in reaching their personal goals, which includes promotional opportunities or the plant reaching its yearly goals for safety, quality, cost containment, and service level.

Managing Operations

LEARNING OUTCOMES

WORST PART OF MY JOB:

Not having the resources sometimes to accomplish everything you want done, which is why as a manager you need to understand the strengths and weaknesses of your people and prioritize tasks that give you the most value.

BEST MANAGEMENT ADVICE EVER RECEIVED:

I have three that come to mind.

▶ Understand where value is being created in your organization, and lead your people or department to add to this value. As a manager, you need to make sure people are working on value-added tasks.

▶ "Management by walking around." Get out of your office and talk to people.

▶ Don't be in a hurry to be promoted to a management position. Management is tough, so learn as much as possible before you take on more responsibilities. You'll know when you're ready.

Using millions of parts as small as rivets and as large as five-story buildings, employees at Hyundai Heavy Industries Inc. build as many as 30 ships at one time.[1] And the "factory" stretches for miles over land and sea. "It's an environment that is too large and complex to be able to keep track of the movement in parts and inventory in real time." Hwang See-young, chief information officer at Hyundai Heavy, knew that production efficiency was limited without real-time data. The solution? High-speed wireless networks that employees can access at anytime and anywhere with notebook computers.

With the new technology, data fly around the shipyard complex at 4 megabits per second. Radio sensors track the movements of parts from fabrication shops to the dry dock and onto a ship being constructed. Also, workers on a ship can access plans using notebook computers or handheld phones. They're also able to hold two-way video conversations with ship designers in the office over a mile away. Eventually, they hope to establish communication capabilities with workers inside a ship that is below ground or at sea level. Now, however, Hyundai Heavy wants to implement the technology in its other construction divisions. Suppose that you were in charge of doing this.

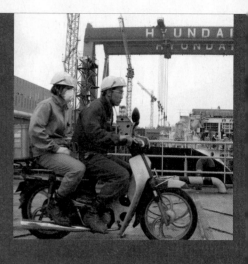

What Would You Do?

As the world's largest maker of ships, Hyundai hopes its new technology helps it reduce expenses and streamline production, an important consideration in today's environment. You've probably never given much thought to how organizations "produce" the goods and services that you buy or use. But it's an important process. Without it, you wouldn't have a car to drive or McDonald's fries to snack on, or even a hiking trail in a local park to enjoy. Organizations need to have well-thought-out and well-designed operating systems, organizational control systems, and quality programs to survive in today's increasingly competitive global environment. And it's the manager's job to manage those systems and programs.

LEARNING OUTCOME 19.1
Explain the role of operations management.

The Role of Operations Management

Inside Intel's factory in New Mexico, employee Trish Roughgarden is known as a "seed"— an unofficial title for technicians who transfer manufacturing know-how from one Intel facility to another.[2] Her job is to make sure that this factory works just like an identical one that opened earlier in Oregon. Then, when a third plant opened in Ireland, several hundred other seeds copied the same techniques. The company's facility in Arizona also benefited from "seeding." What the seeds do is part of a strategy known as "Copy Exactly," which Intel implemented after frustrating variations between factories hurt productivity and product quality. In the intensely competitive chip-making industry, Intel knows that how it manages operations will determine whether it succeeds.

What is **operations management**? The term refers to the transformation process that converts resources into finished goods and services. Exhibit 19-1 portrays this

EXHIBIT 19-1

The Operations System

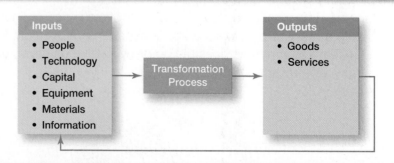

Inputs
- People
- Technology
- Capital
- Equipment
- Materials
- Information

Transformation Process

Outputs
- Goods
- Services

process in a simplified fashion. The system takes in inputs—people, technology, capital, equipment, materials, and information—and transforms them through various processes, procedures, work activities, and so forth into finished goods and services. Because every unit in an organization produces something, managers need to be familiar with operations management concepts in order to achieve goals efficiently and effectively.

Operations management is important to organizations and managers for three reasons: (1) It encompasses both services and manufacturing; (2) it's important in effectively and efficiently managing productivity; and (3) it plays a strategic role in an organization's competitive success.

Services and Manufacturing

With a menu that offers more than 200 items, The Cheesecake Factory restaurants rely on a finely tuned production system. One food-service consultant says, "They've evolved with this highly complex menu combined with a highly efficient kitchen."[3]

Every organization produces something. Unfortunately, this fact is often overlooked except in obvious cases such as in the manufacturing of cars, cell phones, or lawnmowers. After all, **manufacturing organizations** produce physical goods. It's easy to see the operations management (transformation) process at work in these types of organizations because raw materials are turned into recognizable physical products. But the transformation process isn't as readily evident in **service organizations** that produce nonphysical outputs in the form of services. For instance, hospitals provide medical and health care services that help people manage their personal health, airlines provide transportation services that move people from one location to another, a cruise line provides a vacation and entertainment service, military forces provide defense capabilities, and the list goes on and on. These service organizations also transform inputs into outputs, although the transformation process isn't as easily recognizable as that in manufacturing organizations. Take a university, for example. University administrators bring together inputs—professors, books, academic journals, technology materials, computers, classrooms, and similar resources—to transform "unenlightened" students into educated and skilled individuals who are capable of making contributions to society.

The reason we're making this point is that the U.S. economy, and to a large extent the global economy, is dominated by the creation and sale of services. Most of the world's developed countries are predominantly service economies. In the United States, for instance, almost 77 percent of all economic activity is services and in the European Union, it's nearly 73 percent.[4] In lesser-developed countries, the services sector is less important. For instance, in Nigeria, it accounts for only 33 percent of economic activity; in Laos, only 37 percent; and in Vietnam, 38 percent.[5]

Let's Get Real

How our product is produced: *Raw ingredients are assembled, weighed, and cooked in large cookers and then filled in various packaging sizes to meet customer needs.*

Managing Productivity

One jetliner has roughly 4 million parts. Efficiently assembling such a finely engineered product requires intense focus. Boeing and Airbus, the two major global manufacturers, have copied techniques from Toyota. However, not every technique can be copied because airlines demand more customization than do car buyers and significantly more rigid safety regulations apply to jetliners than to cars.[6] At the Evans Findings Company in East Providence, Rhode Island, which makes the tiny cutting devices on dental-floss containers, one production shift each day is run without people.[7] The company's goal is to do as much as possible with no labor. And it's not because they don't care about their employees. Instead, like many U.S. manufacturers, Evans needed to raise productivity in order to survive, especially against low-cost competitors. So they turned to "lights-out" manufacturing

operations management
The transformation process that converts resources into finished goods and services

manufacturing organizations
Organizations that produce physical goods

service organizations
Organizations that produce nonphysical products in the form of services

where machines are designed to be so reliable that they make flawless parts on their own, without people operating them.

Although most organizations don't make products that have 4 million parts and most organizations can't function without people, improving productivity has become a major goal in virtually every organization. For countries, high productivity can lead to economic growth and development. Employees can receive higher wages and company profits can increase without causing inflation. For individual organizations, increased productivity gives them a more competitive cost structure and the ability to offer more competitive prices.

Over the past decade, U.S. businesses have made dramatic improvements to increase their efficiency. For example, at Latex Foam International's state-of-the-art digital facility in Shelton, Connecticut, engineers monitor all of the factory's operations. The facility boosted capacity by 50 percent in a smaller space but with a 30 percent efficiency gain.[8] And it's not just in manufacturing that companies are pursuing productivity gains. Pella Corporation's purchasing office improved productivity by reducing purchase order entry times anywhere from 50 percent to 86 percent, decreasing voucher processing by 27 percent, and eliminating 14 financial systems. Its information technology department slashed e-mail traffic in half and implemented work design improvements for heavy PC users such as call center users. The human resources department cut the time to process benefit enrollment by 156.5 days. And the finance department now takes 2 days instead of 6 to do its end-of-month closeout.[9]

Organizations that hope to succeed globally are looking for ways to improve productivity. For example, McDonald's Corporation drastically reduced the time it takes to cook its french fries—65 seconds as compared to the 210 seconds it once took, saving time and other resources.[10] The Canadian Imperial Bank of Commerce, based in Toronto, automated its purchasing function, saving several million dollars annually.[11] And Skoda, the Czech car company that's a subsidiary of Germany's Volkswagen AG, improved its productivity through an intensive restructuring of its manufacturing process.[12]

Productivity is a composite of people and operations variables. To improve productivity, managers must focus on both. The late W. Edwards Deming, a renowned quality expert, believed that managers, not workers, were the primary source of increased productivity. Some of his suggestions for managers included planning for the long-term future, never being complacent about product quality, understanding whether problems were confined to particular parts of the production process or stemmed from the overall process itself, training workers for the job they're being asked to perform, raising the quality of line supervisors, requiring workers to do quality work, and so forth.[13] As you can see, Deming understood the interplay between people and operations. High productivity can't come solely from good "people management." The truly effective organization will maximize productivity by successfully integrating people into the overall operations system. For instance, at Simplex Nails Manufacturing in Americus, Georgia, employees were an integral part of the company's much-needed turnaround effort.[14] Some production workers were redeployed on a plant-wide cleanup and organization effort, which freed up floor space. The company's sales force was retrained and refocused to sell what customers wanted rather than what was in inventory. The results were dramatic. Inventory was reduced by more than 50 percent, the plant had 20 percent more floor space, orders were more consistent, and employee morale improved. Here's a company that recognized the important interplay between people and the operations system.

Strategic Role of Operations Management

Modern manufacturing originated over 100 years ago in the United States, primarily in Detroit's automobile factories. The success that U.S. manufacturers experienced during World War II led manufacturing executives to believe that troublesome production problems had been conquered. These executives focused, instead, on improving other functional areas such as finance and marketing and paid little attention to manufacturing.

However, as U.S. executives neglected production, managers in Japan, Germany, and other countries took the opportunity to develop modern, computer-based, and technologically advanced facilities that fully integrated manufacturing operations into strategic planning decisions. The competition's success realigned world manufacturing leadership. U.S. manufacturers soon discovered that foreign goods were being made not only less expensively but also with better quality. Finally, by the late 1970s, U.S. executives recognized that they were facing a true crisis and responded. They invested heavily in improving manufacturing technology, increased the corporate authority and visibility of manufacturing executives, and began incorporating existing and future production requirements into the organization's overall strategic plan. Today, successful organizations recognize the crucial role that operations management plays as part of the overall organizational strategy to establish and maintain global leadership.[15]

The strategic role that operations management plays in successful organizational performance can be seen clearly as more organizations move toward managing their operations from a value chain perspective, which we're going to discuss next.

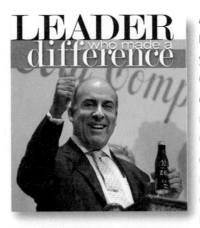

Any guesses as to the world's best global brand . . . for three years running?[16] If you said Coca-Cola, you'd be correct. The company's CEO, Muhtar Kent, recognizes that keeping the Coke family of products number one in customers' minds requires attention to all aspects of production and marketing. Recently, the company worked closely with its biggest bottler to eliminate longstanding "friction points" by creating a joint supply-chain organization. Kent also says that it's important to meet customers' needs and it does that by visiting 20 million shops every week so it can have a pretty good understanding of what's going on with its customers.

What Is Value Chain Management and Why Is It Important?

19.2

LEARNING OUTCOME
Define the nature and purpose of value chain management.

It's 11 P.M., and you're reading a text message from your parents saying they want to buy you a laptop for your birthday this year and to order it. You log on to Dell's Web site and configure your dream machine. You hit the order button and not long after, your dream computer is delivered to your front door, built to your exact specifications, ready to set up and use immediately to type that management assignment due tomorrow. Or consider Siemens AG's Computed Tomography manufacturing plant in Forchheim, Germany, which has established partnerships with about 30 suppliers. These suppliers are partners in the truest sense as they share responsibility with the plant for overall process performance. This arrangement has allowed Siemens to eliminate all inventory warehousing and has streamlined the number of times paper changes hands to order parts from 18 to one. At the Timken's plant in Canton, Ohio, electronic purchase orders are sent across the street to an adjacent "Supplier City" where many of its key suppliers have set up shop. The process takes milliseconds and costs less than 50 cents per purchase order. And when Black & Decker extended its line of hand-held tools to include a glue gun, it totally outsourced the entire design and production to the leading glue gun manufacturer. Why? Because they understood that glue guns don't require motors, which was what Black & Decker did best.[17]

As these examples show, closely integrated work activities among many different players are possible. How? The answer lies in value chain management. The concepts of value chain management have transformed operations management strategies and turned organizations around the world into finely tuned models of efficiency and effectiveness strategically positioned to exploit competitive opportunities.

Let's Get Real

F2F

Understanding operations management is important because *it will give an individual a strong base of knowledge that can be transferred to any future job one might end up in.*

What Is Value Chain Management?

Every organization needs customers if it's going to survive and prosper. Even a not-for-profit organization must have "customers" who use its services or purchase its products. Customers want some type of value from the goods and services they purchase or use, and these customers decide what has value. Organizations must provide that value to attract and keep customers. **Value** is defined as the performance characteristics, features, and attributes, and any other aspects of goods and services for which customers are willing to give up resources (usually money). For example, when you purchase Rihanna's new CD at Best Buy, a new pair of Australian sheepskin Ugg boots online at Zappos, a Wendy's bacon cheeseburger at the drive-through location on campus, or a haircut from your local hair salon, you're exchanging (giving up) money in return for the value you need or desire from these products—providing music during your evening study time, keeping your feet warm *and* fashionable during winter's cold weather, alleviating the lunchtime hunger pangs quickly since your next class starts in 15 minutes, or looking professionally groomed for the job interview you've got next week.

How *is* value provided to customers? Through transforming raw materials and other resources into some product or service that end users need or desire when, where, and how they want it. However, that seemingly simple act of turning varied resources into something that customers value and are willing to pay for involves a vast array of interrelated work activities performed by different participants (suppliers, manufacturers, and even customers)—that is, it involves the value chain. The **value chain** is the entire series of organizational work activities that add value at each step from raw materials to finished product. In its entirety, the value chain can encompass the supplier's suppliers to the customer's customer.[18]

Value chain management is the process of managing the sequence of activities and information along the entire value chain. In contrast to supply chain management, which is *internally* oriented and focuses on efficient flow of incoming materials (resources) to the organization, value chain management is *externally* oriented and focuses on both incoming materials and outgoing products and services. Although supply chain management is efficiency oriented (its goal is to reduce costs and make the organization more productive), value chain management is effectiveness oriented and aims to create the highest value for customers.[19]

Goal of Value Chain Management

Who has the power in the value chain? Is it the suppliers providing needed resources and materials? After all, they have the ability to dictate prices and quality. Is it the manufacturer who assembles those resources into a valuable product or service? Their contribution in creating a product or service is quite obvious. Is it the distributor that makes sure the product or service is available where and when the customer needs it? Actually, it's none of these! In value chain management, ultimately customers are the ones with power.[20] They're the ones who define what value is and how it's created and provided. Using value chain management, managers hope to find that unique combination that offers customers solutions to truly meet their unique needs incredibly fast and at a price that can't be matched by competitors.

With these factors in mind then, the goal of value chain management is to create a value chain strategy that meets and exceeds customers' needs and desires and allows for full and seamless integration among all members of the chain. A good value chain involves a sequence of participants working together as a team, each adding some component of value—such as faster assembly, more accurate information, better customer response and service, and so forth—to the overall process.[21] The better the collaboration among the various chain participants, the better the customer solutions. When value is created for customers and their needs and desires are satisfied, everyone along the chain benefits. For example, at Johnson Controls Inc., managing the value chain started first with improved relationships with internal suppliers, then expanded out to external suppliers and customers. As the company's experience with value chain management improved, so did its connection with its customers, which ultimately paid off for all its value chain partners.[22]

Benefits of Value Chain Management

Collaborating with external and internal partners in creating and managing a successful value chain strategy requires significant investments in time, energy, and other resources, and a serious commitment by all chain partners. Given these demands, why would managers ever choose to implement value chain management? A survey of manufacturers noted four primary benefits of value chain management: improved procurement, improved logistics, improved product development, and enhanced customer order management.[23]

Managing Operations Using Value Chain Management

19.3

LEARNING OUTCOME
Describe how value chain management is done.

Even though it's the world's largest retailer, Walmart Stores still looks for ways to more effectively and efficiently manage its value chain. Its current efforts involve taking over U.S. transportation services from suppliers in an effort to reduce the cost of transporting goods. The goal: "to handle suppliers' deliveries in instances where Walmart can do the same job for less, then use those savings to reduce prices in stores." Walmart believes it has the size and scale to allow it to ship most products more efficiently than the companies that produce the goods.[24]

Even if you're Walmart Stores, managing an organization from a value chain perspective isn't easy. Approaches to giving customers what they want that may have worked in the past are likely no longer efficient or effective. Today's dynamic competitive environment demands new solutions from global organizations. Understanding how and why value is determined by the marketplace has led some organizations to experiment with a new business model, a concept we introduced in Chapter 9. For example, IKEA transformed itself from a small Swedish mail-order furniture operation into one of the world's largest furniture retailers by reinventing the value chain in that industry. The company offers customers well-designed products at substantially lower prices in return for their willingness to take on certain key tasks traditionally done by manufacturers and retailers—assembling furniture and getting it home.[25] The company's creation of a new business model and willingness to abandon old methods and processes has worked well.

Value Chain Strategy

Exhibit 19-2 shows the six main requirements of a successful value chain strategy: coordination and collaboration, technology investment, organizational processes, leadership, employees, and organizational culture and attitudes.

EXHIBIT 19-2

Value Chain Strategy Requirements

---

value
The performance characteristics, features, and attributes, and any other aspects of goods and services for which customers are willing to give up resources

value chain
The entire series of organizational work activities that add value at each step from raw materials to finished product

value chain management
The process of managing the sequence of activities and information along the entire value chain

COORDINATION AND COLLABORATION. For the value chain to achieve its goal of meeting and exceeding customers' needs and desires, collaborative relationships among all chain participants must exist.[26] Each partner must identify things he or she may not value but that customers do. Sharing information and being flexible as far as who in the value chain does what are important steps in building coordination and collaboration. This sharing of information and analysis requires more open communication among the various value chain partners. For example, Kraft Foods believes that better communication with customers and with suppliers has facilitated timely delivery of goods and services.[27]

TECHNOLOGY INVESTMENT. Successful value chain management isn't possible without a significant investment in information technology. The payoff from this investment, however, is that information technology can be used to restructure the value chain to better serve end users. For example, each year the Houston-based food distributor Sysco ships 21.5 million tons of produce, meats, prepared meals, and other food-related products to restaurants, cafeterias, and sports stadiums. To get all that food safely to the right place at the right time, Sysco relies on a complex web of software, databases, scanning systems, and robotics.[28]

ORGANIZATIONAL PROCESSES. At Pactiv Corporation, which manufactures consumer and food-service packaging, the company relied on a planning process that included three-year breakthrough goals, which were then translated into one-year goals, annual improvement priorities, and measurable targets. This disciplined approach to planning has helped the company grow and achieve its goals.[29]

Value chain management radically changes **organizational processes**—that is, the ways that organizational work is done. When managers decide to manage operations using value chain management, old processes are no longer appropriate. All organizational processes must be critically evaluated from beginning to end to see where value is being added. Non-value-adding activities should be eliminated. Questions such as "Where can internal knowledge be leveraged to improve the flow of material and information?" "How can we better configure our product to satisfy both customers and suppliers?" "How can the flow of material and information be improved?" and "How can we improve customer service?" should be asked for each and every process. For example, when managers at Deere and Company implemented value chain management, a thorough process evaluation revealed that work activities needed to be better synchronized and interrelationships between multiple links in the value chain better managed. They changed numerous work processes division-wide in order to realize greater value.[30]

IKEA's value chain management involves collaboration and coordination with customers in processes that enable the company to offer good quality products at low costs. Rather than offering home delivery and product assembly as other furniture retailers do, IKEA expects customers to perform the transport and assembly processes. The retailer facilitates the transportation process by providing customers with tape measures, pencils, and paper while they shop to record product measurements and offers car roof racks for purchase at cost and mini trucks available for rental. The delight of shoppers shown here at IKEA's first store in the Republic of Ireland attest to the retailer's success in providing the value that customers want.

Three important conclusions can be made about organizational processes. First, better demand forecasting is necessary *and* possible because of closer ties with customers and suppliers. For example, in an effort to make sure that Listerine was on the store shelves when customers wanted it (known in the retail industry as *product replenishment rates*), Walmart and Pfizer's Consumer Healthcare Group collaborated on improving product demand forecast information. Through their mutual efforts, the partners boosted Walmart's sales of Listerine, an excellent outcome for both supplier and retailer. Customers also benefited because they were able to purchase the product when and where they wanted it.

Second, selected functions may need to be done collaboratively with other partners in the value chain. This collaboration may even extend to sharing employees. For instance, Saint-Gobain Performance Plastics places its own employees in customer sites and brings in employees of suppliers and customers to work on its premises.[31]

Finally, new measures are needed for evaluating performance of various activities along the value chain. Because the goal in value chain management is meeting and exceeding customers' needs and desires, managers need a better picture of how well this value is being created and delivered to customers. For example, when Nestlé USA implemented value chain management, it redesigned its metrics system to focus on one consistent set of measurements—including, for instance, accuracy of demand forecasts and production plans, on-time delivery, and customer-service levels—that allowed them to more quickly identify problem areas and take actions to resolve them.[32]

LEADERSHIP. Successful value chain management isn't possible without strong and committed leadership. From top organizational levels to lower levels, managers must support, facilitate, and promote the implementation and ongoing practice of value chain management. Managers must seriously commit to identifying what value is, how that value can best be provided, and how successful those efforts have been. A culture where all efforts are focused on delivering superb customer value isn't possible without a serious commitment on the part of the organization's leaders.

Also, it's important that managers outline expectations for what's involved in the organization's pursuit of value chain management. Ideally, managers start with a vision or mission statement that expresses the organization's commitment to identifying, capturing, and providing the highest possible value to customers. For instance, when American Standard began using value chain management, the CEO held dozens of meetings across the United States to explain the new competitive environment and why the company needed to create better working relationships with its value chain partners in order to better serve the needs of its customers.[33]

Then, managers should clarify expectations regarding each employee's role in the value chain. But clear expectations aren't just important for internal partners. Being clear about expectations also extends to external partners. For example, managers at American Standard identified clear requirements for suppliers and were prepared to drop any that couldn't meet them, and did so. The upside, though, was that those suppliers that met the expectations benefited from more business and American Standard had partners willing to work with them in delivering better value to customers.

EMPLOYEES/HUMAN RESOURCES. When new employees at the Thermo Fisher Scientific plant in Marietta, Ohio, have work-related questions, they can consult with a member of the facility's "Tree of Knowledge." The "tree" is actually a bulletin board with pictures of employees who have worked at the plant for decades.[34]

We know from our discussions of management theories throughout this textbook that employees are an organization's most important resource. Without employees, no products are produced and no services are delivered—in fact, no organized efforts in the pursuit of common goals would be possible. So not surprisingly, employees play an

organizational processes
The ways that organizational work is done

important role in value chain management. The three main human resource requirements for value chain management are flexible approaches to job design, effective hiring process, and ongoing training.

Flexibility is the key to job design in value chain management. Traditional functional job roles—such as marketing, sales, accounts payable, customer service, and so forth—won't work. Instead, jobs must be designed around work processes that create and provide value to customers. It takes flexible jobs and flexible employees. For instance, at Nordson Corporation's facility in Swainsboro, Georgia, workers are trained to do several different tasks, which isn't all that uncommon in many manufacturing plants. What's unique about this facility is that even salaried employees are expected to spend four hours every month building products on the shop floor.[35]

In a value chain organization, employees may be assigned to work teams that tackle a given process and may be asked to do different things on different days depending on need. In such an environment where customer value is best delivered through collaborative relationships that may change as customer needs change and where processes or job descriptions are not standardized, an employee's ability to be flexible is critical. Therefore, the organization's hiring process must be designed to identify those employees who have the ability to learn and adapt.

Finally, the need for flexibility also requires a significant investment in continual and ongoing employee training. Whether that training involves learning how to use information technology software, how to improve the flow of materials throughout the chain, how to identify activities that add value, how to make better decisions faster, or how to improve any other number of potential work activities, managers must see to it that employees have the knowledge and tools they need to do their jobs efficiently and effectively.

ORGANIZATIONAL CULTURE AND ATTITUDES. The last requirement for value chain management is having a supportive organizational culture and attitudes. From our extensive description of value chain management, you could probably guess the type of organizational culture that's going to support its successful implementation! Those cultural attitudes include sharing, collaborating, openness, flexibility, mutual respect, and trust. These attitudes encompass not only the internal partners in the value chain, but extend to external partners as well.

Obstacles to Value Chain Management

As desirable as these benefits may be, managers must tackle several obstacles in managing the value chain including organizational barriers, cultural attitudes, required capabilities, and people (see Exhibit 19-3).

ORGANIZATIONAL BARRIERS. At General Cable's manufacturing facility in Manchester, New Hampshire, one of the most interesting challenges faced by managers and employees in maintaining its world-class competitiveness is the 23 different nationalities that speak

EXHIBIT 19-3

Obstacles to Value Chain Management

12 languages besides English. Multiple languages make getting new messages out about anything that comes up especially tricky. But they've made it work using visual cues throughout the plant.[36]

Organizational barriers are among the most difficult obstacles to handle. These barriers include refusal or reluctance to share information, reluctance to shake up the status quo, and security issues. Without shared information, close coordination and collaboration is impossible. And the reluctance or refusal of employees to shake up the status quo can impede efforts toward value chain management and prevent its successful implementation. Finally, because value chain management relies heavily on a substantial information technology infrastructure, system security and Internet security breaches are issues that need to be addressed.

CULTURAL ATTITUDES.   Unsupportive cultural attitudes—especially trust and control— also can be obstacles to value chain management. The trust issue is a critical one, both lack of trust and too much trust. To be effective, partners in a value chain must trust each other. A mutual respect for, and honesty about, each partner's activities all along the chain is essential. When that trust doesn't exist, the partners will be reluctant to share information, capabilities, and processes. But too much trust also can be a problem. Just about any organization is vulnerable to theft of **intellectual property**—that is, proprietary information that's critical to an organization's efficient and effective functioning and competitiveness. You need to be able to trust your value chain partners so your organization's valuable assets aren't compromised.[37] Another cultural attitude that can be an obstacle is the belief that when an organization collaborates with external and internal partners, it no longer controls its own destiny. However, this lack of control just isn't the case. Even with the intense collaboration that's important to value chain management, organizations still control critical decisions such as what customers value, how much value they desire, and what distribution channels are important.[38]

REQUIRED CAPABILITIES.   We know from our earlier discussion of requirements for the successful implementation of value chain management that value chain partners need numerous capabilities. Several of these capabilities—coordination and collaboration, the ability to configure products to satisfy customers and suppliers, and the ability to educate internal and external partners—aren't easy, but they're essential to capturing and exploiting the value chain. Many of the companies we've described throughout this section endured critical, and oftentimes difficult, self-evaluations of their capabilities and processes in order to become more effective and efficient at managing their value chains.

PEOPLE.   The final obstacles to successful value chain management can be an organization's people. Without their unwavering commitment to do whatever it takes, value chain management won't be successful. If employees refuse to be flexible in their work— how and with whom they work—collaboration and cooperation throughout the value chain will be hard to achieve.

In addition, value chain management takes an incredible amount of time and energy on the part of an organization's employees. Managers must motivate those high levels of effort from employees, which is not an easy thing to do.

Finally, a major human resource problem is the lack of experienced managers who can lead value chain management initiatives. It's not that widespread, so there aren't a lot of managers who've done it successfully. However, progressive organizations see the benefits to be gained from value chain management and pursue it despite obstacles.

by the numbers[39]

50 percent of manufacturing companies say that three years from now, competition from low-cost countries will be the biggest market pressure on operations.

8 percent of those same manufacturing companies say that environmental compliance will be the biggest market pressure on operations.

58 percent of companies are looking to connect better with their suppliers.

16 percent of employers prefer using employee referrals to locate quality employees.

12 percent of companies say that sustainability is among their top three supply chain priorities.

64 percent of those companies see sustainability as an opportunity for revenue growth.

intellectual property
Proprietary information that's critical to an organization's efficient and effective functioning and competitiveness

LEARNING OUTCOME **19.4**
Discuss contemporary issues
in managing operations.

Current Issues in Managing Operations

Rowe Furniture had an audacious goal: make a sofa in 10 days. It wanted to "become as efficient at making furniture as Toyota is at making cars." Reaching that goal, however, required revamping its operations management process to exploit technology *and* maintaining quality.[40] Rowe's actions illustrate three of today's most important operations management issues: technology, quality, and mass customization and lean organizations.

Technology's Role in Operations Management

Global positioning systems (GPS) are changing a number of enterprises from shipping to shopping, from health care to law enforcement, and even farming.[41] Like many other technologies, GPS was invented for military use to track weapons and personnel as they moved. Now GPS is being used to track shipping fleets, revitalize consumer products such as watches or photos, and monitor parolees or sex offenders.

As we know from our previous discussion of value chain management, today's competitive marketplace has put tremendous pressure on organizations to deliver products and services that customers value in a timely manner. Smart companies are looking at ways to harness technology to improve operations management. Many fast-food companies are competing to see who can provide faster and better service to drive-through customers. With drive-through now representing a huge portion of sales, faster and better delivery can be a significant competitive edge. For instance, Wendy's has added awnings to some of its menu boards and replaced some of the text with pictures. Others use confirmation screens, a technology that helped McDonald's boost accuracy by more than 11 percent. Technology used by two national chains tells managers how much food they need to prepare by counting vehicles in the drive-through line and factoring in demand for current promotional and popular staple items. Even Domino's is using a new point-of-sale system to attract customers and streamline online orders.[42]

Although an organization's production activities are driven by the recognition that the customer is king, managers still need to be more responsive. For instance, operations managers need systems that can reveal available capacity, status of orders, and product quality while products are in the process of being manufactured, not just after the fact. To connect more closely with customers, production must be synchronized across the enterprise. To avoid bottlenecks and slowdowns, the production function must be a full partner in the entire business system.

What's making such extensive collaboration possible is technology. Technology is also allowing organizations to control costs particularly in the areas of predictive maintenance, remote diagnostics, and utility cost savings. For instance, new Internet-compatible equipment contains embedded Web servers that can communicate proactively—that is, if a piece of equipment breaks or reaches certain preset parameters indicating that it's about to break, it asks for help. But technology can do more than sound an alarm or light up an indicator button. For instance, some devices have the ability to initiate e-mail or signal a pager at a supplier, the maintenance department, or contractor describing the specific problem and requesting parts and service. How much is such e-enabled maintenance control worth? It can be worth quite a lot if it prevents equipment breakdowns and subsequent production downtime.

Managers who understand the power of technology to contribute to more effective and efficient performance know that managing operations is more than the traditional view of simply producing the product. Instead, the emphasis is on working together with all the organization's business functions to find solutions to customers' business problems. Even service providers understand the power of technology for these tasks. For example, Southwest Airlines upgraded its cockpit software, enabling its pilots (who have been extensively trained) to fly precise satellite-based navigation approaches to airports, thus saving fuel, reducing delays, and cutting noise.[43]

Let's Get Real

The impact of technology in my organization *involves increased product quality while lowering costs because front-line supervisors and machine operators now have real-time data on the production floor; production data are collected instantaneously, allowing operators and supervisors the opportunity to make value decisions during the production run.*

Quality Initiatives

Quality problems are expensive. For example, even though Apple has had phenomenal success with its iPod, the batteries in the first three versions died after 4 hours instead of lasting the up-to-12 hours that buyers expected. Apple's settlement with consumers cost close to $100 million. At Schering-Plough, problems with inhalers and other pharmaceuticals were traced to chronic quality control shortcomings, for which the company eventually paid a $500 million fine. And the auto industry paid $14.5 billion to cover the cost of warranty and repair work in one year.[44]

Many experts believe that organizations unable to produce high-quality products won't be able to compete successfully in the global marketplace. What is quality? When you consider a product or service to have quality, what does that mean? Does it mean that the product doesn't break or quit working—that is, that it's reliable? Does it mean that the service is delivered in a way that you intended? Does it mean that the product does what it's supposed to do? Or does quality mean something else? We're going to define **quality** as the ability of a product or service to reliably do what it's supposed to do and to satisfy customer expectations.

How is quality achieved? That's an issue managers must address. A good way to look at quality initiatives is with the management functions—planning, organizing, leading, and controlling—that need to take place.

PLANNING FOR QUALITY.   Managers must have quality improvement goals and strategies and plans to achieve those goals. Goals can help focus everyone's attention toward some objective quality standard. For instance, Caterpillar's goal is to apply quality improvement techniques to help cut costs.[45] Although this goal is specific and challenging, managers and employees are partnering together to pursue well-designed strategies to achieve the goals, and are confident they can do so.

ORGANIZING AND LEADING FOR QUALITY.   Because quality improvement initiatives are carried out by organizational employees, it's important for managers to look at how they can best organize and lead them. For instance, at the Moosejaw, Saskatchewan, plant of General Cable Corporation, every employee participates in continual quality assurance training. In addition, the plant manager believes wholeheartedly in giving employees the information they need to do their jobs better. He says, "Giving people who are running the machines the information is just paramount. You can set up your cellular structure, you can cross-train your people, you can use lean tools, but if you don't give people information to drive improvement, there's no enthusiasm." Needless to say, this company shares production data and financial performance measures with all employees.[46]

Organizations with extensive and successful quality improvement programs tend to rely on two important people approaches: cross-functional work teams, and self-directed or empowered work teams. Because achieving product quality is something that all employees from upper to lower levels must participate in, it's not surprising that quality-driven organizations rely on well-trained, flexible, and empowered employees.

CONTROLLING FOR QUALITY.   Quality improvement initiatives aren't possible without having some way to monitor and evaluate their progress. Whether it involves standards for inventory control, defect rate, raw materials procurement, or other operations management areas, controlling for quality is important. For instance, at the Northrup Grumman Corporation plant in Rolling Meadows, Illinois, several quality controls have been implemented, such as automated testing and IT that integrates product design and

quality
The ability of a product or service to reliably do what it's supposed to do and to satisfy customer expectations

manufacturing and tracks process quality improvements. Also, employees are empowered to make accept/reject decisions about products throughout the manufacturing process. The plant manager explains, "This approach helps build quality into the product rather than trying to inspect quality into the product." But one of the most important things they do is "go to war" with their customers—soldiers preparing for war or in live combat situations. Again, the plant manager says, "What discriminates us is that we believe if we can understand our customer's mission as well as they do, we can help them be more effective. We don't wait for our customer to ask us to do something. We find out what our customer is trying to do and then we develop solutions."[47]

These types of quality improvement success stories aren't just limited to U.S. operations. For example, at a Delphi assembly plant in Matamoros, Mexico, employees worked hard to improve quality and made significant strides. Their customer rejection rate on shipped products is now 10 ppm (parts per million), down from 3,000 ppm—an improvement of almost 300 percent.[48] Quality initiatives at several Australian companies including Alcoa of Australia, Wormald Security, and Carlton and United Breweries have led to significant quality improvements.[49] And at Valeo Klimasystemme GmbH of Bad Rodach, Germany, assembly teams build different climate-control systems for high-end German cars including Mercedes and BMW. Quality initiatives by Valeo's employee teams have led to significant improvements in various quality standards.[50]

Quality Goals

To publicly demonstrate their quality commitment, many organizations worldwide have pursued challenging quality goals—the two best-known being ISO 9000 and Six Sigma.

ISO 9000. **ISO 9000** is a series of international quality management standards established by the International Organization for Standardization (www.iso.org), which set uniform guidelines for processes to ensure that products conform to customer requirements. These standards cover everything from contract review to product design to product delivery. The ISO 9000 standards have become the internationally recognized standard for evaluating and comparing companies in the global marketplace. In fact, this type of certification can be a prerequisite for doing business globally. Achieving ISO 9000 certification provides proof that a quality operations system is in place.

As of 2009, more than 1 million certifications had been awarded to organizations in 175 countries. Almost 40,000 U.S. businesses are ISO 9000 certified. Over 200,000 Chinese firms have received certification.[51]

SIX SIGMA. Motorola popularized the use of stringent quality standards more than 30 years ago, through a trademarked quality improvement program called Six Sigma.[52] Very simply, **Six Sigma** is a quality program designed to reduce defects to help lower costs, save time, and improve customer satisfaction. It's based on the statistical standard that establishes a goal of no more than 3.4 defects per million units or procedures. What does the name mean? Sigma is the Greek letter that statisticians use to define a standard deviation from a bell curve. The higher the sigma, the fewer the deviations from the norm—that is, the fewer the defects. At One Sigma, two-thirds of whatever is being measured falls within the curve. Two Sigma covers about 95 percent. At Six Sigma, you're about as close to defect-free as you can get.[53] It's an ambitious quality goal! Although it is an extremely high standard to achieve, many quality-driven businesses are using it and benefiting from it. For instance, General Electric estimates that it has saved billions in costs since 1995, according to company executives.[54] Other well-known companies pursuing Six Sigma include ITT Industries, Dow Chemical, 3M Company, American Express, Sony Corporation, Nokia Corporation, and Johnson & Johnson. Although manufacturers seem to make up the bulk of Six Sigma users, service companies such as financial institutions, retailers, and health care organizations are beginning to apply it. What impact can Six Sigma have? Let's look at an example.

recognition of the baby boomer demographic by Elliott's Zimmer Holdings are prime examples of identifying environmental opportunities. Remember the discussion in Chapter 9 that opportunities are positive trends in external environmental factors. These trends provide unique and distinct possibilities for innovating and creating value. Entrepreneurs need to be able to pinpoint these pockets of opportunities that a changing context provides. After all, "organizations do not see opportunities, individuals do."[18] And they need to do so quickly, especially in dynamic environments, before those opportunities disappear or are exploited by others.[19]

The late Peter Drucker, a well-known management author, identified seven potential sources of opportunity that entrepreneurs might look for in the external context.[20] These include the unexpected, the incongruous, the process need, industry and market structures, demographics, changes in perception, and new knowledge.

1. *The unexpected.* When situations and events are unanticipated, opportunities can be found. The event may be an unexpected success (positive news) or an unexpected failure (bad news). Either way, it may present opportunities for entrepreneurs to pursue. For instance, the dramatic increase in fuel prices has proved to be a bonanza for companies that offer solutions. For instance, Jeff Pink, CEO of EV Rental Cars, uses only hybrid vehicles. The company's utilization rate—the percentage of days a vehicle is out generating revenue—is about 90 percent.[21] The unexpected increase in fuel prices proved to be an opportunity for this entrepreneur. And for RSA Security, the unexpected opportunity came in the form of identity theft. Art Coviello's company develops software that helps make online transactions more secure. He stated, "A lot of factors are about to turn in RSA's favor, namely the need for more secure, traceable financial transactions in a world beset by online fraud and identity theft."[22]

2. *The incongruous.* When something is incongruous, it exhibits inconsistencies and incompatibilities in the way it appears. Things "ought to be" a certain way, but aren't. When conventional wisdom about the way things should be no longer holds true, for whatever reason, opportunities are present. Entrepreneurs who are willing to "think outside the box"—that is, to think beyond the traditional and conventional approaches—may find pockets of potential profitability. Sigi Rabinowicz, founder and president of Tefron, an Israeli firm, recognized incongruities in the way that women's lingerie was made. He knew that a better way was possible. His company spent more than a decade adapting a circular hosiery knitting machine to make intimate apparel that is nearly seamless.[23] Another example of how the incongruous can be a potential source of entrepreneurial opportunity is Fred Smith, founder of FedEx, who recognized in the early 1970s the inefficiencies in the delivery of packages and documents. His approach was: Why not? Who says that overnight delivery isn't possible? Smith's recognition of the incongruous led to the creation of FedEx, now a multibillion-dollar corporation.

3. *The process need.* What happens when technology doesn't immediately come up with the "big discovery" that's going to fundamentally change the nature of some product or service? What happens is the emergence of pockets of entrepreneurial opportunity in the various stages of the process as researchers and technicians continue to work for the monumental breakthrough. Because the full leap hasn't been possible, opportunities abound in the tiny steps. Take the medical products industry, for example. Although researchers haven't yet discovered a cure for cancer, many successful entrepreneurial biotechnology ventures have been created as knowledge about a possible cure continues to grow.

4. *Industry and market structures.* When changes in technology change the structure of an industry and market, existing firms can become obsolete if they're not attuned to the changes or are unwilling to change. Even changes in social values and consumer tastes can shift the structures of industries and markets. These markets and industries become open targets for nimble and smart entrepreneurs. For instance, while working part-time at an auto body shop while finishing his engineering graduate degree, Joe Born wondered if the industrial paint buffer used to smooth out a car's paint job

could be used to smooth out scratches on CDs. He tried it out on his favorite Clint Black CD that had been ruined and the newly polished CD played flawlessly. After this experience, Born spent almost four years perfecting his disk repair kit invention, the SkipDr.[24] The arena of the Internet provides several good examples of existing industries and markets being challenged by upstart entrepreneurial ventures. For instance, eBay has prospered as an online intermediary between buyers and sellers. eBay's CEO says that the company's job is connecting people, not selling them things. And connect them, they do! The online auction firm has more than 275 million registered users.[25]

5. *Demographics.* The characteristics of the world population are changing. These changes influence industries and markets by altering the types and quantities of products and services desired and customers' buying power. Although many of these changes are fairly predictable if you stay alert to demographic trends, others aren't as obvious. Either way, significant entrepreneurial opportunities can be realized by anticipating and meeting the changing needs of the population. For example, Thay Thida was one of three partners in Khmer Internet Development Services (KIDS) in Phnom Penh, Cambodia. She and her cofounders saw the opportunities in bringing Internet service to Cambodians and profited from their entrepreneurial venture.[26]

6. *Changes in perception.* Perception is one's view of reality. When changes in perception take place, the facts do not vary, but their meanings do. Changes in perception get at the heart of people's psychographic profiles—what they value, what they believe in, and what they care about. Changes in these attitudes and values create potential market opportunities for alert entrepreneurs. For example, think about your perception of healthy foods. Changes in our perception of whether certain food groups are good has brought about product and service opportunities for entrepreneurs to recognize and capture. For example, John Mackey started Whole Foods Market in Austin, Texas, as a place for customers to purchase food and other items free of pesticides, preservatives, sweeteners, and cruelty. Now, as the world's number one natural foods chain, Mackey's entrepreneurial venture consists of about 275 stores in the United States, Canada, and the United Kingdom.[27] Michael and Ellen Diamant changed the perception that baby necessities—diaper bags, bottle warmers, and bottle racks—couldn't be fashionable. Their baby gear company, Skip Hop, offers pricey products that design-conscious new parents have embraced.[28]

7. *New knowledge.* New knowledge is a significant source of entrepreneurial opportunity. Although not all knowledge-based innovations are significant, new knowledge ranks pretty high on the list of sources of entrepreneurial opportunity! It takes more than just having new knowledge, though. Entrepreneurs must be able to do something with that knowledge and to protect important proprietary information from competitors. For example, French scientists are using new knowledge about textiles to develop a wide array of innovative products to keep wearers healthy and smelling good. Neyret, the Parisian lingerie maker, created lingerie products woven with tiny perfume microcapsules that stay in the fabric through about 10 washings. Another French company, Francital, developed a fabric treated with chemicals to absorb perspiration and odors.[29]

Being alert to entrepreneurial opportunities is only part of an entrepreneur's initial efforts. He or she must also understand competitive advantage. As we discussed in Chapter 9, when an organization has a competitive advantage, it has something that other competitors don't; does something better than other organizations; or does something that others can't. Competitive advantage is a necessary ingredient for an entrepreneurial venture's long-term success and survival. Getting and keeping a competitive advantage is tough. However, it is something that entrepreneurs must consider as they begin researching the venture's feasibility.

Researching the Venture's Feasibility—Generating and Evaluating Ideas

On a trip to New York, Miho Inagi got her first taste of the city's delicious bagels. After her palate-expanding experience, she had the idea of bringing bagels to Japan. Five years after her first trip to New York and a subsequent apprenticeship at a New York bagel business, Miho opened Maruichi Bagel in Tokyo. After a struggle to get the store up and running, it now has a loyal following of customers.[30]

It's important for entrepreneurs to research the venture's feasibility by generating and evaluating business ideas. Entrepreneurial ventures thrive on ideas. Generating ideas is an innovative, creative process. It's also one that will take time, not only in the beginning stages of the entrepreneurial venture, but throughout the life of the business. Where do ideas come from?

GENERATING IDEAS. Studies of entrepreneurs have shown that the sources of their ideas are unique and varied. One survey found that "working in the same industry" was the major source of ideas for an entrepreneurial venture (60% of respondents).[31] Other sources included personal interests or hobbies, looking at familiar and unfamiliar products and services, and opportunities in external environmental sectors (technological, sociocultural, demographics, economic, or legal-political).

What should entrepreneurs look for as they explore these idea sources? They should look for limitations of what's currently available, new and different approaches, advances and breakthroughs, unfilled niches, or trends and changes. For example, John C. Diebel, founder of Meade Instruments Corporation, the Irvine, California, telescope maker, came up with the idea of putting computerized attachments on the company's inexpensive consumer models so that amateur astronomers could enter on a keypad the coordinates of planets or stars they wanted to see. The telescope would then automatically locate and focus on the desired planetary bodies. It took the company's engineers two years to figure out how to do it, but Meade now controls more than half the amateur astronomy market.[32]

EVALUATING IDEAS. Evaluating entrepreneurial ideas revolves around personal and marketplace considerations. Each of these assessments will provide an entrepreneur with key information about the idea's potential. Exhibit A-1 describes some questions that entrepreneurs might ask as they evaluate potential ideas.

Personal Considerations	Marketplace Considerations
• Do you have the capabilities to do what you've selected?	• Who are the potential customers for your idea: who, where, how many?
• Are you ready to be an entrepreneur?	• What similar or unique product features does your proposed idea have compared to what's currently on the market?
• Are you prepared emotionally to deal with the stresses and challenges of being an entrepreneur?	• How and where will potential customers purchase your product?
• Are you prepared to deal with rejection and failure?	• Have you considered pricing issues and whether the price you'll be able to charge will allow your venture to survive and prosper?
• Are you ready to work hard?	• Have you considered how you will need to promote and advertise your proposed entrepreneurial venture?
• Do you have a realistic picture of the venture's potential?	
• Have you educated yourself about financing issues?	
• Are you willing and prepared to do continual financial and other types of analyses?	

EXHIBIT A-1

Evaluating Potential Ideas

A. Introduction, historical background, description of product or service
1. Brief description of proposed entrepreneurial venture
2. Brief history of the industry
3. Information about the economy and important trends
4. Current status of the product or service
5. How you intend to produce the product or service
6. Complete list of goods or services to be provided
7. Strengths and weaknesses of the business
8. Ease of entry into the industry, including competitor analysis

B. Accounting considerations
1. Pro forma balance sheet
2. Pro forma profit and loss statement
3. Projected cash flow analysis

C. Management considerations
1. Personal expertise—strengths and weaknesses
2. Proposed organizational design
3. Potential staffing requirements
4. Inventory management methods
5. Production and operations management issues
6. Equipment needs

D. Marketing considerations
1. Detailed product description
2. Identify target market (who, where, how many)
3. Describe place product will be distributed (location, traffic, size, channels, etc.)
4. Price determination (competition, price lists, etc.)
5. Promotion plans (role of personal selling, advertising, sales promotion, etc.)

E. Financial considerations
1. Start-up costs
2. Working capital requirements
3. Equity requirements
4. Loans—amounts, type, conditions
5. Breakeven analysis
6. Collateral
7. Credit references
8. Equipment and building financing—costs and methods

F. Legal considerations
1. Proposed business structure (type; conditions, terms, liability, responsibility; insurance needs; buyout and succession issues)
2. Contracts, licenses, and other legal documents

G. Tax considerations: sales/property/employee; federal, state, and local

H. Appendix: charts/graphs, diagrams, layouts, résumés, etc.

A more structured evaluation approach that an entrepreneur might want to use is a **feasibility study**—an analysis of the various aspects of a proposed entrepreneurial venture designed to determine its feasibility. Not only is a well-prepared feasibility study an effective evaluation tool to determine whether an entrepreneurial idea is a potentially successful one, it can serve as a basis for the all-important business plan.

A feasibility study should give descriptions of the most important elements of the entrepreneurial venture and the entrepreneur's analysis of the viability of these elements. Exhibit A-2 provides an outline of a possible approach to a feasibility study. Yes, it covers a lot of territory and takes a significant amount of time, energy, and effort to prepare it. However, an entrepreneur's potential future success is worth that investment.

Researching the Venture's Feasibility—Competitors

Part of researching the venture's feasibility is looking at the competitors. What would entrepreneurs like to know about their potential competitors? Here are some possible questions:

What types of products or services are competitors offering?

What are the major characteristics of these products or services?

What are their products' strengths and weaknesses?

How do they handle marketing, pricing, and distributing?

What do they attempt to do differently from other competitors?

Do they appear to be successful at it? Why or why not?

What are they good at?

What competitive advantage(s) do they appear to have?

What are they not so good at?

What competitive disadvantage(s) do they appear to have?

How large and profitable are these competitors?

For instance, the CEO of The Children's Place carefully examined the competition as he took his chain of children's clothing stores nationwide. Although he faces stiff competition from the likes of GapKids, J.C. Penney, and Gymboree, he feels that his company's approach to manufacturing and marketing will give it a competitive edge.[33]

Once an entrepreneur has this information, he or she should assess how the proposed entrepreneurial venture is going to "fit" into this competitive arena. Will the entrepreneurial venture be able to compete successfully? This type of competitor analysis becomes an important part of the feasibility study and the business plan. If, after all this analysis, the situation looks promising, the final part of researching the venture's feasibility is to look at the various financing options. This step isn't the final determination of how much funding the venture will need or where this funding will come from but is simply gathering information about various financing alternatives.

Researching the Venture's Feasibility—Financing

Getting financing isn't always easy. For instance, when William Carey first proposed building a liquor distributor business in Poland, more than 20 investment banking houses in New York passed on funding his idea. Carey recalls, "They didn't know Poland, and the business was small. We were ready to give up." Then, a New York investment banking boutique agreed to fund the venture. Today, Carey's company, CEDC (Central European Distribution), has more than 3,000 employees and sales revenues that top $1.1 billion.[34]

Because funds likely will be needed to start the venture, an entrepreneur must research the various financing options. Possible financing options available to entrepreneurs are shown in Exhibit A-3.

- Entrepreneur's personal resources (personal savings, home equity, personal loans, credit cards, etc.)
- Financial institutions (banks, savings and loan institutions, government-guaranteed loan, credit unions, etc.)
- **Venture capitalists**—external equity financing provided by professionally managed pools of investor money
- **Angel investors**—a private investor (or group of private investors) who offers financial backing to an entrepreneurial venture in return for equity in the venture
- **Initial public offering (IPO)**—the first public registration and sale of a company's stock
- National, state, and local governmental business development programs
- Unusual sources (television shows, judged competitions, etc.)

feasibility study
An analysis of the various aspects of a proposed entrepreneurial venture designed to determine its feasibility

venture capitalists
External equity financing provided by professionally managed pools of investor money

angel investors
A private investor (or group of private investors) who offers financial backing to an entrepreneurial venture in return for equity in the venture

initial public offering (IPO)
The first public registration and sale of a company's stock

Planning the Venture—Developing a Business Plan

Planning is also important to entrepreneurial ventures. Once the venture's feasibility has been thoroughly researched, the entrepreneur then must look at planning the venture. The most important thing that an entrepreneur does in planning the venture is developing a **business plan**—a written document that summarizes a business opportunity and defines and articulates how the identified opportunity is to be seized and exploited.

For many would-be entrepreneurs, developing and writing a business plan seems like a daunting task. However, a good business plan is valuable. It pulls together all of the elements of the entrepreneur's vision into a single coherent document. The business plan requires careful planning and creative thinking. But if done well, it can be a convincing document that serves many functions. It serves as a blueprint and road map for operating the business. And the business plan is a "living" document, guiding organizational decisions and actions throughout the life of the business, not just in the start-up stage.

If an entrepreneur has completed a feasibility study, much of the information included in it becomes the basis for the business plan. A good business plan covers six major areas: executive summary, analysis of opportunity, analysis of the context, description of the business, financial data and projections, and supporting documentation.

EXECUTIVE SUMMARY.   The executive summary summarizes the key points that the entrepreneur wants to make about the proposed entrepreneurial venture. These points might include a brief mission statement; primary goals; brief history of the entrepreneurial venture, maybe in the form of a timeline; key people involved in the venture; nature of the business; concise product or service descriptions; brief explanations of market niche, competitors, and competitive advantage; proposed strategies; and selected key financial information.

ANALYSIS OF OPPORTUNITY.   In this section of the business plan, an entrepreneur presents the details of the perceived opportunity. Essentially, details include (1) sizing up the market by describing the demographics of the target market, (2) describing and evaluating industry trends, and (3) identifying and evaluating competitors.

ANALYSIS OF THE CONTEXT.   Whereas the opportunity analysis focuses on the opportunity in a specific industry and market, the context analysis takes a much broader perspective. Here, the entrepreneur describes the broad external changes and trends taking place in the economic, political-legal, technological, and global environments.

DESCRIPTION OF THE BUSINESS.   In this section, an entrepreneur describes how the entrepreneurial venture is going to be organized, launched, and managed. It includes a thorough description of the mission statement; a description of the desired organizational culture; marketing plans including overall marketing strategy, pricing, sales tactics, service-warranty policies, and advertising and promotion tactics; product development plans such as an explanation of development status, tasks, difficulties and risks, and anticipated costs; operational plans including a description of proposed geographic location, facilities and needed improvements, equipment, and work flow; human resource plans including a description of key management persons, composition of board of directors including their background experience and skills, current and future staffing needs, compensation and benefits, and training needs; and an overall schedule and timetable of events.

FINANCIAL DATA AND PROJECTIONS.   Every effective business plan contains financial data and projections. Although the calculations and interpretation may be difficult, they are absolutely critical. No business plan is complete without financial information. Financial plans should cover at least three years and contain projected income statements, pro forma cash flow analysis (monthly for the first year and quarterly for the next two), pro forma balance sheets, breakeven analysis, and cost controls. If major equipment or other capital purchases are expected, the items, costs, and available collateral should be listed. All financial projections and analyses should include explanatory notes, especially where the data seem contradictory or questionable.

SUPPORTING DOCUMENTATION.   For this important component of an effective business plan, the entrepreneur should back up his or her descriptions with charts, graphs, tables, photographs, or other visual tools. In addition, it might be important to include information (personal and work-related) about the key participants in the entrepreneurial venture.

Just as the idea for an entrepreneurial venture takes time to germinate, so does the writing of a good business plan. It's important for the entrepreneur to put serious thought and consideration into the plan. It's not an easy thing to do. However, the resulting document should be valuable to the entrepreneur in current and future planning efforts.

Organizing Issues

Donald Hannon, president of Graphic Laminating Inc. in Solon, Ohio, redesigned his organization's structure by transforming it into an employee-empowered company. He wanted to drive authority down through the organization so employees were responsible for their own efforts. One way he did this was by creating employee teams to handle specific projects. Employees with less experience were teamed with veteran employees. He says, "I want to build a good team and give people the ability to succeed. Sometimes that means giving them the ability to make mistakes, and I have to keep that in perspective. The more we allow people to become better at what they do, the better they will become—and the better we all will do."[35]

Once the start-up and planning issues for the entrepreneurial venture have been addressed, the entrepreneur is ready to begin organizing the entrepreneurial venture. Then, the entrepreneur must address five organizing issues: the legal forms of organization, organizational design and structure, human resource management, stimulating and making changes, and the continuing importance of innovation.

Legal Forms of Organization

The first organizing decision that an entrepreneur must make is a critical one. It's the form of legal ownership for the venture. The two primary factors affecting this decision are taxes and legal liability. An entrepreneur wants to minimize the impact of both of these factors. The right choice can protect the entrepreneur from legal liability as well as save tax dollars, in both the short run and the long run.

What alternatives are available? The three basic ways to organize an entrepreneurial venture are sole proprietorship, partnership, and corporation. However, when you include the variations of these basic organizational alternatives, you end up with six possible choices, each with its own tax consequences, liability issues, and pros and cons. These six choices are sole proprietorship, general partnership, limited liability partnership (LLP), C corporation, S corporation, and limited liability company (LLC). Let's briefly look at each one with their advantages and drawbacks. (Exhibit A-4 summarizes the basic information about each organizational alternative.)

SOLE PROPRIETORSHIP.   A sole proprietorship is a form of legal organization in which the owner maintains sole and complete control over the business and is personally liable for business debts. The legal requirements for establishing a sole proprietorship consist of obtaining the necessary local business licenses and permits. In a sole proprietorship, income and losses "pass through" to the owner and are taxed at the owner's personal income tax rate. The biggest drawback, however, is the unlimited personal liability for any and all debts of the business.

business plan
A written document that summarizes a business opportunity and defines and articulates how the identified opportunity is to be seized and exploited

sole proprietorship
A form of legal organization in which the owner maintains sole and complete control over the business and is personally liable for business debts

Structure	Ownership Requirements	Tax Treatment	Liability	Advantages	Drawbacks
Sole proprietorship	One owner	Income and losses "pass through" to owner and are taxed at personal rate	Unlimited personal liability	*Low start-up costs* Freedom from most regulations *Owner has direct control* All profits go to owner *Easy to exit business*	Unlimited personal liability *Personal finances at risk* Miss out on many business tax deductions *Total responsibility* May be more difficult to raise financing
General partnership	Two or more owners	Income and losses "pass through" to partners and are taxed at personal rate; *flexibility in profit-loss allocations to partners*	Unlimited personal liability	*Ease of formation* Pooled talent *Pooled resources* Somewhat easier access to financing *Some tax benefits*	Unlimited personal liability *Divided authority and decisions* Potential for conflict *Continuity of transfer of ownership*
Limited liability partnership (LLP)	Two or more owners	Income and losses "pass through" to partner and are taxed at personal rate; *flexibility in profit-loss allocations to partners*	Limited, although one partner must retain unlimited liability	*Good way to acquire capital from limited partners*	Cost and complexity of forming can be high *Limited partners cannot participate in management of business without losing liability protection*
C corporation	Unlimited number of shareholders; *no limits on types of stock or voting arrangements*	Dividend income is taxed at corporate and personal shareholder levels; *losses and deductions are corporate*	Limited	*Limited liability* Transferable ownership *Continuous existence* Easier access to resources	Expensive to set up *Closely regulated* Double taxation *Extensive record keeping* Charter restrictions
S corporation	Up to 75 shareholders; *no limits on types of stock or voting arrangements*	Income and losses "pass through" to partners and are taxed at personal rate; *flexibility in profit-loss allocation to partners*	Limited	*Easy to set up* Enjoy limited liability protection and tax benefits of partnership *Can have a tax-exempt entity as a shareholder*	Must meet certain requirements *May limit future financing options*
Limited liability company (LLC)	Unlimited number of "members"; *flexible membership arrangements for voting rights and income*	Income and losses "pass through" to partners and are taxed at personal rate; *flexibility in profit-loss allocations to partners*	Limited	*Greater flexibility* Not constrained by regulations on C and S corporations *Taxed as partnership, not as corporation*	Cost of switching from one form to this can be high *Need legal and financial advice in forming operating agreement*

EXHIBIT A-4

Legal Forms of Business Organization

GENERAL PARTNERSHIP.   A general partnership is a form of legal organization in which two or more business owners share the management and risk of the business. Even though a partnership is possible without a written agreement, the potential and inevitable problems that arise in any partnership make a written partnership agreement drafted by legal counsel a highly recommended thing to do.

LIMITED LIABILITY PARTNERSHIP (LLP).   The limited liability partnership (LLP) is a legal organization formed by general partner(s) and limited partner(s). The general partners actually operate and manage the business. They are the ones who have unlimited liability. At least one general partner is necessary in an LLP, but any number of limited partners are allowed. These partners are usually passive investors, although they can make management suggestions to the general partners. They also have the right to inspect the business and make copies of business records. The limited partners are entitled to a share of the business's profits as agreed to in the partnership agreement, and their risk is limited to the amount of their investment in the LLP.

C CORPORATION.   Of the three basic types of ownership, the corporation (also known as a C corporation) is the most complex to form and operate. A corporation is a legal business entity that is separate from its owners and managers. Many entrepreneurial ventures are organized as a closely held corporation which, very simply, is a corporation owned by a limited number of people who do not trade the stock publicly. Whereas the sole proprietorship and partnership forms of organization do not exist separately from the entrepreneur, the corporation does. The corporation functions as a distinct legal entity and, as such, can make contracts, engage in business activities, own property, sue and be sued, and of course, pay taxes. A corporation must operate in accordance with its charter and the laws of the state in which it operates.

S CORPORATION.   The S corporation (also called a subchapter S corporation) is a specialized type of corporation that has the regular characteristics of a corporation but is unique in that the owners are taxed as a partnership as long as certain criteria are met. The S corporation has been the classic organizing approach for getting the limited liability of a corporate structure without incurring corporate tax. However, this form of legal organization must meet strict criteria. If any of these criteria are violated, a venture's S status is automatically terminated.

LIMITED LIABILITY COMPANY (LLC).   The limited liability company (LLC) is a relatively new form of business organization that's a hybrid between a partnership and a corporation. The LLC offers the liability protection of a corporation, the tax benefits of a partnership, and fewer restrictions than an S corporation. However, the main drawback of this approach is that it's quite complex and expensive to set up. Legal and financial advice is an absolute necessity in forming the LLC's operating agreement, the document that outlines the provisions governing the way the LLC will conduct business.

SUMMARY OF LEGAL FORMS OF ORGANIZATION.   The organizing decision regarding the legal form of organization is an important one because it can have significant tax and

general partnership
A form of legal organization in which two or more business owners share the management and risk of the business

limited liability partnership (LLP)
A form of legal organization consisting of general partner(s) and limited liability partner(s)

corporation
A legal business entity that is separate from its owners and managers

closely held corporation
A corporation owned by a limited number of people who do not trade the stock publicly

S corporation
A specialized type of corporation that has the regular characteristics of a C corporation but is unique in that the owners are taxed as a partnership as long as certain criteria are met

limited liability company (LLC)
A form of legal organization that's a hybrid between a partnership and a corporation

operating agreement
The document that outlines the provisions governing the way an LLC will conduct business

liability consequences. Although the legal form of organization can be changed, it's not an easy thing to do. An entrepreneur needs to think carefully about what's important, especially in the areas of flexibility, taxes, and amount of personal liability in choosing the best form of organization.

Organizational Design and Structure

The choice of an appropriate organizational structure is also an important decision when organizing an entrepreneurial venture. At some point, successful entrepreneurs find that they can't do everything alone. More people are needed. The entrepreneur must then decide on the most appropriate structural arrangement for effectively and efficiently carrying out the organization's activities. Without some suitable type of organizational structure, the entrepreneurial venture may soon find itself in a chaotic situation.

In many small firms, the organizational structure tends to evolve with little intentional or deliberate planning by the entrepreneur. For the most part, the structure may be simple—one person does whatever is needed. As the entrepreneurial venture grows and the entrepreneur finds it increasingly difficult to go it alone, employees are brought on board to perform certain functions or duties that the entrepreneur can't handle. These individuals tend to perform those same functions as the company grows. Then, as the entrepreneurial venture continues to grow, each of these functional areas may require managers and employees.

With the evolution to a more deliberate structure, the entrepreneur faces a whole new set of challenges. All of a sudden, he or she must share decision making and operating responsibilities. This transition is typically one of the most difficult things for an entrepreneur to do—letting go and allowing someone else to make decisions. *After all*, he or she reasons, *how can anyone know this business as well as I do*? Also, what might have been a fairly informal, loose, and flexible atmosphere that worked well when the organization was small may no longer be effective. Many entrepreneurs are greatly concerned about keeping that "small company" atmosphere alive even as the venture grows and evolves into a more structured arrangement. But having a structured organization doesn't necessarily mean giving up flexibility, adaptability, and freedom. In fact, the structural design may be as fluid as the entrepreneur feels comfortable with and yet still have the rigidity it needs to operate efficiently.

Organizational design decisions in entrepreneurial ventures revolve around the six key elements of organizational structure discussed in Chapter 10: work specialization, departmentalization, chain of command, span of control, amount of centralization-decentralization, and amount of formalization. Decisions about these six elements will determine whether an entrepreneur designs a more mechanistic or organic organizational structure (concepts also discussed in Chapter 10). When would each be preferable? A mechanistic structure would be preferable when cost efficiencies are critical to the venture's competitive advantage, when more control over employees' work activities is important, if the venture produces standardized products in a routine fashion, and when the external environment is relatively stable and certain. An organic structure would be most appropriate when innovation is critical to the organization's competitive advantage; for smaller organizations where rigid approaches to dividing and coordinating work aren't necessary; if the organization produces customized products in a flexible setting; and where the external environment is dynamic, complex, and uncertain.

Human Resource Management Issues in Entrepreneurial Ventures

As an entrepreneurial venture grows, additional employees will need to be hired to perform the increased workload. As employees are brought on board, the entrepreneur faces certain human resource management (HRM) issues. Two HRM issues of particular importance to entrepreneurs are employee recruitment and employee retention.

EMPLOYEE RECRUITMENT.   An entrepreneur wants to ensure that the venture has the people to do the required work. Recruiting new employees is one of the biggest challenges that entrepreneurs face. In fact, the ability of small firms to successfully recruit appropriate employees is consistently rated as one of the most important factors influencing organizational success.

Entrepreneurs, particularly, are looking for high-potential people who can perform multiple roles during various stages of venture growth. They look for individuals who "buy into" the venture's entrepreneurial culture—individuals who have a passion for the business. Unlike their corporate counterparts who often focus on filling a job by matching a person to the job requirements, entrepreneurs look to fill in critical skills gaps. They're looking for people who are exceptionally capable and self-motivated, flexible, multi-skilled, and who can help grow the entrepreneurial venture. While corporate managers tend to focus on using traditional HRM practices and techniques, entrepreneurs are more concerned with matching characteristics of the person to the values and culture of the organization; that is, they focus on matching the person to the organization.

EMPLOYEE RETENTION.   Getting competent and qualified people into the venture is just the first step in effectively managing the human resources. An entrepreneur wants to keep the people he or she has hired and trained. Sabrina Horn, president of The Horn Group based in San Francisco, understands the importance of having good people on board and keeping them. In the rough-and-tumble, intensely competitive public relations industry, Sabrina knows that the loss of talented employees could harm client services. To contend with this issue, she offers employees a wide array of desirable benefits such as raises each year, profit sharing, trust funds for employees' children, paid sabbaticals, personal development funds, and so forth. But more importantly, Sabrina recognizes that employees have a life outside the office and treats them accordingly. This type of HRM approach has kept her employees loyal and productive.[36]

A unique and important employee retention issue entrepreneurs must deal with is compensation. Whereas traditional organizations are more likely to view compensation from the perspective of monetary rewards (base pay, benefits, and incentives), smaller entrepreneurial firms are more likely to view compensation from a total rewards perspective. For these firms, compensation encompasses psychological rewards, learning opportunities, and recognition in addition to monetary rewards (base pay and incentives).[37]

Stimulating and Making Changes

We know that the context facing entrepreneurs is one of dynamic change. Both external and internal forces (see Chapter 6) may bring about the need for making changes in the entrepreneurial venture. Entrepreneurs need to be alert to problems and opportunities that may create the need to change. In fact, of the many hats an entrepreneur wears, that of change agent may be one of the most important.[38] If changes are needed in the entrepreneurial venture, often it is the entrepreneur who first recognizes the need for change and acts as the catalyst, coach, cheerleader, and chief change consultant. Change isn't easy in any organization, but it can be particularly challenging for entrepreneurial ventures. Even if a person is comfortable with taking risks—as entrepreneurs usually are—change can be hard. That's why it's important for an entrepreneur to recognize the critical role he or she plays in stimulating and implementing change. For instance, Jeff Fluhr, CEO of StubHub, Inc., is well aware of the important role he plays in stimulating and implementing changes. As the leading Internet player in the ticket reselling market, Fluhr had to continually look for ways to keep his company competitive. One change was the creation of an exclusive advertising agreement with the National Hockey League to promote StubHub.com on NHL.com.[39] StubHub is now a division of eBay.

During any type of organizational change, an entrepreneur also may have to act as chief coach and cheerleader. Because organizational change of any type can be disruptive and scary, the entrepreneur must explain the change to employees and encourage change efforts by supporting employees, getting them excited about the change, building them up, and motivating them to put forth their best efforts.

Finally, the entrepreneur may have to guide the actual change process as changes in strategy, technology, products, structure, or people are implemented. In this role, the entrepreneur answers questions, makes suggestions, gets needed resources, facilitates conflict, and does whatever else is necessary to get the change(s) implemented.

The Importance of Continuing Innovation

In today's dynamically chaotic world of global competition, organizations must continually innovate new products and services if they want to compete successfully. Innovation is a key characteristic of entrepreneurial ventures and, in fact, it's what makes the entrepreneurial venture "entrepreneurial."

What must an entrepreneur do to encourage innovation in the venture? Having an innovation-supportive culture is crucial. What does such a culture look like?[40] It's one in which employees perceive that supervisory support and organizational reward systems are consistent with a commitment to innovation. It's also important in this type of culture that employees not perceive their workload pressures to be excessive or unreasonable. And research has shown that firms with cultures supportive of innovation tend to be smaller, have fewer formalized human resource practices, and less abundant resources.[41]

Leading Issues

The employees at designer Liz Lange's company have to be flexible. Many don't have job descriptions, and everyone is expected to contribute ideas and pitch in with tasks in all departments. Lange says, "The phrase 'That's not my job' doesn't belong here." In return, Lange is a supportive leader who gives her employees considerable latitude.[42]

Leading is an important function of entrepreneurs. As an entrepreneurial venture grows and people are brought on board, an entrepreneur takes on a new role—that of a leader. In this section, we want to look at what's involved with the leading function. First, we're going to look at the unique personality characteristics of entrepreneurs. Then we're going to discuss the important role entrepreneurs play in motivating employees through empowerment and leading the venture and employee teams.

Personality Characteristics of Entrepreneurs

Think of someone you know who is an entrepreneur. Maybe it's someone you personally know or maybe it's someone like Bill Gates of Microsoft. How would you describe this person's personality? One of the most researched areas of entrepreneurship has been the search to determine what—if any—psychological characteristics entrepreneurs have in common, what types of personality traits entrepreneurs have that might distinguish them from non-entrepreneurs, and what traits entrepreneurs have that might predict who will be a successful entrepreneur.

Is there a classic "entrepreneurial personality"? Trying to pinpoint specific personality characteristics that all entrepreneurs share has the same problem as identifying the trait theories of leadership—that is, being able to identify specific personality traits that *all* entrepreneurs share. This challenge hasn't stopped entrepreneurship researchers from listing common traits, however. For instance, one list of personality characteristics included the following: high level of motivation, abundance of self-confidence, ability to be involved for the long term, high energy level, persistent problem solver, high degree of initiative, ability to set goals, and moderate risk-taker. Another list of characteristics of "successful" entrepreneurs included high energy level, great persistence, resourcefulness, the desire and ability to be self-directed, and relatively high need for autonomy.

Another development in defining entrepreneurial personality characteristics was the proactive personality scale to predict an individual's likelihood of pursuing entrepreneurial ventures. We introduced the **proactive personality** trait in Chapter 14. Recall that it's a personality trait of individuals who are more prone to take actions to influence their environment—that is, they're more proactive. Obviously, an entrepreneur is likely to exhibit proactivity as he or she searches for opportunities and acts to take advantage of those opportunities. Various items on the proactive personality scale were found to be good indicators of a person's likelihood of becoming an entrepreneur, including gender, education, having an entrepreneurial parent, and possessing a proactive personality. In addition, studies have shown that entrepreneurs have greater risk propensity than do managers. However, this propensity is moderated by the entrepreneur's primary goal. Risk propensity is greater for entrepreneurs whose primary goal is growth versus those whose focus is on producing family income.

Motivating Employees Through Empowerment

At Sapient Corporation (creators of Internet and software systems for e-commerce and automating back-office tasks such as billing and inventory), cofounders Jerry Greenberg and J. Stuart Moore recognized that employee motivation was vitally important to their company's ultimate success.[43] They designed their organization so individual employees are part of an industry-specific team that works on an entire project rather than on one small piece of it. Their rationale was that people often feel frustrated when they're doing a small part of a job and never get to see the whole job from start to finish. They figured people would be more productive if they got the opportunity to participate in all phases of a project.

When you're motivated to do something, don't you find yourself energized and willing to work hard at doing whatever it is you're excited about? Wouldn't it be great if all of a venture's employees were energized, excited, and willing to work hard at their jobs? Having motivated employees is an important goal for any entrepreneur, and employee empowerment is an important motivational tool entrepreneurs can use.

Although it's not easy for entrepreneurs to do, employee empowerment—giving employees the power to make decisions and take actions on their own—is an important motivational approach. Why? Because successful entrepreneurial ventures must be quick and nimble, ready to pursue opportunities and go off in new directions. Empowered employees can provide that flexibility and speed. When employees are empowered, they often display stronger work motivation, better work quality, higher job satisfaction, and lower turnover.

For example, employees at Butler International, Inc., a technology consulting services firm based in Montvale, New Jersey, work at client locations. President and CEO Ed Kopko recognized that employees had to be empowered to do their jobs if they were going to be successful.[44] Another entrepreneurial venture that found employee empowerment to be a strong motivational approach is Stryker Instruments in Kalamazoo, Michigan, a division of Stryker Corporation. Each of the company's production units is responsible for its operating budget, cost reduction goals, customer-service levels, inventory management, training, production planning and forecasting, purchasing, human resource management, safety, and problem solving. In addition, unit members work closely with marketing, sales, and R&D during new product introductions and continuous improvement projects. Says one team supervisor, "Stryker lets me do what I do best and rewards me for that privilege."[45]

Empowerment is a philosophical concept that entrepreneurs have to "buy into." This doesn't come easily. In fact, it's hard for many entrepreneurs to do. Their life is tied up in the business. They've built it from the ground up. But continuing to grow the entrepreneurial venture is eventually going to require handing over more responsibilities to employees. How can entrepreneurs empower employees? For many entrepreneurs, it's a gradual process.

Entrepreneurs can begin by using participative decision making in which employees provide input into decisions. Although getting employees to participate in decisions isn't quite taking the full plunge into employee empowerment, at least it's a way to begin tapping into the collective array of employees' talents, skills, knowledge, and abilities.

proactive personality
A personality trait that describes individuals who are more prone to take actions to influence their environments

Another way to empower employees is through delegation—the process of assigning certain decisions or specific job duties to employees. By delegating decisions and duties, the entrepreneur is turning over the responsibility for carrying them out.

When an entrepreneur is finally comfortable with the idea of employee empowerment, fully empowering employees means redesigning their jobs so they have discretion over the way they do their work. It's allowing employees to do their work effectively and efficiently by using their creativity, imagination, knowledge, and skills.

If an entrepreneur implements employee empowerment properly—that is, with complete and total commitment to the program and with appropriate employee training—results can be impressive for the entrepreneurial venture and for the empowered employees. The business can enjoy significant productivity gains, quality improvements, more satisfied customers, increased employee motivation, and improved morale. Employees can enjoy the opportunities to do a greater variety of work that is more interesting and challenging.

In addition, employees are encouraged to take the initiative in identifying and solving problems and doing their work. For example, at Mine Safety Appliances Company in Pittsburgh, Pennsylvania, employees are empowered to change their work processes in order to meet the organization's challenging quality improvement goals. Getting to this point took an initial 40 hours of classroom instruction per employee in areas such as engineering drawing, statistical process control, quality certifications, and specific work instruction. However, the company's commitment to an empowered workforce has resulted in profitability increasing 57 percent over the last four years and 95 percent of the company's employees achieving multi-skill certifications.[46]

The Entrepreneur as Leader

The last topic we want to discuss in this section is the role of the entrepreneur as a leader. In this role, the entrepreneur has certain leadership responsibilities in leading the venture and in leading employee work teams.

LEADING THE VENTURE.   Today's successful entrepreneur must be like the leader of a jazz ensemble known for its improvisation, innovation, and creativity. Max DePree, former head of Herman Miller, Inc., a leading office furniture manufacturer known for its innovative leadership approaches, said it best in his book, *Leadership Jazz*, "Jazz band leaders must choose the music, find the right musicians, and perform—in public. But the effect of the performance depends on so many things—the environment, the volunteers playing the band, the need for everybody to perform as individuals and as a group, the absolute dependence of the leader on the members of the band, the need for the followers to play well. . . . The leader of the jazz band has the beautiful opportunity to draw the best out of the other musicians. We have much to learn from jazz band leaders, for jazz, like leadership, combines the unpredictability of the future with the gifts of individuals."[47]

The way an entrepreneur leads the venture should be much like the jazz leader—drawing the best out of other individuals, even given the unpredictability of the situation. One way an entrepreneur leads is through the vision he or she creates for the organization. In fact, the driving force through the early stages of the entrepreneurial venture is often the visionary leadership of the entrepreneur. The entrepreneur's ability to articulate a coherent, inspiring, and attractive vision of the future is a key test of his or her leadership. But if an entrepreneur can articulate such a vision, the results can be worthwhile. A study contrasting visionary and nonvisionary companies showed that visionary companies outperformed the nonvisionary ones by six times on standard financial criteria, and their stocks outperformed the general market by 15 times.[48]

LEADING EMPLOYEE WORK TEAMS.   As we know from Chapter 13, many organizations—entrepreneurial and otherwise—are using employee work teams to perform organizational tasks, create new ideas, and resolve problems.

Employee work teams tend to be popular in entrepreneurial ventures. An *Industry Week* Census of Manufacturers showed that nearly 68 percent of survey respondents used teams

that sold almost $2 million worth of skates, skis, snowboards, and other sporting goods on eBay. As the company grows, Otto is finding that he has to be more organized.[53]

Having enough capital is a major challenge facing growing entrepreneurial ventures. The money issue never seems to go away, does it? It takes capital to expand. The processes of finding capital to fund growth are much like going through the initial financing of the venture. Hopefully, at this time the venture has a successful track record to back up the request. If it doesn't, it may be extremely difficult to acquire the necessary capital. That's why we said earlier that the best growth strategy is a planned one.

Part of that planning should be how growth will be financed. For example, The Boston Beer Company, America's largest microbrewer and producer of Samuel Adams beer, grew rapidly by focusing almost exclusively on increasing its top-selling product line. However, the company was so focused on increasing market share that it had few financial controls and an inadequate financial infrastructure. During periods of growth, cash flow difficulties would force company chairman and brewmaster Jim Koch to tap into a pool of unused venture capital funding. However, when a chief financial officer joined the company, he developed a financial structure that enabled the company to manage its growth more efficiently and effectively by setting up a plan for funding growth.[54]

Another important issue that a growing entrepreneurial venture needs to address is finding people. If the venture is growing quickly, this challenge may be intensified because of time constraints. It's important to plan the numbers and types of employees needed as much as possible in order to support the increasing workload of the growing venture. It may also be necessary to provide additional training and support to employees to help them handle the increased pressures associated with the growing organization.

Finally, when a venture is growing, it's important to create a positive, growth-oriented culture that enhances the opportunities to achieve success, both organizationally and individually. Encouraging the culture can sometimes be difficult to do, particularly when changes are rapidly happening. However, the values, attitudes, and beliefs that are established and reinforced during these times are critical to the entrepreneurial venture's continued and future success. Exhibit A-5 lists some suggestions that entrepreneurs might use to ensure that their venture's culture is one that embraces and supports a climate in which organizational growth is viewed as desirable and important. Keeping employees focused and committed to what the venture is doing is critical to the ultimate success of its growth strategies. If employees don't "buy into" the direction the entrepreneurial venture is headed, it's unlikely the growth strategies will be successful.

CONTROLLING FOR GROWTH. Another challenge that growing entrepreneurial ventures face is reinforcing already established organizational controls. Maintaining good financial records and financial controls over cash flow, inventory, customer data, sales orders, receivables, payables, and costs should be a priority of every entrepreneur—whether pursuing growth or not. However, it's particularly important to reinforce these controls

---

EXHIBIT A-5

Achieving a Supportive, Growth-Oriented Culture

- Keep the lines of communication open—inform employees about major issues.
- Establish trust by being honest, open, and forthright about the challenges and rewards of being a growing organization.
- Be a good listener—find out what employees are thinking and facing.
- Be willing to delegate duties.
- Be flexible—be willing to change your plans if necessary.
- Provide consistent and regular feedback by letting employees know the outcomes—good and bad.
- Reinforce the contributions of each person by recognizing employees' efforts.
- Continually train employees to enhance their capabilities and skills.
- Maintain the focus on the venture's mission even as it grows.
- Establish and reinforce a "we" spirit that supports the coordinated efforts of all the employees and helps the growing venture be successful.

when the entrepreneurial venture is expanding. It's all too easy to let things "get away" or to put them off when there's an unrelenting urgency to get things done. Rapid growth—or even slow growth—does not excuse the need to have effective controls in place. In fact, it's particularly important to have established procedures, protocols, and processes and to use them. Even though mistakes and inefficiencies can never be eliminated entirely, an entrepreneur should at least ensure that every effort is being made to achieve high levels of productivity and organizational effectiveness. For example, at Green Gear Cycling, cofounder Alan Scholz recognized the importance of controlling for growth. How? By following a "Customers for Life" strategy, which meant continually monitoring customer relationships and orienting organizational work decisions around their possible impacts on customers. Through this type of strategy, Green Gear hopes to keep customers for life. That's significant because they figured that, if they could keep a customer for life, the value would range from $10,000 to $25,000 per lifetime customer.[55]

Managing Downturns

Although organizational growth is a desirable and important goal for entrepreneurial ventures, what happens when things don't go as planned—when the growth strategies don't result in the intended outcomes and, in fact, result in a decline in performance? Significant challenges can come in managing the downturns.

Nobody likes to fail, especially entrepreneurs. However, when an entrepreneurial venture faces times of trouble, what can be done? How can downturns be managed successfully? The first step is recognizing that a crisis is brewing.

RECOGNIZING CRISIS SITUATIONS.   An entrepreneur should be alert to the warning signs of a business in trouble. Some signals of potential performance decline include inadequate or negative cash flow, excess number of employees, unnecessary and cumbersome administrative procedures, fear of conflict and taking risks, tolerance of work incompetence, lack of a clear mission or goals, and ineffective or poor communication within the organization.[56]

Another perspective on recognizing performance declines revolves around what is known as the **"boiled frog" phenomenon** in which subtly declining situations are difficult to recognize.[57] The "boiled frog" is a classic psychological response experiment. In one case, a live frog that's dropped into a boiling pan of water reacts instantaneously and jumps out of the pan. But in the second case, a live frog that's dropped into a pan of mild water that is gradually heated to the boiling point fails to react and dies. A small firm may be particularly vulnerable to the boiled frog phenomenon because the entrepreneur may not recognize the "water heating up"—that is, the subtle decline of the situation. When changes in performance are gradual, a serious response may never be triggered or may be initiated too late to intervene effectively in the situation.

So what does the boiled frog phenomenon teach us? It teaches us that entrepreneurs need to be alert to signals that the venture's performance may be worsening. Don't wait until the water has reached the boiling point before you react.

DEALING WITH DOWNTURNS, DECLINES, AND CRISES.   Although an entrepreneur hopes to never have to deal with organizational downturns, declines, or crises, a time may come when he or she must do just that. After all, nobody likes to think about things going bad or taking a turn for the worse. But that's exactly what the entrepreneur should do—think about it *before* it happens (remember feedforward control from Chapter 18).[58] It's important to have an up-to-date plan for covering crises. It's like mapping exit routes from

"boiled frog" phenomenon
A perspective on recognizing performance declines that suggests watching out for subtly declining situations

your home in case of a fire. An entrepreneur wants to be prepared before an emergency hits. This plan should focus on providing specific details for controlling the most fundamental and critical aspects of running the venture—cash flow, accounts receivable, costs, and debt. Beyond having a plan for controlling the venture's critical inflows and outflows, other actions would involve identifying specific strategies for cutting costs and restructuring the venture.

Exiting the Venture

Getting out of an entrepreneurial venture may seem to be a strange thing for entrepreneurs to do. However, the entrepreneur may decide at some point that it's time to move on. That decision may be based on the fact that the entrepreneur hopes to capitalize financially on the investment in the venture—called **harvesting**—or that the entrepreneur is facing serious organizational performance problems and wants to get out, or even on the entrepreneur's desire to focus on other pursuits (personal or business). The issues involved with exiting the venture include choosing a proper business valuation method and knowing what's involved in the process of selling a business.

BUSINESS VALUATION METHODS. Valuation techniques generally fall into three categories: (1) asset valuations, (2) earnings valuations, and (3) cash flow valuations.[59] Setting a value on a business can be a little tricky. In many cases, the entrepreneur has sacrificed much for the business and sees it as his or her "baby." Calculating the value of the baby based on objective standards such as cash flow or some multiple of net profits can sometimes be a shock. That's why it's important for an entrepreneur who wishes to exit the venture to get a comprehensive business valuation prepared by professionals.

OTHER IMPORTANT CONSIDERATIONS IN EXITING THE VENTURE. Although the hardest part of preparing to exit a venture is valuing it, other factors also should be considered.[60] These factors include being prepared, deciding who will sell the business, considering the tax implications, screening potential buyers, and deciding whether to tell employees before or after the sale. The process of exiting the entrepreneurial venture should be approached as carefully as the process of launching it. If the entrepreneur is selling the venture on a positive note, he or she wants to realize the value built up in the business. If the venture is being exited because of declining performance, the entrepreneur wants to maximize the potential return.

Managing Personal Life Choices and Challenges

Being an entrepreneur is extremely exciting and fulfilling, yet extremely demanding, often with long hours and high stress. Yet, being an entrepreneur can offer a variety of rewards, as well. In this section, we want to look at how entrepreneurs can make it work—that is, how can they be successful and effectively balance the demands of their work and personal lives?[61]

Entrepreneurs are a special group. They are focused, persistent, hardworking, and intelligent. Because they put so much of themselves into launching and growing their entrepreneurial ventures, many may neglect their personal lives. Entrepreneurs often have to make sacrifices to pursue their entrepreneurial dreams. However, they can make it work. They can balance their work and personal lives. But how?

One of the most important things an entrepreneur can do is *become a good time manager.* Prioritize what needs to be done. Use a planner (daily, weekly, monthly) to help schedule priorities. Some entrepreneurs don't like taking the time to plan or prioritize, or they think it's a ridiculous waste of time. Yet identifying the important duties and distinguishing them from those that aren't so important actually makes an entrepreneur more efficient and effective. In addition, part of being a good time manager is delegating those decisions and actions the entrepreneur doesn't have to be personally involved in to trusted employees. Although it may be hard to let go of some of the things they've always done, entrepreneurs who delegate effectively will see their personal productivity levels rise.

Another suggestion for finding that balance is to *seek professional advice* in those areas of business where it's needed. Although entrepreneurs may be reluctant to spend scarce cash, the time, energy, and potential problems saved in the long run are well worth the investment. Competent professional advisers can provide entrepreneurs with information to make more intelligent decisions. Also, it's important to *deal with conflicts* as they arise—both workplace and family conflicts. If an entrepreneur doesn't deal with conflicts, negative feelings are likely to crop up and lead to communication breakdowns. When communication falls apart, vital information may get lost, and people (employees *and* family members) may start to assume the worst. It can turn into a nightmare situation that feeds upon itself. The best strategy is to deal with conflicts as they come up. Talk, discuss, argue (if you must), but an entrepreneur shouldn't avoid the conflict or pretend it doesn't exist.

Another suggestion for achieving that balance between work and personal life is to *develop a network of trusted friends and peers.* Having a group of people to talk with is a good way for an entrepreneur to think through problems and issues. The support and encouragement offered by these people can be an invaluable source of strength for an entrepreneur.

Finally, *recognize when your stress levels are too high.* Entrepreneurs *are* achievers. They like to make things happen. They thrive on working hard. Yet, too much stress can lead to significant physical and emotional problems (as we discussed in Chapter 12). Entrepreneurs have to learn when stress is overwhelming them and to do something about it. After all, what's the point of growing and building a thriving entrepreneurial venture if you're not around to enjoy it?

REVIEW AND DISCUSSION QUESTIONS

1. What do you think would be the hardest thing about being an entrepreneur? What do you think would be the most fun thing?
2. How does the concept of social entrepreneurship (see Chapter 5) relate to entrepreneurs and entrepreneurial ventures?
3. Would a good manager be a good entrepreneur? Discuss.
4. Why do you think many entrepreneurs find it hard to step aside and let others manage their business?
5. Do you think a person can be taught to be an entrepreneur? Why or why not?
6. What do you think it means to be a successful entrepreneurial venture? How about a successful entrepreneur?

harvesting
Exiting a venture when an entrepreneur hopes
to capitalize financially on the investment in
the venture

Endnotes

Chapter 1

1. P. Bilbrey and B. Jones, "Don't Go It Alone," *Restaurant Hospitality,* February 2010, pp. 38–40; *2010 Pocket Factbook*, National Restaurant Association, www.restaurant.org; F. Glazer, "Select Concepts Managed to Draw Traffic as Recession Hit Hard," *Nation's Restaurant News,* December 21, 2009, p. 22; and A. Martin, "Empty Tables Threaten Some Restaurant Chains," *New York Times Online,* April 4, 2009.

2. J. Welch and S. Welch, "An Employee Bill of Rights," *Bloomberg BusinessWeek,* March 16, 2009, p. 72.

3. A. Taylor III, "Survival on Dealers' Row," *CNNMoney.com,* March 26, 2008.

4. E. Frauenheim, "Managers Don't Matter," *Workforce Management Online,* April 2010; and K. A. Tucker and V. Allman, "Don't Be a Cat-and-Mouse Manager," The Gallup Organization [www.brain.gallup.com], September 9, 2004.

5. "Work USA 2008/2009 Report: Driving Business Results through Continuous Engagement," Watson Wyatt Worldwide, Washington, DC.

6. T. R. Holcomb, R. M. Holmes, Jr., and B. L. Connelly, "Making the Most of What You Have: Managerial Ability as a Source of Resource Value Creation," *Strategic Management Journal,* May 2009, pp. 457–485.

7. By the Numbers box based on J. Yang and S. Ward, "Do You Want To Become a Manager?" *USA Today Snapshots,* May 5, 2009, p. 1B; "Who Needs Rapport with the Boss?" *Training,* February 2010, p. 10; J. Yang and A. Lewis, "People Skills Can Win Jobs," *USA Today Snapshots,* December 1, 2009, p. 1B; J. Yang and K. Gelles, "Would You Lay Off Your Boss If You Could?" *USA Today Snapshots,* November 10, 2009, p. 1B; J. Macintyre, "Industry Insight," *Springfield Business Journal,* November 30/December 6, 2009, p. 16; J. Yang and V. Salazar, "Is Your Boss Likable? *USA Today Snapshots,* December 14, 2009, p. 1B; "Recession Weather-Proofed," *Training,* March/April 2009, p. 8; J. Yang and V. Salazar, "What Makes Good Employees Quit? *USA Today Snapshots,* February 10, 2009, p. 1B; and R. I. Sutton, "Are You Being a Jerk? Again?" *Bloomberg BusinessWeek,* August 25/September 1, 2008, p. 52.

8. http://www.catalyst.org/publication/322/women-ceos-of-the-fortune-1000, September 27, 2010.

9. D. J. Campbell, "The Proactive Employee: Managing Workplace Initiative," *Academy of Management Executive,* August 2000, pp. 52–66.

10. J. S. McClenahen, "Prairie Home Champion," *Industry Week,* October 2005, pp. 45–47.

11. Q. Hardy, "Google Thinks Small," *Forbes,* November 14, 2005, pp. 198–202.

12. Future Vision box based on: Quote attributed to Charles F. Kettering, WikipediaQuote; M. Gladwell, *The Tipping Point* (Little, Brown and Company, 2000); and H. Yen, The Associated Press, "Minorities Making Up Almost Half of Births," *Springfield, Missouri News-Leader,* March 10, 2010, p. 3B.

13. P. Panchak, "Sustaining Lean," *Industry Week,* October 2005, pp. 48–50.

14. H. Fayol, *Industrial and General Administration* (Paris: Dunod, 1916).

15. For a comprehensive review of this question, see C. P. Hales, "What Do Managers Do? A Critical Review of the Evidence," *Journal of Management,* January 1986, pp. 88–115.

16. J. T. Straub, "Put on Your Manager's Hat," *USA Today Online* [www.usatoday.com], October 29, 2002; and H. Mintzberg, *The Nature of Managerial Work* (New York: Harper & Row, 1973).

17. E. C. Dierdorff, R. S. Rubin, and F. P. Morgeson, "The Milieu of Managerial Work: An Integrative Framework Linking Work Context to Role Requirements," *Journal of Applied Psychology,* June 2009, pp. 972–988.

18. H. Mintzberg and J. Gosling, "Educating Managers Beyond Borders," *Academy of Management Learning and Education,* September 2002, pp. 64–76.

19. See, for example, M. J. Martinko and W. L. Gardner, "Structured Observation of Managerial Work: A Replication and Synthesis," *Journal of Management Studies,* May 1990, pp. 330–357; A. I. Kraut, P. R. Pedigo, D. D. McKenna, and M. D. Dunnette, "The Role of the Manager: What's Really Important in Different Management Jobs," *Academy of Management Executive,* November 1989, pp. 286–293; and C. M. Pavett and A. W. Lau, "Managerial Work: The Influence of Hierarchical Level and Functional Specialty," *Academy of Management Journal,* March 1983, pp. 170–77.

20. Pavett and Lau, "Managerial Work."

21. "What Managers Really Do," *Wall Street Journal,* August 17, 2009, p. R2; and H. Mintzberg, *Managing* (San Francisco: Berrett Koehler), 2009.

22. S. J. Carroll and D. A. Gillen, "Are the Classical Management Functions Useful in Describing Managerial Work?" *Academy of Management Review,* January 1987, p. 48.

23. Leader Who Made a Difference box based on information from Panda Express [www.pandaexpress.com], March 10, 2010; D. G. Fleenor, "Full-Service Training," *Stores Magazine,* August 2008, pp. 76–77; and E. Hessel, "Kung Pao Chicken for the Soul," *Forbes,* August 21, 2008, pp. 106–107.

24. E. White, "Firms Step Up Training for Front-Line Managers," *Wall Street Journal,* August 27, 2007, p. B3.

25. See, for example, J. G. Harris, D. W. DeLong, and A. Donnellon, "Do You Have What It Takes to Be an E-Manager?" *Strategy and Leadership,* August 2001, pp. 10–14; C. Fletcher and C. Baldry, "A Study of Individual Differences and Self-Awareness in the Context of Multi-Source Feedback," *Journal of Occupational and Organizational Psychology,* September 2000, pp. 303–319; and R. L. Katz, "Skills of an Effective Administrator," *Harvard Business Review,* September/October 1974, pp. 90–102.

26. W. C. Symonds, S. Baker, M. Arndt, and R. D. Hof, "The Future of Work," *Business Week,* March 22, 2004, pp. 50–52.

27. T. J. Erickson, "Task, Not Time: Profile of a Gen Y Job," *Harvard Business Review,* February 2008, p. 19.

28. C. Ansberry, "Firms Map Routes to Recovery," *Wall Street Journal,* March 2, 2010, pp. B1+.

29. F. F. Reichheld, "Lead for Loyalty," *Harvard Business Review,* July/August 2001, p. 76.

30. Cited in E. Naumann and D. W. Jackson, Jr., "One More Time: How Do You Satisfy Customers?" *Business Horizons,* May/June 1999, p. 73.

31. Data from *The World Factbook 2010,* [www.cia.gov/publications/factbook/index.html], March 7, 2010.

32. D. Dougherty and A. Murthy, "What Service Customers Really Want," *Harvard Business Review,* September 2009, p. 22; and K. A. Eddleston, D. L. Kidder, and B. E. Litzky, "Who's the Boss? Contending With Competing Expectations From Customers and Management," *Academy of Management Executive,* November 2002, pp. 85–95.

33. See, for instance, D. M. Mayer, M. G. Ehrhart, and B. Schneider, "Service Attribute Boundary Conditions of the Service Climate-Customer Satisfaction Link," *Academy of Management Journal,* October 2009, pp. 1034–1050; M. Groth, T. Hennig-Thurau, and G. Walsh, "Customer Reactions to Emotional Labor: The Roles of Employee Acting Strategies and Customer Detection Accuracy," *Academy of Management Journal,* October 2009, pp. 958–974; J. W. Grizzle, A. R. Zablah, T. J. Brown, J. C. Mowen, and J. M. Lee, "Employee Customer Orientation in Context: How the Environment Moderates the Influence of Customer Orientation on Performance Outcomes," *Journal of Applied Psychology,* September 2009, pp. 1227–1242; B. A. Gutek, M. Groth, and B. Cherry, "Achieving Service Success Through Relationships and Enhanced Encounters," *Academy of Management Executive,* November 2002, pp. 132–144; Eddleston, Kidder, and Litzky, "Who's the Boss? Contending With Competing Expectations From Customers and

Management"; S. D. Pugh, J. Dietz, J. W. Wiley, and S. M. Brooks, "Driving Service Effectiveness Through Employee-Customer Linkages," *Academy of Management Executive,* November 2002, pp. 73–84; S. D. Pugh, "Service With a Smile: Emotional Contagion in the Service Encounter," *Academy of Management Journal,* October 2001, pp. 1018–1027; W. C. Tsai, "Determinants and Consequences of Employee Displayed Positive Emotions," *Journal of Management,* vol. 27, no. 4, 2001, pp. 497–512; Naumann and Jackson, Jr., "One More Time: How Do You Satisfy Customers?"; and M. D. Hartline and O. C. Ferrell, "The Management of Customer-Contact Service Employees: An Empirical Investigation," *Journal of Marketing,* October 1996, pp. 52–70.

34. J. Swartz, "Twitter Helps Customer Service," *USA Today,* November 18, 2009, p. 3B; and J. Swartz, "Businesses Get Cheap Help from a Little Birdie," *USA Today,* June 26, 2009, p. 1B.

35. R. A. Hattori and J. Wycoff, "Innovation DNA," *Training and Development,* January 2002, p. 24.

36. R. Wagner, "One Store, One Team at Best Buy," *Gallup Brain,* August 12, 2004 [http://brain.gallup.com/content/], November 28, 2005.

37. M. Kripalani, "Tata Taps A Vast R&D Shop—Its Own," *Bloomberg BusinessWeek/infocus,* April 20, 2009, p. 50.

38. S. Rosenbloom, "Wal-Mart Unveils Plan to Make Supply Chain Greener," *New York Times Online,* February 26, 2010.

39. KPMG Global Sustainability Services, *Sustainability Insights,* October 2007.

40. *Symposium on Sustainability—Profiles in Leadership,* New York, October 2001.

41. J. Sandberg, "Down over Moving Up: Some New Bosses Find They Hate Their Jobs," *Wall Street Journal,* July 27, 2005, p. B1.

42. C. Tuna and K. J. Winstein, "Economy Promises to Fuel Résumé Fraud," *Wall Street Journal,* November 17, 2008, p. B4; K. J. Winstein and T. Audi, "MGM Mirage CEO Resigns Amid Questions About MBA," *Wall Street Journal,* November 14, 2008, pp. 1+; K. J. Winstein, "Inflated Credentials Surface in Executive Suite," *Wall Street Journal,* November 13, 2008, pp. B1+; "Redoing Your Resume? Leave Off the Lies," *Training,* December 2006, p. 9; J. O'Donnell, "CEO Left RadioShack with His Whole Life in Turmoil," *USA Today,* February 27, 2006; and "Lies, Damn Lies, and Statistics," *Wired,* March 2004, p. 60.

43. S. Y. Todd, K. J. Harris, R. B. Harris, and A. R. Wheeler, "Career Success Implications of Political Skill," *Journal of Social Psychology,* June 2009, pp. 179–204; G. R. Ferris, D. C. Treadway, P. L. Perrewé, R. L. Brouer, C. Douglas, and S. Lux, "Political Skill in Organizations," *Journal of Management,* June 2007, pp. 290–329; K. J. Harris, K. M. Kacmar, S. Zivnuska, and J. D. Shaw, "The Impact of Political Skill on Impression Management Effectiveness," *Journal of Applied Psychology,* January 2007, pp. 278–285; and G. R. Ferris, D. C. Treadway, R. W. Kolodinsky, W. A. Hochwarter, C. J. Kacmar, C. Douglas, and D. D. Frink, "Development and Validation of the Political Skill Inventory," *Journal of Management,* February 2005, pp. 126–152.

44. Based on Life is Good® Web site [www.lifeisgood.com]; T. Trespicio, "Good Vibrations," *Body+Soul,* December 2009, pp. 96–101; J. Larson, "Life Is Good: Spreading Happiness to Troubled Kids," Video clip on *NBC Today,* July 29, 2008 [http://www.msnbc.msn.com/id/21134540/vp/25902982]; E. Wilson, "Everything's Fine! My T-Shirt Says So," *New York Times Online,* July 24, 2008; G. Rifkin, "Millions in Sales from 3 Simple Words," *New York Times Online,* November 22, 2007; and L. Buchanan, "Life Lessons," *Inc.,* October 2006, pp. 86–92.

45. D. Tang, "Branson AirExpress Takes Off in May," *USA Today,* March 10, 2010, p. 3B; K. Leiser, "Branson Airport Enjoys Growth," *stltoday.com,* February 28, 2010; D. Tang, "Branson Airport Says City Owes It Thousands," *Springfield, Missouri News-Leader,* January 23, 2010, p. 1A+; News-Leader Staff, "Branson Votes to Pay Airport After Resolutions," *Springfield, Missouri News-Leader,* January 14, 2010, p. 4B; D. Reed, "Branson Takes New Approach to Airport," *USA Today,* May 5, 2009, pp. 1B+; C. Negroni, "In Missouri, Investors Seek a Profit in Branson Airport," *New York Times Online,* April 21, 2009; and P. Blais, "Branson Takes to the Air," *Planning,* November 2008, pp. 14–17.

History Module

1. C. S. George, Jr., *The History of Management Thought,* 2d ed. (Upper Saddle River, NJ: Prentice Hall, 1972), p. 4.

2. Ibid., pp. 35–41.

3. F. W. Taylor, *Principles of Scientific Management* (New York: Harper, 1911), p. 44. For other information on Taylor, see S. Wagner-Tsukamoto, "An Institutional Economic Reconstruction of Scientific Management: On the Lost Theoretical Logic of Taylorism," *Academy of Management Review,* January 2007, pp. 105–117; R. Kanigel, *The One Best Way: Frederick Winslow Taylor and the Enigma of Efficiency* (New York: Viking, 1997); and M. Banta, *Taylored Lives: Narrative Productions in the Age of Taylor, Veblen, and Ford* (Chicago: University of Chicago Press, 1993).

4. See for example, F. B. Gilbreth, *Motion Study* (New York: Van Nostrand, 1911); and F. B. Gilbreth and L. M. Gilbreth, *Fatigue Study* (New York: Sturgis and Walton, 1916).

5. H. Fayol, *Industrial and General Administration* (Paris: Dunod, 1916).

6. M. Weber, *The Theory of Social and Economic Organizations,* ed. T. Parsons, trans. A. M. Henderson and T. Parsons (New York: Free Press, 1947); and M. Lounsbury and E. J. Carberry, "From King to Court Jester? Weber's Fall from Grace in Organizational Theory," *Organization Studies,* vol. 26, no. 4, 2005, pp. 501–525.

7. E. Mayo, *The Human Problems of an Industrial Civilization* (New York: Macmillan, 1933); and F. J. Roethlisberger and W. J. Dickson, *Management and the Worker* (Cambridge, MA: Harvard University Press, 1939).

8. See, for example, G. W. Yunker, "An Explanation of Positive and Negative Hawthorne Effects: Evidence from the Relay Assembly Test Room and Bank Wiring Observation Room Studies," paper presented, Academy of Management Annual Meeting, August 1993, Atlanta, Georgia; S. R. Jones, "Was There a Hawthorne Effect?" *American Sociological Review,* November 1992, pp. 451–468; and S. R. G. Jones, "Worker Interdependence and Output: The Hawthorne Studies Reevaluated," *American Sociological Review,* April 1990, pp. 176–190; J. A. Sonnenfeld, "Shedding Light on the Hawthorne Studies," *Journal of Occupational Behavior,* April 1985, pp. 111–130; B. Rice, "The Hawthorne Defect: Persistence of a Flawed Theory," *Psychology Today,* February 1982, pp. 70–74; R. H. Franke and J. Kaul, "The Hawthorne Experiments: First Statistical Interpretations," *American Sociological Review,* October 1978, pp. 623–643; and A. Carey, "The Hawthorne Studies: A Radical Criticism," *American Sociological Review,* June 1967, pp. 403–416.

9. N. Zamiska, "Plane Geometry: Scientists Help Speed Boarding of Aircraft," *Wall Street Journal,* November 2, 2005, p. A1+.

10. See, for example, J. Jusko, "Tried and True," *IW,* December 6, 1999, pp. 78–84; T. A. Stewart, "A Conversation with Joseph Juran," *Fortune,* January 11, 1999, pp. 168–170; J. R. Hackman and R. Wageman, "Total Quality Management: Empirical, Conceptual, and Practical Issues," *Administrative Science Quarterly,* June 1995, pp. 309–42; T. C. Powell, "Total Quality Management as Competitive Advantage: A Review and Empirical Study," *Strategic Management Journal,* January 1995, pp. 15–37; R. K. Reger, L. T. Gustafson, S. M. Demarie, and J. V. Mullane, "Reframing the Organization: Why Implementing Total Quality Is Easier Said Than Done," *Academy of Management Review,* July 1994, pp. 565–584; C. A. Reeves and D. A. Bednar, "Defining Quality: Alternatives and Implications," *Academy of Management Review,* July 1994, pp. 419–445; J. W. Dean Jr. and D. E. Bowen, "Management Theory and Total Quality: Improving Research and Practice through Theory Development," *Academy of Management Review,* July 1994, pp. 392–418; B. Krone, "Total Quality Management: An American Odyssey," *The Bureaucrat,* Fall 1990, pp. 35–38; and A. Gabor, *The Man Who Discovered Quality* (New York: Random House, 1990).

11. M. Barbaro, "A Long Line for a Shorter Wait at the Supermarket," *New York Times Online,* June 23, 2007.

12. S. Haines, "Become a Strategic Thinker," *Training,* October/November 2009, p. 64; and K. B. DeGreene, *Sociotechnical Systems: Factors in Analysis, Design, and Management* (Upper Saddle River, NJ: Prentice Hall, 1973), p. 13.

Chapter 2

1. D. Stodder, "Customer Insights," *Information Week,* February 1, 2010, p. 35; M. Bush, "JetBlue," *Advertising Age,* November 16, 2009, p. 12; D. W. Crain, "Only the Right People Are Strategic Assets of the Firm," *Strategy & Leadership,* 2009, vol. 37, no. 6, pp. 33–38; M. Gunther, "Nothing Blue About This Airline," *Fortune,* September 14, 2009, pp. 114–118; N. Zmuda, "Five Brands Doing It Right," *Advertising Age,* April 6, 2009, p. 10; and "JetBlue Hears the Voice of the Customer," *KMWorld,* February 2009, p. 13.

2. S. Terlep and N. E. Boudette, "Feeling Heat from Ford, GM Reshuffles Managers," *Wall Street Journal Online,* March 3, 2010.

3. B. McKay, "Cott Says Chief Will Be Leaving Amid Firm Woes," *Wall Street Journal,* March 25, 2008, p. B6.

4. P. Rozenzweig, "The Halo Effect and Other Managerial Delusions," *The McKinsey Quarterly Online Journal,* no. 1, March 9, 2007.

5. For insights into the symbolic view, see "Why CEO Churn Is Healthy," *BusinessWeek,* November 13, 2000, p. 230; S. M. Puffer and J. B. Weintrop, "Corporate Performance and CEO Turnover: The Role of Performance Expectations," *Administrative Science Quarterly,* March 1991, pp. 1–19; C. R. Schwenk, "Illusions of Management Control? Effects of Self-Serving Attributions on Resource Commitments and Confidence in Management," *Human Relations,* April 1990, pp. 333–347; J. R. Meindl and S. B. Ehrlich, "The Romance of Leadership and the Evaluation of Organizational Performance," *Academy of Management Journal,* March 1987, pp. 91–109; J. A. Byrne, "The Limits of Power," *BusinessWeek,* October 23, 1987, pp. 33–35; D. C. Hambrick and S. Finkelstein, "Managerial Discretion: A Bridge between Polar Views of Organizational Outcomes," in L. L. Cummings and B. M. Staw (eds.), *Research in Organizational Behavior,* vol. 9 (Greenwich, CT: JAI Press, 1987), pp. 369–406; and J. Pfeffer, "Management as Symbolic Action: The Creation and Maintenance of Organizational Paradigms," in L. L. Cummings and B. M. Staw (eds.), *Research in Organizational Behavior,* vol. 3 (Greenwich, CT: JAI Press, 1981), pp. 1–52.

6. T. M. Hout, "Are Managers Obsolete?" *Harvard Business Review,* March–April 1999, pp. 161–168; and Pfeffer, "Management as Symbolic Action."

7. C. Ansberry, "Firms Map Routes to Recovery," *Wall Street Journal,* March 2, 2010, pp. B1+.

8. S. Thurm, "Creativity, Meet Destruction," *Wall Street Journal,* December 21, 2009, p. R4.

9. D. Das, Gaea News Network, "Men Lost More Jobs than Women Worldwide: Accenture," *Reuters,* March 9, 2010; P. Izzo, "Economists Expect Shifting Work Force," *Wall Street Journal Online,* February 11, 2010; and BBC News, "Recession May See 25m Jobs Lost," *BBC News Online,* September 16, 2009.

10. S. Reddy, M. Walker, and A. Batson, "Factories Revive Economy," *Wall Street Journal,* April 2, 2010, pp. A1+; and S. Shinn, "Banking on Customers," *BizEd,* March/April 2010, pp. 16–21.

11. S. Jayson, "iGeneration Has No Off Switch," *USA Today,* February 10, 2010, pp. 1D+; and L. Rosen, *Rewired: Understanding the iGeneration and the Way They Learn* (Palgrave-McMillan), 2010.

12. S. Cardwell, "Where Do Babies Come From?" *Newsweek,* October 19, 2009, p. 56.

13. Y. Hori, J-P. Lehmann, T. Ma Kam Wah, and V. Wang, "Facing Up to the Demographic Dilemma," *Strategy & Business Online,* Spring 2010; and E. E. Gordon, "Job Meltdown or Talent Crunch?" *Training,* January 2010, p. 10.

14. P. Izzo, "Economists Expect Shifting Work Force," *Wall Street Journal Online,* February 11, 2010; and J. Lanhart, "Even In a Recovery, Some Jobs Won't Return," *Wall Street Journal,* January 12, 2010, p. A15.

15. P. Davidson, "More Temp Workers Are Getting Hired," *USA Today,* March 8, 2010, p. 1B; S. Reddy, "Wary Companies Rely on Temporary Workers," *Wall Street Journal,* March 6/7, 2010, p. A4; P. Davidson, "Cuts in Hours Versus Cuts in Jobs," *USA Today,* February 25, 2010, p. 1B; and S. A. Hewlett, L. Sherbin, and K. Sumberg, "How Gen Y and Boomers Will Reshape Your Agenda," *Harvard Business Review,* July–August, 2009, pp. 71–76.

16. Leader Who Made a Difference box based on J. O'Donnell, "Hot Topic CEO's 2 Worlds," *USA Today,* March 22, 2010, p. 1B+; *Fast Company* Staff, "The World's 50 Most Innovative Companies," *Fast Company,* March 2010, p. 105; E. Smith, "Disney Invites 'Goths' to the Party," *Wall Street Journal,* February 19, 2010, p. B8; K. Rockwood, "How Hot Topic's Culture-Heavy Strategy Helped It Sizzle During the Downturn," *Fast Company Online,* September 1, 2009; and K. High, "6 Questions with Betsy McLaughlin," *Billboard,* December 13, 2008, p. 10.

17. J. P. Walsh, "Book Review Essay: Taking Stock of Stakeholder Management," *Academy of Management Review,* April 2005, pp. 426–438; R. E. Freeman, A. C. Wicks, and B. Parmar, "Stakeholder Theory and 'The Corporate Objective Revisited,'" *Organization Science,* 15, 2004, pp. 364–369; T. Donaldson and L. E. Preston, "The Stakeholder Theory of the Corporation: Concepts, Evidence, and Implications," *Academy of Management Review,* January 1995, pp. 65–91; and R. E. Freeman, *Strategic Management: A Stakeholder Approach* (Boston: Pitman/Ballinger), 1984.

18. J. S. Harrison and C. H. St. John, "Managing and Partnering With External Stakeholders," *Academy of Management Executive,* May 1996, pp. 46–60.

19. S. L. Berman, R. A. Phillips, and A. C. Wicks, "Resource Dependence, Managerial Discretion, and Stakeholder Performance," *Academy of Management Proceedings* Best Conference Paper, August 2005; A. J. Hillman and G. D. Keim, "Shareholder Value, Stakeholder Management, and Social Issues: What's the Bottom Line?" *Strategic Management Journal,* March 2001, pp. 125–139; J. S. Harrison and R. E. Freeman, "Stakeholders, Social Responsibility, and Performance: Empirical Evidence and Theoretical Perspectives," *Academy of Management Journal,* July 1999, pp. 479–487; and J. Kotter and J. Heskett, *Corporate Culture and Performance* (New York: The Free Press, 1992).

20. M. Moskowitz, R. Levering, and C. Tkaczyk, "The List," *Fortune,* February 8, 2010, pp. 75–88; E. Ruth, "Gore-Tex Maker Decides It's Time to Demand Some Attention," The Wilmington, DE *News Journal, USA Today,* October 24, 2007, p. 5B; and A. Deutschman, "The Fabric of Creativity," *Fast Company,* December 2004, pp. 54–62.

21. K. Shadur and M. A. Kienzle, "The Relationship Between Organizational Climate and Employee Perceptions of Involvement," *Group & Organization Management,* December 1999, pp. 479–503; M. J. Hatch, "The Dynamics of Organizational Culture," *Academy of Management Review,* October 1993, pp. 657–693; D. R. Denison, "What Is the Difference between Organizational Culture and Organizational Climate? A Native's Point of View on a Decade of Paradigm Wars," paper presented at Academy of Management Annual Meeting, 1993, Atlanta, GA; and L. Smircich, "Concepts of Culture and Organizational Analysis," *Administrative Science Quarterly,* September 1983, p. 339.

22. J. A. Chatman and K. A. Jehn, "Assessing the Relationship between Industry Characteristics and Organizational Culture: How Different Can You Be?" *Academy of Management Journal,* June 1994, pp. 522–553; and C. A. O'Reilly III, J. Chatman, and D. F. Caldwell, "People and Organizational Culture: A Profile Comparison Approach to Assessing Person-Organization Fit," *Academy of Management Journal,* September 1991, pp. 487–516.

23. Y. Berson, S. Oreg, and T. Dvir, "CEO Values, Organizational Culture, and Firm Outcomes," *Journal of Organizational Behavior,* July 2008, pp. 615–633; and E. H. Schien, *Organizational Culture and Leadership* (San Francisco: Jossey-Bass, 1985), pp. 314–315.

24. A. E. M. Va Vianen, "Person-Organization Fit: The Match Between Newcomers' and Recruiters' Preferences for Organizational Cultures," *Personnel Psychology,* Spring 2000, pp. 113–149; K. Shadur and M. A. Kienzle, *Group & Organization Management;* P. Lok and J. Crawford, "The Relationship Between Commitment and Organizational Culture, Subculture, and Leadership Style," *Leadership & Organization Development Journal,* vol. 20, no. 6/7, 1999, pp. 365–374; C. Vandenberghe, "Organizational Culture, Person-Culture Fit, and Turnover: A Replication in the Health Care Industry," *Journal of Organizational Behavior,* March 1999, pp. 175–184; and C. Orphen, "The Effect of Organizational Cultural Norms on the Relationships between Personnel Practices and Employee Commitment," *Journal of Psychology,* September 1993, pp. 577–579.

25. See, for example, J. B. Sorensen, "The Strength of Corporate Culture and the Reliability of Firm Performance," *Administrative Science Quarterly*, 2002, vol. 47, no. 1, pp. 70–91; R. Goffee and G. Jones, "What Holds the Modern Company Together?" *Harvard Business Review*, November–December 1996, pp. 133–148; Collins and Porras, "Building Your Company's Vision," *Harvard Business Review*, September–October 1996, pp. 65–77; J. C. Collins and J. I. Porras, *Built to Last* (New York: HarperBusiness, 1994); G. G. Gordon and N. DiTomaso, "Predicting Corporate Performance from Organizational Culture," *Journal of Management Studies*, November 1992, pp. 793–798; J. P. Kotter and J. L. Heskett, *Corporate Culture and Performance* (New York: Free Press, 1992), pp. 15–27; and D. R. Denison, *Corporate Culture and Organizational Effectiveness* (New York: Wiley, 1990).

26. Sorensen, pp. 70–91; and L. B. Rosenfeld, J. M. Richman, and S. K. May, "Information Adequacy, Job Satisfaction, and Organizational Culture in a Dispersed-Network Organization," *Journal of Applied Communication Research*, vol. 32, 2004, pp. 28–54.

27. C. Edwards, "Why Tech Bows to Best Buy," *BusinessWeek Online*, December 10, 2009.

28. S. E. Ante, "The New Blue," *BusinessWeek*, March 17, 2003, p. 82.

29. C. C. Miller, "Now at Starbucks: A Rebound," *New York Times Online*, January 21, 2010; J. Jargon, "Latest Starbucks Buzzword: 'Lean' Japanese Techniques," *Wall Street Journal*, August 4, 2009, pp. A1+; P. Kafka, "Bean Counter," *Forbes*, February 28, 2005, pp. 78–80; A. Overholt, "Listening to Starbucks," *Fast Company*, July 2004, pp. 50–56; and B. Filipczak, "Trained by Starbucks," *Training*, June 1995, pp. 73–79.

30. P. Guber, "The Four Truths of the Storyteller," *Harvard Business Review*, December 2007, pp. 53–59; S. Denning, "Telling Tales," *Harvard Business Review*, May 2004, pp. 122–129; T. Terez, "The Business of Storytelling," *Workforce*, May 2002, pp. 22–24; J. Forman, "When Stories Create an Organization's Future," *Strategy & Business*, Second Quarter 1999, pp. 6–9; C. H. Deutsch, "The Parables of Corporate Culture," *New York Times*, October 13, 1991, p. F25; and D. M. Boje, "The Storytelling Organization: A Study of Story Performance in an Office-Supply Firm," *Administrative Science Quarterly*, March 1991, pp. 106–126.

31. G. Colvin, "Value Driven," *Fortune*, November 23, 2009, p. 24.

32. J. Useem, "Jim McNerney Thinks He Can Turn 3M From a Good Company Into a Great One—With a Little Help From His Former Employer, General Electric," *Fortune*, August 12, 2002, pp. 127–132.

33. Denning, 2004; and A. M. Pettigrew, "On Studying Organizational Cultures," *Administrative Science Quarterly*, December 1979, p. 576.

34. J. E. Vascellaro, "Facebook CEO in No Rush to 'Friend' Wall Street," *Wall Street Journal*, March 4, 2010, p. A1+.

35. E. H. Schein, "Organizational Culture," *American Psychologist*, February 1990, pp. 109–119.

36. M. Zagorski, "Here's the Drill," *Fast Company*, February 2001, p. 58.

37. "Slogans That Work," *Forbes.com Special*, January 7, 2008, p. 99.

38. P. Keegan, "Best Companies to Work For: Maxine Clark and Kip Tindell Exchange Jobs," *Fortune*, February 8, 2010, pp. 68–72.

39. By the Numbers box based on D. Middleton, "Workers Perceive Little Opportunity," *Wall Street Journal*, March 16, 2010, p. D6; J. Yang and J. Snider, "Employees Believe in Their Companies," *USA Today*, July 27, 2009, p. 1B; M. B. Marklein, "Freshmen Have Making Money on Their Minds," *USA Today*, January 21, 2010, p. 7D; K. O'Sullivan, "Disciplinarians' Dilemma," *CFO*, June 2009, p. 27; and R. Wartzman, "Executives Are Wrong to Devalue Values," *Bloomberg BusinessWeek Online*, October 30, 2009.

40. C. Palmeri, "The Fastest Drill in the West," *BusinessWeek*, October 24, 2005, pp. 86–88.

41. J. Levine, "Dare to Be Boring," *Time*, February 1, 2010, pp. Global Business 1–2.

42. "The World's 50 Most Innovative Companies," *Fast Company*, March 2010, p. 90; L. Tischler, "A Designer Takes On His Biggest Challenge," *Fast Company*, February 2009, pp. 78+; T. Kelley and J. Littman, *The Ten Faces of Innovation: IDEO's Strategies for Defeating the Devil's Advocate and Driving Creativity Throughout Your Organization* (New York: Currency, 2005); C. Fredman, "The IDEO Difference," *Hemispheres*, August 2002, pp. 52–57; and T. Kelley and J. Littman, *The Art of Innovation* (New York: Currency, 2001).

43. D. Lyons, "Think Really Different," *Newsweek*, April 5, 2010, pp. 46–51; and R. Brands, "Innovation Made Incarnate," *Bloomberg BusinessWeek Online*, January 11, 2010.

44. J. Yang and R. W. Ahrens, "Culture Spurs Innovation," *USA Today*, February 25, 2008, p. 1B.

45. J. Cable, "Building an Innovative Culture," *Industry Week*, March 2010, pp. 32–37; M. Hawkins, "Create a Climate of Creativity," *Training*, January 2010, p. 12; and L. Simpson, "Fostering Creativity," *Training*, December 2001, p. 56.

46. M. Millstein, "Customer Relationships Make Playing the Odds Easy," *Chain Store Age*, December 2007, p. 22A; and L. Gary, "Simplify and Execute: Words to Live By in Times of Turbulence," *Harvard Management Update*, January 2003, p. 12.

47. Based on J. McGregor, "Customer Service Champs," *BusinessWeek*, March 3, 2008, pp. 37–57; B. Schneider, M. G. Ehrhart, D. M. Mayer, J. L. Saltz, and K. Niles-Jolly, "Understanding Organization-Customer Links in Service Settings," *Academy of Management Journal*, December 2006, pp. 1017–1032; B. A. Gutek, M. Groth, and B. Cherry, "Achieving Service Success Through Relationships and Enhanced Encounters," *Academy of Management Executive*, November 2002, pp. 132–144; K. A. Eddleston, D. L. Kidder, and B. E. Litzky, "Who's the Boss? Contending With Competing Expectations From Customers and Management," *Academy of Management Executive*, November 2002, pp. 85–95; S. D. Pugh, J. Dietz, J. W. Wiley, and S. M. Brooks, "Driving Service Effectiveness Through Employee-Customer Linkages," *Academy of Management Executive*, November 2002, pp. 73–84; L. A. Bettencourt, K. P. Gwinner, and M. L. Mueter, "A Comparison of Attitude, Personality, and Knowledge Predictors of Service-Oriented Organizational Citizenship Behaviors," *Journal of Applied Psychology*, February 2001, pp. 29–41; M. D. Hartline, J. G. Maxham III, and D. O. McKee, "Corridors of Influence in the Dissemination of Customer-Oriented Strategy to Customer Contact Service Employees," *Journal of Marketing*, April 2000, pp. 35–50; L. Lengnick-Hall and C. A. Lengnick-Hall, "Expanding Customer Orientation in the HR Function," *Human Resource Management*, Fall 1999, pp. 201–214; M. D. Hartline and O. C. Ferrell, "The Management of Customer-Contact Service Employees: An Empirical Investigation," *Journal of Marketing*, October 1996, pp. 52–70; and M. J. Bitner, B. H. Booms, and L. A. Mohr, "Critical Service Encounters: The Employee's Viewpoint," *Journal of Marketing*, October 1994, pp. 95–106.

48. R. A. Giacalone and C. L. Jurkiewicz (eds.), *Handbook of Workplace Spirituality and Organizational Performance* (New York: M. E. Sharp, 2003).

49. M. B. Marklein, "Study: College Students Seeking Meaning of Life," USA Today, *Springfield News-Leader*, December 22, 2007, p. 6C.

50. This section is based on L. Lambert III, "God Goes to the Office," *USA Today*, February 8, 2010, p. 7A; B. S. Pawar, "Workplace Spirituality Facilitation: A Comprehensive Model," *Journal of Business Ethics*, December 2009, pp. 375–386; "Faith and Spirituality in the Workplace," *Walton Business Perspective*, Fall 2009, p. 22; B. S. Pawar, "Some of the Recent Organizational Behavior Concepts as Precursors to Workplace Spirituality," *Journal of Business Ethics*, August 2009, pp. 245–261; L. Lambert III, *Spirituality Inc: Religion in the American Workplace*, (New York University Press), 2009; A. Gross-Schaefer, "Reaching for the Stars: Effective Tools for the Creation of a More Spiritual Workplace," *Employee Relations Law Journal*, Summer 2009, pp. 25–42; D. Grant, "What Should a Science of Workplace Spirituality Study? The Case for a Relational Approach," *Academy of Management Proceedings* Best Paper, August 2005; C. D. Pielstick, "Teaching Spirituality Synchronicity in a Business Leadership Class," *Journal of Management Education*, February 2005, pp. 153–168; H. Ashar and M. Lane-Maher, "Success and Spirituality in the New Business Paradigm," *Journal of Management Inquiry*, June 2004, pp. 249–260; G. A. Gull and J. Doh, "The 'Transmutation' of the Organization: Toward a More Spiritual Workplace," *Journal of Management Inquiry*, June 2004, pp. 128–139; K. C. Cash and G. R. Gray, "A Framework for Accommodating Religion and Spirituality in the Workplace," *Academy of Management Executive*, August 2000, pp. 124–133; F. Wagner-Marsh and J. Conley, "The Fourth Wave: The Spiritually-Based Firm," *Journal of Organizational Change Management*, vol. 12, no. 3, 1999, pp. 292–302; E. H. Burack, "Spirituality in the Workplace," *Journal of Organizational*

Change Management, vol. 12, no. 3, 1999, pp. 280–291; J. Milliman, J. Ferguson, D. Trickett, and B. Condemi, "Spirit and Community at Southwest Airlines: An Investigation of a Spiritual Values-Based Model," *Journal of Organizational Change Management,* vol. 12, no. 3, 1999, pp. 221–233; and I. A. Mitroff and E. A. Denton, *A Spiritual Audit of Corporate America: A Hard Look at Spirituality, Religion, and Values in the Workplace* (San Francisco: Jossey-Bass, 1999).

51. J. Reingold, "Walking the Walk," *Fast Company,* November 2005, p. 82.

52. M. Lips-Wiersma, K. L. Dean, and C. J. Fornaciari, "Theorizing the Dark Side of the Workplace Spirituality Movement," *Journal of Management Inquiry,* December 2009, pp. 288–300; P. Paul, "A Holier Holiday Season," *American Demographics,* December 2001, pp. 41–45; and M. Conlin, "Religion in the Workplace: The Growing Presence of Spirituality in Corporate America," *Business Week,* November 1, 1999, pp. 151–158.

53. Cited in M. Conlin, "Religion in the Workplace," p. 153.

54. C. P. Neck and J. F. Milliman, "Thought Self-Leadership: Finding Spiritual Fulfillment in Organizational Life," *Journal of Managerial Psychology,* vol. 9, no. 8, 1994, p. 9.

55. J. Marques, "Toward Greater Consciousness in the 21st Century Workplace: How Buddhist Practices Fit In," *Journal of Business Ethics,* March 2010, pp. 211–225; L. Kim, "Improving the Workplace with Spirituality," *Journal for Quality and Participation,* October 2009, pp. 32–35; M. Stevenson, "Toward a Greater Understanding of Spirit at Work: A Model of Spirit at Work and Outcomes," *Academy of Management Proceedings Online,* August 2009; P. D. Corner, "Workplace Spirituality and Business Ethics: Insights from an Eastern Spiritual Tradition," *Journal of Business Ethics,* March 2009, pp. 377–389; M. L. Lynn, M. J. Naughton, and S. VanderVeen, "Faith at Work Scale (FWS): Justification, Development, and Validation of a Measure of Judaeo-Christian Religion in the Workplace," *Journal of Business Ethics,* March 2009, pp. 227–243; R. W. Kolodinsky, R. A. Giacalone, and C. L. Jurkiewicz, "Workplace Values and Outcomes: Exploring Personal, Organizational, and Interactive Workplace Spirituality," *Journal of Business Ethics,* August 2008, pp. 465–480; and J. Millman, A. Czaplewski, and J. Ferguson, "An Exploratory Empirical Assessment of the Relationship Between Spirituality and Employee Work Attitudes," paper presented at Academy of Management, Washington, DC, August 2001.

56. M. V. Copeland, "Can the Ski Suit Make the Man (and Woman)?" *Fortune Online,* February 16, 2010; C. Hausman, "New and Old Technologies Keep Officials, Ethicists, Debating Questions of Fairness," *Global Ethics Newsline Online,* February 8, 2010; and S. Sataline, "Some Aging Competitors Call High-Tech Swimsuits Dirty Pool," *Wall Street Journal,* November 3, 2009, p. A1.

57. Based on C. K. Prahalad, "Best Practices Get You Only So Far," *Harvard Business Review,* April 2010, p. 32; J. R. Oreja-Rodriguez and V. Yanes-Estévez, "Environmental Scanning: Dynamism with Rack and Stack Rasch Model," *Management Decision,* vol. 48, no. 2, 2010, pp. 260–276; C. Heavey, Z. Simsek, F. Roche, and A. Kelly, "Decision Comprehensiveness and Corporate Entrepreneurship: The Moderating Role of Managerial Uncertainty Preferences and Environmental Dynamism," *Journal of Management Studies,* December 2009, pp. 1289–1314; R. Subramanian, N. Fernandes, and E. Harper, "Environmental Scanning in U.S. Companies: Their Nature and Their Relationship to Performance," *Management International Review,* July 1993, pp. 271–286; E. H. Burack and N. J. Mathys, "Environmental Scanning Improves Strategic Planning," *Personnel Administrator,* 1989, pp. 82–87; and L. M. Fuld, *Monitoring the Competition* (New York: Wiley, 1988).

58. J. Katz, "Lean Times for 'The Toyota Way,'" *Industry Week,* April 2010, pp. 20–21; H. Tabuchi, "Toyota Vows Change as Quality Panel Meets," *New York Times Online,* March 30, 2010; A. Ohnsman, J. Green, and K. Inoue, "The Humbling of Toyota," *Bloomberg BusinessWeek,* March 22 and 29, 2010, pp. 32–36; D. Searcey and K. Linebaugh, "Toyota Moves to Discredit Its Critics," *Wall Street Journal,* March 6/March 7, 2010, pp. B1+; M. Maynard, "An Apology from Toyota's Leader," *New York Times Online,* February 25, 2010; B. Rooney, "Toyoda: Our Rush to Grow Led to Safety Issues," *CNNMoney.com,* February 23, 2010; and K. Linebaugh, D. Searcey, and N. Shirouzu, "Secretive Culture Led Toyota Astray," *Wall Street Journal,* February 10, 2010, pp. A1+.

59. "Britney Spears Re-ups with Candie's and Kohl's," *Home Textiles Today,* January 25, 2010, p. 6; M. Bustillo and R. Dodes, "As Rivals Fall, Wal-Mart, Kohl's Gain Market Share," *Wall Street Journal,* May 15, 2009, p. B1; S. Rosenbloom, "The Hills Star to Design Clothing for Kohl's," *New York Times Online,* April 22, 2009; S. Rosenbloom, "Handful of Niche Chains Stay Alive in Retailing," *New York Times Online,* December 20, 2008; C. Lu-Lien Tan, "Kohl's Makes Grab for Market Share," *Wall Street Journal,* October 1, 2008, p. B1; and C. Coolidge, "Discount Chic," *Forbes,* April 7, 2008, p. 108.

Chapter 3

1. E. Bellman, "Novelty of Mexican Food in India Is a Hit for Yum," *Wall Street Journal,* March 30, 2010, p. B8; J. Jargon and A. Chang, "Yum Brands Bets on India's Young for Growth," *Wall Street Journal,* December 17, 2009, p. B1; and "Fast Food in Asia-Pacific: Industry Profile," *Datamonitor,* August 2009.

2. G. Koretz, "Things Go Better with Multinationals—Except Jobs," *BusinessWeek,* May 2, 1994, p. 20.

3. The idea for this quiz was adapted from R. M. Hodgetts and F. Luthans, *International Management,* 2d ed. (New York: McGraw-Hill, 1994).

4. Reuters Limited, *USA Today Online* [www.usatoday.com], February 21, 2006; and "Learning the Lingo," *USA Today,* January 26, 2006, p. 1A.

5. Ibid.

6. N. Adler, *International Dimensions of Organizational Behavior,* 5th ed. (Cincinnati: South-Western, 2008).

7. M. R. F. Kets De Vries and E. Florent-Treacy, "Global Leadership From A to Z: Creating High Commitment Organizations," *Organizational Dynamics,* Spring 2002, pp. 295–309; P. R. Harris and R. T. Moran, *Managing Cultural Differences,* 4th ed. (Houston: Gulf Publishing Co., 1996); R. T. Moran, P. R. Harris, and W. G. Stripp, *Developing the Global Organization: Strategies for Human Resource Professionals,* (Houston: Gulf Publishing Co., 1993); Y. Wind, S. P. Douglas, and H. V. Perlmutter, "Guidelines for Developing International Marketing Strategies," *Journal of Marketing,* April 1973, pp. 14–23; and H. V. Perlmutter, "The Tortuous Evolution of the Multinational Corporation," *Columbia Journal of World Business,* January–February 1969, pp. 9–18.

8. T. K. Grose, "When in Rome, Do as Roman CEOs Do," *U.S. News & World Report,* November 2009, pp. 38–41.

9. Leader Who Made a Difference box based on J. Shambora and B. Kowitt, "50 Most Powerful Women," *Fortune,* September 28, 2009, pp. 99–106; P. Sellers, "The Queen of Pop," *Fortune,* September 28, 2009, p. 108; M. Egan and others, "The Top 100," *Forbes,* September 7, 2009, pp. 72–76; I. K. Nooyi, "Leading to the Future," *Vital Speeches of the Day,* September 2009, pp. 404–410; B. Einhorn, "Pepsi Chief on Trip to China," *BusinessWeek Online,* July 3, 2009; G. Fairclough and V. Bauerlein, "Pepsi CEO Tours China to Get a Feel for Market," *Wall Street Journal,* July 1, 2009, p. B5; H. Jackson, "America's Best CEOs," *Institutional Investor,* April 2009, pp. 66–70; "Women to Watch: The 50 Women to Watch," *Wall Street Journal,* November 10, 2008, p. R3; B. McKay, "Boss Talk: PepsiCo CEO Adapts to Tough Climate," *Wall Street Journal,* September 11, 2008, p. B1; and H. Schultz, "Indra Nooyi," *Time,* May 12, 2008, pp. 116–117.

10. S. Kotkin, "The World as an Imperfect Globe," *New York Times Online,* December 2, 2007.

11. "On Course to Be Next EU Member," *Emerging Europe Monitor: South East Europe Monitor,* April 2010, pp. 1–11.

12. Europa [europa.eu/index_en.htm].

13. Ibid.

14. C. Forelle, "After Irish 'Yes,' EU Pushes for a President," *Wall Street Journal,* October 5, 2009, p. A8; Europa Treaty of Lisbon [europa.eu/lisbon/treaty/index_en.htm]; N. Knox, "Leaders of Embattled EU Head to Washington," *USA Today,* June 20, 2005, p. A8; and N. Knox, "European Union Struggles with Constitution Rejection," *USA Today,* May 31, 2005, p. A10.

15. Ibid.

16. S. Erlanger and S. Castle, "Growing Economic Crisis Threatens the Idea of One Europe," *New York Times Online,* March 2, 2009.

17. M. Walker and A. Galloni, "Europe's Choice: Growth or Safety Net," *Wall Street Journal,* March 26, 2010, p. A1.

18. D. Macshane, "Europe Agrees to Disagree on Foreign Policy," *Newsweek,* April 12, 2010, p. 6; and C. Forelle and M. Walker,

"Europeans Agree on Bailout for Greece," *Wall Street Journal,* March 26, 2010, p. A1.

19. *CIA World Factbook* [http://www.cia.gov/library/publications/the-world-factbook/index.html], 2010.

20. A. Selko, "NAFTA: Learning to Love Thy Neighbor," *Industry Week,* February 2009, pp. 38–41.

21. E. Malkin, "NAFTA's Promise, Unfulfilled," *New York Times Online,* March 24, 2009.

22. J. Lyons, "Costa Rica CAFTA Vote Bolsters U.S. Policy," *Wall Street Journal,* October 9, 2007, p. A2.

23. J. Forero, "U.S. and Colombia Reach Trade Deal After 2 Years of Talks," *New York Times Online* [www.nytimes.com], February 28, 2006.

24. "Free Trade Area of the Americas" [en.wikipedia.org], April 6, 2010; "Ministerial Declaration," Web site of the Free Trade Area of the Americas [www.ftaa-alca.org], January 23, 2006; and M. Moffett and J. D. McKinnon, "Failed Summit Casts Shadow on Global Trade Talks," *Wall Street Journal,* November 7, 2005, pp. A1+.

25. "ASEAN Stats" [www.aseansec.org], March 15, 2010.

26. J. Hookway, "Asian Nations Push Ideas for Trade," *Wall Street Journal,* October 26, 2009, p. A12; and Bloomberg News, "Southeast Asian Nations Talk of Economic Union," *New York Times Online,* March 2, 2009.

27. "Asia's Never-Closer Union," *Economist,* February 6, 2010, p. 48; "East Asia Summit: Regional Unity Decades Away," *Business Monitor International* [www.asia-monitor.com], 2009/2010; and "Southeast Asian Nations Talk of Economic Union."

28. "China-ASEAN FTA: Winners and Losers," *China & North East Asia,* February 2010, p. 2.

29. "2004–2007 Strategic Plan," *Commission of the African Union* [www.africa-union.org]; and D. Kraft, "Leaders Question, Praise African Union," *Springfield News-Leader,* July 10, 2002, p. 8A.

30. J. Guo, "Africa Is Booming Like Never Before," *Newsweek,* March 1, 2010, p. 6.

31. "It Really May Happen," *Economist,* January 2, 2010, p. 36; and "Five Into One?" *Business Africa,* December 1, 2009, p. 1.

32. SAARC Official Web site [www.saarc-sec.org]; and N. George, "South Asia Trade Zone in Works," *Springfield News-Leader,* January 4, 2004, p. 1E+.

33. This section is based on materials from the World Trade Organization Web site [www.wto.org]; "What's Up at the WTO?" *Industry Week,* February 2010, p. 20; and D. A. Irwin, "GATT Turns 60," *Wall Street Journal,* April 9, 2007, p. A13.

34. J. W. Miller and M. Dalton, "WTO Finds EU Aid to Airbus Is Illegal," *Wall Street Journal,* March 24, 2010, p. A10; and C. Drew and N. Clark, "WTO Affirms Ruling of Improper Airbus Aid," *New York Times Online,* March 23, 2010.

35. "Internet Censorship: Showdown at the WTO?" *Bloomberg BusinessWeek,* March 15, 2010, p. 12.

36. 2010 Press Release, "Trade to Expand by 9.5 Percent in 2010 After a Dismal 2009, WTO Reports" [www.wto.org], March 26, 2010.

37. International Monetary Fund Web site [www.imf.org], March 15, 2010.

38. World Bank Group Web site [web.worldbank.org], March 15, 2010.

39. News Release, "World Bank Group: Record US $100 Billion Response Lays Foundation for Recovery from Global Economic Crisis" [web.worldbank.org], April 7, 2010.

40. Organization for Economic Cooperation and Development Web site [www.oecd.org], March 15, 2010.

41. D. Searcey, "Small-Scale Bribes Targeted by OECD," *Wall Street Journal,* December 10, 2009, p. A4.

42. By the Numbers box based on A. R. Carey and S. Ward, "What Are the Most Common Foreign Languages Taught in U.S. Schools?" *USA Today,* February 16, 2010, p. 1A; J. Yang and V. Salazar, "Foreign Relations," *USA Today,* December 5, 2007, p. 1B; D. Stuckey and S. Parker, "Young Americans Staying Home," *USA Today,* August 4, 2006, p. 1A; A. R. Carey and A. Lewis, "Bilingual Growth," *USA Today,* December 9, 2008, p. 1A; J. Yang and K. Simmons, "Global Travel and Career," *USA Today,* November 26, 2008, p. 1B; and J. MacIntyre, "Workplace Attitudes," *Springfield Business Journal,* August 12, 2008, p. 14.

43. D. Jolly, "Daimler, Nissan, and Renault Unveil Partnership," *New York Times Online,* April 7, 2010; M. Tanikawa, "Japanese Food Companies Seek Growth Abroad," *New York Times Online,* April 2, 2010;

B. Becht, "Building a Company Without Borders," *Harvard Business Review,* April 2010, pp. 103–106; and "Statistical Information" [www.mosers.org], March 15, 2010.

44. C. A. Bartlett and S. Ghoshal, *Managing Across Borders: The Transnational Solution,* 2d ed. (Boston: Harvard Business School Press), 2002; and N. J. Adler, *International Dimensions of Organizational Behavior,* 4th ed. (Cincinnati, OH: South-Western, 2002), pp. 9–11.

45. M. Bustillo, "After Early Errors, Wal-Mart Thinks Locally to Act Globally," *Wall Street Journal,* August 14, 2009, pp. A1+.

46. P. F. Drucker, "The Global Economy and the Nation-State," *Foreign Affairs,* September–October, 1997, pp. 159–171.

47. P. Dvorak, "Why Multiple Headquarters Multiply," *Wall Street Journal,* November 19, 2007, pp. B1+.

48. B. Becht, "Building a Company Without Borders"; D. A. Aaker, *Developing Business Strategies,* 5th ed. (New York: John Wiley & Sons, 1998); and J.A. Byrne et al., "Borderless Management," *BusinessWeek,* May 23, 1994, pp. 24–26.

49. B. Davis, "Migration of Skilled Jobs Abroad Unsettles Global-Economy Fans," *Wall Street Journal,* January 26, 2004, p. A1.

50. J. Teresko, "United Plastics Picks China's Silicon Valley," *Industry Week,* January 2003, p. 58.

51. F. Mutsaka and P. Wonacott, "Mugabe Presses Law Requiring Foreign Entities to Cede Control," *Wall Street Journal,* February 19, 2010, p. A9.

52. D. Roberts, "Closing for Business," *Bloomberg BusinessWeek,* April 5, 2010, pp. 32–37; and A. Browne and J. Dean, "Business Sours on China," *Wall Street Journal,* March 17, 2010, pp. A1+.

53. J. Bush, "Ikea in Russia: Enough Is Enough," *Bloomberg BusinessWeek,* July 13, 2009, p. 33.

54. News Release, "Elevated Political Risk Levels to Continue Into 2010, Says Aon," *Aon Corporation* [ir.aon.com], January 27, 2010.

55. Roberts, "Closing for Business"; and Browne and Dean, "Business Sours on China."

56. "Leading Indicator," *Newsweek,* September 14, 2009, p. 14.

57. M. Landler, "Germany's Export-Led Economy Finds Global Niche," *New York Times Online,* April 13, 2007.

58. *CIA World Factbook* [http://www.cia.gov/library/publications/the-world-factbook/index.html], 2010.

59. J. McGregor and S. Hamm, "Managing the Global Workforce," *Bloomberg BusinessWeek,* January 28, 2008, pp. 34–51.

60. These examples taken from L. Khosla, "You Say Tomato," *Forbes,* May 21, 2001, p. 36; and T. Raphael, "Savvy Companies Build Bonds with Hispanic Employees," *Workforce,* September 2001, p. 19.

61. See G. Hofstede, *Culture's Consequences: International Differences in Work-Related Values,* 2d ed. (Thousand Oaks, CA: Sage Publications, 2001), pp. 9–15.

62. S. Bhaskaran and N. Sukumaran, "National Culture, Business Culture and Management Practices: Consequential Relationships?" *Cross Cultural Management: An International Journal,* vol. 14, no. 7, 2007, pp. 54–67; G. Hofstede, *Culture's Consequences;* and G. Hofstede, "The Cultural Relativity of Organizational Practices and Theories," *Journal of International Business Studies,* Fall 1983, pp. 75–89.

63. R. R. McCrae, A. Terracciano, A. Realo, and J. Allik, "Interpreting GLOBE Societal Practices Scale," *Journal of Cross-Cultural Psychology,* November 2008, pp. 805–810; J. S. Chhokar, F. C. Brodbeck, and R. J. House, *Culture and Leadership Across the World: The GLOBE Book of In-Depth Studies of 25 Societies,* (Philadelphia: Lawrence Erlbaum Associates), 2007; and R. J. House, P. J. Hanges, M. Javidan, P. W. Dorfman, and V. Gupta, *Culture, Leadership, and Organizations: The GLOBE Study of 62 Societies* (Thousand Oaks, CA: Sage Publications), 2004.

64. D. Yergin, "Globalization Opens Door to New Dangers," *USA Today,* May 28, 2003, p. 11A; K. Lowrey Miller, "Is It Globaloney?" *Newsweek,* December 16, 2002, pp. E4–E8; L. Gomes, "Globalization Is Now a Two-Way Street—Good News for the U.S.," *Wall Street Journal,* December 9, 2002, p. B1; J. Kurlantzick and J. T. Allen, "The Trouble With Globalism," *U.S. News and World Report,* February 11, 2002, pp. 38–41; and J. Guyon, "The American Way," *Fortune,* November 26, 2001, pp. 114–120.

65. Guyon, "The American Way," p. 114.

66. H. Seligson, "For American Workers in China, a Culture Clash," *New York Times Online,* December 24, 2009.

67. G. N. Powell, A. M. Francesco, and Y. Ling, "Toward Culture-Sensitive Theories of the Work-Family Interface," *Journal of Organizational Behavior,* July 2009, pp. 597–616.

68. "Are You Cued in to Cultural Intelligence?" *Industry Week,* November 2009, p. 24; M. Blasco, "Cultural Pragmatists? Student Perspectives on Learning Culture at a Business School," *Academy of Management Learning & Education,* June 2009, pp. 174–187; and D. C. Thomas and K. Inkson, "Cultural Intelligence: People Skills for a Global Workplace," *Consulting to Management,* vol. 16, no. 1, pp. 5–9.

69. M. Javidan, M. Teagarden, and D. Bowen, "Making It Overseas," *Harvard Business Review,* April 2010, pp. 109–113.

70. Ethics Dilemma based on D. Goldman, "IBM Stands for 'I've Been Moved'" *CNNMoney.com,* March 31, 2009.

71. J. Marquez, "French Hostage Situations Have Some Wondering if U.S. Is Next," *Workforce Management Online,* April 3, 2009; D. Gauthier-Villars and L. Abboud, "In France, Boss Can Become a Hostage," *Wall Street Journal,* April 3, 2009, pp. B1+; L. Abboud and M. Colchester, "French Bosses Besieged as Worker Anger Rises," *Wall Street Journal,* April 1, 2009, pp. B1+; D. Gauthier-Villars, "French Business Leaders Vow To Give Up 'Abusive' Benefits," *Wall Street Journal,* October 8, 2008, p. A14; and F. Coleman, "Take A Hostage, Save Your Job," *U.S. News & World Report,* February 3, 1997, p. 43.

72. A. Tudor, "Bhattal's Goal; Keep Lehman Talent," *Wall Street Journal,* April 19, 2010, p. C5; A. Tudor, "Lehman Defections Continue at Nomura," *Wall Street Journal,* March 23, 2010, p. C5; A. Tudor, "Nomura Turns to a Foreigner from Lehman," *Wall Street Journal,* March 18, 2010, p. C1; A. Or, "More Quit Nomura as Bonuses Lapse," *Wall Street Journal,* March 12, 2010, p. C2; A. Rozens, "The Return of Nomura," *Investment Dealers' Digest,* February 12, 2010, p. 1+; "Nomura Set for Fight on All Fronts," *Euroweek,* December 4, 2009, p. 49; L. Peacock, untitled, *Personnel Today,* November 10, 2009, p. 25; and A. Tudor, "Nomura Stumbles in New Global Push," *Wall Street Journal,* July 29, 2009, pp. A1+.

Chapter 4

1. L. Stevens and J. Espinoza, "Deutsche Telekom Sets Women-Manager Quota," *Wall Street Journal Online,* March 22, 2010; J. Blaue, "Deutsche Telekom Launches Quota for Top Women Managers" [www.german-info.com/business_shownews]; N. Clark, "Goal at Deutsche Telekom: More Women as Managers," *New York Times Online,* March 15, 2010; R. Foroohar and S. H. Greenberg, "Working Women Are Poised to Become the Biggest Economic Engine the World Has Ever Known," *Newsweek,* November 2, 2009, pp. B2–B5; News Release, "Women Still Hold Less Than a Quarter of Senior Management Positions in Privately Held Businesses," *Grant Thornton International* [www.gti.org], March 5, 2009; and Catalyst Research Report, "Different Cultures, Similar Perceptions: Stereotyping of Western European Business Leaders Catalyst" [www.catalyst.org], 2006.

2. N. M. Carter and C. Silva, "Pipeline's Broken Promise," *Catalyst* [www.catalyst.org], 2010, p. 1; and "Women in Management in the United States, 1950–Present," *Catalyst* [www.catalyst.org], April, 2010.

3. S. Caminiti, "The Diversity Factor," *Fortune,* October 19, 2007, pp. 95–105; and B. Velez, "People and Places," *DiversityInc Online* [www.diversityinc.com], October 2006.

4. R. Anand and M. Frances Winters, "A Retrospective View of Corporate Diversity Training from 1964 to the Present," *Academy of Management Learning & Education,* September 2008, pp. 356–372.

5. State Farm [www.statefarm.com/about/diversity/], April 14, 2010.

6. Society for Human Resource Management [www.shrm.org], April 14, 2010.

7. M. L. Wheeler, "Diversity: Business Rationale and Strategies," The Conference Board, Report No. 1130-95-RR, 1995, p. 14.

8. S. P. Robbins and P. L. Hunsaker, *Training in Interpersonal Skills: TIPS for Managing People at Work* (Upper Saddle River, NJ: Pearson Prentice Hall, 2009), p. 285.

9. This section is based on S. P. Robbins and T. A. Judge, *Organizational Behavior,* 14th ed. (Upper Saddle River, NJ: Pearson Prentice Hall, 2011), pp. 41–42.

10. "Top 50 Companies for Diversity," *Diversity Inc.,* May/June 2009, p. 42.

11. J. Rosenthal, "Strength in Diversity—Large Corporations Find Working with Minority-Owned Firms Is Good Business," *Workforce Management Online,* February 2010.

12. A. Joshi and H. Roh, "The Role of Context in Work Team Diversity Research: A Meta-Analytic Review," *Academy of Management Journal,* June 2009, pp. 599–627.

13. M. Bello, USA Today, "Controversy Shrouds Scarves," *Springfield, Missouri News-Leader,* April 17, 2010, p. 8A.

14. "Workplace Bias Claims Second Highest Ever in 2009," *Workforce Management Online* [www.workforce.com], January 6, 2010.

15. D. Gilgoff, "Investing in Diversity," *U.S. News & World Report,* November 2009, pp. 72–74.

16. Ernst & Young, "The New Global Mindset: Driving Innovation Through Diversity," EYGM Limited, 2010, p. 1.

17. Ibid.

18. Information in this section from: H. El Nasser, "U.S. Hispanic Population to Triple by 2050," *USA Today Online* [www.usatoday.com], February 12, 2008; "U.S. Population Projections: 2005–2050," Pew Research Center [pewhispanic.org/reports/], February 11, 2008; U.S. Department of Labor, The Bureau of Labor Statistics, "Report of the Taskforce on the Aging of the American Workforce" [www.bls.gov], 2008; and L. B. Shrestha, "The Changing Demographic Profile of the United States," *Congressional Research Service/The Library of Congress,* May 5, 2006.

19. CIA *World Factbook* [http://www.cia.gov/library/publications/the-world-factbook/index.html], 2010.

20. "The Changing Demographic Profile of the United States," p. CRS-16.

21. L. Visconti, "The Business Case for Diversity," *DiversityInc Online* [www.diversityinc.com], July/August 2009.

22. "Report of the Taskforce on the Aging of the American Workforce."

23. S. Roberts, "Census Finds Rise in Foreign Workers," *New York Times Online,* December 8, 2009.

24. J. Preston, "Immigrants in Work Force: Study Belies Image," *New York Times Online,* April 15, 2010.

25. Ernst & Young, "The New Global Mindset: Driving Innovation Through Diversity."

26. Y. Hori, J-P Lehmann, T. Ma Kam Wah, and V. Wang, "Facing Up to the Demographic Dilemma," *Strategy + Business Online,* Issue 58 [www.strategy-business.com/article], Spring 2010.

27. Information in this section from "Facing Up to the Demographic Dilemma," International Data Base Information Gateway, U.S. Census Bureau [www.census.gov/ipc/www/idb/worldpopgraph.php], December 2009; K. Kinsella and W. He, "An Aging World: 2008," U.S. Census Bureau/International Population Reports, June 2009; and J. Hookway, "Affirmative Action Spurs Asian Debate," *Wall Street Journal,* July 8, 2009, pp. A1+.

28. Hori, Lehmann, and Wah, "Facing Up to the Demographic Dilemma."

29. Kinsella and He, "An Aging World: 2008."

30. Material in this section adapted from Robbins and Judge, *Organizational Behavior,* 14th ed., p. 44.

31. L. Wolgemuth, "How to Stand Out from the Crowd and Kick-Start Your Own Recovery," *U.S. News & World Report,* May 2010, pp. 14–16.

32. R. B. Williams, "Generation Y Poised to Dominate the Workplace" [network.nationalpost.com/np/blogs], June 13, 2009.

33. N. Gibbs, "What Women Want Now," *Time,* October 26, 2009, pp. 24–33.

34. H. Hartmann, A. Hegewisch, H. Liepmann, and C. Williams, "Fact Sheet: The Gender Wage Gap: 2009," *Institute for Women's Policy Research* [www.iwpr.org], March 2010.

35. The Associated Press, "Women with Degrees Equal Men," *Springfield, Missouri News-Leader,* April 21, 2010, p. 4B.

36. N. M. Carter and C. Silva, "Women in Management: Delusions of Progress," *Harvard Business Review,* March 2010, pp. 19–21.

37. Material in this section adapted from Robbins and Judge, *Organizational Behavior,* 14th ed., pp. 45–46.

38. G. N. Powell, D. A. Butterfield, and J. D. Parent, "Gender and Managerial Stereotypes: Have the Times Changed?" *Journal of Management,* vol. 28 (2), 2002, pp. 177–193.

39. "Women Leaders: The Hard Truth About Soft Skills," *Bloomberg BusinessWeek Online,* February 16, 2010; and A. Bryant, "No Doubts: Women Are Better Managers," *New York Times Online,* July 26, 2009.

40. "Women Leaders: The Hard Truth About Soft Skills."

41. H. El Nasser, "Multiracial No Longer Boxed In By the Census," *USA Today,* March 3, 2010, pp. 1A+.

42. Ibid.

43. Material in this section adapted from Robbins and Judge, *Organizational Behavior,* 14th ed., p. 47.

44. U.S. Department of Labor/Office of Disability Employment Policy, "Survey of Employer Perspectives on the Employment of People with Disabilities" [http://www.dol.gov/odep/documents/survey_report_jan_09.doc], November 2008.

45. A. Merrick, "Erasing 'Un' From 'Unemployable'; Walgreen Program Trains the Disabled to Take on Regular Wage-Paying Jobs," *Wall Street Journal,* August 2, 2007, pp. B1+.

46. M. Bello, "Controversy Shrouds Scarves."

47. Material in this section adapted from Robbins and Judge, *Organizational Behavior,* 14th ed., pp. 49–50; and S. Ghumman and L. Jackson, "The Downside of Religious Attire: The Muslim Headscarf and Expectations of Obtaining Employment," *Journal of Organizational Behavior,* January 2010, pp. 4–23.

48. "Facts & Figures: Number of Religious Discrimination Complaints Received," *Diversity Inc.* November/December 2009, p. 52.

49. P. Wang and J. L. Schwartz, "Stock Price Reactions to GLBT Nondiscrimination Policies," *Human Resource Management,* March–April 2010, pp. 195–216.

50. L. Sullivan, "Sexual Orientation—The Last 'Acceptable' Bias," *Canadian HR Reporter,* December 20, 2004, pp. 9–11.

51. F. Colgan, T. Wright, C. Creegan, and A. McKearney, "Equality and Diversity in the Public Services: Moving Forward on Lesbian, Gay and Bisexual Equality?" *Human Resource Management Journal,* vol. 19, no. 3, 2009, pp. 280–301.

52. J. Hempel, "Coming Out in Corporate America," *BusinessWeek,* December 15, 2003, pp. 64–72.

53. Material in this section adapted from Robbins and Judge, *Organizational Behavior,* 14th ed., p. 51.

54. By the Numbers box based on J. McGregor, "Our Performance Reviews, Ourselves," *Bloomberg BusinessWeek,* August 24 & 31, 2009, p. 25; L. Vanderkam, "The Princess Problem," *USA Today,* August 12, 2009, p. 9A; A. Tugend, "Bridging the Workplace Generation Gap: It Starts with a Text," *New York Times Online,* November 7, 2009; J. MacIntyre, "Minority Viewpoints at Work," *Springfield Business Journal,* August 10–16, 2009, p. 15; J. Yang and K. Simmons, "Diversity and Reality," *USA Today,* August 25, 2008, p. 1B; J. Yang and K. Gelles, "Workplace Diversity," *USA Today,* August 13, 2008, p. 1B; and J. Yang and S. Ward, "Top Barriers to Women in the Workplace," *USA Today,* March 1, 2010, p. 1B.

55. "Domestic-Partner Perks Most Likely to Come from Large Companies," *HRFocus,* June 2009, p. 12.

56. B. Leonard, "Transgender Issues Test Diversity Limits," *HRMagazine,* June 2007, pp. 32–34.

57. Ibid.

58. Wang and Schwartz, "Stock Price Reactions to GLBT Nondiscrimination Policies."

59. L. Eaton, "Black Workers' Complaints Advance," *Wall Street Journal,* April 16, 2010, p. B4.

60. Leader Who Made a Difference Box based on American Express, "Recognizing Responsibility to Our Employees" [http://home3.americanexpress.com/corp/gb/cresp/pdf/cresp_employees.pdf], April 22, 2010; J. Colvin, "Kenneth Chenault: CEO, American Express," *Fortune,* October 26, 2009, pp. 53–58; "Top 50 Companies for Diversity: American Express," *DiversityInc.,* May/June 2009, p. 62; S. Alleyne, A. M. Lott, and B. Hutson, "The 100 Most Powerful Executives in Corporate America," *Black Enterprise,* February 2009, pp. 100–118; and M. Useem, "The Ultimate Trial By Fire," *U.S. News & World Report,* November 19, 2007, p. 70.

61. Robbins and Judge, *Organizational Behavior,* 14th ed., p. 42.

62. Catalyst, "Workforce Metrics: Level of First Position," *Workforce Management Online* [www.workforce.com], April 8, 2010.

63. J. M. Hoobler, S. J. Wayne, and G. Lemmon, "Bosses' Perceptions of Family-Work Conflict and Women's Promotability: Glass Ceiling Effects," *Academy of Management Journal,* October 2009, pp. 939–957.

64. C. Hymowitz and T. D. Schellhardt, "The Glass Ceiling," *Wall Street Journal: A Special Report—The Corporate Woman,* March 24, 1986, pp. D1+.

65. Hoobler, Wayne, and Lemmon, "Bosses' Perceptions of Family-Work Conflict and Women's Promotability: Glass Ceiling Effects."

66. "Top 50 Companies for Diversity: Marriott International," *DiversityInc.,* May/June 2009, p. 46.

67. K. A. Cañas and H. Sondak, *Opportunities and Challenges of Workplace Diversity,* 2nd ed. (Upper Saddle River, NJ: Pearson Prentice Hall, 2011), p. 26.

68. "Leaders Create Sustainable Approaches to Diversity," *DiversityInc.,* February 2010, p. 20.

69. K. E. O'Brien, A. Biga, S. R. Kessler, and T. D. Allen, "A Meta-Analytic Investigation of Gender Differences in Mentoring," *Journal of Management,* March 2010, pp. 537–554.

70. D. Jones, "Often, Men See Women to the Top," *USA Today,* August 5, 2009, pp. 1B+.

71. J. Prime and C. A. Moss-Racusin, "Engaging Men in Gender Initiatives: What Change Agents Need to Know," *Catalyst* [www.catalyst.org], 2009.

72. L. Visconti, "Diversity Is Not in Your DNA, Says White Guy," *DiversityInc Online* [www.diversityinc.com], March 3, 2010.

73. K. L. Allers, "Won't It Be Grand When We Don't Need Diversity Lists?" *Fortune,* August 22, 2005, p. 101.

74. Press release, "Sodexho Named 2010 Straight for Equality in Business Award Winner," *DiversityInc Online* [www.diversityinc.com], April 9, 2010.

75. Kellogg Company, "Our Commitment to Diversity" [www.kelloggcompany.com], April 22, 2010.

76. B. Frankel, Editor's Letter, "The *Most* Critical Diversity Initiative," *DiversityInc.,* September/October 2009, p. 12.

77. DiversityInc. Staff, "Does McDonald's Web Site Stereotype Blacks?" *DiversityInc Online* [www.diversityinc.com], August 25, 2009.

78. Based on P. L. Hunsaker, *Training in Management Skills* (Upper Saddle River, NJ: Prentice Hall, 2009); C. Harvey and J. Allard, *Understanding and Managing Diversity: Readings, Cases, and Exercises,* 3rd ed. (Upper Saddle River, NJ: Prentice Hall, 2005); and J. Greenberg, *Managing Behavior in Organizations: Science in Service to Practice,* 2nd ed. (Upper Saddle River, NJ: Prentice Hall, 1999).

79. "Transforming Untapped Talent into Leaders," *DiversityInc,* February 2010, pp. 62–67; and "What Does Diversity Mean for the U.S. Navy?" *Diversity Inc.,* November/December, 2009, pp. 60–65.

Chapter 5

1. "Ten Companies With Social Responsibility at the Core," *Advertising Age,* April 19, 2010, p. 88; C. Binkley, "Charity Gives Shoe Brand Extra Shine," *Wall Street Journal,* April 1, 2010, p. D7; J. Shambora, "How I Got Started: Blake Mycoskie, Founder of TOMS Shoes," *Fortune,* March 22, 2010, p. 72; and "Making A Do-Gooder's Business Model Work," *BusinessWeek Online,* January 26, 2009.

2. M. L. Barnett, "Stakeholder Influence Capacity and the Variability of Financial Returns to Corporate Social Responsibility," *Academy of Management Review,* July 2007, pp. 794–816; A. Mackey, T. B. Mackey, and J. B. Barney, "Corporate Social Responsibility and Firm Performance: Investor Preferences and Corporate Strategies," *Academy of Management Review,* July 2007, pp. 817–835; and A. B. Carroll, "A Three-Dimensional Conceptual Model of Corporate Performance," *Academy of Management Review,* October 1979, p. 499.

3. See K. Basu and G. Palazzo, "Corporate Social Performance: A Process Model of Sensemaking," *Academy of Management Review,* January 2008, pp. 122–136; and S. P. Sethi, "A Conceptual Framework for Environmental Analysis of Social Issues and Evaluation of Business Response Patterns," *Academy of Management Review,* January 1979, pp. 68–74.

4. M. Friedman, *Capitalism and Freedom* (Chicago: University of Chicago Press, 1962); and Friedman, "The Social Responsibility of Business Is to Increase Profits," *New York Times Magazine,* September 13, 1970, p. 33.

5. S. Liebs, "Do Companies Do Good Well?" *CFO,* July 2007, p. 16.

6. See, for example, D. J. Wood, "Corporate Social Performance Revisited," *Academy of Management Review,* October 1991, pp. 703–708; and S. L. Wartick and P. L. Cochran, "The Evolution

of the Corporate Social Performance Model, *Academy of Management Review,* October 1985, p. 763.

7. N. Bunkley, "Ford Backs Ban on Text Messaging by Drivers," *New York Times Online,* September 11, 2009.

8. J. O'Donnell, "UPS Workers Head to Haiti to Provide Help," *USA Today,* January 25, 2010, p. 4B.

9. See, for example, R. A. Buchholz, *Essentials of Public Policy for Management,* 2d ed. (Upper Saddle River, NJ: Prentice Hall, 1990).

10. I. Brat, "The Extra Step," *Wall Street Journal,* March 24, 2008, p. R12.

11. Wal-Mart [www.walmartstores.com], March 16, 2006; and an advertisement from *USA Today,* March 6, 2006, p. 5A.

12. This section is based on J. D. Margolis and J. P. Walsh, "Misery Loves Companies: Rethinking Social Initiatives by Business," *Administrative Science Quarterly,* vol. 48, no. 2, 2003, pp. 268–305; K. Davis and W. C. Frederick, *Business and Society: Management, Public Policy, Ethics,* 5th ed. (New York: McGraw-Hill, 1984), pp. 28–41; and R. J. Monsen Jr., "The Social Attitudes of Management," in J. M. McGuire (ed.), *Contemporary Management: Issues and Views* (Upper Saddle River, NJ: Prentice Hall, 1974), p. 616.

13. See, for instance, J. Surroca, J. A. Tribo, and S. Waddock, "Corporate Responsibility and Financial Performance: The Role of Intangible Resources," *Strategic Management Journal,* May 2010, pp. 463–490; R. Garcia-Castro, M. A. Ariño, and M. A. Canela, "Does Social Performance Really Lead to Financial Performance? Accounting for Endogeneity," *Journal of Business Ethics,* March 2010, pp. 107–126; J. Peloza, "The Challenge of Measuring Financial Impacts from Investments in Corporate Social Performance," *Journal of Management,* December 2009, pp. 1518–1541; J. D. Margolis and H. Anger Elfenbein, "Do Well by Doing Good? Don't Count on It," *Harvard Business Review,* January 2008, pp. 19–20; M. L. Barnett, "Stakeholder Influence Capacity and the Variability of Financial Returns to Corporate Social Responsibility," 2007; D. O. Neubaum and S. A. Zahra, "Institutional Ownership and Corporate Social Performance: The Moderating Effects of Investment Horizon, Activism, and Coordination," *Journal of Management,* February 2006, pp. 108–131; B. A. Waddock and S. B. Graves, "The Corporate Social Performance–Financial Performance Link," *Strategic Management Journal,* April 1997, pp. 303–319; J. B. McGuire, A. Sundgren, and T. Schneeweis, "Corporate Social Responsibility and Firm Financial Performance," *Academy of Management Journal,* December 1988, pp. 854–872; K. Aupperle, A. B. Carroll, and J. D. Hatfield, "An Empirical Examination of the Relationship Between Corporate Social Responsibility and Profitability," *Academy of Management Journal,* June 1985, pp. 446–463; and P. Cochran and R. A. Wood, "Corporate Social Responsibility and Financial Performance," *Academy of Management Journal,* March 1984, pp. 42–56.

14. Peloza, "The Challenge of Measuring Financial Impacts from Investments in Corporate Social Performance."

15. B. Seifert, S. A. Morris, and B. R. Bartkus, "Having, Giving, and Getting: Slack Resources, Corporate Philanthropy, and Firm Financial Performance," *Business & Society,* June 2004, pp. 135–161; and McGuire, Sundgren, and Schneeweis, "Corporate Social Responsibility and Firm Financial Performance."

16. A. McWilliams and D. Siegel, "Corporate Social Responsibility and Financial Performance: Correlation or Misspecification?" *Strategic Management Journal,* June 2000, pp. 603–609.

17. A. J. Hillman and G. D. Keim, "Shareholder Value, Stakeholder Management, and Social Issues: What's the Bottom Line?" *Strategic Management Journal,* vol. 22, 2001, pp. 125–139.

18. M. Orlitzky, F. L. Schmidt, and S. L. Rynes, "Corporate Social and Financial Performance," *Organization Studies,* vol. 24, no. 3, 2003, pp. 403–441.

19. A. Hughey and P. Villareal, "Socially Responsible Investing," *National Center for Policy Analysis* [www.ncpa.org/pdfs/ba657.pdf], May 11, 2009.

20. Social Investment Forum, "Socially Responsible Mutual Fund Charts: Financial Performance" [www.socialinvest.org/resources/performance.cfm], April 28, 2010.

21. A. Salkever, "Why Are Coke Drinkers Smiling? Vending Machines to Be More Eco-Friendly," *Daily Finance Online* [www.dailyfinance.com], December 3, 2009.

22. "Hive Mentality," *Body + Soul,* December 2009, p. 26.

23. R. Kauffeld, A. Malhotra, and S. Higgins, "Green Is a Strategy," *Strategy + Business Online* [www.strategy-business.com], December 21, 2009.

24. D. A. Lubin and D. C. Esty, "The Sustainability Imperative," *Harvard Business Review,* May 2010, pp. 42–50; J. Pfeffer, "Building Sustainable Organizations: The Human Factor," *Academy of Management Perspectives,* February 2010, pp. 34–45; R. Nidumolu, C. K. Prahalad, and M. R. Rangaswami, "Why Sustainability Is Now the Key Driver of Innovation," *Harvard Business Review,* September 2009, pp. 56–64; A. A. Marcus and A. R. Fremeth, "Green Management Matters Regardless," *Academy of Management Perspectives,* August 2009, pp. 17–27; D. S. Siegel, "Green Management Matters Only If It Yields More Green: An Economic/Strategic Perspective," *Academy of Management Perspectives,* August 2009, pp. 5–16; and A. White, "The Greening of the Balance Sheet," *Harvard Business Review,* March 2006, pp. 27–28.

25. The concept of shades of green can be found in R. E. Freeman, J. Pierce, and R. Dodd, *Shades of Green: Business Ethics and the Environment* (New York: Oxford University Press, 1995).

26. Leader Who Made a Difference box based on M. J. Ybarra, "Book Review: The Fun Hog Expedition Revisited," *Wall Street Journal,* February 19, 2010, p. W8; K. Garber, "Not in the Business of Hurting the Planet," *US News & World Report,* November 2009, p. 63; and T. Foster, "No Such Thing As Sustainability," *Fast Company,* July/August 2009, pp. 46–48.

27. The Global 100 list is a collaborative effort of Corporate Knights Inc. and Innovest Strategic Value Advisors. Information from Global 100 Web site [www.global100.org], April 30, 2010.

28. C. Hausman, "Financial News Focuses on Questions of Ethics," *Ethics Newsline* [www.globalethics.org/newsline], April 20, 2010; C. Hausman, "Privacy Issues Prominent in Week's Tech News," *Ethics Newsline* [www.globalethics.org/newsline], March 9, 2010; and H. Maurer and C. Lindblad, "Madoff Gets the Max," *Bloomberg BusinessWeek,* July 13 & 20, 2009, p. 6.

29. This last example is based on J. F. Viega, T. D. Golden, and K. Dechant, "Why Managers Bend Company Rules," *Academy of Management Executive,* May 2004, pp. 84–90.

30. K. Davis and W. C. Frederick, *Business and Society,* p. 76.

31. F. D. Sturdivant, *Business and Society: A Managerial Approach,* 3rd ed. (Homewood, IL: Richard D. Irwin, 1985), p. 128.

32. L. K. Treviño, G. R. Weaver, and S. J. Reynolds, "Behavioral Ethics in Organizations: A Review," *Journal of Management,* December 2006, pp. 951–990; T. Kelley, "To Do Right or Just to Be Legal," *New York Times,* February 8, 1998, p. BU12; J. W. Graham, "Leadership, Moral Development, and Citizenship Behavior," *Business Ethics Quarterly,* January 1995, pp. 43–54; L. Kohlberg, *Essays in Moral Development: The Psychology of Moral Development,* vol. 2 (New York: Harper & Row, 1984); and L. Kohlberg, *Essays in Moral Development: The Philosophy of Moral Development,* vol. 1 (New York: Harper & Row, 1981).

33. See, for example, J. Weber, "Managers' Moral Reasoning: Assessing Their Responses to Three Moral Dilemmas," *Human Relations,* July 1990, pp. 687–702.

34. W. C. Frederick and J. Weber, "The Value of Corporate Managers and Their Critics: An Empirical Description and Normative Implications," in W. C. Frederick and L. E. Preston (eds.) *Business Ethics: Research Issues and Empirical Studies* (Greenwich, CT: JAI Press, 1990), pp. 123–144; and J. H. Barnett and M. J. Karson, "Personal Values and Business Decisions: An Exploratory Investigation," *Journal of Business Ethics,* July 1987, pp. 371–382.

35. M. E. Baehr, J. W. Jones, and A. J. Nerad, "Psychological Correlates of Business Ethics Orientation in Executives," *Journal of Business and Psychology,* Spring 1993, pp. 291–308; and L. K. Treviño and S. A. Youngblood, "Bad Apples in Bad Barrels: A Causal Analysis of Ethical Decision-Making Behavior," *Journal of Applied Psychology,* August 1990, pp. 378–385.

36. M. E. Schweitzer, L. Ordonez, and B. Douma, "Goal Setting as a Motivator of Unethical Behavior," *Academy of Management Journal,* June 2004, pp. 422–432.

37. M. C. Jensen, "Corporate Budgeting is Broken—Let's Fix It," *Harvard Business Review,* June 2001, pp. 94–101.

38. R. L. Cardy and T. T. Selvarajan, "Assessing Ethical Behavior Revisited: The Impact of Outcomes on Judgment Bias," paper presented at the Annual Meeting of the Academy of Management, Toronto, 2000.

39. By the Numbers box based on J. Yang and V. Salazar, "Healthy Sick Days," *USA Today,* May 4, 2010, p. 1B; M. B. Marklein, "What Employers Want from Grads," *USA Today,* January 21, 2010, p. 7D; J. Yang and V. Salazar, "Green Efforts Stay Steady," *USA Today,* January 13, 2010, p. 1B; J. MacIntyre, "Leadership Honesty," *Springfield Business Journal,* November 30–December 6, 2009, p. 16; National Business Ethics Survey 2009, Ethics Resource Center [www.ethics.org], November 2009, p. 9; "Companies That Act Ethically Have Edge in Recruiting Talent," *Ethics Newsline* [www.globalethics.org], November 2, 2009; and S. B. Welch, "Workers Want Ethical, Socially Responsible Companies, Survey Finds," *Workforce Management Online* [www.workforce.com], October 30, 2009.

40. M. C. Gentile, "Keeping Your Colleagues Honest," *Harvard Business Review,* March 2010, pp. 114–117; J. R. Edwards and D. M. Cable, "The Value of Value Congruence," *Journal of Applied Psychology,* May 2009, pp. 654–677; G. Weaver, "Ethics and Employees: Making the Connection," *Academy of Management Executive,* May 2004, pp. 121–125; V. Anand, B. E. Ashforth, and M. Joshi, "Business as Usual: The Acceptance and Perpetuation of Corruption in Organizations," *Academy of Management Executive,* May 2004, pp. 39–53; J. Weber, L. B. Kurke, and D. W. Pentico, "Why Do Employees Steal?" *Business & Society,* September 2003, pp. 359–380; V. Arnold and J. C. Lampe, "Understanding the Factors Underlying Ethical Organizations: Enabling Continuous Ethical Improvement," *Journal of Applied Business Research,* Summer 1999, pp. 1–19.

41. P. Van Lee, L. Fabish, and N. McCaw, "The Value of Corporate Values," *Strategy & Business,* Summer 2005, pp. 52–65.

42. F. O. Walumba and J. Schaubroeck, "Leader Personality Traits and Employee Voice Behavior: Mediating Roles of Ethical Leadership and Work Group Psychological Safety," *Journal of Applied Psychology,* September 2009, pp. 1275–1286; G. Weaver, "Ethics and Employees: Making the Connection," May 2004; G. Weaver, L. K. Treviño, and P. L. Cochran, "Integrated and Decoupled Corporate Social Performance: Management Commitments, External Pressures, and Corporate Ethics Practices," *Academy of Management Journal,* October 1999, pp. 539–552; G. R. Weaver, L. K. Treviño, and P. L. Cochran, "Corporate Ethics Programs as Control Systems: Influences of Executive Commitment and Environmental Factors," *Academy of Management Journal,* February 1999, pp. 41–57; R. B. Morgan, "Self- and Co-Worker Perceptions of Ethics and Their Relationships to Leadership and Salary," *Academy of Management Journal,* February 1993, pp. 200–214; and B. Z. Posner and W. H. Schmidt, "Values and the American Manager: An Update," *California Management Review,* Spring 1984, pp. 202–216.

43. IBM Corporate Responsibility Report, 2007 [www.ibm.com]; and A. Schultz, "Integrating IBM," *CRO,* March/April 2007, pp. 16–21.

44. T. Barnett, "Dimensions of Moral Intensity and Ethical Decision Making: An Empirical Study," *Journal of Applied Social Psychology,* May 2001, pp. 1038–1057; and T. M. Jones, "Ethical Decision Making by Individuals in Organizations: An Issue-Contingent Model," *Academy of Management Review,* April 1991, pp. 366–395.

45. W. Bailey and A. Spicer, "When Does National Identity Matter? Convergence and Divergence in International Business Ethics," *Academy of Management Journal,* December 2007, pp. 1462–1480; and R. L. Sims, "Comparing Ethical Attitudes Across Cultures," *Cross Cultural Management: An International Journal,* vol. 13, no. 2, 2006, pp. 101–113.

46. BBC News Online, "Legal Review of Overseas Bribery," November 29, 2007.

47. C. Hausman, "British Defense Giant BAE Must Hire Ethics Monitor and Pay Huge Penalties Under Corruption Settlement," *Ethics Newsline* [www.globalethics.org], February 15, 2010.

48. The FCPA Blog [www.fcpablog.com/blog/2009/12/31/2009-fcpa-enforcement-index.html], April 30, 2010.

49. L. Paine, R. Deshpande, J. D. Margolis, and K. E. Bettcher, "Up to Code: Does Your Company's Conduct Meet World-Class Standards?" *Harvard Business Review,* December 2005, pp. 122–133;

G. R. Simpson, "Global Heavyweights Vow 'Zero Tolerance' for Bribes," *Wall Street Journal,* January 27, 2005, pp. A2+; A. Spicer, T. W. Dunfee, and W. J. Bailey, "Does National Context Matter in Ethical Decision Making? An Empirical Test of Integrative Social Contracts Theory," *Academy of Management Journal,* August 2004, pp. 610–620; J. White and S. Taft, "Frameworks for Teaching and Learning Business Ethics Within the Global Context: Background of Ethical Theories," *Journal of Management Education,* August 2004, pp. 463–477; J. Guyon, "CEOs on Managing Globally," *Fortune,* July 26, 2004, p. 169; A. B. Carroll, "Managing Ethically with Global Stakeholders: A Present and Future Challenge," *Academy of Management Executive,* May 2004, pp. 114–120; and C. J. Robertson and W. F. Crittenden, "Mapping Moral Philosophies: Strategic Implications for Multinational Firms," *Strategic Management Journal,* April 2003, pp. 385–392.

50. United Nations Global Compact [www.unglobalcompact.org/AboutTheGC/index.html], April 30, 2010.

51. Organization for Economic Cooperation and Development, "About Bribery in International Business" [www.oecd.org], April 30, 2010.

52. R. M. Kidder, "Can Disobedience Save Wall Street?" *Ethics Newsline* [www.globalethics.org], May 3, 2010.

53. Enron example taken from P. M. Lencioni, "Make Your Values Mean Something," *Harvard Business Review,* July 2002, p. 113; and Sears example taken from series of posters called "Sears Ethics and Business Practices: A Century of Tradition," in *Business Ethics,* May/June 1999, pp. 12–13; and B. J. Feder, "The Harder Side of Sears," *New York Times,* July 20, 1997, pp. BU1+.

54. J. R. Edwards and D. M. Cable, "The Value of Value Congruence," *Journal of Applied Psychology,* May 2009, pp. 654–677; and Treviño and Youngblood, "Bad Apples in Bad Barrels," p. 384.

55. K. Bart, "UBS Lays Out Employee Ethics Code," *Wall Street Journal Online* [online.wsj.com], January 12, 2010; J. L. Lunsford, "Transformer in Transition," *Wall Street Journal,* May 17, 2007, pp. B1+; and J. S. McClenahen, "UTC's Master of Principle," *Industry Week,* January 2003, pp. 30–36.

56. M. Weinstein, "Survey Says: Ethics Training Works," *Training,* November 2005, p. 15.

57. J. E. Fleming, "Codes of Ethics for Global Corporations," *Academy of Management News,* June 2005, p. 4.

58. "Corporate Codes of Ethics Spread," *Ethics Newsline* [www.globalethics.org], October 12, 2009; "Global Ethics Codes Gain Importance As a Tool to Avoid Litigation and Fines," *Wall Street Journal,* August 19, 1999, p. A1; and J. Alexander, "On the Right Side," *World Business,* January/February 1997, pp. 38–41.

59. F. R. David, "An Empirical Study of Codes of Business Ethics: A Strategic Perspective," paper presented at the 48th Annual Academy of Management Conference; Anaheim, California, August 1988.

60. National Business Ethics Survey 2009, *Ethics Resource Center* [www.ethics.org], November 2009.

61. "Codes of Conduct," Center for Ethical Business Cultures [www.cebcglobal .org], February 15, 2006; L. Paine, R. Deshpande, J. D. Margolis, and K. E. Bettcher, "Up to Code: Does Your Company's Conduct Meet World-Class Standards"; and A. K. Reichert and M. S. Webb, "Corporate Support for Ethical and Environmental Policies: A Financial Management Perspective," *Journal of Business Ethics,* May 2000.

62. D. Jones, "CEO's Moral Compass Steers Siemens," *USA Today,* February 15, 2010, p. 3B.

63. V. Wessler, "Integrity and Clogged Plumbing," *Straight to the Point,* newsletter of VisionPoint Corporation, Fall 2002, pp. 1–2.

64. T. A. Gavin, "Ethics Education," *Internal Auditor,* April 1989, pp. 54–57.

65. L. Myyry and K. Helkama, "The Role of Value Priorities and Professional Ethics Training in Moral Sensitivity," *Journal of Moral Education,* 2002, vol. 31, no. 1, pp. 35–50; W. Penn and B. D. Collier, "Current Research in Moral Development as a Decision Support System," *Journal of Business Ethics,* January 1985, pp. 131–136.

66. J. A. Byrne, "After Enron: The Ideal Corporation," *Business Week,* August 19, 2002, pp. 68–71; D. Rice and C. Dreilinger, "Rights and Wrongs of Ethics Training," *Training & Development Journal,* May 1990, pp. 103–109; and J. Weber, "Measuring the Impact of Teaching Ethics to

Future Managers: A Review, Assessment, and Recommendations," *Journal of Business Ethics,* April 1990, pp. 182–190.

67. E. White, "What Would You Do? Ethics Courses Get Context," *Wall Street Journal,* June 12, 2006, p. B3; and D. Zielinski, "The Right Direction: Can Ethics Training Save Your Company," *Training,* June 2005, pp. 27–32.

68. G. Farrell and J. O'Donnell, "Ethics Training As Taught by Ex-Cons: Crime Doesn't Pay," *USA Today,* November 16, 2005, p. 1B+.

69. J. Weber, "The New Ethics Enforcers," *Business Week,* February 13, 2006, pp. 76–77.

70. The Ethics and Compliance Officer Association [www.theecoa.org], April 30, 2010; and K. Maher, "Global Companies Face Reality of Instituting Ethics Programs," *Wall Street Journal,* November 9, 2004, p. B8.

71. "Survey Reveals How Many Workers Commit Office Taboos," *Ethics Newsline* [www.globalethics.org], September 18, 2007.

72. H. Oh, "Biz Majors Get an F for Honesty," *Business Week,* February 6, 2006, p. 14.

73. "Students Aren't Squealers," *USA Today,* March 27, 2003, p. 1D; and J. Merritt, "You Mean Cheating is Wrong?" *Business Week,* December 9, 2002, p. 8.

74. J. Hyatt, "Unethical Behavior: Largely Unreported in Offices and Justified by Teens," *The CRO Online,* February 13, 2008.

75. D. Lidsky, "Transparency: It's Not Just for Shrink Wrap Anymore," *Fast Company,* January 2005, p. 87.

76. W. Zellner, "A Hero—and a Smoking-Gun Letter," *Business Week,* January 28, 2002, pp. 34–35.

77. National Business Ethics Survey, Ethics Resource Center (Arlington, VA), 2007.

78. S. Armour, "More Companies Urge Workers to Blow the Whistle," *USA Today,* December 16, 2002, p. 1B.

79. J. Wiscombe, "Don't Fear Whistleblowers," *Workforce,* July 2002, pp. 26–27.

80. T. Reason, "Whistle Blowers: The Untouchables," *CFO,* March 2003, p. 18; and C. Lachnit, "Muting the Whistle-Blower?" *Workforce,* September 2002, p. 18.

81. J. Hyatt, "Corporate Whistleblowers Might Need a Monetary Nudge, Researchers Suggest," *CRO Newsletter Online,* April 11, 2007; J. O'Donnell, "Blowing the Whistle Can Lead to Harsh Aftermath, Despite Law"; *USA Today,* August 1, 2005, p. 2B; and D. Solomon, "For Financial Whistle-Blowers, New Shield Is An Imperfect One," *Wall Street Journal,* October 4, 2004, pp. A1+.

82. A. Smith, "Bottled Up," *Time,* August 14, 2009, p. Global 6.

83. This definition based on P. Tracey and N. Phillips, "The Distinctive Challenge of Educating Social Entrepreneurs: A Postscript and Rejoinder to the Special Issue on Entrepreneurship Education," *Academy of Management Learning & Education,* June 2007, pp. 264–271; Schwab Foundation for Social Entrepreneurship [www.schwabfound.org], February 20, 2006; and J. G. Dees, J. Emerson, and P. Economy, *Strategic Tools for Social Entrepreneurs* (New York: John Wiley & Sons, Inc.), 2002.

84. D. Bornstein, *How to Change the World: Social Entrepreneurs and the Power of New Ideas* (New York: Oxford University Press), 2004, inside cover jacket.

85. A. Kamenetz, "Five Social Capitalists Who Will Change the World in 2010," *Fast Company Online* [www.fastcompany.com], February 1, 2010.

86. K. H. Hammonds, "Now the Good News," *Fast Company,* December 2007/January 2008, pp. 110–121; C. Dahle, "Filling the Void," *Fast Company,* January/February 2006, pp. 54–57; and PATH [www.path.org].

87. R. J. Bies, J. M. Bartunek, T. L. Fort, and M. N. Zald, "Corporations as Social Change Agents: Individual, Interpersonal, Institutional, and Environmental Dynamics," *Academy of Management Review,* July 2007, pp. 788–793.

88. "The State of Corporate Philanthropy: A McKinsey Global Survey," *The McKinsey Quarterly Online,* February 2008.

89. R. Nixon, The Associated Press, "Bottom Line for (Red)," *New York Times Online,* February 6, 2008; and G. Mulvihill, "Despite Cause, Not Everyone Tickled Pink by Campaign," *Springfield News-Leader,* October 15, 2007, p. 2E.

90. 2008 Highlights, *The Chronicle of Philanthropy* [www.coneinccom], June 30, 2009.

91. K. J. Delaney, "Google: From 'Don't be Evil' to How to Do Good," *Wall Street Journal,* January 18, 2008, pp. B1+; H. Rubin, "Google Offers a Map for Its Philanthropy," *New York Times Online,* January 18, 2008; and K. Hafner, "Philanthropy Google's Way: Not the Usual," *New York Times Online,* September 14, 2006.

92. Committee to Encourage Corporate Philanthropy [www.corporatephilanthropy.org], April 7, 2008; "Investing in Society," *Leaders,* July–September 2007, pp. 12+; M. C. White, "Doing Good on Company Time," *New York Times Online,* May 8, 2007; and M. Lowery, "How Volunteerism is Changing the Face of Philanthropy," *DiversityInc,* December 2006, pp. 45–47.

93. Y. I. Kane and J. S. Lublin, "Jobs Had Liver Transplant," *Wall Street Journal,* June 20, 2009, pp. A1+; and R. M. Kidder, "Do Ailing CEOs of Publicly Traded Firms Have a Right to Medical Privacy?" *Ethics Newsline* [www.globalethics.org/newsline], January 19, 2009.

94. Skills Exercise based on F. Bartolome, "Nobody Trusts the Boss Completely—Now What?" *Harvard Business Review,* March–April 1989, pp. 135–142; and J. K. Butler Jr., "Toward Understanding and Measuring Conditions of Trust: Evolution of a Condition of Trust Inventory," *Journal of Management,* September 1991, pp. 643–663.

95. J. Sterngold, "Who Cares About Another $200 Million?" *Bloomberg BusinessWeek,* May 3–9, 2010, pp. 56–59; L. Story and E. Dash, "Lehman Channeled Risks Through Alter Ego Firm," *New York Time Online,* April 12, 2010; P. M. Barrett, "Cold Case: Lessons From the Lehman Autopsy," *Bloomberg BusinessWeek,* April 5, 2010, pp. 20–22; A. Smith, "What's Left of Lehman: A Plan," *CNNMoney* [money.cnn.com], March 16, 2010; and G. Wong and A. Smith, "What Killed Lehman," *CNNMoney* [money.cnn.com], March 15, 2010.

96. S. Rosenbloom, "Wal-Mart Unveils Plan to Make Supply Chain Greener," *New York Times Online,* February 26, 2010; K. Rockwood, "Attention, Wal-Mart Shoppers: Clean-up in Aisle Nine," *Fast Company,* February 2010, pp. 30–32; D. Johnson, "Gone Green?" *Dealer News,* February 2010, p. 10; N. Richardson, "Can Wal-Mart Save the World?" *Communication World,* September/October 2009, p. 2; "Green Matters," *World Trade,* September 2009, p. 8; "Wal-Mart to Create Sustainability Index," *Institute for Global Ethics* [www.globalethics.org], July 20, 2009; M. Bustillo, "Wal-Mart to Assign New Green Ratings," *Wall Street Journal,* July 16, 2009, p. B1+; and S. Rosenbloom, "At Wal-Mart, Labeling to Reflect Green Intent," *New York Times Online,* July 16, 2009.

Chapter 6

1. A. Pasztor, "Despite Orders, NASA Keeps Funding Projects," *Wall Street Journal,* June 24, 2010, p. A7; A. Pasztor, "Contractors Face Shutdown Costs as NASA Space Program Morphs," *Wall Street Journal,* May 12, 2010, pp. B1+; A. Pasztor, "Feud Over NASA Threatens America's Edge in Space," *Wall Street Journal,* April 15, 2010, pp. A1+; K. Chang, "Aerospace Business Has Its Doubts About Plans to Revamp NASA," *New York Times Online,* April 11, 2010; and B. M. Testa, "New Workforce Orbit—Relaunch at NASA," *Workforce Management Online* [www.workforce.com], August 17, 2009.

2. A. Weintraub and M. Tirrell, "Eli Lilly's Drug Assembly Line," *Bloomberg BusinessWeek,* March 8, 2010, pp. 56–57.

3. L. Dragoni, P. E. Tesluk, J. E. A. Russell, and I. S. Oh, "Understanding Managerial Development: Integrating Developmental Assignments, Learning Orientation, and Access to Developmental Opportunities in Predicting Managerial Competencies," *Academy of Management Journal,* August 2009, pp. 731–743; G. Nadler and W. J. Chandon, "Making Changes: The FIST Approach," *Journal of Management Inquiry,* September 2004, pp. 239–246; and C. R. Leana and B. Barry, "Stability and Change as Simultaneous Experiences in Organizational Life," *Academy of Management Review,* October 2000, pp. 753–759.

4. The idea for these metaphors came from J. E. Dutton, S. J. Ashford, R. M. O'Neill, and K. A. Lawrence, "Moves That Matter: Issue Selling and Organizational Change," *Academy of Management Journal,* August 2001, pp. 716–736; B. H. Kemelgor, S. D. Johnson, and S. Srinivasan, "Forces Driving Organizational Change: A Business School Perspective," *Journal of Education for Business,* January/February 2000, pp. 133–137; G. Colvin, "When It Comes to Turbulence, CEOs Could Learn a Lot from Sailors," *Fortune,* March 29, 1999,

pp. 194–196; and P. B. Vaill, *Managing as a Performing Art: New Ideas for a World of Chaotic Change* (San Francisco: Jossey-Bass, 1989).

5. K. Lewin, *Field Theory in Social Science* (New York: Harper & Row, 1951).

6. D. Lieberman, "Nielsen Media Has Cool Head at the Top," *USA Today,* March 27, 2006, p. 3B.

7. S. Ante, "Change Is Good—So Get Used to It," *BusinessWeek,* June 22, 2009, pp. 69–70; L. S. Lüscher and M. W. Lewis, "Organizational Change and Managerial Sensemaking: Working Through Paradox," *Academy of Management Journal,* April 2008, pp. 221–240; F. Buckley and K. Monks, "Responding to Managers' Learning Needs in an Edge-of-Chaos Environment: Insights from Ireland," *Journal of Management,* April 2008, pp. 146–163; and G. Hamel, "Take It Higher," *Fortune,* February 5, 2001, pp. 169–170.

8. A. Sains and S. Reed, "Electrolux Cleans Up," *BusinessWeek,* February 27, 2006, pp. 42–43.

9. J. Cohen, "Business As Usual," *Training,* February 2010, pp. 46–50.

10. J. Jesitus, "Change Management: Energy to the People," *Industry Week,* September 1, 1997, pp. 37, 40.

11. D. Lavin, "European Business Rushes to Automate," *Wall Street Journal,* July 23, 1997, p. A14.

12. See, for example, B. B. Bunker, B. T. Alban, and R. J. Lewicki, "Ideas in Currency and OD Practice," *The Journal of Applied Behavioral Science,* December 2004, pp. 403–422; L. E. Greiner and T. G. Cummings, "Wanted: OD More Alive Than Dead!" *Journal of Applied Behavioral Science,* December 2004, pp. 374–391; S. Hicks, "What Is Organization Development?" *Training & Development,* August 2000, p. 65; W. Nicolay, "Response to Farias and Johnson's Commentary," *Journal of Applied Behavioral Science,* September 2000, pp. 380–381; and G. Farias, "Organizational Development and Change Management," *Journal of Applied Behavioral Science,* September 2000, pp. 376–379.

13. T. White, "Supporting Change: How Communicators at Scotiabank Turned Ideas into Action," *Communication World,* April 2002, pp. 22–24.

14. M. Javidan, P. W. Dorfman, M. S. deLuque, and R. J. House, "In the Eye of the Beholder: Cross-Cultural Lessons in Leadership from Project GLOBE," *Academy of Management Perspective,* February 2006, pp. 67–90; and E. Fagenson-Eland, E. A. Ensher, and W. W. Burke, "Organization Development and Change Interventions: A Seven-Nation Comparison," *The Journal of Applied Behavioral Science,* December 2004, pp. 432–464.

15. E. Fagenson-Eland, Ensher, and Burke, "Organization Development and Change Interventions: A Seven-Nation Comparison," p. 461.

16. S. Shinn, "Stairway to Reinvention," *BizEd,* January/February 2010, p. 6; M. Scott, "A Stairway to Marketing Heaven," *BusinessWeek,* November 2, 2009, p. 17; and The Fun Theory [http://thefuntheory.com], November 10, 2009.

17. See, for example, J. D. Ford, L. W. Ford, and A. D'Amelio, "Resistance to Change: The Rest of the Story," *Academy of Management Review,* April 2008, pp. 362–377; A. Deutschman, "Making Change: Why Is It So Hard to Change Our Ways?" *Fast Company,* May 2005, pp. 52–62; S. B. Silverman, C. E. Pogson, and A. B. Cober, "When Employees at Work Don't Get It: A Model for Enhancing Individual Employee Change in Response to Performance Feedback," *Academy of Management Executive,* May 2005, pp. 135–147; C. E. Cunningham, C. A. Woodward, H. S. Shannon, J. MacIntosh, B. Lendrum, D. Rosenbloom, and J. Brown, "Readiness for Organizational Change: A Longitudinal Study of Workplace, Psychological and Behavioral Correlates," *Journal of Occupational and Organizational Psychology,* December 2002, pp. 377–392; M. A. Korsgaard, H. J. Sapienza, and D. M. Schweiger, "Beaten Before Begun: The Role of Procedural Justice in Planning Change," *Journal of Management,* 2002, vol. 28, no. 4, pp. 497–516; R. Kegan and L. L. Lahey, "The Real Reason People Won't Change," *Harvard Business Review,* November 2001, pp. 85–92; S. K. Piderit, "Rethinking Resistance and Recognizing Ambivalence: A Multidimensional View of Attitudes Toward an Organizational Change," *Academy of Management Review,* October 2000, pp. 783–794; C. R. Wanberg and J. T. Banas, "Predictors and Outcomes of Openness to Changes in a Reorganizing Workplace," *Journal of Applied Psychology,* February 2000, pp. 132–142; A. A. Armenakis and A. G. Bedeian, "Organizational Change: A Review of Theory and Research in the 1990s," *Journal of Management,* vol. 25,

no. 3, 1999, pp. 293–315; and B. M. Staw, "Counterforces to Change," in P. S. Goodman and Associates (eds.), *Change in Organizations* (San Francisco: Jossey-Bass, 1982), pp. 87–121.

18. A. Reichers, J. P. Wanous, and J. T. Austin, "Understanding and Managing Cynicism about Organizational Change," *Academy of Management Executive,* February 1997, pp. 48–57; P. Strebel, "Why Do Employees Resist Change?" *Harvard Business Review,* May–June 1996, pp. 86–92; and J. P. Kotter and L. A. Schlesinger, "Choosing Strategies for Change," *Harvard Business Review,* March–April 1979, pp. 107–109.

19. A. Foege, "Wii at Work," *CNNMoney* [cnnmoney.com], June 5, 2009.

20. R. Yu, "Korean Air Upgrades Service, Image," *USA Today,* August 24, 2009, pp. 1B+.

21. See P. Anthony, *Managing Culture* (Philadelphia: Open University Press, 1994); P. Bate, *Strategies for Cultural Change* (Boston: Butterworth-Heinemann, 1994); C. G. Smith and R. P. Vecchio, "Organizational Culture and Strategic Management: Issues in the Strategic Management of Change," *Journal of Managerial Issues,* Spring 1993, pp. 53–70; P. F. Drucker, "Don't Change Corporate Culture—Use It!" *Wall Street Journal,* March 28, 1991, p. A14; and T. H. Fitzgerald, "Can Change in Organizational Culture Really Be Managed?" *Organizational Dynamics,* Autumn 1988, pp. 5–15.

22. K. Maney, "Famously Gruff Gerstner Leaves IBM a Changed Man," *USA Today,* November 11, 2002, pp. 1B+; and Louis V. Gerstner, *Who Says Elephants Can't Dance: Inside IBM's Historic Turnaround* (New York: Harper Business, 2002).

23. See, for example, D. C. Hambrick and S. Finkelstein, "Managerial Discretion: A Bridge between Polar Views of Organizational Outcomes," in L. L. Cummings and B. M. Staw (eds.), *Research in Organizational Behavior,* vol. 9 (Greenwich, CT: JAI Press, 1987), p. 384; and R. H. Kilmann, M. J. Saxton, and R. Serpa (eds.), *Gaining Control of the Corporate Culture* (San Francisco: Jossey-Bass, 1985).

24. P. Davidson, "Moonlighting Becomes a Way of Life for Many," *USA Today,* June 24, 2009, p. 3B.

25. L. J. Dugan, "Working Two Jobs and Still Underemployed," *Wall Street Journal,* December 1, 2009, p. A15; N. Parmar, "The New Balancing Act," *Smart Money,* October 2009, p. 59; and Davidson "Moonlighting Becomes a Way of Life for Many."

26. S. Ilgenfritz, "Are We Too Stressed to Reduce Our Stress?" *Wall Street Journal,* November 10, 2009, p. D2; C. Daniels, "The Last Taboo," *Fortune,* October 28, 2002, pp. 137–144; J. Laabs, "Time-Starved Workers Rebel," *Workforce,* October 2000, pp. 26–28; M. A. Verespej, "Stressed Out," *Industry Week,* February 21, 2000, pp. 30–34; and M. A. Cavanaugh, W. R. Boswell, M. V. Roehling, and J. W. Boudreau, "An Empirical Examination of Self-Reported Work Stress Among U.S. Managers," *Journal of Applied Psychology,* February 2000, pp. 65–74.

27. A report on job stress compiled by the American Institute of Stress [www.stress.org/job], 2002–2003.

28. M. Conlin, "Go-Go-Going to Pieces in China," *Business Week,* April 23, 2007, p. 88; V. P. Sudhashree, K. Rohith, and K. Shrinivas, "Issues and Concerns of Health Among Call Center Employees," *Indian Journal of Occupational Environmental Medicine,"* vol. 9, no. 3, 2005, pp. 129–132; E. Muehlchen, "An Ounce of Prevention Goes A Long Way," Wilson Banwell [www.wilsonbanwell.com], January 2004; UnionSafe, "Stressed Employees Worked to Death" [unionsafe.labor.net.au/news], August 23, 2003; O. Siu, "Occupational Stressors and Well-Being Among Chinese Employees: The Role of Organizational Commitment," *Applied Psychology: An International Review,* October 2002, pp. 527–544; O. Siu, P. E. Spector, C. L. Cooper, L. Lu, and S. Yu, "Managerial Stress in Greater China: The Direct and Moderator Effects of Coping Strategies and Work Locus of Control," *Applied Psychology: An International Review,* October 2002, pp. 608–632; A. Oswald, "New Research Reveals Dramatic Rise in Stress Levels in Europe's Workplaces," University of Warwick [www.warwick.ac.uk/news/pr], 1999; and Y. Shimizu, S. Makino, and T. Takata, "Employee Stress Status During the Past Decade [1982–1992] Based on a Nation-Wide Survey Conducted by the Ministry of Labour in Japan," Japan Industrial Safety and Health Association, July 1997, pp. 441–450.

29. G. Kranz, "Job Stress Viewed Differently by Workers, Employers," *Workforce Management* [www.workforce.com], January 15, 2008.

30. Adapted from the UK National Work-Stress Network [www.workstress.net].

31. R. S. Schuler, "Definition and Conceptualization of Stress in Organizations," *Organizational Behavior and Human Performance,* April 1980, p. 191.

32. By the Numbers box based on S. Schomer, "Under Pressure," *Fast Company,* April 2010, p. 112; "Organizational Change: Facebook Poll," *Harvard Business Review,* March 2010, p. 16; J. Yang and S. Ward, "I'd Rather Give Up," *USA Today,* March 4, 2010, p. 1B; M. Weinstein, "Missing Something," *Training,* January 2010, p. 6; J. MacIntyre, "Hard At Work," *Springfield Business Journal,* November 30–December 6, 2009, p. 16; J. MacIntyre, "Accidental Innovation," *Springfield Business Journal,* September 28–October 4, 2009, p. 22; and M. Healy and S. Ward, "Workplace Worries," *USA Today,* August 28, 2008, p. 1D.

33. J. B. Rodell and T. A. Judge, "Can 'Good' Stressors Spark 'Bad' Behaviors? The Mediating Role of Emotions in Links of Challenge and Hindrance Stressors with Citizenship and Counterproductive Behaviors," *Journal of Applied Psychology,* November 2009, pp. 1438–1451; and see, for example, "Stressed Out: Extreme Job Stress: Survivors' Tales," *Wall Street Journal* (January 17, 2001), p. B1.

34. See, for instance, S. Bates, "Expert: Don't Overlook Employee Burnout," *HR Magazine* (August 2003), p. 14.

35. A. Kanai, "Karoshi (Work to Death) in Japan, *Journal of Business Ethics,* January 2009 Supplement 2, pp. 209–216; "Jobs for Life," *The Economist* [www.economist.com], December 19, 2007; and B. L. de Mente, "Karoshi: Death from Overwork," Asia Pacific Management Forum [www.apmforum.com], May 2002.

36. H. Benson, "Are You Working Too Hard?" *Harvard Business Review,* November 2005, pp. 53–58; B. Cryer, R. McCraty, and D. Childre, "Pull the Plug on Stress," *Harvard Business Review,* July 2003, pp. 102–107; C. Daniels, "The Last Taboo;" C. L. Cooper and S. Cartwright, "Healthy Mind, Healthy Organization—A Proactive Approach to Occupational Stress," *Human Relations,* April 1994, pp. 455–471; C. A. Heaney et al., "Industrial Relations, Worksite Stress Reduction and Employee Well-Being: A Participatory Action Research Investigation," *Journal of Organizational Behavior,* September 1993, pp. 495–510; C. D. Fisher, "Boredom at Work: A Neglected Concept," *Human Relations,* March 1993, pp. 395–417; and S. E. Jackson, "Participation in Decision Making as a Strategy for Reducing Job-Related Strain," *Journal of Applied Psychology,* February 1983, pp. 3–19.

37. C. Mamberto, "Companies Aim to Combat Job-Related Stress," *Wall Street Journal,* August 13, 2007, p. B6.

38. J. Goudreau, "Dispatches from the War on Stress," *BusinessWeek,* August 6, 2007, pp. 74–75.

39. Well Workplace 2008 Award Executive Summaries, Wellmark BlueCross BlueShield and Zimmer Holdings, Inc., available on Wellness Councils of America Web site [www.welcoa.org].

40. P. A. McLagan, "Change Leadership Today," *T&D,* November 2002, pp. 27–31.

41. Ibid, p. 29.

42. K. Kingsbury, "Road to Recovery," *Time,* March 18, 2010, pp. Global 14–16; and C. Haddad, "UPS: Can It Keep Delivering?" *BusinessWeek Online Extra* [www.businessweek.com], Spring 2003.

43. W. Pietersen, "The Mark Twain Dilemma: The Theory and Practice for Change Leadership," *Journal of Business Strategy,* September/October 2002, p. 35.

44. P. A. McLagan, "The Change-Capable Organization," *T&D,* January 2003, pp. 50–58.

45. A. Saha-Bubna and M. Jarzemsky, "MasterCard President Is Named CEO," *Wall Street Journal,* April 13, 2010, p. C3; and S. Vandebook, "Quotable," *IndustryWeek,* April 2010, p. 18.

46. R. M. Kanter, "Think Outside the Building," *Harvard Business Review,* March 2010, p. 34; T. Brown, "Change By Design," *BusinessWeek,* October 5, 2009, pp. 54–56; J. E. Perry-Smith and C. E. Shalley, "The Social Side of Creativity: A Static and Dynamic Social Network Perspective," *Academy of Management Review,* January 2003, pp. 89–106; and P. K. Jagersma, "Innovate or Die: It's Not Easy, But It Is Possible to Enhance Your Organization's Ability to Innovate," *Journal of Business Strategy,* January–February 2003, pp. 25–28.

47. E. Brynjolfsson and M. Schrage, "The New Faster Face of Innovation," *Wall Street Journal,* August 17, 2009, p. R3.

48. Ibid.

49. These definitions are based on T. M. Amabile, *Creativity in Context* (Boulder, CO: Westview Press, 1996).

50. U. R. Hülsheger, N. Anderson, and J. F. Salgado, "Team-Level Predictors of Innovation at Work: A Comprehensive Meta-Analysis Spanning Three Decades of Research," *Journal of Applied Psychology,* September 2009, pp. 1128–1145; R. W. Woodman, J. E. Sawyer, and R. W. Griffin, "Toward a Theory of Organizational Creativity," *Academy of Management Review,* April 1993, pp. 293–321.

51. K. Swisher, "A Question of Management," *Wall Street Journal,* June 2, 2009, p. R4.

52. J. van denEnde and G. Kijkuit, "Nurturing Good Ideas," *Harvard Business Review,* April 2009, p. 24; T. M. Egan, "Factors Influencing Individual Creativity in the Workplace: An Examination of Quantitative Empirical Research," *Advances in Developing Human Resources,* May 2005, pp. 160–181; N. Madjar, G. R. Oldham, and M. G. Pratt, "There's No Place Like Home? The Contributions of Work and Nonwork Creativity Support to Employees' Creative Performance," *Academy of Management Journal,* August 2002, pp. 757–767; T. M. Amabile, C. N. Hadley, and S. J. Kramer, "Creativity Under the Gun," *Harvard Business Review,* August 2002, pp. 52–61; J. B. Sorensen and T. E. Stuart, "Aging, Obsolescence, and Organizational Innovation," *Administrative Science Quarterly,* March 2000, pp. 81–112; G. R. Oldham and A. Cummings, "Employee Creativity: Personal and Contextual Factors at Work," *Academy of Management Journal,* June 1996, pp. 607–634; and F. Damanpour, "Organizational Innovation: A Meta-Analysis of Effects of Determinants and Moderators," *Academy of Management Journal,* September 1991, pp. 555–590.

53. J. S. Lublin, "Smart Balance Keeps Tight Focus on Creativity," *Wall Street Journal,* June 8, 2009, p. B4.

54. P. R. Monge, M. D. Cozzens, and N. S. Contractor, "Communication and Motivational Predictors of the Dynamics of Organizational Innovations," *Organization Science,* May 1992, pp. 250–274.

55. D. Dobson, "Integrated Innovation at Pitney Bowes," *Strategy+Business* [www.strategy-business.com], October 26, 2009.

56. T. M. Amabile, C. N. Hadley, and S. J. Kramer, "Creativity Under the Gun."

57. T. Jana, "Dusting Off A Big Idea in Hard Times," *BusinessWeek,* June 22, 2009, pp. 44–46.

58. N. Madjar, G. R. Oldham, and M. G. Pratt, "There's No Place Like Home? The Contributions of Work and Nonwork Creativity Support to Employees' Creative Performance."

59. Leader Who Made a Difference Box based on C. K. Prahalad, "Best Practices Get You Only So Far," *Harvard Business Review,* April 2010, p. 32; A. Graham, "Too Good to Fail," *Strategy+Business Online* [www.strategy-business.com], February 23, 2010; J. Scanlon, "How to Build a Culture of Innovation," *BusinessWeek Online* [www.businessweek.com], August 19, 2009; and J. Scanlon, "Tata Group's Innovation Competition," *BusinessWeek Online* [www.businessweek.com], June 17, 2009.

60. C. Salter, "Mattel Learns to 'Throw the Bunny,'" *Fast Company,* November 2002, p. 22.

61. See, for instance, J. Cable, "Building an Innovation Culture," *Industry Week,* March 2010, pp. 32–37; M. Hawkins, "Create a Climate of Creativity," *Training,* January 2010, p. 12; D. C. Wyld, "Keys to Innovation: The Right Measures and the Right Culture?" *Academy of Management Perspective,* May 2009, pp. 96–98; J. E. Perry-Smith, "Social Yet Creative: The Role of Social Relationships in Facilitating Individual Creativity," *Academy of Management Journal,* February 2006, pp. 85–101; C. E. Shalley, J. Zhou, and G. R. Oldham, "The Effects of Personal and Contextual Characteristics on Creativity: Where Should We Go from Here?" *Journal of Management,* vol. 30, no. 6, 2004, pp. 933–958; J. E. Perry-Smith and C. E. Shalley, "The Social Side of Creativity: A Static and Dynamic Social Network Perspective;" J. M. George and J. Zhou, "When Openness to Experience and Conscientiousness are Related to Creative Behavior: An Interactional Approach," *Journal of Applied Psychology,* June 2001, pp. 513–524; J. Zhou, "Feedback Valence, Feedback Style, Task Autonomy, and Achievement Orientation: Interactive Effects on Creative Behavior," *Journal of Applied Psychology,* 1998, vol. 83, pp. 261–276; T. M. Amabile, R. Conti, H. Coon, J. Lazenby, and M. Herron, "Assessing the Work Environment for Creativity," *Academy of Management Journal,*

October 1996, pp. 1154–1184; S. G. Scott and R. A. Bruce, "Determinants of Innovative People: A Path Model of Individual Innovation in the Workplace," *Academy of Management Journal*, June 1994, pp. 580–607; R. Moss Kanter, "When a Thousand Flowers Bloom: Structural, Collective, and Social Conditions for Innovation in Organization," in B. M. Staw and L. L. Cummings (eds.), *Research in Organizational Behavior*, vol. 10 (Greenwich, CT: JAI Press, 1988), pp. 169–211; and Amabile, *Creativity in Context*.

62. F. Yuan and R. W. Woodman, "Innovative Behavior in the Workplace: The Role of Performance and Image Outcome Expectations," *Academy of Management Journal*, April 2010, pp. 323–342.

63. J. McGregor, "The World's Most Innovative Companies," *BusinessWeek*, April 24, 2006, p. 70.

64. R. L. Martin and J. Riel, "Innovation's Accidental Enemies," *BusinessWeek Online* [www.businessweek.com], January 14, 2010; and McGregor, "The World's Most Innovative Companies," p. 74.

65. X. Zhang and K. M. Bartol, "Linking Empowering Leadership and Employee Creativity: The Influence of Psychological Empowerment, Intrinsic Motivation, and Creative Process Engagement," *Academy of Management Journal*, February 2010, pp. 107–128.

66. J. H. Dyer, H. B. Gregersen, and C. M. Christensen, "The Innovator's DNA," *Harvard Business Review*, December 2009, pp. 60–67; J. Gong, J-C Huang, and J-L. Farh, "Employee Learning Orientation, Transformational Leadership, and Employee Creativity: The Mediating Role of Employee Creative Self-Efficacy," *Academy of Management Journal*, August 2009, pp. 765–778; B. Buxton, "Innovation Calls for I-Shaped People," *BusinessWeek Online* [www.businessweek.com], July 13, 2009; J. Ramos, "Producing Change That Lasts," *Across the Board*, March 1994, pp. 29–33; T. Stjernberg and A. Philips, "Organizational Innovations in a Long-Term Perspective: Legitimacy and Souls-of-Fire as Critical Factors of Change and Viability," *Human Relations*, October 1993, pp. 1193–2023; and J. M. Howell and C. A. Higgins, "Champions of Change," *Business Quarterly*, Spring 1990, pp. 31–32.

67. Ethics Dilemma based on P. F. Weisberg, "Wellness Programs: Legal Requirements and Risks," *Workforce Management Online* [www.workforce.com], March 2010; S. S. Wang, "Workplace Mental-Health Services Expand," *Wall Street Journal*, December 15, 2009, p. D8; and D. Cole, "The Big Chill," *US News & World Report*, December 6, 2004, pp. EE2–EE5.

68. Developing Your Skill box based on J. P. Kotter and L. A. Schlesinger, "Choosing Strategies for Change," *Harvard Business Review*, March–April 1979, pp. 106–114; and T. A. Stewart, "Rate Your Readiness to Change," *Fortune*, February 7, 1994, pp. 106–110.

69. Team Exercise based on M. Fuchs, "Getting Your Organization Ready for Converting to International Financial Reporting Standards," *Workforce Management Online* [www.workforce.com], September 2009.

70. S. Terlep, "New CEO for Revived GM," *Wall Street Journal*, August 13, 2010, p. A1; D. Welch, "Ed Whitacre's Battle to Save GM from Itself," *Bloomberg BusinessWeek*, May 3–9, 2010, pp. 48–55; S. Terlep, "GM's Plodding Culture Vexes Its Impatient CEO," *Wall Street Journal*, April 7, 2010, pp. B1+; J. Smerd, "Back to the Drawing Board—Can A New Company Culture Save Motors?" *Workforce Management Online* [www.workforce.com], October 19, 2009; and N. King and S. Terlep, "GM Collapses into Government's Arms," *Wall Street Journal Online* [online.wsj.com], June 2, 2009.

71. M. Saltmarsh, "France Télécom Suicides Prompt an Investigation," *New York Times Online*, April 9, 2010; C. Stievenard, "France's Approach to Workplace Bullying," *Workforce Management Online* [www.workforce.com], March 2010; R. Bender and M. Colchester, "Morale Is Priority for France Télécom," *Wall Street Journal*, February 4, 2010, p. B2; The Associated Press, "Executive Quits After Suicides at France Télécom," *New York Times Online*, October 6, 2009; and D. Jolly and M. Saltmarsh, "Suicides in France Put Focus on Workplace," *New York Times Online*, September 30, 2009.

Chapter 7

1. J. Sangalang, "Potter Movie Stars Help Christen Wizarding World," *USA Today*, June 18, 2010, p. 6D; R. Searle, "Harry's World to Open in June," *Travel Weekly*, April 2, 2010, p. 16; Universal Orlando Resort News Release [http://media.universalorlando.com/harrypotter/news.php], March 25, 2010; K. Cushing, "What's the Attraction?" *Travel Weekly*, March 19, 2010, pp. 41–44; J. Clark, "Peek at Potter's World As It Takes Shape," *USA Today*, January 28, 2010, p. 8D; and "Universal Park Plans Potter Rides," *Wall Street Journal*, September 16, 2009, p. B5.

2. M. Trottman, "Choices in Stormy Weather," *Wall Street Journal*, February 14, 2006, p. B1+.

3. S. Minter, "The Season of Snap Judgments," *Industry Week*, May 2010, p. 6; and D. A. Garvin and M. A. Roberto, "What You Don't Know About Making Decisions," *Harvard Business Review*, September 2001, pp. 108–116.

4. "A Bold Alternative to the Worst 'Best' Practices," *BusinessWeek Online* [www.businessweek.com], September 15, 2009.

5. W. Pounds, "The Process of Problem Finding," *Industrial Management Review*, Fall 1969, pp. 1–19.

6. R. J. Volkema, "Problem Formulation: Its Portrayal in the Texts," *Organizational Behavior Teaching Review*, 11, No. 3 (1986–1987), pp. 113–26.

7. T. A. Stewart, "Did You Ever Have to Make Up Your Mind?" *Harvard Business Review*, January 2006, p. 12; and E. Pooley, "Editor's Desk," *Fortune*, June 27, 2005, p. 16.

8. J. Pfeffer and R. I. Sutton, "Why Managing by Facts Works," *Strategy & Business*, Spring 2006, pp. 9–12.

9. See A. Langley, "In Search of Rationality: The Purposes Behind the Use of Formal Analysis in Organizations," *Administrative Science Quarterly*, December 1989, pp. 598–631; and H. A. Simon, "Rationality in Psychology and Economics," *Journal of Business*, October 1986, pp. 209–224.

10. J. G. March, "Decision-Making Perspective: Decisions in Organizations and Theories of Choice," in A. H. Van de Ven and W.F. Joyce (eds.), *Perspectives on Organization Design and Behavior* (New York: Wiley-Interscience, 1981), pp. 232–233.

11. See P. Hemp, "Death by Information Overload," *Harvard Business Review*, September 2009, pp. 82–89; D. Heath and C. Heath, "The Gripping Statistic," *Fast Company*, September 2009, pp. 59–60; D. R. A. Skidd, "Revisiting Bounded Rationality," *Journal of Management Inquiry*, December 1992, pp. 343–347; B. E. Kaufman, "A New Theory of Satisficing," *Journal of Behavioral Economics*, Spring 1990, pp. 35–51; and N. M. Agnew and J. L. Brown, "Bounded Rationality: Fallible Decisions in Unbounded Decision Space," *Behavioral Science*, July 1986, pp. 148–161.

12. See, for example, G. McNamara, H. Moon, and P. Bromiley, "Banking on Commitment: Intended and Unintended Consequences of an Organization's Attempt to Attenuate Escalation of Commitment," *Academy of Management Journal*, April 2002, pp. 443–452; V. S. Rao and A. Monk, "The Effects of Individual Differences and Anonymity on Commitment to Decisions," *Journal of Social Psychology*, August 1999, pp. 496–515; C. F. Camerer and R. A. Weber, "The Econometrics and Behavioral Economics of Escalation of Commitment: A Re-examination of Staw's Theory," *Journal of Economic Behavior and Organization*, May 1999, pp. 59–82; D. R. Bobocel and J. P. Meyer, "Escalating Commitment to a Failing Course of Action: Separating the Roles of Choice and Justification," *Journal of Applied Psychology*, June 1994, pp. 360–363; and B. M. Staw, "The Escalation of Commitment to a Course of Action," *Academy of Management Review*, October 1981, pp. 577–587.

13. W. Cole, "The Stapler Wars," *Time Inside Business*, April 2005, p. A5.

14. See E. Dane and M. G. Pratt, "Exploring Intuition and Its Role in Managerial Decision Making," *Academy of Management Review*, January 2007, pp. 33–54; M. H. Bazerman and D. Chugh, "Decisions Without Blinders," *Harvard Business Review*, January 2006, pp. 88–97; C. C. Miller and R. D. Ireland, "Intuition in Strategic Decision Making: Friend or Foe in the Fast-Paced 21st Century," *Academy of Management Executive*, February 2005, pp. 19–30; E. Sadler-Smith and E. Shefy, "The Intuitive Executive: Understanding and Applying 'Gut Feel' in Decision Making," *Academy of Management Executive*, November 2004, pp. 76–91; and L. A. Burke and M. K. Miller, "Taking the Mystery Out of Intuitive Decision Making," *Academy of Management Executive*, October 1999, pp. 91–99.

15. C. C. Miller and R. D. Ireland, "Intuition in Strategic Decision Making: Friend or Foe," p. 20.

16. E. Sadler-Smith and E. Shefy, "Developing Intuitive Awareness in Management Education," *Academy of Management Learning & Education,* June 2007, pp. 186–205.

17. M. G. Seo and L. Feldman Barrett, "Being Emotional During Decision Making—Good or Bad? An Empirical Investigation," *Academy of Management Journal,* August 2007, pp. 923–940.

18. R. B. Briner, D. Denyer, and D. M. Rousseau, "Evidence-Based Management: Concept Cleanup Time?" *Academy of Management Perspective,* November 2009, p. 22.

19. T. Reay, W. Berta, and M. K. Kohn, "What's the Evidence on Evidence-Based Management?" *Academy of Management Perspectives,* November 2009, p. 5.

20. K. R. Brousseau, M. J. Driver, G. Hourihan, and R. Larsson, "The Seasoned Executive's Decision-Making Style," *Harvard Business Review,* February 2006, pp. 111–121.

21. Future Vision box based on D. Jones and A. Shaw, "Slowing Momentum: Why BPM Isn't Keeping Pace with Its Potential," *BPM Magazine,* February 2006, pp. 4–12; B. Violino, "IT Directions," *CFO,* January 2006, pp. 68–72; D. Weinberger, "Sorting Data to Suit Yourself," *Harvard Business Review,* March 2005, pp. 16–18; and C. Winkler, "Getting a Grip on Performance," *CFO-IT,* Winter 2004, pp. 38–48.

22. Leader Who Made a Difference box based on R. Sandomir, "Nets' Likely Owner Faces a Nation," *New York Times Online,* March 28, 2010; Y. Humber, "Your Handy Guide to Russia's Oligarchs," *BusinessWeek,* March 8, 2010, pp. 62–63; and M. Futterman, "Russia Billionaire to Buy NBA's Nets in Deal to Help Save Brooklyn Arena," *Wall Street Journal,* September 24, 2009, p. B1.

23. S. Holmes, "Inside the Coup at Nike," *BusinessWeek,* February 6, 2006, pp. 34–37; and M. Barbaro, "Slightly Testy Nike Divorce Came Down to Data vs. Feel," *New York Times Online* [www.nytimes.com], January 28, 2006.

24. C. M. Vance, K. S. Groves, Y. Paik, and H. Kindler, "Understanding and Measuring Linear–NonLinear Thinking Style for Enhanced Management Education and Professional Practice," *Academy of Management Learning & Education,* June 2007, pp. 167–185.

25. E. Teach, "Avoiding Decision Traps," *CFO,* June 2004, pp. 97–99; and D. Kahneman and A. Tversky, "Judgment Under Uncertainty: Heuristics and Biases," *Science* 185 (1974), pp. 1124–1131.

26. Information for this section taken from S. P. Robbins, *Decide & Conquer* (Upper Saddle River, NJ: Financial Times/Prentice Hall), 2004.

27. L. Margonelli, "How IKEA Designs Its Sexy Price Tags," *Business 2.0,* October 2002, p. 108.

28. P. C. Chu, E. E. Spires, and T. Sueyoshi, "Cross-Cultural Differences in Choice Behavior and Use of Decision Aids: A Comparison of Japan and the United States," *Organizational Behavior & Human Decision Processes,* vol. 77, no. 2 (1999), pp. 147–170.

29. By the Numbers box based on N. Tasler, "Prime Your Mind for Action," *BusinessWeek Online,* November 3, 2009; B. Dumaine, "The Trouble with Teams," *Fortune,* September 5, 1994, pp. 86–92; A. S. Wellner, "A Perfect Brainstorm," *Inc.,* October 2003, pp. 31–35; "Hurry Up and Decide," *BusinessWeek,* May 14, 2001, p. 16; J. MacIntyre, "Bosses and Bureaucracy," *Springfield, Missouri Business Journal,* August 1–7, 2005, p. 29; J. Crick, "Hand Jive," *Fortune,* June 13, 2005, pp. 40–41; and "On the Road to Invention," *Fast Company,* February 2005, p. 16.

30. S. Thurm, "Seldom-Used Executive Power: Reconsidering," *Wall Street Journal,* February 6, 2006, p. B3.

31. J. S. Hammond, R. L. Keeney, and H. Raiffa, *Smart Choices: A Practical Guide to Making Better Decisions* (Boston, MA: Harvard Business School Press, 1999), p. 4.

32. This discussion is based on E. W. Ford, W. J. Duncan, A. G. Bedeian, P. M. Ginter, M. D. Rousculp, and A. M. Adams, "Mitigating Risks, Visible Hands, Inevitable Disasters, and Soft Variables: Management Research That Matters," *Academy of Management Executive,* November 2005, pp. 24–38; K. H. Hammonds, "5 Habits of Highly Reliable Organizations: An Interview with Karl Weick," *Fast Company,* May 2002, pp. 124–128; and K. E. Weick, "Drop Your Tools: An Allegory for Organizational Studies," *Administrative Science Quarterly,* vol. 41, no. 2 (1996), pp. 301–313.

33. D. Ephron, "The Battle over the Battle of Fallujah," *Newsweek,* June 15, 2009, pp. 40–42; and K. Hall, "Konami Pulls Out of Fallujah Video Game," *BusinessWeek Online,* April 28, 2009.

34. Developing Your Creative Skill exercise based on S. P. Robbins, *Essentials of Organizational Behavior,* 8th ed. (Upper Saddle River, NJ: Prentice Hall, 2004); C. W. Wang and R. Y. Horng, "The Effects of Creative Problem Solving Training on Creativity, Cognitive Type, and R & D Performance," *R&D Management* (January 2002), pp. 35–46; S. Caudron, "Creativity 101," *Workforce* (March 2002), pp. 20, 24; and T. M. Amabile, "Motivating Creativity in Organizations," *California Management Review* (Fall 1997), pp. 42–52.

35. S. Schechner, S. Ovide, and L. A. E. Schuker, "O'Brien's Exit to Cost NBC $40 Million," *Wall Street Journal,* January 19, 2010, pp. B1+; T. Arango, "NBC's Slide to Troubled Nightly Punch Line," *New York Times Online,* January 17, 2010; B. Carter and B. Stelter, "NBC Confirms Its Late-Night Shake-Up," *New York Times Online,* January 11, 2010; A. Chozick and S. Schechner, "NBC Puts Jay Leno Back Into Old Time Slot," *Wall Street Journal,* January 11, 2010, pp. B1+; B. Hare, "For NBC, One Bad Decision After Another," *CNNMoney* [www.cnnmoney.com], January 9, 2010; and J. Poniewozik, "Jay Leno Is Shrinking Your TV," *Time,* September 14, 2009, pp. 38–46.

36. N. Clark, "Eurostar Criticized for Winter Breakdowns," *New York Times Online,* February 13, 2010; B. Mellor and S. Rothwell, "Eurostar Cuts Service Amid Cold Snap," *BusinessWeek,* January 11, 2010, p. 10; D. Jolly, "Eurostar Service Disrupted as Train Stalls in Channel Tunnel," *New York Times Online,* January 8, 2010; and G. Corkindale, "Does Your Company's Reputation Matter?" *BusinessWeek Online,* December 29, 2009.

Chapter 8

1. R. Ellinor, "Driven by a Desire to Help," *Supply Management,* February 18, 2010, p. 4; R. G. Edmonson, "Learning from Disaster," *The Journal of Commerce,* February 15, 2010, pp. 40–45; W. B. Cassidy, "Going the Extra Yard in Haiti," *The Journal of Commerce,* February 15, 2010, pp. 44–45; J. Kay, The Associated Press, "Donations for Haiti Relief Sit in Limbo Over Logistics," *Springfield, Missouri, News-Leader,* February 7, 2010, p. 3E; R. Pérez-Peña, "Haiti Added to 'Most Dangerous Paper Routes in the World,'" *New York Times Online,* February 1, 2010; and U.S. Department of Defense, "Logistics Agency Overnights 38,000 Maps for Haiti Relief," *FDCH Regulatory Intelligence Database,* January 20, 2010.

2. P. Sanders, "Boeing Says Flaw Slows 787 Assembly," *Wall Street Journal,* May 18, 2010, p. B1; Boeing News Release, "ANA Pilots First Customer Crew to Fly Boeing 787 Dreamliner" [boeingmediaroom.com], May 13, 2010; *Seattle Times* Business Staff, "25 More Orders Canceled for Boeing's New 787," *Seattle Times Online,* July 5, 2009; J. L. Lunsford, "Boeing Delays Dreamliner Delivery Again," *Wall Street Journal,* April 10, 2008, p. B3; and J. Teresko, "The Boeing 787: A Matter of Materials," *Industry Week,* December 2007, pp. 34–38.

3. See, for example, A. Ghobadian, N. O'Regan, H. Thomas, and J. Liu, "Formal Strategic Planning, Operating Environment, Size, Sector, and Performance," *Journal of General Management,* Winter 2008, pp. 1–19; F. Delmar and S. Shane, "Does Business Planning Facilitate the Development of New Ventures?" *Strategic Management Journal,* December 2003, pp. 1165–1185; R. M. Grant, "Strategic Planning in a Turbulent Environment: Evidence from the Oil Majors," *Strategic Management Journal,* June 2003, pp. 491–517; P. J. Brews and M. R. Hunt, "Learning to Plan and Planning to Learn: Resolving the Planning School/Learning School Debate," *Strategic Management Journal,* December 1999, pp. 889–913; C. C. Miller and L. B. Cardinal, "Strategic Planning and Firm Performance: A Synthesis of More Than Two Decades of Research," *Academy of Management Journal,* March 1994, pp. 1649–1685; N. Capon, J. U. Farley, and J. M. Hulbert, "Strategic Planning and Financial Performance: More Evidence," *Journal of Management Studies,* January 1994, pp. 22–38; D. K. Sinha, "The Contribution of Formal Planning to Decisions," *Strategic Management Journal,* October 1990, pp. 479–492; J. A. Pearce II, E. B. Freeman, and R. B. Robinson Jr., "The Tenuous Link between Formal Strategic Planning and Financial Performance," *Academy of Management Review,* October 1987, pp. 658–675; L. C. Rhyne, "Contrasting Planning Systems in High, Medium, and Low Performance Companies," *Journal of Management Studies,* July 1987, pp. 363–385; and J. A. Pearce II, K. K. Robbins, and R. B. Robinson, Jr.,

"The Impact of Grand Strategy and Planning Formality on Financial Performance," *Strategic Management Journal*, March–April 1987, pp. 125–134.

4. R. Molz, "How Leaders Use Goals," *Long Range Planning*, October 1987, p. 91.

5. C. Hymowitz, "When Meeting Targets Becomes the Strategy, CEO Is on Wrong Path," *Wall Street Journal*, March 8, 2005, p. B1.

6. McDonald's 2010 Proxy Statement [www.mcdonalds.com], May 24, 2010; and McDonald's Annual Report 2007 [www.mcdonalds.com], April 21, 2008.

7. S. Clifford and J. Creswell, "At Bloomberg, Modest Strategy to Rule the World," *New York Times Online*, November 15, 2009.

8. Nike [www.nikebiz.com/crreport/]; Deutsche Bank [www.db.com/en/content/company/mission_and_brand.htm]; and EnCana Corporate Constitution (2010) [www.encana.com].

9. See, for instance, J. Pfeffer, *Organizational Design* (Arlington Heights, IL: AHM Publishing, 1978), pp. 5–12; and C. K. Warriner, "The Problem of Organizational Purpose," Sociological Quarterly, Spring 1965, pp. 139–146.

10. J. D. Hunger and T. L. Wheelen, *Strategic Management and Business Policy*, 10th ed. (Upper Saddle River, NJ: Prentice Hall, 2006).

11. J. L. Roberts, "Signed. Sealed. Delivered?" *Newsweek*, June 20, 2005, pp. 44–46.

12. Leader Who Made a Difference box based on D. Lyons, "Jeff Bezos," *Newsweek*, December 28, 2009/January 4, 2010, pp. 85–86; B. Stone, "Can Amazon Be Wal-Mart of the Web?" *New York Times Online*, September 20, 2009; and K. Kelleher, "Why Amazon Is Bucking the Trend," *CNNMoney.com*, March 2, 2009.

13. J. Jusko, "Unwavering Focus," *Industry Week*, January 2010, p. 26.

14. P. N. Romani, "MBO By Any Other Name is Still MBO," *Supervision*, December 1997, pp. 6–8; and A. W. Schrader and G. T. Seward, "MBO Makes Dollar Sense," *Personnel Journal*, July 1989, pp. 32–37.

15. R. Rodgers and J. E. Hunter, "Impact of Management by Objectives on Organizational Productivity," *Journal of Applied Psychology*, April 1991, pp. 322–336.

16. E. A. Locke and G. P. Latham, "Has Goal Setting Gone Wild, or Have Its Attackers Abandoned Good Scholarship?" *Academy of Management Perspectives*, February 2009, pp. 17–23; and G. P. Latham, "The Motivational Benefits of Goal-Setting," *Academy of Management Executive*, November 2004, pp. 126–129.

17. L. Wayne, "P&G Sees the World as Its Client," *New York Times Online*, December 12, 2009.

18. For additional information on goals, see, for instance, P. Drucker, *The Executive in Action* (New York: HarperCollins Books, 1996), pp. 207–214; and E. A. Locke and G. P. Latham, *A Theory of Goal Setting and Task Performance* (Upper Saddle River, NJ: Prentice Hall, 1990).

19. By the Numbers box based on American Management Association, "Mercer Study Shows Workforce Priorities for 2010" [www.amanet.org], October 21, 2009; M. Weinstein, "Coming Up Short? Join the Club," *Training*, April 2006, p. 14; G. Kranz, "Workers Unprepared," *Workforce Management Online*, March 13, 2008; J. Yang, "Disaster Recovery Plan," *USA Today*, November 13, 2005, p. 1B; and American Management Association, "2003 Survey on Leadership Challenges" [www.amanet.org], April 24, 2004.

20. Several of these factors were suggested by R. K. Bresser and R. C. Bishop, "Dysfunctional Effects of Formal Planning: Two Theoretical Explanations," Academy of Management Review, October 1983, pp. 588–599; and J. S. Armstrong, "The Value of Formal Planning for Strategic Decisions: Review of Empirical Research," Strategic Management Journal, July–September 1982, pp. 197–211.

21. Brews and Hunt, "Learning to Plan and Planning to Learn: Resolving the Planning School/Learning School Debate."

22. R. Farzad, "AT&T's iMess," *Bloomberg BusinessWeek*, February 15, 2010, pp. 34–40.

23. A. Campbell, "Tailored, Not Benchmarked: A Fresh Look at Corporate Planning," *Harvard Business Review*, March–April 1999, pp. 41–50.

24. J. H. Sheridan, "Focused on Flow," *IW*, October 18, 1999, pp. 46–51.

25. A. Taylor III, "Hyundai Smokes the Competition," *Fortune*, January 18, 2010, pp. 62–71.

26. J. Vance, "Ten Cloud Computing Leaders," *IT Management Online*, May 26, 2010; A. Rocadela, "Amazon Looks to Widen Lead in Cloud Computing," *Bloomberg BusinessWeek Online*, April 28, 2010; and S. Lawson, "Cloud Computing Could Be a Boon for Flash Storage," *Bloomberg Business Week Online*, August 24, 2009.

27. Brews and Hunt, "Learning to Plan and Planning to Learn: Resolving the Planning School/Learning School Debate."

28. J. Ribeiro, "Wipro Sees Drop in Outsourcing Revenue," *Bloomberg BusinessWeek Online*, July 22, 2009; S. N. Mehta, "Schooled by China and India," *CNNMoney Online*, May 5, 2009; R. J. Newman, "Coming and Going," *US News and World Report*, January 23, 2006, pp. 50–52; T. Atlas, "Bangalore's Big Dreams," *US News and World Report*, May 2, 2005, pp. 50–52; and K. H. Hammonds, "Smart, Determined, Ambitious, Cheap: The New Face of Global Competition," *Fast Company*, February 2003, pp. 90–97.

29. G. Fairclough and V. Bauerlein, "Pepsi CEO Tours China to Get a Feel for Market," *Wall Street Journal*, July 1, 2009, p. B5.

30. See, for example, P. Tarraf and R. Molz, "Competitive Intelligence," *SAM Advanced Management Journal*, Autumn 2006, pp. 24–34; W. M. Fitzpatrick, "Uncovering Trade Secrets: The Legal and Ethical Conundrum of Creative Competitive Intelligence," *S.A.M Advanced Management Journal*, Summer 2003, pp. 4–12; L. Lavelle, "The Case of the Corporate Spy," *BusinessWeek*, November 26, 2001, pp. 56–58; C. Britton, "Deconstructing Advertising: What Your Competitor's Advertising Can Tell You About Their Strategy," *Competitive Intelligence*, January/February 2002, pp. 15–19; and L. Smith, "Business Intelligence Progress in Jeopardy," *Information Week*, March 4, 2002, p. 74.

31. S. Greenbard, "New Heights in Business Intelligence," *Business Finance*, March 2002, pp. 41–46; K. A. Zimmermann, "The Democratization of Business Intelligence," *KN World*, May 2002, pp. 20–21; and C. Britton, "Deconstructing Advertising: What Your Competitor's Advertising Can Tell You About Their Strategy," *Competitive Intelligence*, January/February 2002, pp. 15–19.

32. L. Weathersby, "Take This Job and ***** It," *Fortune*, January 7, 2002, p. 122.

33. D. Leonard, "The Corporate Side of Snooping," *New York Times Online*, March 5, 2010; B. Acohido, "Corporate Espionage Surges in Tough Times," *USA Today*, July 29, 2009, pp. 1B+; and B. Rosner, "HR Should Get a Clue: Corporate Spying is Real," *Workforce*, April 2001, pp. 72–75.

34. P. Lattman, "Hotel Feud Prompts Probe by Grand Jury," *Wall Street Journal*, October 7, 2009, p. A1+; "Starwood vs. Hilton," *Hotels' Investment Outlook*, June 2009, p. 14; R. Kidder, "Hotel Industry Roiled by Corporate Espionage Claim," *Ethics Newsline* [www.globalethicslorg/newsline]; Reuters, "Hilton Hotels Is Subpoenaed in Espionage Case," *New York Times Online*, April 22, 2009; T. Audi, "U.S. Probes Hilton Over Theft Claims," *Wall Street Journal*, April 22, 2009, p. B1; and T. Audi, "Hilton Is Sued Over Luxury Chain," *Wall Street Journal*, April 17, 2009, p. B1.

35. S. Bergsman, "Corporate Spying Goes Mainstream," *CFO*, December 1997, p. 24; and K. Western, "Ethical Spying," *Business Ethics*, September–October 1995, pp. 22–23.

36. A. Weintraub and A. Gerlin, "Lessons From the Pandemic That Wasn't," *Bloomberg BusinessWeek*, February 15, 2010, pp. 24–25; A. Fisher, "My Hypochondriac Boss Is Swine-Flu Crazy," *CNNMoney.com*, November 13, 2009; B. McKay and D. Mattioli, "Sick Time: Employers Gear Up for Swine Flu," *Wall Street Journal*, November 2, 2009, pp. B1+; and C. Prystay, M. Hiebert, and K. Linebaugh, "Companies Face Ethical Issues Over Tamiflu," *Wall Street Journal*, January 16, 2006, pp. B1+.

37. C. Herring, "Schools' New Math: The Four-Day Week," *Wall Street Journal*, March 8, 2010, pp. A1+.

38. The Associated Press, "Habitat for Humanity Gets $100 Million from Developer," *Wall Street Journal*, May 15, 2009, p. A5; G. Bluestein, The Associated Press, "Record Gift for Habitat for Humanity," *Springfield, Missouri, News-Leader*, May 15, 2009, p. 3B; The Associated Press, "Habitat for Humanity Gets $100 Million Gift," *MSNBC.com* [www.msnbc.msn.com], May 14, 2009; and "$100 Million Commitment Made to Habitat for Humanity by J. Ronald Terwilliger" [www.habitat.org], May 14, 2009.

39. D. Gross, "The Days the Earth Stood Still," *Newsweek,* May 3, 2010, pp. 46–48; D. Michaels, S. Schaefer Muñoz, and B. Orwall, "Airlines, in Flight Again, See Lesson in Crisis," *Wall Street Journal,* April 22, 2010, p. A14; "Volcano Delays Parts to BMW Factory," *USA Today,* April 20, 2010, p. 5B; J. W. Miller, "Detours for Perishable Goods," *Wall Street Journal,* April 20, 2010, p. A11; C. Jones and D. Reed, "Volcano's Burden Adds Up," *USA Today,* April 20, 2010, p. 2B; and S. Hargreaves, "Ash Cloud Grounds U.S. Produce, Fish, and Parts," *CNNMoney.com,* April 20, 2010.

Chapter 9

1. D. Mascai, "Most Influential Women in Technology," *Fast Company Online,* March 23, 2010; K. Rockwood, "The Teen Titan," *Fast Company,* December 2009/January 2010, p. 33; Eric Pankoke blog, "Interview with AddictingGames, Part 1" [www.iphonelife.com/blog], September 7, 2009; and "AddictingGames Launches Quikie Mini-Games for Verizon," *Telephone IP News,* June 2008, pp. 4–6.
2. B. Morris, "Chuck Schwab Is Worried About the Small Investor," *Bloomberg BusinessWeek,* May 31–June 6, 2010, pp. 58–64; P. Lattman and D. Kesmodel, "Pabst's New Owner Built Fortune on Old Brands," *Wall Street Journal,* May 26, 2010, pp. B1+; M. Helft and J. Wortham, "Facebook Bows to Pressure Over Privacy," *New York Times Online,* May 26, 2010; and D. MacMillan, "French E-tailer Vente-privee Designs an Expansion," *Bloomberg BusinessWeek Online,* May 24, 2010.
3. J. W. Dean, Jr. and M. P. Sharfman, "Does Decision Process Matter? A Study of Strategic Decision-Making Effectiveness," *Academy of Management Journal,* April 1996, pp. 368–396.
4. Based on A. A. Thompson Jr., A. J. Strickland III, and J. E. Gamble, *Crafting and Executing Strategy,* 14th ed. (New York: McGraw-Hill Irwin, 2005).
5. J. Magretta, "Why Business Models Matter," *Harvard Business Review,* May 2002, pp. 86–92.
6. S. Schechner, "Fewer Viewers Tune in for Cowell's 'Idol' Finale," *Wall Street Journal,* May 28, 2010, p. B7; B. Keveny, "Idol Ratings Take A Tumble," *USA Today,* May 4, 2010, p. 1D; R. Bianco, "Time for Producers to Fix 'Idol' Franchise," *USA Today,* May 4, 2010, p. 7D; and D. J. Lang, Associated Press *Springfield, Missouri News-Leader,* May 3, 2008, p. 4C.
7. M. Reimann, O. Schilke, and J. S. Thomas, "Customer Relationship Management and Firm Performance: The Mediating Role of Business Strategy," *Journal of the Academy of Marketing Science,* Summer 2010, pp. 326–346; J. Aspara, J. Hietanen, and H. Tikkanen, "Business Model Innovation vs. Replication: Financial Performance Implications of Strategic Emphases," *Journal of Strategic Marketing,* February 2010, pp. 39–56; J. C. Short, D. J. Ketchen Jr., T. B. Palmer, and G. T. M. Hult, "Firm, Strategic Group, and Industry Influences on Performance," *Strategic Management Journal,* February 2007, pp. 147–167; H. J. Cho and V. Pucik, "Relationship Between Innovativeness, Quality, Growth, Profitability, and Market Value," *Strategic Management Journal,* June 2005, pp. 555–575; A. Carmeli and A. Tischler, "The Relationships Between Intangible Organizational Elements and Organizational Performance," *Strategic Management Journal,* December 2004, pp. 1257–1278; D. J. Ketchen, C. C. Snow, and V. L. Street, "Improving Firm Performance by Matching Strategic Decision-Making Processes to Competitive Dynamics," *Academy of Management Executive,* November 2004, pp. 29–43; E. H. Bowman and C. E. Helfat, "Does Corporate Strategy Matter?" *Strategic Management Journal,* 22 (2001), pp. 1–23; P. J. Brews and M. R. Hunt, "Learning to Plan and Planning to Learn: Resolving the Planning School-Learning School Debate," *Strategic Management Journal,* 20 (1999), pp. 889–913; D. J. Ketchen Jr., J. B. Thomas, and R. R. McDaniel Jr., "Process, Content and Context; Synergistic Effects on Performance," *Journal of Management,* 22, no. 2 (1996), pp. 231–257; C. C. Miller and L. B. Cardinal, "Strategic Planning and Firm Performance: A Synthesis of More Than Two Decades of Research," *Academy of Management Journal,* December 1994, pp. 1649–1665; and N. Capon, J. U. Farley, and J. M. Hulbert, "Strategic Planning and Financial Performance: More Evidence," *Journal of Management Studies,* January 1994, pp. 105–110.
8. J. S. Lublin and D. Mattioli, "Strategic Plans Lose Favor," *Wall Street Journal,* January 25, 2010, p. B7.
9. R. E. Schmid, The Associated Press, *Springfield, Missouri News-Leader,* March 3, 2010, pp. 1A+; D. Leinwand, "Postal Service Seeks 5-Day Delivery," *USA Today,* March 2, 2010, p. 3A; and Wire Reports, "Postal Chief Calls for 5-Day Delivery to Save $3.5 Billion Yearly," *USA Today,* March 26, 2009, p. 4A.
10. You can see this document at the United States Postal Service Web site at [www.usps.com/strategicplanning/].
11. J. Wortham, "Cellphones Now Used More for Data Than for Calls," *New York Times Online,* May 13, 2010; S. Murray, "Grads Head to College in Record Numbers," *Wall Street Journal,* April 28, 2010, p. A6; and S. Rosenbloom, "Calorie Data to Be Posted at Most Chains," *New York Times Online,* March 23, 2010.
12. C. K. Prahalad and G. Hamel, "The Core Competence of the Corporation," *Harvard Business Review,* May–June 1990, pp. 79–91.
13. Leader Who Made a Difference box based on G. Colvin, "Ursula Burns," *Fortune,* May 3, 2010, pp. 96–102; E. G. Graves, Jr., "Taking the Reins of Opportunity," *Black Enterprise,* February 2010, p. 8; U. Burns, "Lead with Values," *Leadership Excellence,* February 2010, p. 7; and N. Byrnes, R. O. Crockett, and J. McGregor, "An Historic Succession at Xerox," *BusinessWeek,* June 8, 2009, pp. 18–22.
14. H. Quarls, T. Pernsteiner, and K. Rangan, "Love Your Dogs," *Strategy & Business,* Spring 2006, pp. 58–65; and P. Haspeslagh, "Portfolio Planning: Uses and Limits," *Harvard Business Review,* January–February 1982, pp. 58–73.
15. *Perspective on Experience* (Boston: Boston Consulting Group, 1970).
16. "100 Best Global Brands," *BusinessWeek,* September 28, 2009, pp. 50–56.
17. J. B. Barney, "Looking Inside for Competitive Advantage," *Academy of Management Executive,* November 1995, pp. 49–61; M. A. Peteraf, "The Cornerstones of Competitive Advantage: A Resource-Based View," *Strategic Management Journal,* March 1993, pp. 179–191; J. Barney, "Firm Resources and Sustained Competitive Advantage," *Journal of Management* 17, No. 1 (1991), pp. 99–120; M. E. Porter, *Competitive Advantage: Creating and Sustaining Superior Performance* (New York: Free Press, 1985); and R. Rumelt, "Towards a Strategic Theory of the Firm," in R. Lamb (ed.), *Competitive Strategic Management* (Upper Saddle River, NJ: Prentice Hall, 1984), pp. 556–570.
18. R. D. Spitzer, "TQM: The Only Source of Sustainable Competitive Advantage," *Quality Progress,* June 1993, pp. 59–64; T. C. Powell, "Total Quality Management as Competitive Advantage: A Review and Empirical Study," *Strategic Management Journal,* January 1995, pp. 15–37; and N. A. Shepherd, "Competitive Advantage: Mapping Change and the Role of the Quality Manager of the Future," *Annual Quality Congress,* May 1998, pp. 53–60.
19. See special issue of *Academy of Management Review* devoted to TQM, July 1994, pp. 390–584; B. Voss, "Quality's Second Coming," *Journal of Business Strategy,* March–April 1994, pp. 42–46; R. Krishnan, A. B. Shani, R. M. Grant, and R. Baer, "In Search of Quality Improvement Problems of Design and Implementation," *Academy of Management Executive,* November 1993, pp. 7–20; C. A. Barclay, "Quality Strategy and TQM Policies: Empirical Evidence," *Management International Review,* Special Issue 1993, pp. 87–98; and R. Jacob, "TQM: More Than a Dying Fad?" *Fortune,* October 18, 1993, pp. 66–72; and R. J. Schonenberger, "Is Strategy Strategic? Impact of Total Quality Management on Strategy," *Academy of Management Executive,* August 1992, pp. 80–87.
20. See, for example, A. Brandenburger, "Porter's Added Value: High Indeed!" *Academy of Management Executive,* May 2002, pp. 58–60; N. Argyres and A. M. McGahan, "An Interview with Michael Porter," *Academy of Management Executive,* May 2002, pp. 43–52; D. F. Jennings and J. R. Lumpkin, "Insights between Environmental Scanning Activities and Porter's Generic Strategies: An Empirical Analysis," *Strategic Management Journal,* 18, No. 4 (1992), pp. 791–803; I. Bamberger, "Developing Competitive Advantage in Small and Medium-Sized Firms," *Long Range Planning,* October 1989, pp. 80–88; C. W. L. Hill, "Differentiation versus Low Cost or Differentiation and Low Cost: A Contingency Framework," *Academy of Management Review,* July 1988, pp. 401–412; A. I. Murray, "A Contingency View of Porter's 'Generic Strategies,'" *Academy of Management Review,* July 1988, pp. 390–400; M. E. Porter, "From Competitive Advantage to Corporate Strategy," *Harvard Business Review,* May–June 1987, pp. 43–59; G. G. Dess

and P. S. Davis, "Porter's (1980) Generic Strategies and Performance: An Empirical Examination with American Data—Part II: Performance Implications," *Organization Studies*, No. 3 (1986), pp. 255–261; G. G. Dess and P. S. Davis, "Porter's (1980) Generic Strategies and Performance: An Empirical Examination with American Data—Part I: Testing Porter," *Organization Studies*, no. 1 (1986), pp. 37–55; G. G. Dess and P. S. Davis, "Porter's (1980) Generic Strategies as Determinants of Strategic Group Membership and Organizational Performance," *Academy of Management Journal*, September 1984, pp. 467–488; Porter, *Competitive Advantage: Creating and Sustaining Superior Performance*; and M. E. Porter, *Competitive Strategy: Techniques for Analyzing Industries and Competitors* (New York: Free Press, 1980).

21. By the Numbers box based on M. E. Mangelsdorf, "Interview with Dr. Peter Weill: Getting an Edge from IT," *Wall Street Journal*, November 30, 2009, p. R2; M. E. Raynor, M. Ahmed, and A. D. Henderson, "Are 'Great' Companies Just Lucky?" *Harvard Business Review*, April 2009, pp. 18–19; J. Yang and M. E. Mullins, "Employee's Concerns in Mergers and Acquisitions," *USA Today*, June 6, 2007, p. 1B; and J. Choi, D. Lovallo, and A. Tarasova, "Better Strategy for Business Units: A McKinsey Global Survey," *The McKinsey Quarterly Online* [www.mckinseyquarterly.com], July 2007.

22. J. W. Bachmann, "Competitive Strategy: It's O.K. to Be Different," *Academy of Management Executive*, May 2002, pp. 61–65; S. Cappel, P. Wright, M. Kroll, and D. Wyld, "Competitive Strategies and Business Performance: An Empirical Study of Select Service Businesses," *International Journal of Management*, March 1992, pp. 1–11; D. Miller, "The Generic Strategy Trap," *Journal of Business Strategy*, January–February 1991, pp. 37–41; R. E. White, "Organizing to Make Business Unit Strategies Work," in H. E. Glass (ed.), *Handbook of Business Strategy*, 2d ed. (Boston: Warren Gorham and Lamont, 1991), pp. 1–24; and Hill, "Differentiation versus Low Cost or Differentiation and Low Cost: A Contingency Framework."

23. J. Plambeck, "As CD Sales Wane, Music Retailers Diversify," *New York Times Online*, May 30, 2010.

24. J. Weber, "Hunting for Growth," *BusinessWeek*, June 22, 2009, pp. 36–41.

25. S. Ghoshal and C. A. Bartlett, "Changing the Role of Top Management: Beyond Structure to Process," *Harvard Business Review*, January–February 1995, pp. 86–96.

26. R. Calori, G. Johnson, and P. Sarnin, "CEO's Cognitive Maps and the Scope of the Organization," *Strategic Management Journal*, July 1994, pp. 437–457.

27. R. D. Ireland and M. A. Hitt, "Achieving and Maintaining Strategic Competitiveness in the 21st Century: The Role of Strategic Leadership," *Academy of Management Executive*, February 1999, pp. 43–57.

28. J. P. Wallman, "Strategic Transactions and Managing the Future: A Druckerian Perspective," *Management Decision*, vol. 48, no. 4, 2010, pp. 485–499; D. E. Zand, "Drucker's Strategic Thinking Process: Three Key Techniques," *Strategy & Leadership*, vol. 38, no. 3, 2010, pp. 23–28; and R. D. Ireland and M. A. Hitt, "Achieving and Maintaining Strategic Competitiveness in the 21st Century: The Role of Strategic Leadership."

29. Lublin and Mattioli, "Strategic Plans Lose Favor."

30. Ibid.

31. K. Shimizu and M. A. Hitt, "Strategic Flexibility: Organizational Preparedness to Reverse Ineffective Decisions," *Academy of Management Executive*, November 2004, p. 44.

32. B. Barnes, "Across U.S., ESPN Aims to Be the Home Team," *New York Times Online*, July 20, 2010; P. Sanders and M. Futterman, "Competition Pushes Up Content Costs for ESPN," *Wall Street Journal*, February 23, 2009, pp. B1+; T. Lowry, "ESPN's Cell-Phone Fumble," *BusinessWeek Online*, October 30, 2006; and T. Lowry, "In the Zone," *BusinessWeek*, October 17, 2005, pp. 66–77.

33. E. Kim, D. Nam, and J. L. Stimpert, "The Applicability of Porter's Generic Strategies in the Digital Age: Assumptions, Conjectures, and Suggestions," *Journal of Management*, vol. 30, no. 5 (2004), pp. 569–589; and G. T. Lumpkin, S. B. Droege, and G. G. Dess, "E-Commerce Strategies: Achieving Sustainable Competitive Advantage and Avoiding Pitfalls," *Organizational Dynamics*, Spring 2002, pp. 325–340.

34. Kim, Nam, and Stimpert, "The Applicability of Porter's Generic Strategies in the Digital Age: Assumptions, Conjectures, and Suggestions."

35. J. Gaffney, "Shoe Fetish," *Business 2.0*, March 2002, pp. 98–99.

36. J. O'Donnell, "Hot Topic CEO's 2 Worlds," *USA Today*, March 22, 2010, pp. 1B+; *Fast Company* Staff, "The World's 50 Most Innovative Companies," *Fast Company*, March 2010, p. 105; E. Smith, "Disney Invites 'Goths' to the Party," *Wall Street Journal*, February 19, 2010, p. B8; K. Rockwood, "Rock Solid," *Fast Company*, September 2009, pp. 44–47; and K. High, "6 Questions with Betsy McLaughlin," *Billboard*, December 13, 2008, p. 10; "And the Winners Are . . . the 100 Best Companies To Work For," *Fortune*, January 11, 2006, pp. 89–113; K. L. Allers, "Retail's Rebel Yell," *Fortune*, November 10, 2003, pp. 137–142; and M. Boyle, "Rapid Growth in Tough Times," *Fortune*, September 2, 2002, p. 150.

37. J. Doebele, "The Engineer," *Forbes*, January 9, 2006, pp. 122–124.

38. S. Ellison, "P&G to Unleash Dental Adult-Pet Food," *Wall Street Journal*, December 12, 2002, p. B4.

39. C. Hausman, "Two Weeks After Trainer's Death, SeaWorld Ponders What to Do with Killer Whale," *Ethics Newsline* [www.globalethics.org/newsline], March 15, 2010; and M. Esterl, "Marine Park Operator Faces a Big Dilemma," *Wall Street Journal*, March 9, 2010, p. A6.

40. Materials for developing a business plan can be found at Small Business Administration, *The Business Plan Workbook* (Washington, DC, May 17, 2001); and on the Small Business Administration Web site [www.sba.gov]. In addition, readers may find software such as Business Plan Pro Software, available at [www.businessplanpro.com], useful.

41. D. Macsai, "The 100 Most Creative People in Business," *Fast Company*, June 2010, p. 72; C. Lauper, "Most Influential People: Artists: Lady Gaga," *Time*, May 10, 2010, p. 78; and J. Jurgensen, "The Lessons of Lady Gaga," *Wall Street Journal*, January 29, 2010, pp. W1+.

42. K. J. O'Brien, "Nokia Tries to Undo Blunders in U.S.," *New York Times Online*, October 19, 2009; M. Borden, "iPhone Envy? You Must Be Jöking," *Fast Company*, September 2009, pp. 66+; and A. Smith, "Nokia Plays It (Not Too) Smart," *Time Global Business*, August 24, 2009, pp. Global 1–2.

Chapter 9A

1. J. Brustein, "Star Pitchers in a Duel? Tickets Will Cost More," *New York Times Online*, June 27, 2010; and A. Satariano, "Innovator: Barry Kahn," *Bloomberg BusinessWeek*, May 24–May 30, 2010, p. 39.

2. J. Trotsky, "The Futurists," *US News & World Report*, April 19, 2004, pp. EE4–EE6.

3. F. Vogelstein, "Search and Destroy," *Fortune*, May 2, 2005, pp. 73–82.

4. S. C. Jain, "Environmental Scanning in U.S. Corporations," *Long Range Planning*, April 1984, pp. 117–128; see also L. M. Fuld, *Monitoring the Competition* (New York: John Wiley & Sons, 1988); E. H. Burack and N. J. Mathys, "Environmental Scanning Improves Strategic Planning," *Personnel Administrator*, April 1989, pp. 82–87; R. Subramanian, N. Fernandes, and E. Harper, "Environmental Scanning in U.S. Companies: Their Nature and Their Relationship to Performance," *Management International Review*, July 1993, pp. 271–286; B. K. Boyd and J. Fulk, "Executive Scanning and Perceived Uncertainty: A Multidimensional Model," *Journal of Management*, vol. 22, no. 1, 1996, pp. 1–21; D. S. Elkenov, "Strategic Uncertainty and Environmental Scanning: The Case for Institutional Influences on Scanning Behavior," *Strategic Management Journal*, vol. 18, 1997, pp. 287–302; K. Kumar, R. Subramanian, and K. Strandholm, "Competitive Strategy, Environmental Scanning and Performance: A Context Specific Analysis of Their Relationship," *International Journal of Commerce and Management*, Spring 2001, pp. 1–18; C. G. Wagner, "Top 10 Reasons to Watch Trends," *The Futurist*, March–April 2002, pp. 68–69; and V. K. Garg, B. A. Walters, and R. L. Priem, "Chief Executive Scanning Emphases, Environmental Dynamism, and Manufacturing Firm Performance," *Strategic Management Journal*, August 2003, pp. 725–744.

5. B. Gilad, "The Role of Organized Competitive Intelligence in Corporate Strategy," *Columbia Journal of World Business*, Winter 1989, pp. 29–35; L. Fuld, "A Recipe for Business Intelligence," *Journal of Business Strategy*, January–February 1991, pp. 12–17; J. P. Herring, "The Role of Intelligence in Formulating Strategy," *Journal of Business Strategy*, September–October 1992, pp. 54–60; K. Western, "Ethical

Spying," *Business Ethics,* September–October 1995, pp. 22–23; D. Kinard, "Raising Your Competitive IQ: The Payoff of Paying Attention to Potential Competitors," *Association Management,* February 2003, pp. 40–44; K. Girard, "Snooping on a Shoestring," *Business 2.0,* May 2003, pp. 64–66; and "Know Your Enemy," *Business 2.0,* June 2004, p. 89.

6. C. Davis, "Get Smart," *Executive Edge,* October–November 1999, pp. 46–50.

7. B. Ettore, "Managing Competitive Intelligence," *Management Review,* October 1995, pp. 15–19.

8. A. Serwer, "P&G's Covert Operation," *Fortune,* September 17, 2001, pp. 42–44.

9. B. Rosner, "HR Should Get a Clue: Corporate Spying Is Real," *Workforce,* April 2001, pp. 72–75.

10. Western, "Ethical Spying."

11. W. H. Davidson, "The Role of Global Scanning in Business Planning," *Organizational Dynamics,* Winter 1991, pp. 5–16.

12. T. Smart, "Air Supply," *US News & World Report,* February 28, 2005, p. EE10.

13. "Is Supply Chain Collaboration Really Happening?" *ERI Journal* [www.eri.com], January–February 2006; L. Denend and H. Lee, "West Marine: Driving Growth Through Shipshape Supply Chain Management, A Case Study," *Stanford Graduate School of Business* [www.vics.org], April 7, 2005; N. Nix, A. G. Zacharia, R. F. Lusch, W. R. Bridges, and A. Thomas, "Keys to Effective Supply Chain Collaboration: A Special Report from the Collaborative Practices Research Program," *Neeley School of Business, Texas Christian University* [www.vics.org], November 15, 2004; Collaborative, Planning, Forecasting, and Replenishment Committee Web site [www.cpfr.org], May 20, 2003; and J. W. Verity, "Clearing the Cobwebs From the Stockroom," *BusinessWeek,* October 21, 1996, p. 140.

14. See A. B. Fisher, "Is Long-Range Planning Worth It?" *Fortune,* April 23, 1990, pp. 281–284; J. A. Fraser, "On Target," *Inc.,* April 1991, pp. 113–114; P. Schwartz, *The Art of the Long View* (New York: Doubleday/Currency, 1991); G. Hamel and C. K. Prahalad, "Competing for the Future," *Harvard Business Review,* July–August 1994, pp. 122–128; F. Elikai and W. Hall, Jr., "Managing and Improving the Forecasting Process," *Journal of Business Forecasting Methods & Systems,* Spring 1999, pp. 15–19; L. Lapide, "New Developments in Business Forecasting," *Journal of Business Forecasting Methods & Systems,* Summer 1999, pp. 13–14; and T. Leahy, "Building Better Forecasts," *Business Finance,* December 1999, pp. 10–12.

15. J. Goff, "Start with Demand," *CFO,* January 2005, pp. 53–57.

16. L. Brannen, "Upfront: Global Planning Perspectives," *Business Finance,* March 2006, pp. 12+.

17. V. Ryan, "Future Tense," *CFO,* December 2008, pp. 37–42.

18. R. Durand, "Predicting a Firm's Forecasting Ability: The Roles of Organizational Illusion of Control and Organizational Attention," *Strategic Management Journal,* September 2003, pp. 821–838.

19. J. Katz, "Forecasts Demand Change," *Industry Week,* May 2010, pp. 26–29; A. Stuart, "Imperfect Futures," *CFO,* July–August 2009, pp. 48–53; C. L. Jain and M. Covas, "Thinking About Tomorrow," *Wall Street Journal,* July 7, 2008, p. R10+; T. Leahy, "Turning Managers into Forecasters," *Business Finance,* August 2002, pp. 37–40; M. A. Giullian, M. D. Odom, and M. W. Totaro, "Developing Essential Skills for Success in the Business World: A Look at Forecasting," *Journal of Applied Business Research,* Summer 2000, pp. 51–65; F. Elikai and W. Hall, Jr., "Managing and Improving the Forecasting Process;" and N. Pant and W. H. Starbuck, "Innocents in the Forest: Forecasting and Research Methods," *Journal of Management,* June 1990, pp. 433–460.

20. T. Leahy, "Turning Managers into Forecasters."

21. J. Hope, "Use a Rolling Forecast to Spot Trends," *Harvard Business School Working Knowledge* [hbswk.hbs.edu], March 13, 2006.

22. This section is based on Y. K. Shetty, "Benchmarking for Superior Performance," *Long Range Planning* vol. 1, April 1993, pp. 39–44; G. H. Watson, "How Process Benchmarking Supports Corporate Strategy," *Planning Review,* January–February 1993, pp. 12–15; S. Greengard, "Discover Best Practices," *Personnel Journal,* November 1995, pp. 62–73; J. Martin, "Are You as Good as You Think You Are?" *Fortune,* September 30, 1996, pp. 142–152; R. L. Ackoff, "The Trouble with Benchmarking," *Across the Board,* January 2000, p. 13; V. Prabhu, D. Yarrow, and G. Gordon-Hart, "Best Practice and Performance Within Northeast Manufacturing," *Total Quality Management,* January 2000, pp. 113–121; "E-Benchmarking: The Latest E-Trend," *CFO,* March 2000, p. 7; E. Krell, "Now Read This," *Business Finance,* May 2000, pp. 97–103; and H. Johnson, "All in Favor Say Benchmark!" *Training,* August 2004, pp. 30–34.

23. "Newswatch," *CFO,* July 2002, p. 26.

24. Benchmarking examples from the following: S. Carey, "Racing to Improve," *Wall Street Journal,* March 24, 2006, pp. B1+; D. Waller, "NASCAR: The Army's Unlikely Adviser," *Time,* July 4, 2005, p. 19; A. Taylor, III, "Double Duty," *Fortune,* March 7, 2005, p. 108; P. Gogoi, "Thinking Outside the Cereal Box," *BusinessWeek,* July 28, 2003, pp. 74–75; "Benchmarkers Make Strange Bedfellows," *Industry Week,* November 15, 1993, p. 8; G. Fuchsberg, "Here's Help in Finding Corporate Role Models," *Wall Street Journal,* June 1, 1993, p. B1; and A. Tanzer, "Studying at the Feet of the Masters," *Forbes,* May 10, 1993, pp. 43–44.

25. E. Krell, "The Case Against Budgeting," *Business Finance,* July 2003, pp. 20–25; J. Hope and R. Fraser, "Who Needs Budgets?" *Harvard Business Review,* February 2003, pp. 108–115; T. Leahy, "The Top 10 Traps of Budgeting," *Business Finance,* November 2001, pp. 20–26; T. Leahy, "Necessary Evil," *Business Finance,* November 1999, pp. 41–45; J. Fanning, "Businesses Languishing in a Budget Comfort Zone?" *Management Accounting,* July/August 1999, p. 8; "Budgeting Processes: Inefficiency or Inadequate?" *Management Accounting,* February 1999, p. 5; A. Kennedy and D. Dugdale, "Getting the Most From Budgeting," *Management Accounting,* February 1999, pp. 22–24; G. J. Nolan, "The End of Traditional Budgeting," *Bank Accounting & Finance,* Summer 1998, pp. 29–36; and J. Mariotti, "Surviving the Dreaded Budget Process," *IW,* August 17, 1998, p. 150.

26. See, for example, S. Stiansen, "Breaking Even," *Success,* November 1988, p. 16.

27. S. E. Barndt and D. W. Carvey, *Essentials of Operations Management* (Upper Saddle River, NJ: Prentice Hall, 1982), p. 134.

28. E. E. Adam Jr. and R. J. Ebert, *Production and Operations Management,* 5th ed. (Upper Saddle River, NJ: Prentice Hall, 1992), p. 333.

29. See, for instance, C. Benko and F. W. McFarlan, *Connecting the Dots: Aligning Projects with Objectives in Unpredictable Times* (Boston, MA: Harvard Business School Press, 2003); M. W. Lewis, M. A. Welsh, G. E. Dehler, and S. G. Green, "Product Development Tensions: Exploring Contrasting Styles of Project Management," *Academy of Management Journal,* June 2002, pp. 546–564; C. E. Gray and E. W. Larsen, *Project Management: The Managerial Process* (Columbus, OH: McGraw-Hill Higher Education, 2000); J. Davidson Frame, *Project Management Competence: Building Key Skills for Individuals, Teams, and Organizations* (San Francisco, CA: Jossey-Bass, 1999).

30. For more information, see Project Management Software Directory [http://infogoal.com/pmc/pmcswr.htm].

31. D. Zielinski, "Soft Skills, Hard Truth," *Training,* July 2005, pp. 19–23.

32. H. Collingwood, "Best Kept Secrets of the World's Best Companies: Secret 05, Bad News Folders," *Business 2.0,* April 2006, p. 84.

33. G. Colvin, "An Executive Risk Handbook," *Fortune,* October 3, 2005, pp. 69–70; A. Long and A. Weiss, "Using Scenario Planning to Manage Short-Term Uncertainty," *Outward Insights* [www.outwardinsights.com], 2005; B. Fiora, "Use Early Warning to Strengthen Scenario Planning," *Outward Insights* [www.outwardinsights.com], 2003; L. Fahey, "Scenario Learning," *Management Review,* March 2000, pp. 29–34; S. Caudron, "Frontview Mirror," *Business Finance,* December 1999, pp. 24–30; and J. R. Garber, "What if…?," *Forbes,* November 2, 1998, pp. 76–79.

34. S. Caudron, "Frontview Mirror," p. 30.

Chapter 10

1. P. Loftus, "Eli Lilly Will Take New Path," *Wall Street Journal,* June 8, 2010, p. B6; J. Miller, "The Lilly Way," *Pharmaceutical Technology,* May 2010, pp. 82–84; L. Lallos, "Retired—But in the Game," *Bloomberg BusinessWeek,* April 25, 2010, p. 62; A. Weintraub and M. Tirrell, "Eli Lilly's Drug Assembly Line," *Bloomberg BusinessWeek,* March 8, 2010, pp. 56–57; J. D. Rockoff, "Lilly Taps Contractors to Revive Pipeline," *Wall Street Journal,* January 5, 2010, pp. B1+;

J. Pepitone, "Eli Lilly to Cut 5,500 Jobs," *CNNMoney.com,* September 14, 2009; and P. Loftus, "Lilly to Revamp, Cut Jobs as Patents Expire," *Wall Street Journal,* May 15, 2009, p. B1.

2. B. Fenwick, "Oklahoma Factory Turns Out US Bombs Used in Iraq," *Planet Ark* [www.planetark.com], November 4, 2003; A. Meyer, "Peeking Inside the Nation's Bomb Factory," *KFOR TV* [www.kfor.com], February 27, 2003; G. Tuchman, "Inside America's Bomb Factory," *CNN* [cnn.usnews.com], December 5, 2002; and C. Fishman, "Boomtown, U.S.A.," *Fast Company,* June 2002, pp. 106–114.

3. D. Hudepohl, "Finesse a Flexible Work Schedule," *Wall Street Journal,* February 19, 2008, p. B8.

4. See, for example, R. L. Daft, *Organization Theory and Design,* 10th ed. (Mason, OH: South-Western College Publishing), 2009.

5. S. Peterson, Associated Press, "Wilson Sporting Goods Football Factory" [www.chron.com], February 3, 2010; T. Arbel, Associated Press, "Factory Activity Fuels Economic Recovery," *OnlineAthens Banner-Herald* [www.onlineathens.com], February 2, 2010; and M. Hiestand, "Making a Stamp on Football," *USA Today,* January 25, 2005, pp. 1C+.

6. S. E. Humphrey, J. D. Nahrgang, and F. P. Morgeson, "Integrating Motivational, Social, and Contextual Work Design Features: A Meta-Analytic Summary and Theoretical Expansion of the Work Design Literature," *Journal of Applied Psychology,* September 2007, pp. 1332–1356.

7. D. Drickhamer, "Moving Man," *IW,* December 2002, pp. 44–46.

8. For a discussion of authority, see W. A. Kahn and K. E. Kram, "Authority at Work: Internal Models and Their Organizational Consequences," *Academy of Management Review,* January 1994, pp. 17–50.

9. C. I. Barnard, *The Functions of the Executive,* 30th Anniversary Edition (Cambridge, MA: Harvard University Press, 1968), pp. 165–166.

10. E. P. Gunn, "Who's the Boss?" *Smart Money,* April 2003, p. 121.

11. R. Ashkenas, "Simplicity-Minded Management," *Harvard Business Review,* December 2007, pp. 101–109; and P. Glader, "It's Not Easy Being Lean," *Wall Street Journal,* June 19, 2006, pp. B1+.

12. R. C. Morais, "The Old Lady Is Burning Rubber," *Forbes,* November 26, 2007, pp. 146–150.

13. D. Van Fleet, "Span of Management Research and Issues," *Academy of Management Journal,* September 1983, pp. 546–552.

14. G. Anders, "Overseeing More Employees—With Fewer Managers," *Wall Street Journal,* March 24, 2008, p. B6.

15. Henri Fayol, *General and Industrial Management,* trans. C. Storrs (London: Pitman Publishing, 1949), pp. 19–42.

16. J. Zabojnik, "Centralized and Decentralized Decision Making in Organizations," *Journal of Labor Economics,* January 2002, pp. 1–22.

17. See, for example, H. Mintzberg, *Power In and Around Organizations* (Upper Saddle River, NJ: Prentice Hall, 1983); and J. Child, *Organization: A Guide to Problems and Practices* (London: Kaiser & Row, 1984).

18. See P. Kenis and D. Knoke, "How Organizational Field Networks Shape InterOrganizational Tie-Formation Rates," *Academy of Management Review* (April 2002), pp. 275–293.

19. A. D. Amar, C. Hentrich, and V. Hlupic, "To Be a Better Leader, Give Up Authority," *Harvard Business Review,* December 2009, pp. 22–24.

20. P. Siekman, "Dig It!" *Fortune,* May 3, 2004, pp. 128[B]–128[L].

21. J. Cable, "Operators Lead the Way," *Industry Week,* January 2010, p. 31.

22. E. W. Morrison, "Doing the Job Well: An Investigation of Pro-Social Rule Breaking," *Journal of Management,* February 2006, pp. 5–28.

23. Ibid.

24. By the Numbers Box based on P. Dvorak, "Firms Shift Underused Workers," *Wall Street Journal,* June 22, 2009, p. B2; M. Weinstein, "It's A Balancing Act," *Training,* May 2009, p. 10; J. Yang and A. Lewis, "Is Teleworking a Good Idea?" *USA Today,* October 28, 2008, p. 1B; Drive Time: More Employees Get to Work Remotely," *Workforce Management Online* [www.workforce.com], September 23, 2008; J. Yang and K. Gelles, "Working Remotely vs. In the Office," *USA Today,* April 24, 2008, p. 1B; A. R. Carey and S. Parker, "Workers Take Home Their Offices," *USA Today,* October 7, 2008, p. 1A.

25. M. Boyle, "A Leaner Macy's Tries Catering to Local Tastes," *Bloomberg BusinessWeek,* September 14, 2009, p. 13.

26. D. A. Morand, "The Role of Behavioral Formality and Informality in the Enactment of Bureaucratic versus Organic Organizations," *Academy of* *Management Review,* October 1995, pp. 831–872; and T. Burns and G. M. Stalker, *The Management of Innovation* (London: Tavistock, 1961).

27. D. Dougherty, "Re-imagining the Differentiation and Integration of Work for Sustained Product Innovation," *Organization Science* (September–October 2001), pp. 612–631.

28. R. D. Hof, "Yahoo's Bartz Shows Who's Boss," *BusinessWeek Online,* February 27, 2009; and J. E. Vascellaro, "Yahoo CEO Set to Install Top-Down Management," *Wall Street Journal,* February 23, 2009, p. B1.

29. A. D. Chandler, Jr., *Strategy and Structure: Chapters in the History of the Industrial Enterprise* (Cambridge, MA: MIT Press, 1962).

30. See, for instance, W. Chan Kim and R. Mauborgne, "How Strategy Shapes Structure," *Harvard Business Review,* September 2009, pp. 73–80; L. L. Bryan and C. I. Joyce, "Better Strategy Through Organizational Design," *The McKinsey Quarterly,* 2007, Number 2, pp. 21–29; D. Jennings and S. Seaman, "High and Low Levels of Organizational Adaptation: An Empirical Analysis of Strategy, Structure, and Performance," *Strategic Management Journal,* July 1994, pp. 459–475; D. C. Galunic and K. M. Eisenhardt, "Renewing the Strategy-Structure-Performance Paradigm," in B. M. Staw and L. L. Cummings (eds.), *Research in Organizational Behavior,* vol. 16 (Greenwich, CT: JAI Press, 1994), pp. 215–255; R. Parthasarthy and S. P. Sethi, "Relating Strategy and Structure to Flexible Automation: A Test of Fit and Performance Implications," *Strategic Management Journal,* 14, no. 6 (1993), pp. 529–549; H. A. Simon, "Strategy and Organizational Evolution," *Strategic Management Journal,* January 1993, pp. 131–142; H. L. Boschken, "Strategy and Structure: Re-conceiving the Relationship," *Journal of Management,* March 1990, pp. 135–150; D. Miller, "The Structural and Environmental Correlates of Business Strategy," *Strategic Management Journal,* January–February 1987, pp. 55–76; and R. E. Miles and C. C. Snow, *Organizational Strategy, Structure, and Process* (New York: McGraw-Hill, 1978).

31. See, for instance, R. Z. Gooding and J. A. Wagner III, "A Meta-Analytic Review of the Relationship between Size and Performance: The Productivity and Efficiency of Organizations and Their Subunits," *Administrative Science Quarterly,* December 1985, pp. 462–481; D. S. Pugh, "The Aston Program of Research: Retrospect and Prospect," in A. H. Van de Ven and W. F. Joyce (eds.), *Perspectives on Organization Design and Behavior* (New York: John Wiley, 1981), pp. 135–166; and P. M. Blau and R. A. Schoenherr, *The Structure of Organizations* (New York: Basic Books, 1971).

32. J. Woodward, *Industrial Organization: Theory and Practice* (London: Oxford University Press, 1965).

33. See, for instance, J. Zhang and C. Baden-Fuller, "The Influence of Technological Knowledge Base and Organizational Structure on Technology Collaboration," *Journal of Management Studies,* June 2010, pp. 679–704; C. C. Miller, W. H. Glick, Y. D. Wang, and G. Huber, "Understanding Technology-Structure Relationships: Theory Development and Meta-Analytic Theory Testing," *Academy of Management Journal,* June 1991, pp. 370–399; J. Hage and M. Aiken, "Routine Technology, Social Structure, and Organizational Goals," *Administrative Science Quarterly,* September 1969, pp. 366–377; J. D. Thompson, *Organizations in Action* (New York: McGraw-Hill, 1967); and C. Perrow, "A Framework for the Comparative Analysis of Organizations," *American Sociological Review,* April 1967, pp. 194–208.

34. D. M. Rousseau and R. A. Cooke, "Technology and Structure: The Concrete, Abstract, and Activity Systems of Organizations," *Journal of Management,* Fall–Winter 1984, pp. 345–361; and D. Gerwin, "Relationships between Structure and Technology," in P. C. Nystrom and W. H. Starbuck (eds.), *Handbook of Organizational Design,* vol. 2 (New York: Oxford University Press, 1981), pp. 3–38.

35. Leader Who Made a Difference box based on N. Reilly, "The Foundation for a New Prosperity," *Newsweek,* November 2, 2009, pp. B6+; D. Jones, "Reinvent Yourself and Your Company," *USA Today,* June 15, 2009, p. 3B; and "Ding Dong! Empowerment Calling," *Economist,* May 30, 2009, p. 70.

36. S. Rausch and J. Birkinshaw, "Organizational Ambidexterity: Antecedents, Outcomes, and Moderators," *Journal of Management,* June 2008, pp. 375–409; M. Yasai-Ardekani, "Structural Adaptations to Environments," *Academy of Management Review,* January 1986, pp. 9–21; P. Lawrence and J. W. Lorsch, *Organization and Environment: Managing Differentiation and Integration* (Boston: Harvard Business

School, Division of Research, 1967); and F. E. Emery and E. Trist, "The Causal Texture of Organizational Environments," *Human Relations,* February 1965, pp. 21–32.

37. S. Reed, "He's Brave Enough to Shake Up Shell," *BusinessWeek,* July 18, 2005, p. 53.

38. B. Rochman, "Banning the Bandz," *Time,* June 14, 2010, p. 99.

39. H. Mintzberg, *Structure in Fives: Designing Effective Organizations* (Upper Saddle River, NJ: Prentice Hall, 1983), p. 157.

40. R. J. Williams, J. J. Hoffman, and B. T. Lamont, "The Influence of Top Management Team Characteristics on M-Form Implementation Time," *Journal of Managerial Issues,* Winter 1995, pp. 466–480.

41. C. Hausman, "Technology Poses New Ethical Dilemmas," *Ethics Newsline Online,* June 14, 2010; and H. Yousuf, "BP Buys Google, Yahoo Oil Spill Search Terms," *CNNMoney.com* [money.cnn.com], June 7, 2010.

42. Based on S. P. Robbins and P. L. Hunsaker, *Training in Interpersonal Skills* (Upper Saddle River, New Jersey: Pearson Prentice Hall), 2009, pp. 173–188; S. Caudron, "Delegate for Results," *Industry Week,* February 6, 1995, pp. 27–30; and R. T. Noel, "What You Say to Your Employees When You Delegate," *Supervisory Management,* December 1993, p. 13.

43. B. Morris, "Chuck Schwab Is Worried About the Small Investor," *Bloomberg BusinessWeek,* May 31–June 6, 2010, pp. 58–64; L. Gibbs, "Chuck Would Like a Word With You," *Money,* January/February 2010, pp. 98–103; R. Markey, F. Reichheld, and A. Dullweber, "Closing the Customer Feedback Loop," *Harvard Business Review,* December 2009, pp. 43–47; and R. Farzad and C. Palmeri, "Can Schwab Seize the Day?" *Bloomberg BusinessWeek,* July 27, 2009, pp. 36–39.

44. M. Weinstein, "Retrain and Restructure Your Organization," *Training,* May 2009, p. 36; J. McGregor, "The Chore Goes Offshore," *BusinessWeek,* March 23 & 30, 2009, pp. 50–51; "Pfizer: Making It 'Leaner, Meaner, More Efficient,'" *BusinessWeek Online,* March 2, 2009; and A. Cohen, "Scuttling Scut Work," *Fast Company,* February 2008, pp. 42–43.

Chapter 11

1. A. Fox, "Pave the Way for Volunteers," *HR Magazine,* June 2010, pp. 70–74; G. Morse, "The Power of Unwitting Workers," *Harvard Business Review,* October 2009, p. 27; and S. Lohr, "Customer Service? Ask a Volunteer," *New York Times Online,* April 26, 2009.

2. N. Wingfield, "To Rebuild Windows, Microsoft Razed Walls," *Wall Street Journal,* October 20, 2009, p. B9.

3. Q. Hardy, "Google Thinks Small," *Forbes,* November 14, 2005, pp. 198–202.

4. See, for example, D. R. Denison, S. L. Hart, and J. A. Kahn, "From Chimneys to Cross-Functional Teams: Developing and Validating a Diagnostic Model," *Academy of Management Journal,* December 1996, pp. 1005–1023; D. Ray and H. Bronstein, *Teaming Up: Making the Transition to a Self-Directed Team-Based Organization* (New York: McGraw Hill, 1995); J. R. Katzenbach and D. K. Smith, *The Wisdom of Teams* (Boston: Harvard Business School Press, 1993); J. A. Byrne, "The Horizontal Corporation," *BusinessWeek,* December 20, 1993, pp. 76–81; B. Dumaine, "Payoff from the New Management," *Fortune,* December 13, 1993, pp. 103–110; and H. Rothman, "The Power of Empowerment," *Nation's Business,* June 1993, pp. 49–52.

5. J. Hyatt, "Engineering Inspiration," *Newsweek,* June 14, 2010, p. 44; T. McKeough, "Blowing Hot and Cold," *Fast Company,* December 2009–January 2010, p. 66; H. Walters, "Inside the Design Thinking Process," *BusinessWeek Online,* December 15, 2009; P. Kaihla, "Best-Kept Secrets of the World's Best Companies," *Business 2.0,* April 2006, p. 83; C. Taylor, "School of Bright Ideas," *Time Inside Business,* April 2005, pp. A8–A12; and B. Nussbaum, "The Power of Design," *BusinessWeek,* May 17, 2004, pp. 86–94.

6. R. L. Hotz, "More Scientists Treat Experiments as a Team Sport," *Wall Street Journal,* November 20, 2009, p. A23.

7. See, for example, G. G. Dess, A. M. A. Rasheed, K. J. McLaughlin, and R. L. Priem, "The New Corporate Architecture," *Academy of Management Executive,* August 1995, pp. 7–20.

8. For additional readings on boundaryless organizations, see Rausch and Birkinshaw, June 2008; M. F. R. Kets de Vries, "Leadership Group Coaching in Action: The Zen of Creating High-Performance Teams,"

Academy of Management Executive, February 2005, pp. 61–76; J. Child and R. G. McGrath, "Organizations Unfettered: Organizational Form in an Information-Intensive Economy," *Academy of Management Journal,* December 2001, pp. 1135–1148; M. Hammer and S. Stanton, "How Process Enterprises Really Work," *Harvard Business Review,* November–December 1999, pp. 108–118; T. Zenger and W. Hesterly, "The Disaggregation of Corporations: Selective Intervention, High-Powered Incentives, and Modular Units," *Organization Science,* 1997, vol. 8, pp. 209–222; R. Ashkenas, D. Ulrich, T. Jick, and S. Kerr, *The Boundaryless Organization: Breaking the Chains of Organizational Structure* (San Francisco: Jossey-Bass, 1997); R. M. Hodgetts, "A Conversation with Steve Kerr," *Organizational Dynamics,* Spring 1996, pp. 68–79; and J. Gebhardt, "The Boundaryless Organization," *Sloan Management Review,* Winter 1996, pp. 117–119. For another view of boundaryless organizations, see B. Victor, "The Dark Side of the New Organizational Forms: An Editorial Essay," *Organization Science,* November 1994, pp. 479–482.

9. J. Marte, "An Internship from Your Couch," *Wall Street Journal,* September 9, 2009, pp. D1+.

10. See, for instance, R. J. King, "It's a Virtual World," *Strategy+Business* [www.strategy-business.com], April 21, 2009; Y. Shin, "A Person-Environment Fit Model for Virtual Organizations," *Journal of Management,* December 2004, pp. 725–743; D. Lyons, "Smart and Smarter," *Forbes,* March 18, 2002, pp. 40–41; W. F. Cascio, "Managing a Virtual Workplace," *Academy of Management Executive,* August 2000, pp. 81–90; G. G. Dess, A. M. A. Rasheed, K. J. McLaughlin, and R. L. Priem, "The New Corporate Architecture"; H. Chesbrough and D. Teece, "When Is Virtual Virtuous: Organizing for Innovation," *Harvard Business Review,* January–February 1996, pp. 65–73; and W. H. Davidow and M. S. Malone, *The Virtual Corporation* (New York: Harper Collins, 1992).

11. StrawberryFrog Web site [www.strawberryfrog.com], June 15, 2010; S. Elliott, "A Pitch for Hummus Goes Nationwide," *New York Times Online,* June 6, 2010; "Over There," *Marketing Magazine,* February 9, 2009, p. 19; M. Maddever, "The New School: An Inconvenient Truth" [www.strategymag.com], April 2007; J. Ewing, "Amsterdam's Red-Hot Ad Shops," *BusinessWeek,* December 18, 2006, p. 52; and T. Howard, "Strawberry Frog Hops to a Different Drummer," *USA Today,* October 10, 2005 p. 4B.

12. R. Reisner, "A Smart Balance of Staff and Contractors," *BusinessWeek Online,* June 16, 2009; and J. S. Lublin, "Smart Balance Keeps Tight Focus on Creativity," *Wall Street Journal,* June 8, 2009, p. B4.

13. R. Merrifield, J. Calhoun, and D. Stevens, "The Next Revolution in Productivity," *Harvard Business Review,* June 2008, pp. 73–80; R. E. Miles et al., "Organizing in the Knowledge Age: Anticipating the Cellular Form," *Academy of Management Executive,* November 1997, pp. 7–24; C. Jones, W. Hesterly, and S. Borgatti, "A General Theory of Network Governance: Exchange Conditions and Social Mechanisms," *Academy of Management Review,* October 1997, pp. 911–945; R. E. Miles and C. C. Snow, "The New Network Firm: A Spherical Structure Built on Human Investment Philosophy," *Organizational Dynamics,* Spring 1995, pp. 5–18; and R. E. Miles and C. C. Snow, "Causes of Failures in Network Organizations," *California Management Review,* 1992, vol. 34, no. 4, pp. 53–72.

14. G. Hoetker, "Do Modular Products Lead to Modular Organizations?" *Strategic Management Journal,* June 2006, pp. 501–518; C. H. Fine, "Are You Modular or Integral?" *Strategy & Business,* Summer 2005, pp. 44–51; D. A. Ketchen, Jr. and G. T. M. Hult, "To Be Modular or Not to Be? Some Answers to the Question," *Academy of Management Executive,* May 2002, pp. 166–167; M. A. Schilling, "The Use of Modular Organizational Forms: An Industry-Level Analysis," *Academy of Management Journal,* December 2001, pp. 1149–1168; D. Lei, M. A. Hitt, and J. D. Goldhar, "Advanced Manufacturing Technology: Organizational Design and Strategic Flexibility," *Organization Studies,* 1996, vol. 17, pp. 501–523; R. Sanchez and J. Mahoney, "Modularity Flexibility and Knowledge Management in Product and Organization Design," *Strategic Management Journal,* 1996, vol. 17, pp. 63–76; and R. Sanchez, "Strategic Flexibility in Product Competition," *Strategic Management Journal,* 1995, vol. 16, pp. 135–159.

15. J. Fortt, "The Chip Company That Dares to Battle Intel," *Fortune,* July 20, 2009, pp. 51–56.

16. C. Hymowitz, "Have Advice, Will Travel," *Wall Street Journal,* June 5, 2006, pp. B1+.

17. S. Reed, A. Reinhardt, and A. Sains, "Saving Ericsson," *BusinessWeek,* November 11, 2002, pp. 64–68.

18. P. Engardio, "The Future of Outsourcing," *BusinessWeek,* January 30, 2006, pp. 50–58.

19. P. Sonne, "Tesco's CEO-to-Be Unfolds Map for Global Expansion," *Wall Street Journal,* June 9, 2010, p. B1; T. Shifrin, "Grocery Giant Tesco Is Creating a Storm in the US Market with Its Tesco in a Box Set of Systems" [www.computerworlduk.com], January 14, 2008; P. Olson, "Tesco's Landing," *Forbes,* June 4, 2007, pp. 116–118; and P. M. Senge, *The Fifth Discipline: The Art and Practice of Learning Organizations* (New York: Doubleday, 1990).

20. A. C. Edmondson, "The Competitive Imperative of Learning," *Harvard Business Review,* July–August 2008, pp. 60–67.

21. S. A. Sackmann, P. M. Eggenhofer-Rehart, and M. Friesl, "Long-Term Efforts Toward Developing a Learning Organization," *Journal of Applied Behavioral Science,* December 2009, pp. 521–549; D. A. Garvin, A. C. Edmondson, and F. Gino, "Is Yours a Learning Organization?" *Harvard Business Review,* March 2008, pp. 109–116; A. N. K. Chen and T. M. Edgington, "Assessing Value in Organizational Knowledge Creation: Considerations for Knowledge Workers," *MIS Quarterly,* June 2005, pp. 279–309; K. G. Smith, C. J. Collins, and K. D. Clark, "Existing Knowledge, Knowledge Creation Capability, and The Rate of New Product Introduction in High-Technology Firms," *Academy of Management Journal,* April 2005, pp. 346–357; R. Cross, A. Parker, L. Prusak, and S. P. Borgati, "Supporting Knowledge Creation and Sharing in Social Networks," *Organizational Dynamics,* Fall, 2001, pp. 100–120; M. Schulz, "The Uncertain Relevance of Newness: Organizational Learning and Knowledge Flows," *Academy of Management Journal,* August 2001, pp. 661–681; G. Szulanski, "Exploring Internal Stickiness: Impediments to the Transfer of Best Practice within the Firm," *Strategic Management Journal,* Winter Special Issue, 1996, pp. 27–43; and J. M. Liedtka, "Collaborating across Lines of Business for Competitive Advantage," *Academy of Management Executive,* April 1996, pp. 20–37.

22. J. Scanlon, "How 3M Encourages Collaboration," *BusinessWeek Online,* September 2, 2009.

23. "Meet the New Steel," *Fortune,* October 1, 2007, pp. 68–71.

24. J. Appleby and R. Davis, "Teamwork Used to Save Money; Now It Saves Lives," *USA Today* [www.usatoday.com], March 1, 2001.

25. C. Kauffman, "Employee Involvement: A New Blueprint for Success," *Journal of Accountancy,* May 2010, pp. 46–49; and R. L. Daft, *Management,* 9th ed. (Mason, OH: South-Western Cengage Learning, 2010), p. 262.

26. S. F. Gale, "The Power of Community," *Workforce Management Online,* March 2009.

27. C. G. Cataldo, "Book Review," *Academy of Management Learning & Education,* June 2009, pp. 301–303; E. Wenger, R. McDermott, and W. Snyder, *Cultivating Communities of Practice: A Guide to Managing Knowledge* (Boston: Harvard Business School Press, 2002), p. 4.

28. E. Wenger, R. McDermott, and W. Snyder, *Cultivating Communities of Practice: A Guide to Managing Knowledge* (Boston: Harvard Business School Press, 2002), p. 39.

29. R. McDermott and D. Archibald, "Harnessing Your Staff's Informal Networks," *Harvard Business Review,* March 2010, pp. 82–89.

30. M. Hemmasi and C. M. Csanda, "The Effectiveness of Communities of Practice: An Empirical Study," *Journal of Managerial Issues,* Summer 2009, pp. 262–279.

31. R. Jana, "How Intuit Makes a Social Network Pay," *BusinessWeek Online,* July 2, 2009.

32. R. A. Guth, "Glaxo Tries a Linux Approach," *Wall Street Journal,* May 26, 2010, p. B4.

33. J. Winsor, "Crowdsourcing: What It Means for Innovation," *BusinessWeek Online,* June 15, 2009.

34. S. Morrison, "Yahoo Chief Defends Her Site, Strategy," *Wall Street Journal,* June 25, 2010, p. B5.

35. D. Lavie, U. Stettner, and M. L. Tushman, "Exploration and Exploitation Within and Across Organizations," *Academy of Management Annals,* June 2010, pp. 109–155; H. Mitsuhashi and H. R. Greve, "A Matching Theory of Alliance Formation and Organizational Success: Complementarity and Compatibility," *Academy of Management Journal,* October 2009, pp. 975–995; D. Durfee, "Try Before You Buy," *CFO,* May 2006, pp. 48–54; B. McEvily and A. Marcus, "Embedded Ties and the Acquisition of Competitive Capabilities," *Strategic Management Journal,* November 2005, pp. 1033–1055; R. D. Ireland, M. A. Hitt, and D. Vaidyanath, "Alliance Management as a Source of Competitive Advantage," *Journal of Management,* 2002, vol. 28, no. 3, pp. 413–446; E. Krell, "The Alliance Advantage," *Business Finance,* July 2002, pp. 16–23; D. Sparks, "Partners," *BusinessWeek,* October 25, 1999, pp. 106–112; and D. Brady, "When Is Cozy Too Cozy?," *BusinessWeek,* October 25, 1999, pp. 127–130.

36. J. Marquez, "Connecting a Virtual Workforce," *Workforce Management Online,* February 3, 2009.

37. By the Numbers box based on J. Schramm, "At Work in a Virtual World," *HR Magazine,* June 2010, p. 152; J. Yang and A. Gonzalez, "Top Peeves About Someone Working from Home," *USA Today,* May 27, 2010, p. 1B; J. Jusko, "A Team Effort," *Industry Week,* January 2007, pp. 42+; P. Coy, M. Conlin, and M. Herbst, "The Disposable Worker," *Bloomberg BusinessWeek,* January 18, 2010, p. 36; "Employee Loyalty Increases During Recession," *Workforce Management Online,* March 9, 2010; "Study: Flexibility Programs Gain Ground in Hard Times," *Workforce Management Online,* July 23, 2009; and J. Hyatt, "Taking It Personally," *CFO,* July–August 2009, p. 29.

38. M. Conlin, "Home Offices: The New Math," *BusinessWeek,* March 9, 2009, pp. 66–68.

39. Ibid.

40. J. Marquez, "Connecting a Virtual Workforce."

41. S. Jayson, "Working At Home: Family-Friendly," *USA Today,* April 15, 2010, pp. 1A+; T. D. Hecht and N. J. Allen, "A Longitudinal Examination of the Work-Nonwork Boundary Strength Construct," *Journal of Organizational Behavior,* October 2009, pp. 839–862; and G. E. Kreiner, E. C. Hollensbe, and M. L. Sheep, "Balancing Borders and Bridges: Negotiating the Work-Home Interface via Boundary Work Tactics," *Academy of Management Journal,* August 2009, pp. 704–730.

42. J. T. Marquez, "The Future of Flex," *Workforce Management Online,* January 2010.

43. B. Walsh, "Thank God It's Thursday," *Time,* September 7, 2009, p. 58.

44. J. Sahadi, "Flex-time, Time Off—Who's Getting These Perks?" *CNNMoney.com,* June 25, 2007.

45. M. Arndt, "The Family That Flips Together . . ." *BusinessWeek,* April 17, 2006, p. 14.

46. S. Greenhouse, "Work-Sharing May Help Companies Avoid Layoffs," *New York Times Online,* June 16, 2009.

47. M. Korn, "Making a Temporary Stint Stick," *Wall Street Journal,* February 9, 2010, p. D6.

48. I. Speizer, "Special Report on Contingency Staffing—The Future of Contingent Staffing Could Be Like Something Out of a Movie," *Workforce Management Online,* October 19, 2009.

49. E. Frauenheim, "Special Report on HR Technology: Tracking the Contingents," *Workforce Management Online,* April 2010.

50. S. Greenhouse, "U.S. Cracks Down on 'Contractors' As a Tax Dodge," *New York Times Online,* February 18, 2010; and M. Orey, "They're Employees. No, They're Not," *BusinessWeek,* November 16, 2009, pp. 73–74.

51. M. Orey, "They're Employees. No, They're Not."

52. Ibid.

53. V. Smith and E. B. Neuwirth, "Temporary Help Agencies and the Making of a New Employment Practice," *Academy of Management Perspectives,* February 2009, pp. 56–72.

54. E. Frauenheim, "Special Report on HR Technology: Tracking the Contingents."

55. C. E. Connelly and D. G. Gallagher, "Emerging Trends in Contingent Work Research," *Journal of Management,* November, 2004, pp. 959–983.

56. K. Holland, "The Anywhere, Anytime Office," *New York Times Online,* September 28, 2008.

57. Leader Who Made a Difference box based on M. T. Hansen et al., "The Best-Performing CEOs in the World," *Harvard Business Review,* January–February 2010, pp. 104–113; P. Burrows, "Cisco's Extreme Ambitions," *BusinessWeek,* November 30, 2009, pp. 26–27; P. Burrows and A. Ricadela, "Cisco Seizes the Moment," *BusinessWeek,* May 25, 2009, pp. 46–48; and "Cisco Systems Layers It On," *Fortune,* December 8, 2008, p. 24.

58. E. Frauenheim, "Special Report on HR Technology: Tracking the Contingents"; A. P. McAfee, "How a Connected Workforce Innovates," *Harvard Business Review,* December 2009, p. 80; R. Yu, "Work Away from Work Gets Easier with Technology," *USA Today,* November 28, 2006, p. 8B; M. Weinstein, "GOing Mobile," *Training,* September 2006, pp. 24–29; C. Cobbs, "Technology Helps Boost Multitasking," *Springfield, Missouri News-Leader,* June 15, 2006, p. 5B; C. Edwards, "Wherever You Go, You're on the Job," *BusinessWeek,* June 20, 2005, pp. 87–90; and S. E. Ante, "The World Wide Work Space," *BusinessWeek,* June 6, 2005, pp. 106–108.

59. N. M. Adler, *International Dimensions of Organizational Behavior,* 5th ed. (Cincinnati, OH: South-Western), 2008, p. 62.

60. P. B. Smith and M. F. Peterson, "Demographic Effects on the Use of Vertical Sources of Guidance by Managers in Widely Differing Cultural Contexts," *International Journal of Cross Cultural Management,* April 2005, pp. 5–26.

61. C. Hausman, "Was AT&T's iPad Security Breach 'Ethical' Hacking?" *Ethics Newsline* [www.globalethics.org], June 21, 2010; S. E. Ante and B. Worthen, "FBI to Probe iPad Breach—Group That Exposed AT&T Flaw to See Addresses Says It Did a Public Service," *Wall Street Journal,* June 11, 2010, p. B1; and S. E. Ante, "AT&T Discloses Breach of iPad Owner Data," *Wall Street Journal Online,* June 9, 2010.

62. Based on H. Mintzberg, *Power In and Around Organizations* (Upper Saddle River, NJ: Prentice Hall, 1983), p. 24; P. L. Hunsaker, *Training in Management Skills* (Upper Saddle River, NJ: Prentice Hall, 2001), pp. 339–364; G. Ferris, S. Davidson, and P. Perrewé, "Developing Political Skill at Work," *Training,* November 2005, pp. 40–45; B. Uzzi and S. Dunlap, "How to Build Your Network," *Harvard Business Review,* December 2005, pp. 53–60; and B. Brim, "The Best Way to Influence Others," *Gallup Management Journal,* February 9, 2006 [http://gmj.gallup.com].

63. B. Vlasic, "Ford's Bet: It's a Small World After All," *New York Times Online,* January 10, 2010; D. Kiley, "Putting Ford on Fast-Forward," *BusinessWeek,* October 26, 2009, pp. 56–57; A. Taylor III, "Fixing Up Ford," *Fortune,* May 25, 2009, pp. 44–51; and M. Dola, "Ford Brings New Focus to Small-Car Market," *Wall Street Journal,* May 6, 2009, pp. B1+.

64. C. Edwards, "Hounding the Hackers," *BusinessWeek,* September 14, 2009, p. 30; A. Vance, "For Symantec and McAfee, 'Arms Race' for Security," *New York Times Online,* July 6, 2009; J. Cox, "Cyber Threats Get Personal," *CNNMoney.com,* September 18, 2007; N. Rothbaum, "The Virtual Battlefield," *Smart Money,* January 2006, pp. 76–80; S. H. Wildstrom, "Viruses Get Smarter—and Greedy," *BusinessWeek Online,* November 22, 2005; and S. Kirsner, "Sweating in the Hot Zone," *Fast Company,* October 2005, pp. 60–65.

Chapter 12

1. C. Dougherty, "A Happy Family of 8,000, But For How Long?" *New York Times Online,* July 12, 2009; J. Marquez, "Harsh Reality: HR on the Edge as Economic Downturn, Layoffs Generate Stress," *Workforce Management Online,* June 22, 2009; M. Luo, "For Small Employers, Shedding Workers and Tears," *New York Times Online,* May 7, 2009; M. Elias, "Those Doing Layoffs Can Feel the Pain," *USA Today,* April 23, 2009, p. 5D; K. O'Sullivan, "How to Talk About Layoffs," *CFO,* February 2009, pp. 44–51; and M. Cooper, "Handing Out the Pink Slips Can Hurt, Too," *New York Times Online,* February 1, 2009.

2. L'Oreal advertisement, *Diversity Inc.,* November 2006, p. 9.

3. A. Carmeli and J. Shaubroeck, "How Leveraging Human Resource Capital With Its Competitive Distinctiveness Enhances the Performance of Commercial and Public Organizations," *Human Resource Management,* Winter 2005, pp. 391–412; L. Bassi and D. McMurrer, "How's Your Return on People?" *Harvard Business Review,* March 2004, p. 18; C. J. Collins and K. D. Clark, "Strategic Human Resource Practices, Top Management Team Social Networks, and Firm Performance: The Role of Human Resource Practices in Creating Organizational Competitive Advantage," *Academy of Management Journal,* December 2003, pp. 740–751; J. Pfeffer, *The Human Equation* (Boston: Harvard Business School Press, 1998); J. Pfeffer, *Competitive Advantage Through People* (Boston: Harvard Business School Press, 1994); A. A. Lado and M. C. Wilson, "Human Resource Systems and

Sustained Competitive Advantage," *Academy of Management Review,* October 1994, pp. 699–727; and P. M. Wright and G. C. McMahan, "Theoretical Perspectives for Strategic Human Resource Management," *Journal of Management* 18, no. 1 (1992), pp. 295–320.

4. "Maximizing the Return on Your Human Capital Investment: The 2005 Watson Wyatt Human Capital Index® Report," "WorkAsia 2004/2005: A Study of Employee Attitudes in Asia," and "European Human Capital Index 2002," Watson Wyatt Worldwide (Washington, DC).

5. See, for example, C. H. Chuang and H. Liao, "Strategic Human Resource Management in Service Context: Taking Care of Business by Taking Care of Employees and Customers," *Personnel Psychology,* Spring 2010, pp. 153–196; M. Subramony, "A Meta-Analytic Investigation of the Relationship Between HRM Bundles and Firm Performance," *Human Resource Management,* September–October 2009, pp. 745–768; M. M. Butts et al., "Individual Reactions to High Involvement Work Practices: Investigating the Role of Empowerment and Perceived Organizational Support," *Journal of Occupational Health Psychology,* April 2009, pp. 122–136; L. Sun, S. Aryee, and K. S. Law, "High-Performance Human Resource Practices, Citizenship Behavior, and Organizational Performance: A Relational Perspective," *Academy of Management Journal,* June 2007, pp. 558–577; A. Carmeli and J. Shaubroeck, "How Leveraging Human Resource Capital with Its Competitive Distinctiveness Enhances the Performance of Commercial and Public Organizations," 2005; Y. Y. Kor and H. Leblebici, "How Do Interdependencies Among Human-Capital Deployment, Development, and Diversification Strategies Affect Firms' Financial Performance?" *Strategic Management Journal,* October 2005, pp. 967–985; D. E. Bowen and C. Ostroff, "Understanding HRM–Firm Performance Linkages: The Role of the 'Strength' of the HRM System," *Academy of Management Review,* April 2004, pp. 203–221; A. S. Tsui, J. L. Pearce, L. W. Porter, and A. M. Tripoli, "Alternative Approaches to the Employee-Organization Relationship: Does Investment in Employees Pay Off?" *Academy of Management Journal,* October 1997, pp. 1089–1121; M. A. Huselid, S. E. Jackson, and R. S. Schuler, "Technical and Strategic Human Resource Management Effectiveness as Determinants of Firm Performance," *Academy of Management Journal,* January 1997, pp. 171–188; J. T. Delaney and M. A. Huselid, "The Impact of Human Resource Management Practices on Perceptions of Organizational Performance," *Academy of Management Journal,* August 1996, pp. 949–969; B. Becker and B. Gerhart, "The Impact of Human Resource Management on Organizational Performance: Progress and Prospects," *Academy of Management Journal,* August 1996, pp. 779–801; M. J. Koch and R. G. McGrath, "Improving Labor Productivity: Human Resource Management Policies Do Matter," *Strategic Management Journal,* May 1996, pp. 335–354; and M. A. Huselid, "The Impact of Human Resource Management Practices on Turnover, Productivity, and Corporate Financial Performance," *Academy of Management Journal,* June 1995, pp. 635–672.

6. "Human Capital a Key to Higher Market Value," *Business Finance,* December 1999, p. 15.

7. M. Boyle, "Happy People, Happy Returns," *Fortune,* January 11, 2006, p. 100.

8. M. Luo, "$13 an Hour? 500 Sign Up, 1 Wins a Job," *New York Times Online,* October 22, 2009.

9. J. Clenfield, "A Tear in Japan's Safety Net," *Bloomberg BusinessWeek,* April 12, 2010, pp. 60–61.

10. "EU: Not Working," *Business Europe,* March 1, 2010, p. 1.

11. A. Kohpaiboon et al., "Global Recession: Labour Market Adjustment and International Production Networks," *ASEAN Economic Bulletin,* April 2010, pp. 98–120.

12. C. Isidore, "Say Goodbye to Full-Time Jobs with Benefits," *CNNMoney.com,* June 1, 2010; C. Rampell, "In a Job Market Realignment, Some Left Behind," *New York Times Online,* May 12, 2010; and P. Izzo, "Economists Expect Shifting Work Force," *Wall Street Journal Online,* February 11, 2010.

13. F. Hansen, "Jobless Recovery Is Leaving a Trail of Recession-Weary Employees in Its Wake," *Compensation & Benefits Review,* May/June 2010, pp. 135–136; J. Hollon, "Worker 'Deal' Is Off," *Workforce Management,* April 2010, p. 42; and "The New Employment Deal: How Far, How Fast, and How Enduring? The 2010 Global Workforce Study," *Towers Watson* [www.towerswatson.com], April 2010.

14. K. Niththyananthan, "BA, Union Set to Restart Talks," *Wall Street Journal Online,* June 1, 2010; The Associated Press, "No Deal in Talks on British Airway," *MSNBC.com,* May 27, 2010; D. Cameron and D. Michaels, "BA Crews Begin Walkout," *Wall Street Journal,* May 25, 2010, p. B2; and J. Brustein, "British Airways Cabin Crew Walks Out," *New York Times Online,* May 24, 2010.

15. K. Bradsher and D. Barboza, "Strike in China Highlights Gap in Workers' Pay," *New York Times Online,* May 28, 2010.

16. P. Korkki, "A Long Slide in Union Membership," *New York Times Online,* February 14, 2010.

17. "Union Membership in Canada – 2008," *Labour Program, Human Resources and Skills Development Canada* [www.labour.gc.ca], June 29, 2010; C. Barratt, "Trade Union Membership 2008," *Department for Business Enterprise and Regulatory Reform* [www.stats.berr.gov.au], April 2009; and J. Visser, "Union Membership Statistics in 24 Countries," *Monthly Labor Review,* January 2006, pp. 38–49.

18. C. Hausman, "Novartis Hit With Punitive Damages in Sex Discrimination Case," *Ethics Newsline* [www.globalethics.org/newsline], May 24, 2010.

19. S. Greenhouse, "Report Warned Wal-Mart of Risks Before Bias Suit," *New York Times Online,* June 3, 2010.

20. S. Armour, "Lawsuits Pin Target on Managers," *USA Today* [www.usatoday.com], October 1, 2002.

21. S. G. Stolberg and R. Pear, "Obama Signs Health Care Overhaul Bill, With a Flourish," *New York Times Online,* March 23, 2010.

22. B. Leonard, "Whistle-Blower Protections Tucked Into Health Care Reform Law," *HR Magazine,* June 2010, p. 16.

23. A. D. Wright, "Congress Weighs Rewards for Innovation in Work/Life Policies," *HR Magazine,* June 2010, p. 132.

24. J. Cable, "Is EFCA's Time Now?" *Industry Week,* April 2010, pp. 26–28; and M. Schoeff, Jr., "Employee Free Choice Act Supporters Press On Despite Longer Senate Odds," *Workforce Management Online,* January 20, 2010.

25. Leader Who Made a Difference box based on M. V. Rafter, "Microsoft Does a Benefits Makeover," *Workforce Management Online,* December 2009; M. Conlin, "The Return of the House Call," *BusinessWeek,* November 16, 2009, pp. 70–71; M. Conlin, "Making the Case for Unequal Pay and Perks," *BusinessWeek Online,* March 12, 2009; "Good Job, Microsoft," *The Bing Blog* [stanleybing.blogs.fortune.cnn.com], February 24, 2009; M. Conlin and J. Greene, "How to Make a Microserf Smile," *BusinessWeek,* September 10, 2007, pp. 56–59; M. Conlin, "Online Extra: Microsoft's Meet-My-Mood Offices," *BusinessWeek Online,* September 10, 2007; and M. Conlin and J. Greene, "Online Extra: Reshaping Microsoft's HR Agenda," *BusinessWeek Online,* September 10, 2007.

26. C. H. Loch, F. J. Sting, N. Bauer, and J. Mauermann, "How BMW Is Defusing the Demographic Time Bomb," *Harvard Business Review,* March 2010, pp. 99–102.

27. C. Rampell, "As Layoffs Surge, Women May Pass Men in Job Force," *New York Times Online,* February 6, 2009.

28. B. Tulgan, "Generation Y Defined: The New Young Workforce," *HR Tools Online* [www.hrtools.com/insights/bruce_tulgan], February 25, 2009.

29. M. A. Costonis and R. Salkowitz, "The Tough Match of Young Workers and Insurance," *New York Times Online,* June 11, 2010.

30. E. Seubert, "What Are Your Organization's Critical Positions," *Workforce Management Online,* December 2009; F. Hansen, "Strategic Workforce Planning in an Uncertain World," *Workforce Management Online,* July 2009; and J. Sullivan, "Workforce Planning: Why to Start Now," *Workforce,* September 2002, pp. 46–50.

31. N. Byrnes, "Star Search," *BusinessWeek,* October 10, 2005, pp. 68–78.

32. J. W. Boudreau and P. M. Ramstad, "Where's Your Pivotal Talent?" *Harvard Business Review,* April 2005, pp. 23–24.

33. B. Einhorn and K. Gokhale, "Bangalore's Paying Again to Keep the Talent," *Bloomberg BusinessWeek,* May 24–May 30, 2010, pp. 14–16; D. A. Thoppil, "Pay War Breaks Out as India's Tech Firms Vie for Talent," *Wall Street Journal,* April 27, 2010, p. B8; and C. Tuna, J. E. Vascellaro, and P-W. Tam, "Tech Sector in Hiring Drive," *Wall Street Journal,* April 16, 2010, pp. A1+.

34. A. S. Bargerstock and G. Swanson, "Four Ways to Build Cooperative Recruitment Alliances," *HRMagazine,* March 1991, p. 49; and T. J. Bergmann and M. S. Taylor, "College Recruitment: What Attracts Students to Organizations?" *Personnel,* May–June 1984, pp. 34–46.

35. J. R. Gordon, *Human Resource Management: A Practical Approach* (Boston: Allyn and Bacon, 1986), p. 170.

36. J. Walker, "Firms Invest Big in Career Sites," *Wall Street Journal Online,* June 8, 2010.

37. L. Petrecca, "With 3,000 Applications a Day, Google Can Be Picky," *USA Today,* May 19, 2010, p. 2B; and M. Helft, "In Fierce Competition, Google Finds Novel Ways to Feed Hiring Machine," *New York Times Online,* May 28, 2007.

38. K. Plourd, "Lights, Camera, Audits!" *CFO,* November 2007, p. 18.

39. S. Burton and D. Warner, "The Future of Hiring—Top 5 Sources for Recruitment Today," *Workforce Vendor Directory 2002,* p. 75.

40. See, for example, L. G. Klaff, "New Internal Hiring Systems Reduce Cost and Boost Morale," *Workforce Management,* March 2004, pp. 76–79; M. N. Martinez, "The Headhunter Within," *HR Magazine,* August 2001, pp. 48–55; R. W. Griffeth, P. W. Hom, L. S. Fink, and D. J. Cohen, "Comparative Tests of Multivariate Models of Recruiting Sources Effects," *Journal of Management,* vol. 23, no. 1, 1997, pp. 19–36; and J. P. Kirnan, J. E. Farley, and K. F. Geisinger, "The Relationship between Recruiting Source, Applicant Quality, and Hire Performance: An Analysis by Sex, Ethnicity, and Age," *Personnel Psychology,* Summer 1989, pp. 293–308.

41. J. McGregor, "Background Checks That Never End," *BusinessWeek,* March 20, 2006, p. 40.

42. A. Fisher, "For Happier Customers, Call HR," *Fortune,* November 28, 2005, p. 272.

43. J. Greenwald, "Judge Rules New York City Fire Department Exams Showed Racial Bias," *Workforce Management Online,* July 28, 2009.

44. A. Douzet, "Quality of Fill an Emerging Recruitment Metric," *Workforce Management Online,* June 24, 2010; and "Quality of Hire Metrics Help Staffing Unit Show Its Contribution to Bottom Line," *Society for Human Resource Management Online,* January 25, 2009.

45. A. Shadday, "Assessments 101: An Introduction to Candidate Testing," *Workforce Management Online,* January 2010; A. M. Ryan and R. E. Ployhart, "Applicants' Perceptions of Selection Procedures and Decisions: A Critical Review and Agenda for the Future," *Journal of Management,* vol. 26, no. 3 (2000), pp. 565–606; C. Fernandez-Araoz, "Hiring Without Firing," *Harvard Business Review,* July–August, 1999, pp. 108–120; A. K. Korman, "The Prediction of Managerial Performance: A Review," *Personnel Psychology,* Summer 1986, pp. 295–322; G. C. Thornton, *Assessment Centers in Human Resource Management* (Reading, MA: Addison-Wesley, 1992); I. T. Robertson and R. S. Kandola, "Work Sample Tests: Validity, Adverse Impact, and Applicant Reaction," *Journal of Occupational Psychology,* vol. 55, no. 3 (1982), pp. 171–183; E. E. Ghiselli, "The Validity of Aptitude Tests in Personnel Selection," *Personnel Psychology,* Winter 1973, p. 475; G. Grimsley and H. F. Jarrett, "The Relation of Managerial Achievement to Test Measures Obtained in the Employment Situation: Methodology and Results," *Personnel Psychology,* Spring 1973, pp. 31–48; J. J. Asher, "The Biographical Item: Can It Be Improved?" *Personnel Psychology,* Summer 1972, p. 266; and G. W. England, *Development and Use of Weighted Application Blanks,* rev. ed. (Minneapolis: Industrial Relations Center, University of Minnesota, 1971).

46. See, for example, Y. Ganzach, A. Pazy, Y. Ohayun, and E. Brainin, "Social Exchange and Organizational Commitment: Decision-Making Training for Job Choice as an Alternative to the Realistic Job Preview," *Personnel Psychology,* Autumn 2002, pp. 613–637; B. M. Meglino, E. C. Ravlin, A. S. DeNisi, "A Meta-Analytic Examination of Realistic Job Preview Effectiveness: A Test of Three Counterintuitive Propositions," *Human Resource Management Review,* vol. 10, no. 4 (2000), pp. 407–434; J. A. Breaugh and M. Starke, "Research on Employee Recruitment: So Many Studies, So Many Remaining Questions," *Journal of Management,* vol. 26, no. 3 (2000), pp. 405–434; and S. L. Premack and J. P. Wanous, "A Meta-Analysis of Realistic Job Preview Experiments," *Journal of Applied Psychology,* November 1985, pp. 706–720.

47. G. Kranz, "Tourism Training Takes Flight in Miami," *Workforce Management Online,* May 2010.

48. K. Gustafson, "A Better Welcome Mat," *Training,* June 2005, pp. 34–41.

49. M. Jokisaari and J-E. Nurmi, "Change in Newcomers' Supervisor Support and Socialization Outcomes After Organizational Entry," *Academy of Management Journal,* June 2009, pp. 527–544; D. G. Allen, "Do Organizational Socialization Tactics Influence Newcomer

Embeddedness and Turnover?" *Journal of Management,* April 2006, pp. 237–256; C. L. Cooper, "The Changing Psychological Contract at Work: Revisiting the Job Demands-Control Model," *Occupational and Environmental Medicine,* June 2002, p. 355; D. M. Rousseau and S. A. Tijoriwala, "Assessing Psychological Contracts: Issues, Alternatives and Measures," *Journal of Organizational Behavior,* vol. 19 (1998), pp. 679–695; S. L. Robinson, M. S. Kraatz, and D. M. Rousseau, "Changing Obligations and the Psychological Contract: A Longitudinal Study," *Academy of Management Journal,* February 1994, pp. 137–152.

50. By the Numbers box based on "Survey: 21 Percent of Job Seekers Dropped After Reference Checks," *Workforce Management Online,* June 23, 2010; J. Yang and A. Lewis, "Doing Jobs Without Training," *USA Today,* October 20, 2008, p. 1B; F. DiMeglio, "Dream Jobs: College Students Get Real," *Bloomberg BusinessWeek Online,* April 30, 2010; E. A. Grant, "Cookie Monster," *Fast Company,* June 2010, pp. 58–60; "Hiring for Fit," *Workforce Management Online,* May 28, 2010; J. Yang and A. Gonzalez, "Most Appealing Career Model for Me Is To...," *USA Today,* May 5, 2010, p. 1B; J. Yang and V. Salazar, "Most Neglected Grooming for Interviews," *USA Today,* December 31, 2009, p. 1B; and J. Yang and K. Simmons, "Preferred Résumé Format," *USA Today,* November 16, 2009, p. 1B.

51. See, for instance, E. G. Tripp, "Aging Aircraft and Coming Regulations: Political and Media Pressures Have Encouraged the FAA to Expand Its Pursuit of Real and Perceived Problems of Older Aircraft and Their Systems. Operators Will Pay," *Business and Commercial Aviation,* March 2001, pp. 68–75.

52. "A&S Interview: Sully's Tale," *Air & Space Magazine* [www.airspacemag.com], February 18, 2009; A. Altman, "Chesley B. Sullenberger III," *Time* [www.time.com], January 16, 2009; and K. Burke, Pete Donohue, and C. Siemaszko, "US Airways Airplane Crashes in Hudson River—Hero Pilot Chesley Sullenberger III Saves All Aboard," *New York Daily News* [www.nydailynews.com], January 16, 2009.

53. D. Heath and C. Heath, "The Power of Razzle-Dazzle," *Fast Company,* December 2009–January 2010, pp. 69–70.

54. T. Raphael, "It's All in the Cards," *Workforce,* September 2002, p. 18.

55. "Training Expenditures," *Training,* October/November 2009, p. 33.

56. B. Hall, "The Top Training Priorities for 2003," *Training,* February 2003, p. 40.

57. D. Heath and C. Heath, "The Power of Razzle-Dazzle."

58. J. McGregor, "The Midyear Review's Sudden Impact," *BusinessWeek,* July 6, 2009, pp. 50–52.

59. K. Sulkowicz, "Straight Talk at Review Time," *BusinessWeek,* September 10, 2007, p. 16.

60. J. Pfeffer, "Low Grades for Performance Appraisals," *BusinessWeek,* August 3, 2009, p. 68.

61. J. D. Glater, "Seasoning Compensation Stew," *New York Times,* March 7, 2001, pp. C1+.

62. This section based on R. I. Henderson, *Compensation Management in a Knowledge-Based World,* 10th ed. (Upper Saddle River, NJ: Prentice Hall, 2006).

63. M. P. Brown, M. C. Sturman, and M. J. Simmering, "Compensation Policy and Organizational Performance: The Efficiency, Operational and Financial Implications of Pay Levels and Pay Structure," *Academy of Management Journal,* December 2003, pp. 752–762; J. D. Shaw, N. P. Gupta, and J. E. Delery, "Pay Dispersion and Workforce Performance: Moderating Effects of Incentives and Interdependence," *Strategic Management Journal,* June 2002, pp. 491–512; E. Montemayor, "Congruence between Pay Policy and Competitive Strategy in High-Performing Firms," *Journal of Management,* vol. 22, no. 6 (1996), pp. 889–908; and L. R. Gomez-Mejia, "Structure and Process of Diversification, Compensation Strategy, and Firm Performance," *Strategic Management Journal,* 13 (1992), pp. 381–397.

64. M. Moskowitz, R. Levering, and C. Tkaczyk, "100 Best Companies to Work For," *Fortune,* February 8, 2010, pp. 75–88.

65. J. D. Shaw, N. Gupta, A. Mitra, and G. E. Ledford, Jr., "Success and Survival of Skill-Based Pay Plans," *Journal of Management,* February 2005, pp. 28–49; C. Lee, K. S. Law, and P. Bobko, "The Importance of Justice Perceptions on Pay Effectiveness: A Two-Year Study of a Skill-Based Pay Plan," *Journal of Management,* vol. 26, no. 6 (1999), pp. 851–873; G. E. Ledford, "Paying for the Skills, Knowledge and Competencies of Knowledge Workers," *Compensation and Benefits*

Review, July–August 1995, pp. 55–62; and E. E. Lawler III, G. E. Ledford Jr., and L. Chang, "Who Uses Skill-Based Pay and Why," *Compensation and Benefits Review,* March–April 1993, p. 22.

66. J. D. Shaw, N. Gupta, A. Mitra, and G. E. Ledford Jr., "Success and Survival of Skill-Based Pay Plans."

67. Information from Hewitt Associates Studies: "Aftermath of the Recession on 2009–2010 Compensation Spending," February 2010; "As Fixed Costs Increase, Employers Turn to Variable Pay Programs as Preferred Way to Reward Employees," August 21, 2007; "Hewitt Study Shows Pay-for-Performance Plans Replacing Holiday Bonuses," December 6, 2005; "Salaries Continue to Rise in Asia Pacific, Hewitt Annual Study Reports," November 23, 2005; and "Hewitt Study Shows Base Pay Increases Flat for 2006 With Variable Pay Plans Picking Up the Slack," Hewitt Associates, LLC [www.hewittassociates.com], August 31, 2005.

68. T. J. Erickson, "The Leaders We Need Now," *Harvard Business Review,* May 2010, pp. 63–66.

69. S. Thurm, "Recalculating the Cost of Big Layoffs," *Wall Street Journal,* May 5, 2010, pp. B1+; and J. Pfeffer, "Lay Off the Layoffs," *Newsweek,* February 15, 2010, pp. 32–37.

70. W. F. Cascio, "Use and Management of Downsizing as a Corporate Strategy," *HR Magazine,* June 2010, special insert; D. K. Datta, J. P. Guthrie, D. Basuil, and A. Pandey, "Causes and Effects of Employee Downsizing: A Review and Synthesis," *Journal of Management,* January 2010, pp. 281–348; B. Conaty, "Cutbacks: Don't Neglect the Survivors," *Bloomberg BusinessWeek,* January 11, 2010, p. 68; and P. Korkki, "Accentuating the Positive After a Layoff," *New York Times Online,* August 16, 2009;

71. R. Ceniceros, "Court Finds McDonald's Liable in Employee's Sexual Assault Case," *Workforce Management Online,* November 25, 2009.

72. U.S. Equal Employment Opportunity Commission, "Sexual Harassment Charges" [www1.eeoc.gov//eeoc/statistics/], July 1, 2010; and D. Mattioli, "More Men Make Harassment Claims," *Wall Street Journal,* March 24, 2010, p. D1.

73. A. B. Fisher, "Sexual Harassment, What to Do," *Fortune,* August 23, 1993, pp. 84–88.

74. M. Velasquez, "Sexual Harassment Today: An Update—Looking Back and Looking Forward," *Diversity Training Group* [www.diversitydtg.com], 2004.

75. "Quick Takes: Sex Discrimination and Sexual Harassment," *Catalyst* [www.catalyst.org], November 9, 2007; P. M. Buhler, "The Manager's Role in Preventing Sexual Harassment," *Supervision,* April 1999, p. 18; and "Cost of Sexual Harassment in the U.S.," *The Webb Report: A Newsletter on Sexual Harassment* (Seattle, WA: Premier Publishing, Ltd.), January 1994, pp. 4–7, and April 1994, pp. 2–5.

76. "Effects of Sexual Harassment," *Stop Violence Against Women* [www.stopvaw.org], May 9, 2007; and V. Di Martino, H. Hoel, and C. L. Cooper, "Preventing Violence and Harassment in the Workplace," *European Foundation for the Improvement of Living and Working Conditions,* 2003, p. 39.

77. The Associated Press, "Corruption, Sexual Harassment Charges Cloud Oxford Debating Club Presidential Election," *International Herald Tribune* [www.iht.com], February 6, 2008; G. L. Maatman, Jr., "A Global View of Sexual Harassment: Global Human Resource Strategies," *HR Magazine,* July 2000, pp. 151–156; and W. Hardman and J. Heidelberg, "When Sexual Harassment Is a Foreign Affair," *Personnel Journal,* April 1996, pp. 91–97.

78. "Sexual Harassment," *The U.S. Equal Employment Opportunity Commission* [www.eeoc.gov].

79. Ibid.

80. A. R. Karr, "Companies Crack Down on the Increasing Sexual Harassment by E-Mail," *Wall Street Journal,* September 21, 1999, p. A1; and A. Fisher, "After All This Time, Why Don't People Know What Sexual Harassment Means?" *Fortune,* January 12, 1998, p. 68.

81. See T. S. Bland and S. S. Stalcup, "Managing Harassment," *Human Resource Management,* Spring 2001, pp. 51–61; K. A. Hess and D. R. M. Ehrens, "Sexual Harassment—Affirmative Defense to Employer Liability," *Benefits Quarterly,* Second Quarter 1999, p. 57; J. A. Segal, "The Catch-22s of Remedying Sexual Harassment Complaints," *HR Magazine,* October 1997, pp. 111–117; S. C. Bahls and J. E. Bahls, "Hand-Off Policy," *Entrepreneur,* July 1997, pp. 74–76; J. A. Segal, "Where Are We Now?" *HR Magazine,* October 1996, pp. 69–73;

B. McAfee and D. L. Deadrick, "Teach Employees to Just Say No," *HR Magazine*, February 1996, pp. 86–89; G. D. Block, "Avoiding Liability for Sexual Harassment," *HR Magazine*, April 1995, pp. 91–97; and J. A. Segal, "Stop Making Plaintiffs' Lawyers Rich," *HR Magazine*, April 1995, pp. 31–35. Also, it should be noted here that under the Title VII and the Civil Rights Act of 1991, the maximum award that can be given, under the Federal Act, is $300,000. However, many cases are tried under state laws that permit unlimited punitive damages, such as the $7.1 million that Rena Weeks received in her trial based on California statutes.

82. S. Shellenbarger, "Supreme Court Takes on How Employers Handle Worker Harassment Complaints," *Wall Street Journal*, April 13, 2006, p. D1.

83. S. Jayson, "Workplace Romance No Longer Gets the Kiss-Off," *USA Today*, February 9, 2006, p. 9D.

84. J. Yang and V. Salazar, "Would You Date a Co-Worker?" *USA Today*, February 14, 2008, p. 1B.

85. Jayson, "Workplace Romance No Longer Gets the Kiss-off."

86. S. Shellenbarger, "For Office Romance, The Secret's Out," *Wall Street Journal*, February 10, 2010, pp. D1+.

87. R. Mano and Y. Gabriel, "Workplace Romances in Cold and Hot Organizational Climates: The Experience of Israel and Taiwan," *Human Relations*, January 2006, pp. 7–35; J. A. Segal, "Dangerous Liaisons," *HR Magazine*, December 2005, pp. 104–108; "Workplace Romance Can Create Unforeseen Issues for Employers," *HR Focus*, October 2005, p. 2; C. A. Pierce and H. Aguinis, "Legal Standards, Ethical Standards, and Responses to Social-Sexual Conduct At Work," *Journal of Organizational Behavior*, September 2005, pp. 727–732; and C. A. Pierce, B. J. Broberg, J. R. McClure, and H. Aguinis, "Responding to Sexual Harassment Complaints: Effects of a Dissolved Workplace Romance on Decision-Making Standards," *Organizational Behavior and Human Decision Processes*, September 2004, pp. 66–82.

88. J. A. Segal, "Dangerous Liaisons."

89. E. Zimmerman, "When Cupid Strikes at the Cubicle," *New York Times Online*, April 9, 2010.

90. S. Ali and B. Frankel, "The Work/Life Balancing Act: How 4 Companies Do It," *DiversityInc*, May 18, 2010, pp. 62–68.

91. J. Miller and M. Miller, "Get a Life!" *Fortune*, November 28, 2005, pp. 108–124.

92. L. Vanderkam, "Graduates, You Can Have It All," *USA Today*, May 27, 2010, p. 11A; and M. Elias, "The Family-First Generation," *USA Today*, December 13, 2004, p. 5D.

93. M. Mandel, "The Real Reasons You're Working So Hard . . . and What You Can Do About It," *BusinessWeek*, October 3, 2005, pp. 60–67.

94. C. Farrell, "The Overworked, Networked Family," *BusinessWeek*, October 3, 2005, p. 68.

95. F. Hansen, "Truths and Myths about Work/Life Balance," *Workforce*, December 2002, pp. 34–39.

96. P. Brough and T. Kalliath, "Work-Family Balance: Theoretical and Empirical Advancements," *Journal of Organizational Behavior*, July 2009, pp. 581–585; E. F. Van Steenbergen and N. Ellemers, "Is Managing the Work-Family Interface Worthwhile? Benefits for Employee Health and Performance," *Journal of Organizational Behavior*, July 2009, pp. 617–642; K. Palmer, "The New Mommy Track," *US News and World Report*, September 3, 2007, pp. 40–45; and J. H. Greenhaus and G. N. Powell, "When Work and Family Are Allies: A Theory of Work-Family Enrichment," *Academy of Management Review*, January 2006, pp. 72–92.

97. Ibid., p. 73.

98. S. Shellenbarger, "What Makes A Company A Great Place to Work Today," *Wall Street Journal*, October 4, 2007, p. D1; and L. B. Hammer, M. B. Neal, J. T. Newsom, K. J. Brockwood, and C. L. Colton, "A Longitudinal Study of the Effects of Dual-Earner Couples' Utilization of Family-Friendly Workplace Supports on Work and Family Outcomes," *Journal of Applied Psychology*, July 2005, pp. 799–810.

99. M. M. Arthur, "Share Price Reactions to Work-Family Initiatives: An Institutional Perspective," *Academy of Management Journal*, August 2003, pp. 497–505.

100. L. B. Hammer et al., "Development and Validation of a Multidimensional Measure of Family Supportive Supervisor Behaviors," *Journal of Management*, August 2009, pp. 837–856; and N. P. Rothbard,

T. L. Dumas, and K. W. Phillips, "The Long Arm of the Organization: Work-Family Policies and Employee Preferences for Segmentation," paper presented at the 61st Annual Academy of Management meeting, Washington, DC, August 2001.

101. R. King, "Slimming Down Employees to Cut Costs," *Bloomberg BusinessWeek Online*, April 26, 2010.

102. R. King, "Slimming Down Employees to Cut Costs"; C. Tkaczyk, "Lowering Health-Care Costs," *Fortune*, November 23, 2009, p. 16; and A. W. Matthews, "When All Else Fails: Forcing Workers into Healthy Habits," *Wall Street Journal*, July 8, 2009, pp. D1+.

103. L. Cornwell, "More Companies Penalize Workers with Health Risks," The Associated Press, *Springfield, Missouri News-Leader*, September 10, 2007, p. 10A.

104. B. Pyenson and K. Fitch, "Smoking May Be Hazardous to Your Bottom Line," *Workforce Management Online* [www.workforce.com], December 2007; and L. Cornwell, The Associated Press, "Companies Tack on Fees on Insurance for Smokers," *Springfield, Missouri News-Leader*, February 17, 2006, p. 5B.

105. M. Scott, "Obesity More Costly to U.S. Companies Than Smoking, Alcoholism," *Workforce Management Online* [www.workforce.com], April 9, 2008.

106. "Obesity Weighs Down Production," *Industry Week*, March 2008, pp. 22–23.

107. J. Appleby, "Companies Step Up Wellness Efforts," *USA Today*, August 1, 2005, pp. 1A+.

108. G. Kranz, "Prognosis Positive: Companies Aim to Get Workers Healthy," *Workforce Management Online* [www.workforce.com], April 15, 2008.

109. M. Conlin, "Hide the Doritos! Here Comes HR," *BusinessWeek*, April 28, 2008, pp. 94–96.

110. J. Fox, "Good Riddance to Pensions," *CNN Money*, January 12, 2006.

111. M. Adams, "Broken Pension System in Crying Need of a Fix," *USA Today*, November 15, 2005, p. 1B+.

112. J. Appleby, "Traditional Pensions Are Almost Gone. Is Employer-Provided Health Insurance Next?" *USA Today*, November 13, 2007, pp. 1A+; S. Kelly, "FedEx, Goodyear Make Big Pension Plan Changes," *Workforce Management Online* [www.workforce.com], March 1, 2007; G. Colvin, "The End of a Dream," *Fortune* [www.cnnmoney.com], June 22, 2006; E. Porter and M. Williams Nash, "Benefits Go the Way of Pensions," *NY Times Online*, February 9, 2006; and J. Fox, "Good Riddance to Pensions."

113. D. S. Urban, "What to Do About 'Body Art' at Work?" *Workforce Management Online*, March 2010.

114. J. Levitz, "UPS Thinks Outside the Box on Driver Training," *Wall Street Journal*, April 6, 2010, pp. B1+; and K. Kingsbury, "Road to Recovery," *Time*, March 8, 2010, pp. Global 14–Global 16.

115. B. Dybwad, "Facebook Passes the 400 Million User Mark" [http://mashable.com], February 4, 2010; L. Gerdes, "Best Places to Intern," *BusinessWeek Online*, December 11, 2010; M. Weinstein, "Virtual Handshake," *Training*, September 2009, pp. 18–22; F. Hansen, "Discriminatory Twist in Networking Sites Puts Recruiters in Peril," *Workforce Management Online*, September 2009; A. Samuel, "Hire Smarter with Social Media," *BusinessWeek Online*, July 13, 2009; and R. Zeidner, "Employers Give Facebook a Poke," *HR Magazine*, December 2008, p. 54.

Chapter 12A

1. J. S. Lublin, "Three Who Thrived After Early Gaffes," *Wall Street Journal*, May 4, 2010, p. D4.

2. S. E. Sullivan and Y. Baruch, "Advances in Career Theory and Research: A Critical Review and Agenda for Future Exploration," *Journal of Management*, December 2009, pp. 1542–1571.

3. "Occupational Employee Statistics (OES) Highlights: An Overview of U.S. Occupational Employment and Wages in 2009," U.S. Bureau of Labor Statistics [http://www.bls.gov/oes/highlight_2009.htm], June 2010.

4. "Management and Business and Financial Occupations," *Occupational Outlook Handbook, 2010–11 Edition* [http://www.bls.gov/oco/oco1001.htm#management].

5. J. Sandberg, "Sometimes an Office Visit Can Feel Like a Visit to a Very Foreign Land," *Wall Street Journal*, October 20, 2005, p. B1; D. Sacks,

"Scout's Honor," *Fast Company,* April 2005, p. 94; D. W. Brown, "Searching for Clues," *Black Enterprise,* November 2002, pp. 114–120; L. Bower, "Weigh Values to Decide If Working for 'Beasts' Worthwhile," *Springfield Business Journal,* November 4, 2002, p. 73; S. Shellenbarger, "How to Find Out If You're Going to Hate a New Job Before You Agree to Take It," *Wall Street Journal,* June 13, 2002, p. D1; and M. Boyle, "Just Right," *Fortune,* June 10, 2002, pp. 207–208.

6. S. Caudron, "Some New Rules for the New World of Work," *Business Finance,* October 2001, p. 24; C. Kanchier, *Dare to Change Your Job and Your Life,* 2d ed. (Indianapolis, IN: Jist Publishing, 2000); and S. Hagevik, "Responsible Risk Taking," *Journal of Environmental Health,* November 1999, pp. 29+.

7. A. Feldman, "The Road to Reinvention," *Bloomberg BusinessWeek,* March 8, 2010, pp. 68–70; E. Zimmerman, "Making Yourself Indispensable," *New York Times Online,* February 14, 2010; S. E. Needleman, "Revving a Career While It's in Neutral," *Wall Street Journal,* January 19, 2010, p. D5; and D. Schawbel, "Upping Your Value at Work," *BusinessWeek Online,* December 18, 2009.

8. D. Nishi, "What To Do If Your Boss Is the Problem," *Wall Street Journal,* April 20, 2010, p. D4; M. Weinstein, "Mind Your Manners," *Training,* July–August 2009, pp. 24–29; M. Solomon, *Working With Difficult People* (Upper Saddle River, NJ: Prentice Hall, 2002); M. Gaskill, "Bigger Bullies," *American Way,* August 2001, pp. 92–96; R. Cooper, "Dealing Effectively with Difficult People," *Nursing,* September 1993, pp. 97–100; and R. M. Bramson, *Coping with Difficult People* (Garden City, NY: Anchor Press/Doubleday, 1981).

9. A. Ebron, "All Work and No Play," *Woman's Day,* October 6, 2009, p. 50; and J. Yang and K. Simmons, "Work–Life Balance Tops Pay," *USA Today,* March 13, 2008, p. 1B.

10. D. Hannah, "Just Out of School? Six Ways You Can Get Ahead at Work," *Diversity Inc.,* May 2008, pp. 46–47.

11. S. Lohr, "How Privacy Vanishes Online," *New York Times Online,* March 16, 2010; and A. Bruzzese, "Online Postings Can Sabotage One's Career," Gannett News Service, *Springfield, Missouri, News-Leader,* August 11, 2009, p. 9B; and D. Hannah, "Just Out of School? Six Ways You Can Get Ahead at Work."

12. J. Hempel, "How LinkedIn Will Fire Up Your Career," *Fortune,* April 12, 2010, pp. 74–82; and J. S. Lublin, "A Networking Pro Learns Some New Tricks," *Wall Street Journal,* March 2, 2010, p. D4.

Chapter 13

1. J. Pugmire, "Outraged Blanc Prepares to Rebuild France Team," The Associated Press [www.google.com/hostednews/ap], July 6, 2010; D. Gauthier-Villars, "France's Bad Case of Les Bleus," *Wall Street Journal,* June 22, 2010, p. A11; and T. Panja, "France's World Cup Squad Quarrels As England Team Holds Crisis Meeting," *Bloomberg.com,* June 20, 2010.

2. B. Mezrich, *Bringing Down the House: The Inside Story of Six MIT Students Who Took Vegas for Millions* (New York: Free Press, 2002). The 2008 film *21* was a fictional work based loosely on the story.

3. M. F. Maples, "Group Development: Extending Tuckman's Theory," *Journal for Specialists in Group Work,* Fall 1988, pp. 17–23; and B. W. Tuckman and M. C. Jensen, "Stages of Small-Group Development Revisited," *Group and Organizational Studies,* December 1977, pp. 419–427.

4. D. Coutou, interview with J. R. Hackman, "Why Teams Don't Work," *Harvard Business Review,* May 2009, pp. 99–105; M. Kaeter, "Repotting Mature Work Teams," *Training,* April 1994, pp. 54–56; and L. N. Jewell and H. J. Reitz, *Group Effectiveness in Organizations* (Glenview, IL: Scott, Foresman, 1981).

5. A. Sobel, "The Beatles Principles," *Strategy & Business,* Spring 2006, p. 42.

6. This model is based on the work of P. S. Goodman, E. Ravlin, and M. Schminke, "Understanding Groups in Organizations," in L. L. Cummings and B. M. Staw (eds.), *Research in Organizational Behavior,* vol. 9 (Greenwich, CT: JAI Press, 1987), pp. 124–128; J. R. Hackman, "The Design of Work Teams," in J. W. Lorsch (ed.), *Handbook of Organizational Behavior* (Upper Saddle River, NJ: Prentice Hall, 1987), pp. 315–342; G. R. Bushe and A. L. Johnson, "Contextual and Internal Variables Affecting Task Group Outcomes in Organizations," *Group and Organization Studies,* December 1989, pp. 462–482; M. A. Campion, C. J. Medsker, and A. C. Higgs, "Relations Between Work Group Characteristics and Effectiveness: Implications for Designing Effective Work Groups," *Personnel Psychology,* Winter 1993, pp. 823–850; D. E. Hyatt and T. M. Ruddy, "An Examination of the Relationship Between Work Group Characteristics, and Performance: Once More into the Breach," *Personnel Psychology,* Autumn 1997, pp. 553–585; and P. E. Tesluk and J. E. Mathieu, "Overcoming Roadblocks to Effectiveness: Incorporating Management of Performance Barriers into Models of Work Group Effectiveness," *Journal of Applied Psychology,* April 1999, pp. 200–217.

7. G. L. Stewart, "A Meta-Analytic Review of Relationships Between Team Design Features and Team Performance," *Journal of Management,* February 2006, pp. 29–54; T. Butler and J. Waldroop, "Understanding 'People' People," *Harvard Business Review,* June 2004, pp. 78–86; J. S. Bunderson, "Team Member Functional Background and Involvement in Management Teams: Direct Effects and the Moderating Role of Power Centralization," *Academy of Management Journal,* August 2003, pp. 458–474; and M. J. Stevens and M. A. Campion, "The Knowledge, Skill, and Ability Requirements for Teamwork: Implications for Human Resource Management," *Journal of Management,* Summer 1994, pp. 503–530.

8. V. U. Druskat and S. B. Wolff, "The Link between Emotions and Team Effectiveness: How Teams Engage Members and Build Effective Task Processes," *Academy of Management Proceedings*, August 1999; D. C. Kinlaw, *Developing Superior Work Teams: Building Quality and the Competitive Edge* (San Diego, CA: Lexington, 1991); and M. E. Shaw, *Contemporary Topics in Social Psychology* (Morristown, NJ: General Learning Press, 1976), pp. 350–351.

9. By the Numbers box based on J. Yang and K. Gelles, "Workplace Friendships," *USA Today,* April 13, 2010, p. 1B; K. Merriman, "Low-Trust Teams Prefer Individualized Pay," *Harvard Business Review,* November 2008, p. 32; M. Weinstein, "Coming Up Short? Join the Club," *Training,* April 2006, p. 14; B. J. West, J. L. Patera, and M. K. Carsten, "Team Level Positivity: Investigating Positive Psychological Capacities and Team Level Outcomes"; L. G. Boiney, "Gender Impacts Virtual Work Teams," *The Graziadio Business Report,* Fall 2001, Pepperdine University; and J. Yang and K. Simmons, "Traits of Good Team Players," *USA Today,* November 21, 2007, p. 1B.

10. McMurry, Inc., "The Roles Your People Play," *Managing People at Work,* October 2005, p. 4; G. Prince, "Recognizing Genuine Teamwork," *Supervisory Management*, April 1989, pp. 25–36; R. F. Bales, *SYMLOG Case Study Kit* (New York: Free Press, 1980); and K. D. Benne and P. Sheats, "Functional Roles of Group Members," *Journal of Social Issues,* vol. 4 (1948), pp. 41–49.

11. A. Erez, H. Elms, and E. Fong, "Lying, Cheating, Stealing: Groups and the Ring of Gyges," paper presented at the Academy of Management Annual meeting, Honolulu: HI: August 8, 2005.

12. S. E. Asch, "Effects of Group Pressure upon the Modification and Distortion of Judgments," in H. Guetzkow (ed.), *Groups, Leadership and Men* (Pittsburgh: Carnegie Press, 1951), pp. 177–190; and S. E. Asch, "Studies of Independence and Conformity: A Minority of One Against a Unanimous Majority," *Psychological Monographs: General and Applied,* vol. 70, no. 9 (1956), pp. 1–70.

13. R. Bond and P. B. Smith, "Culture and Conformity: A Meta-Analysis of Studies Using Asch's [1952, 1956] Line Judgment Task," *Psychological Bulletin,* January 1996, pp. 111–137.

14. M. E. Turner and A. R. Pratkanis, "Mitigating Groupthink by Stimulating Constructive Conflict," in C. DeDreu and E. Van deVliert (eds.), *Using Conflict in Organizations* (London: Sage, 1997), pp. 53–71.

15. A. Deutschman, "Inside the Mind of Jeff Bezos," *Fast Company,* August 2004, pp. 50–58.

16. See, for instance, E. J. Thomas and C. F. Fink, "Effects of Group Size," *Psychological Bulletin,* July 1963, pp. 371–384; and M. E. Shaw, *Group Dynamics: The Psychology of Small Group Behavior*, 3rd ed. (New York: McGraw-Hill, 1981).

17. A. Jassawalla, H. Sashittal, and A. Malshe, "Students' Perceptions of Social Loafing: Its Antecedents and Consequences in Undergraduate Business Classroom Teams," *Academy of Management Learning & Education,* March 2009, pp. 42–54; R. C. Liden, S. J. Wayne, R. A. Jaworski, and N. Bennett, "Social Loafing: A Field Investigation,"

Journal of Management, April 2004, pp. 285–304; and D. R. Comer, "A Model of Social Loafing in Real Work Groups," *Human Relations,* June 1995, pp. 647–667.

18. S. G. Harkins and K. Szymanski, "Social Loafing and Group Evaluation," *Journal of Personality and Social Psychology,* December 1989, pp. 934–941.

19. C. R. Evans and K. L. Dion, "Group Cohesion and Performance: A Meta-Analysis," *Small Group Research,* May 1991, pp. 175–186; B. Mullen and C. Copper, "The Relation between Group Cohesiveness and Performance: An Integration," *Psychological Bulletin,* March 1994, pp. 210–227; and P. M. Podsakoff, S. B. MacKenzie, and M. Ahearne, "Moderating Effects of Goal Acceptance on the Relationship between Group Cohesiveness and Productivity," *Journal of Applied Psychology,* December 1997, pp. 974–983.

20. See, for example, L. Berkowitz, "Group Standards, Cohesiveness, and Productivity," *Human Relations,* November 1954, pp. 509–519; and B. Mullen and C. Copper, "The Relation between Group Cohesiveness and Performance: An Integration."

21. S. E. Seashore, *Group Cohesiveness in the Industrial Work Group* (Ann Arbor: University of Michigan, Survey Research Center, 1954).

22. C. Shaffran, "Mind Your Meeting: How to Become the Catalyst for Culture Change," *Communication World,* February–March 2003, pp. 26–29.

23. I. L. Janis, *Victims of Groupthink* (Boston: Houghton Mifflin, 1972); R. J. Aldag and S. Riggs Fuller, "Beyond Fiasco: A Reappraisal of the Groupthink Phenomenon and a New Model of Group Decision Processes," *Psychological Bulletin,* May 1993, pp. 533–552; and T. Kameda and S. Sugimori, "Psychological Entrapment in Group Decision Making: An Assigned Decision Rule and a Groupthink Phenomenon," *Journal of Personality and Social Psychology,* August 1993, pp. 282–292.

24. See, for example, L. K. Michaelson, W. E. Watson, and R. H. Black, "A Realistic Test of Individual vs. Group Consensus Decision Making," *Journal of Applied Psychology,* vol. 74, no. 5 (1989), pp. 834–839; R. A. Henry, "Group Judgment Accuracy: Reliability and Validity of Postdiscussion Confidence Judgments," *Organizational Behavior and Human Decision Processes,* October 1993, pp. 11–27; P. W. Paese, M. Bieser, and M. E. Tubbs, "Framing Effects and Choice Shifts in Group Decision Making," *Organizational Behavior and Human Decision Processes,* October 1993, pp. 149–165; N. J. Castellan Jr. (ed.), *Individual and Group Decision Making* (Hillsdale, NJ: Lawrence Erlbaum Associates, 1993); and S. G. Straus and J. E. McGrath, "Does the Medium Matter? The Interaction of Task Type and Technology on Group Performance and Member Reactions," *Journal of Applied Psychology,* February 1994, pp. 87–97.

25. E. J. Thomas and C. F. Fink, "Effects of Group Size," *Psychological Bulletin,* July 1963, pp. 371–384; F. A. Shull, A. L. Delbecq, and L.L. Cummings, *Organizational Decision Making* (New York: McGraw-Hill, 1970), p. 151; A. P. Hare, *Handbook of Small Group Research* (New York: Free Press, 1976); M. E. Shaw, *Group Dynamics: The Psychology of Small Group Behavior,* 3rd ed. (New York: McGraw-Hill, 1981); and P. Yetton and P. Bottger, "The Relationships Among Group Size, Member Ability, Social Decision Schemes, and Performance," *Organizational Behavior and Human Performance,* October 1983, pp. 145–159.

26. This section is adapted from S. P. Robbins, *Managing Organizational Conflict: A Nontraditional Approach* (Upper Saddle River, NJ: Prentice Hall, 1974), pp. 11–14. Also, see D. Wagner-Johnson, "Managing Work Team Conflict: Assessment and Preventative Strategies," Center for the Study of Work Teams, University of North Texas [www.workteams.unt .edu/reports], November 3, 2000; and M. Kennedy, "Managing Conflict in Work Teams," Center for the Study of Work Teams, University of North Texas [www.workteams.unt.edu/reports], November 3, 2000.

27. See M. A. Korsgaard et al., "A Multilevel View of Intragroup Conflict," *Journal of Management,* December 2008, pp. 1222–1252; C. K. W. DeDreu, "The Virtue and Vice of Workplace Conflict: Food for (Pessimistic) Thought," *Journal of Organizational Behavior,* January 2008, pp. 5–18; K. A. Jehn, "A Multimethod Examination of the Benefits and Detriments of Intragroup Conflict," *Administrative Science Quarterly,* June 1995, pp. 256–282; K. A. Jehn, "A Qualitative Analysis of Conflict Type and Dimensions in Organizational Groups,"

Administrative Science Quarterly, September 1997, pp. 530–557; K. A. Jehn, "Affective and Cognitive Conflict in Work Groups: Increasing Performance Through Value-Based Intragroup Conflict," in C. DeDreu and E. Van deVliert (eds.), *Using Conflict in Organizations* (London: Sage Publications, 1997), pp. 87–100; K. A. Jehn and E. A. Mannix, "The Dynamic Nature of Conflict: A Longitudinal Study of Intragroup Conflict and Group Performance," *Academy of Management Journal,* April 2001, pp. 238–251; C. K. W. DeDreu and A. E. M. Van Vianen, "Managing Relationship Conflict and the Effectiveness of Organizational Teams," *Journal of Organizational Behavior,* May 2001, pp. 309–328; and J. Weiss and J. Hughes, "Want Collaboration? Accept—and Actively Manage—Conflict," *Harvard Business Review,* March 2005, pp. 92–101.

28. C. K. W. DeDreu, "When Too Little or Too Much Hurts: Evidence for a Curvilinear Relationship Between Task Conflict and Innovation in Teams," *Journal of Management,* February 2006, pp. 83–107.

29. A. Somech, H. S. Desivilya, and H. Lidogoster, "Team Conflict Management and Team Effectiveness: The Effects of Task Interdependence and Team Identification," *Journal of Organizational Behavior,* April 2009, pp. 359–378; K. W. Thomas, "Conflict and Negotiation Processes in Organizations," in M. D. Dunnette and L. M. Hough (eds.), *Handbook of Industrial and Organizational Psychology,* 2 ed., vol. 3 (Palo Alto, CA: Consulting Psychologists Press, 1992), pp. 651–717.

30. A. Li and R. Cropanzano, "Fairness at the Group Level: Justice Climate and Intraunit Justice Climate," *Journal of Management,* June 2009, pp. 564–599.

31. K. E. Culp, "Improv Teaches Work Team Building," *Springfield, Missouri News-Leader,* December 9, 2005, p. 5B; T. J. Mullaney and A. Weintraub, "The Tech Guru: Dr. Gerard Burns," *BusinessWeek,* March 28, 2005, p. 84; and J. S. McClenahen, "Lean and Teams: More Than Blips," *Industry Week,* October 2003, p. 63.

32. See, for example, J. R. Hackman and C. G. Morris, "Group Tasks, Group Interaction Process, and Group Performance Effectiveness: A Review and Proposed Integration," in L. Berkowitz (ed.), *Advances in Experimental Social Psychology* (New York: Academic Press, 1975), pp. 45–99; R. Saavedra, P. C. Earley, and L. Van Dyne, "Complex Interdependence in Task-Performing Groups," *Journal of Applied Psychology,* February 1993, pp. 61–72; M. J. Waller, "Multiple-Task Performance in Groups," *Academy of Management Proceedings* on Disk, 1996; and K. A. Jehn, G. B. Northcraft, and M. A. Neale, "Why Differences Make A Difference: A Field Study of Diversity, Conflict, and Performance in Workgroups," *Administrative Science Quarterly,* December 1999, pp. 741–763.

33. B. J. West, J. L. Patera, and M. K. Carsten, "Team Level Positivity: Investigating Positive Psychological Capacities and Team Level Outcomes," *Journal of Organizational Behavior,* February 2009, pp. 249–267; T. Purdum, "Teaming, Take 2," *Industry Week,* May 2005, p. 43; and C. Joinson, "Teams at Work," *HRMagazine,* May 1999, p. 30.

34. See, for example, S. A. Mohrman, S. G. Cohen, and A. M. Mohrman, Jr., *Designing Team-Based Organizations* (San Francisco: Jossey-Bass, 1995); P. MacMillan, *The Performance Factor: Unlocking the Secrets of Teamwork* (Nashville, TN: Broadman & Holman, 2001); and E. Salas, C. A. Bowers, and E. Eden (eds.), *Improving Teamwork in Organizations: Applications of Resource Management Training* (Mahwah, NJ: Lawrence Erlbaum, 2002).

35. P. Alpern, "Spreading the Light," *Industry Week,* January 2010, p. 35.

36. See, for instance, E. Sundstrom, K. P. DeMeuse, and D. Futrell, "Work Teams: Applications and Effectiveness," *American Psychologist,* February 1990, pp. 120–133.

37. M. Fitzgerald, "Shine a Light," *Fast Company,* April 2009, pp. 46–48; J. S. McClenahen, "Bearing Necessities," *Industry Week,* October 2004, pp. 63–65; P. J. Kiger, "Acxiom Rebuilds from Scratch," *Workforce,* December 2002, pp. 52–55; and T. Boles, "Viewpoint—Leadership Lessons from NASCAR," *Industry Week* [www.industryweek.com], May 21, 2002.

38. M. Cianni and D. Wanuck, "Individual Growth and Team Enhancement: Moving Toward a New Model of Career Development," *Academy of Management Executive,* February 1997, pp. 105–115.

39. "Teams," *Training,* October 1996, p. 69; and C. Joinson, "Teams at Work," p. 30.

40. G. M. Spreitzer, S. G. Cohen, and G. E. Ledford, Jr., "Developing Effective Self-Managing Work Teams in Service Organizations," *Group & Organization Management,* September 1999, pp. 340–366.

41. "Meet the New Steel," *Fortune,* October 1, 2007, pp. 68–71.

42. J. Appleby and R. Davis, "Teamwork Used to Save Money; Now It Saves Lives," *USA Today* [www.usatoday.com], March 1, 2001.

43. A. Malhotra, A. Majchrzak, R. Carman, and V. Lott, "Radical Innovation without Collocation: A Case Study at Boeing-Rocketdyne," *MIS Quarterly,* June 2001, pp. 229–249.

44. A. Stuart, "Virtual Agreement," *CFO,* November 2007, p. 24.

45. F. Siebdrat, M. Hoegl, and H. Ernst, "How to Manage a Virtual Team," *MIT Sloan Management Review,* Summer 2009, pp. 63–68; A. Malhotra, A. Majchrzak, and B. Rosen, "Leading Virtual Teams," *Academy of Management Perspectives,* February 2007, pp. 60–70; B. L. Kirkman and J. E. Mathieu, "The Dimensions and Antecedents of Team Virtuality," *Journal of Management,* October 2005, pp. 700–718; J. Gordon, "Do Your Virtual Teams Deliver Only Virtual Performance?" *Training,* June 2005, pp. 20–25; L. L. Martins, L. L. Gilson, and M. T. Maynard, "Virtual Teams: What Do We Know and Where Do We Go From Here?" *Journal of Management,* December 2004, pp. 805–835; S. A. Furst, M. Reeves, B. Rosen, and R. S. Blackburn, "Managing the Life Cycle of Virtual Teams," *Academy of Management Executive,* May 2004, pp. 6–20; B. L. Kirkman, B. Rosen, P. E. Tesluk, and C. B. Gibson, "The Impact of Team Empowerment on Virtual Team Performance: The Moderating Role of Face-to-Face Interaction," *Academy of Management Journal,* April 2004, pp. 175–192; F. Keenan and S. E. Ante, "The New Teamwork," *Business Week e.biz,* February 18, 2002, pp. EB12–EB16; and G. Imperato, "Real Tools for Virtual Teams?" *Fast Company,* July 2000, pp. 378–387.

46. B. L. Kirkman, C. B. Gibson, and D. L. Shapiro, "Exporting Teams: Enhancing the Implementation and Effectiveness of Work Teams in Global Affiliates," *Organizational Dynamics,* Summer 2001, pp. 12–29; J. W. Bing and C. M. Bing, "Helping Global Teams Compete," *Training & Development,* March 2001, pp. 70–71; C. G. Andrews, "Factors That Impact Multi-Cultural Team Performance," Center for the Study of Work Teams, University of North Texas [www.workteams.unt.edu/reports/], November 3, 2000; P. Christopher Earley and E. Mosakowski, "Creating Hybrid Team Cultures: An Empirical Test of Transnational Team Functioning," *Academy of Management Journal,* February 2000, pp. 26–49; J. Tata, "The Cultural Context of Teams: An Integrative Model of National Culture, Work Team Characteristics, and Team Effectiveness," *Academy of Management Proceedings,* 1999; D. I. Jung, K. B. Baik, and J. J. Sosik, "A Longitudinal Investigation of Group Characteristics and Work Group Performance: A Cross-Cultural Comparison," *Academy of Management Proceedings,* 1999; and C. B. Gibson, "They Do What They Believe They Can? Group-Efficacy Beliefs and Group Performance across Tasks and Cultures," *Academy of Management Proceedings,* 1996.

47. D. Coutou, interview with J. R. Hackman, "Why Teams Don't Work."

48. G. A. Van Kleef et al., "Searing Sentiment or Cold Calculation? The Effects of Leader Emotional Displays on Team Performance Depend on Followers Epistemic Motivation," *Academy of Management Journal,* June 2009, pp. 562–580.

49. Leader Who Made a Difference box based on H. Walters, "Google Did," *Bloomberg BusinessWeek,* May 10–16, 2010, pp. 56–62; "Creative Tension," *Economist,* vol. 392, no. 8649, pp. 74–75; and "Google's Lessons for Employers: Put Your Employees First," *HR Focus,* September 2008, pp. 8–9.

50. R. Bond and P. B. Smith, "Culture and Conformity: A Meta-Analysis of Studies Using Asch's [1952, 1956] Line Judgment Task," *Psychological Bulletin,* January 1996, pp. 111–137.

51. I. L. Janis, *Groupthink,* 2nd ed. (New York: Houghton Mifflin Company, 1982), p. 175.

52. See P. C. Earley, "Social Loafing and Collectivism: A Comparison of the United States and the People's Republic of China," *Administrative Science Quarterly,* December 1989, pp. 565–581; and P. C. Earley, "East Meets West Meets Mideast: Further Explorations of Collectivistic and Individualistic Work Groups," *Academy of Management Journal,* April 1993, pp. 319–348.

53. N. J. Adler, *International Dimensions of Organizational Behavior,* 4th ed. (Cincinnati, OH: Southwestern, 2002), p. 142.

54. Ibid., p. 144.

55. K. B. Dahlin, L. R. Weingart, and P. J. Hinds, "Team Diversity and Information Use," *Academy of Management Journal,* December 2005, pp. 1107–1123.

56. Adler, *International Dimensions of Organizational Behavior,* p. 142.

57. P. S. Hempel, Z-X. Zhang, and D. Tjosvold, "Conflict Management Between and Within Teams for Trusting Relationships and Performance in China," *Journal of Organizational Behavior,* January 2009, pp. 41–65; and S. Paul, I. M. Samarah, P. Seetharaman, and P. P. Mykytyn, "An Empirical Investigation of Collaborative Conflict Management Style in Group Support System-Based Global Virtual Teams," *Journal of Management Information Systems,* Winter 2005, pp. 185–222.

58. S. Chang and P. Tharenou, "Competencies Needed for Managing a Multicultural Workgroup," *Asia Pacific Journal of Human Resources* vol. 42, no. 1 (2004), pp. 57–74; and Adler, *International Dimensions of Organizational Behavior,* p. 153.

59. C. E. Nicholls, H. W. Lane, and M. Brehm Brechu, "Taking Self-Managed Teams to Mexico," *Academy of Management Executive,* August 1999, pp. 15–27.

60. A. Gilley, J. W. Gilley, C. W. McConnell, and A. Veliquette, "The Competencies Used by Effective Managers to Build Teams: An Empirical Study," *Advances in Developing Human Resources,* February 2010, pp. 29–45.

61. B. V. Krishnamurthy, "Use Downtime to Enhance Skills," *Harvard Business Review,* December 2008, pp. 29–30.

62. "Women Leaders: The Hard Truth About Soft Skills," *BusinessWeek Online,* February 17, 2010, p. 8.

63. J. Reingold and J. L. Yang, "The Hidden Workplace: What's Your OQ?" *Fortune,* July 23, 2007, pp. 98–106; and P. Balkundi and D. A. Harrison, "Ties, Leaders, and Time in Teams: Strong Inference About Network Structures' Effects on Team Viability and Performance," *Academy of Management Journal,* February 2006, pp. 49–68.

64. T. Casciaro and M. S. Lobo, "Competent Jerks, Lovable Fools, and the Formation of Social Networks," *Harvard Business Review,* June 2005, pp. 92–99.

65. Balkundi and Harrison, "Ties, Leaders, and Time in Teams: Strong Inference About Network Structures' Effects on Team Viability and Performance."

66. P. Dvorak, "Engineering Firm Charts Ties," *Wall Street Journal,* January 26, 2009, p. B7; and J. McGregor, "The Office Chart That Really Counts," *Business Week,* February 27, 2006, pp. 48–49.

67. E. Bernstein, "You Did *What?* Spare the Office the Details," *Wall Street Journal,* April 6, 2010, pp. D1+.

68. N. Byrnes, "Pepsi Brings in the Health Police," *Bloomberg BusinessWeek,* January 25, 2010, pp. 50–51.

69. P. Harris, "Colombia's Biggest Bank Meshes Diverse Corporate Culture," *Latin Trade,* November–December 2009, p. 43; "Country Award Winners," *The Banker,* December 1, 2006; and B. Sills and J. Marshall, "Bancolombia Aims Higher," *Euromoney,* February 2005, p. 28.

70. C. Sullenberger, "Ushering in Relief By Air," *Time,* May 10, 2010, p. 154; and M. M. Phillips, "U.S. Team Directs Traffic in Crowded Skies," *Wall Street Journal,* January 19, 2010, p. A10.

Chapter 14

1. V. Nayar, "A Maverick CEO Explains How He Persuaded His Team to Leap into the Future," *Harvard Business Review,* June 2010, pp. 110–113; B. Einhorn and K. Gokhale, "Bangalore's Paying Again to Keep the Talent," *Bloomberg BusinessWeek,* May 24, 2010, pp. 14–16; M. Srivastava and S. Hamm, "Using the Slump to Get Bigger in Bangalore," *BusinessWeek,* September 3, 2009, pp. 50–51; and S. Lauchlan, "HCL Embraces *Slumdog* Effect," *Computer Weekly,* June 23, 2009, p. 8.

2. K. O'Toole, "Cold-Calling Van Horne," *Stanford Business Magazine* [www.gsb.stanford.edu], May 2005; and S. Orenstein, "Feeling Your Way to the Top," *Business 2.0,* June 2004, p. 146.

3. "Unplanned Absence Costs Organizations 8.7 Percent of Payroll, Mercer/Kronos Study" [www.mercer.com], June 28, 2010; and K. M. Kroll, "Absence-Minded," *CFO Human Capital,* 2006, pp. 12–14.

4. D. W. Organ, *Organizational Citizenship Behavior: The Good Soldier Syndrome* (Lexington, MA: Lexington Books, 1988), p. 4. See also

J. L. Lavell, D. E. Rupp, and J. Brockner, "Taking a Multifoci Approach to the Study of Justice, Social Exchange, and Citizenship Behavior: The Target Similarity Model," *Journal of Management,* December 2007, pp. 841–866; and J. A. LePine, A. Erez, and D. E. Johnson, "The Nature and Dimensionality of Organizational Citizenship Behavior: A Critical Review and Meta-Analysis," *Journal of Applied Psychology,* February 2002, pp. 52–65.

5. R. Ilies, B. A. Scott, and T. A. Judge, "The Interactive Effects of Personal Traits and Experienced States on Intraindividual Patterns of Citizenship Behavior," *Academy of Management Journal,* June 2006, pp. 561–575; P. Cardona, B. S. Lawrence, and P. M. Bentler, "The Influence of Social and Work Exchange Relationships on Organizational Citizenship Behavior," *Group & Organization Management,* April 2004, pp. 219–247; M. C. Bolino and W. H. Turnley, "Going the Extra Mile: Cultivating and Managing Employee Citizenship Behavior," *Academy of Management Executive,* August 2003, pp. 60–73; M. C. Bolino, W. H. Turnley, and J. J. Bloodgood, "Citizenship Behavior and the Creation of Social Capital in Organizations," *Academy of Management Review,* October 2002, pp. 505–522; and P. M. Podsakoff, S. B. MacKenzie, J. B. Paine, and D. G. Bachrach, "Organizational Citizenship Behaviors: A Critical Review of the Theoretical and Empirical Literature and Suggestions for Future Research," *Journal of Management,* vol. 26, no. 3, 2000, pp. 543–548.

6. M. C. Bolino and W. H. Turnley, "The Personal Costs of Citizenship Behavior: The Relationship Between Individual Initiative and Role Overload, Job Stress, and Work-Family Conflict," *Journal of Applied Psychology,* July 2005, pp. 740–748.

7. This definition adapted from R. W. Griffin and Y. P. Lopez, "Bad Behavior in Organizations: A Review and Typology for Future Research," *Journal of Management,* December 2005, pp. 988–1005.

8. S. J. Breckler, "Empirical Validation of Affect, Behavior, and Cognition as Distinct Components of Attitude," *Journal of Personality and Social Psychology,* May 1984, pp. 1191–1205; and S. L. Crites, Jr., L. R. Fabrigar, and R. E. Petty, "Measuring the Affective and Cognitive Properties of Attitudes: Conceptual and Methodological Issues," *Personality and Social Psychology Bulletin,* December 1994, pp. 619–634.

9. D. R. May, R. L. Gilson, and L. M. Harter, "The Psychological Conditions of Meaningfulness, Safety and Availability and the Engagement of the Human Spirit at Work," *Journal of Occupational and Organizational Psychology,* March 2004, pp. 11–37; R. T. Keller, "Job Involvement and Organizational Commitment as Longitudinal Predictors of Job Performance: A Study of Scientists and Engineers," *Journal of Applied Psychology,* August 1997, pp. 539–545; W. Kahn, "Psychological Conditions of Personal Engagement and Disengagement at Work," *Academy of Management Journal,* December 1990, pp. 692–794; and P. P. Brooke, Jr., D. W. Russell, and J. L. Price, "Discriminant Validation of Measures of Job Satisfaction, Job Involvement, and Organizational Commitment," *Journal of Applied Psychology,* May 1988, pp. 139–145.

10. P. Korkki, "With Jobs Few, Most Workers Aren't Satisfied," *New York Times Online,* January 10, 2010.

11. The Conference Board, "U.S. Job Satisfaction Keeps Falling, the Conference Board Reports Today" [www.conference-board.org], February 28, 2005.

12. A. B. Krueger, "Job Satisfaction Is Not Just a Matter of Dollars," *New York Times,* December 8, 2005, p. C3.

13. "Six Nation Survey Finds Satisfaction with Current Job," *Harris Interactive* [www.harrisinteractive.com], October 9, 2007; and SwissInfo, "Swiss Like Work, But Not Their Salaries" [www.swissinfo.org], June 7, 2005.

14. Watson Wyatt Worldwide, "A Comparison of Attitudes Around the Globe" [www.watsonwyatt.com/research], 2006.

15. "Overstretched," *The Economist* [www.economist.com], May 20, 2010.

16. T. A. Judge, C. J. Thoresen, J. E. Bono, and G. K. Patton, "The Job Satisfaction-Job Performance Relationship: A Qualitative and Quantitative Review," *Psychological Bulletin,* May 2001, pp. 376–407.

17. J. K. Harter, F. L. Schmidt, and T. L. Hayes, "Business-Unit Level Relationship Between Employee Satisfaction, Employee Engagement, and Business Outcomes: A Meta-Analysis," *Journal of Applied Psychology,* April 2002, pp. 268–279; A. M. Ryan, M. J. Schmit, and R. Johnson, "Attitudes and Effectiveness: Examining Relations at an Organizational Level," *Personnel Psychology,* Winter 1996, pp. 853–882; and C. Ostroff, "The Relationship Between Satisfaction, Attitudes, and Performance: An Organizational Level Analysis," *Journal of Applied Psychology,* December 1992, pp. 963–974.

18. E. A. Locke, "The Nature and Causes of Job Satisfaction," in M. D. Dunnette (ed.), *Handbook of Industrial and Organizational Psychology* (Chicago: Rand McNally, 1976), p. 1331; S. L. McShane, "Job Satisfaction and Absenteeism: A Meta-Analytic Re-Examination," *Canadian Journal of Administrative Science,* June 1984, pp. 61–77; R. D. Hackett and R. M. Guion, "A Reevaluation of the Absenteeism-Job Satisfaction Relationship," *Organizational Behavior and Human Decision Processes,* June 1985, pp. 340–381; K. D. Scott and G. S. Taylor, "An Examination of Conflicting Findings on the Relationship Between Job Satisfaction and Absenteeism: A Meta-Analysis," *Academy of Management Journal,* September 1985, pp. 599–612; R. D. Hackett, "Work Attitudes and Employee Absenteeism: A Synthesis of the Literature," paper presented at the 1988 National Academy of Management Meeting, Anaheim, CA, August 1988; and R. Steel and J. R. Rentsch, "Influence of Cumulation Strategies on the Long-Range Prediction of Absenteeism," *Academy of Management Journal,* December 1995, pp. 1616–1634.

19. P. W. Hom and R. W. Griffeth, *Employee Turnover* (Cincinnati, OH: Southwestern, 1995); R. W. Griffith, P. W. Hom, and S. Gaertner, "A Meta-Analysis of Antecedents and Correlates of Employee Turnover: Update, Moderator Tests, and Research Implications for the Next Millennium," *Journal of Management,* vol. 26, no. 3, 2000, p. 479; and P. W. Hom and A. J. Kinicki, "Toward a Greater Understanding of How Dissatisfaction Drives Employee Turnover," *Academy of Management Journal,* October 2001, pp. 975–987.

20. See, for example, J. M. Carsten and P. E. Spector, "Unemployment, Job Satisfaction, and Employee Turnover: A Meta-Analytic Test of the Muchinsky Model," *Journal of Applied Psychology,* August 1987, pp. 374–381; and C. L. Hulin, M. Roznowski, and D. Hachiya, "Alternative Opportunities and Withdrawal Decisions: Empirical and Theoretical Discrepancies and an Integration," *Psychological Bulletin,* July 1985, pp. 233–250.

21. T. A. Wright and D. G. Bonett, "Job Satisfaction and Psychological Well-Being as Nonadditive Predictors of Workplace Turnover," *Journal of Management,* April 2007, pp. 141–160; and D. G. Spencer and R. M. Steers, "Performance as a Moderator of the Job Satisfaction-Turnover Relationship," *Journal of Applied Psychology,* August 1981, pp. 511–514.

22. See, for instance, M. Schulte, C. Ostroff, S. Shmulyian, and A. Kinicki, "Organizational Climate Configurations: Relationships to Collective Attitudes, Customer Satisfaction, and Financial Performance," *Journal of Applied Psychology,* May 2009, pp. 618–634; S. P. Brown and S. K. Lam, "A Meta-analysis of Relationships Linking Employee Satisfaction to Customer Responses," *Journal of Retailing,* vol. 84, 2008, pp. 243–255; X. Luo and C. Homburg, "Neglected Outcomes of Customer Satisfaction," *Journal of Marketing,* April 2007, pp. 133–149; P. B. Barger and A. A. Grandey, "Service With a Smile and Encounter Satisfaction: Emotional Contagion and Appraisal Mechanisms," *Academy of Management Journal,* December 2006, pp. 1229–1238; C. Homburg and R. M. Stock, "The Link Between Salespeople's Job Satisfaction and Customer Satisfaction in a Business-to-Business Context: A Dyadic Analysis," *Journal of the Academy of Marketing Science,* Spring 2004, pp. 144–158; J. K. Harter, F. L. Schmidt, and T. L. Hayes, "Business-Unit-Level Relationship Between Employee Satisfaction, Employee Engagement, and Business Outcomes: A Meta-Analysis," *Journal of Applied Psychology,* April 2002, pp. 268–279; J. Griffith, "Do Satisfied Employees Satisfy Customers? Support-Services Staff Morale and Satisfaction Among Public School Administrators, Students, and Parents," *Journal of Applied Social Psychology,* August 2001, pp. 1627–1658; D. J. Koys, "The Effects of Employee Satisfaction, Organizational Citizenship Behavior, and Turnover on Organizational Effectiveness: A Unit-Level, Longitudinal Study," *Personnel Psychology,* Spring 2001, pp. 101–114; E. Naumann and D. W. Jackson, Jr., "One More Time: How Do You Satisfy Customers?" *Business Horizons,* May–June 1999, pp. 71–76; W. W. Tornow and J. W. Wiley, "Service Quality and Management Practices: A Look at Employee Attitudes, Customer Satisfaction, and Bottom-Line

Consequences," *Human Resource Planning,* vol. 4, no. 2, 1991, pp. 105–116; and B. Schneider and D. E. Bowen, "Employee and Customer Perceptions of Service in Banks: Replication and Extension," *Journal of Applied Psychology,* August 1985, pp. 423–433.

23. M. J. Bittner, B. H. Blooms, and L. A. Mohr, "Critical Service Encounters: The Employees' Viewpoint," *Journal of Marketing,* October 1994, pp. 95–106.

24. J. M. O'Brien, "Zappos Knows How to Kick It," *Fortune,* February 2, 2009, pp. 55–60.

25. See J. A. LePine, A. Erez, and D. E. Johnson, "The Nature and Dimensionality of Organizational Citizenship Behavior: A Critical Review and Meta-Analysis," 2002; P. Podsakoff, S. B. Mackenzie, J. B. Paine, and D. G. Bachrach, "Organizational Citizenship Behaviors: A Critical Review of the Theoretical and Empirical Literature and Suggestions for Future Research," *Journal of Management,* May 2000, pp. 513–563; T. S. Bateman and D. W. Organ, "Job Satisfaction and the Good Soldier: The Relationship between Affect and Employee 'Citizenship'," *Academy of Management Journal,* December 1983, pp. 587–595.

26. B. J. Hoffman, C. A. Blair, J. P. Maeriac, and D. J. Woehr, "Expanding the Criterion Domain? A Quantitative Review of the OCB Literature," *Journal of Applied Psychology,* vol. 92, no. 2, 2007, pp. 555–566; J. A. LePine, A. Erez, and D. E. Johnson, "The Nature and Dimensionality of Organizational Citizenship Behavior: A Critical Review and Meta-Analysis," 2002; and D. W. Organ and K. Ryan, "A Meta-Analytic Review of Attitudinal and Dispositional Predictors of Organizational Citizenship Behavior," *Personnel Psychology,* Winter 1995, pp. 775–802.

27. N. A. Fassina, D. A. Jones, and K. L. Uggerslev, "Relationship Clean-Up Time: Using Meta-Analysis and Path Analysis to Clarify Relationships Among Job Satisfaction, Perceived Fairness, and Citizenship Behaviors," *Journal of Management,* April 2008, pp. 161–188; M. A. Konovsky and D. W. Organ, "Dispositional and Contextual Determinants of Organizational Citizenship Behavior," *Journal of Organizational Behavior,* May 1996, pp. 253–266; R. H. Moorman, "Relationship Between Organization Justice and Organizational Citizenship Behaviors: Do Fairness Perceptions Influence Employee Citizenship?" *Journal of Applied Psychology,* December 1991, pp. 845–855; and J. Fahr, P. M. Podsakoff, and D. W. Organ, "Accounting for Organizational Citizenship Behavior: Leader Fairness and Task Scope versus Satisfaction," *Journal of Management,* December 1990, pp. 705–722.

28. W. H. Bommer, E. C. Dierdorff, and R. S. Rubin, "Does Prevalence Mitigate Relevance? The Moderating Effect of Group-Level OCB on Employee Performance," *Academy of Management Journal,* December 2007, pp. 1481–1494.

29. See, for example, S. Rabinowitz and D. T. Hall, "Organizational Research in Job Involvement," *Psychological Bulletin,* March 1977, pp. 265–288; G. J. Blau, "A Multiple Study Investigation of the Dimensionality of Job Involvement," *Journal of Vocational Behavior,* August 1985, pp. 19–36; and N. A. Jans, "Organizational Factors and Work Involvement," *Organizational Behavior and Human Decision Processes,* June 1985, pp. 382–396.

30. D. A. Harrison, D. A. Newman, and P. L. Roth, "How Important Are Job Attitudes?: Meta-Analytic Comparisons of Integrative Behavioral Outcomes and Time Sequences," *Academy of Management Journal,* April 2006, pp. 305–325; G. J. Blau, "Job Involvement and Organizational Commitment as Interactive Predictors of Tardiness and Absenteeism," *Journal of Management,* Winter 1986, pp. 577–584; and K. Boal and R. Cidambi, "Attitudinal Correlates of Turnover and Absenteeism: A Meta-Analysis," paper presented at the meeting of the American Psychological Association, Toronto, Canada, 1984.

31. G. J. Blau and K. Boal, "Conceptualizing How Job Involvement and Organizational Commitment Affect Turnover and Absenteeism," *Academy of Management Review,* April 1987, p. 290.

32. See, for instance, P. W. Hom, R. Katerberg, and C. L. Hulin, "Comparative Examination of Three Approaches to the Prediction of Turnover," *Journal of Applied Psychology,* June 1979, pp. 280–290; R. T. Mowday, L. W. Porter, and R. M. Steers, *Employee Organization Linkages: The Psychology of Commitment, Absenteeism, and Turnover* (New York: Academic Press, 1982); H. Angle and J. Perry, "Organizational Commitment: Individual and Organizational Influence," *Work and Occupations,* May 1983, pp. 123–145; and J. L. Pierce and

R. B. Dunham, "Organizational Commitment: Pre-Employment Propensity and Initial Work Experiences," *Journal of Management,* Spring 1987, pp. 163–178.

33. L. W. Porter, R. M. Steers, R. T. Mowday, and V. Boulian, "Organizational Commitment, Job Satisfaction, and Turnover among Psychiatric Technicians," *Journal of Applied Psychology,* October 1974, pp. 603–609.

34. D. M. Rousseau, "Organizational Behavior in the New Organizational Era," in J. T. Spence, J. M. Darley, and D. J. Foss (eds.), *Annual Review of Psychology,* vol. 48 (Palo Alto, CA: Annual Reviews, 1997), p. 523.

35. P. Eder and R. Eisenberger, "Perceived Organizational Support: Reducing the Negative Influence of Coworker Withdrawal Behavior," *Journal of Management,* February 2008, pp. 55–68; R. Eisenberger, F. Stinglhamber, C. Vandenberghe, I. L. Sucharski, and L. Rhoades, "Perceived Supervisor Support: Contributions to Perceived Organizational Support and Employee Retention," *Journal of Applied Psychology,* June 2002, pp. 565–573; L. Rhoades and R. Eisenberger, "Perceived Organizational Support: A Review of the Literature," *Journal of Applied Psychology,* August 2002, pp. 698–714; J. L. Kraimer and S. J. Wayne, "An Examination of Perceived Organizational Support as a Multidimensional Construct in the Context of an Expatriate Assignment," *Journal of Management,* vol. 30, no. 2, 2004, pp. 209–237; J. W. Bishop, K. D. Scott, J. G. Goldsby, and R. Cropanzano, "A Construct Validity Study of Commitment and Perceived Support Variables," *Group & Organization Management,* April 2005, pp. 153–180; and J. A-M. Coyle-Shapiro and N. Conway, "Exchange Relationships: Examining Psychological Contracts and Perceived Organizational Support," *Journal of Applied Psychology,* July 2005, pp. 774–781.

36. J. Marquez, "Disengaged Employees Can Spell Trouble at Any company," *Workforce Management* [www.workforce.com], May 13, 2008.

37. J. Smythe, "Engaging Employees to Drive Performance," *Communication World,* May–June 2008, pp. 20–22; A. B. Bakker and W. B. Schaufeli, "Positive Organizational Behavior: Engaged Employees in Flourishing Organizations," *Journal of Organizational Behavior,* February 2008, pp. 147–154; U. Aggarwal, S. Datta, and S. Bhargava, "The Relationship between Human Resource Practices, Psychological Contract, and Employee Engagement—Implications for Managing Talent," *IIMB Management Review,* September 2007, pp. 313–325; M. C. Christian and J. E. Slaughter, "Work Engagement: A Meta-Analytic Review and Directions for Research in an Emerging Area," *AOM Proceedings,* August 2007, pp. 1–6; C. H. Thomas, "A New Measurement Scale for Employee Engagement: Scale Development, Pilot Test, and Replication," *AOM Proceedings,* August 2007, pp. 1–6; A. M. Saks, "Antecedents and Consequences of Employee Engagement," *Journal of Managerial Psychology,* vol. 21, no. 7, 2006, pp. 600–619; and A. Parsley, "Road Map for Employee Engagement," *Management Services,* Spring 2006, pp. 10–11.

38. "Driving Employee Engagement in a Global Workforce," *Watson Wyatt Worldwide,* 2007–2008, p. 2.

39. A. J. Elliott and P. G. Devine, "On the Motivational Nature of Cognitive Dissonance: Dissonance as Psychological Discomfort," *Journal of Personality and Social Psychology,* September 1994, pp. 382–394.

40. L. Festinger, *A Theory of Cognitive Dissonance* (Stanford, CA: Stanford University Press, 1957); and C. Crossen, "Cognitive Dissonance Became a Milestone in 1950s Psychology," *Wall Street Journal,* December 4, 2006, p. B1.

41. See, for example, S. V. Falletta, "Organizational Intelligence Surveys," *T&D,* June 2008, pp. 52–58; R. Fralicx, P. Foley, H. Friedman, P. Gilberg, D. P. McCauley, and L. F. Parra, "Point of View: Using Employee Surveys to Drive Business Decisions," Mercer Human Resource Consulting, July 1, 2004; L. Simpson, "What's Going on in Your Company? If You Don't Ask, You'll Never Know," *Training,* June 2002, pp. 30–34; and B. Fishel, "A New Perspective: How to Get the Real Story from Attitude Surveys," *Training,* February 1998, pp. 91–94.

42. A. Kover, "And the Survey Says . . . ," *Industry Week,* September 2005, pp. 49–52.

43. See J. Welch and S. Welch, "Employee Polls: A Vote in Favor," *BusinessWeek,* January 28, 2008, p. 90; E. White, "How Surveying Workers Can Pay Off," *Wall Street Journal,* June 18, 2007, p. B3; A. Kover, "And the Survey Says . . . ," R. Fralicx, P. Foley,

H. Friedman, P. Gilberg, D. P. McCauley, and L. F. Parra, "Point of View: Using Employee Surveys to Drive Business Decisions"; and S. Shellenbarger, "Companies Are Finding It Really Pays to be Nice to Employees," *Wall Street Journal,* July 22, 1998, p. B1.

44. L. Saari and T. A. Judge, "Employee Attitudes and Job Satisfaction," *Human Resource Management,* Winter 2004, pp. 395–407; and T. A. Judge and A. H. Church, "Job Satisfaction: Research and Practice," in C. L. Cooper and E. A. Locke (eds.), *Industrial and Organizational Psychology: Linking Theory with Practice* (Oxford, UK: Blackwell, 2000).

45. Harrison, Newman, and Roth, "How Important Are Job Attitudes?" pp. 320–321.

46. Leader Who Made a Difference Box based on L. Heracleous and J. Wirtz, "Singapore Airlines' Balancing Act," *Harvard Business Review,* July–August 2010, pp. 145–149; S. Cendrowski, "Singapore Airlines," *Fortune,* June 14, 2010, p. 22; and S. Govindasamy, "A State of Mind," *Airline Business,* February 2010, pp. 18–21.

47. A. Tugend, "Blinded by Science in the Online Dating Game," *New York Times Online,* July 18, 2009; and C. Arnst, "Better Loving Through Chemistry," *BusinessWeek,* October 24, 2005, p. 48.

48. I. Briggs-Myers, *Introduction to Type* (Palo Alto, CA: Consulting Psychologists Press, 1980); W. L. Gardner and M. J. Martinko, "Using the Myers-Briggs Type Indicator to Study Managers: A Literature Review and Research Agenda," *Journal of Management,* vol. 22, no. 1, 1996, pp. 45–83; and N. L. Quenk, *Essentials of Myers-Briggs Type Indicator Assessment* (New York: Wiley, 2000).

49. R. D. Meyer, R. S. Dalal, and S. Bonaccio, "A Meta-Analytic Investigation into the Moderating Effects of Situational Strength on the Conscientiousness–Performance Relationship," *Journal of Organizational Behavior,* November 2009, pp. 1077–1102; C. G. DeYoung, L. C. Quilty, and J. B. Peterson, "Between Facets and Domains: 10 Aspects of the Big Five," *Journal of Personality and Social Psychology,* November 2007, pp. 880–896; T. A. Judge, D. Heller, and M. K. Mount, "Five-Factor Model of Personality and Job Satisfaction: A Meta-Analysis," *Journal of Applied Psychology,* June 2002, pp. 530–541; G. M. Hurtz and J. J. Donovan, "Personality and Job Performance: The Big Five Revisited," *Journal of Applied Psychology,* December 2000, pp. 869–879; M. K. Mount, M. R. Barrick, and J. P. Strauss, "Validity of Observer Ratings of the Big Five Personality Factors," *Journal of Applied Psychology,* April 1996, pp. 272–280; O. P. John, "The Big Five Factor Taxonomy: Dimensions of Personality in the Natural Language and in Questionnaires," in L. A. Pervin (ed.), *Handbook of Personality Theory and Research* (New York: Guilford Press, 1990), pp. 66–100; and J. M. Digman, "Personality Structure: Emergence of the Five-Factor Model," in M. R. Rosenweig and L. W. Porter (eds.), *Annual Review of Psychology,* vol. 41 (Palo Alto, CA: Annual Review, 1990), pp. 417–440.

50. M. R. Barrick and M. K. Mount, "The Big Five Personality Dimensions and Job Performance: A Meta-Analysis," *Personnel Psychology,* vol. 44, 1991, pp. 1–26; A. J. Vinchur, J. S. Schippmann, F. S. Switzer III, and P. L. Roth, "A Meta-Analytic Review of Predictors of Job Performance for Salespeople," *Journal of Applied Psychology,* August 1998, pp. 586–597; G. M. Hurtz and J. J. Donovan, "Personality and Job Performance Revisited," *Journal of Applied Psychology,* December 2000, pp. 869–879; T. A. Judge and J. E. Bono, "Relationship of Core Self-Evaluations Traits—Self Esteem, Generalized Self-Efficacy, Locus of Control, and Emotional Stability—With Job Satisfaction and Job Performance: A Meta-Analysis," *Journal of Applied Psychology,* February 2001, pp. 80–92; T. A. Judge, D. Heller, and M. K. Mount, "Five-Factor Model of Personality and Job Satisfaction: A Meta-Analysis"; and D. M. Higgins, J. B. Peterson, R. O. Pihl, and A. G. M. Lee, "Prefrontal Cognitive Ability, Intelligence, Big Five Personality, and the Prediction of Advanced Academic and Workplace Performance," *Journal of Personality and Social Psychology,* August 2007, pp. 298–319.

51. I-S. Oh and C. M. Berry, "The Five-Factor Model of Personality and Managerial Performance: Validity Gains Through the Use of 360 Degree Performance Ratings," *Journal of Applied Psychology,* November 2009, pp. 1498–1513.

52. A. E. Poropat, "A Meta-Analysis of the Five-Factor Model of Personality and Academic Performance," *Psychological Bulletin,* vol. 135, no. 2, 2009, pp. 322–338.

53. J. B. Rotter, "Generalized Expectancies for Internal versus External Control of Reinforcement," *Psychological Monographs* 80, no. 609, 1966.

54. See, for instance, D. W. Organ and C. N. Greene, "Role Ambiguity, Locus of Control, and Work Satisfaction," *Journal of Applied Psychology,* February 1974, pp. 101–102; and T. R. Mitchell, C. M. Smyser, and S. E. Weed, "Locus of Control: Supervision and Work Satisfaction," *Academy of Management Journal,* September 1975, pp. 623–631.

55. W. Amelia, "Anatomy of a Classic: Machiavelli's Daring Gift," *Wall Street Journal,* August 30–31, 2008, p. W10; R. G. Vleeming, "Machiavellianism: A Preliminary Review," *Psychological Reports,* February 1979, pp. 295–310; and S. A. Snook, "Love and Fear and the Modern Boss," *Harvard Business Review,* January 2008, pp. 16–17.

56. See J. Brockner, *Self-Esteem at Work: Research, Theory, and Practice* (Lexington, MA: Lexington Books, 1988), chapters 1–4; and N. Branden, *Self-Esteem at Work* (San Francisco: Jossey-Bass, 1998).

57. "Social Studies," *Bloomberg BusinessWeek,* June 14–20, 2010, pp. 72–73.

58. See M. Snyder, *Public Appearances/Private Realities: The Psychology of Self-Monitoring* (New York: W. H. Freeman, 1987); and D. V. Day, D. J. Schleicher, A. L. Unckless, and N. J. Hiller, "Self-Monitoring Personality at Work: A Meta-Analytic Investigation of Construct Validity," *Journal of Applied Psychology,* April 2002, pp. 390–401.

59. Snyder, *Public Appearances/Private Realities*; and J. M. Jenkins, "Self-Monitoring and Turnover: The Impact of Personality on Intent to Leave," *Journal of Organizational Behavior,* January 1993, pp. 83–90.

60. M. Kilduff and D. V. Day, "Do Chameleons Get Ahead? The Effects of Self-Monitoring on Managerial Careers," *Academy of Management Journal,* August 1994, pp. 1047–1060; and A. Mehra, M. Kilduff, and D. J. Brass, "The Social Networks of High and Low Self-Monitors: Implications for Workplace Performance," *Administrative Science Quarterly,* March 2001, pp. 121–146.

61. N. Kogan and M. A. Wallach, "Group Risk Taking as a Function of Members' Anxiety and Defensiveness," *Journal of Personality,* March 1967, pp. 50–63; and J. M. Howell and C. A. Higgins, "Champions of Technological Innovation," *Administrative Science Quarterly,* June 1990, pp. 317–341.

62. By the Numbers box based on E. Frauenheim, "Recession Unleashes Boss Bullying," *Workforce Management Online,* April 2010; D. Smith, "Surviving a Down Economy With an Upbeat Attitude," *T&D,* November 2009, pp. 16–17; S. Jayson, "A Detailed Look at Millennials," *USA Today,* February 24, 2010, p. 10B; T. Janisch, "Digital Marketplace: Welcoming Gen Y to the Workforce" [wistechnology.com/articles/], May 19, 2009; J. Yang and J. Snider, "Most Do Nothing When Co-Worker Takes Credit," *USA Today,* December 29, 2009, p. 1B; J. Yang and S. Ward, "Executives Who Are Satisfied With Their Job," *USA Today,* September 1, 2009, p. 1B; and J. Yang and S. Ward, "What Makes Workers Happy?" *USA Today,* September 23, 2009, p. 1B.

63. M. Friedman and R. H. Rosenman, *Type A Behavior and Your Heart* (New York: Alfred A. Knopf, 1974).

64. S. K. Parker and C. G. Collins, "Taking Stock: Integrating and Differentiating Multiple Proactive Behaviors," *Journal of Management,* May 2010, pp. 633–662; J. D. Kammeyer-Mueller and C. R. Wanberg, "Unwrapping the Organizational Entry Process: Disentangling Multiple Antecedents and Their Pathways to Adjustment," *Journal of Applied Psychology,* October 2003, pp. 779–794; S. E. Seibert, M. L. Kraimer, and J. M. Crant, "What Do Proactive People Do? A Longitudinal Model Linking Proactive Personality and Career Success," *Personnel Psychology,* Winter 2001, pp. 845–874; J. M. Crant, "Proactive Behavior in Organizations," *Journal of Management,* vol. 26, no. 3, 2000, pp. 435–462; J. M. Crant and T. S. Bateman, "Charismatic Leadership Viewed from Above: The Impact of Proactive Personality," *Journal of Organizational Behavior,* February 2000, pp. 63–75; S. E. Seibert, J. M. Crant, and M. L. Kraimer, "Proactive Personality and Career Success," *Journal of Applied Psychology,* June 1999, pp. 416–427; R. C. Becherer and J. G. Maurer, "The Proactive Personality Disposition and Entrepreneurial Behavior Among Small Company Presidents," *Journal of Small Business Management,* January 1999,

R. R. Reilly, "Does Performance Improve Following Multisource Feedback? A Theoretical Model, Meta-Analysis, and Review of Empirical Findings," *Personnel Psychology,* Spring 2005, pp. 171–203.

28. Y. Gong, J-C. Huang, and J-L. Farh, "Employee Learning Orientation, Transformational Leadership, and Employee Creativity: The Mediating Role of Employee Self-Efficacy," *Academy of Management Journal,* August 2009, pp. 765–778; M. E. Gist, "Self-Efficacy: Implications for Organizational Behavior and Human Resource Management," *Academy of Management Review,* July 1987, pp. 472–485; and A. Bandura, *Self-Efficacy: The Exercise of Control* (New York: Freeman, 1997).

29. E. A. Locke, E. Frederick, C. Lee, and P. Bobko, "Effect of Self-Efficacy, Goals, and Task Strategies on Task Performance," *Journal of Applied Psychology,* May 1984, pp. 241–251; M. E. Gist and T. R. Mitchell, "Self-Efficacy: A Theoretical Analysis of Its Determinants and Malleability," *Academy of Management Review,* April 1992, pp. 183–211; A. D. Stajkovic and F. Luthans, "Self-Efficacy and Work-Related Performance: A Meta-Analysis," *Psychological Bulletin,* September 1998, pp. 240–261; and A. Bandura, "Cultivate Self-Efficacy for Personal and Organizational Effectiveness," in E. Locke (ed.), *Handbook of Principles of Organizational Behavior* (Malden, MA: Blackwell, 2004), pp. 120–136.

30. A. Bandura and D. Cervone, "Differential Engagement in Self-Reactive Influences in Cognitively-Based Motivation," *Organizational Behavior and Human Decision Processes,* August 1986, pp. 92–113; and R. Ilies and T. A. Judge, "Goal Regulation Across Time: The Effects of Feedback and Affect," *Journal of Applied Psychology,* May 2005, pp. 453–467.

31. See J. C. Anderson and C. A. O'Reilly, "Effects of an Organizational Control System on Managerial Satisfaction and Performance," *Human Relations,* June 1981, pp. 491–501; and J. P. Meyer, B. Schacht-Cole, and I. R. Gellatly, "An Examination of the Cognitive Mechanisms by Which Assigned Goals Affect Task Performance and Reactions to Performance," *Journal of Applied Social Psychology* vol. 18, no. 5, 1988, pp. 390–408.

32. K. Maher and K. Hudson, "Wal-Mart to Sweeten Bonus Plans for Staff," *Wall Street Journal,* March 22, 2007, p. A11; and Reuters, "Wal-Mart Workers to Get New Bonus Plan," *CNNMoney.com,* March 22, 2007.

33. B. F. Skinner, *Science and Human Behavior* (New York: Free Press, 1953); and Skinner, *Beyond Freedom and Dignity* (New York: Knopf, 1972).

34. The same data, for instance, can be interpreted in either goal-setting or reinforcement terms, as shown in E. A. Locke, "Latham vs. Komaki: A Tale of Two Paradigms," *Journal of Applied Psychology,* February 1980, pp. 16–23. Also, see M. O. Ambrose and C. T. Kulik, "Old Friends, New Faces: Motivation Research in the 1990s."

35. J. Katz, "Cozy Up to Customers," *Industry Week,* February 2010, p. 16.

36. See, for example, A. M. Grant and S. K. Parker, "Redesigning Work Design Theories: The Rise of Relational and Proactive Perspectives," in *The Academy of Management Annals,* J. P. Walsh and A. P. Brief (eds.), 2009, pp. 317–375; R. W. Griffin, "Toward an Integrated Theory of Task Design," in L. L. Cummings and B. M. Staw (eds.), *Research in Organizational Behavior,* vol. 9 (Greenwich, CT: JAI Press, 1987), pp. 79–120; and M. Campion, "Interdisciplinary Approaches to Job Design: A Constructive Replication with Extensions," *Journal of Applied Psychology,* August 1988, pp. 467–481.

37. N. Tasler, "Help Your Best People Do a Better Job," *BusinessWeek Online,* March 26, 2010; S. Caudron, "The De-Jobbing of America," *Industry Week,* September 5, 1994, pp. 31–36; W. Bridges, "The End of the Job," *Fortune,* September 19, 1994, pp. 62–74; and K. H. Hammonds, K. Kelly, and K. Thurston, "Rethinking Work," *BusinessWeek,* October 12, 1994, pp. 75–87.

38. M. A. Campion and C. L. McClelland, "Follow-Up and Extension of the Interdisciplinary Costs and Benefits of Enlarged Jobs," *Journal of Applied Psychology,* June 1993, pp. 339–351; and M. L. Ambrose and C. T. Kulik, "Old Friends, New Faces: Motivation Research in the 1990s."

39. See, for example, J. R. Hackman and G. R. Oldham, *Work Redesign* (Reading, MA: Addison-Wesley, 1980); Miner, *Theories of Organizational Behavior,* pp. 231–266; R. W. Griffin, "Effects of Work Redesign on Employee Perceptions, Attitudes, and Behaviors: A Long-Term Investigation," *Academy of Management Journal,* June 1991, pp. 425–435; J. L. Cotton, *Employee Involvement*

(Newbury Park, CA: Sage, 1993), pp. 141–172; and M. L. Ambrose and C. T. Kulik, "Old Friends, New Faces: Motivation Research in the 1990s."

40. J. R. Hackman and G. R. Oldham, "Development of the Job Diagnostic Survey," *Journal of Applied Psychology,* April 1975, pp. 159–170; and J. R. Hackman and G. R. Oldham, "Motivation through the Design of Work: Test of a Theory," *Organizational Behavior and Human Performance,* August 1976, pp. 250–279.

41. J. R. Hackman, "Work Design," in J. R. Hackman and J. L. Suttle (eds.), *Improving Life at Work* (Glenview, IL: Scott, Foresman, 1977), p. 129; and M. L. Ambrose and C. T. Kulik, "Old Friends, New Faces: Motivation Research in the 1990s."

42. D. J. Holman, C. M. Axtell, C. A. Sprigg, P. Totterdell, and T. D. Wall, "The Mediating Role of Job Characteristics in Job Redesign Interventions: A Serendipitous Quasi-Experiment," *Journal of Organizational Behavior,* January 2010, pp. 84–105.

43. J. L. Pierce, I. Jussila, and A. Cummings, "Psychological Ownership Within the Job Design Context: Revision of the Job Characteristics Model," *Journal of Organizational Behavior,* May 2009, pp. 477–496.

44. A. M. Grant and S. K. Parker, "Redesigning Work Design Theories: The Rise of Relational and Proactive Perspectives."

45. J. Camps and R. Luna-Arocas, "High Involvement Work Practices and Firm Performance," *The International Journal of Human Resource Management,* May 2009, pp. 1056–1077; M. M. Butts, R. J. Vandenberg, D. M. DeJoy, B. S. Schaffer, and M. G. Wilson, "Individual Reactions to High Involvement Work Practices: Investigating the Role of Empowerment and Perceived Organizational Support," *Journal of Occupational Health Psychology,* April 2009, pp. 122–136; P. Boxall and K. Macky, "Research and Theory on High-Performance Work Systems: Progressing the High-Involvement Stream," *Human Resource Management Journal,* vol. 19, no. 1, 2009, pp. 3–23; R. D. Mohr and C. Zoghi, "High-Involvement Work Design and Job Satisfaction," *Industrial and Labor Relations Review,* April 2008, pp. 275–296; and C. D. Zatzick and R. D. Iverson, "High-Involvement Management and Workforce Reduction: Competitive Advantage or Disadvantage?" *Academy of Management Journal,* October 2006, pp. 999–1015.

46. J. S. Adams, "Inequity in Social Exchanges," in L. Berkowitz (ed.), *Advances in Experimental Social Psychology,* vol. 2 (New York: Academic Press, 1965), pp. 267–300; M. L. Ambrose and C. T. Kulik, "Old Friends, New Faces: Motivation Research in the 1990s"; and T. Menon and L. Thompson, "Envy at Work," *Harvard Business Review,* April 2010, pp. 74–79.

47. See, for example, P. S. Goodman and A. Friedman, "An Examination of Adams' Theory of Inequity," *Administrative Science Quarterly,* September 1971, pp. 271–288; M. R. Carrell, "A Longitudinal Field Assessment of Employee Perceptions of Equitable Treatment," *Organizational Behavior and Human Performance,* February 1978, pp. 108–118; E. Walster, G. W. Walster, and W. G. Scott, *Equity: Theory and Research* (Boston: Allyn & Bacon, 1978); R. G. Lord and J. A. Hohenfeld, "Longitudinal Field Assessment of Equity Effects on the Performance of Major League Baseball Players," *Journal of Applied Psychology,* February 1979, pp. 19–26; J. E. Dittrich and M. R. Carrell, "Organizational Equity Perceptions, Employee Job Satisfaction, and Departmental Absence and Turnover Rates," *Organizational Behavior and Human Performance,* August 1979, pp. 29–40; and J. Greenberg, "Cognitive Reevaluation of Outcomes in Response to Underpayment Inequity," *Academy of Management Journal,* March 1989, pp. 174–184.

48. P. S. Goodman, "An Examination of Referents Used in the Evaluation of Pay," *Organizational Behavior and Human Performance,* October 1974, pp. 170–195; S. Ronen, "Equity Perception in Multiple Comparisons: A Field Study," *Human Relations,* April 1986, pp. 333–346; R. W. Scholl, E. A. Cooper, and J. F. McKenna, "Referent Selection in Determining Equity Perception: Differential Effects on Behavioral and Attitudinal Outcomes," *Personnel Psychology,* Spring 1987, pp. 113–127; and C. T. Kulik and M. L. Ambrose, "Personal and Situational Determinants of Referent Choice," *Academy of Management Review,* April 1992, pp. 212–237.

49. See, for example, R. C. Dailey and D. J. Kirk, "Distributive and Procedural Justice as Antecedents of Job Dissatisfaction and Intent to Turnover," *Human Relations,* March 1992, pp. 305–316; D. B. McFarlin

and P. D. Sweeney, "Distributive and Procedural Justice as Predictors of Satisfaction with Personal and Organizational Outcomes," *Academy of Management Journal,* August 1992, pp. 626–637; M. A. Konovsky, "Understanding Procedural Justice and Its Impact on Business Organizations," *Journal of Management,* vol. 26, no. 3, 2000, pp. 489–511; J. A. Colquitt, "Does the Justice of One Interact With the Justice of Many? Reactions to Procedural Justice in Teams," *Journal of Applied Psychology,* August 2004, pp. 633–646; J. Brockner, "Why It's So Hard to be Fair," *Harvard Business Review,* March 2006, pp. 122–129; and B. M. Wiesenfeld, W. B. Swann, Jr., J. Brockner, and C. A. Bartel, "Is More Fairness Always Preferred? Self-Esteem Moderates Reactions to Procedural Justice," *Academy of Management Journal,* October 2007, pp. 1235–1253.

50. V. H. Vroom, *Work and Motivation* (New York: John Wiley, 1964).

51. See, for example, H. G. Heneman III and D. P. Schwab, "Evaluation of Research on Expectancy Theory Prediction of Employee Performance," *Psychological Bulletin,* July 1972, pp. 1–9; and L. Reinharth and M. Wahba, "Expectancy Theory as a Predictor of Work Motivation, Effort Expenditure, and Job Performance," *Academy of Management Journal,* September 1975, pp. 502–537.

52. See, for example, V. H. Vroom, "Organizational Choice: A Study of Pre- and Postdecision Processes," *Organizational Behavior and Human Performance,* April 1966, pp. 212–225; L. W. Porter and E. E. Lawler III, *Managerial Attitudes and Performance* (Homewood, IL: Richard D. Irwin, 1968); W. Van Eerde and H. Thierry, "Vroom's Expectancy Models and Work-Related Criteria: A Meta-Analysis," *Journal of Applied Psychology,* October 1996, pp. 575–586; and M. L. Ambrose and C. T. Kulik, "Old Friends, New Faces: Motivation Research in the 1990s."

53. See, for instance, M. Siegall, "The Simplistic Five: An Integrative Framework for Teaching Motivation," *The Organizational Behavior Teaching Review,* vol. 12, no. 4, 1987–1988, pp. 141–43.

54. I. Mount, "Building a Community—and Staff Loyalty," *CNNMoney.com,* June 5, 2009.

55. J. M. O'Brien, "Zappos Know How to Kick It," *Fortune,* February 2, 2009, pp. 54–60.

56. T. Barber, "Inspire Your Employees Now," *Bloomberg BusinessWeek Online,* May 18, 2010; D. Mattioli, "CEOs Welcome Recovery to Look After Staff," *Wall Street Journal,* April 5, 2010, p. B5; J. Sullivan, "How Do We Keep People Motivated Following Layoffs?" *Workforce Management Online,* March 2010; S. Crabtree, "How to Bolster Employees' Confidence," *The Gallup Management Journal Online,* February 25, 2010; S. E. Needleman, "Business Owners Try to Motivate Employees," *Wall Street Journal,* January 14, 2010, p. B5; H. Mintzberg, "Rebuilding Companies as Communities," *Harvard Business Review,* July–August 2009, pp. 140–143; and R. Luss, "Engaging Employees Through Periods of Layoffs," *Towers Watson* [www.towerswatson.com], March 3, 2009.

57. J. W. Miller and D. Kesmodel, "Drinking on the Job Comes to a Head at Carlsberg," *Wall Street Journal,* April 10–11, 2010, pp. A1+; and Associated Press, "Carlsberg Workers Balk At Loss of On-the-Job Beer," *Wall Street Journal,* April 9, 2010, p. B2.

58. N. J. Adler with A. Gundersen, *International Dimensions of Organizational Behavior,* 5th ed. (Cincinnati, OH: South-Western College Pub., 2008).

59. G. Hofstede, "Motivation, Leadership and Organization: Do American Theories Apply Abroad?" *Organizational Dynamics,* Summer 1980, p. 55.

60. Ibid.

61. J. K. Giacobbe-Miller, D. J. Miller, and V. I. Victorov, "A Comparison of Russian and U.S. Pay Allocation Decisions, Distributive Justice Judgments and Productivity under Different Payment Conditions," *Personnel Psychology,* Spring 1998, pp. 137–163.

62. S. L. Mueller and L. D. Clarke, "Political-Economic Context and Sensitivity to Equity: Differences between the United States and the Transition Economies of Central and Eastern Europe," *Academy of Management Journal,* June 1998, pp. 319–329.

63. S. D. Sidle, "Building a Committed Global Workforce: Does What Employees Want Depend on Culture?" *Academy of Management Perspective,* February 2009, pp. 79–80; and G. A. Gelade, P. Dobson, and K. Auer, "Individualism, Masculinity, and the Sources of Organizational Commitment," *Journal of Cross-Cultural Psychology,* vol. 39, no. 5, 2008, pp. 599–617.

64. I. Harpaz, "The Importance of Work Goals: An International Perspective," *Journal of International Business Studies,* First Quarter 1990, pp. 75–93.

65. G. E. Popp, H. J. Davis, and T. T. Herbert, "An International Study of Intrinsic Motivation Composition," *Management International Review,* January 1986, pp. 28–35.

66. R. W. Brislin, B. MacNab, R. Worthley, F. Kabigting Jr., and B. Zukis, "Evolving Perceptions of Japanese Workplace Motivation: An Employee-Manager Comparison," *International Journal of Cross-Cultural Management,* April 2005, pp. 87–104.

67. J. T. Marquez, "Tailor-Made Careers," *Workforce Management Online,* January 2010.

68. J. R. Billings and D. L. Sharpe, "Factors Influencing Flextime Usage Among Employed Married Women," *Consumer Interests Annual,* 1999, pp. 89–94; and I. Harpaz, "The Importance of Work Goals: An International Perspective," *Journal of International Business Studies,* First Quarter 1990, pp. 75–93.

69. N. Ramachandran, "New Paths At Work," *US News & World Report,* March 20, 2006, p. 47; S. Armour, "Generation Y: They've Arrived at Work With a New Attitude," *USA Today,* November 6, 2005, pp. B1+; and R. Kanfer and P. L. Ackerman, "Aging, Adult Development, and Work Motivation," *Academy of Management Review,* July 2004, pp. 440–458.

70. T. D. Golden and J. F. Veiga, "The Impact of Extent of Telecommuting on Job Satisfaction: Resolving Inconsistent Findings," *Journal of Management,* April 2005, pp. 301–318.

71. See, for instance, M. Alpert, "The Care and Feeding of Engineers," *Fortune,* September 21, 1992, pp. 86–95; G. Poole, "How to Manage Your Nerds," *Forbes ASAP,* December 1994, pp. 132–136; T. J. Allen and R. Katz, "Managing Technical Professionals and Organizations: Improving and Sustaining the Performance of Organizations, Project Teams, and Individual Contributors," *Sloan Management Review,* Summer 2002, pp. S4–S5; and S. R. Barley and G. Kunda, "Contracting: A New Form of Professional Practice," *Academy of Management Perspectives,* February 2006, pp. 45–66.

72. J. P. Broschak and A. Davis-Blake, "Mixing Standard Work and Nonstandard Deals: The Consequences of Heterogeneity in Employment Arrangements," *Academy of Management Journal,* April 2006, pp. 371–393; M. L. Kraimer, S. J. Wayne, R. C. Liden, and R. T. Sparrowe, "The Role of Job Security in Understanding the Relationship Between Employees' Perceptions of Temporary Workers and Employees' Performance," *Journal of Applied Psychology,* March 2005, pp. 389–398; and C. E. Connelly and D. G. Gallagher, "Emerging Trends in Contingent Work Research," *Journal of Management,* November 2004, pp. 959–983.

73. C. Haddad, "FedEx: Gaining on the Ground," *BusinessWeek,* December 16, 2002, pp. 126–128; and L. Landro, "To Get Doctors to Do Better, Health Plans Try Cash Bonuses," *Wall Street Journal,* September 17, 2004, pp. A1+.

74. K. E. Culp, "Playing Field Widens for Stack's Great Game," *Springfield, Missouri, News-Leader,* January 9, 2005, pp. 1A+.

75. J. Case, "The Open-Book Revolution," *Inc.,* June 1995, pp. 26–50; J. P. Schuster, J. Carpenter, and M. P. Kane, *The Power of Open-Book Management* (New York: John Wiley, 1996); J. Case, "Opening the Books," *Harvard Business Review,* March–April 1997, pp. 118–127; and D. Drickhamer, "Open Books to Elevate Performance," *Industry Week,* November 2002, p. 16.

76. J. Ruhlman and C. Siegman, "Boosting Engagement While Cutting Costs," *The Gallup Management Journal Online,* June 18, 2009.

77. By the Numbers box based on J. Yang and S. Ward, "Who Appreciates You the Most at Work?" *USA Today,* June 2, 2010, p. 1B; E. Frauenheim, "Bosses Don't Drive Workers Away, Poll Concludes," *Workforce Management Online,* April 2010; J. Yang and K. Simmons, "What Primary Motivation Does Your Employer Provide?" *USA Today,* February 22, 2010, p. 1B; A. R. Carey and S. Ward, "What Small Perks Workers Want," *USA Today,* March 31, 2010, p. 1A; J. Yang and A. Gonzalez, "Most Preferred Forms of Recognition at Workplace," *USA Today,* May 4, 2009, p. 1B; A. Ebron, "All Work and No Play," *Woman's Day,* October 6, 2009, p. 50; and A. R. Carey and S. Parker, "Underpaid for Work We Do," *USA Today,* September 15, 2008, p. 1A.

78. P. Lencioni, "The No-Cost Way to Motivate," *BusinessWeek,* October 5, 2009, p. 84; and F. Luthans and A. D. Stajkovic, "Provide Recognition for Performance Improvement," in E. A. Locke (ed.), *Principles of Organizational Behavior* (Oxford, England: Blackwell, 2000), pp. 166–180.
79. C. Huff, "Recognition That Resonates," *Workforce Management Online,* April 1, 2008.
80. D. Drickhamer, "Best Plant Winners: Nichols Foods Ltd.," *Industry Week,* October 1, 2001, pp. 17–19.
81. M. Littman, "Best Bosses Tell All," *Working Woman,* October 2000, p. 54; and Hoover's Online [www.hoovers.com], June 20, 2003.
82. E. White, "Praise From Peers Goes a Long Way," *Wall Street Journal,* December 19, 2005, p. B3.
83. Ibid.
84. K. J. Dunham, "Amid Sinking Workplace Morale, Employers Turn to Recognition," *Wall Street Journal,* November 19, 2002, p. B8.
85. Cited in S. Caudron, "The Top 20 Ways to Motivate Employees," *Industry Week,* April 3, 1995, pp. 15–16. See also B. Nelson, "Try Praise," *Inc.,* September 1996, p. 115; and J. Wiscombe, "Rewards Get Results," *Workforce,* April 2002, pp. 42–48.
86. R. Flandez, "Vegetable Gardens Help Morale Grow," *Wall Street Journal Online,* August 18, 2009; "Pay Raise Alternatives = Motivated Employees," *Training,* July/August 2009, p. 11; D. Koeppel, "Strange Brew: Beer and Office Democracy," *CNNMoney.com,* June 9, 2009; and B. Brim and T. Simon, "Strengths on the Factory Floor," *The Gallup Management Journal Online,* March 10, 2009.
87. V. M. Barret, "Fight the Jerks," *Forbes,* July 2, 2007, pp. 52–54.
88. E. White, "The Best vs. the Rest," *Wall Street Journal,* January 30, 2006, pp. B1+.
89. R. K. Abbott, "Performance-Based Flex: A Tool for Managing Total Compensation Costs," *Compensation and Benefits Review,* March–April 1993, pp. 18–21; J. R. Schuster and P. K. Zingheim, "The New Variable Pay: Key Design Issues," *Compensation and Benefits Review,* March–April 1993, pp. 27–34; C. R. Williams and L. P. Livingstone, "Another Look at the Relationship between Performance and Voluntary Turnover," *Academy of Management Journal,* April 1994, pp. 269–298; A. M. Dickinson and K. L. Gillette, "A Comparison of the Effects of Two Individual Monetary Incentive Systems on Productivity: Piece Rate Pay versus Base Pay Plus Incentives," *Journal of Organizational Behavior Management,* Spring 1994, pp. 3–82; and C. B. Cadsby, F. Song, and F. Tapon, "Sorting and Incentive Effects of Pay for Performance: An Experimental Investigation," *Academy of Management Journal,* April 2007, pp. 387–405.
90. E. White, "Employers Increasingly Favor Bonuses to Raises," *Wall Street Journal,* August 28, 2006, p. B3.
91. "More Than 20 Percent of Japanese Firms Use Pay Systems Based on Performance," *Manpower Argus,* May 1998, p. 7; and E. Beauchesne, "Pay Bonuses Improve Productivity, Study Shows," *Vancouver Sun,* September 13, 2002, p. D5.
92. H. Rheem, "Performance Management Programs," *Harvard Business Review,* September–October 1996, pp. 8–9; G. Sprinkle, "The Effect of Incentive Contracts on Learning and Performance," *Accounting Review,* July 2000, pp. 299–326; and "Do Incentive Awards Work?," *HRFocus,* October 2000, pp. 1–3.
93. R. D. Banker, S. Y. Lee, G. Potter, and D. Srinivasan, "Contextual Analysis of Performance Impacts on Outcome-Based Incentive Compensation," *Academy of Management Journal,* August 1996, pp. 920–948.
94. T. Reason, "Why Bonus Plans Fail," *CFO,* January 2003, p. 53; and "Has Pay For Performance Had Its Day?" *The McKinsey Quarterly,* no. 4, 2002, accessed on Forbes Web site [www.forbes.com].
95. R. Dodes and D. Mattioli, "Retailers Try on New Sales Tactics," *Wall Street Journal,* April 19, 2010, p. B9; and A. Kadet, "Rise of the Retail Robot," *Smart Money,* November 2009, p. 96.
96. L. Petrecca, "With 3,000 Applications a Day, Google Can Be Picky," *USA Today,* May 19, 2010, p. 2B; S. E. Ante and K. Weisul, "And Google Begat . . . ," *Bloomberg BusinessWeek,* March 8, 2010, pp. 39–42; R. Levering and M. Moskowitz, "And the Winners Are . . . ," *Fortune,* February 2, 2009, pp. 67+; A. Lashinsky, "Where Does Google Go Next?" *CNNMoney.com,* May 12, 2008; K. Hafner, "Google

Options Make Masseuse a Multimillionaire," *New York Times Online,* November 12, 2007; Q. Hardy, "Close to the Vest," *Forbes,* July 2, 2007, pp. 40–42; K. J. Delaney, "Start-Ups Make Inroads with Google's Work Force," *Wall Street Journal Online,* June 28, 2007; and "Perk Place: The Benefits Offered by Google and Others May Be Grand, But They're All Business," *Knowledge @ Wharton* [knowledge.wharton.upenn.edu/article], March 21, 2007.
97. M. Conlin, "Is Optimism a Competitive Advantage?" *BusinessWeek,* August 24 & 31, 2009, pp. 52–53; "New ROLE," *Training,* June 2009, p. 4; C. Ressler and J. Thompson, *Why Work Sucks and How to Fix It* (New York: Penguin Group, 2008); J. Marquez, "Changing A Company's Culture, Not Just Its Schedules, Pays Off," *Workforce Management Online,* November 17, 2008; S. Brown, "Results Should Matter, Not Just Working Late," *USA Today,* June 16, 2008, p. 4B; and J. Thottam, "Reworking Work," *Time,* July 25, 2005, pp. 50–55.

Chapter 17

1. S. Ali, "How to Build the Next Generation of Global Leaders," *Diversity Inc.,* May 2010, pp. 82–85; and P. O'Connell, "How Companies Develop Great Leaders," *Bloomberg BusinessWeek Online,* February 16, 2010.
2. "Selected Results From Best Companies for Leadership Survey," *Bloomberg BusinessWeek Online,* February 16, 2010.
3. Most leadership research has focused on the actions and responsibilities of managers and extrapolated the results to leaders and leadership in general.
4. "Study: Long Finger Equals Success," *Springfield, Missouri, News-Leader,* January 13, 2009, p. 4B.
5. See T. A. Judge, J. E. Bono, R. Ilies, and M. W. Gerhardt, "Personality and Leadership: A Qualitative and Quantitative Review," *Journal of Applied Psychology,* August 2002, pp. 765–780; and S. A. Kirkpatrick and E. A. Locke, "Leadership: Do Traits Matter?" *Academy of Management Executive,* May 1991, pp. 48–60.
6. "Ensemble Acting in Business," *New York Times Online,* June 7, 2009; and J. M. O'Brien, "Ousted Seagate CEO Provocative to the End," *CNNMoney.com,* January 13, 2009.
7. K. Lewin and R. Lippitt, "An Experimental Approach to the Study of Autocracy and Democracy: A Preliminary Note," *Sociometry,* vol. 1, 1938, pp. 292–300; K. Lewin, "Field Theory and Experiment in Social Psychology: Concepts and Methods," *American Journal of Sociology,* vol. 44, 1939, pp. 868–896; K. Lewin, L. Lippitt, and R. K. White, "Patterns of Aggressive Behavior in Experimentally Created Social Climates," *Journal of Social Psychology,* vol. 10, 1939, pp. 271–301; and L. Lippitt, "An Experimental Study of the Effect of Democratic and Authoritarian Group Atmospheres," *University of Iowa Studies in Child Welfare,* vol. 16, 1940, pp. 43–95.
8. B. M. Bass, *Stogdill's Handbook of Leadership* (New York: Free Press, 1981), pp. 289–299.
9. R. M. Stogdill and A. E. Coons (eds.), *Leader Behavior: Its Description and Measurement,* Research Monograph no. 88 (Columbus: Ohio State University, Bureau of Business Research, 1951). For an updated literature review of Ohio State research, see S. Kerr, C. A. Schriesheim, C. J. Murphy, and R. M. Stogdill, "Toward a Contingency Theory of Leadership Based upon the Consideration and Initiating Structure Literature," *Organizational Behavior and Human Performance,* August 1974, pp. 62–82; and B. M. Fisher, "Consideration and Initiating Structure and Their Relationships with Leader Effectiveness: A Meta-Analysis," in F. Hoy (ed.), *Proceedings* of the 48th Annual Academy of Management Conference, Anaheim, California, 1988, pp. 201–205.
10. R. Kahn and D. Katz, "Leadership Practices in Relation to Productivity and Morale," in D. Cartwright and A. Zander (eds.), *Group Dynamics: Research and Theory,* 2d ed. (Elmsford, NY: Row, Paterson, 1960).
11. R. R. Blake and J. S. Mouton, *The Managerial Grid III* (Houston: Gulf Publishing, 1984).
12. L. L. Larson, J. G. Hunt, and R. N. Osborn, "The Great Hi-Hi Leader Behavior Myth: A Lesson from Occam's Razor," *Academy of Management Journal,* December 1976, pp. 628–641; and P. C. Nystrom, "Managers and the Hi-Hi Leader Myth," *Academy of Management Journal,* June 1978, pp. 325–331.
13. W. G. Bennis, "The Seven Ages of the Leader," *Harvard Business Review,* January 2004, p. 52.

14. F. E. Fiedler, *A Theory of Leadership Effectiveness* (New York: McGraw-Hill, 1967).

15. R. Ayman, M. M. Chemers, and F. Fiedler, "The Contingency Model of Leadership Effectiveness: Its Levels of Analysis," *Leadership Quarterly,* Summer 1995, pp. 147–167; C. A. Schriesheim, B. J. Tepper, and L. A. Tetrault, "Least Preferred Coworker Score, Situational Control, and Leadership Effectiveness: A Meta-Analysis of Contingency Model Performance Predictions," *Journal of Applied Psychology,* August 1994, pp. 561–573; and L. H. Peters, D. D. Hartke, and J. T. Pholmann, "Fiedler's Contingency Theory of Leadership: An Application of the Meta-Analysis Procedures of Schmidt and Hunter," *Psychological Bulletin,* March 1985, pp. 274–285.

16. See E. H. Schein, *Organizational Psychology*, 3rd ed. (Upper Saddle River, NJ: Prentice Hall, 1980), pp. 116–117; and B. Kabanoff, "A Critique of Leader Match and Its Implications for Leadership Research," *Personnel Psychology*, Winter 1981, pp. 749–764.

17. P. Hersey and K. Blanchard, "So You Want to Know Your Leadership Style?" *Training and Development Journal*, February 1974, pp. 1–15; and P. Hersey and K. H. Blanchard, *Management of Organizational Behavior: Leading Human Resources*, 8th ed. (Englewood Cliffs, NJ: Prentice Hall, 2001).

18. See, for instance, E. G. Ralph, "Developing Managers' Effectiveness: A Model with Potential," *Journal of Management Inquiry*, June 2004, pp. 152–163; C. L. Graeff, "Evolution of Situational Leadership Theory: A Critical Review," *Leadership Quarterly*, vol. 8, no. 2, 1997, pp. 153–170; and C. F. Fernandez and R. P. Vecchio, "Situational Leadership Theory Revisited: A Test of an Across-Jobs Perspective," *Leadership Quarterly*, vol. 8, no. 1, 1997, pp. 67–84.

19. R. J. House, "A Path-Goal Theory of Leader Effectiveness," *Administrative Science Quarterly*, September 1971, pp. 321–338; R. J. House and T. R. Mitchell, "Path-Goal Theory of Leadership," *Journal of Contemporary Business*, Autumn 1974, p. 86; and R. J. House, "Path-Goal Theory of Leadership: Lessons, Legacy, and a Reformulated Theory," *Leadership Quarterly,* Fall 1996, pp. 323–352.

20. J. C. Wofford and L. Z. Liska, "Path-Goal Theories of Leadership: A Meta-Analysis," *Journal of Management*, Winter 1993, pp. 857–876; and A. Sagie and M. Koslowsky, "Organizational Attitudes and Behaviors as a Function of Participation in Strategic and Tactical Change Decisions: An Application of Path-Goal Theory," *Journal of Organizational Behavior*, January 1994, pp. 37–47.

21. R. M. Dienesch and R. C. Liden, "Leader–Member Exchange Model of Leadership: A Critique and Further Development," *Academy of Management Review,* July 1986, pp. 618–634; G. B. Graen and M. Uhl-Bien, "Relationship-Based Approach to Leadership: Development of Leader–Member Exchange (LMX) Theory of Leadership Over 25 Years: Applying a Multi-Domain Perspective," *Leadership Quarterly,* Summer 1995, pp. 219–247; R. C. Liden, R. T. Sparrowe, and S. J. Wayne, "Leader–Member Exchange Theory: The Past and Potential for the Future," in G. R. Ferris (ed.), *Research in Personnel and Human Resource Management*, vol. 15 (Greenwich, CT: JAI Press, 1997), pp. 47–119; and C. P. Schriesheim, S. L. Castro, X. Zhou, and F. J. Yammarino, "The Folly of Theorizing 'A' but Testing 'B': A Selective Level-of-Analysis Review of the Field and a Detailed Leader–Member Exchange Illustration," *Leadership Quarterly,* Winter 2001, pp. 515–551.

22. R. C. Liden and G. Graen, "Generalizability of the Vertical Dyad Linkage Model of Leadership," *Academy of Management Journal,* September 1980, pp. 451–465; R. C. Liden, S. J. Wayne, and D. Stilwell, "A Longitudinal Study of the Early Development of Leader–Member Exchanges," *Journal of Applied Psychology,* August 1993, pp. 662–674; S. J. Wayne, L. J. Shore, W. H. Bommer, and L. E. Tetrick, "The Role of Fair Treatment and Rewards in Perceptions of Organizational Support and Leader–Member Exchange," *Journal of Applied Psychology,* June 2002, pp. 590–598; and S. S. Masterson, K. Lewis, and B. M. Goldman, "Integrating Justice and Social Exchange: The Differing Effects of Fair Procedures and Treatment on Work Relationships," *Academy of Management Journal,* August 2000, pp. 738–748.

23. D. Duchon, S. G. Green, and T. D. Taber, "Vertical Dyad Linkage: A Longitudinal Assessment of Antecedents, Measures, and Consequences," *Journal of Applied Psychology,* February 1986, pp. 56–60; R. C. Liden, S. J. Wayne, and D. Stilwell, "A Longitudinal Study of the Early Development of Leader–Member Exchanges"; M. Uhl-Bien, "Relationship Development as a Key Ingredient for Leadership Development," in S. E. Murphy and R. E. Riggio (eds.), *Future of Leadership Development* (Mahwah, NJ: Lawrence Erlbaum, 2003), pp. 129–147; R. Vecchio and D. M. Brazil, "Leadership and Sex-Similarity: A Comparison in a Military Setting," *Personnel Psychology,* vol. 60, 2007, pp. 303–335; and V. L. Goodwin, W. M. Bowler, and J. L. Whittington, "A Social Network Perspective on LMX Relationships: Accounting for the Instrumental Value of Leader and Follower Networks," *Journal of Management,* August 2009, pp. 954–980.

24. See, for instance, C. R. Gerstner and D. V. Day, "Meta-analytic Review of Leader–Member Exchange Theory: Correlates and Construct Issues," *Journal of Applied Psychology,* December 1997, pp. 827–844; R. Ilies, J. D. Nahrgang, and F. P. Morgerson, "Leader–Member Exchange and Citizenship Behaviors: A Meta-analysis," *Journal of Applied Psychology,* January 2007, pp. 269–277; and Z. Chen, W. Lam, and J. A. Zhong, "Leader–Member Exchange and Member Performance: A New Look at Individual-Level Negative Feedback-Seeking Behavior and Team-Level Empowerment Culture," *Journal of Applied Psychology,* January 2007, pp. 202–212.

25. Leader Who Made a Difference box based on R. Sidel, "Banga to Be MasterCard's Protector," *Wall Street Journal,* May 29–30, 2010, pp. B1+; A. Saha-Bubna and M. Jarzemsky, "MasterCard President Is Named CEO," *Wall Street Journal,* April 13, 2010, p. C3; "Why Banga Quit Citi," *Euromoney,* July 2009, p. 41; and E. Wilson, "Banga Demolishes Citi's Asia-Pac Silos," *Euromoney,* May 2009, p. 49.

26. B. M. Bass and R. E. Riggio, *Transformational Leadership,* 2d ed. (Mahwah, NJ: Lawrence Erlbaum Associates, Inc., 2006), p. 3.

27. B. M. Bass, "Leadership: Good, Better, Best," *Organizational Dynamics,* Winter 1985, pp. 26–40; and J. Seltzer and B. M. Bass, "Transformational Leadership: Beyond Initiation and Consideration," *Journal of Management*, December 1990, pp. 693–703.

28. B. J. Avolio and B. M. Bass, "Transformational Leadership, Charisma, and Beyond." Working paper, School of Management, State University of New York, Binghamton, 1985, p. 14.

29. S. J. Peterson and F. O. Walumba, "CEO Positive Psychological Traits, Transformational Leadership, and Firm Performance in High-Technology Start-up and Established Firms," *Journal of Management,* April 2009, pp. 348–368; R. S. Rubin, D. C. Munz, and W. H. Bommer, "Leading from Within: The Effects of Emotion Recognition and Personality on Transformational Leadership Behavior," *Academy of Management Journal,* October 2005, pp. 845–858; T. A. Judge and J. E. Bono, "Five-Factor Model of Personality and Transformational Leadership," *Journal of Applied Psychology,* October 2000, pp. 751–765; B. M. Bass and B. J. Avolio, "Developing Transformational Leadership: 1992 and Beyond," *Journal of European Industrial Training*, January 1990, p. 23; and J. J. Hater and B. M. Bass, "Supervisors' Evaluation and Subordinates' Perceptions of Transformational and Transactional Leadership," *Journal of Applied Psychology,* November 1988, pp. 695–702.

30. Y. Ling, Z. Simsek, M. H. Lubatkin, and J. F. Veiga, "Transformational Leadership's Role in Promoting Corporate Entrepreneurship: Examining the CEO-TMT Interface," *Academy of Management Journal,* June 2008, pp. 557–576; A. E. Colbert, A. L. Kristof-Brown, B. H. Bradley, and M. R. Barrick, "CEO Transformational Leadership: The Role of Goal Importance Congruence in Top Management Teams," *Academy of Management Journal,* February 2008, pp. 81–96; R. F. Piccolo and J. A. Colquitt, "Transformational Leadership and Job Behaviors: The Mediating Role of Core Job Characteristics," *Academy of Management Journal,* April 2006, pp. 327–340; O. Epitropaki and R. Martin, "From Ideal to Real: A Longitudinal Study of the Role of Implicit Leadership Theories on Leader–Member Exchanges and Employee Outcomes," *Journal of Applied Psychology,* July 2005, pp. 659–676; J. E. Bono and T. A. Judge, "Self-Concordance at Work: Toward Understanding the Motivational Effects of Transformational Leaders," *Academy of Management Journal,* October 2003, pp. 554–571; T. Dvir, D. Eden, B. J. Avolio, and B. Shamir, "Impact of Transformational Leadership on Follower Development and Performance: A Field Experiment," *Academy of Management Journal,* August 2002, pp. 735–744; N. Sivasubramaniam, W. D. Murry, B. J. Avolio, and D. I. Jung, "A Longitudinal Model of the Effects of

Team Leadership and Group Potency on Group Performance," *Group and Organization Management,* March 2002, pp. 66–96; J. M. Howell and B. J. Avolio, "Transformational Leadership, Transactional Leadership, Locus of Control, and Support for Innovation: Key Predictors of Consolidated-Business-Unit Performance," *Journal of Applied Psychology,* December 1993, pp. 891–911; R. T. Keller, "Transformational Leadership and the Performance of Research and Development Project Groups," *Journal of Management,* September 1992, pp. 489–501; and Bass and Avolio, "Developing Transformational Leadership."

31. F. Vogelstein, "Mighty Amazon," *Fortune,* May 26, 2003, pp. 60–74.

32. A. Pentland, "We Can Measure the Power of Charisma," *Harvard Business Review,* January–February 2010, pp. 34–35; J. M. Crant and T. S. Bateman, "Charismatic Leadership Viewed From Above: The Impact of Proactive Personality," *Journal of Organizational Behavior,* February 2000, pp. 63–75; G. Yukl and J. M. Howell, "Organizational and Contextual Influences on the Emergence and Effectiveness of Charismatic Leadership," *Leadership Quarterly,* Summer 1999, pp. 257–283; and J. A. Conger and R. N. Kanungo, "Behavioral Dimensions of Charismatic Leadership," in J. A. Conger, R. N. Kanungo and Associates, *Charismatic Leadership* (San Francisco: Jossey-Bass, 1988), pp. 78–97.

33. J. A. Conger and R. N. Kanungo, *Charismatic Leadership in Organizations* (Thousand Oaks, CA: Sage, 1998).

34. F. Walter and H. Bruch, "An Affective Events Model of Charismatic Leadership Behavior: A Review, Theoretical Investigation, and Research Agenda," *Journal of Management,* December 2009, pp. 1428–1452; K. S. Groves, "Linking Leader Skills, Follower Attitudes, and Contextual Variables via An Integrated Model of Charismatic Leadership," *Journal of Management,* April 2005, pp. 255–277; J. J. Sosik, " The Role of Personal Values in the Charismatic Leadership of Corporate Managers: A Model and Preliminary Field Study," *Leadership Quarterly,* April 2005, pp. 221–244; A. H. B. deHoogh, D. N. den Hartog, P. L. Koopman, H. Thierry, P. T. van den Berg, J. G. van der Weide, and C. P. M. Wilderom, "Leader Motives, Charismatic Leadership, and Subordinates' Work Attitudes in the Profit and Voluntary Sector," *Leadership Quarterly,* February 2005, pp. 17–38; J. M. Howell and B. Shamir, "The Role of Followers in the Charismatic Leadership Process: Relationships and Their Consequences," *Academy of Management Review,* January 2005, pp. 96–112; J. Paul, D. L. Costley, J. P. Howell, P. W. Dorfman, and D. Trafimow, "The Effects of Charismatic Leadership on Followers' Self-Concept Accessibility," *Journal of Applied Social Psychology,* September 2001, pp. 1821–1844; J. A. Conger, R. N. Kanungo, and S. T. Menon, "Charismatic Leadership and Follower Effects," *Journal of Organizational Behavior,* vol. 21, 2000, pp. 747–767; R. W. Rowden, "The Relationship Between Charismatic Leadership Behaviors and Organizational Commitment," *Leadership & Organization Development Journal,* January 2000, pp. 30–35; G. P. Shea and C. M. Howell, "Charismatic Leadership and Task Feedback: A Laboratory Study of Their Effects on Self-Efficacy," *Leadership Quarterly,* Fall 1999, pp. 375–396; S. A. Kirkpatrick and E. A. Locke, "Direct and Indirect Effects of Three Core Charismatic Leadership Components on Performance and Attitudes," *Journal of Applied Psychology,* February 1996, pp. 36–51; D. A. Waldman, B. M. Bass, and F. J. Yammarino, "Adding to Contingent-Reward Behavior: The Augmenting Effect of Charismatic Leadership," *Group & Organization Studies,* December 1990, pp. 381–394; and R. J. House, J. Woycke, and E. M. Fodor, "Charismatic and Noncharismatic Leaders: Differences in Behavior and Effectiveness," in Conger and Kanungo, *Charismatic Leadership,* pp. 103–104.

35. B. R. Agle, N. J. Nagarajan, J. A. Sonnenfeld, and D. Srinivasan, "Does CEO Charisma Matter? An Empirical Analysis of the Relationships Among Organizational Performance, Environmental Uncertainty, and Top Management Team Perceptions of CEO Charisma," *Academy of Management Journal,* February 2006, pp. 161–174.

36. R. Birchfield, "Creating Charismatic Leaders," *Management,* June 2000, pp. 30–31; S. Caudron, "Growing Charisma," *Industry Week,* May 4, 1998, pp. 54–55; and J. A. Conger and R. N. Kanungo, "Training Charismatic Leadership: A Risky and Critical Task," in Conger and Kanungo, *Charismatic Leadership,* pp. 309–323.

37. J. G. Hunt, K. B. Boal, and G. E. Dodge, "The Effects of Visionary and Crisis-Responsive Charisma on Followers: An Experimental Examination," *Leadership Quarterly,* Fall 1999, pp. 423–448; R. J. House and R. N. Aditya, "The Social Scientific Study of Leadership: Quo Vadis?" *Journal of Management,* vol. 23, no. 3, 1997, pp. 316–323; and R. J. House, "A 1976 Theory of Charismatic Leadership."

38. This definition is based on M. Sashkin, "The Visionary Leader," in Conger and Kanungo et al., *Charismatic Leadership,* pp. 124–125; B. Nanus, *Visionary Leadership* (New York: Free Press, 1992), p. 8; N. H. Snyder and M. Graves, "Leadership and Vision," *Business Horizons,* January–February 1994, p. 1; and J. R. Lucas, "Anatomy of a Vision Statement," *Management Review,* February 1998, pp. 22–26.

39. Nanus, *Visionary Leadership,* p. 8.

40. By the Numbers box based on "Selected Results from Best Companies for Leadership Survey," *BusinessWeek Online,* February 16, 2010; J. M. Kouzas and B. Z. Posner, "To Lead, Create a Shared Vision," *Harvard Business Review,* January 2009, pp. 20–21; "Still Haven't Closed the Gap," *Training,* March–April 2009, p. 9; and P. Cappelli, H. Singh, J. V. Singh, and M. Useem, "Leadership Lessons from India," *Harvard Business Review,* March 2010, pp. 90–97.

41. S. Caminiti, "What Team Leaders Need to Know," *Fortune,* February 20, 1995, pp. 93–100.

42. Ibid., p. 93.

43. Ibid., p. 100.

44. N. Steckler and N. Fondas, "Building Team Leader Effectiveness: A Diagnostic Tool," *Organizational Dynamics,* Winter 1995, p. 20.

45. R. S. Wellins, W. C. Byham, and G. R. Dixon, *Inside Teams* (San Francisco: Jossey-Bass, 1994), p. 318.

46. Steckler and Fondas, "Building Team Leader Effectiveness," p. 21.

47. G. Colvin, "The FedEx Edge," *Fortune,* April 3, 2006, pp. 77–84.

48. See J. R. P. French Jr. and B. Raven, "The Bases of Social Power," in D. Cartwright and A. F. Zander (eds.), *Group Dynamics: Research and Theory* (New York: Harper & Row, 1960), pp. 607–623; P. M. Podsakoff and C. A. Schriesheim, "Field Studies of French and Raven's Bases of Power: Critique, Reanalysis, and Suggestions for Future Research," *Psychological Bulletin,* May 1985, pp. 387–411; R. K. Shukla, "Influence of Power Bases in Organizational Decision Making: A Contingency Model," *Decision Sciences,* July 1982, pp. 450–470; D. E. Frost and A. J. Stahelski, "The Systematic Measurement of French and Raven's Bases of Social Power in Workgroups," *Journal of Applied Social Psychology,* April 1988, pp. 375–389; and T. R. Hinkin and C. A. Schriesheim, "Development and Application of New Scales to Measure the French and Raven (1959) Bases of Social Power," *Journal of Applied Psychology,* August 1989, pp. 561–567.

49. J. M. Kouzes and B. Z. Posner, *Credibility: How Leaders Gain and Lose It, and Why People Demand It* (San Francisco: Jossey-Bass, 1993), p. 14.

50. Based on F. D. Schoorman, R. C. Mayer, and J. H. Davis, "An Integrative Model of Organizational Trust: Past, Present, and Future," *Academy of Management Review,* April 2007, pp. 344–354; G. M. Spreitzer and A. K. Mishra, "Giving Up Control Without Losing Control," *Group & Organization Management,* June 1999, pp. 155–187; R. C. Mayer, J. H. Davis, and F. D. Schoorman, "An Integrative Model of Organizational Trust," *Academy of Management Review,* July 1995, p. 712; and L. T. Hosmer, "Trust: The Connecting Link between Organizational Theory and Philosophical Ethics," *Academy of Management Review,* April 1995, p. 393.

51. P. L. Schindler and C. C. Thomas, "The Structure of Interpersonal Trust in the Workplace," *Psychological Reports,* October 1993, pp. 563–573.

52. H. H. Tan and C. S. F. Tan, "Toward the Differentiation of Trust in Supervisor and Trust in Organization," *Genetic, Social, and General Psychology Monographs,* May 2000, pp. 241–260.

53. H. H. Brower, S. W. Lester, M. A. Korsgaard, and B. R. Dineen, "A Closer Look at Trust Between Managers and Subordinates: Understanding the Effects of Both Trusting and Being Trusted on Subordinate Outcomes," *Journal of Management,* April 2009, pp. 327–347; R. C. Mayer and M. B. Gavin, "Trust in Management and Performance: Who Minds the Shop While the Employees Watch the Boss?" *Academy of Management Journal,* October 2005, pp. 874–888; and K. T. Dirks and D. L. Ferrin, "Trust in Leadership: Meta-Analytic Findings and Implications for Research and Practice," *Journal of Applied Psychology,* August 2002, pp. 611–628.

54. See, for example, Dirks and Ferrin, "Trust in Leadership: Meta-Analytic Findings and Implications for Research and Practice"; J. K. Butler Jr., "Toward Understanding and Measuring Conditions of Trust: Evolution of a Conditions of Trust Inventory," *Journal of Management,* September 1991, pp. 643–663; and F. Bartolome, "Nobody Trusts the Boss Completely—Now What?" *Harvard Business Review,* March–April 1989, pp. 135–142.

55. P. H. Kim, K. T. Dirks, and C. D. Cooper, "The Repair of Trust: A Dynamic Bilateral Perspective and Multilevel Conceptualization," *Academy of Management Review,* July 2009, pp. 401–422; R. Zemke, "The Confidence Crisis," *Training,* June 2004, pp. 22–30; J. A. Byrne, "Restoring Trust in Corporate America," *BusinessWeek,* June 24, 2002, pp. 30–35; S. Armour, "Employees' New Motto: Trust No One," *USA Today,* February 5, 2002, p. 1B; J. Scott, "Once Bitten, Twice Shy: A World of Eroding Trust," *New York Times,* April 21, 2002, p. WK5; J. Brockner, P. A. Siegel, J. P. Daly, T. Tyler, and C. Martin, "When Trust Matters: The Moderating Effect of Outcome Favorability," *Administrative Science Quarterly,* September 1997, p. 558; and J. Brockner, P. A. Siegel, J. P. Daly, T. Tyler, and C. Martin, "When Trust Matters: The Moderating Effect of Outcome Favorability," *Administrative Science Quarterly,* September 1997, p. 558.

56. "Weathering the Storm: A Study of Employee Attitudes and Opinions," *WorkUSA 2002 Study,* Watson Wyatt [www.watsonwyatt.com].

57. T. Vinas, "DuPont: Safety Starts at the Top," *Industry Week,* July 2002, p. 55.

58. A. Srivastava, K. M. Bartol, and E. A. Locke, "Empowering Leadership in Management Teams: Effects on Knowledge Sharing, Efficacy, and Performance," *Academy of Management Journal,* December 2006, pp. 1239–1251; P. K. Mills and G. R. Ungson, "Reassessing the Limits of Structural Empowerment: Organizational Constitution and Trust as Controls," *Academy of Management Review,* January 2003, pp. 143–153; W. A. Rudolph and M. Sashkin, "Can Organizational Empowerment Work in Multinational Settings?" *Academy of Management Executive,* February 2002, pp. 102–115; C. Gomez and B. Rosen, "The Leader–Member Link Between Managerial Trust and Employee Empowerment," *Group & Organization Management,* March 2001, pp. 53–69; C. Robert and T. M. Probst, "Empowerment and Continuous Improvement in the United States, Mexico, Poland, and India," *Journal of Applied Psychology,* October 2000, pp. 643–658; R. C. Herrenkohl, G. T. Judson, and J. A. Heffner, "Defining and Measuring Employee Empowerment," *Journal of Applied Behavioral Science,* September 1999, p. 373; R. C. Ford and M. D. Fottler, "Empowerment: A Matter of Degree," *Academy of Management Executive,* August 1995, pp. 21–31; and W. A. Rudolph, "Navigating the Journey to Empowerment," *Organizational Dynamics,* Spring 1995, pp. 19–32.

59. T. A. Stewart, "Just Think: No Permission Needed," *Fortune,* January 8, 2001, pp. 190–192.

60. M. Elliott, "Who Needs Charisma?" *Time,* July 20, 2009, pp. 35–38.

61. F. W. Swierczek, "Leadership and Culture: Comparing Asian Managers," *Leadership & Organization Development Journal,* December 1991, pp. 3–10.

62. House, "Leadership in the Twenty-First Century," p. 443; M. F. Peterson and J. G. Hunt, "International Perspectives on International Leadership," *Leadership Quarterly,* Fall 1997, pp. 203–231; and J. R. Schermerhorn and M. H. Bond, "Cross-Cultural Leadership in Collectivism and High Power Distance Settings," *Leadership & Organization Development Journal,* vol. 18, issue 4/5, 1997, pp. 187–193.

63. R. J. House, P. J. Hanges, S. A. Ruiz-Quintanilla, P. W. Dorfman, and Associates, "Culture Specific and Cross-Culturally Generalizable Implicit Leadership Theories: Are the Attributes of Charismatic/Transformational Leadership Universally Endorsed?" *Leadership Quarterly,* Summer 1999, pp. 219–256; and D. E. Carl and M. Javidan, "Universality of Charismatic Leadership: A Multi-Nation Study," paper presented at the National Academy of Management Conference, Washington, DC, August 2001.

64. D. E. Carl and M. Javidan, "Universality of Charismatic Leadership, p. 29.

65. See, for instance, R. Lofthouse, "Herding the Cats," *EuroBusiness,* February 2001, pp. 64–65; and M. Delahoussaye, "Leadership in the 21st Century," *Training,* September 2001, pp. 60–72.

66. See, for example, D. S. DeRue and N. Wellman, "Developing Leaders via Experience: The Role of Developmental Challenge, Learning Organization, and Feedback Availability," *Journal of Applied Psychology,* July 2009, pp. 859–875; A. A. Vicere, "Executive Education: The Leading Edge," *Organizational Dynamics,* Autumn 1996, pp. 67–81; J. Barling, T. Weber, and E. K. Kelloway, "Effects of Transformational Leadership Training on Attitudinal and Financial Outcomes: A Field Experiment," *Journal of Applied Psychology,* December 1996, pp. 827–832; and D. V. Day, "Leadership Development: A Review in Context," *Leadership Quarterly,* Winter 2000, pp. 581–613.

67. K. Y. Chan and F. Drasgow, "Toward a Theory of Individual Differences and Leadership: Understanding the Motivation to Lead," *Journal of Applied Psychology,* June 2001, pp. 481–498.

68. M. Sashkin, "The Visionary Leader," in J. A. Conger, R. N. Kanungo and Associates (eds.), *Charismatic Leadership* (San Francisco: Jossey-Bass, 1988), p. 150.

69. S. Kerr and J. M. Jermier, "Substitutes for Leadership: Their Meaning and Measurement," *Organizational Behavior and Human Performance,* December 1978, pp. 375–403; J. P. Howell, P. W. Dorfman, and S. Kerr, "Leadership and Substitutes for Leadership," *Journal of Applied Behavioral Science* 22, No. 1 (1986), pp. 29–46; J. P. Howell, D. E. Bowen, P. W. Dorfman, S. Kerr, and P. M. Podsakoff, "Substitutes for Leadership: Effective Alternatives to Ineffective Leadership," *Organizational Dynamics,* Summer 1990, pp. 21–38; and P. M. Podsakoff, B. P. Niehoff, S. B. MacKenzie, and M. L. Williams, "Do Substitutes for Leadership Really Substitute for Leadership? An Empirical Examination of Kerr and Jermier's Situational Leadership Model," *Organizational Behavior and Human Decision Processes,* February 1993, pp. 1–44.

70. "Rhode Island Board Backs Off Firings: Teachers Keep Their Jobs," *Education Week,* June 9, 2010, p. 4; R. Weingarten, "Don't Scapegoat the Teachers," *USA Today Online,* March 11, 2010; G. Toppo, "Firing Teachers: A First Step to Reform or a Step . . . ," *USA Today Online,* March 10, 2010; C. Hausman, "Does Poor School Performance Justify Clean Sweep of Staff?" *Ethics Newsline Online* [www.globalethics.org], March 1, 2010; and G. Toppo, "Mass Firings at R.I. School May Signal a Trend," *USA Today Online,* February 25, 2010.

71. A. Bernasek, "World's Most Admired Companies," *Fortune,* March 22, 2010, pp. 121+; "Selected Results from Best Companies for Leadership Survey," *Bloomberg BusinessWeek Online,* February 16, 2010; J. Kerr and R. Albright, "Finding and Cultivating Finishers," *Leadership Excellence,* July 2009, p. 20; D. Jones, "3M CEO Emphasizes Importance of Leaders," *USA Today,* May 18, 2009, p. 4B; G. Colvin, "World's Most Admired Companies 2009," *Fortune,* March 16, 2009, pp. 75+; and M. C. Mankins and R. Steele, "Turning Great Strategy into Great Performance," *Harvard Business Review,* July–August 2005, pp. 64–72.

72. "Inbox," *Time,* April 5, 2010, p. 7; M. Thompson, "The Sea Witch," *Time,* March 22, 2010, pp. 30–33; B. H. Johnsen, J. Eid, S. Pallesen, P. T. Bartone, and O. A. Nissestad, "Predicting Transformational Leadership in Naval Cadets: Effects of Personality Hardiness and Training," *Journal of Applied Social Psychology,* September 2009, pp. 2213–2235; and P. Thunholm, "Military Leaders and Followers—Do They Have Different Decision Styles?" *Scandinavian Journal of Psychology,* August 2009, pp. 317–324.

Chapter 18

1. R. Albergotti, "World News: Luger's Death Blamed on 'Series of Events,'" *Wall Street Journal,* April 20, 2010, p. A17; N. Köhler, A. Wherry, and N. MacDonald, "Who's to Blame?" *Macleans,* March 1, 2010, pp. 37–38; G. A. Fowler, "The Winter Olympics; Rogge Says Luge Death Casts 'Shadow,'" *Wall Street Journal,* February 26, 2010, p. W5; D. Crawford, R. Albergotti, and I. Johnson, "Speed and Commerce Skewed Track's Design," *Wall Street Journal Online,* February 16, 2010; and A. Thompson, M. Futterman, and R. Albergotti, "Death Casts Pall Over Olympics," *Wall Street Journal,* February 13, 2010, p. A1.

2. B. Hagenbaugh, "State Quarters Extra Leaf Grew Out of Lunch Break," *USA Today,* January 20, 2006, p. 1B.

3. K. A. Merchant, "The Control Function of Management," *Sloan Management Review,* Summer 1982, pp. 43–55.

4. E. Flamholtz, "Organizational Control Systems Managerial Tool," *California Management Review,* Winter 1979, p. 55.

5. D. Heath and C. Heath, "The Telltale Brown M&M," *Fast Company,* March 2010, pp. 36–38.

6. T. Vinas and J. Jusko, "5 Threats That Could Sink Your Company," *Industry Week,* September 2004, pp. 52–61; "Workplace Security: How Vulnerable Are You?" Special section in *Wall Street Journal,* September 29, 2003, pp. R1–R8; P. Magnusson, "Your Jitters Are Their Lifeblood," *BusinessWeek,* April 14, 2003, p. 41; and T. Purdum, "Preparing for the Worst," *Industry Week,* January 2003, pp. 53–55.

7. A. Dalton, "Rapid Recovery," *Industry Week,* March 2005, pp. 70–71.

8. S. Kerr, "On the Folly of Rewarding A, While Hoping for B," *Academy of Management Journal,* December 1975, pp. 769–783.

9. D. Heath and C. Heath, "Watch the Game Film," *Fast Company,* June 2010, pp. 52–54.

10. M. Starr, "State-of-the-Art Stats," *Newsweek,* March 24, 2003, pp. 47–49.

11. "Domino's Delivered Free Pizzas," *Springfield, Missouri, News-Leader,* April 3, 2009, p. 3B; L. Robbins, "Goggle Error Sends Warning Worldwide," *New York Times Online,* February 1, 2009; and V. O'Connell, "Stores Count Seconds to Cut Labor Costs," *Wall Street Journal,* November 17, 2008, pp. A1+.

12. H. Koontz and R. W. Bradspies, "Managing Through Feedforward Control," *Business Horizons,* June 1972, pp. 25–36.

13. M. Helft, "The Human Hands Behind the Google Money Machine," *New York Times Online,* June 2, 2008.

14. B. Caulfield, "Shoot to Kill," *Forbes,* January 7, 2008, pp. 92–96.

15. T. Laseter and L. Laseter, "See for Yourself," *Strategy+Business* [www.strategy-business.com], November 29, 2007.

16. W. H. Newman, *Constructive Control: Design and Use of Control Systems* (Upper Saddle River, NJ: Prentice Hall, 1975), p. 33.

17. T. L. Albright, C. M. Burgess, A. R. Hibbets, and M. L. Roberts, "Four Steps to Simplify Multimeasure Performance Evaluations Using the Balanced Scorecard," *Journal of Corporate Accounting & Finance,* July–August 2010, pp. 63–68; H. Sundin, M. Granlund, and D. A. Brown, "Balancing Multiple Competing Objectives with a Balanced Scorecard," *European Accounting Review,* vol. 19, no. 2, 2010, pp. 203–246; R. S. Kaplan and D. P. Norton, "How to Implement a New Strategy Without Disrupting Your Organization," *Harvard Business Review,* March 2006, pp. 100–109; L. Bassi and D. McMurrer, "Developing Measurement Systems for Managers in the Knowledge Era," *Organizational Dynamics,* May 2005, pp. 185–196; G. M. J. DeKoning, "Making the Balanced Scorecard Work (Part 2)," *Gallup Brain* [brain.gallup.com], August 12, 2004; G. J. J. DeKoning, "Making the Balanced Scorecard Work (Part 1)," *Gallup Brain* [brain.gallup.com], July 8, 2004; K. Graham, "Balanced Scorecard," *New Zealand Management,* March 2003, pp. 32–34; K. Ellis, "A Ticket to Ride: Balanced Scorecard," *Training,* April 2001, p. 50; and T. Leahy, "Tailoring the Balanced Scorecard," *Business Finance,* August 2000, pp. 53–56.

18. T. Leahy, "Tailoring the Balanced Scorecard."

19. Ibid.

20. B. Worthen, "Private Sector Keeps Mum on Cyber Attacks," *Wall Street Journal,* January 19, 2010, p. B4; G. Bowley, "Ex-Worker Said to Steal Goldman Code," *New York Times Online,* July 7, 2009; and R. King, "Lessons from the Data Breach at Heartland," *BusinessWeek Online,* July 6, 2009.

21. Deloitte & Touche and the Ponemon Institute, "Research Report: Reportable and Multiple Privacy Breaches Rising at Alarming Rate," *Ethics Newsline* [ethicsnewsline.wordpress.com], January 1, 2008.

22. B. Grow, K. Epstein, and C-C. Tschang, "The New E-Spionage Threat," *BusinessWeek,* April 21, 2008, pp. 32–41; S. Leibs, "Firewall of Silence," *CFO,* April 2008, pp. 31–35; J. Pereira, "How Credit-Card Data Went Out Wireless Door," *Wall Street Journal,* May 4, 2007, pp. A1+; and B. Stone, "Firms Fret as Office E-Mail Jumps Security Walls," *New York Times Online,* January 11, 2007.

23. D. Whelan, "Google Me Not," *Forbes,* August 16, 2004, pp. 102–104.

24. V. Fuhrmans, "Replicating Cleveland Clinic's Success Poses Major Challenges," *Wall Street Journal,* July 23, 2009, p. A4.

25. R. Pear, "A.M.A. to Develop Measure of Quality of Medical Care," *New York Times Online,* February 21, 2006; and A. Taylor III, "Double Duty," *Fortune,* March 7, 2005, pp. 104–110.

26. S. Minter, "How Good Is Your Benchmarking?" *Industry Week,* October 2009, pp. 24–26; and T. Leahy, "Extracting Diamonds in the Rough," *Business Finance,* August 2000, pp. 33–37.

27. B. Bruzina, B. Jessop, R. Plourde, B. Whitlock, and L. Rubin, "Ameren Embraces Benchmarking As a Core Business Strategy," *Power Engineering,* November 2002, pp. 121–124.

28. Leader Who Made a Difference box based on A. Bernasek, "The World's Most Admired Companies," *Fortune,* March 22, 2010, pp. 121+; P. Sanders, "Disney Angles for Cash, Loyalty," *Wall Street Journal,* March 11, 2009, p. B4; and R. Siklos, "Bob Iger Rocks Disney," *CNN Online* [www.cnnmoney.com], January 5, 2009.

29. J. Yaukey and C. L. Romero, "Arizona Firm Pays Big for Workers' Digital Downloads," Associated Press, *Springfield, Missouri, News-Leader,* May 6, 2002, p. 6B.

30. D. Mattioli and J. Espinoza, "World Cup Poses Challenge to Bosses," *Wall Street Journal,* June 14, 2010, p. B9; "March Madness Leads to Drop in Productivity," *Delaware County Daily Times Online,* March 16, 2010; and "March Madness at Work Raises Questions of Priorities, Productivity," *FoxSports Online,* March 15, 2010.

31. L. Petrecca, "Feel Like Someone's Watching? You're Right," *USA Today,* March 17, 2010, pp. 1B+.

32. S. Armour, "Companies Keep an Eye on Workers' Internet Use," *USA Today,* February 21, 2006, p. 2B.

33. B. White, "The New Workplace Rules: No Video-Watching," *Wall Street Journal,* March 4, 2008, pp. B1+.

34. P-W. Tam, E. White, N. Wingfield, and K. Maher, "Snooping E-Mail by Software Is Now a Workplace Norm," *Wall Street Journal,* March 9, 2005, pp. B1+; D. Hawkins, "Lawsuits Spur Rise in Employee Monitoring," *U.S. News & World Report,* August 13, 2001, p. 53; and L. Guernsey, "You've Got Inappropriate Mail," *New York Times,* April 5, 2000, pp. C1+.

35. S. Armour, "More Companies Keep Track of Workers' E-Mail," *USA Today,* June 13, 2005, p. 4B; and E. Bott, "Are You Safe? Privacy Special Report," *PC Computing,* March 2000, pp. 87–88.

36. B. Acohido, "An Invitation to Crime," *USA Today,* March 4, 2010, pp. A1+; W. P. Smith and F. Tabak, "Monitoring Employee E-mails: Is There Any Room for Privacy?" *Academy of Management Perspectives,* November 2009, pp. 33–38; and S. Boehle, "They're Watching You," *Training,* September 2008, pp. 23–29.

37. By the Numbers box based on J. Yang and P. Trap, "Participating in Office Pools," *USA Today,* April 5, 2010, p. 1B; J. Yang and S. Parker, "Unproductive Work Hours Cost Billions," *USA Today,* September 29, 2009, p. 1B; M. Leone, "Something Wicked This Way Comes," *CFO,* June 2010, pp. 14–15; "Light-Fingered Employees Lift Laptops, Hardware," *Workforce Management Online,* July 22, 2008; J. Casale, "Data Breach Threats from Within Growing," *Workforce Management Online,* April 2009; M. Conlin, "To Catch a Corporate Thief," *BusinessWeek,* February 16, 2009, p. 52; A. R. Carey and S. Ward, "Have a Boss Who Plays Games at Work?" *USA Today,* May 6, 2009, p. 1A; and S. L. Mintz, "The Gauge of Innocence," *CFO,* April 2009, pp. 52–57.

38. S. Greenhouse, "Shoplifters? Studies Say Keep an Eye on Workers," *New York Times Online,* December 30, 2009.

39. A. M. Bell and D. M. Smith, "Theft and Fraud May Be an Inside Job," *Workforce Online* [www.workforce.com], December 3, 2000.

40. C. C. Verschoor, "New Evidence of Benefits from Effective Ethics Systems," *Strategic Finance,* May 2003, pp. 20–21; and E. Krell, "Will Forensic Accounting Go Mainstream?" *Business Finance,* October 2002, pp. 30–34.

41. J. Greenberg, "The STEAL Motive: Managing the Social Determinants of Employee Theft," in R. Giacalone and J. Greenberg (eds.), *Antisocial Behavior in Organizations* (Newbury Park, CA: Sage, 1997), pp. 85–108.

42. B. E. Litzky, K. A. Eddleston, and D. L. Kidder, "The Good, the Bad, and the Misguided: How Managers Inadvertently Encourage Deviant Behaviors," *Academy of Management Perspective,* February 2006, pp. 91–103; "Crime Spree," *BusinessWeek,* September 9, 2002, p. 8; B. P. Niehoff and R. J. Paul, "Causes of Employee Theft and Strategies That HR Managers Can Use for Prevention," *Human Resource Management,* Spring 2000, pp. 51–64; and G. Winter, "Taking at the Office Reaches New Heights: Employee Larceny Is Bigger and Bolder," *New York Times,* July 12, 2000, pp. C1+.

43. This section is based on J. Greenberg, *Behavior in Organizations: Understanding and Managing the Human Side of Work,* 8th ed. (Upper Saddle River, NJ: Prentice Hall, 2003), pp. 329–330.

44. A. H. Bell and D. M. Smith, "Why Some Employees Bite the Hand That Feeds Them," *Workforce Management Online,* December 3, 2000.

45. B. E. Litzky et al., "The Good, the Bad, and the Misguided"; A. H. Bell and D. M. Smith, "Protecting the Company Against Theft and Fraud," *Workforce Management Online,* December 3, 2000; J. D. Hansen, "To Catch a Thief," *Journal of Accountancy,* March 2000, pp. 43–46; and J. Greenberg, "The Cognitive Geometry of Employee Theft," in *Dysfunctional Behavior In Organizations: Nonviolent and Deviant Behavior* (Stamford, CT: JAI Press, 1998), pp. 147–193.

46. R. Rivera and L. Robbins, "Troubles Preceded Connecticut Workplace Killing," *New York Times Online,* August 3, 2010; J. Griffin, "Workplace Violence News" [workplaceviolencenews.com], July 16, 2010; J. Smerd, "Workplace Shootings in Florida, Texas Again Put Focus on Violence on the Job," *Workforce Management Online,* November 6, 2009; R. Lenz, Associated Press, "Gunman Kills Five, Himself At Plant," *Springfield, Missouri, News-Leader,* June 26, 2008, p. 6A; CBS News, "Former Postal Worker Kills 5, Herself" [www.cbsnews.com/stories], January 31, 2006; CBS News, "Autoworker's Grudge Turns Deadly" [www.cbsnews.com/stories], January 27, 2005; D. Sharp, "Gunman Just Hated a Lot of People," *USA Today,* July 10, 2003, p. 3A; and M. Prince, "Violence in the Workplace on the Rise; Training, Zero Tolerance Can Prevent Aggression," *Business Insurance,* May 12, 2003, p. 1.

47. "Workplace Shootings: Fact Sheet," U.S. Bureau of Labor Statistics [www.bls.gov/data/], July 2010; Occupational Health and Safety, "BLS: Workplace Homicides Drop to Lowest Number on Record" [www.ohsonline.com], August 17, 2007.

48. J. McCafferty, "Verbal Chills," *CFO,* June 2005, p. 17; S. Armour, "Managers Not Prepared for Workplace Violence," July 15, 2004, pp. 1B+; and "Workplace Violence," OSHA Fact Sheet, U.S. Department of Labor, Occupational Safety and Health Administration, 2002.

49. "Ten Tips on Recognizing and Minimizing Violence," *Workforce Management Online,* December 3, 2000.

50. "Bullying Bosses Cause Work Rage Rise," *Management Issues News* [www.management-issues.com], January 28, 2003.

51. R. McNatt, "Desk Rage," *BusinessWeek,* November 27, 2000, p. 12.

52. M. Gorkin, "Key Components of a Dangerously Dysfunctional Work Environment," *Workforce Management Online,* December 3, 2000.

53. "Ten Tips on Recognizing and Minimizing Violence"; M. Gorkin, "Five Strategies and Structures for Reducing Workplace Violence"; "Investigating Workplace Violence: Where Do You Start?"; and "Points to Cover in a Workplace Violence Policy," all articles from *Workforce Management Online,* December 3, 2000.

54. A. Taylor, "Enterprise Asks What Customer's Thinking and Acts," *USA Today,* May 22, 2006, p. 6B; and A. Taylor, "Driving Customer Satisfaction," *Harvard Business Review,* July 2002, pp. 24–25.

55. S. D. Pugh, J. Dietz, J. W. Wiley, and S. M. Brooks, "Driving Service Effectiveness Through Employee–Customer Linkages," *Academy of Management Executive,* November 2002, pp. 73–84; J. L. Heskett, W. E. Sasser, and L. A. Schlesinger, *The Service Profit Chain* (New York: Free Press, 1997); and J. L. Heskett, T. O. Jones, G. W. Loveman, W. E. Sasser, Jr., and L. A. Schlesinger, "Putting the Service Profit Chain to Work," *Harvard Business Review,* March–April 1994, pp. 164–170.

56. T. Buck and A. Shahrim, "The Translation of Corporate Governance Changes Across National Cultures: The Case of Germany," *Journal of International Business Studies,* January 2005, pp. 42–61; and "A Revolution Where Everyone Wins: Worldwide Movement to Improve Corporate-Governance Standards," *BusinessWeek,* May 19, 2003, p. 72.

57. J. S. McClenahen, "Executives Expect More Board Input," *Industry Week,* October 2002, p. 12.

58. D. Salierno, "Boards Face Increased Responsibility," *Internal Auditor,* June 2003, pp. 14–15.

59. A. Vanacore, "Cameras Scan Store Lines for 'Sweethearting,'" The Associated Press, *Springfield, Missouri News-Leader,* May 11, 2009, p. 9A.

60. A. Andors, "Keeping Teen Workers Safe," *HR Magazine,* June 2010, pp. 76–80.

61. R. Brown, "Oil Rig's Siren Was Kept Silent, Technician Says," *New York Times Online,* July 23, 2010; I. Urbina, "Workers on Doomed Rig Voiced Concern About Safety," *New York Times Online,* July 21, 2010; R. Gold, "Rig's Final Hours Probed," *Wall Street Journal,* July 19, 2010, pp. A1+; S. Lyall, "In BP's Record, a History of Boldness and Costly Blunders," *New York Times Online,* July 12, 2010; B. Casselman and R. Gold, "Unusual Decisions Set Stage for BP Disaster," *Wall Street Journal,* May 27, 2010, pp. A1+; H. Fountain and T. Zeller, Jr., "Panel Suggests Signs of Trouble Before Rig Explosion," *New York Times Online,* May 25, 2010; and R. Gold and N. King Jr., "The Gulf Oil Spill: Red Flags Were Ignored Aboard Doomed Rig," *Wall Street Journal,* May 13, 2010, p. A6.

62. K. Kühn, "How Has T5 Taken Off?" *Caterer & Hotelkeeper,* March 12, 2010, pp. 22–25; C. Dosh, "Debunking T5 Terror," *Successful Meetings,* April 2009, p. 99; M. Frary, "A Tale of Two Terminals," *Business Travel World,* August 2008, pp. 16–19; K. Capell, "British Airways Hit by Heathrow Fiasco," *BusinessWeek,* April 3, 2008, p. 6; The Associated Press, "Problems Continue at Heathrow's Terminal 5," *International Herald Tribune* [www.iht.com], March 31, 2008; M. Scott, "New Heathrow Hub: Slick, but No Savior," *BusinessWeek,* March 28, 2008, p. 11; and G. Katz, "Flights Are Canceled, Baggage Stranded, as London's New Heathrow Terminal Opens," *The Seattle Times Online* [seattletimes.nwsource.com], March 27, 2008.

Chapter 19

1. K. Baxter, "Seoul Showcases Its Talent," *MEED: Middle East Economic Digest,* May 14, 2010, pp. 13–24; E. Ramstad, "High-Speed Wireless Transforms a Shipyard," *Wall Street Journal,* March 16, 2010, p. B6; and Datamonitor, "Company Profile: Hyundai Heavy Industries Co., Ltd." [www.datamonitor.com], November 27, 2009.

2. D. Clark, "Inside Intel, It's All Copying," *Wall Street Journal,* October 28, 2002, pp. B1+.

3. D. McGinn, "Faster Food," *Newsweek,* April 19, 2004, pp. E20–E22.

4. *World Factbook 2010,* available online at [www.ocdi.gov/cia/publications].

5. Ibid.

6. D. Michaels and J. L. Lunsford, "Streamlined Plane Making," *Wall Street Journal,* April 1, 2005, pp. B1+.

7. T. Aeppel, "Workers Not Included," *Wall Street Journal,* November 19, 2002, pp. B1+.

8. A. Aston and M. Arndt, "The Flexible Factory," *BusinessWeek,* May 5, 2003, pp. 90–91.

9. P. Panchak, "Pella Drives Lean Throughout the Enterprise," *Industry Week,* June 2003, pp. 74–77.

10. J. Ordonez, "McDonald's to Cut the Cooking Time of Its French Fries," *Wall Street Journal,* May 19, 2000, p. B2.

11. C. Fredman, "The Devil in the Details," *Executive Edge,* April–May, 1999, pp. 36–39.

12. Information from [http://new.skoda-auto.com/Documents/AnnualReports/skoda_auto_annual_report_2007_%20EN_FINAL.pdf], July 8, 2008; and T. Mudd, "The Last Laugh," *Industry Week,* September 18, 2000, pp. 38–44.

13. W. E. Deming, "Improvement of Quality and Productivity Through Action by Management," *National Productivity Review,* Winter 1981–1982, pp. 12–22.

14. T. Vinas, "Little Things Mean a Lot," *Industry Week,* November 2002, p. 55.

15. "The Future of Manufacturing 2009," *Industry Week,* November 2009, pp. 25–31; T. D. Kuczmarski, "Remanufacturing America's Factory Sector," *BusinessWeek Online,* September 9, 2009; P. Panchak, "Shaping the Future of Manufacturing," *Industry Week,* January 2005, pp. 38–44; M. Hammer, "Deep Change: How Operational Innovation Can Transform Your Company," *Harvard Business Review,* April 2004, pp. 84–94; S. Levy, "The Connected Company," *Newsweek,* April 28, 2003, pp. 40–48; and J. Teresko, "Plant Floor Strategy," *Industry Week,* July 2002, pp. 26–32.

16. Leader Who Made a Difference box based on "100 Best Global Brands," *BusinessWeek,* September 28, 2009, p. 50; V. Bauerlein, "Coca-Cola CEO Defends Bottling System," *Wall Street Journal,* April 22, 2009, p. B3; and J. Shambora, A. Lashinsky, B. Gimbel, and J. Schlosser, "A View from the Top," *Fortune,* March 16, 2009, pp. 105–110.

17. T. Laseter, K. Ramdas, and D. Swerdlow, "The Supply Side of Design and Development," *Strategy+Business,* Summer 2003, p. 23; J. Jusko, "Not All Dollars and Cents," *Industry Week,* April 2002, p. 58; and D. Drickhamer, "Medical Marvel," *Industry Week,* March 2002, pp. 47–49.

18. J. H. Sheridan, "Managing the Value Chain," *Industry Week* [www.industryweek.com], September 6, 1999, pp. 1–4.

19. Ibid, p. 3.

20. J. Teresko, "Forward, March!" *Industry Week,* July 2004, pp. 43–48; D. Sharma, C. Lucier, and R. Molloy, "From Solutions to Symbiosis: Blending with Your Customers," *Strategy+Business,* Second Quarter 2002, pp. 38–48; and S. Leibs, "Getting Ready: Your Suppliers," *Industry Week* [www.industryweek.com], September 6, 1999.

21. D. Bartholomew, "The Infrastructure," *Industry Week* [www.industryweek.com], September 6, 1999, p. 1.

22. T. Stevens, "Integrated Product Development," *Industry Week,* June 2002, pp. 21–28.

23. T. Vinas, "A Map of the World: IW Value-Chain Survey," *Industry Week,* September 2005, pp. 27–34.

24. C. Burritt, C. Wolf, and M. Boyle, "Why Wal-Mart Wants to Take the Driver's Seat," *Bloomberg BusinessWeek,* May 31–June 6, 2010, pp. 17–18.

25. R. Normann and R. Ramirez, "From Value Chain to Value Constellation," *Harvard Business Review on Managing the Value Chain* (Boston, MA: Harvard Business School Press, 2000), pp. 185–219.

26. "Collaboration Is the Key to Reducing Costs," *Industry Week,* October 2009, p. 35; J. Teresko, "The Tough Get Going," *Industry Week,* March 2005, pp. 25–32; D. M. Lambert and A. M. Knemeyer, "We're in This Together," *Harvard Business Review,* December 2004, pp. 114–122; and V. G. Narayanan and A. Raman, "Aligning Incentives in Supply Chains," *Harvard Business Review,* November 2004, pp. 94–102.

27. D. Drickhamer, "Looking for Value," *Industry Week,* December 2002, pp. 41–43.

28. J. L. Yang, "Veggie Tales," *Fortune,* June 8, 2009, pp. 25–30.

29. J. Jusko, "Focus. Discipline. Results," *Industry Week,* June 2010, pp. 16–17.

30. J. H. Sheridan, "Managing the Value Chain," p. 3.

31. S. Leibs, "Getting Ready: Your Customers," *Industry Week* [www.industryweek.com], September 6, 1999, p. 1.

32. G. Taninecz, "Forging the Chain," *Industry Week,* May 15, 2000, pp. 40–46.

33. S. Leibs, "Getting Ready: Your Customers."

34. J. Katz, "Empowering the Workforce," *Industry Week,* January 2009, p. 43.

35. D. Blanchard, "In the Rotation," *Industry Week,* January 2009, p. 42.

36. N. Zubko, "Mindful of the Surroundings," *Industry Week,* January 2009, p. 38.

37. "Top Security Threats and Management Issues Facing Corporate America: 2003 Survey of *Fortune* 1000 Companies," ASIS International and Pinkerton [www.asisonline.org].

38. J. H. Sheridan, "Managing the Value Chain," p. 4.

39. By the Numbers box based on "The Future of Manufacturing 2009," *Industry Week,* November 2009, p. 26; First-Hand Accounts," *Industry Week,* July 2008, p. 28; "State of the Workforce Report," *Industry Week,* November 2008, p. 18; and "Sustainable Supply Chains," *Industry Week,* December 2008, p. 57.

40. R. Russell and B. W. Taylor, *Operations Management,* 5th ed. (New York: Wiley, 2005); C. Liu-Lien Tan, "U.S. Response: Speedier Delivery," *Wall Street Journal,* November 18, 2004, pp. D1+; and C. Salter, "When Couches Fly," *Fast Company,* July 2004, pp. 80–81.

41. D. Joseph, "The GPS Revolution: Location, Location, Location," *BusinessWeek Online,* May 27, 2009.

42. J. Jargon, "Domino's IT Staff Delivers Slick Site, Ordering System," *Wall Street Journal,* November 24, 2009, p. B5; and S. Anderson, The Associated Press, "Restaurants Gear Up for Window Wars," *Springfield, Missouri, News-Leader,* January 27, 2006, p. 5B.

43. S. McCartney, "A Radical Cockpit Upgrade Southwest Fliers Will Feel," *Wall Street Journal,* April 1, 2010, p. D1.

44. D. Bartholomew, "Quality Takes a Beating," *Industry Week,* March 2006, pp. 46–54; J. Carey and M. Arndt, "Making Pills the Smart Way," *BusinessWeek,* May 3, 2004, pp. 102–103; and A. Barrett, "Schering's Dr. Feelbetter?" *BusinessWeek,* June 23, 2003, pp. 55–56.

45. T. Vinas, "Six Sigma Rescue," *Industry Week,* March 2004, p. 12.

46. J. S. McClenahen, "Prairie Home Companion," *Industry Week,* October 2005, pp. 45–46.

47. T. Vinas, "Zeroing In on the Customer," *Industry Week,* October 2004, pp. 61–62.

48. W. Royal, "Spotlight Shines on Maquiladora," *Industry Week,* October 16, 2000, pp. 91–92.

49. See B. Whitford and R. Andrew (eds.), *The Pursuit of Quality* (Perth: Beaumont Publishing, 1994).

50. D. Drickhamer, "Road to Excellence," *Industry Week,* October 16, 2000, pp. 117–118.

51. J. Heizer and B. Render, *Operations Management,* 10th ed. (Upper Saddle River, NJ: Prentice Hall, 2011), p. 193.

52. G. Hasek, "Merger Marries Quality Efforts," *Industry Week,* August 21, 2000, pp. 89–92.

53. M. Arndt, "Quality Isn't Just for Widgets," *BusinessWeek,* July 22, 2002, pp. 72–73.

54. E. White, "Rethinking the Quality Improvement Program," *Wall Street Journal,* September 19, 2005, p. B3.

55. M. Arndt, "Quality Isn't Just for Widgets."

56. S. McMurray, "Ford's F-150: Have It Your Way," *Business 2.0,* March 2004, pp. 53–55; "Made-to-Fit Clothes Are on the Way," *USA Today,* July 2002, pp. 8–9; and L. Elliott, "Mass Customization Comes a Step Closer," *Design News,* February 18, 2002, p. 21.

57. E. Schonfeld, "The Customized, Digitized, Have-it-Your-Way Economy," *Fortune,* October 28, 1998, pp. 114–120.

58. Heizer and Render, *Operations Management,* p. 636; and S. Minter, "Measuring the Success of Lean," *Industry Week,* February 2010, pp. 32–35.

59. Heizer and Render, *Operations Management,* p. 636.

60. C. Burritt, C. Wolf, and M. Boyle, "Why Wal-Mart Wants to Take the Driver's Seat;" V. O'Connell, "Wal-Mart Program Will Aid Suppliers," *Wall Street Journal,* November 14–15, 2009, p. B4; and M. Boyle, "Wal-Mart Keeps the Change," *Fortune,* November 10, 2003, p. 46.

61. Skills Exercise based on M. H. Bazerman and M. A. Neale, *Negotiating Rationally* (New York: The Free Press, 1992); J. A. Wall Jr. and M. W. Blum, "Negotiations," *Journal of Management,* June 1991, pp. 278–282; L. Babcock, S. Laschever, M. Gelfand, and D. Small, "Nice Girls Don't Ask," *Harvard Business Review,* October 2003, pp. 14–15; and M. Kaplan, "How to Negotiate Anything," *Money,* May 2005, pp. 117–119.

62. S. Berfield, "Starbucks: Howard Schultz vs. Howard Schultz," *BusinessWeek Online,* August 6, 2009; J. Jargon, "Latest Starbucks Buzzword: 'Lean' Japanese Techniques," *Wall Street Journal,* August 4, 2009, p. A1; and "Starbucks Opens LEED Certified Coffee Roasting Plant," News Release [www.starbucks.com], February 19, 2009.

63. Press Release, "Blue Bird Corporation to Centralize Large Bus Assembly Operations in Fort Valley" [www.blue-bird.com/pressrelease], June 24, 2001; D. Blanchard, "Lean In for a Smooth Ride," *Industry Week,* January 2008, p. 38; and D. Blanchard, "Blue Bird North Georgia: IW Best Plants Profile 2007" [www.industryweek.com], January 1, 2008.

Appendix

1. R. Schmidt and P. O'Connor, "Def Jam's Founder Out-Lobbies Big Banks," *Bloomberg BusinessWeek,* June 28, 2010, pp. 21–22; R. A. Smith, "From Phat to Skinny," *Wall Street Journal,* May 1, 2010, p. W7; J. Dean, "The Endless Flow of Russell Simmons," *Entrepreneur,* September 2009, pp. 24–28; S. Page, "Top 25 Influential People," *USA Today,* September 4, 2007, p. A10; S. Berfield, "Hip-Hop Nation," *BusinessWeek,* June 13, 2005, p. 12; R. Kurtz, "Russell Simmons, Rush Communications," *Inc.,* April 2004, p. 137; J. Reingold, "Rush Hour," *Fast Company,* November 2003, pp. 68–80; S. Berfield, "The CEO of Hip Hop," *BusinessWeek,* October 27, 2003, pp. 90–98; J. L. Roberts, "Beyond Definition," *Newsweek,* July 28, 2003, pp. 40–43; and C. Dugas, "Hip-Hop Legend Far Surpassed Financial Goals," *USA Today,* May 15, 2003, p. 6B.

2. P. Burrows, "Ringing Off the Hook in China," *BusinessWeek,* June 9, 2003, pp. 80–82.

3. J. W. Carland, F. Hoy, W. R. Boulton, and J. C. Carland, "Differentiating Entrepreneurs from Small Business Owners: A Conceptualization," *Academy of Management Review,* vol. 9, no. 2, 1984, pp. 354–359.

4. J. McDowell, "Small Business Continues to Drive U.S. Economy," Office of Advocacy, U.S. Small Business Administration [www.sba.gov/advo/press], October 3, 2005.

5. P. Almeida and B. Kogut, "The Exploration of Technological Diversity and Geographic Localization in Innovation: Start-Up Firms in the Semiconductor Industry," *Small Business Economics*, vol. 9, no. 1, 1997, pp. 21–31.

6. R. J. Arend, "Emergence of Entrepreneurs Following Exogenous Technological Change," *Strategic Management Journal*, vol. 20, no. 1, 1999, pp. 31–47.

7. U.S. Small Business Administration Office of Advocacy, "Frequently Asked Questions," *Small Business Administration* [www.sba.gov], April 16. 2007.

8. "The Small Business Economy: A Report to the President," U.S. Small Business Administration, Office of Advocacy [www.sba.gov/advo/].

9. Press release, "Where Do Jobs Come From? New Analysis of Job Gains and Losses from the Office of Advocacy," U.S. Small Business Administration, Office of Advocacy [www.sba.gov/advo/].

10. N. Bosma, J. Levie et al., "Global Entrepreneurship Monitor: 2009 Executive Report" [www.gemconsortium.org], pp. 5–8.

11. W. Royal, "Real Expectations," *Industry Week*, September 4, 2000, pp. 31–34.

12. "Creating a Sustainable Business Among South Africa's Poor One Bite at a Time," *Knowledge @ Wharton* [http://knowledge.wharton.upenn.edu], July 13, 2006.

13. T. Purdum, "25 Growing Companies," *Industry Week*, November 20, 2000, p. 82.

14. C. Sandlund, "Trust Is a Must," *Entrepreneur*, October 2002, pp. 70–75.

15. B. I. Koerner, "Cereal in the Bowl, Not on the Floor," *New York Times Online* [www.nytimes.com], June 18, 2006.

16. "Facts for Features," *U.S. Census Bureau Newsroom*, January 3, 2006; and M. Arndt, "Zimmer: Growing Older Gracefully," *BusinessWeek*, June 9, 2003, pp. 82–84.

17. G. B. Knight, "How Wall Street Whiz Found a Niche Selling Books on the Internet," *Wall Street Journal*, May 15, 1996, pp. A1+.

18. N. F. Krueger, Jr., "The Cognitive Infrastructure of Opportunity Emergence," *Entrepreneurship Theory and Practice*, Spring 2000, p. 6.

19. D. P. Forbes, "Managerial Determinants of Decision Speed in New Ventures," *Strategic Management Journal*, April 2005, pp. 355–366.

20. P. Drucker, *Innovation and Entrepreneurship* (New York: Harper & Row, 1985).

21. G. Bounds, "Hybrids Fuel Agency's Fast Ride," *Wall Street Journal*, July 11, 2006, pp. B1+.

22. B. Bergstein, The Associated Press, "RSA Security Finds Future in Threat of Identity Theft," *Springfield News-Leader*, August 22, 2005, p. 5B.

23. B. McClean, "This Entrepreneur Is Changing Underwear," *Fortune*, September 18, 2000, p. 60.

24. S. Schubert, "The Ultimate Music Buff," *Business 2.0*, March 2006, p. 64.

25. Latest figures on registered users from Hoover's Online [www.hoovers.com], July 13, 2008; and A. Cohen, "eBay's Bid to Conquer All," *Time*, February 5, 2001, pp. 48–51.

26. S. McFarland, "Cambodia's Internet Service Is in Kids' Hands," *Wall Street Journal*, May 15, 2000, p. A9A.

27. Information on Whole Foods Market from Hoovers Online [www.hoovers.com], July 13, 2008.

28. D. Fahmy, "Making Necessities Stylish and Getting a Higher Price," *New York Times Online* [www.nytimes.com], March 9, 2006.

29. A. Eisenberg, "What's Next: New Fabrics Can Keep Wearers Healthy and Smelling Good," *New York Times*, February 3, 2000, pp. D1+.

30. A. Morse, "An Entrepreneur Finds Tokyo Shares Her Passion for Bagels," *Wall Street Journal*, October 18, 2005, pp. B1+.

31. S. Greco, "The Start-Up Years," *Inc. 500*, October 21, 1997, p. 57.

32. T. Stevens, "Master of His Universe," *Industry Week*, January 15, 2001, pp. 76–80; and R. Grover, "Back from a Black Hole," *BusinessWeek*, May 29, 2000, p. 186.

33. E. Neuborne, "Hey, Good-Looking," *BusinessWeek*, May 29, 2000, p. 192.

34. A. Barrett, B. Turek, and C. Faivre d'Arcier, "Bottoms Up—and Profits, Too," *BusinessWeek*, September 12, 2005, pp. 80–82; and C. Hajim, "Growth in Surprising Places," *Fortune*, September 5, 2005, bonus section.

35. J. Hovey, "25 Growing Companies," *Industry Week*, November 20, 2000, p. 66.

36. "Best Employer," *Working Woman*, May 1999, p. 54.

37. R. L. Heneman, J. W. Tansky, and S. J. Camp, "Human Resource Management Practices in Small and Medium-Sized Enterprises: Unanswered Questions and Future Research Perspectives," *Entrepreneurship Theory and Practice*, vol. 25, no. 1, pp. 11–26.

38. Based on G. Fuchsberg, "Small Firms Struggle with Latest Management Trends," *Wall Street Journal*, August 26, 1993, p. B2; M. Barrier, "Reengineering Your Company," *Nation's Business*, February 1994, pp. 16–22; J. Weiss, "Reengineering the Small Business," *Small Business Reports*, May 1994, pp. 37–43; and K. D. Godsey, "Back on Track," *Success*, May 1997, pp. 52–54.

39. S. Stecklow, "StubHub's Ticket to Ride," *Wall Street Journal*, January 17, 2006, pp. B1+.

40. G. N. Chandler, C. Keller, and D. W. Lyon, "Unraveling the Determinants and Consequences of an Innovation-Supportive Organizational Culture," *Entrepreneurship Theory and Practice*, Fall 2000, pp. 59–76.

41. Ibid.

42. P. Gogoi, "Pregnant with Possibility," *BusinessWeek*, December 26, 2005, p. 50.

43. Information from company's Web site [www.sapient.com], July 7, 2003; and S. Herrera, "People Power," *Forbes*, November 2, 1998, p. 212.

44. "Saluting the Global Awards Recipients of Arthur Andersen's Best Practices Awards 2000," *Fortune Online* [www.fortune.com], January 16, 2001.

45. T. Purdum, "Winning with Empowerment," *Industry Week*, October 16, 2000, pp. 109–110.

46. Company financial information from Hoover's Online [www.hoovers.com], July 13, 2006; and P. Strozniak, "Rescue Operation," *Industry Week*, October 16, 2000, pp. 103–104.

47. M. Depree, *Leadership Jazz* (New York: Dell, 1993).

48. J. C. Collins and J. I. Porras, *Built to Last: Successful Habits of Visionary Companies* (New York: Harper-Business, 1994).

49. P. Strozniak, "Teams at Work," *Industry Week*, September 18, 2000, pp. 47–50.

50. Ibid.

51. T. Siegel Bernard, "Scooter's Popularity Offers A Chance for Growth," *Wall Street Journal*, September 20, 2005, p. B3.

52. J. Bailey, "Growth Needs a Plan or Only Losses May Build," *Wall Street Journal*, October 29, 2002, p. B9; and L. Beresford, "Growing Up," *Entrepreneur*, July 1995, pp. 124–128.

53. R. D. Hof, "EBay's Rhine Gold," *BusinessWeek*, April 3, 2006, pp. 44–45.

54. J. Summer, "More, Please!" *Business Finance*, July 2000, pp. 57–61.

55. T. Stevens, "Pedal Pushers," *Industry Week*, July 17, 2000, pp. 46–52.

56. P. Lorange and R. T. Nelson, "How to Recognize—and Avoid—Organizational Decline," *Sloan Management Review*, Spring 1987, pp. 41–48.

57. S. D. Chowdhury and J. R. Lange, "Crisis, Decline, and Turnaround: A Test of Competing Hypotheses for Short–Term Performance Improvement in Small Firms," *Journal of Small Business Management*, October 1993, pp. 8–17.

58. C. Farrell, "How to Survive a Downturn," *BusinessWeek*, April 28, 1997, pp. ENT4–ENT6.

59. R. W. Pricer and A. C. Johnson, "The Accuracy of Valuation Methods in Predicting the Selling Price of Small Firms," *Journal of Small Business Management*, October 1997, pp. 24–35.

60. J. Bailey, "Selling the Firm and Letting Go of the Dream," *Wall Street Journal*, December 10, 2002, p. B6; P. Hernan, "Finding the Exit," *Industry Week*, July 17, 2000, pp. 55–61; D. Rodkin, "For Sale by Owner," *Entrepreneur*, January 1998, pp. 148–53; A. Livingston, "Avoiding Pitfalls When Selling a Business," *Nation's Business*, July 1998, pp. 25–26; and G. Gibbs Marullo, "Selling Your Business: A Preview of the Process," *Nation's Business*, August 1998, pp. 25–26.

61. K. Stringer, "Time Out," *Wall Street Journal*, March 27, 2002, p. R14; T. Stevens, "Striking a Balance," *Industry Week*, November 20, 2000, pp. 26–36; and S. Caudron, "Fit to Lead," *Industry Week*, July 17, 2000, pp. 63–68.

Name Index

Gull, G. A., 60n50
Gundersen, A., 446n58
Gunn, E. P., 270n10
Gunther, M., 44n1
Guo, J., 76n30
Gupta, N. P., 326n63, 327n65–66
Gupta, V., 82n63
Gustafson, K., 324n48
Gustafson, L. T., 35n10
Gutek, B. A., 15n33, 58n47, 419n53
Guth, R. A., 296n32
Guthrie, J. P., 329n70
Guyon, J., 85n64–65, 134n49
Gwinner, K. P., 58n47

H

Hachiya, D., 376n20
Hackett, R. D., 375n18
Hackman, J. R., 35n10, 348n4, 348n6, 356n32, 359n47, 438n39–41, 439, 440
Haddad, C., 164n42, 449n73
Hadley, C. N., 166n52, 167n56
Hafner, K., 142n92, 417n40, 455n96
Hage, J., 276n33
Hagenbaugh, B., 486n2
Hagevik, S., 341n6
Haggerman, L., 410n19
Haight, D., 406
Haines, S., 36n12
Haines, T., 208
Hajim, C., 545n34
Hales, C. P., 10n15
Hall, B., 325n56
Hall, D. T., 377n29, 432n9
Hall, K., 196n33
Hall, W., Jr., 250n14, 251n19
Halvorsen, F., 219
Hambrick, D. C., 45n5, 160n23
Hamby, A., 161
Hamel, G., 23, 41, 154n7, 228n12, 244, 250n14, 283, 306
Hamm, S., 81n59, 372n1, 400n99
Hammer, L. B., 332n98, 332n100
Hammer, M., 291n8, 519n15
Hammond, J. S., 193n31, 198
Hammonds, K. H., 141n87, 193n32, 213n28, 438n37
Hanges, P. J., 82n63, 475n63
Hannah, D., 342n10–11
Hannon, D., 547
Hansen, F., 314n13, 318–319n30, 331n95, 339n115
Hansen, J. D., 501, 501n45
Hansen, M. T., 293, 301n57
Haque, A., 384n67
Hardman, W., 329n77
Hardy, Q., 7n11, 289n3, 455n96
Hare, A. P., 353n25
Hare, B., 198n35
Hargreaves, S., 220n39
Harkins, S. G., 352n18, 436n25
Harpaz, I., 447n64, 448n68
Harper, E., 63n57, 248n4
Harris, J. G., 12n25
Harris, K. J., 22n43
Harris, P., 368n69
Harris, P. R., 71n7
Harris, R. B., 22n43
Harrison, D. A., 363n63, 363n65, 377n30, 380n45, 418n50

Harrison, J. S., 50n18, 50n19
Hart, S. L., 289n4
Hartel, C. E. J., 385n71, 386n73
Härtel, C. E. J., 386n74
Harter, J. K., 23, 375n17, 376n22
Harter, L. M., 374n9
Hartke, D. D., 466n15
Hartline, M. D., 15n33, 58n47
Hartmann, H., 106n34
Harvey, C., 118n78, 119
Hasek, G., 528n52
Haslam, S. A., 430n5
Haspeslagh, P., 230n14
Hatch, M. J., 52n21
Hater, J. J., 470n29
Hatfield, J. D., 126n13
Hatsukano, K., 107
Hattori, R. A., 16n35
Hausman, C., 63n56, 130n28, 134n47, 242n39, 281n41, 304n61, 315n18, 479n70
Havilland, J. M., 385n70
Hawkins, D., 500n34
Hawkins, N., 58n45, 168n61
Hayes, T. L., 375n17, 376n22
He, W., 103n27, 104, 104n29
Healy, M., 162n32
Heaney, C. A., 163n36
Heath, C., 173, 183n11, 324n53, 325n57, 486n5, 490n9
Heath, D., 173, 183n11, 324n53, 325n57, 486n5, 490n9
Heaton, C. P., 419–420n54
Heavey, C., 63n57
Hecht, T. D., 298n41
Heffner, J. A., 474n58
Hegewisch, A., 106n34
Heidelberg, J., 329n77
Heil, G., 432n8, 433n11
Heizer, J., 528n51, 530n58–59
Helfat, C. A., 226n7
Helft, M., 224n2, 320n37, 494n13
Helkama, K., 138n66
Heller, D., 382n49–50
Hemmasi, M., 295n30
Hemp, P., 183n11
Hempel, J., 109n52, 342–343n12
Hempel, P. S., 362n57
Henderson, A. D., 234n22
Henderson, A. M., 31n6
Henderson, F., 174
Henderson, R. I., 326n62
Heneman, H. G., III, 442n51
Heneman, R. L., 551n37
Henneman, T., 416n35
Hennig-Thurau, T., 15n33
Henry, R. A., 353n24
Hentrich, C., 273n19
Henwood, C. I., 404n2
Heracleous, L., 380n46
Herbert, T. T., 447n65
Herbst, M., 297n36
Hermerling, J. W., 91
Hernan, P., 558n60
Herrenkohl, R. C., 474n58
Herrera, S., 553n43
Herring, C., 218n37
Herring, J. P., 249n5
Herron, M., 168n61
Hersey, P., 466–467, 466n17
Hershcovis, M. S., 395n96
Herson, M., 399

Herzberg, F., 433–434, 433n13, 447
Heskett, J., 50n19
Heskett, J. L., 54n25, 504n55, 534
Hess, K. A., 330n81
Hessel, E., 12n23
Hesterly, W., 291n8, 291n13
Hewlett, S. A., 48n15, 393n89
Hibbets, A. R., 496n17
Hicks, S., 156n12
Hiebert, M., 217n36
Hiestand, M., 265n5
Hietanen, J., 226n7
Higgins, C. A., 169n66, 383n61
Higgins, D. M., 382n50
Higgins, L. H., 389n83
Higgins, S., 127n23
Higgs, A. C., 348n6
High, K., 50n16, 238n36
Hill, C. W. L., 232n20
Hiller, N. J., 383n58
Hillman, A. J., 50n19, 126n17
Hilton, J. L., 389n84
Hinds, P. J., 362n55
Hinkin, T. R., 430n1, 472n48
Hitt, M. A., 235n27–28, 235, 236n31, 291n14, 296n35
Hlupic, V., 273n19
Hochwarter, W. A., 22n43
Hodgetts, R. M., 70n3, 291n8
Hoegl, M., 359n45
Hoel, H., 329n76
Hoetker, G., 291n14
Hof, R. D., 12n26, 274n28, 556n53
Hoffman, B. J., 376n26
Hoffman, J., 398n97
Hoffman, J. J., 278n40
Hofstede, G., 82–84, 82n61–62, 446n59
Hohenfeld, J. A., 441n47
Holcomb, T. R., 5n6
Holland, J., 386
Holland, J. L., 386n77
Holland, K., 301n56
Hollenbeck, J. R., 436n27
Hollender, J., 340
Hollensbe, E. C., 298n41
Hollon, J., 314n13
Holman, D. J., 440n42
Holmes, R. M., Jr., 5n6
Holmes, S., 190n23
Hom, P. W., 320n40, 376n19, 377n32
Homburg, C., 376n22
Hoobler, J. M., 112n62, 112n64
Hooker, J., 91
Hookway, J., 75n26, 103n27
Hope, J., 251n21, 253n25
Hori, Y., 48n13, 103n26, 104n28
Horn, S., 551
Horng, R. Y., 197n34
Horovitz, B., 426n66
Horwitz-Bennett, B., 414n30
Hosmer, L. T., 473n50
Hotz, R. L., 291n6
Hough, L. J., 356
Hough, L. M., 355n29
Hough-Dunnette, L., 356
Hourihan, G., 186n21
House, R. J., 82, 82n63, 84, 157n14, 467, 467n19, 470n34, 471n37, 475, 475n63, 478
Hout, T. M., 45n6
Hovey, J., 547n35
Howard, A., 475

Warriner, C. K., 206n9
Wartick, S. L., 125n6
Wartzman, R., 57n39
Watkins, B., 462
Watkins, S., 140
Watson, G. H., 251n22
Watson, W. E., 353n24
Wattenberg, B. J., 82
Wayne, L., 210n17
Wayne, S. J., 112n62, 112n64, 352n17, 377n35, 449n72, 469n22–24
Weathersby, L., 214n32
Weaver, G., 132n40, 132n42
Weaver, G. R., 130n32
Webb, M. S., 137n61
Weber, J., 131n33–34, 132n40, 138n67, 139n70, 235n24
Weber, M., 29, 31–32, 31n6, 39, 264
Weber, R. A., 184n12
Weber, T., 476n66
Weed, S. E., 382n54
Weeks, R., 330n81
Weick, K., 193–194, 193n32
Weill, P., 234n22
Weinberger, D., 187n20
Weingart, L. R., 362n55
Weinstein, M., 136n56, 162n32, 211n19, 273n24, 284n44, 301n58, 339n115, 342n8, 349n9
Weintraub, A., 152n2, 217n36, 264n1, 356n31
Weintrop, J. B., 45n5
Weisberg, P. F., 171n67
Weiss, A., 259n33
Weiss, H. M., 385n72
Weiss, J., 354n27, 551n38
Weissenberger, B., 425n65
Weisul, K., 455n96
Weitz, E., 395n96, 399
Welch, D., 174n71
Welch, J., 4n2, 291, 380n43
Welch, S., 4n2, 380n43
Welch, S. B., 132n39
Wellins, R. S., 472n45
Wellman, N., 476n66
Wellner, A. S., 193n29
Welsh, M. A., 258n29
Wenger, E., 295, 295n27–28
Wessler, V., 138n64
West, B. J., 349n9, 357n33
Western, K., 215n35, 249n5
Wheatley, M. J., 481
Wheelen, T. L., 207n10
Wheeler, A. R., 22n43
Wheeler, D. L., 414n26
Wheeler, M. L., 99n7
Whelan, D., 497–498n23
Wherry, A., 486n1
Whitacre, E., 175
White, A., 127n25
White, B., 417n39, 500n33
White, E., 12n24, 138n68, 380n43, 418n44, 450n82, 450n88, 451n90, 500n34, 528n54
White, J., 134n49
White, M. C., 142n93
White, P., 390n85
White, R. E., 234n21
White, R. K., 462n7
White, T., 156n13
Whiteside, K., 404n1
Whitford, B., 528n49

Whiting, S., 154
Whitlock, B., 498n27
Whittington, J. L., 469n24
Wicks, A. C., 50n17, 50n19
Wiesenfeld, B. M., 442n49
Wilderom, C. P. M., 470n34
Wildstrom, S. H., 308n64, 418n49
Wiley, J., 275n31, 433n13
Wiley, J. W., 15n33, 58n47, 376n22, 420n56, 504n55
Williams, A., 409n13
Williams, C., 106n34
Williams, C. R., 436n27, 450n89
Williams, E., 404
Williams, J. E., 384n67
Williams, M. L., 476n69
Williams, R. B., 106n32
Williams, R. J., 278n40
Williams Nash, M., 333n112
Willyerd, K., 394n93
Wilson, E., 23n45, 469n21
Wilson, M. C., 312n3
Wilson, M. G., 441n45
Wind, Y., 71n7
Wingfield, N., 288n2, 500n34
Winkler, C., 187n20
Winsor, J., 296, 296n33
Winstein, K. J., 21n42
Winter, G., 500n42
Winters, M. F., 99, 99n4
Winters, R., 387n79
Wirtz, J., 380n46
Wiscombe, J., 140n80, 450n85
Wise, R., 243
Woehr, D. J., 376n26
Wofford, J. C., 436n27, 468n20
Wolf, C., 521n24, 533n60
Wolff, S. B., 349n8
Wolgemuth, L., 106n31
Wonacott, P., 80n51
Wong, C., 386n74
Wong, G., 147n96
Wood, D. J., 125n6
Wood, R. A., 126n13
Woodman, R. W., 166n50, 168n62
Woodward, C., 416n35
Woodward, C. A., 158n17
Woodward, J., 276, 276n32
Wortham, J., 224n2, 227n11
Worthen, B., 304n61, 497n20
Worthley, R., 447n66
Woycke, J., 470n34
Wright, A. D., 316n23
Wright, P., 234n21
Wright, P. M., 312n3
Wright, T., 109n51
Wright, T. A., 376n21
Wycoff, J., 16n35
Wyld, D., 234n21
Wyld, D. C., 168n61

X

Xiaojuan, H., 56

Y

Yach, D., 368
Yamaji, H., 93
Yammarino, F. J., 469n22, 470n34
Yanes-Estévez, V., 63n57

Yang, J., 5n7, 57n39, 58n44, 77n42, 110n58, 132n39, 162n32, 211n19, 234n22, 273n24, 297n36, 324n50, 330n84, 342n9, 349n9, 383n62, 418n50, 449n77, 500n37
Yang, J. L., 363n63, 522n28
Yang-Ho, C., 159–160
Yarrow, D., 251n22
Yasai-Ardekani, M., 276n35
Yaukey, J., 499n29
Ybarra, M. J., 127n24
Yen, H., 7n12
Yergin, D., 85n64
Yetton, P., 353n25
Young, M., 411n21
Youngblood, S. A., 131n35, 135n54
Youngs, R., 540
Yousuf, H., 281n41
Yu, J., 384n67
Yu, R., 159n20, 301n58
Yu, S., 161n28
Yuan, F., 168n62
Yukl, G., 470n32
Yunker, G. W., 34n8

Z

Zablah, A. R., 15n33
Zabojnik, J., 272n16
Zacharia, A. G., 250n13
Zagorski, M., 56n36
Zahra, S. A., 126n13
Zald, M. N., 141n88
Zamiska, N., 34n9
Zand, D. E., 235n28, 235
Zander, A., 463n10
Zander, A. F., 472n48
Zapp, J., 4
Zaslow, J., 385n69
Zatzick, C. D., 441n45
Zeidner, R., 339n115
Zeldin, Z., 188
Zeller, T., J R., 510n61
Zellner, W., 140n77
Zemke, R., 474n55
Zenger, J. H., 481
Zenger, T., 291n8
Zhang, J., 276n33
Zhang, X., 169n65
Zhang, Z-X., 362n57
Zhong, J. A., 469n25
Zhou, J., 168n61
Zhou, X., 469n22
Zielinski, D., 138n68, 259n31, 407n10
Zimmerman, E., 330n89, 341n7, 425n65
Zimmermann, K. A., 214n31
Zingheim, P. K., 450n89
Zivnuska, S., 22n43
Zmuda, N., 44n1
Zogby, J., 91
Zoghi, C., 441n45
Zoroya, G., 406n8
Zubko, N., 525n36
Zuckerberg, M., 55, 238
Zukis, B., 447n66

Organization Index

Glindex

A

Absenteeism *The failure to show up for work,* 373

Acceptance theory of authority *The view that authority comes from the willingness of subordinates to accept it,* 268–269

Achievement, in national cultures, 83E3-5

Achievement-oriented leader, 467

Active listening *Listening for full meaning without making premature judgments or interpretations,* 411

behaviors, 411E15-3

Activist (or dark green) approach to going green, 128

Activities *The time or resources needed to progress from one event to another in a PERT network,* 254, 255

Ad hoc committee, 294–295

Adjourning *The final stage of group development for temporary groups during which group members are concerned with wrapping up activities rather than task performance,* 348, 349

Affective component *That part of an attitude that's the emotional or feeling part,* 374, 375

Affinity groups, 115–116

Affirmative action *Organizational programs that enhance the status of members of protected groups,* 315, 316

African Union (AU), 76

Age Discrimination in Employment Act, 316E12-3

Aggressive individuals, 342

Aging workforce, 47, 105–106, 318

Agreeableness, in Big Five Model, 382

Americans with Disabilities Act, 316E12-3

Anchoring effect, 190–191, 191E7-11

Angel investors *A private investor (or group of private investors) who offers financial backing to an entrepreneurial venture in return for equity in the venture,* 545

Anti-Bribery Convention, 135

Artificial intelligence software, 187

Asch's cards, 350–351, 351E13-4

Assertiveness, in national cultures, 83, 84E3-6

Association of Southeast Asian Nations (ASEAN) *A trading alliance of ten Southeast Asian nations,* 75–76, 75E3-2

Assumed similarity *The assumption that others are like oneself,* 389

Attentional processes, in social learning, 391

Attitudes *Evaluative statements, either favorable or unfavorable, concerning objects, people, or events,* 374, 375

cognitive dissonance and, 379

consistency and, 378

cultural, 525

ethnocentric, 71

geocentric, 72, 73

global perspective and, 71–72

implications for managers, 380

polycentric, 72, 73

value chain management and, 524

Attitude surveys *Surveys that elicit responses from employees through questions about how they feel about their jobs, work groups, supervisors, or the organization,* 379–380

sample of, 379E14-3

Attractiveness of reward, 443

Attribution theory *A theory used to explain how we judge people differently depending on what meaning we attribute to a given behavior,* 388–389, 389E14-7

Audio/videotapes, 408E15-2

Audit committee, 505

Australian laws pertaining to HRM, 317

Authority *The rights inherent in a managerial position to tell people what to do and to expect them to do it,* 268, 269

acceptance theory of, 268–269

line, 269–270, 270E10-5

staff, 270, 270E10-5

Autocratic style *A leader who dictates work methods, makes unilateral decisions, and limits employee participation,* 462, 463

Automation, 156

Autonomy *The degree to which a job provides substantial freedom, independence, and discretion to the individual in scheduling work and determining the procedures to be used in carrying it out,* 439

stress and, 162

Availability bias, 191, 191E7-11

B

Baby boomers, 47–48, 318, 394

Balanced scorecard *A performance measurement tool that looks at more than just the financial perspective,* 496–497

BARS performance appraisal, 327E12-10

Basic corrective action *Corrective action that looks at how and why performance deviated before correcting the source of deviation,* 490, 491

BCG matrix *A strategy tool that guides resource allocation decisions on the basis of market share and growth rate of SBUs,* 230–231, 231E9-4

Behavior *The actions of people,* 372, 373

negative, in workplace, 394–395

shaping, 391–392

See also Ethical behavior; Organizational behavior (OB)

Behavioral component *That part of an attitude that refers to an intention to behave in a certain way toward someone or something,* 374, 375

Behavioral theories *Leadership theories that identify behaviors that differentiated effective leaders from ineffective leaders,* 462–464, 462E17-2

Behavioral theories of leadership, 462–464, 462E17-2

managing power, 472–473

Ohio State studies and, 463

University of Iowa studies and, 462–463

University of Michigan studies and, 463

Benchmark *The standard of excellence against which to measure and compare,* 498, 499

Benchmarking *The search for the best practices among competitors or noncompetitors that lead to their superior performance,* 251, 498, 499

internal, suggestions for, 498E18-10

steps in, 252EMP-2

Big Five Model *Personality trait model that includes extraversion, agreeableness, conscientiousness, emotional stability, and openness to experience,* 382, 383

Blogs, 320, 416, 418, 497, 499

Board of directors, role of, 505

Board representatives *Employees who sit on a company's board of directors and represent the interests of the firm's employees,* 317, 318

Body language *Gestures, facial configurations, and other body movements that convey meaning,* 407

"Boiled frog" phenomenon *A perspective on recognizing performance declines that suggests watching out for subtly declining situations,* 557

Boundaryless organization *An organization whose design is not defined by, or limited to, the horizontal, vertical, or external boundaries imposed by a predefined structure,* 291

advantages/disadvantages of, 289E11-1

internal/external, 291

network organizations, 291–292

virtual organizations, 291

Bounded rationality *Decision making that's rational, but limited (bounded) by an individual's ability to process information,* 183

Breakeven analysis *A technique for identifying the point at which total revenue is just sufficient to cover total costs,* 256, 256EMP-10, 257

Budget *A numerical plan for allocating resources to specific activities,* 252–253

improving, 253EMP-4

types of, 252EMP-3

Bulletin boards, 408E15-2

Bureaucracy *A form of organization characterized by division of labor, a clearly defined hierarchy, detailed rules and regulations, and impersonal relationships,* 31, 38

Weber's, 31, 32EMH-4

Business model *How a company is going to make money,* 225

Business plan *A written document that summarizes a business opportunity and defines and articulates how the identified opportunity is to be seized and exploited*, 546, 547
analysis of the context, 546
analysis of opportunity, 546
description of the business, 546
executive summary, 546
financial data and projections, 546–547
supporting documentation, 547

C

Calm waters metaphor, 152–153
Canadian Human Rights Act, 316–317
Canadian laws pertaining to HRM, 316–317
Capabilities *An organization's skills and abilities in doing the work activities needed in its business*, 228, 229
Career module, managing, 340–343
career opportunities in management, 340
cultural fit, finding, 340–341
getting along with people, 341–342
job fulfillment, 342
reinventing yourself, 341
risk taking, 341
successful career, path to, 341–342
Center for Creative Leadership study, 357
Central America Free Trade Agreement (CAFTA), 74
Centralization *The degree to which decision making is concentrated at upper levels of the organization*, 272, 273
today's view of, 272–273
vs. decentralization, 272E10-7
Certainty *A situation in which a manager can make accurate decisions because all outcomes are known*, 187
Chain of command *The line of authority extending from upper organizational levels to the lowest levels, which clarifies who reports to whom*, 268, 269
authority and, 268–270, 269E10-4, 270E10-5
dual, in matrix structure, 290
information technology and, 271
responsibility and, 270
today's view of, 270–271
unity of command and, 270
Change agent *Someone who acts as a catalyst and assumes the responsibility for managing the change process*, 155
Change-capable organizations, 164–165, 165E6-8
Change process, 152–154
calm waters metaphor and, 152–153
in entrepreneurial ventures, 551–552
external and internal forces for, 152, 153E6-1
Lewin's three-step change process and, 153, 153E6-2
resistance to, 158–159, 159E6-5
white-water rapids metaphor and, 153, 154
See also Organizational change
Channel *The medium a message travels along*, 406, 407
Charismatic leader *An enthusiastic, self-confident leader whose personality and actions influence people to behave in certain ways*, 470–471
Civil Rights Act of 1964, 316E12-3

Classical approach *First studies of management, which emphasized rationality and making organizations and workers as efficient as possible*, 29, 38
Classical view *The view that management's only social responsibility is to maximize profits*, 124, 125
Clicks-and-bricks strategy, 237
Closed system *Systems that are not influenced by and do not interact with their environment*, 36, 38
Closely held corporation *A corporation owned by a limited number of people who do not trade the stock publicly*, 548EA-4, 549
Code of ethics *A formal statement of an organization's primary values and the ethical rules it expects its employees to follow*, 136–137
Coercion, to reduce resistance to change, 159, 159E6-5
Coercive power *The power a leader has to punish or control*, 472, 473
Cognitive component *That part of an attitude that's made up of the beliefs, opinions, knowledge, or information held by a person*, 374, 375
Cognitive dissonance *Any incompatibility or inconsistency between attitudes or between behavior and attitudes*, 379
Collaboration, organizing for, 293–297
benefits and drawbacks of, 293E11-3
external collaboration, 295–297
internal collaboration, 294–295
value chain management in, 522
Collectivism, in national cultures
in GLOBE framework, 84, 84E3-6
in Hofstede's framework, 83E3-5
in-group, 84, 84E3-6
institutional, 84, 84E3-6
Command groups, 347E13-1
Commitment concept *The purpose of an organization*, 211–212
Committee to Encourage Corporate Philanthropy, 142
Communication *The transfer and understanding of meaning*, 404–405
functions of, 405–406
information technology and, 416–417
interpersonal, 406–411
nature of, 404–405
organizational, 412–415
to reduce resistance to change, 158, 159E6-5
Communication issues, 417–421
customer service and, 419–420
e-mail, 416, 417–418
employee input, 420, 420E15-5
ethical communication, 420–421
Internet, 417–418
knowledge resources, 418–419
Communication networks *The variety of patterns of vertical and horizontal flows of organizational communication*, 413–414
Communication process *The seven elements involved in transferring meaning from one person to another*, 406, 407
Communities of practice *Groups of people who share a concern, a set of problems, or a passion about a topic, and who deepen their knowledge and expertise in that area by interacting on an ongoing basis*, 295, 295E11-4

Compensation and benefits, 326, 327–328
determining factors for, 327, 328E12-11
family-friendly, 330
laws for, 316E12-3
skill-based pay, 327
types of, 326
variable pay systems, 327–328
Competence, 473
Competitive advantage *What sets an organization apart; its distinctive edge*, 232, 233
in entrepreneurial ventures, 542
five forces model and, 233, 233E9-5
quality as, 232
sustaining, 232
Competitive strategy *An organizational strategy for how an organization will compete in its business(es)*, 231
choosing, 233–234
competitive advantage in, 231–232
cost leadership, 233
differentiation, 234
focus, 234
functional, 234
Competitor intelligence *Environmental scanning activity by which organizations gather information about competitors*, 214–215, 249
Competitors, in entrepreneurial ventures, 544–545
Complainers, 342
Compressed workweek *A workweek where employees work longer hours per day but fewer days per week*, 299
Computer conference, 408E15-2
Computerization, 156
Computer software, decision-making, 187
Concentration, 229
Conceptual skills *The ability to think and to conceptualize about abstract and complex situations*, 13
Concurrent control *Control that takes place while a work activity is in progress*, 494, 495, 503E18-12
Confirmation bias, 191, 191E7-11
Conflict *Perceived incompatible differences that result in interference or opposition*, 354, 355
functional *vs.* dysfunctional, 354–355
future, 356
group performance and, 355E13-7
human relations view of, 354, 355
management, 354–356, 356E13-8
views regarding, 354
Conformity
in global work teams, 362
in group structure, 350–351
Conscientiousness, in Big Five Model, 382
Consideration *The extent to which a leader has work relationships characterized by mutual trust and respect for group members' ideas and feelings*, 463
Consistency, 473
Consolidated Omnibus Reconciliation Act (COBRA), 316E12-3
Contingency approach *A management approach that recognizes organizations as different, which means they face different situations (contingencies) and require different ways of managing*, 37, 38
contingency variables in, 38EMH-8
Contingency planning, 259–260

Least-preferred coworker (LPC) questionnaire *A questionnaire that measures whether a leader is task or relationship oriented,* 464–465

Legal (or light green) approach to going green, 128

Legal aspects of workforce diversity, 113–114, 113E4-8

Legal environment of HRM, 80, 315–317, 316E12-3
  affirmative action and, 315
  in Australia, 317
  in Canada, 316–317
  in Germany, 317
  major HRM laws in, 316E12-3
  in Mexico, 317
  in U.S., 316

Legal forms of organizations, 547–550, 548EA-4

Legal issues in Internet usage, 418, 525

Legitimate power *The power a leader has as a result of his or her position in the organization,* 472, 473

Lewin's three-step change process, 153, 153E6-2

Licensing *An organization gives another organization the right to make or sell its products using its technology or product specifications,* 79

Life-long learning, 156

Lilly Ledbetter Fair Pay Act, 316E12-3

Limited liability company (LLC) *A form of legal organization that's a hybrid between a partnership and a corporation,* 548EA-4, 549

Limited liability partnership (LLP) *A form of legal organization consisting of general partner(s) and limited liability partner(s),* 548EA-4, 549

Linear programming *A mathematical technique that solves resource allocation problems,* 257
  example of, 257–258, 257EMP-11
  graphical solution to, 258EMP-12

Linear thinking style *Decision style characterized by a person's preference for using external data and facts and processing this information through rational, logical thinking,* 190, 191

Line authority *Authority that entitles a manager to direct the work of an employee,* 269
  chain of command and, 269E10-4
  vs. staff authority, 270, 270E10-5

Load chart *A modified Gantt chart that schedules capacity by entire departments or specific resources,* 254, 254EMP-6, 255

Locus of control *The degree to which people believe they are masters of their own fate,* 131, 382, 383

Long-term plans *Plans with a time frame beyond three years,* 207

Low-skilled employees, motivating, 449

Loyalty, 473

M

Machiavellianism *A measure of the degree to which people are pragmatic, maintain emotional distance, and believe that ends justify means,* 383

Management *Coordinating and overseeing the work activities of others so that their activities are completed efficiently and effectively,* 8, 9

approaches to, 28–29, 29EMH-1 (*See also* Management theories)
career opportunities in, 340
early, 28
efficiency and effectiveness of, 8, 8E1-3
functions of, 8–10, 9E1-4
in global environment (*See* Global management)
levels of, 6, 6E1-1
omnipotent view of, 44–45
operations, 516–530
of organizational change, contemporary issues in, 159–165
reality of work and, 18
skills, 12–13, 12E1-6, 13E1-7
symbolic view of, 45
of teams, 345–364
universality of, 17–18, 17E1-9
value chain, 519–525
workforce diversity and, 100E4-2, 101, 110–112, 114

Management by objectives (MBO) *A process of setting mutually agreed-upon goals and using those goals to evaluate employee performance,* 209–210
steps in, 210E8-3

Management by walking around *A term used to describe when a manager is out in the work area interacting directly with employees,* 494, 495, 503E18-12

Management information system (MIS) *A system used to provide management with needed information on a regular basis,* 497

Management science. *See* Quantitative approach

Management theories, 28–38, 29EMH-1
  behavioral approach, 32–33
  classical approach, 29–32
  contemporary approaches, 36–38
  contingency approach, 37–38, 38MH-8
  quantitative approach, 34–35
  systems approach, 36–37, 36EMH-7

Manager *Someone who coordinates and oversees the work of other people so that organizational goals can be accomplished,* 5–6
  changing nature of, 13–14, 14E1-8
  contemporary model of, 10–12
  customer service and, 14–16
  as decision maker, 182–194
  discretion of, constraints on, 45E2-1
  general administrative theory used by, 32
  of global work teams, role in, 362
  importance of, 4–5
  innovation and, 16
  organizational behavior used by, 34
  organizational culture and, 56–57, 57E2-9
  organizations and, 6–8
  quantitative approach used by, 45
  rewards of challenges of, 18–19, 19E1-10
  scientific management used by, 30–31
  sustainability and, 16
  vs. nonmanagerial employees, 5
  See also Management

Managerial grid *A two-dimensional grid for appraising leadership styles,* 462E17-2, 463–464

Managerial roles *Specific actions or behaviors expected of and exhibited by a manager,* 10–12

Manipulation, to reduce resistance to change, 159, 159E6-5

Manufacturing organizations *Organizations that produce physical goods,* 517

Market approach to going green, 128

Marshall Plan, 77

Mass customization *Providing customers with a product when, where, and how they want it,* 529–530

Mass production *The production of items in large batches,* 276, 277

Material artifacts and symbols used to teach organizational culture, 55–56

Matrix structure *An organizational structure that assigns specialists from different functional departments to work on one or more projects,* 290, 291
  advantages/disadvantages of, 289E11-1
  example of, 290E11-2

Maximax/maximin choice, 188–189, 189E7-9

MBO performance appraisal, 327E12-10

Means-ends chain *An integrated network of goals in which the accomplishment of goals at one level serves as the means for achieving the goals, or ends, at the next level,* 209

Mechanistic organization *An organizational design that's rigid and tightly controlled,* 274, 275
  vs. organic organizations, 274E10-8

Memos, 408E15-2, 410

Mercosur, 75

Message *A purpose to be conveyed,* 406, 407

Mexican Federal Labor Law, 317

Mexican laws pertaining to HRM, 317

Microchronometer, 30

Middle managers *Managers between the lowest level and top levels of the organization who manage the work of first-line managers,* 6, 7

Minimum-wage employees, motivating, 449

Mintzberg's managerial roles, 10–12, 11E1-5

Mission *A statement of an organization's purpose,* 210, 211
  identifying, 227, 227E9-2

Modular organization, 291–292

Monolingualism, 71

Moral development, stages of, 130–131, 131E5-4

Motivating jobs, designing, 438–441
  job characteristics model for, 438–440
  job enlargement for, 438–441
  job enrichment for, 438
  redesigning approaches to, 440–441, 440E17-7

Motivation *The process by which a person's efforts are energized, directed, and sustained toward attaining a goal,* 430–431
  of contingent workers, 448–449
  current issues in, 445–451
  of diverse workforce, 448
  economic circumstances and, 445
  entrepreneurs and, 553
  of low-skilled, minimum-wage employees, 449
  managing cross-cultural challenges in, 445–447
  motivating unique groups of workers, 447–449
  of professionals, 448
  rewards programs for, 449–451

Motivation, theories of, 431–437
  equity theory, 441–442, 442E16-8
  expectancy theory, 442–443, 442E16-9
  goal-setting theory, 435–437, 437E16-5

Photo Credits